Snakes: Ecology and Evolutionary Biology

EDITORS

Richard A. Seigel
Savannah River Ecology Laboratory
Aiken, South Carolina

Joseph T. Collins
Museum of Natural History
The University of Kansas, Lawrence
Kansas

Susan S. Novak
Savannah River Ecology Laboratory
Aiken, South Carolina

McGraw-Hill Publishing Company

New York   St. Louis   San Francisco   Auckland
Bogotá   Hamburg   London   Madrid   Milan   Mexico
Montreal   New Delhi   Panama   Paris   São Paulo
Singapore   Sydney   Tokyo   Toronto

Dedication

For every major undertaking there are those whose influence, love, and friendship go beyond the scope of the project and give the work a much deeper significance. It is to those people in our lives that we dedicate this volume.

For Nadia, and in memory of
James D. Anderson   RAS

For Suzanne, and in memory of
Doc and Lou   JTC

For Jim, for my parents,
but mostly, Nuel, for you.   SSN

ISBN 0-07-056046-3

For more information about other McGraw-Hill materials, call 1-800-2-MCGRAW in the United States. In other countries, call your nearest McGraw-Hill office.

Library of Congress Cataloging-in-Publication Data

Snakes — ecology and evolutionary biology.

Bibliography: p.
Includes index.
1. Snakes—Ecology.   2. Snakes—Evolution.   3. Reptiles
—Ecology.   4. Reptiles—Evolution.   I. Seigel, Richard A.
II. Collins, Joseph T.   III. Novak, Susan S.
QL666.06S66   1987   597.96′045   86–31212
ISBN 0-07-056046-3

Printing: 2   3   4   5   6   7   8   Year: 8   9   5   4   3   2   1   0   9

Contents

Preface   ix
Acknowledgment   x
Introduction   xi
Contributors   xiii

Section I • Evolutionary Biology and Morphology   1

Chapter 1 • Systematics   3
   Samuel B. McDowell
   Infraorder Cholophidia 5
   Infraorder Scolecophidia 13
   Infraorder Alethinophidia 16
      Classification of the Alethinophidia 17 • Superfamily
         Acrochordoidea Bonaparte (ex Acrochordina) 18 • Superfamily
         Anilioidea Stejneger 21 • Superfamily Tropidopheoidea
         Brongersma (ex Tropidophinae) 24 • Superfamily Bolyerioidea
         Hoffstetter (ex Bolyerinae) 26 • Superfamily Booidea Gray (ex
         Boidae) 27 • Superfamily Colubroidea Oppel (ex Colubrini) 30
   Future Research 43

Chapter 2 • Fossil History   51
   Jean-Claude Rage
   The Origin of Snakes 52
      Phyletic Aspects 52 • The Mode of Life of the Snake Ancestor 53
   The Adopted Phylogeny and Systematics 54
   The Tempo of Snake History 56
      The Emergence of Snakes 56 • Eocene Times: The Climax of the
         Booidea and the Emergence of the Colubroidea 59 • A
         Transitional Epoch: The Oligocene 61 • Miocene Times:
         Expansion of the Colubroidea 62 • Plio-Pleistocene 66
   An Overview of the Paleobiogeographic History of Snakes 67
   Summary 69

**Chapter 3 • Geographic Distribution: Problems in Phylogeny and
        Zoogeography**   77
John E. Cadle
Phylogenetic Relationships of Snake Lineages 78
Temporal Framework for the Radiation of Extant Snakes 82
Fossil Snakes, Phylogeny, and Neontology 83
The Composition of Extant Snake Faunas 84
    North America 84 • The Neotropical Region, Including the West
        Indies 88 • Africa, Madagascar, the Seychelles, and the
        Mascarene Islands 90 • Europe and Temperate Asia 93 • Southern
        Asia, the Indo-Australian Archipelago, and the Philippine Islands
        94 • Australian Region, Including New Guinea and the Islands of
        Melanesia 96
A Summary of Patterns in the Extant Snake Fauna 97
Future Research 99

Chapter 4 • Functional Morphology   106
David Cundall
Locomotion 107
    Kinematic Properties 109 • Structural Considerations 109 • Lateral
        Undulation 111 • Concertina and Sidewinding Locomotion
        115 • Rectilinear Motion 117 • Locomotion and the Axial
        Musculoskeletal System 117 • Other Aspects of the Form and
        Function of the Trunk 120
Feeding 121
    Musculoskeletal Structure of the Head 122 • The Strike 125 • Prey
        Transport 126 • The Evolution of Prey Transport Mechanisms in
        Snakes 131 • Venom Glands and Teeth 133
Summary 134

Section II • Techniques 141

Chapter 5 • Collecting and Life-History Techniques   143
Henry S. Fitch
Methods of Obtaining Snakes 144
    Clues for Finding Snakes 144 • Road Sampling 145 • Trapping 145
Marking Snakes 148
    Radioactive Tags and Radiotelemetry 148 • Scale Clipping
        150 • Natural Markings 151 • Tattooing, Tagging, Painting, and
        Branding 151
Measuring 152
Sex and Breeding Condition 153
Censusing 155
Feeding 156
Handling Venomous Snakes 157
Restraint and Anesthesia 160
Enclosures 160
Summary 161

Chapter 6 • Captive Maintenance 165
James B. Murphy and Jonathan A. Campbell
Quarantine and Medical Care 165
Thermoregulation 166
Shedding 167
Water 167
Light 168
Feeding 168
  Family Viperidae 168 • Family Boidae 172 • Family Colubridae
    172 • Feeding of Neonates 173 • Summary on Feeding 174
Reproduction 175
Neonates 175
Hibernation 176
Summary and Future Research 176

Section III • Life History and Ecology 183

Chapter 7 • Social Behavior 184
James C. Gillingham
The Domain of Social Behavior 184
Social Behavior in a Solitary Reptile 184
Conspecific Intersexual Behavior 185
  Precourtship Behavior 185 • Courtship Behavior 186 • Postmating
    Behavior 192 • Intersexual Combat Behavior 192
Conspecific Intrasexual Behavior 192
  Combat Bouts 193
Aggregation 197
  Seasonal Aggregations197 • Daily Aggregations 198
Recording and Analyzing Snake Social Behavior 198
Future Research 200

Chapter 8 • Reproductive Ecology 210
Richard A. Seigel and Neil B. Ford
Male Reproductive Cycles 210
  Spermatogenic Cycle 211 • Hormonal Cycles 213 • Environmental
    Control of Male Reproduction 214
Female Reproductive Cycles 215
  Temperate Zone Cycles: Seasonal Reproduction 215 • Timing of
    Vitellogenesis 216 • Tropical Zone Cycles: Seasonal and
    Aseasonal Reproduction 218 • Fat Body Cycling 221 • Endocrine
    Cycles 221
Viviparity and Parental Care 222
  Origins of Viviparity 222 • Placentation 224 • Parental Care 225
Fecundity 226
  Clutch and Litter Size 227 • Frequency of Reproduction
    227 • Relative Clutch Mass 235 • Offspring Size 236 • Body Size
    239 • Temporal Variation 240 • Geographic Variation 241
Summary and Future Research 242

Chapter 9 • Population Ecology   **253**
William S. Parker and Michael V. Plummer
Abundance 254
   Patterns of Abundance 259
Age and Growth 263
   Aging Techniques 263 • Introduction to Growth 263 • Post-natal
   Growth 263
Population Structure 268
   Sex Ratio 268 • Size and Age Structure 272 • Intergroup Comparisons
   of Size and Age 272 • Intraspecific Comparisons 277
   Maturity and Fecundity 277
   Maturity 277 • Fecundity 279
Mortality and Survivorship 279
   Identifying Sources of Mortality 279 • Seasonal and Annual
   Differences in Mortality 280 • Differential Mortality
   281 • Problems of Post-natal and Juvenile Survivorship 281 • Effect
   of Hatchling Size on Survivorship 284 • Age-Specific Survivorship
   284 • Comparative Survivorship Patterns. 285
Life Tables 285
Future Research 287
   Criteria for the Selection of Populations 287 • Experimental
   Population Biology 288
Summary 289

Chapter 10 • Foraging Ecology   **302**
Henry R. Mushinsky
Morphological Adaptations of the Feeding Apparatus 306
Behavioral Traits Associated with Feeding 307
Ontogeny, Body Size, and Energetic Constraints on Snake Foraging
   308
Optimal Foraging and Prey Size 311
Tongue Flicking and Snake Foraging Ecology 312
Foraging Ecology of Venomous Snakes 313
Foraging in Water 315
Food as a Partitioned Resource 317
Future Research 321

Chapter 11 • Communities   **335**
Laurie J. Vitt
Species Richness 337
   Latitudinal Patterns of Species Richness 337 • Elevational Patterns of
   Species Richness 339 • Habitat Patterns of Species Richness
   341 • Determinants of Snake Species Richness 345
Species Diversity 347
Niche Relationships 349
   Temperate Zone Snakes 349 • Tropical Snakes 350
Morphological Analyses 354
Life-History Diversity 357
   Temperate Zones 357 • Tropics 358
Summary and Future Research 358

Chapter 12 • Spatial Patterns and Movements   **366**
  Patrick T. Gregory, J. Malcolm Macartney, and Karl W. Larsen
  Spatial Patterns 367
    Kinds of Patterns and Their Measurement 367 • Snake Behavior and
      Communication 368 • Spatial Patterns in Snakes 368
  Movements and Home Ranges 374
    Introductory Comments 374 • Patterns of Movements in Snakes
      374 • Methods and Concepts 375 • Home Range 376 • Factors
      Influencing Movements and Home Ranges 379
  Orientation and Navigation 381
    Introductory Comments 381 • Terminology 382 • Evidence for
      Orientation and Navigation in Snakes 382 • Possible Mechanisms
      and Sensory Cues 383
  Future Research 386
  Summary 386

Chapter 13 • Activity Patterns   **396**
  J. Whitfield Gibbons and Raymond D. Semlitsch
  Seasonal Activity Patterns 397
    Seasonal Activity Peaks 397 • Activity Associated With Hibernacula
      404 • Activity Associated With Habitat Selection 406 • Sexual
      Differences in Activity Patterns 408
  Daily Activity Patterns 410
  Discussion and Conclusions 412
  Future Research 415

Chapter 14 • Temperature, Energetics, and Physiological Ecology **422**
  Harvey B. Lillywhite
  Thermal Relations of Snakes 424
    Historical Aspects 424 • Behavioral Thermoregulation
      425 • Plasticity of Thermal Preferenda 433 • Physiological
      Thermoregulation 435 • Tolerance Limits and the Distribution of
      Species 439
  Thermal Dependence of Physiology and Behavior 441
    Metabolic Rates 441 • Digestive Functions and Growth
      444 • Neuromuscular Performance 446 • Cardiorespiratory
      Function 449 • Acid-Base Regulation 453 • Water Relations
      454 • Reproduction 455
  Energetics 455
    Resting Metabolism 456 • Activity Energetics 457 • Muscle and
      Locomotory Energetics 461 • Energy Budgets 463
  Summary and Future Research 465

Chapter 15 • Status, Conservation, and Management   **478**
  C. Kenneth Dodd, Jr.
  Literature on the Status of Snakes 478
    Europe 488 • North America 488 • Asia 489 • Australia
      490 • Caribbean and Other Islands 491 • Africa and South
      America 492

Threats to Snake Populations 493
  Habitat Destruction 493 • Malicious Killing 494 • Rattlesnake
  Roundups 495 • Biocides 496
Exotic Species Introductions 497
Trade 497
Biological Considerations for Snake Conservation 499
  Extinction and Genetic Diversity 500 • Susceptibility to Decline 500
Management of Snakes 502
  Prohibition on Take 502 • Habitat Protection 503 • Captive
  Propagation 503 • Education 503
Summary 504
Index   **514**

Preface

This volume had its origins in 1979, when one of us (RAS) made the "transition" from turtle to snake ecology. It quickly became apparent that, in comparison with turtles or lizards, the literature on snakes was distressingly scattered. Especially lacking were review works such as those available for other taxa (e.g., *Turtles: Perspectives and Research*). A few texts are available for snakes, but these are either badly out of date (*Handbook of Snakes*) or limited to a single taxon (*Biology of Sea Snakes*). Snakes were of course included in the fine *Biology of the Reptilia* series, but the reviews rarely focused specifically (or even primarily) on snakes. The need for a more general and up-to-date volume that concentrated on snakes became even more apparent over the next several years, as the number and quality of publications and oral presentations on snake biology continued to increase. It occurred to us that, if we were having difficulty in locating and keeping track of the burgeoning literature on snakes, perhaps our colleagues were too. Conversations with other researchers reinforced this view, and we began to plan a text that focused mainly on snakes, rather than one that treated them as a sub-group of the lizards.

Our primary goals for this present volume were (1) to draw together, for the first time, a summary of what is known about some of the major aspects of snake ecology and evolutionary biology, (2) to summarize the primary literature on snakes, both for the experienced investigator who is overwhelmed by the mass of citations available and for the researcher just starting to work with these animals, and (3) to stimulate new and innovative research on snakes by drawing attention to those areas of snake biology badly in need of additional attention and by making reasonable speculations concerning provocative questions that remain inadequately addressed. Our primary audience is the professional researcher, but we hoped to include material that would interest other groups (resource managers, amateur naturalists) as well.

Early in our planning for this volume, it became apparent that the coverage could not be as broad as we had hoped. For one thing, the length of any text is limited by the financial realities of publishing. To adequately cover *all* aspects of snake biology would require a "Biology of the Serpentes" series, which neither we nor our publishers were willing to consider. Thus the length of each chapter had to be constrained, sometimes below that which the author would have preferred. Second, not all of the chapters we would have liked to have included were feasible, both because of space constraints and because some authors were unavailable to take on such a large commitment. Even with these constraints, we feel we have produced a text that will be of considerable value to the biological community. For the first time, the interested reader can find, under one cover, extensive material on the systematics, zoogeography, and fossil history of snakes and then turn a few pages and see how this information relates to the details of foraging ecology, reproductive biology, or conservation. To this end, we have strongly encouraged our authors to exchange information and to note where other related chapters should be consulted. In addition, we did not discourage overlap among chapters, as long as redundance was avoided. Thus different perspectives on the same subject can be found in various chapters. Clearly, these perspectives are not always in agreement. To us, this indicates a lively, vibrant field with many open questions. We hope that the availability of a text such as this will help stimulate additional research on this fascinating, but relatively neglected group of organisms.

Acknowledgment

Our primary debt is to the authors of the individual chapters, without whom this volume would not have been possible. Throughout lengthy delays and constant editorial demands for revisions, they have responded with unfailing good humor and have succeeded in producing superb contributions. We thank them all.

We would also like to acknowledge those colleagues who served as reviewers for the individual contributions. In addition to those who wished to remain anonymous, we would like to thank the following; A. F. Bennett, W. S. Brown, K. V. Kardong, J. L. Knight, H. Quinn, and S. Sweet. Many of the authors for the text also served as reviewers for other chapters, and we appreciate their assistance. Finally, the comments of the anonymous reviewers who critiqued the initial proposal for Macmillan are appreciated.

Our colleagues at the Savannah River Ecology Laboratory and at the University of Kansas provided us with much-needed support, both logistical and moral. At SREL, the support of J. W. Gibbons, head of the Division of Stress and Wildlife Ecology, and M. H. Smith, director of SREL, was invaluable. The secretarial pool, headed by M. Stapleton, gallantly typed and re-typed many of these chapters, often on short notice; special thanks go to P. Davis, S. Hemmer, J. Hinton, C. Houck, and C. Turnipseed for their assistance. J. L. Knight and L. A. Brandt served as *de facto* editorial assistants for the volume, helping with much of the xeroxing, proofreading and mailing, and we owe them a special debt of gratitude that they no doubt will frequently remind us of. At the University of Kansas, we would like to express our appreciation to F. B. Cross, Curator of Ichthyology, W. E. Duellman, Curator of Herpetology, and P. S. Humphrey, Director of the Museum of Natural History. Our editors at Macmillan—S. George, S. Greene, M. Horowitz, G. Payne, E. Penati, and J. Snyder—have been a pleasure to work with, and we deeply appreciate their support and cooperation.

Preparation of this manuscript was partially supported by Department of Energy Contract DE-AC09-76SR00819 to the University of Georgia's Institute of Ecology (SREL).

Introduction

This volume is divided into three sections: Evolutionary Biology and Morphology, Techniques, and Life History and Ecology. Although each section was designed to address different concerns, there are considerable interrelationships among and within sections.

An in-depth knowledge of the systematics, origins, and morphology of snakes is an obvious prerequisite to an understanding of their biology. In the section on Evolutionary Biology and Morphology, S. B. McDowell attempts the monumental task of synthesizing the systematics of snakes. His classification scheme is both elegant and novel and will undoubtedly stimulate considerable comment and interest. The fossil record for snakes is widely perceived as rare and difficult to study, but J. C. Rage points out that much of this belief is unfounded and summarizes what is currently known about the origins and fossil history of snakes. In his chapter on geographic distribution, J. E. Cadle points out the dependence of zoogeography on systematics and fossil history and provides a perspective on these topics slightly different from that of Rage and McDowell. Finally, D. Cundall discusses the functional morphology of snakes, with special emphasis on locomotion and feeding, the two areas of snake functional morphology that have received the most attention in the literature.

Field or laboratory studies on snake ecology and life history are clearly dependent on being able to find, collect, and maintain these animals under a variety of conditions. H. S. Fitch summarizes over 40 years' experience in working with snakes in his chapter on collecting and life-history techniques. In their chapter on laboratory maintenance, J. B. Murphy and J. A. Campbell discuss the techniques used at the Dallas Zoo to successfully maintain and breed an impressive variety of serpents.

The final section of the text focuses on ecology and behavior, areas that are receiving increasing attention by researchers. Although snakes are widely believed to be relatively asocial, J. C. Gillingham shows that the complexity of snake social behavior has been underestimated. The diverse literature on reproductive ecology is summarized by R. A. Seigel and N. B. Ford. The reproductive cycles of many Temperate Zone snakes are now well known, but much additional research is needed on tropical species, and important problems such as clutch frequency need additional attention. W. S. Parker and M. V. Plummer tackle the difficult topic of snake population ecology. In addition to summarizing data on survivorship and growth, these authors provide a number of specific suggestions for improving future studies on population ecology. The ability of snakes to subdue and swallow extremely large prey has long fascinated biologists, and H. R. Mushinsky synthesizes the massive literature on this subject. He shows that snakes are potentially quite important in the food chain and that snakes make excellent subjects for studies on foraging ecology. As shown by L. J. Vitt, our knowledge of the community ecology of snakes remains sparse. Although Vitt demonstrates some interesting patterns of diversity and species richness, he also suggests that much additional work is necessary to fully understand the community ecology of this group. The related fields of spatial patterns and movements and activity patterns are summarized by P. T. Gregory and co-workers and by J. W. Gibbons and R. D. Semlitsch. Gregory et al. show that many of the spatial patterns of snakes are related to the distribution of critical resources, especially food and hibernacula. Gibbons and Semlitsch focus on *why* snakes are active from the viewpoint that movements are not random but are under the control of natural selection. H. B. Lillywhite discusses the broad field of physiological ecology, especially in reference to reproduction, foraging, and energetics. The text closes with a discussion of the conservation and management of snakes. As C. K. Dodd, Jr., points out, the management of snakes is hampered by a lack of information on snake ecology and life history. However, it is clear that the harvest of many snakes is extremely high and that the continued survival of some species is in doubt unless some action is taken in the near future.

The message that comes from most of these chapters is that we have barely begun to scratch the surface in terms of assessing the diversity and complexity of snake biology. It is our hope that this text will help stimulate additional research on this group and that the various chapters will help encourage new researchers to use snakes as subjects when considering ecological and evolutionary questions. To this end, specific lists of open questions and recommendations for areas of future research that could profitably be pursued are provided in most of these contributions, although these lists are far from exhaustive.

We are very excited about the future of research on snakes: The unique morphological attributes of this group may provide us with some fascinating insights into both ecology and evolutionary biology. We hope that other researchers will share this excitement and that this text will help both new and established investigators pursue additional studies on this diverse group of reptiles.

Contributors

Editors:

Richard A. Seigel, Savannah River Ecology Laboratory, P.O. Drawer E, Aiken, South Carolina 29802

Joseph T. Collins, Museum of Natural History, The University of Kansas, Lawrence, Kansas 66045

Susan S. Novak, Savannah River Ecology Laboratory, P.O. Drawer E, Aiken, South Carolina 29802

Authors (listed alphabetically):

John E. Cadle, Department of Biochemistry, Louisiana State University Medical Center, 1901 Perdido Street, New Orleans, Louisiana 70112

Jonathan A. Campbell, Department of Biology, The University of Texas at Arlington, Arlington, Texas 76019

David Cundall, Department of Biology, Lehigh University, Bethlehem, Pennsylvania 18015

C. Kenneth Dodd, Jr., U.S. Fish and Wildlife Service, 412 N.E. 16th Avenue, Room 250, Gainesville, Florida 32609

Henry S. Fitch, Division of Biological Sciences, The University of Kansas, Lawrence, Kansas 66045

Neil B. Ford, School of Sciences and Mathematics, The University of Texas at Tyler, Tyler, Texas 75701

J. Whitfield Gibbons, Savannah River Ecology Laboratory, P.O. Drawer E, Aiken, South Carolina 29802

James C. Gillingham, Department of Biology, Central Michigan University, Mt. Pleasant, Michigan 48859

Patrick T. Gregory, Department of Biology, The University of Victoria, Victoria, British Columbia, Canada V8W 2Y2

Karl W. Larsen, Department of Biology, The University of Victoria, Victoria, British Columbia, Canada V8W 2Y2

Harvey B. Lillywhite, Department of Zoology, The University of Florida, Gainesville, Florida 32611

J. Malcolm Macartney, Department of Biology, The University of Victoria, Victoria, British Columbia, Canada V8W 2Y2

Samuel B. McDowell, Department of Zoology and Physiology, Rutgers University, Newark, New Jersey 07102

James B. Murphy, Department of Herpetology, Dallas Zoo, 621 East Clarendon Drive, Dallas, Texas 75203

Henry R. Mushinsky, Department of Biology, The University of South Florida, Tampa, Florida 33620

William S. Parker, Division of Science and Mathematics, Mississippi University for Women, Columbus, Mississippi 39701

Michael V. Plummer, Department of Biology, Harding University, Searcy, Arkansas 72143

Jean-Claude Rage, Laboratoire de Paléontologie des Vertébrés et de Paléontologie Humaine, Université Pierre et Marie Curie (Paris VI), 4, place Jussieu, 75230 Paris, France

Richard A. Seigel, Savannah River Ecology Laboratory, P.O. Drawer E, Aiken, South Carolina 29802

Raymond D. Semlitsch, Department of Biology, Memphis State Univerity, Memphis, Tennessee 38152

Laurie J. Vitt, Department of Biology, The University of California, Los Angeles, California 90024

Evolutionary Biology and Morphology

CHAPTER ONE

Systematics

Samuel B. McDowell

The classification of snakes in the nineteenth century was based completely on living forms but approached them entirely as specimens in museum jars. External structure was the criterion, and families were diagnosed on subtleties of body shape. Although Schlegel's *Essai sur la physionomie des serpens,* published in 1837, contains much information on visceral anatomy, the use of internal anatomy for classification did not come until Duméril's (1853) classification based on the skull and, particularly, dentition. Duméril thus accepted the idea that it might not be possible to classify a snake without removing the specimen from its jar and making certain dissections on it, the starting point in modern snake taxonomy. Cope added to the required dissections by introducing, as characters, vertebral hypapophyses, hemipenial structure, and lungs, his work culminating in a posthumously edited classification (Cope, 1900) based entirely on internal anatomy. Boulenger's classification, using osteology but not soft anatomy, was simpler and more influential. That still more information might be necessary, such as chromosome counts and analyses of serum and tissue proteins, is a twentieth century extension of Duméril's acceptance of the necessity of processing a specimen in the laboratory before valid systematic conclusions could be reached.

It is generally accepted today that a classification, to be natural, should express the evolutionary history of the classified group, and one often forgets that no such idea motivated Schlegel or Duméril. A major difference between modern classifications and those of the nineteenth century is the implicit assumption today that there was a real historical sequence of species giving rise to other species in a definite place, at a definite time, and in response to definable ecological factors. This precise historical sequence of events is very difficult to determine (some would say impossible), but it should leave clues that are accessible to a variety of different disciplines.

Among these clues is a fossil record discussed elsewhere in this volume by Rage. Rage and I do not agree on all points in the interpretation of the fossil record of snakes, because it is an extremely difficult record to interpret. It is based almost entirely on vertebrae and, to judge from living species of snakes that seem closely related on such grounds as soft anatomy and tertiary structure of serum proteins, considerable evolution may produce no detectable change in vertebrae. Closely related forms, however, may sometimes have quite different vertebrae, and differences within the column of a single individual may exceed those between corresponding vertebrae of different genera. In spite of difficulties in interpretation, and the resulting differences of opinion, the importance of the fossil record in reconstructing the history of the diversification of snakes—and in the classification expressing this history—cannot be denied. Yet no use was made of the fossil record in snake classification until the twentieth century.

Hoffstetter attempted a general classification of snakes consistent with the fossil record (see Hoffstetter, 1955, 1962). Hoffstetter's classification was necessarily "horizontal," indicating general levels of specialization, and could be considered phenetic. It divided living snakes into Scolecophidia (typhlopids and leptotyphlopids), Henophidia (boidlike snakes) and Caenophidia (= Colubroidea). It has been followed, with minor modifications, by Romer (1956) and Underwood (1967). Rieppel (1979a) presented a similar horizontal classification but termed it "cladistic."

The most recent complete classification of snakes (Dowling and Duellman, 1978) is somewhat similar to Hoffstetter's but considers the Typhlopoidea (= Scolecophidia) to be derived from boidlike snakes through the uropeltines and places the Typhlopoidea (including Uropeltidae) after the Booidea (= Henophidia) and before the Colubroidea (= Hoffstetter's Caenophidia). A point of difference between various authors is the proper placement of *Acrochordus*. Hoffstetter and Gayrard (1965) removed *Acrochordus* from the Colubridae and placed it in the Henophidia; they were followed in this by Underwood (1967). Dowling and Duellman (1978), on the other hand, placed *Acrochordus* within the subfamily Natricinae of the Colubridae; later, Dowling et al. (1983) transferred *Acrochordus* to the Homalopsinae within the Colubridae. Obviously, there is no consensus yet on the higher classification of snakes.

Part of the difficulty in reaching such a consensus results from conflicting or almost unintelligible evidence, or from a lack of critical evidence. But there is also an ideological disagreement between three schools of taxonomy as to what a classification attempts and what sort of evidence leads to rejecting a particular classification. The pure *pheneticist* considers classification to have one purpose: expressing degrees of resemblance between the objects classified; underlying causes of resemblance are irrelevant, and a classification is rejected only when it is shown that two forms placed apart are more similar to each other (by the measurements chosen) than to the forms with which they have been placed in close association. The pure *cladist* regards classification as an expression of pairings, by shared derived characters, in hierarchical order; the "purest" cladists regard any historical narrative or scenario accounting for this hierarchical pairing as irrelevant and reject a classification only if a more parsimonious pattern of dichotomous branching can be found to account for the associations of derived characters. Most taxonomists probably think of themselves as members of a third school, which may be called the *biological*, whose purpose of classification is to express the true historical scenario of what happened and reject a classification if evidence from any source, including historical geology, makes the scenario implied by the classification seem improbable.

In practice, a taxonomist is not always free to chose his school; the method is thrust upon him by the nature of the data. Data on "immunological distance" are necessarily phenetic; they tell (approximately) how many antigenic sites on a molecule differ between taxa, but not which particular sites are similar and which are different, the information necessary for cladistic analysis. If the data were DNA nucleotide sequence, only a cladistic analysis would be possible. Nearly all the data available to me are morphological, but I hesitate to attempt a cladistic analysis because of uncertainty as to how observations are to be coded into the abstract "character states." Just how an observation of form is symbolized in character states has a great effect on the cladogram that results. Too much present theory of cladistics underestimates the problems of determining whether two organisms share the same character and of determining how many characters are really involved in a difference of structural patterns. For this reason I cannot regard myself as a cladist, and because I have attempted to include recent, necessarily phenetic, immunological comparisons, a purely cladistic classification is impossible. The following attempts to express a general scenario of what seems to have happened, but to avoid implying events for which there is no evidence at present. In particular, I have tried to avoid implying that modern snakes that are not colubroid are, therefore, part of the adaptive radiation of boa- and pythonlike snakes; such may indeed turn out to be true, but at the moment there is no evidence from anatomy, paleontology, or molecular systematics for this traditional view. I have tried to maintain monophyletic suprageneric groups but have not attempted a critique of genera (see Table 1–1). The authorship of names for the higher categories used here is given by Smith et al. (1977).

INFRAORDER CHOLOPHIDIA

This group is here expanded beyond its original contents (Nopcsa, 1923), the Simoliopheidae, to include all fossil snakes that do not appear to be referable to either the Scolecophidia or the Alethinophidia, but represent earlier and more primitive adaptive radiations. More precision is now impossible because the fossils are imperfectly preserved and it is not possible to make full comparisons, either with one another or with living snakes.

Table 1–1. A Proposed Classification
of Snakes

Infraorder Cholophidia
    Family Simoliopheidae
    Family Madtsoiidae
    Family Dinilysiidae
Infraorder Scolecophidia
    Family Anomalepididae
    Family Typhlopidae
    Family Leptotyphlopidae
Infraorder Alethinophidia
    Superfamily Acrochordoidea
        Family Nigeropheidae
        Family Palaeopheidae
        Family Anomalopheidae
        Family Acrochordidae
    Superfamily Anilioidea
        Family Loxocemidae
        Family Xenopeltidae
        Family Aniliidae
        Family Uropeltidae
    Superfamily Tropidopheoidea
        Family Tropidopheidae
    Superfamily Bolyerioidea
        Family Bolyeriidae
    Superfamily Booidea
        Family Pythonidae
        Family Boidae
    Superfamily Colubroidea
      Series Proteroglypha
        Family Atractaspididae
        Family Elapidae
      Series Opisthoglypha
        Family Colubridae
        Family Viperidae

Family Simoliopheidae. Included are *Lapparentophis* Hoffstetter (1959a) vertebrae, freshwater Neocomian or Albian Cretaceous of Algeria; *Pachyophis* Nopcsa (including *Mesophis* Bolkay) articulated vertebral column (fragmentary mandible and maxilla), marine Cenomanian Cretaceous of Jugoslavia; *Pachyrhachis* Haas (1979, 1980a) vertebral column with considerable portions of the skull, marine lower Cenomanian near Jerusalem; *Simoliophis* Sauvage ribs and vertebrae, marine Cenomanian of Europe and Egypt.

Excluded is *Estesius* Wallach (1984), a substitute name for the lower Cenomanian reptile described by Haas (1980a) as *Ophiomorphus* (preoccupied), with nearly complete trunk, hind limb and pelvis and a skull either ventral to or within the anterior rib cage. The continuity of the vertebral column is interrupted anteriorly by the edge of the block, and it is not certain whether this skull is that of the animal represented by the vertebrae or that of prey swallowed head-first. This skull suggests mosasaurs and *Varanus* rather than snakes; there is a temporal arch, the teeth are swollen basally, and the parietal lacks a large descending process. Although "vestigial" by lizard standards (it is small and without digits), the leg of *Estesius* is far better developed than in any known snake and shows distinct femur, tibia, and fibula, as well as a transverse distal bone representing tarsals. The pelvis has pubis, ischium, and ilium (this last expanded dorsally to suggest sacral attachment) and is external to the ribs. No snake is known to have more than a single leg bone (the femur), and pelvic vestiges are internal to the ribs. What is now visible in *Estesius* indicates that it cannot be included in the Simoliopheidae and perhaps should not even be referred to the Serpentes.

Simoliophis, Pachyophis, and *Pachyrhachis* seem to have been an aberrant early line of snakes from marine deposits and specially characterized by pachyostosis of middle-trunk vertebrae. They are linked to the remainder of the Serpentes through the earlier non-marine *Lapparentophis,* which did not show evidence of this pachyostosis but was clearly related by details of the zygosphene and zygapophyses to *Simoliophis* (Hoffstetter, 1959b).

In *Pachyrhachis* some of the upper teeth were furrowed along the anterior face of their (recurved, acute, and quite snakelike) crown. It has been assumed that furrowed teeth are an advanced condition associated with a novel adaptation within the Colubroidea, the venom apparatus. Grooved teeth in *Pachyrhachis* does not disprove this assumption but raises a second possibility not considered previously; grooved teeth (and associated venom-secreting oral glands?) are primitive for snakes, and their absence is secondary reduction among apparently primitive living snakes. Haas (1979) interpreted the maxilla as bearing fewer than 10 teeth, with its *posterior* end meeting the prefrontal (i.e., the maxilla was confined to the muzzle, as in varanoids, not extended back beneath the orbit as in living snakes); the anterior end is not sutured to the premaxilla, which bears two pairs of teeth. The lower jaw shows the snakelike loose attachment, rather than symphysis, of the dentaries. As in most living snakes (and varanoids), an intramandibular hinge separates splenial plus dentary from angular plus compound bone. The high coronoid process is formed entirely by the coronoid bone, as in lizards and Scolecophidia. The quadrate and ear is alethinophidian-like (Haas, 1980b, *contra* Haas, 1979), a slender stapedial shaft meeting a facet on the upper end of the quadrate and the quadrate suspended entirely from a *Python*-like tabular ("squamosal" of Haas).

Family Madtsoiidae. (Madtsoiinae of Boidae, Hoffstetter, 1961). *Madtsoia* Simpson (1933), Upper Cretaceous of Africa and Madagascar, upper Paleocene–lower Eocene of Brazil and Argentina; *Gigantophis* Andrews, upper Eocene of Africa; *Wonambi* Meredith Smith (1976), Pleistocene (70,000 to 37,000 yr old) of southern Australia. Although previously referred to the Boidae, these snakes are here referred to the Cholophidia because what is known of them (vertebrae) suggests that they were less like living snakes than was *Dinilysia,* and the skull of *Dinilysia* indicates it was more primitive than any living group of snakes. All three genera represent giant snakes with vertebrae as large as those of very large specimens of *Python* and *Eunectes*.

The vertebrae resemble those of *Lapparentophis* (Hoffstetter 1959a) in most respects, but the zygosphene is dorsal to the zygapophysial articulations and its facets do not converge anteriorly; they have paracotylar foramina (present in many modern snakes but not in boids) and also large parazygantral foramina ventrolateral to the zygantrum (Hoffstetter, 1961), diagnostic of the Madtsoiidae, at least in large size and constancy throughout the column. As in Simoliopheidae, but not in *Dinilysia* or modern snakes (except immediately behind the skull), the diapophysis of Madtsoiidae projects at least as far laterally as the prezygapophysis directly above it, and the latter lacks any accessory process extending beyond its articular surface. Thus no portion of the vertebra directly overhangs the rib articulation. Just behind the skull, where the longissimus is represented by a continuous longissimus capitis, rather than separate costal levators and isolated bellies, modern snakes may show the same lateral projection of the diapophysis that Madtsoiidae have throughout the column. This suggests that in Madtsoiidae (and Simoliopheidae) the longissimus column of musculature was essentially uninterrupted, as in lizards, and a characteristic of all living snakes had not been achieved.

The dentary referred to *Madtsoia* (Hoffstetter, 1959b) is unusually deep and has three mental foramina, not the single foramen (rarely, as in *Acrochordus*, two foramina) of extant snakes.

Family Dinilysiidae. (Romer, 1956). For the Upper Cretaceous *Dinilysia* of southern Argentina, known from the skull (Estes et al., 1970; Frazzetta, 1970) and the vertebrae and ribs (Hecht, 1982); provisionally, *Coniophis* (Upper Cretaceous to Eocene of North America), known only from vertebrae, is included here. In the vertebrae, Dinilysiidae differ from the previous families and resemble modern snakes in that (1) the prezygapophysis overhangs the rib articulation; (2) the diapophysial facet for the rib is more clearly divided into an hemispherical dorsal portion and a ventral saddle-shaped portion; (3) the zygapophysial articular plane is moved ventrally to about the level of the floor (rather than the roof) of the neural canal; and (4) there is a small prezygapophysial process. A feature noted by Hecht (1982) as uniting *Coniophis* and *Dinilysia* and setting them apart from most other snakes [shown for the anterior, but not the posterior, vertebrae of the uropeltid *Rhinophis* by Hoffstetter and Gasc (1969)] is the transverse posterior edge of the neural arch, without a triangular median emargination.

The skull of *Dinilysia* leads me (McDowell, 1974) to place this genus in the Cholophidia because it appears to combine the lizardlike features of the Scolecophidia and Alethinophidia without showing the characteristic specializations of either major group of living snakes. This is essentially the same phylogenetic assessment given by Hecht (1982). Rieppel (1979a) places *Dinilysia* in a "plesion" of its own, diverging from a common ancestry with the Alethinophidia after the divergence of the Scolecophidia; Rage (1977a), however, derives *Din-ilysia* from a common ancestry with Xenopeltidae and Boidea after divergence of the Aniliidae, thus placing it within the Alethinophidia.

The most peculiar features of *Dinilysia*, as described by Estes et al. (1970), concern the paroccipital process, the suspension of the quadrate, and the fenestra ovalis. The latter is very large, containing a similarly large and closely fitting footplate of the stapes, and is not surrounded by a bony rim or chamber to enclose an external extension of the perilymphatic sac lying on the external surface of the stapes. All living snakes have this extension of the perilymphatic sac over the outer face of the stapes and, except for Acrochordidae, have at least a partial bony rim, the crista circumfenestralis, around this extension. The paroccipital process of *Dinilysia* is unlike the small posterolateral projection so named in living snakes; instead, it is a large, horizontal shelf on the side of the braincase, extending from the posterolateral corner of the skull to above the anterior rim of the fenestra ovalis like an eave overhanging the fenestra; the proötic forms the anterior edge of this eave, and the tabular (supratemporal of Estes et al., 1970) fits over the lateral edge of the exoccipital portion of the process, forming the surface to which the upper end of the quadrate is attached. Frazzetta (1970) restored the entire dorsal edge of the quadrate as applied against this surface of the tabular but, as preserved (Estes et al., 1970), the posterior end of the dorsal edge of the quadrate projects behind the tabular; this tablike projection seems very similar to the process of the quadrate receiving the cartilaginous processus internus of the stapes in *Acrochordus, Anomalepis* (see Haas, 1968), and *Lio-typhlops* (see Haas, 1964). The tabular of *Dinilysia* has, in addition to the lobe along the lateral edge of the paroccipital process suspending the quadrate, a dorsomedial lobe on the dorsal surface of the paroccipital process that overlaps a process from the posterolateral corner of the parietal. This tabular-parietal arch is similar to the arch of lizards that forms the dorsal rim of the posterior temporal fenestra and the posterior rim of the superior temporal fenestra; but in *Dinilysia* this arch is pressed against the dorsal surface of the paroccipital process, oc-cluding the posterior temporal fenestra. The tabular of *Dinilysia* is thus forked anteriorly into a rounded lateral lobe (along the lateral edge of the paroccipital process) and a pointed dorsomedial lobe (sutured to the parietal).

This same bilobate anterior border of the tabular is seen in a number of living Alethinophidia (e.g., *Cylindrophis, Loxocemus,* and such colubrids as *Boaedon* (Figure 1–1); the dorsomedial lobe extends to the parietal, as in *Dinilysia,* but the lateral lobe extends onto the dorsal part of the crista circumfenestralis. It appears that the dorsal part of the crista circumfenestralis of living snakes is the direct homolog of the more anterior part of the shelflike paroccipital process of *Dinilysia*; the thick eave overhanging the fenestra ovalis in *Dinilysia* has been thinned to a shell-like lamina and crimped down over the external perilymphatic sac; what is called the "paroccipital process" in living snakes is only the pos-terolateral corner of the complete paroccipital process (as the term is used for lizards and *Dinilysia*) and most or all of the paroccipital process of living snakes

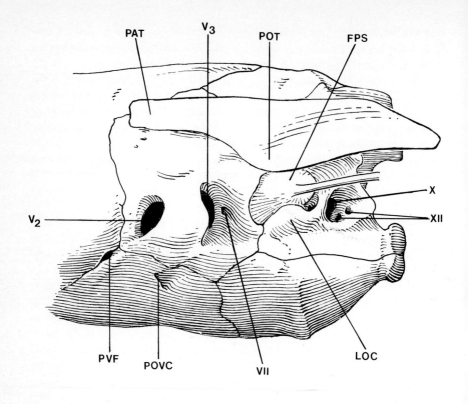

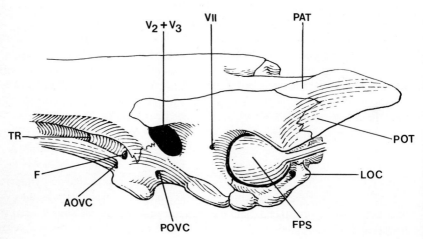

is converted to the crista circumfenestralis, a bony housing around a peculiarity of (at least, living) snakes, the perilymphatic sac external to the stapes.

In *Acrochordus* (see McDowell, 1979) no such bony housing exists; this may be primitive but may be one of many persistently embryonic features of the ear of *Acrochordus*. In *Acrochordus*, the external projection of the perilymphatic sac is present, but with a wall of flexible tissue only, and extends forward to reach the level of the facial nerve foramen; the hyomandibular ramus of the facial is embedded in the lateral connective tissue wall of the perilymphatic sac. Whether primitive or paedomorphic, the ear of *Acrochordus* probably gives an estimate of the soft structures in this region of *Dinilysia*.

Although the dorsal portion of the crista circumfenestralis appears homologous to the anterior portion of the paroccipital process of *Dinilysia* (and *Acrochordus*) in both Alethinophidia and Scolecophidia, these two groups differ in the details of the position of the crista circumfenestralis (McDowell, 1979; Rieppel, 1979b). This observation suggests that conversion of the paroccipital process into a bony housing for the perilymphatic sac took place independently in the two groups but took much the same general course because it was built around a feature common to both alethinophidian and scolecophidian snakes, an extension of the perilymphatic sac external to the stapes. In Scolecophidia, the bony housing is bent down lateral to the hyomandibular ramus of the facial nerve, which is thus enclosed within the "juxtastapedial fossa" for the perilymphatic extension, emerging from this chamber with the shaft of the stapes. In Alethinophidia, the bony housing separates the perilymphatic sac (within the juxtastapedial fossa) from hyomandibular VII, which is entirely outside the chamber. As noted by Rieppel (1979b), the scolecophidian *Liotyphlops* as described by Haas (1964) seems to be an exception to this and in need of restudy; Haas described the lateral wall of the external perilymphatic chamber as fenestrated, and the homolog of the paroccipital process possibly does not descend far enough to take either an "alethinophidian" or a "scolecophidian" position.

Figure 1–1. Ear region of *Boaedon virgatus* (AMNH 50638) (above) and *Dinilysia patagonica* (below), based on Estes et al. (1970). Not to same scale. AOVC, Anterior orifice of "Vidian canal" (for emergence of *VII pal.*); F, "unknown foramen" of Estes et al. (1970), here interpreted as for the exit of V_4 *levator bulbi* from the cavum epeptericum; FPS, footplate of stapes; LOC, longissimus crest; PAT, parietotabular arch process of tabular bone; POT, paroccipital process lobe of tabular bone; POVC, posterior orifice of Vidian canal (for entry of *VII pal.*); PVF, pituitary vein foramen (giving entry into the cavum epeptericum of V_4 *levator bulbi* in *Boaedon*); TR, foramen for trabecular cartilage; V_2, foramen for maxillary ramus of trigeminal nerve; V_3, foramen for mandibular ramus of trigeminal nerve; $V_2 + V_3$, undivided foramen for maxillary and mandibular nerves of *Dinilysia*, probably also including PVF of *Boaedon;* VII, foramen for facial nerve; X, foramen for vagus nerve; XII, foramina for hypoglossal nerve.

In the preceding discussion, *Dinilysia* has been considered primitive, following the assessment of Estes et al. (1970). However, *Pachyrhachis* (see Simoliopheidae, described previously) is a considerably older form, and Haas (1980a) found it to be more like certain Alethinophidia (boids, most colubrids) in the tabular-quadrate region. The quadrate of *Dinilysia* is much shorter than that of *Pachyrhachis* and most Alethinophidia and is quite peculiar in its broad and simply convex head for the mandible; but in its major features, such as an inverted L-shape with the stapedial facet extended directly posterior to the cranial attachment, it is most similar to that of anomalepidid scolecophidians. It is thus possible (but not probable) that *Dinilysia* stands near the divergence, but within the Scolecophidia.

As described by Estes et al. (1970) and Frazzetta (1970), *Dinilysia* shows several features that are more lizardlike than the corresponding structure in either Scolecophidia or Alethinophidia:

1. The presence of a jugal forming the lower end of the postorbital arch (not certain, because both ectopterygoids are damaged anteriorly and the "jugal" on the dorsal side of each maxilla might be a fragment of the ectopterygoid).

2. The palatine and pterygoid bear teeth that are tiny compared with the maxillary teeth. In living snakes, the palate is either toothless (scolecophidians, *Calabaria,* uropeltines, etc.) or has large teeth similar to those of the maxilla except that the dental lamina of replacement teeth lies lateral, rather than medial, to the functioning row. Many lizards have a "shagreen" of tiny teeth, without any obvious replacement series, on the pterygoid and (less often) on the palatine. The palatal dentition of *Dinilysia,* mainly on the pterygoid, is much more like that of lizards than that of any living snake.

3. The presence of two lachrymal foramina, as in the varanoid lizards *Varanus* and *Lanthanotus*. Estes et al. (1970) used the terminology of Bahl's description of *Varanus* in calling these foramina "lacrimal foramen" (for the smaller, more lateral foramen between the prefrontal and the palatine) and "orbitonasal canal" (for the larger, more medial foramen between the prefrontal and the palatine). In scolecophidians there is no lachrymal foramen because the lachrymal duct has become free of the prefrontal and the palatine. In Alethinophidia there is one lachrymal foramen, apparently a homolog of the "orbitonasal canal" of Estes et al (1970). However, there is frequently (usually, in Colubroidea) a second foramen in the prefrontal, for a vein from the nasal capsule, dorsal to, dorsolateral to, or just within the orbital orifice of the canal containing the lachrymal duct; it is thus uncertain whether *Dinilysia* had two lachrymal ducts, as in varanoid lizards, or a single duct and a separate foramen for the vein, as in most colubroids.

In the firm parietal-sphenoid suture and in the frontal-sphenoid suture *anterior* to the optic nerve, *Dinilysia* shares departures from the lizard condition with Alethinophidia but not with Scolecophidia. Otherwise, the alethinophidian and scolecophidian features of *Dinilysia* seem to consist of the lack of specialized features seen in one group and not the other. In this category may be listed the following scolecophidian features: (1) failure of the proötic to form a vertical bar between the maxillary (V_2) and mandibular (V_3) nerves; (2) a coronoid process (of unknown height and shape, because of breakage) formed by the coronoid bone alone without a supporting lamina of the surangular; and (3) a lack of interolfactory pillars of the frontal or any other obvious modifications for kinesis of the snout anterior to the frontals. It should be noted that *Acrochordus* shows the alethinophidian condition in all these features, making it unlikely that the Acrochordoidea represent a pre-*Dinilysia* evolutionary divergence. The following alethinophidian features of *Dinilysia* appear to be merely the absence of scolecophidian specializations: (1) the presence of a lateral wing of the sphenoid, bearing the basipterygoid process and with canals for the palatine nerve and carotid artery well within its border; and (2) the presence of a distinct paroccipital process supporting a large tabular bone.

INFRAORDER SCOLECOPHIDIA

In the following diagnosis, based on McDowell (1967a, 1974), characters that appear primitive, making derivation from Alethinophidia unlikely, are followed by (p); characters that seem to be specializations ruling out Scolecophidia as likely ancestors of the Alethinophidia are followed by (s).

Coronoid bone rising high above prearticular and surangular as a coronoid process of the mandible (p); mouth small, its angle below or anterior to the eye, the mandible (excluding retroarticular process) less than half as long as the skull (s); basipterygoid process (and portion of sphenoid that would support it) absent, so that the canal for the palatine nerve is at the extreme lateral edge of the sphenoid (s); no frontal pillars between olfactory nerves (p); all branches of the trigeminal nerve (including V_4 rami) emerging through a simple proötic notch completed as a foramen by the parietal (p); prefrontal without lachrymal foramen (s); quadrate with simple attachment to side of the otic capsule, without differentiated paroccipital process or participation of the (usually absent) tabular (s); extensive to complete bony enclosure of the extracapsular perilymph by a crista circumfenestralis (true also of most Alethinophidia), but this bony enclosure (except in *Liotyphlops*) enclosing the hyomandibular ramus of VII (s).

My interpretation is that the Scolecophidia and Alethinophidia diverged from a *Dinilysia*-like ancestor (see previous discussion), and a basal split between Scolecophidia and Alethinophidia is expressed in most, but not all, classifications. Dowling (1975; also Dowling and Duellman, 1978) argues for a close relationship between Scolecophidia and Uropeltidae (= my Uropeltinae). Without denying that (his) Uropeltidae are related to *Cylindrophis* (an aniliid in his classification), he places the scolecophidian families and (his) Uropeltidae in a superfamily Typhlopoidea, between the Booidea and Colubroidea, implying that the Scolecophidia are derived from a boa- or pythonlike ancestor through aniliid-like intermediates and that the seemingly primitive features of the Scolecophidia indicate degenerative evolution. This seems unlikely to me but cannot be completely ruled out. Looking through the characters marked (p) in the diagnosis, one feature is common to all of them: a structure that is bony in Alethinophidia is unrepresented in Scolecophidia (e.g., the surangular lamina supporting the coronoid). Possibly, the apparent primitive characters of the Scolecophidia result from secondary loss of bone.

In some features of the skull and head muscles, it is not the anilioids but *Acrochordus* that makes the nearest approach, among Alethinophidia, to the Anomalepididae (seemingly the most primitive family of Scolecophidia). Haas (1930) has shown that the "retractor maxillae" muscle of *Typhlops* has the same position, relative to the branches of the trigeminal nerve, as the levator pterygoideus of lizards and most snakes, but with its insertion shifted to the rear of the maxilla, rather than on the pterygoid, and its belly greatly enlarged and extending onto the dorsal aspect of the skull. After studying *Liotyphlops* (Haas, 1964) and *Anomalepis* (Haas, 1968), he retracted this interpretation (Haas, 1973) because anomalepidids have a large retractor maxillae like that of *Typhlops* but inserting on the ectopterygoid bone adjacent to the pterygoideus attachment and, in addition, have a normal levator pterygoideus. Haas (1973) identified the retractor maxillae of anomalepidids as part of the pterygoideus, shifted from the lower jaw to the dorsal part of the braincase. It is very hard to imagine an intermediate condition for such a radical shift of a muscle.

However, *Acrochordus* (Haas, 1931) has *two* levator pterygoideus muscles: (1) a deeper muscle, similar to the single levator of other Alethinophidia and to the levator pterygoideus of anomalepidids; and (2) a more superficial levator inserting on the ectopterygoid. Enlargement of this superficial levator pterygoideus would produce the retractor maxillae of anomalepidids, and transfer of its insertion anteriorly onto the maxilla (accompanying the loss of the ectopterygoid) would yield the retractor maxillae of typhlopids. Typhlopidae (and Leptotyphlopidae) are peculiar in lacking the usual (deep) levator inserting on the pterygoid. This resemblance between *Acrochordus* and Anomalepididae, two separate levators, might be a primitive feature of snakes that has been lost in other living forms.

Haas (1964, 1968) showed that the bone suspending the maxilla in Anomalepididae is the prefrontal, not a palpebral, borne on a long pedicle of the frontal. A prefrontal pedicle of the frontal is diagnostic of *Acrochordus* among Alethinophidia and of Anomalepididae among Scolecophidia.

The simplest interpretation is that Scolecophidia and Alethinophidia (including *Acrochordus*) have diverged from some common ancestor, probably not unlike *Dinilysia*.

Osteological study by List (1966) revealed important skull differences between the Anomalepididae and the Typhlopidae (with which the anomalepidids had been classified) and showed that the Leptotyphlopidae share a number of specializations with the Typhlopidae. Although List clearly defined these families by skull structure, he found no identifying vertebral characters; and so the fossil record (back to the Belgian early Eocene) of the Scolecophidia cannot be assigned more definitely than to an infraorder.

The following classification is based on skull structure (see Haas, 1964, 1968; List, 1966; McDowell, 1967b, Rieppel, 1979a, b), head muscles (see previous discussion and Haas, 1973, for a review), and the hyobranchium [following McDowell (1972); for a different interpretation, that the hyobranchium of Anomalepididae is largely non-homologous with that of Typhlopidae and Leptotyphlopidae, see Langebartel (1968)]. This arrangement is consistent with visceral anatomy [see Brongersma (1959) for lungs and Robb and Smith (1966) for oviducts] and suggests an evolutionary sequence of (1) a primitive group, the Anomalepididae, that gives rise to a typhlopid-leptotyphlopid stem form; and (2) divergence from this stem of Typhlopidae (losing mandibular teeth) and Leptotyphlopidae (losing maxillary mobility and teeth). One aspect of the anatomy does not support this sequence; many Leptotyphlopidae have the most complete vestiges of a pelvic girdle and femur among Scolecophidia, in spite of their advanced position in the phylogeny based on head structure, and the Anomalepididae (the basal group, on the basis of head structure) have the pelvic girdle absent or represented only by a pair of cartilaginous bars (List, 1966). This conflict between the evidence of the head and the evidence of the pelvis cannot be completely resolved at present.

Family Anomalepididae (Taylor, as Anomalepidae). Postorbital ("jugal") present, isolated; an ectopterygoid extending from pterygoid to maxilla; prefrontal a crescent of bone posterolateral to the (exposed) lateral nasal gland, its posterior end articulated to a pedicle of the frontal, its anterior end articulated to the mobile maxilla; maxilla and dentary toothed; retroarticular process long; hyobranchium M-shaped between the jaws; deep levator pterygoideus present, inserted on pterygoid; superficial levator pterygoideus present, greatly enlarged as a retractor maxillae, inserted on the ectopterygoid; a tracheal lung; usually (exception, *Helminthophis frontalis:* Robb and Smith, 1966) with both left and right oviducts; first supralabial scute wedged between rostral and nasal. *Anomalepis, Liotyphlops, Helminthophis, Typhlophis.* Continental Central and South America.

The next two families have no postorbital and no free ectopterygoid (maxilla free of pterygoid); prefrontal a broad lamina firmly built into the lateral wall of the snout (thus concealing the lateral nasal gland) without an articular facet for maxilla; frontal without a pedicle for prefrontal; hyobranchium Y-shaped, well posterior to head; deep levator pterygoideus absent; left oviduct absent in female (but male *Ramphotyphlops* have paired and symmetric retrocloacal sacs that may be homologs of female oviducts); first supralabial reduced and overlapped by nasal or absent.

Family Typhlopidae. Superficial levator pterygoideus present as a retractor maxillae inserted on the toothed and mobile maxilla; dentary toothless; retroarticular process long; a tracheal lung; supralabials separating lateral head scutes from edge of lip. *Typhlops, Ramphotyphlops* (= *Typhlina*, suppressed). Almost world-wide in tropics and subtropics, including islands; barely into Europe and not north of Mexico [much of the distribution on scattered Pacific islands represents records of *Ramphotyphlops braminus,* an all-female (McDowell, 1974) species commensal with man and easily introduced accidentally].

Family Leptotyphlopidae. No superficial levator pterygoideus (retractor maxil-lae), maxilla toothless and immobile; dentary toothed; retroarticular process very short; no tracheal lung; supralabial series incomplete or absent, lateral head scutes reaching edge of lip. *Leptotyphlops, Rhinoleptus.* Continental North and South America, West Indies, Africa (not Madagascar), Arabia, and Pakistan.

INFRAORDER ALETHINOPHIDIA

Each of the following characters distinguishes this infraorder from the Scole-cophidia, but each requires comment:

1. Coronoid bone, if present, equaled or exceeded in dorsal extent by a surangular lamina of the compound bone. The coronoid may form part of the apex of the coronoid process, supported by an equally high surangular lamina; the surangular lamina may form the entire coronoid process; in most colubroids, there is neither a coronoid process nor coronoid bone.

2. Mouth large to very large, with the mandible (excluding the retroarticular process) much more than half as long as the skull.

3. Sphenoid with a lateral wing, (i.e., the part of the sphenoid bearing the basipterygoid process in lizards and *Dinilysia*), sometimes with a basipterygoid process. The palatine ramus of VII and the carotid lie medial to this lateral wing, usually in a bony canal representing the usual reptilian canal for palatine VII through the base of the basipterygoid process. This lateral wing of the sphenoid is, at least, the base of the reptilian basipterygoid process.

4. Frontals forming a pillar between the olfactory nerves. This interolfactory pillar may articulate with the nasals and the cartilaginous nasal capsule, per-mitting some lateral snout movement, but in most alethinophidians, the snout-frontal joint is displaced ventral to the interolfactory pillar, permitting vertical flexion of the snout; the pillar is retained when the snout becomes secondarily rigid (e.g., *Xenocalamus*) and is strong in *Acrochordus,* with movable frontal bones. The interolfactory pillar is absent in lizards, *Dinilysia,* and Scolecophidia and is a diagnostic specialization of the Alethinophidia.

5. An ossification across the trigeminal notch (or foramen) in the proötic, fused to the proötic lateral to the trigeminal ganglion. Usually, this "alethino-phidian bridge" divides the trigeminal aperture into separate V_2 and V_3 foramina. Brock (1929) termed it "Gaupp's bone." Rieppel (1976) called it the "lateros-phenoid," elsewhere (e.g., Camp, 1942) used for an ossification of the orbital

cartilage in lizards. The alethinophidian bridge may or may not be preformed in cartilage (Haluska and Alberch, 1983) and shows some variation and asymmetry in extent, but its presence is diagnostic and constant.

6. Prefrontal with a lachrymal notch or foramen. See the previous discussion of *Dinilysia*.

7. Quadrate suspended from the tabular (usual), from the tabular and a distinct paroccipital process, or only from a distinct paroccipital process. This appears to be primitive but, as noted previously, the paroccipital process may form part of the crista circumfenestralis in both Scolecophidia and Alethinophidia.

8. Any closure of the bony chamber around the extrastapedial perilymph is medial to the hyomandibular ramus of VII, and so that nerve is not enclosed in the "juxtastapedial" chamber. This difference in detail from the Scolecophidia suggests that a juxtastapedial chamber has arisen independently in the two infraorders.

Classification of the Alethinophidia

The majority of living Alethinophidia belong to a well-characterized superfamily Colubroidea showing distinctive rib ends, a unique cranioquadrate muscle, and a general loss of some obviously primitive features seen in many alethinophidians that are not Colubroidea. Because the non-colubroid Alethinophidia form a small (but highly varied) group, it has been convenient to regard them as a distinct group (the Henophidia) characterized by an absence of the distinctive features of the Colubroidea. This conceals very considerable differences among the lineages of "henophidians" and complicates the determination of "caenophidian" ancestry.

The assumption that Boidae are the most primitive alethinophidians is suspect, and no such assumption is made here; rather, *Dinilysia* is taken as primitive when evaluating osteological differences. By this criterion, a restricted superfamily Booidea is a rather specialized group, in spite of certain undeniably primitive features (e.g., pelvic limb and girdle vestiges). In lacking some of these specializations, certain other henophidians (such as *Acrochordus*) resemble Colubroidea, and some authors interpret these non-booid henophidians as showing a special affinity with Colubroidea.

The classification proposed here is essentially that of McDowell (1975) and Smith et al. (1977), but with the Acrochordoidea provisionally expanded to include several thoroughly aquatic fossil snakes.

Particularly in the classification of Colubroidea, the components of the adductor mandibulae externus provide important taxonomic characters (Haas, 1973, and references therein; Rieppel, 1980). The homologies with lizard muscles used previously seem incorrect (McDowell, 1986), and corrected homologies are:

1. The *levator anguli oris* of lizards is represented in snakes by *both* the "levator anguli oris" and "superficialis" of authors (the "1a" and "1b" of

Haas's 1973 review). All snakes have a levator anguli oris, which may be a single sheet of fibers or split into two or three sections.

2. The lizard *adductor externus superficialis* is represented in snakes by the "adductor externus profundus" (Haas's "3"), arising on the quadrate and inserting on the outer side of the mandible.

3. The lizard *adductor externus medialis* is represented in snakes by the muscle with the same name (Haas's "2").

4. The lizard *adductor externus profundus* is absent in snakes. The facial artery in snakes lies close to V_3 and V_2, with no muscle fibers between the artery and the nerves, and the posterior temporal fenestra has been closed by the appression of its roof (the tabular-parietal arch) against its floor (the exoccipital portion of the ear capsule), a closure that is apparent in *Dinilysia*. Thus the space occupied by the profundus in lizards does not exist in snakes.

Superfamily Acrochordoidea Bonaparte (ex Acrochordina)

Accessory process of prezygapophysis a dorsoventral keel along the buttress of the prezygapophysis, extending from just beneath the prezygapophysial articular surface to (or nearly to) the diapophysial facet for the rib; ribs (where known) without well-defined tuber costae.

This diagnosis, limited by referred fossils to vertebral characters, distinguishes this group from other Alethinophidia, in which the accessary prezygapophysial process is tubercle-like, horizontally expanded, or absent; the absence of a distinct tuber costae is equally diagnostic. Since *Dinilysia* had a tubercle-like accessory prezygapophysial process and a tuber costae, the characters of the Acrochordoidea are here interpreted as specialized, probably for a totally aquatic life. The resemblance of the fossils to *Acrochordus* may be the convergent result of aquatic adaptation. The Anomalopheidae (as here defined) are interpreted by Rage (1978a, 1983a) as primitive Colubroidea but are here considered Acrochordoidea. Unfortunately, the most distinctive features of the Acrochordoidea are in the cranial and soft anatomy and known only for the living family Acrochordidae.

Family Nigeropheidae Rage. Vertebrae; ribs unknown; for *Nigerophis* (Paleocene, Africa); *Woutersophis* (middle Eocene, Belgium). Articular surface for rib a simple, vertically oval convexity, about half of it below level of attachment to centrum; centrum of *Nigerophis* (not *Woutersophis*) showing a somewhat triangular cross section; no distinct pterapophysis; vertebrae deeper than broad (even when the strong neural spine is ignored); lateral nutrient foramina absent or sporadic; no foramina flanking zygosphene; hypapophyses reduced to strong keels on middle and posterior dorsals; anterior dorsals with a mound, but not a distinct process, beneath the cotyle; condyle facing backward and slightly upward.

Rage (1983a) has discussed the relationships of this marine family, which is undeniably close to the Acrochordidae and also to the Palaeopheidae. Palaeopheidae are known from the Upper (Maestrichtian) Cretaceous (Rage and Wouters, 1979), predating *Nigerophis*, yet are more specialized. Rage refers the Palaeopheidae to the lineage including the Boidae, rather than to the acrochordid lineage, but from a stage when these two lineages were not yet greatly divergent. Nigeropheidae may have originated much earlier than their known occurrences, and derivation of the Palaeopheidae (and Acrochordidae) from the Nigeropheidae seems morphologically plausible.

Family Palaeopheidae Lydekker. Vertebrae, ribs and, for *Archaeophis*, partial skull. Differ from Nigeropheidae as follows: (1) pterapophysis a distinct projection; (2) vertebral condyle directed straight backward (unique among snakes); (3) rib facets more depressed; (4) anterior(?) dorsals with the mound beneath the cotyle hypertrophied into a second hypapophysis; and (5) proportions shorter and deeper relative to width across zygapophyses.

Following Rage (1983a), two subfamilies: (1) Subfamily Archaeopheinae, for the lower Eocene *Archaeophis proavus* Massalongo (type) and *A. turkmenicus* Tatarinov (better preserved and the basis for taxonomic placement of the genus). See Rage (1978a, 1983a, and this volume); and (2) Subfamily Palaeopheinae, for *Palaeophis* Owen (Upper Cretaceous of Morocco to middle Eocene of Europe, North America, and North Africa) and *Pterosphenus* Lucas (upper Eocene of North America, Ecuador, and North Africa), the two genera grading into one another (Rage, 1983b).

The fragmentary skull of *Archaeophis proavus* (Janensch, 1906; Auffenberg, 1959) is very peculiar. The rod-shaped bone identified as the quadrate by Janensch extends downward and strongly *forward* from its suspension on the projecting tabular. The shape and slant of this element are not seen elsewhere in postembryonic Alethinophidia but are approached by *Leptotyphlops* (suspension from a projecting tabular is unknown among Scolecophidia). This is very unlike *Acrochordus*, where the long, dorsally expanded quadrate slants *backward*. The toothed maxilla is exceptionally long, as in *Acrochordus*, but the very narrow premaxilla is peculiar.

Although Rage (1978a, 1983a) interprets the Palaeopheinae as having the closest affinity with the Boidae, features shared by Boidae and Palaeopheinae are either primitive or also shared with Acrochordidae; several peculiarities indicate a special affinity with Acrochordidae: (1) presence in some *Palaeophis* (Rage, 1978a, 1983b) of parazygosphenal foramina, known elsewhere only in *Acrochordus*, (2) absence or irregular appearance of lateral foramina, (3) absence of tuber costae, and (4) form of the prezygapophysial accessory process. However, the disagreement with Rage (and Hoffstetter, 1955) is not so great as the taxonomy makes it appear, because "basal boid" in Rage's classification is essentially equivalent to "basal alethinophidian" in mine. We agree that the palaeopheids are close to modern snakes and are not derived from Simoliopheidae.

Family Anomalopheidae Auffenberg. Including Russellopheidae Rage; the only specimen of *Anomalophis bolcensis* is considerably fractured, and many of its apparent differences from the much smaller *Russellophis* may result from faulty reconstruction. *Anomalophis* (ribs, vertebrae) and *Russellophis* (vertebrae); early Eocene of Europe. Differing from other Acrochordoidea as follows: (1) conspicuously longer and less deepened vertebrae, the proportions as usual in Colubroidea; (2) at least in *Russellophis,* a distinct lateral nutrient foramen on each vertebra; (3) middle and posterior dorsals with only a weak ventral ridge; (4) diapophyses only slightly (*Russellophis*) or not (*Anomalophis*) extended below centrum; and (5) no trace of a pterapophysis.

Because the absence of a tuber costae (*Anomalophis*) and the form of the prezygapophysial processes seem to be specializations of the Acrochordoidea, I interpret the very colubrid general form of the vertebrae as an indication of evolutionary convergence. The simple rib facets, lack of paracotylar foramina, and nearly straight backward direction of the condyle, which lacks a sharp bordering lip, are unlike modern Colubroidea. However, a close relationship to the ancestry of Colubroidea (Rage's position) cannot be ruled out, and the Anomalopheidae may be precolubroids that were convergent to Acrochordoidea as a result of aquatic adaptation.

Family Acrochordidae Bonaparte. For *Acrochordus,* Miocene to Recent (India to Australia and the Solomons). Vertebrae differing from those of other Acrochordoidea in (1) constant presence of paracotylar foramina; and (2) articular surface for rib clearly divided into a hemispherical dorsal portion and a wider, saddle-shaped ventral portion.

The peculiar soft and cranial anatomy of *Acrochordus* is the chief reason for recognizing a superfamily Acrochordoidea. The osteological peculiarities were first appreciated by Hoffstetter and Gayrard (1965); Underwood (1967) noted soft anatomical features (e.g., presence of two carotids) indicating henophidian rather than colubroid affinities of *Acrochordus*; Brongersma (1957) noted the very large compound tracheal lung; Schmidt (1918) described the skin, unique among snakes in having microscopic hairlike projections (seen also in many lizards and perhaps representing the prototrichia of Elias and Bortner, 1957). The ear region (McDowell, 1979) is very peculiar, largely through retention of embryonic features. McDowell (1979) reviewed the anatomy and distinguished three living species of *Acrochordus, A. javanicus, A. arafurae,* and *A. granulatus.* The great difference between *Acrochordus* and Colubroidea transferrin was demonstrated by Schwaner and Dessauer (1982); *Acrochordus* transferrin showed no detectable reaction with antisera to the transferrins of the colubrids compared.

However, Dowling et al. (1983) refer *Acrochordus* to a tribe Acrochordini within the subfamily Homalopsinae of the Colubridae. This is not so inconsistent with Schwaner and Dessauer's transferrin evidence as it might seem, because Schwaner and Dessauer also failed to obtain a detectable reaction of *Homalopsis* transferrin with antisera to other colubroid transferrins (no *Acrochordus-Homalopsis* comparison of transferrins was reported by Schwaner and Dessauer). However, the morphological difference between *Acrochordus* and *Homalopsis* is so great that the classifications of Dowling et al. (1983) seem unconvincing.

Acrochordus has a number of resemblances to Anomalepididae (see Scolecophidia, above) that are not seen in other Alethinophidia and certainly cannot be accounted for as the result of similar habitat or general body form; I regard these resemblances as primitive features retained by *Acrochordus* but lost in other Alethinophidia.

Acrochordus is less primitive than some other Alethinophidia (e.g., *Python*) in loss of coronoid, pelvic vestiges, basipterygoid process, and premaxillary teeth. The levator bulbi musculature is divided into two portions, with the larger posterolateral to the Vidian (VII palatine + sympathetic) nerve; unlike the booid and colubroid pattern, the smaller part, medial to the Vidian nerve, also inserts on the palatine and not on the vomer as a retractor vomeris.

Anilioidea, Tropidopheoidea, and Bolyerioidea differ from other Alethinophidia in having a retractor arcus palatini muscle that is anteromedial (rather than posterolateral) to the Vidian nerve. The lizard depressor palpebrae, the probable homolog of the retractor arcus palatini of (at least most) snakes, lies posterolateral to the Vidian nerve (see Willard, 1915), and the anilioids, tropidopheoids, and bolyerioids share a common specialization that may indicate a special common ancestry, in spite of (convergent?) resemblances of some of them to other superfamilies. This and the following common characters of Anilioidea, Tropidopheoidea, and Bolyerioidea are not repeated in diagnoses of these superfamilies: V_4 levator bulbi nerve joining VII palatine deep within Vidian canal to form Vidian nerve; lateral nasal gland exposed, the facial wing of the prefrontal lying ventrolateral to the gland (and to the aditus conchae of the nasal capsule); stapes-quadrate contact near dorsal end of latter, with no muscle fibers passing through the space above the stapedial shaft; ribs with tuber costae; terminal cartilages of ribs simple and conical; no protractor quadrati muscle; and dorsal scales arranged in transverse rows that meet the ventrals, without irregularly intercalated transverse rows.

Superfamily Anilioidea Stejneger

Accessory prezygapophysial process a small tubercle or barely developed; anterior dentigerous process of palatine underlapping ventral surface of vomer (this dentigerous process is toothless in uropeltines); tabular (lost in Uropeltinae) with well-defined lateral lobe bordering juxtastapedial fossa; foot plate of stapes very large and extended posterior to base of shaft, the fenestra ovalis protruding so deeply into the recessus scalae tympani that the apertura interna lies anterior to the rear of the fenestra ovalis [Note: because of the different proportions of the recessus scalae tympani produced by posterior expansion of the fenestra ovalis, as compared by Boidae and most colubroids, Rieppel (1979b,c) gives a different name, "fenestra pseudorotunda," to the posterior portion of the recessus scalae tympani of Aniliidae and Uropeltidae, even though it has the normal contents of a recessus scalae tympani, the perilymphatic foramen of the otic capsule and nerve IX; *Loxocemus* and *Xenopeltis* (well figured by Rieppel, 1979c) are less extreme in this proportional difference, but strongly approach *Anilius* and *Cylindrophis,* making clear the homologies]; coronoid present (usually fused to adjacent bones in *Xenopeltis*); levator anguli oris broad, with anterior fibers that curve downward and forward around corner of mouth; no tracheal lung.

Four families are recognized here, with the upper Eocene *Eoanilius* the earliest known fossil (*Coniophis* is here referred tentatively to the Dinilysiidae in the Cholophidia).

Family Loxocemidae Cope (*ex* Loxocemi). A supraorbital bone excluding frontal from orbital rim; tabular projecting beyond braincase; large splenial, angular, and coronoid, but coronoid fails to extend onto the well-defined coronoid process; dentigerous process of dentary ending opposite rear of ventral border of dentary, only slightly behind splenial-angular hinge; premaxilla toothed; pelvis of two bones, and a femur; hemipenis bilobate, with flounces grading distally into coarse calyces (Dowling, 1975), with strongly forked sulcus running in a centrolineal position (i.e., on dorsal face of each lobe, halfway between medial and lateral faces of the lobe) to the flat discoidal end of each lobe; left lung more than half as long as right; a large retractor arcus palatini but no retractor vomeris. *Loxocemus,* of southern Mexico and Central America.

Family Xenopeltidae Bonaparte (*ex* Xenopeltina). No supraorbital or postorbital, the frontal entering orbital rim; roof of muzzle differing from that of *Loxocemus* (and *Dinilysia*) in approximation of prefrontals behind the nasals and in a long anterior extension of prefontal along dorsal edge of maxilla (as in Bolyeriidae); tabular projecting behind braincase; splenial large; angular minute or absent; coronoid slender, usually fused into compound bone; coronoid process absent; dentigerous process of dentary extended far backward, well posterior to splenial-angular hinge and ventral edge of dentary; premaxilla toothed; no pelvic or femoral vestiges; hemipenis (see Dowling, 1975) as in *Loxocemus* but with only a few flounces and no calyces; left lung about half the length of the right; a retractor arcus palatini; no retractor vomeris. *Xenopeltis,* of Indo-Chinese, Malaysian, and Indonesian regions, to Sulawesi.

Dowling (1975) and Dowling and Duellman (1978) refer *Xenopeltis* and *Loxocemus* to a subfamily Xenopeltinae of the Boidae and also include West

African *Calabaria* in spite of its very different hemipenis, skull, and scutellation. Underwood (1967) placed *Xenopeltis* in its own family and placed *Loxocemus* by itself in a subfamily Loxoceminae of the Boidae; but Underwood (1976) placed *Xenopeltis* and *Loxocemus* together in the Xenopeltinae of the Boidae. *Xenopeltis* and *Loxocemus* do agree with Booidea in having a large left lung. The large left lung of Booidea, *Xenopeltis,* and *Loxocemus* is usually considered primitive, telling very little about the phyletic lineage; but booids and at least *Xenopeltis* have been shown by Brongersma (1951a) to have this large left lung considerably vascularized by the right pulmonary artery (as is the vestigial left lung of many colubroids, *Anilius,* and *Cylindrophis*). This vascularization suggests the large left lung could be secondary enlargement of a "vestigial" lung; if so, it would represent a shared specialization of *Loxocemus, Xenopeltis,* and Booidea.

Loxocemus and *Xenopeltis* seem to be quite primitive snakes, but on the phylogenetic line to Aniliidae rather than the line to Booidea. The Loxocemidae and Xenopeltidae are kept distinct in part because of the considerable anatomical differences (mostly specializations of *Xenopeltis*) and the absence of intermediates.

Family Aniliidae Stejneger. No supraorbital or postorbital, but frontal nearly or quite excluded from orbit by parietal; tabular not extending past paroccipital process; splenial and angular absent; dentary with equal posterior extent on dorsal and ventral borders, extended back over lateral surface of compound bone; coronoid bone reaching summit of strong coronoid process; premaxilla toothed; a femur and a pelvic bone; hemipenis forked for half its length (i.e., more deeply than in preceding families), with numerous transverse flounces grading into calyces at the tip of each lobe (Dowling and Duellman, 1978), the sulcus forked in the crotch and running centripetally (i.e., along side each lobe facing midline of organ), to the discoidal end of each lobe; left lung vestigial; a retractor vomeris and a larger retractor arcus palatini (pattern most nearly approached by *Ungaliophis*). *Anilius,* tropical South America.

Provisionally, because of geography, *Colombophis* Hoffstetter and Rage (1977), from the La Venta (middle Miocene) of Colombia, is referred here. This genus, known only from vertebrae, is anilioid-like, but much larger than any known anilioid. The weakness of the neural spine suggests Aniliidae and Uropeltidae, but it is the Asiatic uropeltids that it more resembles in details of morphology. In the presence of paracotylar foramina on some vertebrae and simple rib articulations, *Colombophis* differs from all living Anilioidea and may not even be alethinophidian as here restricted.

Family Uropeltidae Muller (*ex* Uropeltana). Postorbital present in some genera; free supraorbital absent in adult, but at least sometimes contained in an anterior projection of the parietal excluding frontal from orbital rim (see Rieppel, 1977); tabular absent or not extending beyond paroccipital process; splenial, angular, and coronoid present, the coronoid process (absent in *Melanophidium;* Rieppel,

1977) with coronoid bone to its apex; dentigerous process of dentary exceeding ventral border of dentary and extending behind level of splenial-angular hinge (but not as far as in Xenopeltidae); premaxilla without teeth; hemipenis simple, with simple sulcus, smooth, longitudinally plicate, papillose, or spinose but without flounces or calyces; left lung vestigial or absent; no retractor vomeris; retractor arcus palatini small, its fibers nearly vertical.

Subfamily *Cylindropheinae*. A pelvic girdle with pubis, ilium, ischium, and femur. The following are characteristic of the subfamily, but are not known for *Anomochilus:* tabular present; orbital foramen about equally bordered by frontal and parietal; axis with odontoid process; occipital condyle sessile; palatine and pterygoid toothed; hemipenis without spines. The oviparous *Anomochilus* (Malaya–East Indies), and live-bearing *Cylindrophis* (Sri Lanka, Burma through Indo-China and East Indies to Aru Island). On geographic grounds, *Eoanilius* Rage (1974), vertebrae and a quadrate from the upper Eocene of France, is referred here, in spite of important differences (the quadrate more resembles that of *Anilius*).

Subfamily *Uropeltinae*. No pelvis; no tabular; frontal forming most (*Melanophidium, Teretrurus:* Underwood, 1967; Rieppel, 1977) or all of border of orbital foramen; apex dentis, its ligament to basioccipital, and odontoid process of axis absent; occipital condyle with greatly elongated pedicle; pterygoid toothless, as is (except in *Platyplectrurus* and some *Melanophidium*) palatine; hemipenis usually with spines (not in *Melanophidium* and *Platyplectrurus:* Smith, 1943); live-bearing. *Melanophidium, Teretrurus, Platyplectrurus, Plectrurus, Uropeltis, Rhinophis, Pseudotyphlops*. Sri Lanka and peninsular India.

Although the Uropeltinae have many peculiarities (notably in the occipital articulation), they are related to *Cylindrophis*, and Rieppel (1977, 1979c, 1980) has documented the transitional nature of *Melanophidium* and (in jaw muscles) *Cylindrophis maculatus* between the two groups. The hemipenis and cranial details indicate clearly that it is *Cylindrophis*, not *Anilius* or other anilioids, that is in the clade with uropeltines. This is expressed here in the vertical classification that attempts to distinguish identifiable clades. Rieppel (1979b,c, 1980) placed *Anilius* and *Cylindrophis* together in one family, because of their shared primitive features, and places the Uropeltinae in a separate family. This is perhaps good phenetics, but violates the cladistics that Rieppel claims to follow. My classification is not quite cladistic, because the Sri Lankan *maculatus* is left in *Cylindrophis*, even though its loss of the apex dentis and ligament (Williams, 1959), and its distribution, suggest that it is at the base of the uropeltine phyletic line; by strict cladistics, it should be included in the subfamily Uropeltinae.

Superfamily Tropidopheoidea Brongersma (ex Tropidophinae)

Accessory prezygapophysial process a minute tubercle; palatine failing to reach vomer beneath choanal passage; levator bulbi musculature in *Ungaliophis*, much as in Aniliidae, with a small retractor vomeris and a larger retractor arcus palatini (AMNH 93813); in *Tropidophis,* as in *Loxocemus* and *Xenopeltis,* with a broad retractor palatini, no retractor vomeris; tabular with lateral lobe extending nearly or quite to rim of juxtastapedial fossa; coronoid reduced (not contributing to coronoid process) or absent; levator anguli oris represented by only the most posterior portion, without fibers to the corner of the mouth; left lung vestigial or absent; a large tracheal lung, almost to head; one transverse scale row for each ventral; except for *Tropidophis semicinctus,* with pelvic vestiges, at least in male; no premaxillary teeth; hemipenis forked for from one-third to two-thirds its length, with strongly forked sulcus.

Family Tropidopheidae Brongersma (*ex* Tropidophinae). The four living genera separate clearly into two groups, here proposed as subfamilies, and some fossil genera seem referable to these groups:

Subfamily Ungaliopheinae (New). Hemipenis bilobate, the sulcus forking well proximal to the crotch to run centrolineally on each lobe to the smooth, discoidal tip; organ with smooth, fleshy flounces, irregularly cross-connected to define calyces (see Dowling, 1975); kidneys lobulated; middle and posterior dorsals nearly flat ventrally; no paracotylar foramina; coronoid process high. *Ungaliophis* (Mexico to Ecuador) and *Exiliboa* (southern Mexico); see Bogert (1968a) for externals, viscera, vertebrae, and the probable relationship to this group of *Dunnophis* [vertebrae from the middle Eocene of North America and (Rage, 1974) upper Eocene of Europe]. *Platyspondylia* Rage (1974), upper Oligocene of France, is known from the vertebrae, quadrate, palatine, and compound bone; particularly, the palatine and compound bone so strongly resemble those of *Ungaliophis* that they are referred to this subfamily.

Subfamily Tropidopheinae Brongersma. Hemipenis more deeply forked (for slightly less than half its length in *Trachyboa* to almost two-thirds its length in *Tropidophis*), with sulcus forking in the crotch to run centripetally along each lobe, which lacks terminal discoidal area; organ with numerous closely packed flounces denticulated along their edges to suggest (uncalcified) spines, these forming soft but spine-shaped papillae at the level of organ furcation and on lips of sulcus branch in *Tropidophis* (Dowling, 1975); kidneys not divided into lobules; middle and posterior dorsals with hypapophysis or a strongly projecting keel; paracotylar foramina present; coronoid process of mandible reduced, lower than inner lip of adductor fossa. *Tropidophis* (Greater Antilles, Bahamas, tropical South America) and *Trachyboa* (northwestern South America); see Brongersma (1951b) for viscera, Bogert (1968a,b) for vertebrae, and McDowell (1975) for figure of skull. The middle Eocene North American *Boavus* appears to belong here, on the basis of skull characters as figured by Gilmore (1938) and strong keels on the ventral surface of all the dorsal vertebrae; however, Gilmore does not indicate paracotylar foramina in *Boavus* and shows a larger splenial and coronoid for *Boavus* than are known for any living tropidopheid.

The well-developed tracheal lung of Tropidopheidae distinguishes them from

Anilioidea, Bolyerioidea, and Booidea, and from most Colubroidea. It is uncertain whether the tracheal lung is a specialization or primitive, but the presence of a tracheal lung in the most primitive Scolecophidia, *Acrochordus*, and a number of colubroids that seem primitive within their respective phyletic lines, suggests the latter. That the tropidopheids are more colubroid-like than are Booidea in many ways may be the result of retaining primitive alethinophidian features also retained in colubroids.

Superfamily Bolyeroidea Hoffstetter (ex Bolyerinae)

Accessory prezygapophysial process a strongly projecting conical tuberosity (as in Colubroidea, which they also resemble in strong differentiation of articular surface of diapophysis into a dorsal hemispherical and ventral saddle-shaped portion, and in the presence of paracotylar foramina). Skull as in Tropidophoidea, but unique in form of maxilla; it is divided into anterior and posterior portions by a joint; anterior portion suspended, by its medial process, from a lateral flange of palatine; posterior portion with its own medial process extending from its anteromedial corner to attach by ligament to apex of lateral process of palatine; thus the two parts of the maxilla together have both an anterior and a posterior medial process, as in most Colubroidea; at least in *Casarea,* with both retractor vomeris and retractor arcus palatini [F. Irish (Pers. comm., based on a well-preserved but juvenile specimen); Frazzetta (1971) failed to find the retractor vomeris in a poorly preserved adult]; levator anguli oris as in Tropidophoidea; left lung vestigial; no tracheal lung, but *Casarea* (BM 70.11.30.40) with extension of right lung forward of heart along trachea for about a heart length; no pelvic vestiges in either sex; two transverse scale rows for each ventral; hemipenis extremely elongated, forked for 80% or more of its length [such deep forking seen elsewhere only in some Colubroidea; for *Casarea,* BM 70.11.30.40, organ to C47, forked at C5, the sulcus forked at C3-C4 suture and running centrolineally on lobes, but gradually spiraling around each lobe to end on smooth tip (a terminal disk as in *Loxocemus* and *Exiliboa* when everted?); proximal half of each lobe with scattered low papillae, followed on middle of lobe by fleshy transverse flounces; then, to the bare tip, tripelike calyces; the organ most nearly matched by the colubrid *Achalinus*]. *Casarea* (Pleistocene of Mauritius to Recent of Round Island) and *Bolyeria* (Round Island, perhaps extinct), forming Family Bolyeriidae Hoffstetter.

Underwood (1976) places these two peculiar Mascarene snakes in a subfamily of the Tropidopheidae, and this may be their true position; certainly, most features of the skull, apart from the maxilla, show close similarity between the Bolyeriidae and *Ungaliophis*. However, it seems possible that these resemblances are largely the primitive characters of Alethinophidia. There are a number of special resemblances between Bolyeriidae and Colubroidea: the strong prezygapophysial process and form of the costal articulation of the vertebrae, the *Achalinus*-like hemipenis, lack of pelvic vestiges, and posterior medial process of the maxilla. Haluska and Alberch (1983) show that, in the development of the colubrid *Elaphe,* the maxilla has anterior and posterior ossification centers and the bone passes through a bolyeriid-like stage when it is formed of distinct anterior and posterior portions. Critical—and at present unavailable—information for interpreting the bolyeriid maxilla is whether Tropidophoidea, Anilioidea, and Booidea also have multiple ossification centers in the maxilla. However, the relations of the levator bulbi muscles to the Vidian nerve suggest that Anilioidea, Tropidophoidea, and Bolyerioidea are all closely related and that the resemblances of some of them to Colubroidea or to Booidea are convergent.

Undoubtedly, the position of the bolyeriids will be better understood when F. Irish and P. Alberch complete their ongoing studies of the anatomy of these snakes. I am indebted to F. Irish for unpublished information on the head muscles of *Casarea.*

Superfamily Booidea Gray (ex Boidae)

Ribs with tuber costae, the terminal cartilages simple; accessory prezygapophysial process a small and inconspicuous tubercle (but in the fossil *Cadurceryx,* horizontally expanded); palatine separated from vomer beneath choanal passage; prefrontal with a triangular anterior facial process that fits directly over the aditus conchae to conceal the lateral nasal gland (except for its anterior duct to nostril region) (see note following diagnosis); anastomosis of palatine VII and V_4 nerve (to form true Vidian nerve) either entirely external and anterior to Vidian canal (lizardlike) or just within a funnellike anterior orifice of the canal (as in *Acrochordus*); all levator bulbi muscle fibers that lie anteromedial to path of true Vidian nerve go to vomer as a retractor vomeris; levator bulbi fibers inserting on palatine as a retractor arcus palatini (absent in *Calabaria, Lichanura, Charina*) passing posterolateral to Vidian nerve; tabular without lateral lobe, well separated from rim of juxtastapedial fossa; stapes with abruptly, but only moderately, enlarged footplate, the fenestra ovalis anterior to the recessus scalae tympani; stapes articulating with middle or lower end of quadrate, the more dorsal part of the medial face of the quadrate being occupied by the extended origin of the adductor mandibulae posterior, fibers of which pass dorsal to the shaft of the stapes from the tabular and quadrate to the mandible (unique in detail); coronoid bone (absent in *Charina*) extending onto coronoid process; levator anguli oris as in Tropidopheoidea; no protractor quadrati; no tracheal lung, but left lung large (as in Loxocemidae and Xenopeltidae); pelvic vestiges and a femur, at least in males; dorsal scales with irregularly intercalated transverse rows that do not involve the lowermost longitudinal rows (suggested by a few colubroids and difficult to compare in *Acrochordus,* but otherwise unique).

[*Note on the facial wing of the prefrontal of Booidea:* It is the position of this wing, overlying the lateral nasal gland and concha, not its size or roofing of the muzzle, that is diagnostic of booids. The colubrid *Oxyrhabdium* has a larger anterior wing of the prefrontal than that of any booid, but the prefrontal of *Oxyrhabdium,* as in other colubroids, leaves the lateral nasal gland exposed, dorsomedial to the wing. The facial wing of the prefrontal does *not* seem to be a primitive feature of booids, in spite of Rieppel's (1979b) interpretation; it is not sutured to either the nasal or maxilla but is movable and usually overlaps the nasal bone. It lies in a region that is not roofed by bone in *Dinilysia,* and it is not usual in lizards for the prefrontal to contribute to the (rigid) roof of the muzzle in this region, normally occupied in lizards by a dorsal extension of the maxilla.]

This is a sharply defined group without clear relationships to any other. Removal of Madtsoiidae to the Cholophidia leaves the Booidea without clear paleontological evidence of being particularly ancient, but the occurrence of pelvic vestiges and, in some genera, of premaxillary teeth and a basipterygoid process in real articulation with the pterygoid suggest this is an old group. In spite of Underwood's (1976) cladogram, many genera have a rectal cecum, found also in Scolecophidia, Anilioidea, and a few colubroids, but not in Tropidophoidea, Bolyerioidea, or *Acrochordus* [the cecum of booids is easily missed because it lies much farther forward than in anilioids and scolecophidians; Cope (1900, pl. 7) figures its position in *Charina*].

I make fuller use here of the taxonomic hierarchy to express degrees of relationship within the Booidea than previously (McDowell, 1975, 1979) and recognize Pythonidae and Boidae as families, the latter divided into Boinae and Erycinae.

Family Pythonidae Fitzinger (*ex* Pythonidea). A supraorbital bone; anterior end of Meckelian cartilage free of dentary; palatine not independently erectile, its lateral process underlapped by an anteroposteriorly long medial process of maxilla; palatine enters infraorbital fenestra between maxilla and pterygoid; palatine tooth row (absent in *Calabaria*) continuous with that of pterygoid; rectus capitis dorsalis inserted on a transverse nuchal crest of supraoccipital; oviparous. *Aspidites, Liasis* (= *Bothrochilus*), *Chondropython, Python, Calabaria;* Australia through East Indies and tropical Asia; also, Africa (not Madagascar); *Python* in Miocene of Africa and Pakistan.

Underwood (1976) places *Calabaria* in a monotypic subfamily Calabariinae, relating it (in his cladogram) more closely to Boinae (and tropidophoids and bolyerioids) than to Pythoninae. The hemipenis (Doucet, 1963) is peculiar in having a simple sulcus and a domelike terminal capitation [no suggestion of terminal disks, such as seen in *Loxocemus* and *Xenopeltis,* in spite of Dowling and Duellman's (1978) classification of *Calabaria* with these genera]. Peculiar as it is, the hemipenis of *Calabaria* is most easily derived from that of *Python regius* (figure in Doucet, 1963) by loss of sulcus furcation. The skull peculiarities of *Calabaria* seem to involve imposition of *Charina*-like burrowing modifications on a *Python regius* skull. Because this classification makes no attempt to express the quantity of morphological difference, but merely attempts to distinguish phyletic lineages, the Calabariinae is not recognized here.

Family Boidae Gray. No supraorbital bone; tip of Meckelian cartilage enclosed by dentary; palatine erectile independently of maxilla (immobile in *Lichanura* and *Charina*, where retractor palatini muscle is lost), the medial process of the maxilla meeting only extreme rear of palatine and nearly or quite meeting pterygoid to exclude palatine from infraorbital fenestra; palatine dentition (reduced in *Lichanura* and *Charina*) set off from the pterygoid tooth row and more medially placed; rectus capitis dorsalis insertion converging medially on a sagittal crest of supraoccipital produced backward dorsal to exoccipitals (unique); live-bearing.

Subfamily Boinae Gray (*ex* Boidae). Prefrontals nearly or quite in contact; hemipenis strongly bilobated except in *Xenoboa* (which has papillose terminal lobes and conspicuous labial pits); caudal vertebrae with simple neural spines and strong zygosphene-zygantral articulations. *Boa, Acrantophis, Sanzinia, Xenoboa, Corallus, Epicrates, Eunectes, Candoia;* Neotropical (and Antillean) region; Malagasy-Mascarene region; Pacific region (including Sulawesi, New Guinea). *Palaeopython,* upper Eocene of Europe, is associated with a pterygoid bone (Rage, 1974) that indicates it belongs in this subfamily.

Subfamily Erycinae Bonaparte (*ex* Erycina). Prefrontals widely separated, the nasals broad posteriorly; hemipenis feebly or not bilobate, without papillae, flounced and calyculate; no labial pits; at least posterior caudals with forked neural spine, frequently with accessory lateral process, and zygosphene-zygantral articulation reduced or absent. The North American *Lichanura* and *Charina,* with large choanal process of palatine, no retractor arcus palatini (the palatine dentition reduced and bone only feebly mobile), seem quite distinct from the Old World (continental Africa and Eurasia) *Eryx* and *Gongylophis* (strong palatine dentition, the bone mobile and its choanal process reduced, the retractor arcus palatini present). Hoffstetter and Rage (1972) discussed the fossil record, which goes back to the lower Paleocene in North America (predating the known record for Pythonidae and Boinae).

McDowell (1979) gives a more extended discussion of relationships in Boinae. Schwaner and Dessauer (1981) made a general blood protein immunological comparison of the Pacific boine *Candoia* with *Corallus, Epicrates, Charina, Eryx, Lichanura,* several Australasian pythons, and *Python regius;* their findings support the basic division into Boidae and Pythonidae, because the immunological distances between *Candoia* and other Boidae (including erycines) were less than those between *Candoia* and the pythons, and their more precise comparisons of albumin and transferrin showed a great difference between *Candoia* and pythons.

Superfamily Colubroidea Oppel (ex Colubrini)

Ribs with tuber costae, the terminal cartilage expanded and with anterior and posterior recurrent processes (Hardaway and Williams, 1976; Persky et al., 1976); except in *Xenodermus,* accessory prezygapophysial process strongly projecting, conical or horizontally expanded; except in *Xenocalamus,* palatine separated from vomer ventral to choanal passage; prefrontal leaves lateral nasal gland exposed; Vidian canal, if present, with or without anterior continuation around true Vidian nerve; a retractor vomeris, anteromedial to true Vidian nerve; retractor arcus palatini posterolateral to true Vidian nerve; tabular, in some, with lateral lobe reaching margin of juxtastapedial fossa; stapes-quadrate contact usually displaced ventrally, to middle or lower end of quadrate (as in Booidea), but this displacement by the depressor mandibulae, the adductor mandibulae posterior not entering the suprastapedial space; no coronoid bone; except in *Homoroselaps, Atractaspis,* and relatives, no coronoid process; levator anguli oris may include homolog of anteriormost fibers of Anilioidea; protractor pterygoideus with its posterior portion split off as a protractor quadrati inserting on quadrate or retroarticular process (unique); left lung vestigial or absent; tracheal lung often present; no pelvic vestiges; one transverse scale row for each ventral (but intercalated lateralmost transverse rows may occur in Xenoderminae and fusion of transverse rows in some proteroglyphs).

An additional character of this group, absent in some (probably secondarily), is development of some lateral dental lamina of the maxilla as venom-secreting tissue, in a thick-walled venom gland, deep to the quadratomaxillary ligament, or in a more superficial Duvernoy's gland in the supralabial gland; *Atractaspis* has a Duvernoy's gland in the rear of the supralabial gland and, deep to it, a thick-walled muscular venom gland. Certain maxillary teeth deliver these secretions and are often (not always) grooved or canaliculate; earlier classifications were based on the position of these fangs. The evolution of fangs was reviewed by Anthony (1955); the glands were reviewed by Smith and Bellairs (1947), Taub (1966), and Kochva (1978); Taub (1957) detailed the differences in Duvernoy's gland among colubrids.

All these authors assume a phylogeny from colubrids without fangs or venomous tissue, to those with rear fangs and a Duvernoy's gland, to (separately) elapids and viperids with a venom gland compressed by fibers of the mandibular adductor. This assumption has been questioned: Underwood (1967) derived colubrids without fangs from rear-fanged genera; McDowell (1975) attributed a lack of Duvernoy's gland in colubrids to secondary loss; Cadle (1982) showed immunologically that the "advanced" venomous snakes must be derived from the base of the colubroid lineage, suggesting that venom-secreting tissue was present in the common ancestor of colubroids.

Considering the entire venom apparatus, the "sophisticated" apparatus of proteroglyphs is easier to derive from the lizard and "henophidian" pattern than is that of the "primitive" rear-fanged snakes (McDowell, 1986). The venom gland of proteroglyphs is the rictal fold (Mundplatte) of lizards, connected (as in lizards) to the levator anguli oris. New venomous epithelium is lodged in an old pocket with old muscle connections. Smith and Bellairs (1947) found the homologous rictal pocket to be lined with glandular (probably not venomous) epithelium in *Cylindrophis*. In proteroglyphs, the anterior attachment of the pterygoideus is, as in lizards and henophidians, on the rear of the ectopterygoid, remote from the fangs; the pterygoideus cannot manipulate and drive in the fangs. Kardong (1979, 1980, 1982) and Cundall (1983) discuss the importance of the pterygoideus in manipulating the rear maxillary teeth of colubrids and the fangs of viperids (derived from posteriormost maxillary teeth); proteroglyphs have no such ability to manipulate the fangs.

As argued in more detail in McDowell (1986), colubroids form two series: (1) a more primitive series Proteroglypha, containing elapids and (linked by intermediates called *Calliophis*) *Atractaspis* and certain African genera usually placed in the Colubridae (the "Aparallactinae" but neither *Aparallactus* nor *Macrelaps*); and (2) a series Opisthoglypha, containing Colubridae and Viperidae, either with a venom apparatus using teeth under the control of the pterygoideus or linked by intermediates to species with such a venom apparatus. Secondary reduction of the venom apparatus in some colubrids makes this definition untidy; another character comes closer to "keying out" the two series—in the series Proteroglypha, as in henophidians, the cervicomandibularis, to the lips and throat, merely overlies the jaw articulation. In the series Opisthoglypha (except *Duberria*), the cervicomandibularis inserts on the jaw articulation to be the functional retractor quadrati and is so named by some authors (but the cervicoquadratus is the retractor quadrati of older literature).

Series Proteroglypha. Not a formal taxon; see previous discussion of Colubroidea.

Family Atractaspididae Günther. Posterior dorsal vertebrae with flat ventral platform covered by broad ligament without muscle fibers. At least a low keel (often a strong crest) forming a coronoid process anterior to adductor fossa; postorbital vestigial or absent; most posterior fibers of levator anguli oris ending ventrally on lower jaw; dentary not extending behind splenial-angular hinge. Africa and Middle East. *Atractaspis, Homoroselaps* (with fangs only on maxilla); *Amblyodipsas, Xenocalamus, Chilorhinophis, Polemon, Micrelaps* (with teeth anterior to fangs).

Immunological study by Cadle (1982) indicates divergences within this group as old as colubroid families; yet there are strong morphological similarities between (for example) *Atractaspis* and *Amblyodipsas*. This is consistent with a very old separation of this group from the colubroid stem. The coronoid process (also in a few Elapidae) is a henophidian feature of this group. Cadle's (1982) albumin comparisons show that this group is not derived from Colubridae but do not confirm its naturalness; it may be several very primitive lineages.

Family Elapidae Boie. Posterior dorsals with hypapophyses or, at least, strongly compressed median keels, with subvertebral muscle fibers; no maxillary teeth anterior to fangs. The next two subfamilies form a transition between the preceding family and the "euproteroglyphs".

Subfamily Calliopheinae (New). A coronoid process; posterior fibers of levator anguli oris to lower jaw; Harderian gland extends back over lateral surface of levator anguli oris (as in Atractaspididae); dentary not extending behind splenial-angular hinge. Indian and Malay-Sunda regions. *Calliophis gracilis* (type of genus), *C. bibroni,* and *C. melanurus.*

Subfamily Maticorinae Smith, Smith and Sawin (*ex* Maticorini). No coronoid process and posterior fibers of levator anguli oris ending on venom gland (as in all following Proteroglypha); Harderian gland as in preceding subfamilies; dentary not extending behind splenial-angular hinge. India to Sunda and Philippine Islands. *Maticora* (including *"Calliophis" nigrescens* and *"C." maculiceps,* in spite of lack of backward prolongation of the venom gland).

Subfamily Elapinae Boie (*ex* Elapidae). Harderian gland confined to orbit (as in all following Proteroglypha); dentary not extending behind splenial-angular hinge. Eastern Asia, Bougainville Island, and warm temperate to tropical continental New World. This subfamily begins the euproteroglyph series and includes New World *Micrurus, Leptomicrurus,* and *Micruroides,* as well as *"Calliophis" macclellandi, "C." kelloggi,* and *"C." japonicus,* all lacking a postorbital and having a strongly bilobate hemipenis with spinose lobes (*Micrurus* might be expanded to include all these); also the Philippine *Hemibungarus* (for *"Calliophis" calligaster*), with a simple hemipenis (sulcus forked) with papillose calyces and a large postorbital. *Parapistocalamus* (Bougainville Island) is similar to *Hemibungarus,* but has a much reduced mandibular dentition and has lost the choanal process of the palatine (as have *Laticauda* and Hydropheinae).

Intermediates between the Atractaspididae and euproteroglyphs are noted by McCarthy (1985) and discussed by McDowell (1986).

Subfamily Laticaudinae Cope. As in Elapinae, but: lining of narial vestibule with rugae or papillae; palatine forked posteriorly to clasp the pterygoid (as in Hydropheinae, but vertical rotation of palatine permitted); and stapes fused to exoccipital. Marine, but coming ashore; tropical eastern Indian and western Pacific oceans.

Laticauda. The snout is not modified in the same way as in marine Hydropheinae, and *Laticauda* appears less closely related to the marine Hydropheinae than are terrestrial Australasian Hydropheinae such as *Notechis,* as evidenced by transferrin immunoassay (T. Schwaner, Pers. comm.). However, the form (but not the mobility) of the palatine-pterygoid articulation is similar to that of all Hydropheinae. *Laticauda* may share ancestry with Hydropheinae but has unique marine adaptations.

Subfamily Bungarinae Eichwald (*ex* Bungaroidei). As in Elapinae, but dentigerous process of dentary extended behind level of splenial-angular hinge; pterygoid and palatine meet in simple overlap, permitting a slight (*Bungarus*) to extensive (e.g., *Naja*) erection of the palatine; except in *Dendroaspis*, at least a flangelike vestige of the choanal process of the palatine. Africa and Asia (Miocene-Pliocene of Europe). Species diversity is greatest in Africa, but the Asiatic *Bungarus* and *Ophiophagus* are each so peculiar in anatomy as to suggest an ancient divergence. *Elapsoidea, Boulengerina, Paranaja, Pseudohaje, Dendroaspis, Aspidelaps, Hemachatus* (Africa only); *Ophiophagus, Bungarus* (Asia only); *Walterinnesia, Naja* (Asia and Africa).

Subfamily Hydropheinae Fitzinger (*ex* Hydrophes). As in Bungarinae, but: palatine clasping the pterygoid by medial and lateral processes and locked into a horizontal position to function as an anterior prolongation of the pterygoid ("palatine draggers" of McDowell, 1970); and palatine without choanal process, its lateral process small and imperforate or absent. Australia and Tasmania to New Guinea, the Moluccas, Solomons, and Fiji (terrestrial forms); coastal waters of Australia and Asia and even (*Pelamis*) to tropical America and Africa. *Salomonelaps, Loveridgelaps, Ogmodon, Vermicella, Pseudechis, Micropechis, Suta, Cryptophis, Hemiaspis, Rhinoplocephalus, Demansia, Aspidomorphus, Simoselaps, Neelaps, Cacophis, Glyphodon, Toxicocalamus, Oxyuranus, Pseudonaja, Echiopsis, Acanthophis, Hoplocephalus, Notechis, Tropidechis, Elapognathus* (terrestrial); *Ephalophis, Parahydrophis, Hydrelaps, Aipysurus, Emydocephalus, Disteira, Hydrophis, Thalassophis, Acalyptophis, Lapemis, Pelamis* (marine).

Smith et al. (1977) make this group a family, divided into Oxyuraninae (terrestrial genera) and Hydrophiinae (marine genera). Recent work (in Grigg et al., 1985) by Schwaner, Mengden, and others on proteins and karyotypes support the close relationship of Australasian terrestrial elapids to sea snakes but makes it seem unlikely that terrestrial versus marine represents the primary phyletic split within this group.

Series Opisthoglypha. Not a formal taxon; see previous discussion of Colubroidea.

Family Colubridae Oppel (*ex* Colubrini). Solid maxillary teeth anterior to fangs (if fangs are present), the fangs with open groove (not closed canal), below or behind pterygoideus attachment to ectopterygoid; if a thick-walled and muscularized venom gland is present (*Mehelya* and *Gonionotophis*), the attached muscle is the pterygoideus, not the levator anguli or oris or the adductor externus superficialis; venom secretion (lost in some) normally by Duvernoy's gland (in the supralabial gland, external to the quadratomaxillary ligament) supplying teeth (grooved or not) on rear of maxilla (opposite or behind posterior medial process of maxilla, adjacent to anterior attachment of pterygoideus superficialis). Distribution nearly equals that of terrestrial snakes.

The classification of Colubridae by morphological characters has so far been unsuccessful if predicting the results of some independent test of relationship, such as immunological comparison, is taken as the measure of success. Underwood (1967) divided them into Dipsadidae, Homalopsidae, Natricidae, and Colubridae. Dowling and Duellman (1978) recognized a single Colubridae but divided it into Xenodontinae, Lycodontinae, Colubrinae, and Natricinae; the Lycodontinae seem particularly heterogeneous, and the inclusion of *Lycodon* and its relatives, with simple sulcus spermaticus, in a subfamily characterized by a forked sulcus, appears to have been a lapse; the Natricinae, including *Acrochordus* and Homalopsinae, also seems heterogeneous.

The Natricidae of Underwood (1967) included many genera placed in the Xenodontinae by Dowling and Duellman, and his Homalopsidae included Boiginae and *Dasypeltis* (placed in the Colubrinae by Dowling and Duellman). Neither classification agrees well with the other, and neither has shown much predictive value for subsequent immunochemical comparisons. Thus Schwaner and Dessauer (1982) found that the transferrins supported most of Dowling and Duellman's Natricinae, but not the inclusion of *Acrochordus* or the Homalopsinae (*sensu stricto*) in this group. Dowling et al. (1983), using albumin, found little support for the "Lycodontinae" and separated a subfamily Boodontinae from Lycodontinae, mainly to accommodate *Madagascarophis* and *Boaedon* in the same group; although the relationship was distant, *Boaedon* came closer to *Madagascarophis* than did any other genus tested.

Cadle (1984a–c, 1985) has made extensive serum albumin comparisons among Neotropical snakes, particularly the Xenodontinae (*sensu* Dowling and Duellman, 1978), allowing more precise evaluation of the morphological characters used for genera and tribes. The results suggest that there is much convergence in morphological details. All West Indian xenodontines except *Tretanorhinus* are closely related but have come to resemble several different mainland groups in features of dentition, skull, and hemipenis. *Heterodon* is isolated, but closer to *Diadophis* than to *Xenodon* (which it resembles in feeding apparatus).

Almost any morphological innovation appearing once in colubrids appears at least once again in some other geographic region. In a large and actively speciating group, with general homogeneity in developmental pattern (so that similar modification of this pattern is likely to produce similar effects), this is not surprising, particularly if there has been no extensive "editing away" of troublesome convergent forms by extinction. The problems of identifying lineages do not seem insurmountable, however, when a single geographic area is considered. Most of the convergences Cadle has revealed are between a Central American and South American or Antillean lineage. Within Central America,

Cadle's work seems, indeed, to simplify the identification of *Hypsiglena, Leptodeira*, etc.

My own (entirely morphological) observations suggest that among Colubridae there are a few strongly characterized, but small, groups, and also a very large main group in which it is impossible to find unique specializations distinguishing the various clades. The small groups are probably well defined because they are old and the forms tying them to the rest have become extinct; but, although these groups are probably old, they may not be the oldest; their isolation by extinction of annectents is probably accidental. Further, some of these "old, isolated" groups seem joined to one another, not by shared anatomical peculiarities allowing tidy diagnosis, but by peculiarities shared by some—but not all—members of a pair of groups. The following attempts to identify clusters of related forms.

Subfamily Homalopsinae. With posterior hypapophyses; hemipenis bilobate with forked, strictly centripetal sulcus, with numerous small spines but calyces— if suggested at all—merely defined by webbing between bases of spinules, without rearrangement of the spinules; snout attached to frontals by the septomaxillae; frontals in long contact with trabeculae; tabular well separated from rim of juxtastapedial fossa; live-bearing. Mostly rear-fanged aquatic forms, with large tracheal lung (*Gerarda, Cantoria, Fordonia, Enhydris, Cerberus, Myron, Homolopsis, Bitia, Erpeton*), but the terrestrial *Brachyorrhos*, without rear fangs, but similar hemipenis, vertebrae and skull, and live-bearing, probably belongs here. Asia, from India through East Indies and Philippines to northern Australia.

Subfamily Xenoderminae. With posterior hypapophyses; hemipenis deeply to very deeply forked, with forked sulcus that is partially centrolineal (organ unknown for *Stoliczkaia*); in *Achalinus* and *Xylophis*, hemipenis without spines and much as in the bolyeriid *Casarea* (see previous discussion), but the flounced region longer; septomaxilla, if touching frontal at all, not articulating with it, the suspension of the snout by the trabecular cartilage (*Oxyrhabdium*) or nasal (*Xylophis*) or [*Xenodermus, Stoliczkaia* (Underwood, 1967), *Achalinus, Fimbrios*] by the vomer; frontals in long contact with trabecular cartilage and (except in *Xylophis* and *Oxyrhabdium*) meeting parietal below orbital foramen to exclude sphenoid (as in most henophidians and many proteroglyphs); at least in *Oxyrhabdium, Xylophis, Achalinus,* and *Fimbrios*, anterior medial process of maxilla suspended from ventral side of lateral process of palatine, not directly from prefrontal, the more lateral maxilloprefrontal articulation by a loose elastic ligament [as in Tropidophoidea, Bolyerioidea, Booidea, and *Dinilysia;* in most Colubroidea, there is direct and tight attachment of the anterior medial process of the maxilla to the prefrontal and the palatine either articulates with the prefrontal medial to this attachment or (e.g., *Lycophidion*) the palatine is suspended by its lateral process from the maxilla]. India and southeastern Asia.

I expand the Xenoderminae of Underwood (1967) (but exclude *Nothopsis*) by including *Xylophis* and *Oxyrhabdium*. This is mainly because they share with

Achalinus and *Fimbrios* the suspension of the maxilla from the palatine (perhaps merely primitive). *Xylophis* is remarkably similar to *Achalinus* in hemipenis, snout skeleton, and head muscles; the nasal and prefrontal bones meet, as in *Fimbrios*. Inclusion of *Xylophis* in this subfamily suggests further relationships, because *Xylophis perroteti* is unusual in having the kidneys nearly reaching the cloaca and in having a distinct rectal cecum, suggesting the next two subfamilies (which lack posterior hypapophyses). *Xylophis* seems annectent to them (otherwise, these next two subfamilies are quite isolated).

Subfamily *Calamariinae*. Specially characterized by the orbital foramen (Underwood, 1967); the frontal and sphenoid form the border, excluding (or nearly so, in *Macrocalamus*) the parietal. The hemipenis lacks spines and is only shallowly bilobate or simple, the sulcus simple (*Rhabdion*) or centrolineal. The nasal and prefrontal bones meet; suspension of the snout is by nasal-frontal contact; frontals in long contact with trabeculae; kidneys near cloaca but no rectal cecum. In some *Calamaria* (e.g., *C. gervaisi*) and *Macrocalamus*, the levator anguli oris is superficial to the rear of the infralabial gland, as in *Achalinus spinalis* and Pareatinae; in *Macrocalamus*, the maxilla extends freely behind its ectopterygoid articulation, as in *Fimbrios* (and a few other, probably unrelated, snakes such as *Bothrolycus*), but this rear extension is lost in the other genera. East Asia, to Ceram. *Macrocalamus, Rhabdion, Pseudorhabdion, Calamaria* (and probably other, undissected genera).

Inger and Marx (1965) discussed the relationships of *Calamaria* and its relatives (but not *Macrocalamus*) and reached no conclusions except that the *Calamaria* group was likely to be independent of African burrowers and of Indian–southeastern Asian forms. But *Macrocalamus lateralis* (BM 98.9.22.38 examined) and *Xylophis* seem to bridge the otherwise broad gap between Calamariinae and Xenoderminae.

Subfamily *Pareatinae*. Specially characterized by forward projection of the interolfactory pillar of the frontals into the snout, rigidly bracing it (*Xylophis* approaches this in the long contact of the median descending process of the nasal and the distinctly forethrust interolfactory pillar of the frontals); rectal cecum as in *Xylophis;* hemipenis moderately to deeply bilobate, with centrolineal sulcus and no spines (in *Aplopeltura,* with many flounces, suggestive of *Xylophis*); kidneys far posterior. Contact of frontals with trabeculae ranges from long to extremely short (*Aplopeltura*); the orbital foramen is small (with a sphenoid entry) or a large fenestra reaching nearly to the dorsal limit of the orbit (as in *Xylophis*). Unlike Xenoderminae and Calamariinae, the palatine has a long choanal process reaching the vomer. Reduction of the pterygoid, combined with a long quadrate, causes the pterygoid to fall short of the jaw joint, as in Neotropical relatives of *Dipsas* (probably as a convergent adaptation for snail eating, because the hemipenis and snout skeleton are very different in the Neotropical forms and suggest *Rhadinaea*). Southeastern Asia. *Pareas, Aplopeltura*.

The above are isolated but anatomically well-defined groups of uncertain relationships because of conflicting resemblances. In the remainder of the Colubridae, there is a different problem; the anatomical differences are minor and, if convergence takes place, there are few alternative characters to reveal it by their discordance. The following appear to be major lineages, but their precise membership is uncertain and Cadle's (1984a–c, 1985) immunological results make clear that morphology by itself is inadequate to identify the clades.

Subfamily Boodontinae (sensu Dowling et al., 1983). African and Madagascan colubrids with centrolineal sulcus, posterior hypapophyses, and either no suggestion of hemipenial calyces (most) or with fleshy interconnections of the spines, forming "calyces" that do not disarrange the spines. This includes most Madagascan colubrids, both aglyphous (Pseudoxyrhopus, Liophidium, Liopholidophis, Lioheterodon, Dromicodryas, Micropisthodon examined) and rearfanged (Langaha, Madagascarophis, Ithycyphus, Lycodryas; also Ditypophis of Socotra). The whole-serum immunological comparisons of Domergue et al. (1969), using anti-Lioheterodon and counting precipitation rings, gave surprising results, putting Mimophis (with simple sulcus on a greatly reduced hemipenis and poorly distinguished from Psammophis) close to Lioheterodon, along with Langaha and Dromicodryas, but placing Ithycyphus far distant; there was no indication of a division between those with rear fangs against those without rear fangs. This technique does not give results directly comparable with comparisons of single proteins.

The continental African snakes related to Boaedon (Lamprophis, Lycodonomorphus, Pseudoboodon, Bothrophthalmus), to Lycophidion (Chamaelycus, Hormonotus, Dendrolycus—Bothrolycus belongs here, not to the Boaedon cluster) and to Duberria belong to this assemblage. In these African forms, the chromosome count is elevated into the 40s, rather than being 36 as in most booid and colubroid snakes (W. Branch, Pers. comm.), not an important character in itself, but ruling out the group as ancestral to 36-chromosome lineages except by remarkable coincidence. Otherwise, these appear to be very primitive colubrids; in the Boaedon cluster (not Lycodonomorphus bicolor and L. whytii) and in Duberria shirana (not D. lutrix) there is a distinct rectal cecum, lost in most Colubridae [also retained in Pseudoxyrhopus, Liopholidophis sexlineatus (but not L. lateralis), and Liophidium]. In such features as lack of hemipenial flounces, Duberria is more like the Madagascan group than like other African genera, and in one seemingly primitive feature (a secondary loss?) it differs from other Colubridae; the cervicomandibularis makes no direct attachment to the jaw articulation. I have no karyotype data on Madagascan colubrids.

Mehelya and Gonionotophis seem to belong to this group but have a thick-walled venom gland, receiving pterygoideus fibers, have Stoliczkaia-like vertebrae with wings on the pre- and postzygapophyses, and have the sulcus spermaticus almost centrifugal (i.e., running, on each branch of the organ, on the side farthest from the midline of the organ). In most, the hemipenis is forked, but in Gonionotophis granti it is hardly bilobate (BM 1938.3.1.95); further, in G. granti (AMNH 96099) the anterior subcaudals have pits, an unusual feature suggesting two African genera, Afronatrix and Hydraethiops, that seem to link in turn with (at least some) Asiatic natricines. *Afronatrix* and *Hydraethiops* have a feebly bilobate organ, with a smooth terminal basin in the crotch. The sulcus has lost one branch, but the other extends, centrolineally, on to one lobe to join the distal end of the terminal basin. A similar entirely spinose hemipenis, with a simple sulcus produced by the loss of one branch and the other centrolineal, also occurs in the Oriental *Sinonatrix, Rhabdops, Opisthotropis,* and *Pseudagkistrodon* (for *"Macropisthodon" rudis,* not congeneric with *Macropisthodon,* which has a *Rhabdophis*-like hemipenis and skull). Whether these Oriental snakes are related to *Afronatrix* and *Hydraethiops,* or are merely convergent, is uncertain; if the relationship is real, would this indicate an African origin for the lineage or that *Afronatrix* and *Hydraethiops* represent an Oriental invasion of Africa? Rossman and Elberle (1977) discuss the hemipenis and chromosomes of natricines and report a $2n$ of 46 in *Pseudagkistrodon* and a $2n$ of 42 in *Sinonatrix* (no data for *Hydraethiops* and *Afronatrix*).

In *Natriciteres* the hemipenis is very asymmetrically bilobate, with the outer lobe short and asulcate; the medial lobe ends in a narrow extension bearing the tip of the sulcus [figured by Dowling and Duellman (1978), but miscaptioned; the figures of *Natriciteres olivacea* and *Hydraethiops melanogaster* are transposed; Bogert (1940) figures *N. fuliginoides,* without narrowed tip, perhaps not fully everted]. The sulcus does not extend to the crotch side of the longer lobe and so is centrolineal. Asymmetry of the lobes is also seen in *Liophidium trilineatum* (see Domergue, 1983), but with the lateral lobe the longer and both lobes sulcate (centrolineally). *Limnophis* is similar to *Natriciteres olivacea* but lacks the short lateral lobe. Although it lacks posterior hypapophyses, the African *Grayia* seems related to *Natriciteres* but with symmetrical hemipenial lobes with long, distal, narrowed portions carrying the centrolineal sulcus.

In *Pseudaspis* and *Pythonodipsas* the sulcus is centrifugal at the base of each lobe, and then spirals distally into centripetal position. *Pythonodipsas* is rear-fanged, but *Pseudaspis* has variable rear maxillary teeth. In *Pythonodipsas,* posterior hypapophyses are unambiguous; in *Pseudaspis,* they are keels not extending below the condyle, but the hypapophysial muscle is present (as in *Duberria,* like *Pseudaspis* in live-bearing). The chromosomes are $2n = 42$ in *Pseudaspis* and (W. Branch, Pers. comm.) *Pythonodipsas.*

Aparallactus also has small but quite distinct posterior hypapophyses and hypapophysial muscle (*contra* literature); the palatine and pterygoid articulate and the choanal process of the palatine is absent; there is typical colubrid attachment of the pterygoideus to the ectopterygoid just above the rear maxillary teeth. It does not fit with the other Aparallactinae of Bourgeois (1968), which are here referred to the Atractaspididae. Sulcus furcation is a minute divergence at the extreme tip and cannot be classified as centrolineal or centripetal. There are important differences (see Bourgeois, 1968), but the skull suggests *Lycophidion* and, tentatively, *Aparallactus* is placed in the Boodontinae.

Subfamily Pseudoxenodontinae (New). Oriental colubrids with posterior hypapophyses and forked centrolineal sulcus: *Pseudoxenodon, Plagiopholis.* The hemipenial structure could easily be modified into that of Natricinae, Xenodontinae, or Colubrinae; distinct calyces on the lobes of the organ and a centrolineal sulcus are nonnatricine features to be expected in a primitive xenodontine; loss of one sulcus branch would yield the colubrine hemipenis. In spite of hemipenial differences from natricines, the vertebrae have natricine posterior hypapophyses and the septomaxillary-frontal articulation is well lateral to the trabecular cartilage, as in natricines and most xenodontines, and also in *Hydraethiops, Afronatrix*, the *Sinonatrix-Opisthotropis* series of Asia, *Limnophis*, and *Natriciteres*, here considered Boodontinae because the hemipenis lacks calyces and seems derived (by loss of a sulcus branch) from a centrolineal organ. The Pseudoxenodontinae, rather than the Boodontinae, may be ancestral to *Hydraethiops*, etc. or may be close relatives of the Boodontinae that have retained calyces. No karyological or immunological data are available. If xenodontines and natricines are closely related, as implied by Underwood (1967), the Pseudoxenodontinae might share the common ancestry. In having tracheal air sacs both *Plagiopholis* and *Pseudoxenodon* resemble some of the natricine *Rhabdophis*, but also *Pseudagkistrodon*, the Asiatic colubrines *Stegonotus, Gonyosoma*, and *Xenelaphis*, and the elapid *Ophiophagus*. The conflict of morphological clues and lack of an independent check (such as proteins) makes it impossible to place *Pseudoxenodon* and *Plagiopholis* with any assurance.

Subfamily Natricinae. With centripetal sulcus spermaticus (when forked) or simple sulcus that extends to the center of the distal end of the organ, the hemipenis spinose, without calyces, and usually with asymmetrically placed enlarged spines at the base; strong posterior hypapophyses; contact of frontals with trabeculae short or absent.

This definition excludes *Hydraethiops, Afronatrix, Sinonatrix, Rhabdops, Opisthotropis, Limnophis, Natriciteres* (possible Boodontinae), and *Pseudoxenodon* and *Plagiopholis* (Psuedoxenodontinae). The strictly centripetal sulcus of *Xenochrophis* is a resemblance to Homalopsinae, but immunological comparisons by Schwaner and Dessauer (1982) do not support a close relationship. Schwaner and Dessauer did not compare Boodontinae or Pseudoxenodontinae but showed that *Afronatrix*, Asiatic water snakes, American Thamnophini (*sensu* Rossman and Eberle, 1977), and *Natrix* form a natural group when compared with colubrines. This is reinforced by Dowling et al. (1983); between *Natriciteres olivacea* and *Thamnophis sirtalis*, they found an albumin immunological distance (ID) of 46—the same as between *Thamnophis sirtalis* and *T. mendax* but considerably greater than the ID between *Thamnophis sirtalis* and other American natricines (Thamnophini) or the ID of 39 between *T. sirtalis* and *Xenochrophis flavipunctatus*. The ID between *T. sirtalis* and *Madagascarophis* (Boodontinae, following Dowling et al., 1983) was 80, greater than the ID of 67 between *T. sirtalis* and the homalopsine *Enhydris enhydris* or the ID of 54 between *T. sirtalis* and the colubrine *Elaphe obsoleta*. It seems impossible to resolve the precise limits of the Natricinae without much more information on various Boodontinae.

Morphology cannot now be resolved with immunology or with karyotyping.

Rossman and Eberle (1977) report $2n = 36$ for all American genera examined and for *Amphisema stolata* and *A. vibakari;* 36 chromosomes, found in most snakes (including henophidians), might be achieved by secondary reduction from the high counts of African Boodontinae or the 40 to 44 observed in *Rhabdophis, Sinonatrix,* and *Xenochrophis,* but such coincidence seems implausible.

The broad "centripetal sulcus" extending only halfway along each lobe in *Rhabdophis* (see Rossman and Eberle, 1977) seems to be a simple true sulcus opening into a smooth crotch region; but *Amplorhinus* of southern Africa and *Psammodynastes* of southeastern Asia have a true sulcus branch running centropetally along each lobe (both are live bearers with a tracheal lung, thus are like Homalopsinae, and the centripetal sulcus might be directly inherited from a homalopsine ancestor). In *Xenochrophis cerasogaster* (Indian region), the sulcus forks in the crotch and gradually thickens its tissue, broadens, and loses lips as it extends to the tips of the blunt lobes; in *X. piscator,* the furcation of the sulcus itself becomes thick tissue, and the tips of the lobes become nonsulcate nipples; this could lead to what is seen in Asiatic *Amphisema,* North American Thamnophini, and European–western Asian *Natrix:* a terminal basin of thick, smooth tissue receiving the simple sulcus near the midline of the organ. The Seychelles *Lycognathophis,* with a simple sulcus and simple organ, with numerous spines distally but some enlarged and asymmetrically placed spines proximally, also appears natricine, with a skull very similar to that of *Amphiesma. Geodipsas* of Africa and Madagascar and the Madagascan *Alluaudina* have an entirely spinulose simple organ, with a furcate sulcus (at the extreme tip in Madagascan *Geodipsas*); even when sulcus furcation is deep (*G. depressiceps, Alluaudina*), the branches of the sulcus do not diverge but run close to the midline of the organ, suggesting a centripetal sulcus.

No South American colubrid appears definitely natricine. Posterior hypapophyses (the conventional diagnostic character of the subfamily) are known for some *Helicops, Ninia,* etc., referred here to Xenodontinae on hemipenial evidence. *Hydrops* approaches a natricine hemipenis but lacks hypapophyses posteriorly.

The Asiatic *Cyclocorus, Aspidura, Haplocercus, Blythia, Trachischium,* and *Elapoidis* seem to be Colubrinae related to *Lycodon.*

Subfamily Xenodontinae. With sulcus spermaticus forked (except in some genera with a capitate hemipenis) and centrolineal, or centripetal near the crotch but becoming centrolineal distally, or (the majority) centrifugal (i.e., its branches taking the position farthest from the midline of the organ); most genera with well-defined calyces; some (e.g., *Nothopsis, Amastridium*) with natricine posterior hypapophyses but most with posterior hypapophyses reduced to keels.

Jenner and Dowling (1985) have classified this group on hemipenial structure and albumin comparisons. Cadle's (1984a–c, 1985) extensive serum albumin comparisons show that even some genera (e.g., *Rhadinaea*) are polyphyletic and destroy any confidence that a simple morphological key will reflect the true phylogeny. It is a working assumption that the Xenodontinae are a New Worldgroup, but this has not been proven—or even extensively tested. The African *Grayia* would key out to this subfamily as a colubrid with forked sulcus spermaticus and without posterior hypapophyses. Such *Ahaetulla* (= *Dryophis*) as *A. prasina* (AMNH 58525, *A. nasuta* (AMNH 87456), and *A. pulverulenta* (AMNH 85526), but not *A. fasciolata* (AMNH 2918), have a small left side branch of the sulcus (either organ, inverted) ending short of the terminus of the main sulcus and also falling short of the tip of the organ. Such an asymmetrically forked sulcus is seen in some *Rhadinaea,* and *Ahaetulla* may be an Asiatic relative of that genus.

Aside from these questionable Old World relatives, the naturalness of the Xenodontinae (but not of its tribes and genera) is supported by immunological comparisons; all xenodontines compared come out closer to some other xenodontine than to a non-xenodontine—but only when *Leptodeira* and its close relatives are accepted as Xenodontinae. The key character of Xenodontinae, sulcus furcation, is poorly, if at all, developed in the *Leptodeira* group; they are assigned to the Xenodontinae because the hemipenis is capitate as in some unequivocal Xenodontinae (e.g., *Rhadinaea, Coniophanes, Dipsas*). The range of Xenodontinae may be given, tentatively, as temperate and tropical New World, including the West Indies and the Galapagos Islands.

Subfamily Colubrinae. Hemipenis with simple sulcus, but usually weakly bilobate with the sulcus extending to the right lobe (either everted organ); organs (usually) not mirror images distally, and the sulcus may be asymmetric for most of their length; calyces usually present distally. Posterior hypapophyses usually merely keels (present throughout column in some; may be present posteriorly but absent from midbody in *Boiga irregularis*). Usually, frontal facet for septomaxilla less distant from interolfactory pillar and from trabecular ridge of frontal than in Natricinae and Xenodontinae, the nasal and septomaxilla usually sharing this facet. Range as for the family.

The albumin comparisons of Cadle (1984c) and of Dowling et al. (1983) indicate that there is a natural nucleus to this group, found in both the New World and Old World. However, certain groups here included within the Colubrinae, but not yet compared serologically with this nucleus, show morphological differences that make their inclusion uncertain.

Oligodon and *Dryocalamus* have a symmetrically bilobate distal end of the hemipenis with a nude terminal basin on the centripetal face of the lobes; the simple sulcus extends into the crotch of this organ, in natricine fashion, rather than onto the right lobe; however, some *Oligodon* and *Dryocalamus* have distal calyces or flounces, rather than the entirely spinose armature of Natricinae. *Oligodon* and *Dryocalamus* lack posterior hypapophyses, have a small splenial with the Meckelian canal completely closed over, and have a strong dorsoanterior lobe of the crista circumfenestralis nearly concealing the footplate of the stapes; all of these are common colubrine characters not observed in natricines. The distal symmetry of the hemipenis of *Oligodon* and *Dryocalamus* may be secondarily superimposed on a typically colubrine organ.

In *Lycodon aulicus*, I found strong posterior hypapophyses, with accompanying muscle, in AMNH 66777 (Philippines), but no posterior hypapophyses or hypapophysial muscle in AMNH 99391 (Sri Lanka); strong posterior hypapophyses, with muscle, were observed in *L. osmanhilli* (AMNH 96070) and *L. travancoricus* (AMNH 43387); no posterior hypapophyses were found in *L. albofuscus* (Duméril and Bibron) (= *"Lepturophis borneensis"* Boulenger) (FMNH 148894, 148896), *L. subcinctus* (AMNH 27755), *L. striatus* (AMNH 89286), or *L. ruhstrati* (AMNH 34584). The hemipenis of *L. albofuscus* (FMNH 148896) is clearly colubrine, with a distinctly bilobate distal end bearing calyces and a simple sulcus extending centrifugally to the right (as everted) lobe, but other species are equivocal; the sulcus is definitely simple, but the distal end is not clearly bilobate and, in *L. ruhstrati* and *L. striatus,* not clearly calyculate.

Cyclocorus agrees generally with *Lycodon,* and especially as follows: long and simply pointed parasphenoid rostrum; anterior orifice of Vidian canal in parietal; suspension of the rostral complex by a nasal-frontal condyle-cotyle joint, the septomaxilla meeting the frontal but not expanded into a distinct articular surface. The hemipenis is very narrow, entirely spinose (no calyces), with a simple sulcus, and no indication of distal bilobation; it could be either natricine or colubrine. The strong posterior hypapophyses are natricine, but the skull, compared bone by bone, makes a relationship to *Lycodon* seem more probable, and the posterior hypapophyses of some *Lycodon* gives derivation of *Cyclocorus* from *Lycodon* plausibility.

Some small burrowing snakes with a simple sulcus, an entirely spinose and cylindroid hemipenis and posterior hypapophyses, have been regarded as "degenerate natricines" but seem more likely to be derived from the *Lycodon-Cyclocorus* lineage, perhaps independently. These genera are the Indonesian *Elapoidis,* the Burmese–northern Indian *Trachischium* and *Blythia,* and the Sri Lankan *Haplocercus* and *Aspidura.* They agree with *Lycodon* in the articulation of the snout to the frontals mainly by the nasals, the septomaxillary-frontal contact either resting on the trabecular cartilage and lacking formed articular surfaces or (Sri Lankan genera) quite absent, whereas natricines (except *Psammodynastes*) have a particularly well-developed septomaxillary-frontal articulation set off from the trabecular cartilage and with well-defined articular surfaces. Except for *Elapoidis,* they are more like *Lycodon* than like natricines in having the Meckelian cartilage enclosed by the dentary anteriorly. In all of them, the parasphenoid tapers to a point anteriorly and the frontals cover the trabeculae laterally, as in *Lycodon* and unlike natricines.

Family Viperidae Bonaparte. Maxilla much shortened, not extending anterior to its prefrontal articulation, its dentition reduced to a pair of fangs (with enclosed canal, not an open groove) at its rear, just behind its ectopterygoid articulation; a thick-walled venom gland, homologous to that of Proteroglypha and to the small "anterior temporal" or "posterior" gland of Colubridae, but with novel muscular connections; the levator anguli oris, although present, does not attach to the gland, which is instead attached to fibers of the adductor externus super-ficialis (sometimes also to the pterygoideus).

The classification of this family follows Liem et al. (1971). Cadle (1982) showed that the albumin differences between viperids and colubrids are so great that it is unlikely that viperids are descended from any present-day colubrid lineage.

Subfamily Azemiopinae. No loreal pit; palatine with long and slender choanal process; prefrontal with ventral part of its medial edge drawn back as a pos-teromedial process, forming a partial medial wall for orbit. *Azemiops,* south-eastern Asia.

Subfamily Crotalinae. A deep loreal (heat-sensory) pit lodged in a fossa on prefrontal and maxilla; palatine with at least low flange representing choanal process, long and fingerlike in *Deinagkistrodon* and *Calloselasma;* no postero-medial process of prefrontal. *Agkistrodon, Hypnale, Calloselasma, Trimeresu-rus, Bothrops, Tropidolaemus, Lachesis, Sistrurus, Crotalus.* Asia, eastern Eu-rope, and New World.

Subfamily Viperinae. No loreal pit; no trace of choanal process on palatine; no posteriomedial process of prefrontal. *Vipera, Bitis, Causus, Atheris, Echis, Eristicophis, Cerastes, Pseudocerastes.* Eurasia and Africa (not Madagascar).

FUTURE RESEARCH

As the above summary indicates, much is uncertain about the phylogeny of snakes. A great deal remains to be discovered by the techniques already in use—comparative morphology, immunology, and karyology. In comparative mor-phology, not only of the living forms but particularly of the fossils, the obvious problem is choosing between conflicting evidence, and independent evidence of immunology and karyology is invaluable in making a choice. Just a few well selected (or simply lucky) immunological comparisons might clarify the clas-sification of many species by telling us how to read the large body of morpho-logical data accumulated over two centuries. We already know enough of the morphology of living snakes to draw up several hundred conflicting phylogenies. Identifying the correct one (the one expressing what really happened, not nec-essarily the most parsimonious) would be much easier if more comparisons of transferrins or serum albumins were available, or even gross chromosome counts, particularly for Asiatic and Madagascar forms.

A less obvious need for the correct interpretation of anatomical data is some developmental perspective. At present, almost all information is about adult structure and phrased as "characters," statements about the presence or absence of some anatomical feature that has so impressed us (or our predecessors) that we have given it a name. This is forced upon us by the nature of our material, but it is plainly unrealistic.

There is no biological mechanism for inheriting a character. Rather, genes can somehow regulate developmental processes so that the probability of an anatomical character resulting from development is increased or decreased.

The anatomy is a clue to the development that produced it, and whether or not the genes favoring a particular development become fixed in a population is largely dependent on whether the anatomy resulting from this development meets functional demands imposed by the environment. It would be very foolish not to exploit the information that can be obtained from the anatomy of museum specimens; such study still remains the most efficient means of obtaining clues to phylogeny in any particular case—its value is taken for granted in the identification of the specimens used and in the choice of taxa to be compared in biochemical, or karyological systematics.

The anatomy is *not* a totem pole. There is no evidence that development has a purpose of producing tidy credentials of ancestry, even though close common ancestry can be deduced from close anatomical resemblances. We know virtually nothing about the interactions in development of the anatomical characters used in the classification of snakes. How much does the development of a newly acquired character modify the development of other characters and perhaps disguise them? How "independent" are characters from different regions of the body that happen to develop at the same time?

None of these questions of development are directly answerable by examining fossils, but the interpretation of the anatomy of fossils is as dependent on a developmental perspective as the interpretation of the anatomy of living forms (indeed, paleontologists seem to be more aware of ontogenetic change than most neontologists). The discovery of more fossil material, particularly skulls, will certainly advance our understanding of snake phylogeny and may change our concepts radically. Such discoveries need good luck, but such luck requires hard work in the quarries.

The systematic method that will give accuracy and certainty when data are incomplete has not yet been devised.

LITERATURE CITED

Anthony, J. 1955. Essai sur l'évolution anatomique de l'appareil venimeux des ophidiens, *Ann. Sci. Nat. Zool.* 17:7–53.

Auffenberg, W. 1959. *Anomalophis bolcensis* (Massalongo), a new genus of fossil snake from the Italian Eocene, *Breviora* 114:1–16.

Bogert, C. M. 1940. Herpetological results of the Vernay Angola Expedition with notes on African reptiles in other collections. I. Snakes, including an arrangement of African Columbridae, *Bull. Am. Mus. Nat. Hist.* 57:1–107, pl. I.

Bogert, C. M. 1968a. The variations and affinities of the dwarf boas of the genus *Ungaliophis, Am. Mus. Novit.* 2340:1–26.

Bogert, C. M. 1968b. A new genus and species of dwarf boa from southern Mexico, *Am. Mus. Novit.* 2353:1–38.

Brock G. T. 1929. On the development of the skull of *Leptodeira hotamboia*, *Q. J. Microsc. Sci.* (N. S.) 73:239–333, pls. 12–13.

Brongersma, L. D. 1951a. Some remarks on the pulmonary artery in snakes with two lungs, *Zool. Verh.* (*Leiden*) 14:1–36.

Brongersma, L. D. 1951b. Some notes upon the anatomy of *Tropiophis* and *Trachyboa* (Serpentes), *Zool. Meded.* (*Leiden*) 31:107–124.

Brongersma, L. D. 1957. Les organes de respiration et l'artère pulmonaire chez les serpents, *C. R. Assoc. Anat.* 44:206–210.

Brongersma, L. D. 1959. Upon some features of the respiratory and circulatory systems in the Typhlopidae and some other snakes, *Arch. Néerl. Zool.* 13 (suppl. 1):120–127.

Bourgeois, M. 1968. Contribution à la morphologie comparée du crane des ophidiens de l'Afrique Centrale, *Publ. Univ. Off. Congo (Lubumbashi)* 13:1–295.

Cadle, J. E. 1982. Problems and approaches in the interpretation of the evolutionary history of venomous snakes, *Mem. Inst. Butantan (Sao Paulo)* 46:255–274.

Cadle, J. E. 1984a. Molecular systematics of Neotropical xenodontine snakes. I. South American xenodontines, *Herpetologica* 40:8–20.

Cadle, J. E. 1984b. Molecular systematics of Neotropical xenodontine snakes. II. Central American xenodontines, *Herpetologica* 40:21–30.

Cadle, J. E. 1984c. Molecular systematics of Neotropical xenodontine snakes. III. Overview of xenodontine phylogeny and the history of New World snakes, *Copeia* 1984:641–652.

Cadle, J. E. 1985. The Neotropical colubrid snake fauna (Serpentes: Colubridae): Lineage components and biogeography, *Syst. Zool.* 34:1–20.

Camp, C. L. 1942. California mosasaurs, *Mem. Univ. California* 13:i–vi, 1–68, pls. 1–7.

Cope, E. D. 1900. The crocodilians, lizards, and snakes of North America, *Rep. U. S. Nat. Mus.* 1898:153–1270, pls. 1–35.

Cundall, D. 1983. Activity of head muscles during feeding by snakes; A comparative study, *Am. Zool.* 23:383–396.

Domergue, C. A. 1983. Notes sur les serpents de la région malgache III. Description de trois espèces nouvelles rapportées au genre *Liophidium* Boulenger, 1896, *Bull. Mus. Nat. Hist. Nat.*, Paris, (ser. 4) 5 [A]:1109–1122.

Domergue, C., Dodin, A., Pinon, J.-M., and Brygoo, E. R. 1969. Première application des techniques sérologiques à l'étude de la systématique des serpentes de Madagascar, *Arch. Inst. Pasteur Madagascar* 38:175–180.

Doucet, J. 1963. Les serpents de la République de Côte d'Ivoire, *Acta Trop.* 20:201–259, 297–340.

Dowling, H. G. 1975. The nearctic snake fauna, in: 1974 Yearbook of Herpetology (H. G. Dowling, ed.) pp. 191–202, HISS Publications, New York.

Dowling, H. G. and Duellman, W. E. 1978. Systematic herpetology: A synopsis of families and higher categories, HISS Publications, New York.

Dowling, H. G., Highton, R., Maha, G. C., and Maxson, L. R. 1983. Biochemical evaluation of colubrid snake phylogeny, *J. Zool. (Lond.)* 201:309–329.

Duméril, A.-M.-C. 1853. Prodrome de la classification des reptiles ophidiens, *Mem. Acad. Sci. Inst. Fr.* (ser. ii) 23:399–536, 2 pls.

Elias, H. and Bortner, S. 1957. On the phylogeny of hair. *Am. Mus. Novit.* 1820:1–15.

Estes, R., Frazzetta, T. H., and Williams, E. E. 1970. Studies of the fossil snake *Dinilysia patagonica* Woodward. I. Cranial morphology, *Bull. Mus. Comp. Zool. Harv. Univ.* 140:25–74.

Frazzetta, T. H. 1970. Studies on the fossil snake *Dinilysia patgonica* Woodward. II. Jaw machinery in the earliest snakes, *Forma Functio* 3:205–221.

Frazzetta, T. H. 1971. Notes upon the jaw musculature of the bolyerine snake, *Casarea dussumieri, J. Herpetol.* 5:61–63.

Gilmore, C. W. 1938. Fossil snakes of North America, *Spec. Pap. Geol. Soc. Amer.* 9:vii + 96, pls. 1–4.

Grigg, G., Shine, R., and Ehmann, H. (eds.). 1985. The Biology of Australasian Frogs and Reptiles, Surrey Beatty, Chipping Norton, N.S.W., Australia.

Haas, G. 1930. Über das kopfskelett und die Kaumuskulatur der Typhlopiden und Glauconiiden, *Zool. Jahrb. Abt. Anat.* 52:1–94.

Haas, G. 1931. Uber die Morphologie der Kiefermuskulatur und die Schädelmechanik einiger Schlangen, *Zool. Jahrb. Abt. Anat.* 54:333–416.

Haas G. 1964. Anatomical observations on the head of *Liotyphlops albirostris* (Typhlopidae, Ophidia), *Acta Zool.* 45:1–62.

Haas, G. 1968. Anatomical observations on the head of *Anomalepis aspinosus* (Typhlopidae, Ophidia), *Acta Zool.* 49:63–139.

Haas, G. 1973. Muscles of the jaws and associated structures in the Rhynchocephalia and Squamata, in: Biology of the Reptilia, vol. 4 (C. Gans and T. S. Parsons, eds.) pp. 285–490, Academic Press, New York.

Haas, G. 1979. On a new snakelike reptile from the lower Cenomanian of Ein Jabrud, near Jerusalem, *Bull. Mus. Nat. Hist. Nat.,* Paris (ser. 4), Tome 1, Sect. C:51–64.

Haas, G. 1980a. Remarks on a new ophiomorph reptile from the lower Cenomanian of Ein Jabrud Israel, in: Aspects of Vertebrate History (L. L. Jacobs, ed.) pp. 177–192, Museum of Northern Arizona Press, Flagstaff, Arizona.

Haas, G. 1980b. *Pachyrhachis problemticus* Haas, snake-like reptile from the lower Cenomanian: Ventral view of the skull, *Bull. Mus. Nat. Hist. Nat.,* Paris (ser. 4), tome 2, sect. C:87–104.

Haluska, F. and Alberch, P. 1983. The cranial development of *Elaphe obsoleta* (Ophidia, Colubridae), *J. Morphol.* 178:37–55.

Hardaway, T. E. and Williams, K. L. 1976. Costal cartilages in snakes and their phylogenetic significance, *Herpetologica* 32:378–387.

Hecht, M. K. 1982. The vertebral morphology of the Cretaceous snake, *Dinilysia patagonica* Woodward, *Neues Jahrb. Geol. Palaeont. Monatsh.* 1982 (Heft 9):523–532.

Hoffstetter, R. 1955. Squamates de type moderne, in: Traité de Paléontologie (J. Piveteau, ed.) tome V, pp. 606–662, Masson, Páris.

Hoffstetter, R. 1959a. Un serpent terrestre dans le Crétacé inférieur du Sahara, *Bull. Soc. Geol. Fr.* (ser. 7), Tome 1:897–902.

Hoffstetter, R. 1959b. Un dentaire de *Madtsoia* (serpent géant du Paléocène de Patagonie), *Bull. Mus. Nat. Hist. Nat.* Pàris, (ser. 2) tome 31 (no. 4):379–386.

Hoffstetter, R. 1961. Nouveaux restes d'un serpent Boïdé (*Madtsoia madagascariensis* nov. sp.) dans le Crétacé supérieur de Madagascar, *Bull. Mus. Natl. Hist. Nat.* Paris, (ser. 2) tome 33 (no. 2):152–160.

Hoffstetter, R. 1962. Revue des récentes acquisitions concernant l'histoire et la systématique des squamates, *Colloq. Int. Cent. Natl. Rech. Sci.* 104:243–279.

Hoffstetter, R. and Gasc, J. P. 1969. Vertebrae and ribs of modern reptiles, in: Biology of the Reptilia, vol. 1 (C. Gans A. d'A. Bellairs and T. S. Parsons, eds.) pp. 201–309, Academic Press, New York.

Hoffstetter, R. and Gayrard, Y. 1965. Observations sur l'ostéologie et la classification des Acrochordidae (Serpentes), *Bull. Mus. Natl. Hist. Natl., Paris,* (ser. 2), 36:677–696.

Hoffstetter, R. and Rage, J. C. 1972. Les *Erycinae* fossiles de France (Serpentes, Boidae) Compréhension et histoire de la sousfamille, *Ann. Paléontol. (Vert.)* 58:81–124, pls. i–ii.

Hoffstetter, R. and Rage, J. C. 1977. Le gisement de vertébrés miocènes de la Venta (Colombie) et sa faune de serpents, *Ann. Paléontol.* (Ver.), 63:161–190.

Inger, R. F. and H. Marx. 1965. The systematics and evolution of the Oriental colubrid snakes of the genus *Calamaria, Fieldiana Zool.* 49:1–304.

Janensch, W. 1906. Über *Archaeophis proavus* Mass., eine Schlange aus dem Eocan des Monte Bolca, *Beitr. Palaeontol. Oesterr.* 19:1–33.

Jenner, J. V. and Dowling, H. G. 1985. Taxonomy of American xenodontine snakes: The tribe Pseudoboini, *Herpetologica,* 41:161–172.

Kardong, K. V. 1979. "Protovipers" and the evolution of snake fangs, *Evolution* 33:433–443.

Kardong, K. V. 1980. Evolutionary patterns in advanced snakes, *Am. Zool.* 20:269–282.

Kardong, K. V. 1982. The evolution of the venom apparatus in snakes from colubrids to viperids and elapids, *Mem. Inst. Butantan (Sao Paulo)* 46:105–118.

Kochva, E. 1978. Oral glands of the Reptilia, in: Biology of the Reptilia, vol. 8 (C. Gans and K. A. Gans, eds.) pp. 43–161, Academic Press, New York.

Langebartel, D. 1968. The hyoid and its associated muscles in snakes, Illinois Biol. Monogr. 38, University of Illinois Press, Urbana.

Liem, K. F., H. Marx, and G. Rabb. 1971. The viperid snake *Azemiops:* Its comparative cephalic anatomy and phylogenetic position in relation to Viperinae and Crotalinae, *Fieldiana Zool.* 59(2):64–126.

List, J. C. 1966. Comparative osteology of the snake families Typhlopidae and Leptotyphlopidae, Illinois Biol. Monogr. 36, University of Illinois Press, Urbana.

McCarthy, C. J. 1985. Monophyly of elapid snakes (Serpentes: Elapidae). An assessment of the evidence, *Zool. J. Linn. Soc.* 83:79–93.

McDowell, S. B. 1967a. Osteology of the Typhlopidae and Leptotyphlopidae: A critical review, *Copeia* 1967:686–692.

McDowell, S. B. 1967b. The extracolumella and tympanic cavity of the "earless" monitor lizard, *Lanthanotus borneensis, Copeia* 1967:154–159.

McDowell, S. B 1970. The status and relationships of the Solomon Island elapid snakes, *J. Zool. (Lond.)* 161:145–190.

McDowell, S. B. 1972. The evolution of the tongue of snakes and its bearing on snake origins, in: Evolutionary Biology, vol. 6 (T. Dobzhansky, M. K. Hecht, and W. C. Steere, eds.) pp. 191–273, Appleton-Century-Crofts, New York.

McDowell, S. B. 1974. A catalogue of the snakes of New Guinea and the Solomons, with special reference to those in the Bernice P. Bishop Museum. I. Scolecophidia, *J. Herpetol.* 8:1–57.

McDowell, S. B. 1975. A catalogue of the snakes of New Guinea and the Solomons, with special reference to those in the Bernice P. Bishop Museum. II. Anilioidea and Pythoninae, *J. Herpetol.* 9:1–80.

McDowell, S. B. 1979. A catalogue of the snakes of New Guinea and the Solomons, with special reference to those in the Bernice P. Bishop Museum. III. Boinae and Acrochordoidea (Reptilia; Serpentes), *J. Herpetol.* 13:1–92.

McDowell, S. B. 1986. The architecture of the corner of the mouth of colubroid snakes, *J. Herpetol.* 20:349–403.

Nopcsa, F. 1923. *Eidolosaurus* und *Pachyophis,* zwei neue Neocom Reptilien, *Palaeontogr.* 65 (4):97–154.

Persky, B., Smith, H. M., and Williams, K. L. 1976. Additional observations on ophidian costal cartilages, *Herpetologica* 32:399–401.

Rage, J. C. 1974. Les serpents des phosphorites du Quercy, *Palaeovertebrata* 6:274–303.

Rage, J. C. 1977a. La position phylétique de *Dinilysia patagonica,* serpent du Crétacé supérieur, *C.R. Acad. Sci. Paris,* 284 (ser. D):1765–1768.

Rage, J. C. 1978a. L'origine des Colubroides et des Acrochordoides (Reptilia, Serpentes), *C.R. Acad. Sci. Paris,* 286 (ser. D):595–597.

Rage, J. C. 1978b. La poche à phosphate de Ste.-Neboule (Let) et sa faune de vertebres du Ludian supérieur. 5. Squamates, *Palaeovertebrata* 8:201–215.

Rage, J. C. 1983a. Les serpents aquatiques de l'Eocène européen: Dèfinition des espèces et aspects stratigraphiques, *Bull. Mus. Natl. Hist. Natl.,* Paris, (4) 5 (sect. C):213–241.

Rage, J. C. 1983b. *Palaeophis colossaeus* nov. sp. (le plus grand Serpent connu?) de l'Eocène du Mali et le problème du genre chez les Palaeopheinae, *C.R. Acad. Sci. Paris,* 296 (ser. II):1741–1744.

Rage, J. C. and Wouters, G. 1979. Dècouverte du plus ancien Palaeopheidé (Reptilia, Serpentes) dans le Maestrichtien du Màroc, *Geobios* 12:293–296.

Rieppel, O. 1976. The homology of the laterosphenoid bone in snakes, *Herpetologica* 32:426–429.

Rieppel, O. 1977. Studies on the skull of the Henophidia (Reptilia: Serpentes), *J. Zool. (Lond.)* 181:145–173.

Rieppel, O. 1979a. A cladistic classification of primitive snakes based on skull structure, *Z. Zool. Syst. Evolutionsforsch.* 17:140–150.

Rieppel, O. 1979b. The braincase of *Typhlops* and *Leptotyphlops* (Reptilia: Serpentes), *Zool. J. Linn. Soc.* 65:161–176.

Rieppel, O. 1979c. The evolution of the basicranium in the Henophidia (Reptilia: Serpentes), *Zool. J. Linn. Soc.* 66:411–431.

Rieppel, O. 1980. The trigeminal jaw adductors of primitive snakes and their homologies with the lacertilian jaw adductors, *J. Zool. (Lond.)* 190: 447–471.

Robb, J. and Smith H. M. 1966. The systematic position of the group of snake genera allied to *Anomalepis, Nat. Hist. Misc.* (Chic.) 184:1–8.

Romer, A. S. 1956. Osteology of the Reptiles, University of Chicago Press, Chicago.

Rossman, D. A. and Eberle, W. G. 1977. Partition of the genus *Natrix*, with preliminary observations on evolutionary trends in natricine snakes, *Herpetologica* 33:34–43.

Schmidt, W. J. 1918. Studien am Integument der Reptilien. VIII. Uber die Haut der Acrochordinen, *Zool. Jahrb. Abt. Anat.* 40:155–202, pls. 4–5.

Schwaner, T. D. and Dessauer, H. C. 1981. Immunodiffusion evidence for the relationships of Papuan boids, *J. Herpetol.* 15:250–253.

Schwaner, T. D. and Dessauer, H. C. 1982. Comparative immunodiffusion survey of snake transferrins focused on the relationships of the natricines, *Copeia* 1982:541–549.

Simpson, G. G. 1933. A new fossil snake from the *Notostylops* beds of Patagonia, *Bull. Am. Mus. Natl. Hist.* 67:1–22.

Smith, H. M., Smith, R. B., and Sawin, H. L. 1977. A summary of snake classification (Reptilia, Serpentes), *J. Herpetol.* 11:115–121.

Smith, M. A. 1943. The Fauna of British India, Ceylon and Burma, Including the Whole of the Indo-Chinese Subregion: Reptilia and Amphibia, vol. III, Serpentes, Taylor and Francis, London.

Smith, M. A. and Bellairs, A. d'A. 1947. The head glands of snakes, with remarks on the evolution of the parotid gland and teeth of the opisthoglypha, *J. Linn. Soc. Lond. Zool.* 41:351–368, pls. 4–5.

Smith, M. J. 1976. Small fossil vertebrates from Victoria Cave, Naracoorte, South Australia. IV. Reptiles, *Trans. R. Soc. R. Aust.* 100:39–51.

Taub, A. M. 1957. Comparative histological studies on Duvernoy's gland of colubrid snakes, *Bull. Am. Mus. Natl. Hist.* 138:1–50, pls. 1–8.

Taub, A. M. 1966. Ophidian cephalic glands, *J. Morphol.* 118:529–542.

Underwood, G. 1967. A Contribution to the Classification of Snakes, British Museum (Natural History), London.

Underwood, G. 1976. A systematic analysis of boid snakes, in: Morphology and Biology of Reptiles (A. d'A. Bellairs and C. B. Cox, eds.) pp. 151–175, Linn. Soc. Symp. Ser. 3, Academic Press, London.

Wallach, V. 1984. A new name for *Ophiomorphus colberti* Haas, 1980, *J. Herpetol.* 18:329.

Willard, W. A. 1915. The cranial nerves of *Anolis carolinensis, Bull. Mus. Comp. Zool. Harv. Univ.* 59:17–116, pls. 1–7.

Williams, E. E. 1959. The occipito-vertebral joint in the burrowing snakes of the Family Uropeltidae, *Breviora* 106:1–10.

CHAPTER TWO

Fossil History

Jean-Claude Rage

In paleontology, it is said that fossil snakes are rare and difficult to study. This assertion is largely untrue. Articulated fossil snakes are infrequent, and from this observation comes the belief that fossil snakes are rare. But isolated snake bones are not infrequently found in deposits bearing vertebrates; they are even common. Obviously, vertebrae are by far the most prevalent remains. At first sight, the study of vertebrae is an uphill battle, the difficulty arising chiefly from the lack of an appropriate bibliography. However, when the student makes comparisons between fossil and recent vertebrae, he or she becomes aware that the difficulties are not insurmountable and that determinations are often easy (except within the Scolecophidia).

Although the usefulness of vertebrae for purposes of identification is well established, their significance in phyletic reconstruction is sometimes questioned. It is clear that the vertebrae of related living snakes are similar. On the other hand, snakes with similar modes of life but that are not related have dissimilar vertebrae. At most, modes of life slightly modify the vertebral morphology, and in spite of these adaptative modifications the vertebral type remains perceivable. Non-experts in snake vertebrae often believe that vertebrae are especially liable to parallelism. This idea comes from the fact that they are attracted by vertebral projecting parts whose variations are easily observed, and it is true that these parts (processes, neural spine) more or less undergo variations connected with the mode of life. But phyletic inferences are based on the general structure of the vertebrae, not on these projecting parts. Moreover, vertebral morphology is rather conservative; this is awkward for phyletic analyses at a low taxonomic level but favorable for phyletic analyses at a higher phyletic level; for such a purpose, snake vertebrae are reliable.

The first descriptions of fossil snakes were made in the 1830s and 1840s. Since that time, articles have accumulated in geological and biological journals.

It is not possible to cite all these works in this short review; literature concerning fossil snakes has been well documented by Gilmore (1938), Kuhn (1939, 1963), Hoffstetter (1955, 1962), Mlynarski (1961), Auffenberg (1963), Holman (1979a, 1981a), Rage (1984a), and Szyndlar (1984).

THE ORIGIN OF SNAKES

Phyletic Aspects

Paleontology does not afford unquestionable annectent forms between generalized tetrapodous reptiles and typical snakes. The oldest known snake, *Lapparentophis*, reveals no information about the origin of snakes. Even *Dinilysia*, a well-preserved snake from the late Cretaceous, is equally unavailing. Therefore, discussions dealing with this question generally rest on comparative anatomy.

Some fossil Lepidosauria might be related to snake ancestry. *Pachyophis* and *Mesophis*, from the lowermost late Cretaceous, are both known by rather complete though badly crushed skeletons (Nopcsa, 1923; Bolkay, 1925). I do not think that it is really possible to draw inferences from these fossils, which might be either primitive snakes or merely peculiar varanoid lizards. *Pachyrhachis problematicus*, approximately contemporaneous with *Pachyophis* and *Mesophis*, is another snakelike fossil; posterior limb rudiments might have been present (Haas, 1979, 1980a). Vertebrae and ribs of the mid-body were pachyostotic, as in *Pachyophis*. The maxillae, mandibles, and suspensorial apparatus appear clearly snakelike. *Pachyrhachis* may be a primitive snake but, because of peculiarities of its skull, such a designation cannot be accepted without reservations, and the opinion of Haas (1979), who regards *Pachyrhachis* as a snakelike varanoid, cannot be absolutely ruled out. *Estesius colberti* is another elongate squamate from the earliest late Cretaceous (Haas, 1980b; Wallach, 1984). In spite of the elongation of the body, a rather well-developed hind limb and a rudimentary pelvic girdle were present. Vertebrae and ribs were not pachyostotic. The skull [if it is actually the skull of *Estesius;* see McDowell (this volume)] is partly concealed by the axial skeleton and apparently retains an upper temporal arch. Because the major observable features of *Estesius* are primitive, I am unable to infer its relationships and it remains an enigmatic fossil.

Research on living forms may provide another means of determining the ancestry of snakes. It is clear that snakes display much closer affinities with lizards than with any other group. From this observation two opinions have arisen: (1) Snakes may have originated from lizards, and (2) snakes and lizards may be more or less independent squamatan groups (Rage, 1984a).

Bellairs and Underwood (1951), McDowell and Bogert (1954), Underwood (1957), and Bellairs (1972) supported an origin of snakes within the lizard group. The varanoids have been generally considered close to the snake ancestry, especially various extinct varanoid groups regarded as possible ancestors of, or closely related to, the unknown snake ancestor (for a review see Rage, 1984a). McDowell and Bogert (1954) believe that the living *Lanthanotus* represents a "structural ancestor" of snakes. Close relationships between *Lanthanotus* and snakes have been also admitted by McDowell (1967, 1972) and Bellairs (1972), but Rieppel (1983) has rejected these views. Underwood (1957) has put forward an alternative to the varanoid hypothesis; an equal case could be made relating snakes to Gekkota.

Contrary to these beliefs, Hoffstetter (1962, 1968) suggested that snakes did not originate from lizards but that both originated from a common ancestor. Rieppel (1980, 1983) has also contended that snakes are clearly distinct from lizards and that they may have evolved from a "pre-lacertilian stage." He has also wondered whether snakes and lizards are sister groups. Whatever the precise relationships between snakes and lizards may be (sister groups or otherwise), early "lizards" should be taken into account. By late Permian–early Triassic times (i.e., the Paleozoic-Mesozoic transition), some lizards already displayed modern characteristics and apparently were already involved in the evolution of modern lizards. If snakes did not evolve from lizards, then they must have originated at a very early date (this date could not have been later than that of these early lizards), approximately at the Paleozoic-Mesozoic transition. However, the monophyly of lizards has not yet been demonstrated (Rage, 1982a; Estes et al., in press), and thus it is unsafe to regard snakes and lizards as sister groups. On the other hand, snakes and amphisbaenians might be sister groups (Rage, 1982a). Relations of this possible snake-amphisbaenian assemblage with lizards have been investigated by Estes et al. (in press), who placed snakes and amphisbaenians (along with the Dibamidae) within the Autarchoglossa, without more precision; both groups seem unsuited to this analysis.

In conclusion, both the origin of snakes and the relationships between snakes and lizards at this time remains unknown. Apparently, the notion that snakes originated within lizards seems to have been revived.

The Mode of Life of the Snake Ancestor

Another aspect of the origin of snakes should be considered: Under what environmental pressure did a generalized lepidosaur evolve into a snake? Fossils do not cast light on this problem. According to Nopcsa (1923), snake ancestors were aquatic, but Janensch (1906) and Camp (1923) suggested that these ancestors were terrestrial. Mahendra (1938) hypothesized that snakes evolved from fossorial ancestors. Brock (1941), Walls (1942), Bellairs and Underwood (1951), Underwood (1967, 1970), and Senn (1966) have endorsed Mahendra's opinion. This theory rests partly on ophthalmological data first disclosed by Walls indicating that snakes passed through a phase during which the role of vision was reduced. However, Hoffstetter (1968) and Rieppel (1978) correctly showed that several characters of snakes are inconsistent with a "burrowing origin." Moreover, various characters that, according to the advocates of the burrowing theory, would be the consequence of a fossorial phase may in fact be adaptations to diet or feeding habits (Berman and Regal, 1967). Finally, only the ophthalmological characters require a subterranean phase. Therefore, Hoffstetter (1968) suggested that snake ancestors were not active burrowers in hard ground but were merely animals that lived in loose soils (mud, humus, sand); Bellairs (1972) set forth a similar point of view. Rieppel (1978) concurred with Hoffstetter and Bellairs but suggested that the primitive mode of life of snakes might have been secretive or semi-burrowing. He also suggested that vision reduction could be the result of the hunting habits of snake ancestors. The first mammals were small, lived in holes or crevices, and were probably crepuscular and nocturnal; hunting such prey required improved olfaction, whereas the role of vision was reduced. Moreover, passage through crevices might have been related to body elongation (Gans, 1974), a possible "protoadaptation" for burrowing (Gans, 1975).

From this set of proposals, it is difficult to infer a coherent scenario. I propose the following early history of snakes: (1) A sheltering behavior (crevice or hole dwellers) caused elongation of the body; the subsequent limb reduction, a secondary result, might have occurred during the following phase, (2) a subterranean, or at least secretive, phase (favored by the elongate body) caused the peculiar ophthalmological characteristics of snakes, and (3) the re-emergence allowed the adaptation, in Alethinophidia, to feeding on large prey.

THE ADOPTED PHYLOGENY AND SYSTEMATICS

The recognized phylogeny of snakes (Figure 2–1) will not be discussed at length (for details see Rage, 1984a). Only the points that are inconsistent with McDowell's classification (this volume) are stressed here.

1. An initial dichotomy has led to the Scolecophidia on one hand and to the Alethinophidia on the other. All known fossil snakes, with some doubts about the Simoliopheoidea, may be referred to these two lineages (*Pachyophis, Mesophis, Pachyrhachis,* and *Estesius* are not considered snakes). Therefore, the Cholophidia are not recognized as a natural assemblage.

2. *Lapparentophis* may have originated from very early Alethinophidia, before the dichotomy leading to the Anilioidea and Booidea. Hoffstetter (1959a) considered *Simoliophis* a marine descendant of *Lapparentophis*-like snakes, which is probably correct. Haas (1979) believed that *Simoliophis* and *Pachyrhachis* are related, but pachyostosis, the only character that supports this opinion, is not reliable.

3. The Aniliidae are probably the most primitive extant snakes, and they are perhaps not very different from the early snakes. Although McDowell (1975) may be correct, I retain *Anilius* and *Cylindrophis* (and also *Anomochilus*) in the same family. The vertebrae of *Coniophis* are reminiscent of those of the Aniliidae,

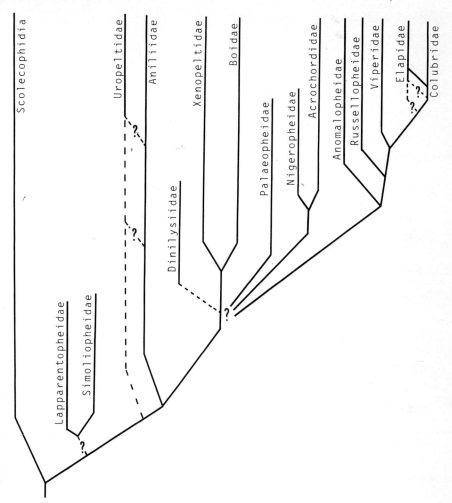

Figure 2–1. Proposed interrelationships of snakes.

but they lack the posterior median emargination of the neural arch. This morphology is that of a primitive alethinophidian and perhaps that of a form intermediate between the Scolecophidia and Alethinophidia. *Coniophis* is provisionally included in the Aniliidae.

4. *Dinilysia* is placed on the alethinophidian lineage, and it even appears more advanced than the anilioids. The booid characters incipient in *Dinilysia* are well established in *Xenopeltis* and *Loxocemus*.

5. The Boidae, as they are defined here, include several divergent lineages leading to groups that are today somewhat different from each another. However, this assemblage is apparently monophyletic or paraphyletic and, even if the

familial status does not express the diversity of its components, I retain the traditional acceptance. Besides the typical boids, Boinae (boas and pythons), Erycinae, and Calabariinae, the "atypical" Bolyeriinae and Tropidopheinae are maintained in the family. The extinct Madtsoiinae, regarded as very primitive snakes by McDowell (this volume), are also referred to the Boidae.

6. *Anomalophis* and *Russellophis* branched from the colubroid line of evolution before the origin of recent families.

I adopt the following classification:

Suborder Scolecophidia
  (Subdivision useless for paleontological purposes)
Suborder Alethinophidia
  Superfamily Simoliopheoidea
    Families Lapparentopheidae, Simoliopheidae
  Superfamily Anilioidea
    Families Aniliidae, Uropeltidae
  Superfamily Booidea
    Families Dinilysiidae, Xenopeltidae, Boidae (Boinae, Erycinae, Calabariinae, Bolyeriinae, Tropidopheinae, Madtsoiinae), Palaeopheidae (Palaeopheinae, Archaeopheinae)
  Superfamily Acrochordoidea
    Families Acrochordidae, Nigeropheidae
  Superfamily Colubroidea
    Families Anomalopheidae, Russellopheidae, Colubridae, Elapidae, Viperidae.

THE TEMPO OF SNAKE HISTORY

Although snakes probably originated well before the Cretaceous, the oldest known snake comes from the early Cretaceous, and representatives of the group become comparatively frequent only in uppermost Cretaceous sediments.

The Emergence of Snakes

The Oldest Undoubted Snakes: The Simoliopheoidea. The oldest snake, *Lapparentophis defrennei* (sole member of the Lapparentopheidae) comes from continental deposits of the Algerian early Cretaceous whose precise age remains unknown. It has a primitive character that is strikingly reminiscent of the lizards: The articular surfaces of the zygapophyses are strongly slanting and the level of the prezygapophysial tips lies above the level of the neural arch roof. *Lapparentophis* was a terrestrial snake (Hoffstetter, 1959a).

The marine beds of the European and African Cenomanian (early late Cre-

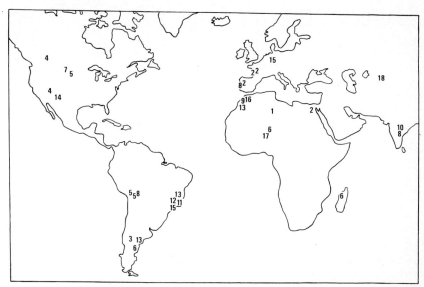

Figure 2–2. Geographical distribution of the oldest known snakes (Cretaceous and Paleocene). 1, early Cretaceous (*Lapparentophis*); 2, early late Cretaceous (*Simoliophis*); 3, late Cretaceous, ante-Maastrichtian (*Dinilysia*); 4, late Cretaceous possible aniliids; 5, late Cretaceous supposed aniliids (*Coniophis*); 6, late Cretaceous Madtsoiinae; 7, late Cretaceous possible Erycinae; 8, late Cretaceous other Boidae; 9, late Cretaceous Palaeopheidae; 10, late Cretaceous or early Paleocene boid; 11, Paleocene supposed aniliid (*Coniophis*); 12, Paleocene aniliid; 13, Paleocene Madtsoiinae; 14, Paleocene Erycinae; 15, Paleocene other Boidae; 16, Paleocene Palaeopheidae; 17, Paleocene Nigeropheidae; 18, Paleocene or early Eocene Palaeopheidae.

taceous) have yielded vertebrae of *Simoliophis,* a single representative of the Simoliopheidae (Figure 2–2). The vertebrae and ribs of the mid-trunk region are pachyostotic, and the strong slanting of the zygapophyses is retained. Anterior ribs display a very reduced tuber costae (vestigial or incipient?), whereas more posterior ribs lack any trace of such an element (Nopcsa, 1925). *Simoliophis* was a marine snake, and the pachyostosis was probably a consequence of this mode of life.

The First Radiation of Snakes. During the post-Turonian part of the late Cretaceous (Figure 2–3), snakes became more numerous and diversified. *Dinilysia patagonica* has been found in Argentina in beds that have not been precisely dated (Senonian ante-Maastrichtian). The holotype of this snake has been studied by Estes et al. (1970) and Hecht (1982), but its phyletic position is still disputed (Rage, 1977, 1984a). The oldest known Boidae (if the Madtsoiinae are really boid snakes) appeared at that time. *Madtsoia madagascariensis* is known in the Campanian (or perhaps Santonian) of Madagascar (Hoffstetter, 1961a); a closely

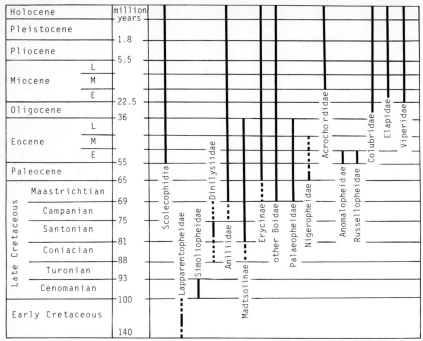

Figure 2–3.   Stratigraphic range of snakes (ages of Lapparentopheidae, Dinilysiidae, and oldest Madtsoiinae not precisely known). E, early; M, middle; L, late.

related form (*M*. aff. *madagascariensis*) comes from beds in Niger that are perhaps slightly older (Broin et al., 1974). Madtsoiinae are also known in the Campanian or early Maastrichtian of South America (A. Albino, unpublished data). Supposed Aniliidae, referred to the genus *Coniophis,* have been found in the Campanian of North America (*C. cosgriffi:* Armstrong-Ziegler, 1978; *Coniophis* sp.: Fox, 1975); the referral of both fossils to *Coniophis* has not been actually ascertained.

A richer fauna took form during the Maastrichtian (Figure 2–3); snakes began to thrive at that time. *Coniophis* was still present: *C. precedens* in North America (Rage, 1984a) and *Coniophis* sp. in South America (Rage, 1981; Muizon et al., 1983). Boidae were well represented and are known in North America (perhaps an erycine snake: Estes et al., 1969), South America (Muizon et al., 1983), Europe (Portugal: J. C. Rage, unpublished data), and India (Jain and Sahni, 1983). Moreover, at that time, the first representative of the Palaeopheidae, a highly aquatic group, appeared (Morocco: Rage, 1984a). In India, sediments that may be uppermost Cretaceous or lowermost Paleocene in age have yielded indeterminate boid snakes (Sahni et al., 1982).

Fossils from the Paleocene are not numerous, but this paucity is not a reflection of the actual number of snakes present. It is probable that snakes were then in expansion, but Paleocene deposits bearing tetrapods are rather rare. Aniliidae, *Coniophis* included, have been reported from South America (Rage, 1981). Madtsoiinae are known in the South American Paleocene (Hoffstetter, 1959b; Báez and Gasparini, 1979; Rage, 1981). An indeterminate madtsoiine snake has been found in the Paleocene of Morocco (J. C. Rage, unpublished data). A *Dunnophis*-like snake (Tropidopheinae) occurred in the Brazilian Paleocene where other Boidae are well represented (Rage, 1981). Boidae have been also reported from the Paleocene of Eastern Germany (Kuhn, 1940). The oldest undoubted erycine, *Helagras prisciformis,* appeared in the Paleocene of New Mexico (Hoffstetter and Rage, 1972). The Palaeopheidae are still rare. *Palaeophis* was reported from the Paleocene of Morocco, and *Vialovophis zhylan* has been found in the late Paleocene or early Eocene of Southern Kazakhstan (Nessov and Udovitschenko, 1984). Nessov regarded *Vialovophis* as a nigeropheid, but I consider it a probable palaeopheid and even as a possible synonym of *Palaeophis*. The Paleocene marine beds of Niger have yielded *Nigerophis mirus* (Nigeropheidae), which is considered a close relative of the Acrochordidae (Rage, 1984a).

Eocene Times: The Climax of the Booidea and the Emergence of the Colubroidea

The Eocene sediments have offered rich and varied snake faunas.

Scolecophidia. The oldest known representative of the Scolecophidia appeared very early in the Eocene of Europe (Rage, 1984a). Fossil Scolecophidia are poorly represented among fossil snakes because of their small size and brittle bones. This group unquestionably originated long before the Eocene, but no ante-Eocene fossil has been found.

Aniliidae. Coniophis was still present in the middle and late Eocene of North America (Hecht, 1959; Holman, 1979b) and was also known in the European late Eocene (Rage, 1984a). *Eoanilius* comes from the English and French late Eocene (Rage, 1984a), and an undescribed aniliid has been reported from the middle Eocene of Central Asia (Zerova and Chkhikvadze, 1984).

Boidae. A set of boid genera may be referred to the Boinae (*Boavus, Cheilophis,* and *Paraepicrates* in North America; *Palaeopython,* and *Paleryx* in Europe). A more precise assignment requires certain skull bones that remain generally unknown. However, adequate skull bones are known in *Palaeopython* from the late and perhaps middle Eocene; I place this snake within the boas. Underwood (1976) considered *Paraepicrates* a boa; however, only vertebrae are available, therefore this opinion may be questioned. Because of the morphology of its maxilla, *Cheilophis* could be also regarded as a boa (Rage, 1984b). Two late Eocene Boidae, *Dawsonophis* (Holman, 1979b) and *Cadurcoboa* (Rage, 1984a) could be referred to the Boinae. In Asia, an unidentified boine is known in the middle Eocene (from Pakistan: J. C. Rage, unpublished data).

The Erycinae underwent great diversification in the North American-European geographic unit during the Eocene. They expanded in number and diversity throughout this epoch: *Calamagras* and *Ogmophis* (these might be congeneric: Rage, 1984a), *Lithophis* and *Huberophis* (Holman, 1979a) in North America; *Calamagras* and *Cadurceryx* in Europe. *Dunnophis* (Tropidopheinae) was first reported in the fossil record in the European early Eocene (Antunes and Russell, 1981; Rage, 1984a); it is also known from the late Eocene (Rage, 1984a). In North America the genus has been recorded from the middle and late Eocene (Hecht, 1959; Holman, 1979b).

The Last Madtsoiinae. The Madtsoiinae were still present in the Eocene, but *Madtsoia* was lacking in Africa where a large form, *Gigantophis garstini,* has been reported from the late Eocene (Andrews, 1906; Hoffstetter, 1961b). The early Eocene of Argentina has yielded *Madtsoia bai* (Simpson, 1933). The Madtsoiinae did not survive beyond the late Eocene (Figure 2–3).

Palaeopheidae. Representatives of the family have been often recorded in Eocene deposits. The Archaeopheinae are known by only two specimens. *Archaeophis proavus* comes from the uppermost lower Eocene beds of Italy (Janensch, 1906; Auffenberg, 1959). Tatarinov (1963) described *Archaeophis turkmenicus* from the early Eocene of the Turkmen SSR, but this species might belong to a distinct genus (Rage, 1984a). From the Eocene, 18 species (of which 13 are valid) referred to the Palaeopheinae have been described. Because fossil snakes are little studied, this number shows that palaeopheine snakes are not rare in Eocene sediments. They include snakes of all sizes (Holman, 1982a; Rage, 1984a), and they form a morphological series in which the primitive morphology is similar to that of the boids (Rage, 1983a). This series is subdivided into two phenotypic genera: *Palaeophis* (early and middle Eocene) for the primitive species, and *Pterosphenus* (late Eocene) for the advanced ones. Both *Palaeophis* and *Pterosphenus* inhabited estuaries, lagoons, and shallow marine waters (Westgate and Ward, 1981; Rage, 1983b; Hutchison, 1985).

Acrochordoidea. From the Eocene only one snake is referable to the Acrochordoidea. This snake, *Woutersophis novus,* was aquatic and restricted to the middle Eocene Belgian shallow sea. *Woutersophis* undoubtedly belongs to the Palaeopheidae-Acrochordoidea complex, but within this assemblage its precise relationship remains doubtful. I tentatively assigned it to the Nigeropheidae on the basis of some characters not consistent with the Palaeopheidae (Rage, 1983b).

Colubroidea. Several Colubridae have been reported from the Eocene, but these fossils are either non-colubrid snakes or actually come from later stratigraphic levels. At the present time, no colubrid snake is known from the Eocene, but forms that are considered Colubroidea appeared during that epoch. *Anomalophis bolcensis* (Anomalopheidae), from the late early Eocene of Italy, was probably an aquatic snake (Auffenberg, 1959). Its vertebrae retain primitive features known in Booidea and Anilioidea, but both the lengthening of the vertebrae and the narrowing of the centrum represent a step toward colubroid vertebral morphology (Rage, 1984a). The genus *Russellophis* (Russellopheidae) is known from the early Eocene of France (Rage, 1984a) and Portugal (Antunes and Russell, 1981). Like *Anomalophis, Russellophis* has primitive characters, but the highly lightened structure of the vertebrae demonstrates that this snake is a more advanced colubroid than *Anomalophis*. The upper Eocene beds of England have yielded *Vectophis wardi*, a snake of uncertain affinities that might be a primitive colubroid (Milner et al., 1982; Rage, 1984a). From the same beds, Milner et al. (1982) have also reported the presence of a possible other colubroid ("Caenophidia 2").

Conclusion. It should be noted that the Eocene appears to have been a period during which snakes thrived. Especially, the Boidae flourished and climaxed during that time. During that epoch, there also arose the first Colubroidea, a group that would replace the Booidea as dominant about 13 million years later.

A Transitional Epoch: The Oligocene

Only Oligocene snakes from European and North American localities have been studied. There is only one report of an Oligocene snake from another continent (Asia, see below). The Oligocene is characterized by impoverished faunas which contrast sharply with the rich assemblages of the Eocene. Though apparently unfavorable for snakes, the Oligocene was marked by an important event, the appearance of the oldest known Colubridae. The known faunas from that epoch comprise only Boidae, Colubridae, and one snake *incertae sedis*.

Boidae. The boid fauna was rather unbalanced in North America where the Erycinae represented the main part of the snake fauna. These Erycinae comprised *Calamagras* and *Ogmophis* (Holman, 1979a), an early *Geringophis* (Holman, 1982b), and a tiny snake that would be a late *Helagras* (Holman, 1983). No non-erycine boid has yet been described from the North American Oligocene. In Europe, Boidae were rare during the early Oligocene, but their number somewhat increased during the middle and late Oligocene. The last *Dunnophis* (an unnamed species) was present in the lowermost Oligocene (Rage, 1984a). One erycine, *Bransateryx vireti*, thrived during the middle and late Oligocene (Hoffstetter and Rage, 1972). The other Oligocene Boidae from Europe are still undescribed except for *Platyspondylia lepta* (Rage, 1984a). Chkhikvadze et al. (1983) reported undescribed Erycinae from the Asian Oligocene.

Alethinophidia Incertae Sedis. Coprophis dakotaensis is the only described Oligocene snake of henophidian grade from North America that is apparently not referable to the Erycinae (Parris and Holman, 1978).

The Oldest Known Colubridae. During the middle Oligocene (Figure 2–3), the Colubridae appeared suddenly, and almost simultaneously, in Europe and North America. In Europe, *Coluber cadurci* occurred during the middle and late Oligocene (Rage, 1984a). It should be noted that *C. cadurci* belongs to a group of colubrid genera whose vertebrae cannot be determined at the generic level; therefore, I only symbolically referred the species to the genus *Coluber*. *Texasophis galbreathi* is known from the middle (or late?) Oligocene of Colorado (Holman, 1984a,b). In both Europe and North America, no potential ancestors for these colubrids were present; therefore *C. cadurci* and *T. galbreathi* were probably immigrants.

A supposed colubrid, *Coluber atavus,* from the uppermost Oligocene, is known in western Germany (Rage, 1984a).

Miocene Times: Expansion of the Colubroidea

Following the rather depauperate Oligocene, the Miocene corresponded to a period of revival for snakes. An astonishing variety of snakes (mainly Colubridae) burst upon the North American and European scenes (fossils from other continents are still poorly known). The frequency of snake occurrences in Miocene sediments is so great that Stanley (1979) wrote that the Neogene (Miocene plus Pliocene) was the "age of snakes"; in fact, it could be more appropriately labeled the "age of Colubroidea." As early as the early Miocene, the Elapidae and Viperidae appeared in the fossil record (Figure 2–3). During the Miocene in North America (Holman, 1976) and Europe, colubroid snakes replaced the Boidae as the dominant constituents of the snake fauna. By early Miocene times, Boidae still outnumbered colubroid snakes in North America, whereas in Europe the latter were apparently already slightly more numerous than the former. At the end of the Miocene, the Colubroidea markedly outnumbered the Boidae on both continents. During the Miocene, probable representatives of extant species began to occur.

A note about stratigraphy is appropriate here. Most North American workers traditionally place the Miocene-Pliocene boundary at approximately 12 MYA, whereas European paleontologists generally place it at approximately 5.5 MYA. In consequence, for the Neogene, the same stratigraphic terms have different meanings in North America and Europe. Here, the European meaning is adopted

million years	Traditional use in North America		Use in Europe		million years
	Mammal Ages	Epochs	Epochs	Mammal Ages	
1.8		Pleistocene	Pleistocene		1.8
	Blancan	late Pliocene	Pliocene	Villanyian	
5.5				Ruscinian	5.5
	Hemphillian	middle Pliocene	late Miocene	Turolian	
	Clarendonian	early Pliocene		Vallesian	
	Barstovian	late Miocene	middle Miocene	Astaracian	
	Hemingfordian	middle Miocene	early Miocene	Orleanian	
		early Miocene		Agenian	
22.5	Arikareean				22.5
		Oligocene	Oligocene	Arvernian	

Figure 2–4. Correlation between neogene stratigraphic terms used in Europe and their traditional use in North America.

more especially because North American workers increasingly use it (see Figure 2–4).

Scolecophidia. The Scolecophidia are generally present in the European Miocene. One species has been described from the French middle Miocene and has been tentatively referred to *Typhlops* (*Typhlops grivensis*: Hoffstetter, 1946). An unidentified form has been reported from the middle Miocene of North Africa (Rage, 1976).

Aniliidae. An aniliid snake, *Colombophis portai,* is known from the middle Miocene of South America (Hoffstetter and Rage, 1977). It is markedly larger than the living aniliids.

Boidae. Several extinct boid genera have been erected (they chiefly belong to the Erycinae), but extinct species referred to living genera are also known. During the early Miocene in North America, non-erycine boids remained rather rare; only *Pseudoepicrates* (Auffenberg, 1963) and *Anilioides* (Auffenberg, 1963; Holman, 1979a) have been described. Inversely, erycine snakes still flourished (Holman, 1979a). The living genus *Charina* appeared during the early Miocene (*C. prebottae:* Holman, 1979a). In Europe, although some non-erycine boids were present, only Erycinae have been described in the early Miocene. *Bransateryx* maintained a niche (Rage, 1984a), and remains from the Czechoslovak early Miocene are tentatively assigned to the living oriental genus *Gongylophis* (Szyndlar, in press a). One palatine demonstrates that a python was present in

Europe (J. C. Rage, unpublished data). Some indeterminate boid vertebrae are known from the early Miocene of East Africa (Rage, 1979).

By middle Miocene times, Erycinae strongly outnumbered other boids in North America. Only one non-erycine boid (unnamed) has been reported (Holman, 1979a). In Europe, boid snakes were rare at that time; a tiny erycine, *Albaneryx*, was probably more or less distantly related to the North American *Lichanura* (Rage, 1984a). In Africa, *Eryx* (or *Gongylophis*) was present, as was a medium-sized form, *Python maurus* (Rage, 1976). *Eunectes stirtoni* is the only boid snake described from the Miocene of South America (Hoffstetter and Rage, 1977).

Late Miocene Boidae are still poorly known. From North America, two species have been reported: the erycine *Ogmophis pliocompactus* and the strange *Tregophis brevirachis* (Holman, 1979a). The latter genus is known by only one vertebra that lacks the zygantral roof, and this feature might be a pathological one. In Europe, only one erycine has been recorded in the late Miocene (Demarcq et al., 1983). In Asia, *Python* is known from the upper Miocene beds of the Siwalik group (J. C. Rage, unpublished data).

Acrochordidae. The only described extinct acrochordid, *Acrochordus dehmi*, comes from the middle Miocene of India and Pakistan. Hoffstetter (1964) considered, not without some reservations, that it was present in the middle and upper Miocene and lower Pliocene levels of the Siwalik deposits. However, a thorough study (J. C. Rage, unpublished data) demonstrates that *A. dehmi*, as defined by Hoffstetter, was present only during the middle Miocene. In the upper Miocene and lower Pliocene levels, the vertebrae are different and tend toward the morphology of the extant *A. javanicus*.

Colubridae. After their somewhat inconspicuous appearance during the Oligocene, Colubridae underwent impressive diversification by Miocene times. Colubridae have been the ruling group within snakes since that epoch.

By the early Miocene (Figure 2–5), various extinct genera appeared in North America; however, extant genera, represented by extinct species, had already made their appearance (Holman, 1979a). In Europe, extinct genera occurred during the early Miocene (Rage, 1984a; Szyndlar, in press a); the living genus *Coluber* has been reported (but see comments about assignments to *Coluber*). At least one colubrid has been recorded in the lower Miocene beds of Africa (Rage, 1979).

Middle Miocene colubrids are numerous in North America. Several genera were inherited from the early Miocene, and they were joined by other extinct genera (Figure 2–5). Extant genera have also been recorded (Holman, 1979a). In Europe, extinct genera were known at that time (Mlynarski et al., 1982; Rage, 1984a), and several extinct forms present in western Europe but related to North American snakes have been described (Rage and Holman, 1984). Living genera were represented by extinct species (Rage, 1984a; Rage and Szyndlar, 1986).

EXTINCT GENERA		EXTANT GENERA		EXTANT SPECIES	
North America	Europe	North America	Europe	N.A.	Europe

late Miocene — North America extinct: Paleoheterodon, Texasophis, Paleofarancia?; Europe extinct: Hispanophis, Nanus, Zelceophis; North America extant: Diadophis, Heterodon, Nerodia, Stilosoma; Europe extant: Elaphe; N.A. species: Coluber constrictor, Lampropeltis triangulum; Europe species: Natrix natrix, Natrix tessellata, Elaphe longissima

middle Miocene — North America extinct: Ameiseophis, Dakotaophis, Neonatrix, Paracoluber, Dryinoides, Nebraskophis, Paleoheterodon, Texasophis; Europe extinct: Neonatrix, Texasophis, Palaeonatrix, Paleoheterodon, Protropidonotus; North America extant: Lampropeltis; Europe extant: Coluber, Natrix

early Miocene — North America extinct: Paraoxybelis, Pseudocemophora, Ameiseophis, Dakotaophis, Neonatrix; Europe extinct: Dolniceophis, Neonatrix, Texasophis; North America extant: Salvadora, Elaphe

Figure 2–5. Stratigraphic occurrence of colubrid taxa reported from North American and European Miocene.

In Africa, two indeterminate colubrids have been reported from the middle Miocene of Morocco (Rage, 1976). In Asia, one genus has been described (Sun Ailin, 1961); rare, unidentified colubrids were present in the middle Miocene of the Siwalik group (J. C. Rage, unpublished data). In South America, one colubrid is known from the middle Miocene (Hoffstetter and Rage, 1977).

Colubridae were still numerous during the late Miocene, but extinct genera diminished in number. More numerous were the extinct species referred to extant genera (Auffenberg, 1963; Holman, 1979a). The oldest known representatives of living species have been reported from that period in North America: *Coluber constrictor* and *Lampropeltis triangulum* (Holman, 1979a; see also Viperidae). The composition of the contemporaneous European fauna is similar, with few extinct genera (Bachmayer and Szyndlar, 1985; Szyndlar, 1984, in press b). European extinct species belonging to living genera were known (Rage, 1984a). Recent species perhaps appeared at that time: *Natrix natrix, N. tessellata* (Bolkay, 1913) and *Elaphe longissima* (Szunyoghy, 1932), but these fossils need revision. Some colubrid vertebrae are known in the late Miocene of Asia (Siwalik group: J. C. Rage, unpublished data).

Elapidae. The oldest known Elapidae appeared abruptly in the early Miocene of France (*Palaeonaja romani:* Hoffstetter, 1939) and Spain (*Palaeonaja* sp.: Alferez Delgado and Brea Lopez, 1981). The generic distinction between *Palaeonaja* and the living related forms needs a reappraisal (Bachmayer and Szyndlar, 1985). Elapids might have been present in the early Miocene of Africa (Rage, 1979).

The middle Miocene marks the appearance of recent elapid genera: *Micrurus* sp. in North America (Holman, 1979a) and *Naja antiqua* in North Africa (Rage, 1976). During the middle Miocene, *Palaeonaja* survived in France (Hoffstetter,

1939). At that time, *Micrurus* spread into Laurasia and reached Europe where it was represented by *M. gallicus* (Rage and Holman, 1984). "Hydropheinae" (here included in the Elapidae) have been reported from the middle Miocene of the USSR (undescribed: Zerova and Chkhikvadze, 1984), but such a designation is questionable because hydropheine vertebrae are not easily distinguished from those of the Colubridae and other Elapidae.

Late Miocene Elapidae have been recorded only in Europe (Alberdi et al., 1981; Bachmayer and Szyndlar, 1985; Szyndlar, in press b).

Viperidae. Viperidae appeared almost simultaneously in Europe and North America during the most early Miocene. They were rather frequent in Europe at that time but have not yet been studied (Hoffstetter, 1962; Rage, 1984a), whereas in North America only one vertebra from this age is known (Holman, 1981b). Two extinct species from later early Miocene were present in Czechoslovakia (Szyndlar, in press a).

Viperidae are frequently encountered in middle Miocene deposits of Europe and North America; they have not yet been studied and remain undescribed except for the poorly known *Vipera kargii* (Rage, 1984a). One extinct species from the middle Miocene of North Africa has been referred to *Vipera* (*V. maghrebiana:* Rage, 1976). Viperids were present in Central Asia in the early or middle Miocene (Chkhikvadze et al., 1983).

In the late Miocene, only extant species have been reported from North America (Holman, 1979a). One extinct species, *Vipera gedulyi,* was described in Europe (Bolkay, 1913).

A Late Enigmatic Snake. Miocene snakes are of a modern type. Nevertheless, a strange snake, *Goinophis minusculus,* has been reported from the early Miocene of North America (Holman, 1979a). Its centrum and synapophyses are reminiscent of those of lizards, but the general morphology of the vertebra is that of a snake. During the early Miocene, *Goinophis* represented a late relict whose relationships within snakes remain unknown.

Plio-Pleistocene

The Pliocene is marked by the dominance of recent forms. Extinct taxa still occurred, but they decreased in number and the Pliocene fauna displayed a modern aspect. Pliocene Scolecophidia have been reported only from Anatolia (Rage and Sen, 1976). Erycine were still numerous; the last *Ogmophis* occurred in North America (Rogers, 1976), and unidentified *Eryx* were present in Mediterranean areas (Hoffstetter and Rage, 1972; Rage and Sen, 1976). One extinct non-erycine boid (*Daunophis langi*) has been described from the Pliocene (Swinton, 1926); this fossil comes from Burma, and the validity of the taxon is doubtful (Rage, 1984a). Boids (*Python*) were present in the Pliocene of East Africa (Rage,

1979), and a boid similar to *Morelia* has been reported from the Australian Pliocene (Archer and Wade, 1976). Only living genera of colubrids were known during the Pliocene, but some extinct species remained. Extant species clearly outnumbered extinct taxa in North America (Holman, 1979a). In Europe, living genera were represented by some extinct species (Szyndlar, 1984). In North America, Pliocene Elapidae have not yet been found, whereas in southern Europe *Palaeonaja depereti* (Hoffstetter, 1939) and *Naja* cf. *naja* (Jaen and Sanchiz, 1985) have been recorded and a large elapid (*Palaeonaja?*) was discovered in Anatolia (Rage and Sen, 1976). Viperids were represented by recent forms.

By Pleistocene times, the faunas definitively displayed a modern composition. Extinct taxa were then quite uncommon in North America and Europe (Holman, 1981a; Szyndlar, 1981; Meylan, 1982). In Africa, the lowermost beds of Olduvai, Tanzania, have yielded, aside from some modern colubrids and elapids, a large *Python* (*P*. aff. *sebae*) and an extinct viper, *Bitis olduvaiensis* (Rage, 1973). Two snakes are known from subrecent deposits of Mauritius Island: a scolecophidian referred with doubt to *Typhlops* (*T. cariei:* Hoffstetter, 1946) and the only known fossil bolyeriine snake (*Casarea* sp.: Hoffstetter, 1960). A large extinct boid snake, *Wonambi naracoortensis,* has been found in the Pleistocene of Australia (Smith, 1976); it might belong to the Madtsoiinae.

AN OVERVIEW OF THE PALEOBIOGEOGRAPHIC HISTORY OF SNAKES

The lack of paleontological data on the early Scolecophidia prevents reconstruction of the global history of snakes. It is only possible to go over the paleobiogeographic events that concerned Alethinophidia; in the following section only the major events are given.

1. Nearly all the Cretaceous terrestrial snakes come from Gondwanan continents. Moreover, the Madtsoiinae are known from the late Cretaceous in Madagascar, Africa, and South America. Such a range suggests that they were distributed on this part of Gondwana before the breakup of the supercontinent, and that the Boidae therefore originated in Gondwana, with the Anilioidea-Booidea dichotomy occurring somewhere on this supercontinent (Rage, 1981). This is corroborated by the presence of *Dinilysia* on a Gondwanan continent. (*Dinilysia,* whatever its precise phyletic position may be, is close to the Anilioidea-Booidea dichotomy.) *Lapparentophis* is also a Gondwanan snake; if it is actually a primitive alethinophidian, then it would represent further proof of this paleobiogeographical location of the early alethinophidian history.

2. During the latest Cretaceous, a terrestrial route connected South and North America for a short time (Rage, 1981). This route permitted faunal exchanges between South America and Laurasia, and aniliids and boids reached North America at that time. Boids and aniliids spread to Europe, to which the latter

continent was then connected. It is quite possible that aniliids and boids entered Asia during the early Cenozoic (or the latest Cretaceous), along with other terrestrial forms, by the Bering filter bridge, but no paleontological evidence is available yet. Concerning the dispersal from Gondwana to Laurasia, two other possibilities must be considered. Rare interchanges occurred between Eurasia and Africa by the latest Cretaceous-Paleocene times (Bonis et al., 1985), and Africa was still joined to South America by a probably discontinuous transoceanic land route (Rage, 1981). This South America–Africa–Laurasia connection was clearly less effective than the South America–North America route. On the other hand, India, which is a fragment of Gondwana, was isolated from other Gond-wanan continents but already connected to Laurasia by a terrestrial route as early as the Cretaceous-Paleocene transition (Sahni et al., 1982). It should be noted, though, that snake dispersal by these two routes has not been demonstrated.

3. The colubrid and viperid appearance was nearly contemporaneous in North America and Europe. This suggests that Asia was the center of origin, or at least the center of dispersal, of both families (Rage, 1982b).

4. By early Miocene times, several groups were able to reach Africa after this continent made contact with Eurasia. This wave of immigrants was probably comprised of Colubridae, Viperidae, Erycinae, and perhaps non-erycine boids and Elapidae.

5. The presence of an unidentified modern-type colubrid in the middle Mio-cene of South America has been regarded by Hoffstetter and Rage (1977) as the result of a waif dispersal from North America. Because exchanges between Africa and South America were theoretically possible until 35 or 40 MYA, Cadle (1984), who is an advocate of an early origin of the Colubridae, has suggested an African origin for some South American colubrids. Such a dispersal route might be documented by mammals (Hoffstetter, 1972), but 35 to 40 MYA seems to be too early a time for such a dispersal; colubrids were probably lacking in Africa before the early Miocene, about 22 MYA. On the other hand, the North America–South America path of waif dispersal during the Miocene is also il-lustrated by mammals (Marshall et al., 1982), and it has been considered for viperids (Duellman, 1979).

6. During the Miocene, some genera were common to both Europe and North America. Because potential ancestors for these forms are lacking on both con-tinents, vicariance may be ruled out. This geographical distribution may be the result either of a dispersal from North America toward Europe by way of Asia and/or of an origin in Asia and a subsequent spread toward both Europe and North America (Rage and Holman, 1984).

7. During its drift, in the Miocene, Australia arrived in the vicinity of Asia. Since that time, some mammals of Asian origin have reached Australia. I sup-pose, without any paleontological evidence, that several Asian snake groups invaded Australia and were added to some autochthonous forms inherited from Gondwana, i.e., snakes of the probable madtsoiine Australian lineage and per-haps Typhlopidae. Nevertheless, Tyler (1979) considered the Australian Ty-phlopidae immigrants. Boidae, which have undergone an important radiation in

Australia, might have reached that country by Miocene times, whereas Australian Colubridae, which are poorly diversified, might have been Pleistocene immigrants (Cogger and Heatwole, 1981).

8. The Panamanian land bridge appeared during the Pliocene. South America, which was isolated for a long time, had by then become connected to North America. This event, the "great interchange," has been thoroughly analyzed for mammals (Marshall et al., 1982), although snake activity is unknown. However, it would be surprising if snakes had not been involved in this interchange.

SUMMARY

The problem of the origin of snakes is not yet settled. Snakes show much closer affinities with lizards than with any other living vertebrate group. From this observation, three possibilities arise: (1) Snakes evolved from a pre-lacertilian stage of evolution; (2) snakes and lizards evolved from a common ancestor (they are sister groups); (3) snakes originated within the lizard group. The latter hypothesis currently seems to be in favor. Some Cretaceous fossils might be related to the snake ancestry: *Pachyophis* (and *Mesophis*), *Estesius,* and chiefly *Pachyrhachis*. The ancestors of snakes were probably secretive or semi-burrowing forms living in loose soils. This subterranean phase, which caused the ophthalmological characteristics of snakes, could have been preceded by a sheltering behavior that induced body elongation and subsequent limb reduction, a morphology that is favorable to subterranean habits.

Within the snake group, the major dichotomy appeared between the Scolecophidia and the Alethinophidia. All the known fossil snake groups seem to have originated after this dichotomy. The oldest known snake, *Lapparentophis,* comes from the early Cretaceous. The late Cretaceous and Paleocene corresponded to the first radiation of snakes. During the Eocene, snakes underwent an important diversification, and snakes of henophidian grade, mainly Boidae, were the dominant forms. The first colubroid snakes appeared during the Eocene. The Oligocene faunas were poor; at that time, however, the Colubridae appeared. During the Miocene, colubroid snakes underwent an impressive diversification, while the Boidae waned; the Elapidae and Viperidae first appeared at that time. Extant species were known as early as the late Miocene.

The early history of Alethinophidia took place in Gondwana. By the end of the Cretaceous, the Aniliidae and the Boidae had reached Laurasia. The Colubridae and the Viperidae probably originated in Asia, or at least widely dispersed from that continent.

LITERATURE CITED

Alberdi, M. T., Morales, J., Moya, S., and Sanchiz, B. 1981. Macrovertebrados (reptilia y mammalia) del yacimiento finimioceno de Librilla (Murcia), *Estud. Geol.* 37:307–312.

Alférez Delgado, F. and Brea López, P. 1981. Estudio preliminar de los restos de peces, anfibios y reptiles del yacimiento mioceno de Córcoles (Guadalajara), *Bol. R. Soc. Esp. Hist. Nat. Secc. Geol.* 79:5–20.

Andrews, C. W. 1906. A Descriptive Catalogue of the Tertiary Vertebrata of the Fayûm, Egypt, British Museum, London.

Antunes, M. T. and Russell, D. E. 1981. Le gisement de Silveirinha (Bas Mondego, Portugal): La plus ancienne faune de vertébrés éocènes connue en Europe, *C. R. Acad. Sci. Paris* 293:1099–1102.

Archer, M. and Wade, M. 1976. Results of the Ray E. Lemley expeditions, I. The Allingham formation and a new Pliocene vertebrate fauna from Northern Queensland, *Mem. Queensl. Mus.* 17:379–397.

Armstrong-Ziegler, G. 1978. An aniliid snake and associated vertebrates from the Campanian of New Mexico, *J. Paleontol.* 52:480–483.

Auffenberg, W. 1959. *Anomalophis bolcensis* (Massalongo), a new genus of fossil snake from the Italian Eocene, *Breviora* 114:1–16.

Auffenberg, W. 1963. The fossil snakes of Florida, *Tulane Stud. Zool.* 10:131–216.

Bachmayer, F. and Szyndlar, Z. 1985. Ophidians (Reptilia: Serpentes) from Kohfidisch fissures of Burgenland, Austria, *Ann. Naturhist. Mus. Wien* 87A:79–100.

Báez, A. M. and Gasparini, Z. B. de. 1979. The South American herpetofauna: An evaluation of the fossil record, in: The South American Herpetofauna: Its Origin, Evolution, and Dispersal (W. E. Duellman, ed.) *Univ. Kans. Mus. Nat. Hist. Monogr.* 7:29–54.

Bellairs, A. d'A. 1972. Comments on the evolution and affinities of snakes, in: Studies in Vertebrate Evolution (K. A. Joysey and T. S. Kemp, eds.) pp. 157–172, Oliver and Boyd, Edinburgh.

Bellairs, A. d'A. and Underwood, G. 1951. The origin of snakes, *Biol. Rev.* 26:193–237.

Berman, D. S. and Regal, P. J. 1967. The loss of the ophidian middle ear, *Evolution* 21:641–643.

Bolkay, S. J. 1913. Additions to the fossil herpetology of Hungary from the Pannonian and Praeglacial period, *Mitt. Jahrb. Kgl. Ungar. Geol. Reichsanst.* 21:217–230.

Bolkay, S. J. 1925. *Mesophis nopcsai* n.g. n.sp. ein neues schlangenähnliches Reptil aus der unteren Kreide (Neocom) von Bilek-Selišta (Ost-Hercegovina), *Glas. Zemal. Muz. Bosni Hercegovini* 37:125–135.

Bonis, L. de, Bouvrain, G., Buffetaut, E., Denys, C., Geraads, D., Jaeger, J. J., Martin, M., Mazin, J. M., and Rage, J. C. 1985. Contribution des Vertébrés a l'histoire de la Téthys et des continents péritéthysiens, *Bull. Soc. Geol. Fr.* 1:781–786.

Brock, G. T. 1941. The skull of *Acontias meleagris,* with a study of the affinities between lizards and snakes, *J. Linn. Soc. (Zool.)* 41:71–88.

Broin, F. de, Buffetaut, E., Koeniguer, J. C., Rage, J. C., Russell, D., Taquet, P., Vergnaud-Grazzini, C., and Wenz, S. 1974. La faune de Vertébrés continentaux du gisement d'In Beceten (Sénonien du Niger), *C.R. Acad. Sci. Paris* 279:469–472.

Cadle, J. E. 1984. Molecular systematics of neotropical xenodontine snakes. III. Overview of xenodontine phylogeny and the history of New World snakes, *Copeia* 1984:641–652.

Camp, C. L. 1923. Classification of the lizards, *Bull. Am. Mus. Nat. Hist.* 48:289–481.

Chkhikvadze, V. M., Shammakov, S. Sh., and Zerova, G. A. 1983. Materials to the formation history of Squamata fauna of Middle Asia and Kazakhstan, *Izv. Akad. Nauk. Turkm. SSR* 2:3–8. (In Russian.)

Cogger, H. G. and Heatwole, H. 1981. The Australian reptiles: Origins, biogeography, distribution patterns and island evolution, in: Ecological Biogeography of Australia (A. Keast, ed.) pp. 1333–1373, W. Junk, The Hague.

Demarcq, G., Ballesio, R., Rage, J. C., Guérin, C., Mein, P., and Méon, H. 1983. Données paléoclimatologiques du Néogène de la Vallée du Rhône (France), *Palaeogeogr. Palaeoclimatol. Palaeoecol.* 42:247–272.

Duellman, W. E. 1979. The South American herpetofauna: A panoramic view, in: The South American Herpetofauna: Its Origin, Evolution, and Dispersal (W. E. Duellman, ed.) *Univ. Kans. Mus. Nat. Hist. Monogr.* 7:1–28.

Estes, R., Berberian, P., and Meszoely, C. A. M. 1969. Lower vertebrates from the late Cretaceous Hell Creek Formation, McCone County, Montana, *Breviora* 337:1–33.

Estes, R., Frazzetta, T. H., and Williams, E. E. 1970. Studies on the fossil snake *Dinilysia patagonica* Woodward: I. Cranial morphology, *Bull. Mus. Comp. Zool.* 140:25–73.

Estes, R., Queiroz, K. de, and Gauthier, J. Phylogenetic relationships of the squamate families, Herpetol. League Spec. Publ. 2 (S. Moody, ed.). In press.

Fox, R. C. 1975. Fossil snakes from the upper Milk River formation (Upper Cretaceous), Alberta, *Can. J. Earth Sci.* 12:1557–1563.

Gans, C. 1974. Biomechanics: An Approach to Vertebrate Biology, J. B. Lippincott, Philadelphia.

Gans, C. 1975. Tetrapod limblessness: Evolution and functional corollaries, *Am. Zool.* 15:455–467.

Gilmore, C. W. 1938. Fossil snakes of North America, *Geol. Soc. Amer. Spec. Pap. (Reg. Stud.)* 9:1–96.

Haas, G. 1979. On a new snakelike reptile from the lower Cenomanian of Ein Jabrud, near Jerusalem, *Bull. Mus. Natl. Hist. Nat.* 1:51–64.

Haas, G. 1980a. *Pachyrhachis problematicus* Haas, snakelike reptile from the lower Cenomanian: Ventral view of the skull, *Bull. Mus. Natl. Hist. Nat.* 2:87–104.

Haas, G. 1980b. Remarks on a new ophiomorph reptile from the lower Cenomanian of Ein Jabrud, Israel, in: Aspects of Vertebrate History (L. L. Jacobs, ed.) pp. 171–192, Museum of Northern Arizona Press, Flagstaff, Arizona.

Hecht, M. K. 1959. Amphibians and reptiles, in: The Geology and Paleontology of the Elk Mountain and Tabernacle Butte Area, Wyoming (P. O. McGrew, ed.) *Bull. Am. Mus. Nat. Hist.* 117:130–146.

Hecht, M. K. 1982. The vertebral morphology of the Cretaceous snake, *Dinilysia patagonica* Woodward, *Neues Jahrb. Geol. Palaeontol. Monatsh.* 9:523–532.

Hoffstetter, R. 1939. Contribution à l'étude des Elapidae actuels et fossiles et de l'ostéologie des ophidiens, *Arch. Mus. Hist. Nat. Lyon* 15:1–78.

Hoffstetter, R. 1946. Les Typhlopidae fossiles, *Bull. Mus. Natl. Hist. Nat.* 18:309–315.

Hoffstetter, R. 1955. Squamates de type moderne, in: Traité de Paléontologie 5 (J. Piveteau, ed.) pp. 606–662, Masson, Paris.

Hoffstetter, R. 1959a. Un serpent terrestre dans le Crétacé inférieur du Sahara, *Bull. Soc. Géol. Fr.* 1:897–902.

Hoffstetter, R., 1959b. Un dentaire de *Madtsoia* (serpent géant du Paléocène de Patagonie), *Bull. Mus. Natl. Hist. Nat.* 31:379–386.

Hoffstetter, R. 1960. Sur la classification des Boïdés de Madagascar et des Mascareignes, *Bull. Mus. Natl. Hist. Nat.* 32:131–138.

Hoffstetter, R. 1961a. Nouveaux restes d'un serpent boïdé (*Madtsoia madagascariensis* nov. sp.) dans le Crétacé supérieur de Madagascar, *Bull. Mus. Natl. Hist. Nat.* 33:152–160.

Hoffstetter, R. 1961b. Nouvelles récoltes de serpents fossiles dans l'Eocène supérieur du désert libyque, *Bull. Mus. Natl. Hist. Nat.* 33:326–331.

Hoffstetter, R. 1962. Revue des récentes acquisitions concernant l'histoire et la systématique des squamates, *Coll. Intern. CNRS* 104:243–278.

Hoffstetter, R. 1964. Les serpents du Néogène du Pakistan (couches des Siwaliks), *Bull. Soc. Géol. Fr.* 6:467–474.

Hoffstetter, R. 1968. Review of "A contribution to the classification of snakes" by G. Underwood, *Copeia* 1968:201–213.

Hoffstetter, R. 1972. Relationships, origins, and history of the ceboid monkeys and caviomorph rodents: A modern reinterpretation, in: Evolutionary Biology, vol. 6 (T. Dobzhansky, M. K. Hecht, and W. C. Steere, eds.) pp. 323–347, Appleton-Century-Crofts, New York.

Hoffstetter, R. and Rage, J. C. 1972. Les Erycinae fossiles de France. Compréhension et histoire de la sous-famille, *Ann. Paléontol. Vertébr.* 58:81–124.

Hoffstetter, R. and Rage, J. C. 1977. Le gisement de vertébrés miocènes de La Venta (Colombie) et sa faune de serpents, *Ann. Paléontol. Vertébr.* 63:161–190.

Holman, J. A. 1976. Snakes and stratigraphy, *Mich. Acad.* 8:387–396.

Holman, J. A. 1979a. A review of North American Tertiary snakes, *Pub. Mus. Mich. State Univ. Paleontol. Ser.* 1:203–260.

Holman, J. A. 1979b. Paleontology and geology of the Badwater Creek area, Central Wyoming. 17. The late Eocene snakes, *Ann. Carnegie Mus.* 48:103–110.

Holman, J. A. 1981a. A review of North American Pleistocene snakes, *Publ. Mus. Mich. State Univ. Paleontol. Ser.* 1:263–306.

Holman, J. A. 1981b. A herpetofauna from an eastern extension of the Harrison Formation (early Miocene: Arikareean), Cherry County, Nebraska, *J. Vertebr. Paleontol.* 1:49–56.

Holman, J. A. 1982a. *Palaeophis casei,* new species, a tiny palaeopheid snake from the early Eocene of Mississippi, *J. Vertebr. Paleontol.* 2:163–166.

Holman, J. A. 1982b. *Geringophis* (Serpentes: Boidae) from the middle Oligocene of Nebraska, *Herpetologica* 38:489–492.

Holman, J. A. 1983. A new species of *Helagras* (Serpentes) from the middle Oligocene of Nebraska, *J. Herpetol.* 17:417–419.

Holman, J. A. 1984a. *Texasophis galbreathi,* new species, the earliest New World colubrid snake, *J. Vertebr. Paleontol.* 3:223–225.

Holman, J. A. 1984b. Erratum to Holman 1984a, *J. Vertebr. Paleontol.* 4:168.

Hutchison, J. H. 1985. *Pterosphenus* cf. *P. schucherti* Lucas (Serpentes, Palaeophidae) from the late Eocene of peninsular Florida, *J. Vertebr. Paleontol.* 5:20–23.

Jaen, M. J. and Sanchiz, B. 1985. Fossil snakes from the Pliocene of Layna, Central Spain, Abstracts Third Meeting Soc. Herpetol. Europ., p. 72.

Jain, S. L. and Sahni, A. 1983. Some upper Cretaceous vertebrates from Central India and their palaeogeographical implications, in: Cretaceous of India (H. K. Maheshwari, ed.) pp. 66–83, Indian Association of Palynostratigraphers, Lucknow, India.

Janensch, W. 1906. Uber *Archaeophis proavus* Mass., eine Schlange aus dem Eocän des Monte Bolca, *Beitr. Palaeontol. Osterr.-Ungarns* 19:1–33.

Kuhn, O. 1939. Squamata: Lacertilia et Ophidia, Fossilium Catalogus. I: Animalia (W. Quenstedt, ed.) pars 86, pp. 1–89, 1–33, W. Junk, The Hague.

Kuhn, O. 1940. Crocodilier-und Squamatenreste aus dem oberen Paleocän von Walbeck, *Zentralbl. Min.* 1:21–25.

Kuhn, O. 1963. Serpentes, Fossilium Catalogus. I: Animalia (F. Westphal, ed.), pars 103, W. Junk, The Hague.

McDowell, S. B. 1967. The extracolumella and tympanic cavity of the "earless" monitor lizard, *Lanthanotus borneensis, Copeia* 1967:154–158.

McDowell, S. B. 1972. The evolution of the tongue of snakes, and its bearing on snake origins, in: Evolutionary Biology, vol. 6 (T. Dobzhansky, M. K. Hecht, and W. C. Steere, eds). pp. 191–273, Appleton-Century-Crofts, New York.

McDowell, S. B. 1975. A catalogue of the snakes of New Guinea and the Solomons with special reference to those in the Bernice P. Bishop Museum. II. Anilioidea and Pythoninae, *J. Herpetol.* 9:1–80.

McDowell, S. B. and Bogert, C. M. 1954. The systematic position of *Lanthanotus* and the affinities of the anguinomorphan lizards, *Bull. Am. Mus. Nat. Hist.* 105:1–142.

Mahendra, B. 1938. Some remarks on the phylogeny of the Ophidia, *Anat. Anz.* 86:347–356.

Marshall, L. G., Webb, S. D., Sepkoski, J. J., Jr., and Raup, D. M. 1982. Mammalian evolution and the Great American interchange, *Science* 215:1351–1357.

Meylan, P. A. 1982. The squamate reptiles of the Inglis IA fauna (Irvingtonian: Citrus County, Florida), *Bull. Fla. State Mus. Biol. Sci.* 27:1–85.

Milner, A. C., Milner, A. R., and Estes, R. 1982. Amphibians and squamates from the upper Eocene of Hordle Cliff, Hampshire: A preliminary report, *Tertiary Res.* 4:149–154.

Mlynarski, M. 1961. Serpents pliocènes et pléistocènes de la Pologne avec la revue critique des Colubridés fossiles, *Folia Quat.* 4:1–45.

Mlynarski, M., Szyndlar, Z., Estes, R., and Sanchiz, F. 1982. Lower vertebrate fauna from the Miocene of Opole (Poland), *Estud. Geol.* 38:103–119.

Muizon, C. de, Gayet, M., Lavenu, A., Marshall, L. G., Sigé, B., and Villaroel, C. 1983. Late Cretaceous vertebrates, including mammals, from Tiupampa, southcentral Bolivia, *Geobios* 16:747–753.

Nessov, L. A. and Udovitschenko, N. I. 1984. Sea snakes and cartilaginous fishes of the Paleogene of South Kazakhstan *Paleont. Sbornik* 21:69–74. (In Russian.)

Nopcsa, F. 1923. *Eidolosaurus* und *Pachyophis,* Zwei neue Neocom-Reptilien, *Palaeontographica* 55:97–154.

Nopcsa, F. 1925. Die *Symoliophis*-Reste, in: Ergebnisse der Forschungsreisen Prof. E. Stromers in den Wüsten Ägyptens, II, *Abh. Bayer. Akad. Wiss., Math.-Naturw. Abt.* 30:1–27.

Parris, D. C. and Holman, J. A. 1978. An Oligocene snake from a coprolite, *Herpetologica* 34:258–264.

Rage, J. C. 1973. Fossil snakes from Olduvai, Tanzania, in: Fossil Vertebrates from Africa, vol. 3 (L. S. B. Leakey, R. J. G. Savage, and S. C. Coryndon, eds.) pp. 1–6, Academic Press, London.

Rage, J. C. 1976. Les Squamates du Miocène de Beni Mellal, Maroc, *Géol. Médit.* 3:57–69.

Rage, J. C. 1977. La position phylétique de *Dinilysia patagonica,* serpent du Crétacé supérieur, *C.R. Acad. Sci. Paris* 284:1765–1768.

Rage, J. C. 1979. Les serpents de la Rift Valley: Un apercu général, *Bull. Soc. Géol. Fr.* 21:329–330.

Rage, J. C. 1981. Les continents péri-atlantiques au Crétacé supérieur: Migrations des faunes continentales et problèmes paléogéographiques, *Cretaceous Res.* 2:65–84.

Rage, J. C. 1982a. La phylogénie des lépidosauriens (Reptilia): Une approche cladistique, *C.R. Acad. Sci. Paris* 294:563–566.

Rage, J. C. 1982b. L'histoire des serpents, *Pour Sci.* 54:16–27.

Rage, J. C. 1983a. *Palaeophis colossaeus* nov. sp. (le plus grand serpent connu?) de l'Eocène du Mali et le problème du genre chez les Palaeopheinae, *C.R. Acad. Sci. Paris* 296:1741–1744.

Rage, J. C. 1983b. Les serpents aquatiques de l'Eocène européen. Définition des espèces et aspects stratigraphiques, *Bull. Mus. Natl. Hist. Nat.* 5:213–241.

Rage, J. C. 1984a. Serpentes, Handbuch der Paläoherpetologie/Encyclopedia of Paleoherpetology, part 11, xii + 80 p., Gustav Fischer, Stuttgart.

Rage, J. C. 1984b. The fossil snake *Cheilophis huerfanoensis* Gilmore, 1938, from Eocene of Colorado: Redescription and reappraisal of relationships, *J. Vertebr. Paleontol.* 3:219–222.

Rage, J. C. and Holman, J. A. 1984. Des serpents (Reptilia, Squamata) de type nord-américain dans le Miocène francais: Evolution parallèle ou dispersion? *Geobios* 17:89–104.

Rage, J. C. and Sen, S. 1976. Les amphibiens et les reptiles du Pliocène supérieur de Calta (Turquie), *Géol. Médit.* 3:127–134.

Rage, J. C. and Szyndlar, Z. 1986. *Natrix longivertebrata* from the European Neogene, a snake with one of the longest known stratigraphic ranges, *Neues Jahrb. Geol. Paläont. Monatsh.* 1:56–64.

Rieppel, O. 1978. The evolution of the naso-frontal joint in snakes and its bearing on snake origin, *Z. Zool. Syst. Evolutionsforsch.* 16:14–27.

Rieppel, O. 1980. The sound-transmitting apparatus in primitive snakes and its phylogenetic significance. *Zoomorphology* 96:45–62.

Rieppel, O. 1983. A comparison of the skull of *Lanthanotus borneensis* (Reptilia: Varanoidea) with the skull of primitive snakes, *Z. Zool. Syst. Evolutionsforsch.* 21:142–153.

Rogers, K. L. 1976. Herpetofauna of the Beck Ranch local fauna (upper Pliocene: Blancan) of Texas, *Publ. Mus. Mich. State Univ. Paleontol. Ser.* 1:167–200.

Sahni, A., Kumar, K., Hartenberger, J. L., Jaeger, J. J., Rage, J. C., Sudre, J., and Vianey-Liaud, M. 1982. Microvertébrés nouveaux des Trapps du Deccan (Inde): Mise en évidence d'une voie de communication terrestre probable entre la Laurasie et l'Inde à la limite Crétacé-Tertiaire, *Bull. Soc. Géol. Fr.* 24:1093–1099.

Senn, D. G. 1966. Über das optische System im Gehirn squamater Reptilien, *Acta Anat. Suppl.* 52:1–87.

Simpson, G. G. 1933, A new fossil snake from the *Notostylops* beds of Patagonia, *Bull. Am. Mus. Nat. Hist.* 67:1–22.

Smith, M. J. 1976. Small fossil vertebrates from Victoria Cave, Naracoorte, South Australia. IV. Reptiles, *Trans. R. Soc. S. Aust.* 100:39–51.

Stanley, S. M. 1979. Macroevolution: Pattern and Process, W. H. Freeman, San Francisco.

Sun Ailin. 1961. Notes on fossil snakes from Shanwang, Shantung, *Vertebr. Palasiat.* 4:310–312.

Swinton, W. E. 1926. *Daunophis langi,* gen. et sp. n. (Pliocene, Burma), *Ann. Mag. Nat. Hist.* 17:342–348.

Szunyoghy, J. von. 1932. Beitrage zur vergleichenden Formenlehre des Colubridenschädels, nebst einer kranialogischen Synopsis der fossilen Schlangen Ungarns, *Acta Zool.* 13:1–56.

Szyndlar, Z. 1981. Early Pleistocene reptile fauna from Kozi Grzbiet in the Holy Cross Mts., *Acta Geol. Pol.* 31:81–101.

Szyndlar, Z. 1984. Fossil snakes from Poland, *Acta Zool. Cracov.* 28:1–156.

Szyndlar, Z. Snakes from the lower Miocene locality of Dolnice (Czechoslovakia), *J. Vertebr. Paleontol.* In press a.

Szyndlar, Z. Ophidian fauna (Reptilia, Serpentes) from the uppermost Miocene of Algora (Spain), *Estud. Geol.* In press b.

Tatarinov, L. P. 1963. The first occurrence in the USSR of the ancient sea snakes, *Paleontol. Zh.* 2:109–115. (In Russian.)

Tyler, M. J. 1979. Herpetofaunal relationships of South America with Australia, in: The South American Herpetofauna: Its Origin, Evolution, and Dispersal (W. E. Duellman, ed.) *Univ. Kans. Mus. Nat. Hist. Monogr.* 7:73–106.

Underwood, G. 1957. On lizards of the family Pygopodidae: A contribution to the morphology and phylogeny of the Squamata, *J. Morphol.* 100:207–268.

Underwood, G. 1967. A Contribution to the Classification of Snakes, Trustees of the British Museum (Natural History), London.

Underwood, G. 1970. The eye, in: Biology of the Reptilia, vol. 2 (C. Gans, and T. S. Parsons, eds.) pp. 1–97, Academic Press, London.

Underwood, G. 1976. A systematic analysis of boid snakes, in: Morphology and Biology of Reptiles (A. d'A. Bellairs and C. B. Cox, eds.) pp. 151–175, Linn. Soc. Symp. Ser. 3, Academic Press, London.

Wallach, V. 1984. A new name for *Ophiomorphus colberti* Haas, 1980, *J. Herpetol.* 18:329.

Walls, G. L. 1942. The vertebrate eye and its adaptative radiation, *Bull. Cranbrook Inst. Sci. Bull.* 19:1–785.

Westgate, J. W. and Ward, J. S. 1981. The giant aquatic snake *Pterosphenus schucherti* (Palaeophidae) in Arkansas and Mississippi, *J. Vertebr. Paleontol.* 1:161–164.

Zerova, G. A. and Chkhikvadze, V. M. 1984. Review of Cenozoic lizards and snakes of the USSR, *Proc. Acad. Sci. Georgian SSR Biol. Ser.* 10:319–326. (In Russian.)

CHAPTER THREE

Geographic Distribution: Problems in Phylogeny and Zoogeography

John E. Cadle

The geographic distribution of snakes has not yet received a comprehensive treatment. The tremendous diversity of snakes, their poor fossil record, and apparently considerable homoplasy in morphological features have retarded progress in understanding phylogenetic relationships among lineages. Thus there has been no firm foundation on which to base testable historical biogeographic hypotheses. Given this limitation, my purpose will not be to provide a definitive synthesis of snake biogeography. By its nature, biogeography depends heavily on systematics and paleontology, and a considerable number of problems must be resolved in these areas before biogeographic studies on snakes can be truly synthetic. At the outset, then, I will discuss these problems, concentrating on those topics that I perceive as most relevant to phylogenetic and biogeographic studies. These include consideration of the age of the various snake lineages (How representative is the fossil record?) and problems in correlating the studies of paleontologists and neontologists (To what extent can lineages be identified from fossil vertebrae?). The chapters by McDowell and Rage in this volume should be referred to for additional information and viewpoints.

I discuss the snake fauna of the world by geographic regions. This approach is somewhat artificial, but because of the uncertainties concerning the phylogenetic relationships for most groups, it is inadvisable to discuss each lineage separately. I review only extant lineages of snakes, and their fossil records will be discussed only as they relate to historical biogeographic patterns. For uniformity I follow the classification of McDowell (this volume) although, as noted below, my interpretation of certain aspects of snake phylogeny differs from his.

PHYLOGENETIC RELATIONSHIPS OF SNAKE LINEAGES

Two major monophyletic groups of snakes, the Scolecophidia and the Alethinophidia (Henophidia plus Caenophidia of some authors), are generally recognized (Figure 3–1) (McDowell, 1974; Rieppel, 1979), but there is little agreement beyond this level. The Scolecophidia appear to be an ancient group of snakes,

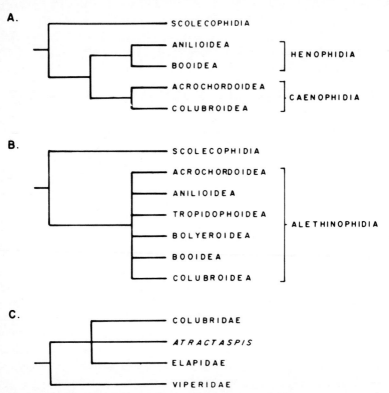

Figure 3–1. Alternative views of the phylogeny of higher taxa of snakes. (A) Modified from Rieppel (1979): Recognizes the Henophidia and Caenophidia as monophyletic groups (both comprising the Alethinophidia). In addition to the features noted by Rieppel, the sister group relationship of the Acrochordoidea and Colubroidea is supported by shared derived features of the carotid circulation and vomer structure (Groombridge, 1979, 1984). Rieppel's Booidea comprises the Booidea, Bolyeroidea, and Tropidophoidea of McDowell (this volume). (B) A phylogeny suggested by McDowell (this volume); the Alethinophidia is monophyletic, but relationships among major groups within it are unresolved. (C) Phylogenetic relationships among Colubroidea supported by some biochemical and morphological evidence (Cadle, 1982a); McDowell's interpretation (this volume) differs in recognizing Viperidae plus Colubridae (modified) as a distinct group relative to Elapidae plus Atractaspididae (including some "colubrids").

and the relationships among species have not been studied comprehensively. Consequently, they are ignored in this discussion.

It is quite possible that the Henophidia as presently constituted (Underwood, 1967; Rieppel, 1979; McDowell, 1975, and this volume) is paraphyletic. For example, most of the derived features characterizing the Booidea as recognized by Rieppel (1979) (*Xenopeltis, Loxocemus, Calabaria,* plus "typical" boas and pythons) (Figure 3–1a) also characterize various caenophidians (Rieppel, 1979). Further work may demonstrate a closer relationship between caenophidians and some henophidian lineages than the latter are *inter se.* This same caveat applies to the relationships between the Anilioidea and the Booidea within the Henophidia. That is, are they monophyletic sister groups? (See McDowell, this volume.) McDowell's classification (this volume) (see Figure 3–1b), although lacking resolution at higher taxonomic levels, is reflective of current uncertainties about relationships among alethinophidian lineages. Clearly, much work remains to be done on the composition and higher-level phylogeny of these groups, an important consideration in discussing the biogeography of these lineages.

McDowell (this volume) proposes a novel arrangement of the Colubroidea, making a basic division between the Proteroglypha (Elapidae plus Atractaspididae) and the Opisthoglypha (Colubridae plus Viperidae). Whereas McDowell considers the Proteroglypha the most primitive of the Colubroidea, and the Viperidae most closely related to his (modified) Colubridae, the available biochemical evidence (and some interpretations of morphological data) suggests that the Viperidae is the sister group to the remaining colubroids tested (including McDowell's Elapidae, Atractaspididae, and Colubridae) (Cadle, 1982a,b) (Figure 3–1c). Thus, within the Colubroidea I recognize four major groups: the Viperidae, Atractaspididae, Elapidae, and Colubridae.

The Viperidae includes the primitive *Azemiops* (Azemiopinae) of southern Asia, the Viperinae of Eurasia and Africa, and the Crotalinae of southern Asia and the New World. Relationships among the viperine genera are not well understood. An immunoelectrophoretic study on venom proteins (Detrait and Saint-Girons, 1979) indicated that the African genera *Bitis, Echis,* and *Cerastes* had more antigens in common than any of them had with several species of Eurasian *Vipera; Atheris* was distinct from both the *Bitis* and *Vipera* groups (no other genera were tested). These data are difficult to interpret phylogenetically, however, and confirmation of the hypothesized relationships must come from other sources. Groombridge (1984) demonstrated that all viperine genera except *Causus* shared a derived feature of the carotid circulation, which suggests that *Causus* may be the sister group of the others. The phylogenetic position of *Azemiops* is unclear (Liem et al., 1971).

Within the Viperidae, the pit vipers (Crotalinae) are clearly monophyletic, although the definition of and relationships among natural groups within the pit vipers are currently debated. The most recent checklist (Hoge and Romano-Hoge, 1978/1979) recognized two groups: (1) *Agkistrodon* s.l. and (2) *Crotalus, Bothrops, Lachesis, Sistrurus,* and *Trimeresurus* s.l. Brattstrom (1964), however, considered the New World species of *Agkistrodon* more closely related to *Crotalus, Sistrurus,* and *Lachesis* than to Asian *Agkistrodon*. In his phylogeny, a separate lineage included *Trimeresurus* s.l. and *Bothrops* s.l. The relationships among these groups clearly need additional study.

The relationships of *Atractaspis* are not clear (see Cadle, 1982b). McDowell's hypothesis of a relationship to *Amblyodipsas,* etc., cannot be falsified, but such molecular data as exist suggest a remote relationship at best (Cadle, 1982b). There is some indication from albumin immunological data of an association between *Atractaspis* and the elapids, although here the data are somewhat equivocal (Cadle, 1982a,b, and unpublished data); an alternative interpretation is that *Atractaspis* diverged from a basic colubroid stock at about the same time as, but independent of, elapids. For the present I recognize the Atractaspididae (including only *Atractaspis*) as a primitive colubroid lineage possibly remotely related to the Elapidae.

I follow the traditionally accepted boundaries of the family Elapidae (McCarthy, 1985). There have been no comprehensive surveys of phylogenetic relationships within the Elapidae. Molecular studies (Cadle and Gorman, 1981; Mao et al., 1983; Schwaner et al., 1985) suggest that the radiation of Australopapuan terrestrial elapids is largely monophyletic. Moreover, these studies also indicate that sea snakes (marine Hydropheinae plus Laticaudinae of McDowell, this volume) are closely related to the Australopapuan terrestrial elapids and that these three groups are derived lineages. There is inadequate resolution of whether the marine Hydropheinae plus Laticaudinae are monophyletic within the broader Hydropheinae-Laticaudinae (in McDowell's classification they are not). However, morphological, karyological, and biochemical data are broadly concordant regarding a close relationship among terrestrial Australopapuan elapids and the two sea snake groups (Mengden, 1983; McDowell, this volume). Some biochemical evidence (J.E. Cadle, unpublished data) suggests that the Elapinae and Bungarinae of McDowell are not monophyletic, but further work is required to determine natural units within these groups.

The Colubridae poses many problems, one being that there is apparently no derived feature that demonstrates the monophyly of all the "colubrid" lineages. Thus there is a possibility that this large group is paraphyletic. The natural units and their relationships within the Colubridae are also subject to much controversy. This precludes all but the most superficial analytic approach to the biogeography of this family. In this review I concentrate on the groups for which we have the most data concerning both intra- and intergroup relationships: the Natricinae, Xenodontinae, and Colubrinae of McDowell (this volume). The following synopsis comments on aspects of colubrid relationships that are not emphasized by McDowell.

1. *Natricines*: As generally recognized (Malnate, 1960; Rossman and Eberle, 1977) this is only a core group of genera. Numerous other African and Asian genera are possible members of this group, but there is little consistency in the

interpretation of the available phylogenetic data for them (reviewed by Mc-Dowell, this volume); these genera are thus ignored in this review. Immunological comparisons of transferrins (Mao and Dessauer, 1971; Schwaner and Dessauer, 1982, and references therein) suggest four major monophyletic groups among the species tested: (a) thamnophiines, comprising the nine New World genera and possibly *Afronatrix*; (b) European *Natrix* (three species); (c) *Sinonatrix*; and (d) other Asian genera (*Xenochrophis, Amphiesma,* and *Rhabdophis* tested). The branching order among these clades has not been resolved. McDowell excludes *Afronatrix* and *Sinonatrix* from the Natricinae in his classification, but they are retained here on the basis of biochemical evidence and Malnate's (1960) studies.

2. *Homalopsines* (Gyi, 1970; McDowell, this volume): This group, which also includes the terrestrial *Brachyorrhos,* are sometimes considered related to or included within the natricines (e.g., Dowling and Duellman, 1978). Immunological comparisons of transferrins and albumins suggest, however, that the groups are two distinct lineages (Schwaner and Dessauer, 1982; Dowling et al., 1983). Their relationships to one another vis-à-vis other colubrid lineages remain to be determined, however.

3. *"Xenodontines"*: The clades recognized here are the South and Central American xenodontine lineages (Cadle, 1984a,b); several North American xenodontine genera appear unrelated to these groups, but their relationships to other snakes are not clear (Cadle, 1984c). I treat these clades separately for zoogeographic analyses or for higher taxonomic phylogenetic analyses of colubrids (contrary to Dowling et al., 1983 and McDowell, this volume) until their monophyly has been demonstrated.

4. *Colubrines*: This group appears reasonably well defined morphologically (McDowell, this volume), and molecular evidence suggests close relationships among the constituent genera (Schwaner and Dessauer, 1982; Dowling et al., 1983; Cadle, 1984c). Except for a few small generic associations, the definition of monophyletic groups within the colubrines is not well established.

5. *Xenodermines, calamariines, pareatines, boodontines, lycodontines, and pseudoxenodontines of McDowell (this volume)*: We have fewer phylogenetic data for these groups than for other colubrids. Most have been included within a composite group, the Lycodontinae (e.g., Dowling and Duellman, 1978), but immunological comparisons of albumins and transferrins suggest that the Lycodontinae is not monophyletic (Schwaner and Dessauer, 1982; Dowling et al., 1983; J. E. Cadle, unpublished data). However, the relationships (and composition) of its constituent groups remain open to question. Presently, there are insufficient molecular data on these snakes to evaluate other comparative evidence of relationships. Among the Boodontinae, micro-complement fixation comparisons of albumins (Dowling et al., 1983; J. E. Cadle, unpublished data) suggest several ancient lineages (not clearly monophyletic), consistent with McDowell's (this volume) view that the Boodontinae includes many very prim-

itive colubrids. McDowell's recognition of the polyphyly of the "Aparallactinae" (Bourgeois, 1965; McDowell, 1968) is consistent with limited immunological comparisons of albumins (Cadle, 1982b), but further work is necessary to evaluate the alternative hypotheses for their relationships presented thus far.

TEMPORAL FRAMEWORK FOR THE RADIATION OF EXTANT SNAKES

To the extent that distributional patterns are related to events in earth history, zoogeographic analyses are ultimately constrained by the ages of the lineages under consideration. With a reasonably representative fossil record the ages could be taken directly from paleontological evidence. This is not true for snakes, and I believe that a judicious interpretation of fossil data and molecular data (presently limited primarily to albumin and transferrin immunological comparisons and electrophoretic data) will provide the best estimates for the ages of extant lineages. However, such data must be calibrated using the fossil record or biogeographic data before they can be used to generate time scales for the evolution of particular lineages. A calibration of the albumin immunological data (Cadle, 1982a) suggests that most of the extant major lineages of colubrids (natricines, colubrines, Central and South American xenodontines, homalopsines, etc.) date back to at least the Oligocene (approximately 30 MYA), and some possibly appreciably further [the earliest colubrids, assigned to the Colubrinae, are from France and Colorado 30 to 32 MYA (Rage, 1982; Holman, 1984)]. It then follows that the basal radiations leading to extant elapids and viperids must be earlier (cf. Figure 3–1c), thus pushing the origin of extant colubroid lineages beyond the documentation provided by fossils [the earliest elapid and viperid fossils appeared in Europe approximately 20 MYA (elapids) or somewhat more recently than this (vipers) (Rage, 1982)]. Consequently, I conclude that some extant colubroid lineages originated possibly as early as 40 to 60 MYA (the earliest colubroid fossils are from the lower Eocene and apparently do not belong to any extant lineage).

It is clear that the molecular differentiation among taxa within the Henophidia and Scolecophidia is very great (approaching the limits, for example, of microcomplement fixation comparisons of albumins). These appear to be ancient groups extending well back into the Mesozoic, as indicated also by the fossil record for some of these groups (Rage, this volume).

As a first approximation, then, we can consider the evolution of colubroid snakes as having occurred within the Cenozoic and that of "lower" Alethinophidian groups to have extended back into the Mesozoic for an undetermined period of time. The distributions of extant lineages will then have been influenced by paleogeographic and paleoclimatic events of the Mesozoic and Cenozoic (for summaries see Raven and Axelrod, 1974; Lillegraven et al., 1979; Tarling, 1980; Audley-Charles et al., 1981).

FOSSIL SNAKES, PHYLOGENY, AND NEONTOLOGY

Ophidian paleontologists and neontologists have generally approached the estimation of snake phylogeny using different sets of characters. Snake fossils are
usually preserved as vertebrae, and vertebral characters are almost the only data
available for classifying and deriving phylogenies from fossils. While vertebrae
are used to some extent by neontologists, there has been a greater reliance on
features of the skull, head musculature, glands, hemipenes, other aspects of soft
anatomy and, more recently, biochemical and molecular data. Clearly, to understand the history of extant lineages of snakes, these approaches must be
integrated. McDowell (this volume) noted some of the ambiguities in interpreting
the relationships of particular fossil snakes. Here I comment on general problems
that must be faced in making phylogenetic statements concerning snake fossils.
My comments should not be seen as a criticism of the paleontological approach
but rather as an exploration of potential problems that may arise from the interpretation of fossil material. I consider two aspects of the fossil record: (1) the
nature of the vertebrae and (2) the possibly biasing influence of the spatial
distribution of fossils.

Surprisingly, we still lack an adequate survey of vertebral morphology and
variation for a single snake taxon (of either a lower or a higher category). This
precludes a rigorous evaluation of the value of vertebral characters in reconstructing phylogenetic relationships among snakes. I suggest that it would be
instructive to attempt to define extant snake lineages on the basis of vertebral
characters. The extent to which vertebrae yield estimates of phylogeny consistent
with those provided by other features could then be evaluated, and one could
thereby assess the variability of vertebral characters within higher taxa containing
numerous living representatives.

My own work with xenodontines illustrates some of the uncertainties regarding the interpretation of vertebral characters. The classically recognized
colubrid subfamily Xenodontinae is possibly non-monophyletic, being defined
by primitive characters of the hemipenes (Cadle, 1984c). Several lineages exist
within this group that are as differentiated from one another as from other colubrid
lineages (Schwaner and Dessauer, 1982; Cadle, 1984a,b; Cadle and Dessauer,
1985). The North American fossil genera *Dryinoides, Paleofarancia,* and *Diadophis* (also with living species) have been suggested to be related to extant
xenodontines s.l. (Auffenberg, 1958, 1963; Holman, 1979) but were placed in
the Colubrinae (Holman, 1979). This raises the question of whether the vertebral
characters used to define colubrid subfamilies (Holman, 1979) are truly indicative
of relationships. For xenodontines in particular it is not clear whether the vertebral
features that characterize the North American Xenodontinae will also characterize
the other extant xenodontines, which include more than 80 Neotropical genera.

The problem for xenodontines (and, I suggest, for other snake lineages) is
that there is inadequate evaluation of which vertebral characters are derived

within particular clades, which have appeared convergently in other lineages, and which are conservative (primitive) for these clades. Some vertebral features, at least, appear to be related to functional characteristics and mode of life (Gasc, 1976). The fact that the vertebrae of the earliest uncontested colubrid fossil, *Coluber cadurci*, from the middle Oligocene of France are identical to those of modern *Coluber* and other related Eurasian colubrine genera (Rage, 1974), suggests that vertebral evolution in this group has either been very conservative or that extant and Oligocene colubrines have attained the same vertebral form independently. This points up the need for a thorough study of vertebral evolution in snakes.

Another factor that will influence inferences about the biogeographic history of extant snakes is fossil distribution. There is a distinctly north temperate bias in the distribution of snake fossils, particularly of colubroids. Most current knowledge comes from western North America and western Europe. Snake fossils are virtually unknown from Asia and Australia. In contrast, many extant lineages have virtually no extra-tropical representives (see following). Indeed, nearly all colubrid fossils known have been assigned to the two primarily temperate lineages living today, the colubrines and the natricines. As shown in the following discussion, the pattern of relationships and distributions of these two lineages is unusual among colubrids; inferences concerning geographic deployment made from these lineages may not be general features of colubrid history.

THE COMPOSITION OF EXTANT SNAKE FAUNAS

The distributions of major lineages of snakes are indicated in Table 3–1. In the following discussion I comment on the composition of present-day snake faunas for each region, indicating hypotheses that could account for the distributional patterns of each lineage. Therefore, some lineages are discussed for more than one area.

North America

All extant North American snake lineages except leptotyphlopids are present in the North American fossil record; extinct groups also present are aniliids, paleophids, boine boids, and several "Henophidia" *incertae sedis*. The elapids (micrurines) and extinct groups are discussed under the Neotropical fauna, where these groups are most diverse today.

The boid fauna of North America is represented by two living erycine genera, *Lichanura* and *Charina*. Fossil erycines are widespread in North America and western Europe from the Paleocene on (Hoffstetter and Rage, 1972; Holman, 1979). Hoffstetter and Rage (1972) and Rage (1977) outlined the history of erycines based on fossil evidence and suggested several scenarios for the history

Table 3–1 Geographic Distribution of Extant Snake Taxa[a]

Taxon	Europe, N.W. Africa	Africa	Madagascar	Mascarene Islands	Temperate E. Asia	Southern Asia	Australian Region	North America	Central America	South America	West Indies
Anomalepididae									X	X	
Leptotyphlopidae		X				X		X	X	X	
Typhlopidae	X	X	X			X	X		X	X	X
Uropeltidae						X					
Aniliidae										X	
Xenopeltidae						X					
Loxocemidae									X		
Acrochordidae						X	X				
Bolyeriidae				X							
Tropidopheinae									X	X	X
Ungaliopheinae									X	X	
Pythonidae		X				X	X				
Erycinae	X	X			X			X			
Boinae			X				X		X	X	X
Viperinae	X	X			X	X					
Azemiopinae						X					
Crotalinae					X	X		X	X	X	
Atractaspididae		X									
Elapinae-Bungarinae- Maticorinae- Calliopheinae		X				X		X	X	X	
Marine Hydropheinae		X	X		X	X	X	X	X	X	
Terrestrial Hydropheinae							X				
Laticaudinae						X	X				
Pareatinae						X					
Xenoderminae						X					
Calamariinae						X					
Homalopsinae						X	X				
Natricinae	X	X			X	X	X	X	X		X
Colubrinae	X	X			X	X	X	X	X	X	
Central American xenodontines								X	X	X	X
South American xenodontines									X	X	X
Xenodontinae *incertae* *sedis*								X	X		
Boodontinae- Lycodontinae		X	X			X					
Pseudoxenodontinae						X					

[a]The classification follows McDowell (this volume) with slight modification as noted in the text.

of this group. Rage's (1977) interpretation included (1) a North American origin followed by migration into western Europe via the North Atlantic route by the lower Eocene; (2) diversification of the North American group, which gave rise to lines that led to *Lichanura* and *Charina* and to a line that migrated westward across Asia during the Oligocene and Miocene to give rise to the European Miocene fossil *Albaneryx*; (3) extinction of the erycines of western Europe, which left no living descendants; and (4) origin of the modern Eurasian species from unspecified ancestral stocks that migrated westward from North America across Asia during the Eocene-Pliocene, which gave rise also to the European Oligocene *Bransateryx* and, during the Miocene, to the living species of *Eryx*.

This scenario involving three separate migrations appears complex in view of the lack of substantiating fossil material from Asia (where the Cenozoic fossil record is poor) and the relatively recent appearance of fossils assigned to the *Eryx* lineage (Miocene: Rage, 1976). A much more parsimonious alternative (not requiring extensive migrations) considered by Hoffstetter and Rage (1972) and Estes and Hutchison (1980) is the divergence of the New and Old World erycine lineages coincident with disruption of the North Atlantic land continuity after the lower Eocene. This alternative interpretation would necessitate modification of Rage's (1977) phylogeny. However, final resolution will depend on the phylogeny ultimately accepted for fossil and recent erycine genera.

Vipers present in North America include the crotalines *Crotalus, Agkistrodon,* and *Sistrurus*. Most authors (e.g., Brattstrom, 1964) have considered *Bothrops* and *Trimeresurus* s.l. a separate lineage from the other Old and New World crotalines, so that at least two phyletic lines are presumed to be present in both the Old World and the New World. Most authors also have assumed an origin of pit vipers in southeastern Asia, followed by at least two dispersals (three, if *Agkistrodon* s.l. is monophyletic) into North America via a Bering land bridge. Present evidence is also consistent with a vicariance explanation if the pit vipers are seen as widely distributed members of an Asiamerican fauna during the early Tertiary. Vicariance by increasingly cooler climates at higher latitudes would then have resulted in present distributional patterns. One problem with this vicariance explanation is the nearly total lack of pre-Pliocene viperid fossils in North America, and these should be present if viperids were present earlier in the Tertiary of North America.

Colubrids are represented in North America by two widespread lineages, colubrines and natricines. Both of these groups are nearly worldwide in distribution, though with limited extension into the Australian region; natricines are not present in South America. Also present are five genera of "xenodontines" (*Carphophis, Contia, Diadophis, Farancia,* and *Heterodon*) whose relationships to one another and to other colubrids are obscure (Cadle, 1984c). The fossil record of these groups in North America extends to the middle Oligocene (colubrines: Holman, 1984), middle Miocene (natricines: Holman, 1979), and upper Miocene (xenodontines: Auffenberg, 1958; Holman, 1979).

Extensive biochemical and other evidence suggest that North American natricines (thamnophiines) are monophyletic relative to Old World forms (Schwaner and Dessauer, 1982, and references therein; Dowling et al., 1983). It is not clear to which of at least four Old World natricine groups the thamnophiines are most closely related. Using micro-complement fixation comparisons of transferrins (not rate-tested), Mao and Dessauer (1971) have determined that thamnophiines are approximately equidistant from *Natrix* and *Sinonatrix* and slightly more removed from Asian *Rhabdophis-Xenochrophis-Amphiesma*. Schwaner and Des-sauer (1982), using qualitative comparisons of transferrins, found thamnophiines closest to *Afronatrix* of West Africa, but these data conflicted somewhat with more quantitative comparisons (Gartside and Dessauer, 1977).

The origin of thamnophiines is generally presumed to have been via Cenozoic dispersal from Asia across the Bering land bridge (e.g., Malnate, 1960), which could have occurred during much of the Cenozoic (Simpson, 1947). If present distributions of the major clades within the natricines were the result of dispersals, however, one might expect to see broad sympatry among members of different monophyletic groups. This is not true for the living fauna; North America, Asia, and Europe appear to have distinct natricine faunas that are monophyletic relative to those of other regions. This pattern of distribution suggests fragmentation of an extensive ancestral range covering much of Europe, Asia, North America, and Africa. A concerted effort to estimate phylogenetic relationships among the natricine groups of these regions might shed considerable light on the historical factors determining their present distributions.

In contrast to natricines, North American colubrines do not appear to be monophyletic, suggesting dispersals of several groups between the Old World and the New World (Cadle, 1984c). Biochemical evidence (George and Des-sauer, 1970; Schwaner and Dessauer, 1982; Dowling et al., 1983; Cadle, 1984c) suggests that, while the colubrine lineage is relatively old (at least 30 MYA, according to fossil remains), divergence between many Old and New World genera is relatively recent. Exchange among elements of the North American and Asian faunas was probably possible up until the relatively late Miocene across the Bering land bridge (Simpson, 1947; Wolfe and Leopold, 1967). This seems the most likely route of entry of colubrines into the New World given the close relationships among these genera worldwide.

The history of North American xenodontines is enigmatic, because their relationships to other colubrids are unclear. Contrary to the conclusion of Dowl-ing et al. (1983) that these forms are related to neotropical xenodontines, this cannot be substantiated with more thorough analyses (Cadle, 1984c). Because the features suggesting xenodontine affinities are primitive characters (Cadle, 1984c), it is possible that they have had a history independent of the neotropical lineages.

Rage and Holman (1984) report four genera of colubroids common to Mio-cene deposits of North America and Europe (*Texasophis, Paleoheterodon, Neo-natrix*, and *Micrurus*), discounting parallelism as an explanation for the similarity in vertebral form of these fossils. Given the difficulties in estimating phylogenetic relationships from vertebrae within this group (Rage, 1984), it is difficult to make a reasonable choice between homoplasy and a true relationship between these forms without some independent evidence [a similar problem exists in interpretation of the mammalian faunas; see Engesser (1979)]. A common finding in extant snakes to which multiple data sets are applied is that genera with distributions spanning the Old World and the New World often have as their closest relatives other genera of the same geographic region (e.g., *Natrix*: Rossman and Eberle, 1977; *Elaphe*: Lawson and Dessauer, 1981; Dowling et al., 1983). For the fossil genera we do not have the option of examining alternative data sets, and in these instances it seems likely that they would exhibit the pattern shown in the living fauna.

The Neotropical Region, Including the West Indies

Neotropical snake biogeography has been summarized by Cadle and Sarich (1981), Rage (1981), Savage (1982), Cadle (1984c, 1985), Estes and Baez (1985), and Vanzolini and Heyer (1985).

The living primitive alethinophidian fauna of the neotropics includes *Loxocemus, Anilius,* boine boids, and tropidophiids (Table 3–1). *Loxocemus* and *Anilius* possibly have their closest relatives in southeast Asia (reviewed by McDowell, this volume), *Xenopeltis* and Uropeltidae (including *Cylindrophis*), respectively. These relationships are not well substantiated, however, and the Anilioidea may simply be a group of primitive lineages without special relationships to one another. Fossil evidence suggests that anilioids were once widespread (North and South America, Europe: Hoffstetter and Rage, 1977), but there are problems in the assignment of some fossil material to this lineage (McDowell, this volume). Thus the present distribution of the Anilioidea may be a relict from a former widespread one, but this conclusion must depend on the demonstration that the group (or components thereof) is monophyletic relative to other Alethinophidia.

As noted by McDowell (this volume), the tropidophiids fall into two distinct groups: *Exiliboa* (Mexico) plus *Ungaliophis* (Mexico to Colombia); and *Tropidophis* (scattered localities on mainland South America, the Greater Antilles, and the Bahama Banks) plus *Trachyboa* (Panama and northwestern South America). All current evidence suggests that these are ancient lineages with possible ties to fossil forms in North America and western Europe (see McDowell, this volume; Rage, this volume). The degree of divergence between the two groups of tropidophiids and between them and other alethinophidian groups is not yet documented (McDowell, 1975, and this volume). The extant genera appear to be patchily distributed on the mainland.

McDowell (1979) concluded that the neotropical boine genera fell into two groups: *Boa* and *Xenoboa,* most closely related to the Malagasy boines; and *Corallus, Epicrates,* and *Eunectes,* most closely related to the southwestern Pacific boine *Candoia.* Some biochemical evidence suggests, however, that the relationships of *Boa* to *Corallus* and *Epicrates* are fairly close (J. E. Cadle, unpublished data). This seems to preclude a special relationship between *Boa* and the Malagasy genera. Further study of these genera is warranted. The distribution of present-day species is basically South American, but *Boa* encompasses the entire range of boines in the New World from northern Mexico to Paraguay and Argentina. *Epicrates* includes one widely distributed species on mainland Central and South America but has eight additional species in the Greater Antilles. Steadman et al. (1984) recovered *Boa* and an unidentified boid from fossil deposits on Antigua, which has no boids today. *Epicrates* and *Tropidophis* may eventually be recovered from fossil deposits in the Lesser Antilles.

The controversy surrounding the origin and relationships of neotropical crotalines has been summarized previously (see NORTH AMERICA). *Bothrops* s.l. is by far the largest group, comprising more than 50 species. South of the Isthmus of Tehuantepec, *Crotalus* is represented only by three species. *Lachesis* is distributed throughout tropical forests in southern Central America and South America. The distributions of *Lachesis* and *Crotalus* are exclusive, with the latter being found only in dry forest or savanna regions (including savanna enclaves within rain forests). This pattern suggests that the present distribution of *Crotalus*, in South America at least, is a retraction of a wider range during drier climatic phases when savannas were more widespread (Hoogmoed, 1982).

Neotropical elapids (*Micrurus* plus the North American *Micruroides*) comprise about 50 species, most of which are in South America, although the group ranges north to the southern United States (see Roze, 1982). The relationship of micrurines to some Asian terrestrial elapids (Elapinae of McDowell, this volume) is supported by morphological studies (cf. McDowell, 1967, 1969), but these postulated relationships remain to be tested in detail biochemically. No special association between micrurines and particular Asian elapids [specifically to *Laticauda*, as suggested by McDowell (1967)] can be demonstrated by albumin comparisons (Cadle and Sarich, 1981; J. E. Cadle, unpublished data; members of McDowell's Calliopheinae, Maticorinae, and some Elapinae have not been compared). It is clear from available comparisons that micrurines are a relatively derived elapid group. Present evidence suggests that micrurines have been in the New World since the late Oligocene or early Miocene (Cadle and Sarich, 1981). Fossil vertebrae identified as *Micrurus* have been reported from the middle Miocene (12 to 14 MYA) of Nebraska (Holman, 1977) and France (Rage and Holman, 1984). However, they have yet to be adequately diagnosed from some Asian genera (Calliopheinae and Maticorinae), many of which have very similar vertebrae (Savitzky, 1978).

The colubrid fauna of the Neotropics is dominated by the Central and South American xenodontines, which have different patterns of diversity and endemism (Cadle, 1985). The sister group of either xenodontine clade is not known. Until their relationships to Old World lineages are clarified, their early history in the Neotropics will remain obscure. Colubrines, while widespread in the Neotropics, do not attain the species or ecological diversity represented in either xenodontine lineage. They are relatively closely related to their North American and Old

World counterparts and most likely entered South America from the north. The limited biochemical data available on the relationships among extant South American colubrines (Cadle, 1984c, and unpublished data) suggest dispersal of several lines within this clade into South America. Thamnophiines penetrate Central America to Costa Rica but are most speciose and ecologically diverse in the eastern United States.

Colubrids appeared in South America in the middle Miocene (Hoffstetter and Rage, 1977), but whether the fossil represents one of the extant lineages or an extinct clade has not been resolved. Hoffstetter and Rage suggested that this fossil may represent one of the earliest colubrid immigrants to South America from the north. However, the pattern of relationships of the living fauna suggests a more ancient emplacement (at least 30 MYA) for at least the xenodontines in South America (Savage, 1982; Cadle, 1985); colubrines probably entered South America later than xenodontines. There is insufficient evidence to choose between a northern origin (via North and Central America) and a southern one (via Africa) for the origin of South American colubrids (Cadle, 1984c, 1985; Estes and Baez, 1985). Among the living faunas of South America and Africa there are some morphological similarities between South American xenodontines and some "lycodontines" (e.g., *Grayia*: McDowell, this volume). However, these similarities, particularly the divided sulcus spermaticus, are primitive features. Thus these groups cannot be allied on this basis, a problem also with the definition of the Xenodontinae (Cadle, 1984c). Nevertheless, given that no strong case has been made allying xenodontines with any other snake lineage, the possibility of an African origin for them presently cannot be ruled out.

Cadle (1985) and Vanzolini and Heyer (1985) concluded that most exchange between the snake faunas of Central and South America occurred long before formation of the Isthmian link during the Pliocene. The degree of molecular differentiation among Central and South American species of micrurines, colubrines, and xenodontines suggests that dispersal occurred in these groups over much of the Neogene (Cadle and Sarich, 1981; Cadle, 1984c, 1985). For xenodontines, Cadle (1985) showed that the pre-Isthmian link exchange between Central and South America was predominantly from Central America into South America. Vanzolini and Heyer (1985) concluded that only two examples among snakes represent cases of dispersal across the Isthmian link: *Crotalus durissus* and *Drymarchon corais*. To these might be added several species of xenodontines and colubrines that have dispersed from lower Central America to northwestern South America, or vice versa, but have not extended their distribution far beyond the Isthmian region (Cadle, 1985).

Africa, Madagascar, the Seychelles, and the Mascarene Islands

The lower Alethinophidia are represented in this region by Pythonidae (*Python* and *Calabaria*, mainland sub-Saharan Africa), Boinae (*Sanzinia* and *Acranto-*

phis, Madagascar), and Bolyeroidea (*Bolyeria* and *Casarea*, Mauritius and Round Island). The relationships of the latter two groups to other Alethinophidia are not understood. The boids have been discussed with reference to Neotropical boines and are further mentioned below in connection with the southwestern Pacific boids (see AUSTRALIAN REGION). Concerning the bolyerioids, little can be added to the comments of McDowell (this volume) until their relationships are clarified. I follow McDowell in regarding *Calabaria* as a pythonid, although its phylogenetic relationships are debated; in addition to the hypotheses discussed by McDowell, Rieppel (1978) considers *Calabaria* closely related to the Erycinae. If this is true, then *Calabaria* is the only extant species with a primarily tropical distribution.

Schwaner and Dessauer (1981), on the basis of transferrin and albumin immunological comparisons, suggest that the African *Python regius* is more distantly related to Australasian species of *Python* than the latter are to *Liasis*. Without knowing quantitatively at the molecular level how divergent the African pythons are from one another and from the species of southern Asia [they are all very similar morphologically (McDowell, 1975)], several scenarios could account for the disjunct distribution of living pythonids between these regions. An ancient separation of the African from the Asian pythons could reflect Gondwanan fragmentation (with Asian species derived from ancestral forms transported via the Indian subcontinent), but a more recent vicariance due to climatic changes in southwestern Asia [increasing aridity during the Neogene (Axelrod, 1979)] could also explain the pattern. It should be possible to obtain a clearer picture of the historical biogeography of pythons when their relationships are studied in greater detail.

There are no adequate studies on the phylogeny of African viperines (here excluding the species of European *Vipera* in northwestern Africa). The fauna includes an endemic, presumably primitive genus (*Causus*); the derived genera *Bitis, Atheris,* and *Adenorhinus,* endemic except that *Bitis* extends marginally into the Arabian peninsula; and *Echis* and *Cerastes,* species of an arid-adapted fauna extending across northern Africa and into southwestern Asia (see below). The African viperine fauna is thus very distinct from that of Europe and eastern Asia, which includes a variety of species of *Vipera* but none of the African genera. Thus, except for *Causus,* which may be the sister group to other viperines (see aforementioned and Groombridge, 1984), the distinction between *Vipera* and the African genera may represent a fundamental phyletic split within the Viperinae. This supposition needs to be substantiated with further phylogenetic studies of this group.

Within Africa and the Middle East, the distributions of *Atractaspis* and the other members of McDowell's (this volume) Atractaspididae are practically co-extensive. *Atractaspis* is also found in the southern portion of the Arabian peninsula. All the Atractaspididae are primitive colubroids with no known relatives outside Africa.

With the exceptions of *Naja* (Africa and southern Asia) and *Walterinnesia*

(Egypt through the Middle East to Iran), the genera of African elapids are endemic to that continent. However, they do not form a monophyletic group relative to Asian genera (J. E. Cadle, unpublished data). The cobralike forms (*Naja, Aspidelaps, Hemachatus, Pseudohaje,* and possibly *Boulengerina*) very likely form one lineage; the remaining genera (*Elapsoidea, Paranaja, Dendroaspis,* and *Homoroselaps*) have complex relationships to one another and to Asian elapids. Fossils related to *Naja* (*Palaeonaja*) from the early Miocene (20 to 22 MYA) of France are the oldest elapids known. Hoffstetter (1939) suggested that both Europe and Africa were invaded independently from Asia during the Miocene by a proto-*Naja* stock; this idea was supported by similarities between the Miocene herpetofaunas of Europe and Asia and their dissimilarity to those of North Africa (Rage, 1976). However, some exchange between Africa and Europe was possible during the Miocene, as indicated by mammalian faunas (Coryndon and Savage, 1973); thus Africa also appears to be a possible source of the Miocene *Palaeonaja* of Europe. We have few indications of the history of the other African elapid genera, but some biochemical data suggest that several of these lineages are very ancient (J. E. Cadle, unpublished data).

The colubrid fauna of Africa includes a diversity of primitive genera [Lycodontinae-Boodontinae (hereafter referred to as boodontines) and possibly Natricinae] and numerous derived genera of colubrines. Also included are the solid-toothed members of McDowell's (this volume) Atractaspididae ("aparallactines" of some authors). With the exceptions of *Boiga* and *Psammophis,* these genera are basically endemic to Africa or Madagascar. It is very likely that many colubrines have close relatives in southern Asia, but there is little indication of close relationships between the boodontines and genera elsewhere, nor are the relationships of the natricines clear (see aforementioned and McDowell, this volume). It is possible that the relatives of some boodontines are among the New World xenodontines, although the limited biochemical comparisons among these groups have thus far failed to demonstrate such relationships (Cadle, 1984c). Nevertheless, if such a relationship were eventually to be established, it would suggest a mechanism for deployment of the xenodontines: early Tertiary dispersal of ancestral forms from Africa, similar to scenarios for the deployment of platyrrhines and hystricognaths in South America (reviewed by Cadle, 1985).

The snake fauna of Madagascar includes only typhlopids (9 species), boine boids (3 species), and boodontine colubrids (43 species in 16 genera) (Brygoo, 1982). Except for the colubrid *Geodipsas,* which is also found in eastern and central Africa, all genera of boids and colubrids are endemic. Unfortunately, virtually nothing is known of the relationships of these genera to one another or to those of Africa where, presumably, their closest relatives are found. This is also true of the endemic colubrids of the Seychelles (*Lycognathophis*) and Socatra (*Ditypophis*).

The fauna of Africa, then, appears to be a mixture of primitive lineages, including pythons, the elapids *Naja* and *Elapsoidea,* the viperid *Causus,* Atractaspididae (of McDowell, this volume), and many boodontine colubrids. There are clear ties among some of these forms to southern Asian faunas (e.g., *Naja, Boiga,* and *Psammophis*), but these are perhaps fairly recent (Neogene) associations. The overall aspect of the African snake fauna is one of old autochthonous groups. This pattern is similar to that of the African mammalian fauna, which was isolated for extensive periods of the Cenozoic and likewise has many autochthonous groups (Cooke, 1972; Maglio, 1978).

In sub-Saharan Africa there is a sharp distinction at the species level between the snake faunas of savanna and forest regions (Hughes, 1983). Despite the disjunction of rain forest areas in Africa, most forest species (70%) are found throughout the forested regions, and likewise a high percentage of savanna species are widely distributed within savanna. These sub-Saharan faunas comprise many widespread, but endemic, genera having both forest and savanna species (e.g., *Bitis, Naja, Dendroaspis,* and *Thelotornis*).

In contrast, the snake faunas of arid regions of northern Africa and southwestern Asia from the Middle East to India share a number of elements among various lineages of snakes (and other vertebrates): *Eryx* (Erycinae), *Cerastes* and *Echis* (Viperinae), *Naja* and *Walterinnesia* (Elapidae), and various colubrids (e.g., *Psammophis, Lytorhynchus, Eirenis, Coluber,* and *Spalerosophis*). These elements comprise a desert-adapted fauna that is distinctive relative to the snake faunas of sub-Saharan Africa, Europe and temperate Asia, and southeastern Asia. Nevertheless, the desert fauna is derived from those of surrounding areas, including temperate European and Asian species (*Eryx, Coluber*), species derived from the African fauna (*Naja, Psammophis*), and autochthonous species whose relationships are unclear (*Cerastes, Echis, Spalerosophis, Lytorhynchus, Eirenis*). This characteristic fauna has probably developed over much of the later Tertiary, particularly from the Miocene onward, as these regions changed from more subtropical to more xeric environments (Axelrod, 1979).

Europe and Temperate Asia

The snake fauna of temperate Eurasia has few snake lineages represented. In addition to living groups present (Table 3–1), boine boids, aniliids, and elapids are present in the fossil record. Szyndlar (1984) summarized aspects of the fossil and recent snake fauna.

The colubrid fauna of Europe and temperate Asia is depauperate in the number of taxa represented. All are members of the Natricinae and Colubrinae, and the widespread genera *Coluber, Elaphe,* and *Natrix* account for most of the species. Several European species of *Coluber, Natrix, Coronella,* and *Malpolon* are found in northern Africa but do not extend into the Sahara. *Macroprotodon* penetrates well into the Sahara, and both *Coluber* and *Malpolon* are represented by species in the savanna regions south of the Sahara (Hughes, 1983). *Telescopus,* present in southern Europe, is widely distributed from the Middle East throughout Africa. In temperate eastern Asia, there are essentially no tropical or subtropical elements present other than several species of *Elaphe* whose ranges extend north into Russia. Thus, at the generic level, the modern colubrid fauna of Europe and northern Asia appears to show little affinity with those of more tropical regions. The major lineages represented, Natricinae and Colubrinae, are the most widespread of all extant snake lineages.

Superficially, then, the modern colubrid fauna of Europe and temperate Asia appears to have a marginal affinity with lineages present in tropical southeastern Asia (*Elaphe, Coluber,* natricines). However, because phylogenetic relationships of clades within the Colubrinae and Natricinae have not been fully resolved, this apparent similarity remains to be substantiated. Certainly, none of the endemic lineages of colubrids in southeastern Asia (xenodermines, calamariines, pareatines, pseudoxenodontines) are represented in the extant or fossil fauna of Europe. Owing to the the extensive distributions of colubrines and natricines (and the probable polyphyly of genera such as *Coluber* and *Elaphe*), much remains to be understood about the relationships within these groups before a special affinity between the faunas of different geographic regions can be discerned. It is likely that extensive dispersal of species within these groups has occurred within the recent past (see Szyndlar, 1984; Thorpe, 1984; Cadle, 1985).

Thorpe (1979, 1984) documented patterns of geographic variation in the European grass snake (*Natrix natrix*) using multivariate morphometrics, and related these patterns to climatic changes during the Pleistocene. Thorpe's studies suggest range retraction of this species into refugia in southeastern and southwestern Europe during glacial periods, with subsequent expansion during more favorable periods.

Southern Asia, the Indo-Australian Archipelago, and the Philippine Islands

Of the lower alethinophidian groups present in this region (Table 3–1), *Acrochordus* appears to be a primitive lineage whose relationships to other extant snakes is remote (see McDowell, this volume; for biochemical data see George and Dessauer, 1970; Schwaner and Dessauer, 1982). *Xenopeltis* also appears to have no close living or fossil relatives and may not be an anilioid (S. McDowell, personal communication).

Anilioids are also represented by the endemic Uropeltidae (including *Cylindrophis* and *Anomochilus*). Currently, their presumed closest relative is *Anilius* of South America, although this relationship is by no means conclusive. Based on fossil evidence, Hoffstetter and Rage (1977) proposed that aniliids arose in North America and later dispersed to Asia (where they gave rise to *Cylindrophis*) and to South America. Rage (1981) modified this view and concluded that aniliids arose in South America, later dispersing to North America and Asia. In view of the uncertainties regarding the nature of the relationship between the uropeltids and aniliids (and of fossils to either of these families), it seems premature to conclude that their deployment involved extensive migration. If uropeltids and aniliids are eventually shown to comprise a monophyletic group of anilioids, then perhaps their present distributions might be more easily viewed as a relict produced by extinction in intervening areas.

The viperid fauna of southern Asia comprises the viperines *Vipera russelli* and *Eristicophis macmahonii*, the primitive viper *Azemiops feae*, and a diversity of crotalines of the genera *Trimeresurus* s.l. and *Agkistrodon* s.l. *Vipera russelli* is widely distributed from India and Sri Lanka across southern Asia but has an apparently fragmented range in southeastern Asia. *Eristicophis* is restricted to arid regions of West Pakistan, Afghanistan, and Iran and is thus part of the desert fauna extending westward into northern Africa. *Azemiops* is considered the most primitive living viper (Liem et al., 1971) and is found in southern China, northern Burma, and Tibet. *Trimeresurus* s.l. and *Agkistrodon* s.l. are widely distributed across southern Asia east of the Caspian Sea (see NORTH AMERICA regarding subdivision of these genera).

The elapid fauna of southern Asia is diverse, including representatives of all six of McDowell's (this volume) subfamilies. Relationships among these forms are not clear, except as noted previously for sea snakes and Australian elapids. It is very likely that both primitive and derived lineages are included in the Elapinae and Bungarinae of McDowell, but details of the relationships among the constituent genera remain to be determined.

The colubrid fauna of southern Asia comprises groups that are endemic or nearly so (Pareatinae, Calamariinae, Xenoderminae, Homalopsinae) and two very widely distributed groups (Natricinae and Colubrinae). Also included is a number of genera whose relationships are uncertain (see McDowell, this volume); one of these (*Psammophis*) extends to Africa and is diverse throughout that continent. It is not clear whether the morphological distinction of the endemics reflects an ancient origin or simply a highly derived morphology (McDowell, this volume). Immunological comparisons of albumins and tranferrins suggest that homalopsines indeed form a lineage that differentiated at least as early as extant natricines, colubrines, and xenodontines (Schwaner and Dessauer, 1982; Dowling et al., 1983; J. E. Cadle, unpublished data). There are no biochemical data for the other endemic groups, and their relationships to other colubrids are unknown. The probable monophyly of Asiatic natricines (reviewed previously) suggests vicariance as the primary mode of deployment of this group, but further studies are required to determine the factors responsible (see NORTH AMERICA). Colubrines of southern Asia are represented by several broadly distributed (possibly non-monophyletic) genera (e.g., *Coluber, Boiga, Elaphe*) and numerous endemic ones. Relationships within the colubrines are not sufficiently understood to suggest their biogeographic history. Present evidence does not suggest a greater affinity between Asian and New World colubrines than between either of these and African or European taxa.

Australian Region, Including New Guinea and the Islands of Melanesia

The snake fauna of the Australian region is perhaps the most unusual of any continental region—as much for what it lacks (viperids and a diversity of colubrids) as for what it contains (typhlopids, pythons, boids, and an endemic and diverse elapid fauna). As with the endemic Australian mammalian (Keast, 1972), lizard (Moody, 1980; Estes, 1983), and frog (Savage, 1973) faunas, it is tempting to suggest that the snake fauna is an ancient one reflecting Australia's Gondwanan origins. This is perhaps true for the Scolecophidia and primitive Alethinophidia in the region, but several lines of evidence argue for a comparatively recent origin for the colubroid groups. Biochemical studies on Australian elapids and sea snakes show that they are both derived members of the elapid clade and closely related to one another (Cadle and Gorman, 1981; Schwaner et al., 1985). Their radiation is probably no older than Miocene. Other possible recent derivatives in the Australasian region are *Stegonotus* (Philippines, Moluccas, New Guinea, northern Australia), almost identical with the Oriental *Dinodon* (McDowell, 1972); the homalopsines *Myron* and *Heurnia,* endemic to Australia and New Guinea; species of the colubrid genera *Tropidonophis* (*sensu* E. V. Malnate and G. Underwood, unpublished data), *Enhydris,* and *Dendrelaphis,* endemic to Australia–New Guinea but with close relatives in southeastern Asia; and species of *Boiga, Cerberus, Fordonia,* and *Acrochordus,* which are widely distributed throughout the Indo-Australian region. For *Tropidonophis,* E. V. Malnate and G. Underwood (unpublished data) show that the species of the Moluccas, New Guinea, and Australia are derived relative to those of the Philippines, suggesting a more recent origin for the former species. All these colubrids are members of lineages showing patterns of recent dispersal (natricines and colubrines) or are estuarine or saltwater forms (homalopsines and *Acrochordus*).

Whether some of the endemic pythons of Australia–New Guinea also show a pattern of recent origin is problematic. Because these lineages are undoubtedly much older than those represented by the elapids and colubrids, it is possible that they have inhabited Australia and New Guinea for much longer. McDowell (1975) suggested that Australian pythonines (*Liasis, Python, Chondropython*) formed a closely related group along with the Asian *P. reticulatus; P. curtus, P. molurus,* and the African *Python* were seen as more distantly related. These conclusions have to some extent been confirmed by qualitative comparisons of albumins and transferrins (Schwaner and Dessauer, 1981). The fact that no spurs were obtained in immunodiffusion cross-reactions involving Australian–New Guinea *Python* and *Liasis* suggests extremely close relationships among these forms. This observation, in turn, strengthens the possibility that the pythonines of the Australian region arrived there more recently than Australia's Gondwanan origins and otherwise ancient fauna would suggest. The critical data needed to test this hypothesis are quantitative estimates of molecular divergence among the various species of *Python* and the endemic Australopapuan pythonines. Until such data become available, present information is consistent with either an ancient emplacement of pythonines in the Australian region or with a more recent history comparable to that of the elapids and colubrids.

The deployment of the boine *Candoia* is an enigma. Although clearly a boine by morphological and biochemical criteria (Underwood, 1976; McDowell, 1979; Schwaner and Dessauer, 1981), there are conflicting data concerning its relationship to other genera. It has been suggested to be the most primitive boine (Underwood, 1976), a specialized relative of coralline boids (*Corallus, Epicrates, Eunectes*: McDowell, 1979), and the closest relative of the Madagascar boids (Branch, 1981). These phylogenetic problems must be resolved before an adequate explanation for the biogeography of *Candoia* can be proposed.

It should be noted that the distributions of boines and of iguanid lizards (assuming each to be monophyletic) coincide almost precisely. Both are most diverse in South America and are present in the southwestern Pacific and in Madagascar. Waif dispersal from South America has been proposed for deployment of the Fiji iguanids (*Brachylophus*: reviewed by Gibbons, 1981). The Malagasy iguanids, on the other hand, have been suggested to represent a relictual distribution resulting from vicariance as Africa and South America separated during the early and middle Cretaceous (Estes, 1983). These hypotheses could be evaluated with adequate data on the relationships among boines.

It would be of considerable interest to obtain estimates of molecular divergence between the Australian colubrids and their closest Asian relatives. If such estimates suggest a comparatively recent origin for these snakes within their respective lineages, it would strengthen the hypothesis that much of the snake fauna of the Australian region has originated since the collision of the Australian and Pacific plates; that is, within the last 20 MYA or so. This scenario would explain why the Australian region lacks an ancient advanced snake fauna (viperids and primitive colubrids and elapids). These groups evolved during the Cenozoic when Australia was largely isolated from other continents.

A SUMMARY OF PATTERNS IN THE EXTANT SNAKE FAUNA

Inspection of the pattern of distribution of major lineages in the extant snake fauna (Table 3–1) reveals that southern Asia far exceeds other regions in the number of lineages represented and also has the largest number of endemic groups. This distinction may be more apparent than real, however, inasmuch as most of the endemic lineages are monotypic groups (*Xenopeltis, Azemiops*) or morphologically specialized groups recognized as subfamilies by McDowell (this volume). Except for these groups, the Uropeltidae, Homalopsinae, and Acrochordidae (the latter two shared with Australia) are the only autochthonous, well-differentiated groups in southern Asia. Similarly, the Neotropical region includes two ancient monotypic groups (*Loxocemus* and *Anilius*) and the autochthonous Tropidophiidae and xenodontines. Undoubtedly, Africa (and perhaps Madagascar as a subdivision) would also emerge as a center of endemism if the component lineages within the Boodontinae-Lycodontinae were better understood. In contrast to these regions, the Holarctic region has only widespread groups, the most notable being erycines, viperids, natricines, and colubrines. Of all extant alethinophidians, natricines and especially colubrines are the only lineages approaching cosmopolitanism.

Also clear from a consideration of the extant snake fauna is the prevalence of primitive groups in the Neotropics, Africa, and southern Asia. These include not only the primitive alethinophidian groups (anilioids, tropidophoids, acrochordids, etc.), but primitive colubroids as well. Primitive colubroids are represented in the Neotropics by xenodontines, particularly the South American xenodontine clade (Cadle, 1984a); in Africa by atractaspidids, primitive viperids (*Causus*), elapids (e.g., *Elapsoidea*), and colubrids (boodontines and lycodontines); and in southern Asia by primitive viperids (*Azemiops*) and perhaps colubrids. All phylogenetic data for these groups suggest that they are ancient lineages and thus have probably been associated with these southern land masses for a considerable period of time. None of these primitive colubroid groups are represented by fossil records, a fact that must be taken into account when reconstructing scenarios for the evolution of colubroids. In contrast, several of the primitive alethinophidian groups on these southern continents (aniliids, boine boids) have fossil records not only on the southern continents but in North America and Europe as well.

I do not believe that paleogeographic reconstructions for snake lineages are currently possible with confidence because of the lack of well-established phylogenetic hypotheses for most groups. Even an accepted relationship such as that between South American aniliids and Asian uropeltids can be questioned. Among groups such as natricines and crotalines, where there are undeniable relationships between Old and New World clades, the relationships among component genera are not clear. These problems must be resolved before accurate reconstructions of the history of the lineages can be made. Those patterns that are apparent from the extant snake fauna can be summarized:

1. Australia shows close ties with southeastern Asia in its colubrid, elapid, and pythonid fauna. *Candoia* is the only snake showing a possible relationship to the South American fauna. All Asian ties were probably established by the early Miocene as the Australian plate approached that of southeastern Asia.

2. Southern Asia has a number of ancient endemic groups showing possible ties with South America (uropeltids), Africa (pythonids), and Central America (*Xenopeltis*). More recent patterns are with North America (crotalines and elapids), Africa (elapids and colubrids), and Europe (*Vipera*). The origin of primitive endemic groups in Asia is enigmatic, as are the relationships of specialized colubrid groups (xenodermines, pareatines, pseudoxenodontines, calamariines).

3. Africa's snake fauna has many autochthonous groups whose relationships to other regions are unclear. The viperid, elapid, and colubrid faunas are largely endemic at the generic level, and also included are such phylogenetically isolated

groups as atractaspidids. Saharan Africa shares some elements with temperate Eurasia (erycines and colubrids). The possible relationship of some colubrids (boodontines) to those of South America (xenodontines) has not yet been established. The Malagasy boines are possible evidence of a more ancient (Gondwanan) relationship with South America. Like Asia, Africa has many primitive colubroid groups of unknown affinities.

4. Temperate Europe and Asia include mostly widespread groups. Elements shared with Africa and North America are natricines and colubrines (also shared with southern Asia) and erycines. No endemic major groups characterize either Europe or northern Asia, although *Vipera* and *Natrix* may be monophyletic within their respective lineages.

5. North America has ancient ties to the fauna of Europe (erycines) and more recent ones to Asia (elapids, crotalines, possibly natricines). The endemic "xenodontines" have unclear affinities.

6. Central and South America have ancient groups with possible relationships to southern Asian taxa (*Loxocemus, Anilius*) and of uncertain relationships (tropidophiids). Boines are possible Gondwanan relicts. More recent ties with Asia (via North America) are also seen (elapids, colubrines, crotalines). The endemic Central and South American xenodontines could be related to either African or Asian colubrid lineages and are ancient components of the Neotropical snake fauna.

FUTURE RESEARCH

The current major problem in interpreting aspects of snake zoogeography is our lack of detailed knowledge of phylogenetic relationships, which thereby precludes more than a largely descriptive biogeography. Many higher snake taxa are of uncertain composition or monophyletic status (e.g., Boodontinae, Lycodontinae, Anilioidea, Colubridae). These problems must be addressed before adequate biogeographic models can be presented for these lineages.

There needs to be a greater integration of paleontological and neontological data as applied to phylogenetic analyses of snakes (see also McDowell, this volume). The ability to accurately correlate fossil vertebrae with lineages defined by multiple characters in the living fauna is clearly prerequisite to making fully effective use of the fossil record in analyzing past distributions of snake lineages. The degree to which such correlations exist has not yet been adequately demonstrated for most extant lineages. Indeed, the conflicting interpretations of different character sets for the extant fauna urge caution in making an unduly narrow interpretation of paleontological data.

As phylogenetic relationships for various snake lineages become more firmly established, it will be possible to outline mechanisms for their geographic deployment. Most scenarios in the literature currently rely heavily on dispersalist interpretations. Vicariance explanations are perhaps more plausible for some lineages, especially for primitive Alethinophidia and some of the more ancient colubroids. There is ample evidence, however, for dispersal in some lineages. Of all major lineages discussed here, the problem posed by colubrine colubrids is perhaps the greatest. This lineage is nearly worldwide in distribution, and its genera are reasonably closely related. Judging from biochemical data on extant forms, genera from one continent may be as closely related to those from remote areas as to other genera from the same continent (e.g., molecular distances between some North American and African genera are as small as those between some North American genera). Other colubrid lineages show more restricted geographic distributions and generally more ancient patterns of divergence among their constituent genera. The only close approach to the pattern in colubrines is seen in natricines, which are also the only other colubrids clearly having both New and Old World representatives. The behavioral, physiological, and ecological characteristics of colubrines that might promote their wide dispersal (and potentially limit dispersal by members of other lineages) are unknown. Exploration of these properties is one area in which biogeographic studies can be integrated with autecological and behavioral studies discussed by others in this volume.

ACKNOWLEDGMENTS

My phylogenetic studies of snakes, which have formed the basis of many of the interpretations presented here, were supported by the National Science Foundation (DEB 80-14101 and BSR 84-00166). I thank R. Estes, W. R. Heyer, E. V. Malnate, and S. B. McDowell for access to unpublished manuscripts. I appreciate the comments of H. C. Dessauer, H. W. Greene, E. V. Malnate, S. B. McDowell, and J. C. Rage, although their agreement with the conclusions presented is not implied.

LITERATURE CITED

Audley-Charles, M. G., Hurley, A. M., and Smith, A. G., 1981. Continental movements in the Mesozoic and Cenozoic, in: Wallace's Line and Plate Tectonics (T. C. Whitemore, ed.) pp. 9–23, Clarendon Press, Oxford.

Auffenberg, W. 1958. A new genus of colubrid snake from the Upper Miocene of North America, Am. Mus. Novit. 1874:1–16.

Auffenberg, W. 1963. The fossil snakes of Florida, Tulane Stud. Zool. 10:131–216.

Axelrod, D. I. 1979. Desert vegetation: Its age and origin, in: Arid Land Plant Resources (J. R. Goodin and D. K. Northington, eds.) pp. 1–72, Texas Tech University, Lubbock.

Bourgeois, M. 1965. Contribution à la morphologie comparée du crâne des ophidiens de l'Afrique Centrale, *Publ. Univ. Off. Congo* (*Lubumbashi*) 28:1–293.

Branch, W. R. 1981. Hemipenes of the Madagascan boas *Acrantophis* and *Sanzinia*, with a review of hemipeneal morphology in the Boinae, *J. Herpetol.* 15:91–99.

Brattstrom, B. H. 1964. Evolution of the pit vipers, *Trans. San Diego Soc. Nat. Hist.* 13:185–268.

Brygoo, E. R. 1982. Les ophidiens de Madagascar, *Mem. Inst. Butantan* (*São Paulo*) 46:19–58.

Cadle, J. E. 1982a. Evolutionary relationships among advanced snakes, Ph.D. dissertation, University of California, Berkeley.

Cadle, J. E. 1982b. Problems and approaches in the interpretation of the evolutionary history of venomous snakes, *Mem. Inst. Butantan* (*São Paulo*) 46:255–274.

Cadle, J. E. 1984a. Molecular systematics of Neotropical xenodontine snakes. I. South American xenodontines, *Herpetologica* 40:8–20.

Cadle, J. E. 1984b. Molecular systematics of Neotropical xenodontine snakes. II. Central American xenodontines, *Herpetologica* 40:21–30.

Cadle, J. E. 1984c. Molecular systematics of Neotropical xenodontine snakes. III. Overview of xenodontine phylogeny and the history of New World snakes, *Copeia* 1984:641–652.

Cadle, J. E. 1985. The Neotropical colubrid snake fauna (Serpentes: Colubridae): Lineage components and biogeography, *Syst. Zool.* 34:1–20.

Cadle, J. E. and Dessauer, H. C. 1985. Biochemical evolution in South Americ ı xenodontine snakes. Abstracts of the meeting of the American Societ Ichthyologists and Herpetologists, Knoxville, Tennessee.

Cadle, J. E. and Gorman, G. C. 1981. Albumin immunological evidence and the relationships of sea snakes, *J. Herpetol.* 15:329–334.

Cadle, J. E. and Sarich, V. M. 1981. An immunological assessment of the phylogenetic position of New World coral snakes, *J. Zool.* (*Lond.*) 195:157–167.

Cooke, H. B. S. 1972. The fossil mammal fauna of Africa, in: Evolution, Mammals, and Southern Continents (A. Keast, F. C. Erk, and B. Glass, eds.) pp. 89–139, State University of New York Press, Albany.

Coryndon, S. C. and Savage, R. J. G. 1973. The origin and affinities of African mammal faunas, in: Organisms and Continents through Time, *Syst. Assoc. Publ.* 9:121–135.

Detrait, J. and Saint-Girons, H. 1979. Communautés antigéniques des venins et systématique des Viperidae, *Bijdr. Dierkde.* 49:71–80.

Dowling, H. G. and Duellman, W. E. 1978. Systematic Herpetology: A Synopsis of Families and Higher Categories, HISS Publications, New York.

Dowling, H. G., Highton, R., Maha, G. C., and Maxson, L. R. 1983. Biochemical evaluation of colubrid snake phylogeny, *J. Zool.* (*Lond.*) 201:309–329.

Engesser, B. 1979. Relationships of some insectivores and rodents from the Miocene of North America and Europe, *Bull. Carnegie Mus. Nat. Hist.* 14:1–45.

Estes, R. 1983. The fossil record and early distribution of lizards, in: Advances in Herpetology and Evolutionary Biology (A. Rhodin and K. Miyata, eds.) pp. 365–398, Museum of Comparative Zoology, Harvard University, Cambridge.

Estes, R. and Baez, A. 1985. Herpetofaunas of North and South America during the Late Cretaceous and Cenozoic: Evidence for interchange? in: The Great American Biotic Interchange (F. Stehli and D. Webb, eds.) pp. 139–197, Plenum Press, New York.

Estes, R. and Hutchison, J. H. 1980. Eocene lower vertebrates from Ellesmere Island, Canadian Arctic Archipelago, *Palaeogeogr. Palaeoclimatol. Palaeoecol.* 30:325–347.

Gartside, D. F. and Dessauer, H. C. 1977. Immunological evidence on affinities of African *Natrix, Copeia* 1977:190–191.

Gasc, J. P. 1976. Snake vertebrae: A mechanism or merely a taxonomist's toy? in: Morphology and Biology of Reptiles (A. d'A. Bellairs and C. B. Cox, eds.) pp. 177–190, Linn. Soc. Symp. Ser. 3, Academic Press, London.

George, D. W. and Dessauer, H. C. 1970. Immunological correspondence of transferrins and the relationships of colubrid snakes, *Comp. Biochem. Physiol.* 33:617–627.

Gibbons, J. R. H. 1981. The biogeography of *Brachylophus* (Iguanidae), including the description of a new species, *B. vitiensis,* from Fiji, *J. Herpetol.* 15:255–273.

Groombridge, B. C. 1979. On the vomer in Acrochordidae (Reptilia: Serpentes), and its cladistic significance, *J. Zool. (Lond.)* 189:559–567.

Groombridge, B. C. 1984. The facial carotid artery in snakes (Reptilia, Serpentes): Variations and possible cladistic significance, *Amphib.-Reptilia* 5:145–155.

Gyi, K. K. 1970. A revision of colubrid snakes of the subfamily Homalopsinae, *Univ. Kans. Publ. Mus. Nat. Hist.* 20:47–223.

Hoffstetter, R. 1939. Contribution à l'étude des Elapidae actuels et fossiles et de l'ostéologie des ophidiens, *Arch. Mus. Hist. Nat. Lyon* 15:1–78.

Hoffstetter, R. and Rage, J. C. 1972. Les Erycinae fossiles de France (Serpentes, Boidae): Comprehension et histoire de la sous-famille, *Ann. Paleontol. (Vertebr.)* 58:81–124.

Hoffstetter, R. and Rage, J. C. 1977. Le gisement de vertébrés Miocènes de La Venta (Colombie) et sa faune de serpents, *Ann. Paleontol. (Vertebr.)* 63:161–190.

Hoge, A. R. and Romano-Hoge, A. 1978/79. Poisonous snakes of the world. I. Checklist of the pit vipers (Viperoidea, Viperidae, Crotalinae), *Mem. Inst. Butantan (São Paulo)* 42/43:179–310.

Holman, J. A. 1977. Upper Miocene snakes (Reptilia, Serpentes) from southeastern Nebraska, *J. Herpetol.* 11:323–335.

Holman, J. A. 1979. A review of North American Tertiary snakes, *Publ. Mus. Mich. State Univ. Paleontol. Ser.* 1:200–260.

Holman, J. A. 1984. *Texasophis galbreathi,* new species, the earliest New World colubrid snake, *J. Vert. Paleontol.* 3:223–225.

Hoogmoed, M. S. 1982. Snakes of the Guianan region, *Mem. Inst. Butantan (São Paulo)* 46:219–254.

Hughes, B. 1983. African snake faunas, *Bonn. Zool. Beitr.* 34:311–356.

Keast, A. 1972. Australian mammals: Zoogeography and evolution, in: Evolution, Mammals, and Southern Continents (A. Keast, F. C. Erk, and B. Glass, eds.) pp. 195–246, State University of New York Press, Albany.

Lawson, R. and Dessauer, H. C. 1981. Electrophoretic evaluation of the colubrid genus *Elaphe* (Fitzinger), *Isozyme Bull.* 14:83.

Liem, K. F., Marx, H., and Rabb, G. B. 1971. The viperid snake *Azemiops:* Its comparative cephalic anatomy and phylogenetic position in relation to Viperinae and Crotalinae, *Fieldiana Zool.,* 59:65–126.

Lillegraven, J. A., Kraus, M. J., and Bown, T. M. 1979. Paleogeography of the world of the Mesozoic, in: Mesozoic Mammals, The First Two-Thirds of Mammalian History (J. A. Lillegraven, Z. Kielan-Jaworowska, and W. A. Clemens, eds.) pp. 277–308, University of California Press, Berkeley.

McCarthy, C. J. 1985. Monophyly of elapid snakes (Serpentes: Elapidae). An assessment of the evidence, *Zool. J. Linn. Soc.* 83:79–93.

McDowell, S. B. 1967. *Aspidomorphus,* a genus of New Guinea snakes of the family Elapidae, with notes on related genera, *J. Zool. (Lond.)* 151:497–543.

McDowell, S. B. 1968. Affinities of the snakes usually called *Elaps lacteus* and *E. dorsalis, J. Linn. Soc. (Zool.)* 47:561–578.

McDowell, S. B. 1969. *Toxicocalamus,* a New Guinea genus of snakes of the family Elapidae, *J. Zool. (Lond.)* 159:443–511.

McDowell, S. B. 1972. The species of *Stegonotus* (Serpentes, Colubridae) in Papua New Guinea, *Zool. Meded.* 47:6–26.

McDowell, S. B. 1974. A catalogue of the snakes of New Guinea and the Solomons, with special reference to those in the Bernice P. Bishop Museum. I. Scolecophidia, *J. Herpetol.* 8:1–57.

McDowell, S. B. 1975. A catalogue of the snakes of New Guinea and the Solomons, with special reference to those in the Bernice P. Bishop Museum. II. Anilioidea and Pythoninae, *J. Herpetol.* 9:1–80.

McDowell, S. B. 1979. A catalogue of the snakes of New Guinea and the Solomons, with special reference to those in the Bernice P. Bishop Museum. III. Boinae and Acrochordoidea (Reptilia, Serpentes), *J. Herpetol.* 13:1–92.

Maglio, V. J. 1978. Patterns of faunal evolution, in: Evolution of African Mammals (V. J. Maglio and H. B. S. Cooke, eds.) pp. 603–619, Harvard University Press, Cambridge.

Malnate, E. V. 1960. Systematic division and evolution of the colubrid snake genus *Natrix,* with comments on the subfamily Natricinae, *Proc. Acad. Nat. Sci. Philadelphia* 112:41–71.

Mao, S.-H. and Dessauer, H. C. 1971. Selectively neutral mutations, transferrins and the evolution of natricine snakes, *Comp. Biochem. Physiol.* 40A:669–680.

Mao, S.-H., Chen, B.-Y., Yin, F.-Y., and Guo, Y.-W. 1983. Immunotaxonomic relationships of sea snakes to terrestrial elapids, *Comp. Biochem. Physiol.* 74A:869–872.

Mengden, G. A. 1983. The taxonomy of Australian elapid snakes: A review, *Rec. Aust. Mus.* 35:195–222.

Moody, S. M. 1980. Phylogenetic and historical biogeographical relationships of the genera in the Family Agamidae (Reptilia: Lacertilia), Ph.D. Dissertation, University of Michigan, Ann Arbor.

Rage, J. C. 1974. Les serpents des phosphorites du Quercy, *Palaeovertebrata* 6:274–303.

Rage, J. C. 1976. Les squamates du Miocène de Beni Mallal, Maroc, *Geol. Mediterr.* 3:57–69.

Rage, J. C. 1977. An erycine snake (Boidae) of the genus *Calamagras* from the French Lower Eocene, with comments on the phylogeny of the Erycinae, *Herpetologica* 33:459–463.

Rage, J. C. 1981. Les continents péri-atlantiques au Crétacé Supérieur: Migrations des faunes continentales et problèmes paleogeographiques, *Cretac. Res.* 2:65–84.

Rage, J. C. 1982. L'histoire des serpents, *Pour la science* 54:16–27.

Rage, J. C. 1984. Serpentes. Handbuch der Paläoherpetology, Gustav Fischer, Stuttgart.

Rage, J. C. and Holman, J. A. 1984. Des serpents (Reptilia, Squamata) de type Nord-Americain dans le Miocène Français: Evolution parallele ou dispersion? *Geobios* 17:89–104.

Raven, P. H. and Axelrod, D. I. 1974. Angiosperm biogeography and past continental movements, *Ann. Mo. Bot. Gard.* 61:539–673.

Rieppel, O. 1978. A functional and phylogenetic interpretation of the skull of the Erycinae (Reptilia, Serpentes), *J. Zool. (Lond.)* 186:185–208.

Rieppel, O. 1979. A cladistic classification of primitive snakes based on skull structure, *Z. Zool. Syst. Evolutionsforsch.* 17:140–150.

Rossman, D. A. and Eberle, W. G. 1977. Partition of the genus *Natrix,* with preliminary observations on evolutionary trends in natricine snakes, *Herpetologica* 33:34–43.

Roze, J. A. 1982. New World coral snakes: A taxonomic and biological summary, *Mem. Inst. Butantan (São Paulo)* 46:305–338.

Savage, J. M. 1973. The geographic distribution of frogs: Patterns and predictions, in: Evolutionary Biology of the Anurans (J. L. Vial, ed.) pp. 351–445, University of Missouri Press, Columbia.

Savage, J. M. 1982. The enigma of the Central American herpetofauna: Dispersals or vicariance?, *Ann. Mo. Bot. Gard.* 69:464–547.

Savitzky, A. H. 1978. The origin of the New World proteroglyphous snakes and its bearing on the study of venom delivery systems in snakes, Ph.D. Dissertation, University of Kansas, Lawrence.

Schwaner, T. D. and Dessauer, H. C. 1981. Immunodiffusion evidence for the relationships of Papuan boids, *J. Herpetol.* 15:250–253.

Schwaner, T. D. and Dessauer, H. C. 1982. Comparative immunodiffusion survey of snake transferrins focused on the relationships of the natricines, *Copeia* 1982:541–549.

Schwaner, T. D., Baverstock, P. R., Dessauer, H. C., and Mengden, G. A. 1985. Immunological evidence for the phylogenetic relationships of Australian elapid snakes, in: Biology of Australasian Frogs and Reptiles (G. Grigg, R. Shine, and N. Ehmann, eds.) Surrey Beatty, Chipping Norton, Australia.

Simpson, G. G. 1947. Holarctic mammalian faunas and continental relationships during the Cenozoic, *Bull. Geol. Soc. Am.* 58:613–688.

Steadman, D. W., Pregill, G. K., and Olson, S. L. 1984. Fossil vertebrates from Antigua, Lesser Antilles: Evidence for late Holocene human-caused extinctions in the West Indies, *Proc. Natl. Acad. Sci. USA* 81:4448–4451.

Szyndlar, Z. 1984. Fossil snakes from Poland, *Acta Zool. Cracov.* 28:3–156.

Tarling, D. H. 1980. The geologic evolution of South America with special reference to the last 200 million years, in: Evolutionary Biology of New World Monkeys and Continental Drift (R. L. Ciochon and A. B. Chiarelli, eds.) pp. 1–41, Plenum Press, New York.

Thorpe, R. S. 1979. Multivariate analysis of the population systematics of the ringed snake *N. natrix* (L.), *Proc. R. Soc. Edinb.* 78B:1–62.

Thorpe, R. S. 1984. Primary and secondary transition zones in speciation and population differentiation: A phylogenetic analysis of range expansion, *Evolution* 38:233–243.

Underwood, G. 1967. A Contribution to the Classification of Snakes, British Museum (Natural History), London.

Underwood, G. 1976. A systematic analysis of boid snakes, in: Morphology and Biology of Reptiles, (A. d'A. Bellairs and C. B. Cox, eds.) pp. 151–175, Linn. Soc. Symp. Ser. 3, Academic Press, London.

Vanzolini, P. E. and Heyer, W. R. 1985. The American herpetofauna and the interchange, in: The Great American Biotic Interchange (F. Stehli and D. Webb, eds.) pp. 475–487, Plenum Press, New York.

Wolfe, J. A. and Leopold, E. B. 1967. Neogene and early Quaternary vegetation of northwestern North America and northeastern Asia, in: The Bering Land Bridge (D. M. Hopkins, ed.) pp. 193–206, Stanford University Press, Stanford, California.

CHAPTER FOUR

Functional Morphology

David Cundall

Functional morphology deals, in theory, with all potential relationships between form and function (Dullemeijer, 1974). The recent renaissance in vertebrate functional morphology (Lauder, 1982; Wake, 1982; Hildebrand et al., 1985) has produced new approaches to the problem of relating form and function, as well as considerable appreciation of the morphological bases of some complex behaviors in selected groups of vertebrates. Snakes are particularly fascinating subjects for functional morphological work because they swallow large prey whole and move through almost any terrestrial or aquatic habitat without limbs. Much of this chapter reviews recent efforts to understand the morphological bases of these two behaviors.

In studying behaviors such as locomotion and feeding, functional morphologists usually must make their observations in a laboratory. When dealing with species whose behaviors in the field are poorly known, it is impossible to know whether behaviors recorded in the laboratory are typical of those exhibited under natural conditions. Further, most studies on functional morphology typically examine only one functional aspect of a particular structural system, providing only a partial view of the potential biological role (in the sense of Bock, 1980) of the structural system being examined. Because one of the ultimate goals of functional morphology is to understand the origin and maintenance of organismic structure in relation to supraorganismic structure (i.e., the structure of communities, ecosystems, etc.), these are serious limitations that are difficult or impossible to surmount despite the arsenal of tools and techniques now available. Nevertheless, recent studies on snakes suggest that some relationships between behavior, organismic structure, and habitat structure can be examined experimentally.

LOCOMOTION

Snakes are limbless musculoskeletal tubes housed in a casing of integument and containing a core of viscera (Figure 4–1). In this regard, they are similar to a variety of other limbless vertebrates but differ from them in displaying a greater diversity of locomotor modes. This suggests that basic body plan probably is not the sole determinant of locomotor pattern. Among snakes, the relative dimensions of the visceral core and the shape of the musculoskeletal tube (length of the head, neck, trunk, and tail regions) vary greatly and must be critical to the mechanics of locomotion. To date, research on locomotion in snakes has dealt solely with the trunk region. Aspects of the cervical region have been explored morphologically (Pregill, 1977; Ruben, 1977a; Ruben and Geddes, 1983) but not functionally, and the tail has been ignored.

Snakes use two kinematically different types of locomotion. The most common, and presumably the most primitive, is lateral undulation, in which there are no points of static contact (regions of the body that are not moving relative to the surrounding medium or substrate) between the body and the medium over or through which the snake is moving. A distinct variant of this mode, slide-pushing, has been described recently by Gans (1984). The second type of locomotion involves the use of static points of contact to generate movement of other parts of the body relative to the substrate or surrounding medium. Snakes use static points of contact in four very different ways, referred to as rectilinear locomotion, concertina locomotion, sidewinding, and saltation (Gans and Mendelssohn, 1972; Gans, 1974). Rectilinear locomotion depends on movements of the ventral skin relative to the rest of the body and does not necessarily involve lateral bending of the vertebral column. On the other hand, concertina, sidewinding, and saltation locomotion share with lateral undulation the property that locomotion arises from lateral bending of the trunk.

Edwards (1985), in a recent review of terrestrial limbless locomotion, concluded that no published studies provide the empirical observations necessary to

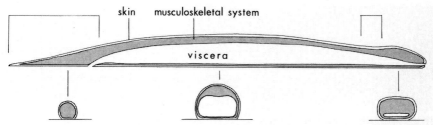

Figure 4–1. The organization of the skin, musculoskeletal system, and viscera in a snake. Mid-sagittal view (above), and representative cross-sectional views (below). Bracketed regions indicate areas for which no detailed functional studies are available.

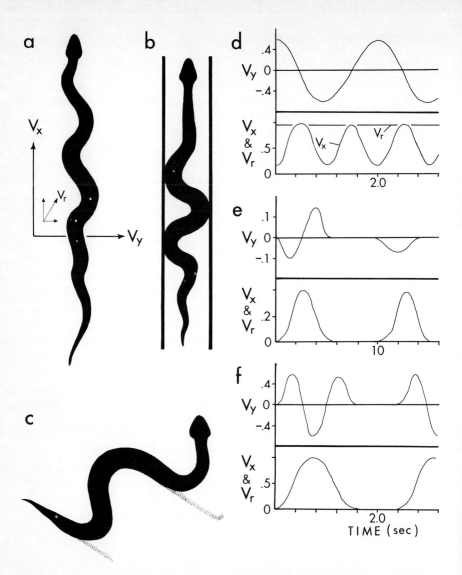

Figure 4–2. Representative views of the trunk during (a) lateral undulation, (b) concertina locomotion, and (c) sidewinding. Direction of travel is toward top of figure in all three cases. Dotted lines in (c) show position of track left by static regions of contact with the substrate. Kinematic variables used by Jayne (1985a, 1986) are shown in (a). White dots represent positions of a point on the trunk at two points in time. Relative and absolute values of V_r, V_x, and V_y are functions of the lengths of the lines shown in the inset vector diagram to the left of the dots. Graphs show the general patterns of the three variables during (d) lateral undulation, (e) concertina locomotion, and (f) sidewinding. All velocities are given as number of total body lengths per second. Although V_x and V_r are shown to overlap perfectly in both (e) and (f), it should be noted that this is frequently not the case for concertina locomotion, and during sidewinding, V_x is slightly less than V_r. See text for further details.

108

understand the actions of the musculoskeletal system during any mode other than rectilinear locomotion, for which some limited data are available. More recent work by Jayne (1985a) has provided the first electromyographic (EMG) evidence of muscle activity in locomotor modes involving bending of the vertebral column. Further, Jayne (1985a, 1986) has provided detailed kinematic descriptions of lateral undulation, sidewinding, and concertina locomotion, permitting objective differentiation of these three modes.

Kinematic Properties

Jayne (1985a, 1986) measured actual velocity of a point on the trunk (V_r), velocity of that point parallel to the direction of travel (V_x), and velocity perpendicular to the direction of travel (V_y) to define a set of kinematic properties for three modes of locomotion in snakes (Figure 4–2a). During one period of activity, if V_r has a coefficient of variation less than 37%, the mode of locomotion is considered to be lateral undulation. During lateral undulation, if V_x and V_y are plotted against time, the period of V_x is one half that of V_y (Figure 4–2b). If the coefficient of variation of V_r exceeds 37% during a single cycle of activity, the snake is performing either concertina or sidewinding locomotion. During sidewinding locomotion, there is always a 1 : 1 : 1 ratio of the periods of V_x, V_y, and V_r, and V_y shows a consistent R,L,R (or L,R,L) pattern between times of static contact (Figure 4–2c). Concertina locomotion never shows a consistent triphasic pattern during a period of V_y, and the ratio of V_y to V_r is often not 1 : 1 (Figure 4–2d). Future use of these operational definitions of the various modes of locomotion should encourage more refined analyses and permit quantification of relationships between kinematic variables and substrate variables.

Structural Considerations

The mechanical behavior of the trunk of snakes is in large part defined and limited by the supporting skeletal elements (Gasc, 1974). Although snakes have large numbers of trunk vertebrae (120 to more than 320 precloacal vertebrae; Hoffstetter and Gasc, 1969), lateral flexion of intervertebral joints is limited, by zygapophyseal ligaments, to angles rarely exceeding 12°, and dorsoventral flexion is limited to a similar extent by various intervertebral ligaments (Gasc, 1974; Jayne, 1985a; Mosauer, 1932a, reported angular displacements of 25°, but this has never been substantiated). Rotation around the long axis of the vertebral column is negligible in most snakes (~2° per joint), resulting in part from the angular relationships between the zygosphene-zygantral and zygapophyseal articulations (Gasc, 1974). Ribs articulate with most of the trunk vertebrae (Hoffstetter and Gasc, 1969). Although the nature of the rib and vertebral articulating surfaces has been noted for a number of species, potential movements of the ribs have not been well defined. Casual observations of live snakes indicate, however, that the ribs of many species can be moved extensively. The cross-sectional shape of the trunk is therefore capable of major changes, including extraordinary degrees of flattening (e.g., the hood of *Naja, Hydrodynastes,* and *Heterodon;* dorsoventral body flattening in many snakes; lateral body flattening in marine hydropheines, *Acrochordus,* and some other aquatic snakes). This behavioral capability undoubtedly has some relevance to the mechanics of locomotion and the types of muscle activity required to optimize patterns of force generation.

The musculoskeletal system of the trunk of snakes is characterized by large numbers of segments interconnected by muscles of different lengths (Mosauer, 1935; Auffenberg, 1958, 1961, 1962; Gasc, 1974, 1981). Considered simplistically, muscles lying close to skeletal elements tend to be relatively short, spanning only one or a few segments, whereas more superficial muscles of both the epaxial and hypaxial series span larger numbers of segments between attachment points. An increase in the length of the superficial epaxial muscles stems primarily from elongation of their tendons, but increased length of the superficial hypaxial muscles is a function of increased length of muscle tissue (Figures 4–3 and 4–4). In both cases, long superficial muscle complexes are wrapped by tendon arches or fascial sheaths that connect directly or indirectly with underlying skeletal elements and limit the extent to which these muscles can pull away from the skeletal axis during flexion.

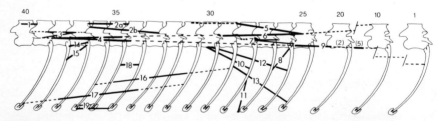

Figure 4–3. Lateral view of postcardiac trunk muscle arrangements in the colubrid genus *Masticophis* (based on the description of Mosauer, 1935; terminology after Gasc, 1981). Muscle tissue indicated by solid lines, tendons by dashed lines. Anterior is to the right. Numbers above vertebrae indicate the number of segments between attachment points. Muscles: 1, interneuralis; 2a, medial head of multifidis; 2b, lateral head of multifidis; 3, interarticularis superior; 4, longissimus dorsi; 5, spinalis; 6, semispinalis; 7, interarticularis inferior; 8, levator costa; 9, iliocostalis; 10, transversus dorsalis; 11, transversus ventralis; 12, obliquus internus dorsalis; 13, obliquus internus ventralis; 14, tuberculocostalis; 15, intercostalis quadrangularis; 16, supracostalis lateralis superior; 17, supracostalis lateralis inferior; 18, intercostalis externus; 19, intercostalis ventralis.

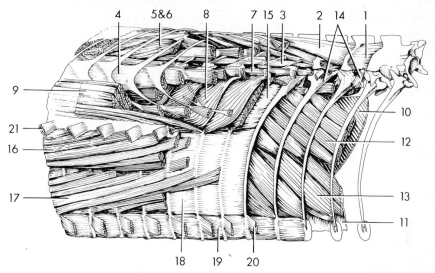

Figure 4–4. Oblique view of the axial trunk muscles of a viperid snake (*Cerastes cerastes*) showing the complexity of muscle and tendon arrangements (redrawn from Gasc, 1974). Numbers indicate same muscles as in Figure 4–3 with the addition of 20, costocutaneus inferior; 21, costocutaneus superior.

The axial muscles and associated skeleton are arranged as an inverted "U" (Figure 4–5). The only axial muscle that extends between the arms of the "U" is the transversus abdominis, pars ventralis, and in most snakes the fibrous portion of this muscle does not extend ventral to the costal cartilages at the tips of the ribs. In all snakes except the Scolecophidia, each rib is attached to the dermis of the skin by a superior costocutaneus muscle extending posteriorly from the rib and an inferior costocutaneus muscle extending anteriorly from the rib. The skin itself contains a complex array of muscles that interconnect the ventral and lower lateral scale rows (Buffa, 1905). The ubiquity of this structural arrangement in alethinophidian snakes implies that muscular control of rib position, skin position, and possibly even scale orientation may be important in most modes of locomotion.

Lateral Undulation

Lateral undulatory locomotion has received the most detailed treatment in the literature (e.g., Mosauer, 1932a,b; Wiedemann, 1932; Gray, 1946, 1953; Rashevsky, 1948; Gans, 1974; Jayne, 1985a,b). Available evidence indicates that all snakes are capable of using lateral undulation when swimming, traversing solid surfaces with evenly or unevenly spaced irregularities, or traversing unevenly

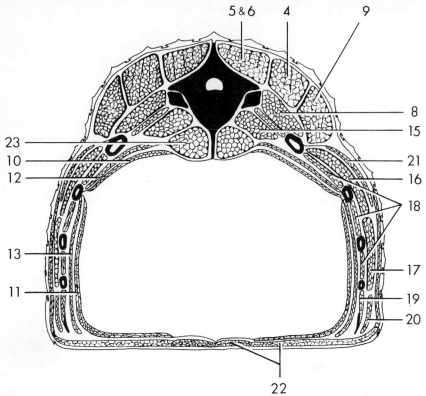

Figure 4–5. Cross-sectional view of the trunk skeleton and muscles (modified from Gasc, 1981). Ventral relationships from dissections of *Agkistrodon*. Numbers indicate same muscles as in Figures 4–3 and 4–4 with the addition of 22, scutali-interscutali complex: 23, parapophyseo-hypapophyseus.

spaced solid surfaces such as branches. In a series of simple but elegant experiments, Gray and Lissmann (1950) determined that forward motion during lateral undulation was produced by the resultant of forces exerted both perpendicular and tangential to lateral (not ventral) regions of the body in direct contact with pivot points (vertically oriented irregularities of the substrate). By measuring the resultant force and determining its orthogonal components, total force directed perpendicular to the lateral body surface was found to approximate closely the total frictional resistance of the ventral body surface in the direction opposite to the direction of motion. Total force exerted tangential to the body surface was assumed to be a measure of friction of the lateral body surface against pivot points. As the number of pivot points increased, or as the extent of the lateral body surface in contact with surface irregularities increased, the force exerted perpendicular to the direction of travel increased, while forces exerted along the direction of travel remained approximately the same.

Gray and Lissmann (1950) speculated on the morphological basis of these patterns of force generation, and Gray (1953) presented idealized models suggesting that alternative waves of contraction passed posteriorly down the body to produce the general pattern of lateral undulation. On solid substrates, this pattern would be modified to permit the snake to utilize irregularly placed lateral points of contact. Of particular significance was Gray's (1953) demonstration that bending of the body to one side had to be initiated by contraction of muscle segments lying immediately posterior to the bend and on the same side of the body toward which the bending was directed. Muscle segments on the opposite side of the body would be stretched in this situation and would begin contraction at their point of maximum stretch to effect straightening of the trunk anterior to the point of lateral contact. Jayne (1985a) later demonstrated that EMG patterns of activity for the superficial epaxial muscles (Mm. spinalis, semispinalis, longissimus, and iliocostalis) during terrestrial lateral undulation largely conformed to Gray's (1953) model. All the muscles on one side tended to become active at the point of maximum stretch (bending toward the opposite side) and remained active to their point of maximum contraction (bending toward the same side) except when the body remained straight between pivot points (Figure 4–6). Of particular interest is the fact that the correspondence between the contraction of muscle segments and their position relative to the site of bending was largely independent of their attachment points which lay anywhere from 10 to 17 segments from the site of electrode implantation. The EMG results also showed muscle activity in large numbers of adjacent muscle segments. By looking at the overlap in EMG activity for ipsilateral homologous muscles located in body segments less than 180° out of phase, Jayne (1985a) determined that as few as 25 segments in the anterior trunk of *Nerodia* were active simultaneously during swimming lateral undulation, whereas as many as 120 segments were simultaneously active in the posterior trunk of swimming *Elaphe*.

Although our understanding of the relationships between bone movement, muscle activity, and patterns of force generation during lateral undulation remains incomplete, I think the following features of Jayne's (1985a) analysis are particularly significant. First, for a given species, the number of segments in a single block of simultaneously active muscle tissue was often smaller during terrestrial lateral undulation than during swimming lateral undulation. Second, the number of segments in a block of simultaneously active muscle tissue in-

Figure 4–6. Approximate amplitude and timing of superficial epaxial muscle activity (hatched areas) during lateral undulation (modified from Jayne, 1985a). Black dots represent pivot points.

Figure 4–7. Placement of pivot points during swimming (a), traversing a solid surface with unevenly spaced pivot points (b), and traversing unevenly spaced solid surfaces (c). Major pivot points in (a) are enclosed by the dotted lines, pivot points in (b) are represented by hatched areas, pivot points in (c) are branches. Differences in body form suggest existence of "search-and-place" control patterns during terrestrial (b and c) lateral undulation.

creased as the wave of muscle contraction passed down the body during swimming lateral undulation. Third, EMG and mechanical waves tended to pass down the body synchronously at a rate equal to the net forward velocity of the snake during terrestrial lateral undulation, whereas there was a phase lag of mechanical to EMG waves and an increase in the caudally directed velocities of both waves during swimming lateral undulation. Fourth, activity of the medial superficial epaxial muscles was more variable during terrestrial lateral undulation than during swimming and did not always match the activity patterns of the lateral epaxial muscles, which correlated well with mechanical events. This suggests that snakes swim using a primitive lateral undulation control system possibly similar to that of fish (Grillner and Kashin, 1976). Lateral undulation on solid surfaces that may be highly heterogeneous in their placement of pivot points (Figure 4–7) may require additional control systems that permit the generation of irregularly spaced waves of varying amplitude.

Concertina and Sidewinding Locomotion

In both concertina and sidewinding locomotion, the trunk establishes static points of contact with the substrate, usually at points of lateral flexion of the trunk. The different kinematic properties of the two modes stem from differences in patterns of muscle activity (Jayne, 1985a). During concertina locomotion, the superficial epaxial muscles usually exhibit alternate unilateral activity of the concave sides of the regions of the trunk maintaining static contact (Figure 4–8). Unlike lateral undulation, these regions of muscle contraction do not progress steadily down the trunk, and they vary in length in direct proportion to the length of the static wave. Regions of the trunk being released from, or incorporated into, the static wave, display descending waves of muscle activity similar to those occurring in lateral undulation. Jayne (1985a) also demonstrated that mechanical events correlated well with the position of spinalis contractile tissue but not with the actual site of attachment of spinalis anterior tendons, which frequently lay in a region of the trunk bending toward the opposite side.

Gans (1973, 1976) has described a unique array of features associated with burrowing in uropeltids. These snakes bend the anterior third of the vertebral column and axial muscles separately from the cutaneous musculature and the skin, causing the surface of the animal to shorten and increase in diameter. This behavior, which presumably anchors the anterior trunk during the penetration phase of burrowing, is correlated with an increase in muscle mass in the anterior trunk and a greater abundance of red fibers (Gans et al., 1978).

Unlike concertina locomotion, sidewinding is powered by continuous and alternating waves of lateral bending propagated posteriorly from the head and produced by alternate large blocks of simultaneously active muscle segments (Jayne, 1985a). Between static contact points, the trunk is lifted by bilateral activity of the semispinalis-spinalis complex (and possibly the multifidis and

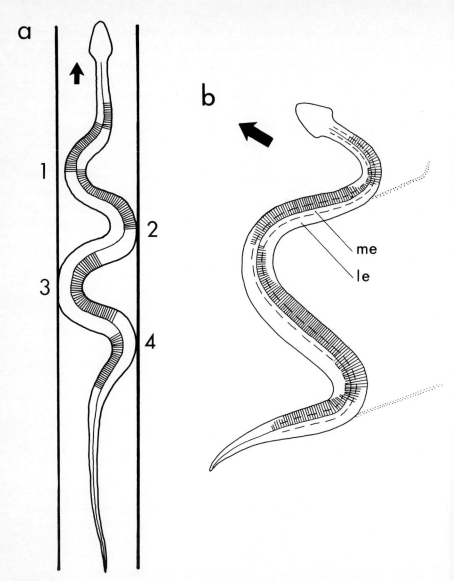

Figure 4–8. Timing of superficial epaxial muscle activity during (a) concertina locomotion and (b) sidewinding (after a description by Jayne, 1985a). Hatched areas indicate regions of muscle activity. Arrows indicate direction of travel. In (a), snake has static contact at points 2, 3, and 4 and has just begun to move away from 1. le, Lateral epaxial muscles, primarily longissimus dorsi and iliocostalis; me, medial epaxial muscles, primarily spinalis-semispinalis and multifidis. Dotted lines in (b) indicate orientation of track left by static regions of the trunk.

other deep intervertebral muscles) in trunk segments lying either anterior (*Crotalus*) or posterior (*Nerodia*) to the nearest static contact point. Regions of active longissimus dorsi and iliocostalis muscles of one side rarely overlapped with active regions of the same muscles on the other side, suggesting that these muscles, but not the spinalis, contribute to lateral bending (Figure 4–8).

Sidewinding has been observed in a variety of snakes (Cowles, 1956; Brain, 1960; Gans and Mendelssohn, 1972; Jayne, 1986), but the most effective practitioners of this mode appear to be small desert-dwelling viperid species and some species of homalopsines that inhabit mud flats. Jayne (1982) found that viperid species that regularly employ sidewinding had relatively short spinalis segments and fewer trunk vertebrae. The same is apparently true of homalopsine genera (*Cerberus, Fordonia, Bitia*) that are proficient sidewinders (B. Jayne, personal communication). Jayne's (1986) demonstration that *Cerberus* may readily combine kinematic features of both sidewinding and lateral undulation (essentially sidewinding with no static contact) suggests that some facultative sidewinders may provide clues to both the evolution and functional morphology of this unique mode of locomotion.

Rectilinear Locomotion

Lissmann (1950) provided the most detailed experimental evidence for rectilinear locomotion and confirmed models previously proposed by Mosauer (1932b), Wiedemann (1932), and Bogert (1947). In essence, this mode of locomotion is presumed to depend on successive waves of bilaterally symmetric contractions of the superior and inferior costocutaneus muscles. The former muscles serve to pull the ventral skin forward relative to the ventral tips of the ribs, whereas the latter serve to pull the ribs and vertebral column forward over the ventral skin after it makes static contact with the substrate. No electromyographic analyses of this mode of locomotion have been published. It seems likely that rectilinear locomotion depends on the maintenance of some rigidity of the vertebral column to prevent protracting regions of the ventral skin from settling onto the substrate. It also seems likely that various cutaneous muscles contribute to the movements of the skin. Rectilinear locomotion is most common in booids and large viperids, although variants of this mode are frequently seen in a variety of smaller species when they move over smooth substrates. Inasmuch as the requisite musculature is present in most alethinophidian snakes, it is not clear why rectilinear locomotion is not used more frequently by more species.

Locomotion and the Axial Musculoskeletal System

Electromyographic results suggest that prevailing views of the mechanical organization of the superficial epaxial muscles may need radical revision. Except during dorsiflexion, which typically occurs along the tendons anterior to the point of activity of spinalis contractile tissue (Jayne, 1985a), the contractile tissue of these muscles behaves as though it were directly attached to vertebrae at either end. The long tendons of origin or insertion often do not flex adjacent vertebrae when the contractile tissue is active. Furthermore, Jayne (1985a) found that the complex tendinous interconnections between epaxial muscles did not result in the interconnected contractile tissues forming a single functional unit. It appears that the extraordinary complexity of tendinous arrangements in the superficial epaxial muscles of snakes has successfully concealed the sites of functional attachment of the contractile tissues.

Given that the most complex axial trunk muscles have patterns of activation similar to patterns seen in the myomeres of fish (Blight, 1977), patterns of motor control and the organization of the ventral motor column in the spinal cord of snakes are of considerable interest. Fetcho (1986a) has recently demonstrated that topographic arrangements of motoneurons in the medial motor column of the ventral horn in *Nerodia* are like arrangements of homologous motoneurons in rats. In particular, motoneurons innervating the superficial epaxial muscles of snakes and mammals are almost identical in their relative positions, but both arrangements differ radically from those of axial muscle motoneurons in anamniotes (Fetcho, 1986b). The extent to which these differences in motoneuron organization influence patterns of muscle control and coordination remains unclear. However, it now seems unlikely that the mechanisms of axial muscle coordination in snakes are similar to those in fishes, despite the similarity in patterns of muscle activation during swimming lateral undulation in the two groups.

Two final points deserve comment. First, virtually all considerations of terrestrial locomotion in snakes, both empirical and theoretical, have ignored a basic structural feature of the system. Snakes crawl on their bellies but produce major propulsive forces along the vertebral axis. These propulsive forces must be transmitted down the body wall to the skin covering the tips of the ribs (Figures 4–5 and 4–9). We need to know how the body wall transmits these forces and to what extent the efficiency of terrestrial locomotion is a function of muscular control of rib position relative to the vertebral column and of skin position relative to the ribs.

Second, swimming and terrestrial lateral undulation clearly involve very different muscular mechanisms and patterns of force generation (Figure 4–7), and it seems fruitless to continue thinking of these as minor variants of the same locomotor mode (Jayne, 1985a; Gans, 1986). The evolutionary success of snakes is undoubtedly due in large measure to the early appearance of locomotor control systems that permitted the use of irregularly placed pivot points in terrestrial environments, as suggested by Gans (1974). Thus it seems possible that the complexity of the axial muscles of the trunk is a reflection of the mechanical basis of the control system as much as it is the structural basis of force generation. In particular, the anterior tendons of the spinalis muscles may serve not only to

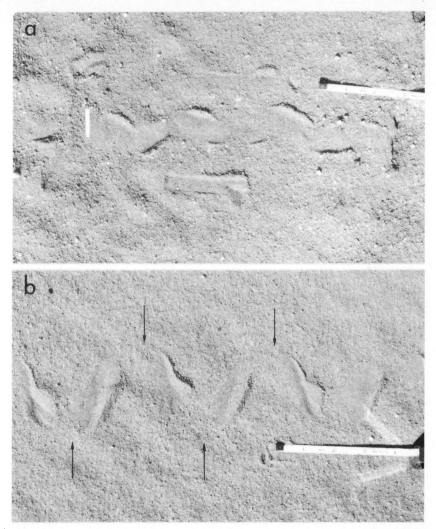

Figure 4–9. Tracks made by *Heterodon platirhinos* during locomotion on sand in the pine barrens of New Jersey. (a) Slow movement appearing superficially similar to rectilinear locomotion but demonstrating numerous alternating pivot points (arrows). Trunk of snake appeared essentially straight but had numerous shallow bends. Width of body is indicated by vertical white bar. Scale on the right is in inches. Snake had a total length of 15.5 in. (39.4 cm). (b) Track made by same animal during an effort to escape. Note that the trunk was raised off the sand at the anterior regions of each bend (shown by black arrows) and that, in order to produce the force patterns indicated by the track, rib displacements or rotation around the long axis of the vertebral column had to occur. This pattern of undulatory locomotion exhibited features of slide-pushing, notably the posterior travel of established waves due to the forced rearward migration of sand particles to produce effective pivot points. More detailed analyses of tracks and the force patterns necessary to produce them could yield much useful information about locomotion under natural conditions.

119

transmit forces anteriorly but also to convey mechanical information posteriorly to stretch receptors in the muscle belly (B. Jayne, personal communication).

Other Aspects of the Form and Function of the Trunk

The trunk of snakes performs various essential functions in addition to locomotion. Ventilation is perhaps the most critical of these. Rosenberg (1973) found that simultaneous activity of the dorsal and ventral transversus and the dorsal and ventral obliquus abdominis internus initiated a ventilatory cycle, effecting exhalation by adducting and retracting the ribs and pulling the ventral body wall dorsally. Relaxation of these muscles followed by combined activity of the iliocostals and costal levators protracted and abducted the ribs, causing inhalation. During exhalation and inhalation, the dilator laryngis remained active. Rosenberg (1973) found that the sphincter laryngis did not become active until shortly after cessation of activity of the levators costae, resulting in a short exhalation before the apneic period between ventilatory cycles. Although the triphasic pattern of airflow described by Rosenberg has since been shown to be an artifact of the Kopfkappe method of measuring air flow (Clark et al., 1978), biphasic activity of the axial trunk muscles presumably produces the currently accepted biphasic airflow.

The muscles involved in ventilation do not appear to be important components of the locomotor system. However, movements of the ribs during ventilation must have some influence on the behavior of the trunk during locomotion, and future work should examine the relationships between ventilatory cycles and locomotor movements.

In many snakes, the trunk performs various types of prey restraint. Constricting behavior has been shown to be highly conservative in henophidian snakes (which include superfamilies Acrochordoidea, Anilioidea, Tropidopheoidea, Bolyerioidea, and Booidea; see McDowell, this volume), whereas colubroid species known to constrict (approximately 80 species) use a variety of different methods (Willard, 1977; Greene and Burghardt, 1978). The functional morphology of this process has not yet been examined in any depth, primarily because snakes tend to remove recording electrodes during constriction. However, a number of morphological features appear to be correlated, albeit somewhat loosely, with constricting behavior. In particular, vertebral number and relative vertebral width at the zygapophyseal joints are directly correlated with constriction (Johnson, 1955; Gasc, 1974), whereas the length of superficial epaxial muscle segments is inversely correlated with constriction (Mosauer, 1935; Gasc, 1974, 1981; Jayne, 1982). In addition, both the relative cross-sectional area and the fiber-to-tendon ratio of the hypaxial muscle mass appear to be larger in constricting species (Gasc, 1981). Ruben (1977b) has suggested that constriction and rapid locomotion may be mutually exclusive, because the number and amplitude of body waves generated during locomotion may be a function of the number of vertebrae and the length of epaxial muscle segments. More detailed correlations between modes of constriction and axial musculoskeletal morphology may provide testable hypotheses concerning the mechanism and evolution of this behavior in snakes.

The skin of snakes provides the mechanical interface between the trunk and the substrate. Gray and Lissmann (1950) found that frictional coefficients for the ventral and lateral skin of *Natrix* approximated 0.4 for most smooth surfaces, but ranged from 0.24 to 2.10 depending on the direction of movement and the nature of the substrate. Frictional coefficients for the skin have not been measured for any snake on a natural substrate. The relationship between the frictional coefficient and scale surface microstructure is also unknown, but Gans and Baic (1977) have shown that the highly regular ridged pattern on precaudal trunk scales of uropeltids may inhibit wetting and adherence of soil particles.

The mechanical properties of snake skin (loading curves, strain, stress, maximum load, maximum stiffness, elastic modulus) have been examined for skin samples from various regions of the trunk of *Nerodia, Ahaetulla, Laticauda, Hydrophis, Enhydrina,* and *Acrochordus* (Jayne, 1985a). Generally, the mechanical properties of snake skin vary greatly but tend to be intermediate between those of shark or eel skin and mammal skin. There appear to be no direct correlations among stiffness, scale morphology, and scale number. Further studies are needed to determine how the elastic properties of the skin may influence the energetics of locomotion.

Models of the evolution of limblessness (Gans, 1962, 1975) and its influence on musculoskeletal morphology (Mosauer, 1932b, 1935; Auffenberg, 1958, 1961, 1962; Gasc, 1981) have relied on morphological properties whose relationships to behavior were only vaguely understood. We still have no understanding of the contribution of the tail to locomotion in snakes or of the basic structural properties of the tail. The mechanics of burrowing in snakes remain virtually unexplored (but see Gans, 1973, 1974, 1976) despite repeated speculations that snakes evolved from fossorial ancestors (Walls, 1940; Bellairs and Underwood, 1951; Senn and Northcutt, 1973). Thus, despite recent major advances in our knowledge of particular aspects of the functional morphology of the trunk of snakes, we remain far from developing a coherent picture of the system.

FEEDING

If one ignores the problem of getting the head to the prey, the head may be considered the major structural component responsible for both prey capture and prey transport. These two functions differ radically in their kinematic properties in snakes. Prey are usually captured by a rapid strike involving bilaterally synchronous motions of the jaw elements (Van Riper, 1953; Frazzetta, 1966; Kardong, 1974), whereas prey are transported through the oral cavity by alternating unilateral motions of the same jaw elements (Albright and Nelson, 1959a,b; Frazzetta, 1966; Kardong, 1977; Cundall and Gans, 1979). Between capture and transport, many species of snakes use complex and usually alternating movements of the right and left jaw elements to manipulate live prey into a position suitable for swallowing. Constricting henophidian and colubroid species restrain their prey using coils of the body while retaining a grasp on the prey with their jaws, and some colubrid, elapid, and viperid species use their jaws alone to restrain prey following a strike. After transporting the prey through the oral cavity, snakes use various movements of the anterior trunk to aid swallowing. Neither prey manipulation nor swallowing has been considered in any detail in the functional morphological literature. In fact, much of our current understanding of the function of the musculoskeletal system of the heads of snakes is based on studies on prey transport.

Musculoskeletal Structure of the Head

The cephalic muscles of snakes have been most recently reviewed by Haas (1973), who cited much of the previous literature but devoted most of his review to the trigeminal musculature. More recent studies on selected taxa or muscle groups include those of McDowell (1972) on the tongue and its associated muscles, Kardong (1973) on *Agkistrodon,* Kramer (1977) on *Vipera,* Groombridge (1979) on intermandibular muscles, Varkey (1979) on North American natricines, Kardong (1980) on *Alsophis,* Rieppel (1980a) on aniliids and uropeltids, and Cundall (1986) on *Opheodrys, Entechinus,* and *Symphimus.* Descriptions of the skull are available for a large variety of species, but they are widely scattered in the literature. Recent accounts that provide access to the older literature include those of Gans (1952), Dullemeijer (1956, 1959), Frazzetta (1959, 1966), Bourgeois (1965), Kardong (1974), and Rieppel (1977a,b, 1978a,b). Bellairs and Kamal (1981) have presented an extensive review of the development of the skull in snakes.

The basic form of the skull and its associated muscles in a generalized colubroid snake is shown in Figures 4–10 through 4–12. Several features are important to note. First, the braincase is quite solid and provides much of the surface area for attachment of the muscles that move both the palatomaxillary arches and the mandibles. Second, each palatomaxillary arch is most closely attached to the snout and the prefrontal, both of which are capable of some movement relative to the braincase. Third, the bones comprising a palatomaxillary arch are movably attached to each other and are functionally and structurally separated from the bones of the other arch. Fourth, in most snakes, the suspensorial elements (quadrate and supratemporal) are movably attached to each other, the braincase, and the rear end of the palatomaxillary arch. The net result of

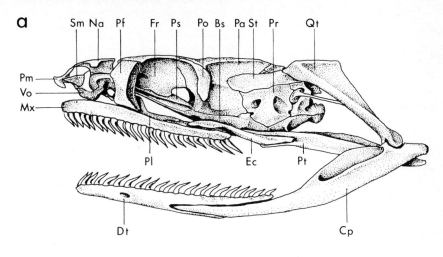

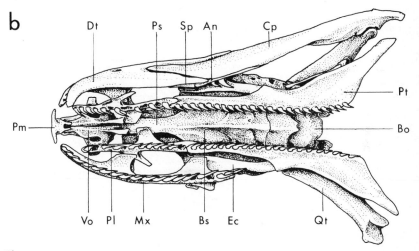

Figure 4–10. Lateral (a) and ventral (b) views of the skull of *Nerodia rhombifera*. An, Angular; Bo, basioccipital; Bs, basisphenoid; Cp, compound bone; Dt, dentary; Ec, ectopterygoid; Fr, frontal, Mx, maxilla; Na, nasal; Pa, parietal; Pf, prefrontal; Pl, palatine; Pm, premaxilla; Po, postorbital, Pr, proötic; Ps, parasphenoid; Pt, pterygoid; Qt, quadrate; Sm, septomaxilla; Sp, splenial; St, supratemporal; Vo, vomer.

this arrangement is that the rear end of the palatomaxillary arch typically may move farther than the anterior end. Finally, when the snake is ingesting prey, the mandible and suspensorium form a relatively slender, curved, bony rod extending diagonally through what is, in essence, a muscular sling that surrounds most of the prey.

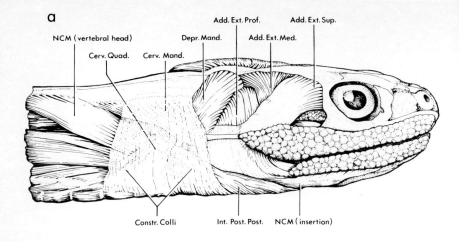

a

NCM (vertebral head)   Depr. Mand.   Add. Ext. Prof.   Add. Ext. Sup.
                                       Add. Ext. Med.
Cerv. Quad.   Cerv. Mand.

Constr. Colli   Int. Post. Post.   NCM (insertion)

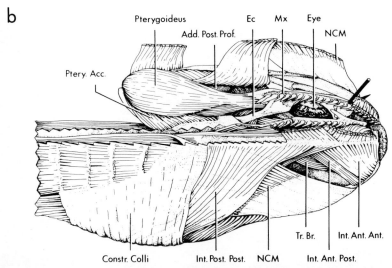

b

Pterygoideus   Ec   Mx   Eye
Add. Post. Prof.   NCM
Ptery. Acc.

Tr. Br.   Int. Ant. Ant.
Constr. Colli   Int. Post. Post.   NCM   Int. Ant. Post.

Figure 4–11. Views of dissections of the head of *Nerodia rhombifera* showing (a) a lateral view of the superficial mandibular adductor muscles and anterior superficial cervical muscles associated with the mandible or quadrate (from Cundall and Gans, 1979), and (b) a ventral view of the superficial and deep intermandibular muscles and the pterygoideus (modified from Cundall and Gans, 1979). Add. Ext. Med., adductor mandibulae externus, pars medialis; Add. Ext. Prof., adductor mandibulae externus, pars profundus; Add. Ext. Sup., adductor mandibulae externus, pars superficialis: Add. Post. Prof., adductor mandibulae posterior, pars profundus; Cerv. Mand., cervicomandibularis; Cerv. Quad., cervicoquadratus; Constr. Colli, constrictor colli; Depr. Mand., depressor mandibulae; Ec, ectopterygoid; Int. Ant. Ant., intermandibularis anterior, pars anterior; Int. Ant. Post., intermandibularis anterior, pars posterior; Int. Post. Post., intermandibularis posterior, pars posterior; Mx, maxilla; NCM, neurocostomandibularis; Ptery. Acc., pterygoideus accessorius; Tr. Br., transversus branchialis.

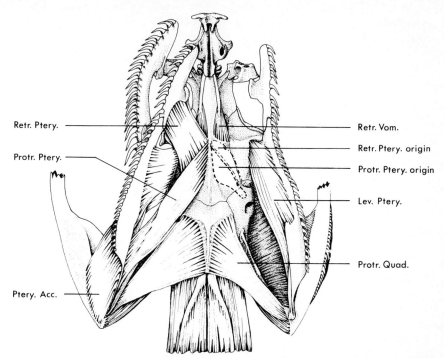

Figure 4–12. Ventral view of the protractors, levator, and retractor of the palatopterygoid bar in *Nerodia rhombifera*. Lev. Ptery., levator pterygoidei; Protr. Ptery., protractor pterygoidei; Protr. Quad., protractor quadrati; Ptery. Acc., pterygoideus accessorius; Retr. Ptery., retractor pterygoideus; Retr. Vom., retractor vomeris. From Cundall and Gans (1979).

The Strike

Although it has long been recognized that many snakes strike at their prey using rapid bilaterally symmetric motions of the jaws, the exact mechanism by which this occurs has proved extraordinarily difficult to demonstrate. Anatomical and high-speed cinematographic analyses of the strike in *Python* (Frazzetta, 1966) and *Agkistrodon* (Kardong, 1974) suggest that there are a number of basic similarities in the strike mechanism of these two very different taxa. First, abduction of both mandibles and protraction of both palatomaxillary arches occur together during the time interval between initiation of the strike and contact with the prey. In both genera, as the head is rapidly accelerated toward the prey, the braincase and snout flex dorsally. This ensures that it is the tooth rows of the upper or lower jaws that first contact the prey.

Protraction of the palatomaxillary arches during the strike is now assumed to be a function of the pterygoid protractors (Boltt and Ewer, 1964; Kardong, 1974). In both *Python* and *Agkistrodon*, protraction of the pterygoid causes anterior displacement of both the palatine and maxilla, the extent of movement being limited primarily by ligaments attaching the palatine to the prefrontal in *Python* and the maxilla to the postorbital in *Agkistrodon*. In addition, Kardong (1974) has pointed out that limits to suspensorial movement in *Agkistrodon* constrain the movements of the pterygoid to directions most effective for fang erection.

When directed at prey, the strike typically culminates in a rapid bite as the jaws contact the prey surface. Adduction of the mandibles is usually bilaterally symmetric, but details of palatomaxillary movements remain obscure. Many prey react vigorously when struck, imposing considerable stress to various parts of the snake's head. Although it is clear that the greatest constraints on the design of the heads of snakes arise from the demands of prey capture, the mechanics of this process and its influence on cephalic form remain poorly understood and virtually unexplored by modern analytical techniques.

Prey Transport

The mechanisms that snakes use to transport prey through the oral cavity have been examined in detail in a number of species (*Python:* Frazzetta, 1966; *Elaphe:* Albright and Nelson, 1959b; Cundall, 1983; *Nerodia:* Cundall and Gans, 1979; Cundall, 1983; *Heterodon:* Cundall, 1983; *Bitis:* Boltt and Ewer, 1964; *Vipera:* Dullemeijer, 1956; *Agkistrodon:* Kardong, 1977; Cundall, 1983) and found to be similar in many respects. Based on synchronized cinematographic and electromyographic analyses (Cundall and Gans, 1979; Cundall, 1983), the motions of the various skull bones in colubroid snakes are as follows during a single cycle for the right side (Figure 4–13).

The cycle begins with release of the prey by a slight depression of the right mandible and rotation of the braincase about its long axis, which slightly lifts the right upper jaw. The palatomaxillary protractors and levator become active at this time (Figure 4–14), their activity gradually increasing as rotation of the braincase continues. These muscles collectively elevate and protract the palatopterygoid bar, causing both the palatopterygoid joint and the maxilla to move laterally and anteriorly. Precise movements of the upper jaws are dependent not only on features of the intrinsic palatomaxillary joints but also on the mobility of the prefrontal bone and snout complex.

As the advance phase progresses, the mandibular depressor becomes active, causing continued abduction of the mandible as the distal end of the quadrate is pulled anteriorly and medially by movement of the palatopterygoid bar and activity of the quadrate protractor. At the same time, the pterygoid retractor on the opposite side of the head becomes active, causing the braincase to slide forward over the left upper jaw which remains fixed on the surface of the prey. Usually this motion is accompanied by continued rotation of the braincase about its longitudinal axis, combined with rotation about its transverse axis. The latter

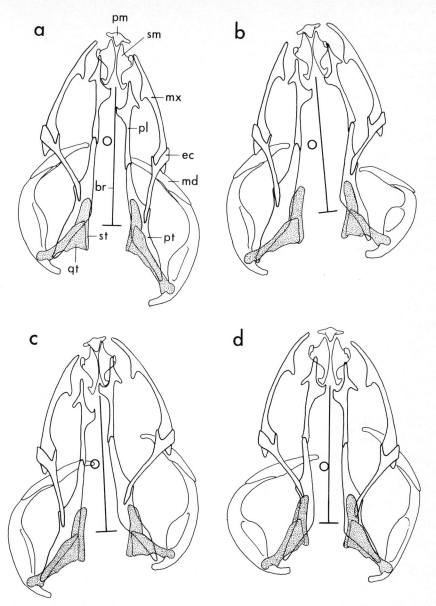

Figure 4–13. Diagrammatic summary of bone movements during the transport process showing (a) beginning of right side advance, (b) end of advance of the right jaws, (c) end of fast period of closing of the right side, (d) middle of slow period of advance of the left jaws. Circle near left palatopterygoid joint denotes a fixed point on the surface of the prey. br, Axis of braincase, posterior end of braincase denoted by line perpendicular to axis; ec, ectopterygoid; md, mandible; mx, maxilla; pl, palatine; pm, premaxilla; pt, pterygoid; qt, quadrate; sm, septomaxilla; st, supratemporal. Modified from Cundall and Gans (1979).

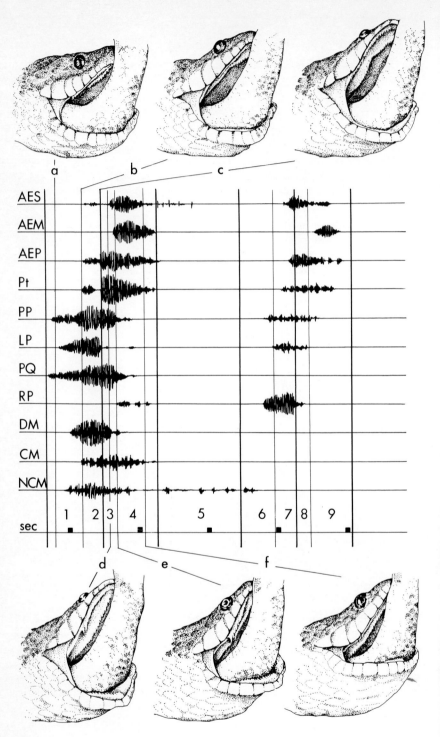

rotation moves the snout to the left and swings the posterior end of the braincase anterior to, and to the right of, its starting position relative to the left pterygoid (Figure 4–13). All these movements maximize the distance traveled by the advancing right upper jaw along the long axis of the prey.

Closing is initiated by marked protraction of the quadratomandibular joint and/or depression of the rear end of the maxilla (or backward rotation of the fang in viperid snakes). At the same time the palatopterygoid joint drops onto the surface of the prey (Cundall and Gans, 1979; Cundall, 1983). These movements are correlated with a burst of activity in the pterygoideus muscle (Figure 4–14) which connects the distal end of the ectopterygoid and associated posterior end of the maxilla with the caudomedial end of the mandible. With the exception of the pterygoid levator, which displays a reduction in or cessation of activity at this time, the protractors of the palatomaxillary arch continue their activity unabated throughout this early part of closing. As the right palatopterygoid teeth contact the prey, the braincase reverses its rotational movement and the mandible lifts, both motions serving to fix the teeth of the palatopterygoid bar on the prey surface. These latter motions are accompanied by high but gradually decreasing levels of activity in all the mandibular adductors on the right side, and lower levels of activity in the adductors on the left side.

When snakes transport prey with pliable integuments, continued closing of the right side often carries the right quadratomandibular joint posteriorly, with associated retraction of the mandible and palatomaxillary arch. These movements, presumably powered by contractions of the mandibular adductors and several cervical muscles, notably the cervicomandibularis and neurocostomandibularis, are less evident when snakes feed on large prey with stiff integuments. It now seems clear that the jaw apparatus is designed to move the head of the snake over the prey. Retraction movements that would draw the prey into the

---

Figure 4–14.   Representative activity of selected cephalic muscles during transport of a fish by *Nerodia rhombifera*. Tracings from Super-8 film showing (a) early stage of slow period (1) of advance phase of the right jaws; (b) beginning of fast period (2) of right side advance; (c) end of right side advance; (d) approximate mid-point of fast period (3) of right closing; (e) end of fast period of right closing; (f) later point in slow period (4) of right closing. EMG traces show right side muscles. Vertical lines separate behavioral periods and phases of transport. 1 to 4, given above; 5, relaxation of right side; 6, slow period of left advance; 7, fast period of left advance; 8, fast period of left closing; 9, slow period of left closing. AES, Adductor mandibulae externus, pars superficialis; AEM, adductor mandibulae externus, pars medialis; AEP, adductor mandibulae externus, pars profundus; Pt, pterygoideus; PP, protractor pterygoidei; LP, levator pterygoidei; PQ, protractor quadrati; RP, retractor pterygoidei; DM, depressor mandibulae; CM, cervicomandibularis; NCM, neurocostomandibularis. Lowermost trace shows a time marker in 1-s intervals. Data from Cundall and Gans (1979).

oral cavity are energetically efficient only when the prey mass is small relative to the mass of the snake's head (Cundall, 1983).

Although electromyographic data are currently available for only four colubroid taxa (Cundall and Gans, 1979; Cundall, 1983), evidence suggests that the protractor muscles of the palatopterygoid bar (Figure 4–12) have relatively conservative patterns of activity (Figure 4–14) consistent with the conservative nature of the movements of these bones. With one exception, the muscles attached to the mandible and its suspensorium (Figure 4–11) have much more variable patterns of activity, which correlate with the diversity of movements that these bones may exhibit during advance and closing phases of transport. The exception is the pterygoideus muscle (Figure 4–11). This muscle displays a relatively conservative pattern of activity (Figure 4–14) that correlates well with movements of the palatopterygoid joint seen during the initial phase of closing.

Despite the apparent unilateral nature of jaw movements, asymmetric bilateral activity is exhibited by various mandibular adductor muscles, the protractors and levator of the palatomaxillary arch, and the intermandibular muscles. Generally, activity of muscles on the closed side peaks at the end of advance and the beginning of closing of the active side and seems to function in preventing the closed side from opening when the opposite jaws are maximally abducted. However, all these muscles occasionally display unilateral activity, illustrating that muscular control of the feeding apparatus is both variable and complex. Any real understanding of the contribution of individual muscles to particular bone movements during prey transport must await the measurement of forces generated by individual muscles.

In colubroid taxa that have been carefully observed (Boltt and Ewer, 1964; Kardong, 1977; Cundall, 1983), neither the maxillary nor the dentary teeth appear to be essential for prey transport and frequently fail to contact the surface of the prey. Based on these observations and patterns of muscle activity during prey transport in four colubroid species, I suggested (Cundall, 1983) that each upper jaw in colubroid snakes is divided into a medial component that functions in prey transport and a lateral component that may respond to a variety of functional demands. Release of the maxilla from a necessary role in prey transport permits it to respond to selection associated primarily with the demands of prey capture. On the other hand, variations in mandibular movement and in the activity of mandibular muscles reflect a loose relationship between the functions of the mandible and those of the palatopterygoid bar. Because the mandibular teeth frequently do not contact the prey during transport, the mandible may function primarily in pressing the prey against the palatopterygoid teeth. Conceivably it does this by orienting the position of the muscular sling, particularly the intermandibular muscles that usually lie beneath the prey. This function can be satisfied by a variety of mandibular and suspensorial movements produced by an equivalent variety of muscle activity patterns.

The Evolution of Prey Transport Mechanisms in Snakes

Gans (1961) suggested that the critical first step in the evolution of the feeding apparatus of alethinophidian snakes was liberation of the mandibular tips and a departure from the inertial feeding mechanics typical of many lizards. These changes, which presumably followed an increase in the relative mass of the trunk as a result of elongation, permitted engulfment of prey of larger diameter and of greater mass relative to the head of the snake. Subsequent structural modifications involved mobilization of the various attachments between the suspensorial elements and the skull and between the palatomaxillary arches and the skull.

The problem of determining which alethinophidian groups are the most primitive (see Cadle, this volume; McDowell, this volume; Rage, this volume) and the absence of information on the functional properties of the head in primitive snakes have made Gans' (1961) model difficult to evaluate. If we assume that the feeding apparatus of living anilioids is structurally and functionally representative of the primitive condition for alethinophidian snakes, then Gans' (1961) model may be examined in light of the studies previously described plus the morphological works of Haas (1930, 1931, 1955, 1962), Frazzetta (1959, 1966), Estes et al. (1970), and Rieppel (1977 a,b, 1978a,b, 1979, 1980a,b) and recent unpublished studies of mine on feeding mechanics in the aniliid species *Cylindrophis rufus*.

In the anilioids (e.g., *Cylindrophis* and *Loxocemus:* Groombridge, 1979; D. Cundall, personal observations) there is a loosening of the mandibular symphysis that permits the dentaries to undergo various angular displacements relative to each other but does not allow any significant separation of their tips. However, a highly mobile intramandibular joint exists (Figure 4–15), permitting deformation of the mandible to fit the conformation of the prey surface (seen in *Cylindrophis* and *Loxocemus*). This has little effect on gape size, limiting these snakes to prey of relatively small diameter (Greene, 1983).

Colubroid snakes share one property of the skull that is critical to prey transport, namely, a high degree of mobility of the palatomaxillary arches. On the basis of skull form, this appears to be the case even in fossorial taxa (experimental confirmation of this contention might clarify many assumptions regarding the influence of fossoriality on the form and function of the skull) that display relatively short suspensoria and mandibles and relatively rigid snouts (Savitzky, 1983). Most henophidian species, on the other hand, share a different pattern of bone and joint relationships in both the palatomaxillary arch and the snout. The henophidian ectopterygoid is quite short and relatively immobile, and the origin of the pterygoideus muscle is limited primarily to the lateral edge of the pterygoid. This structural relationship should cause the medial and lateral elements of the palatomaxillary arch to act more or less as a unit (Cundall and Greene, 1982), a conclusion largely supported by Frazzetta's (1966) analysis of

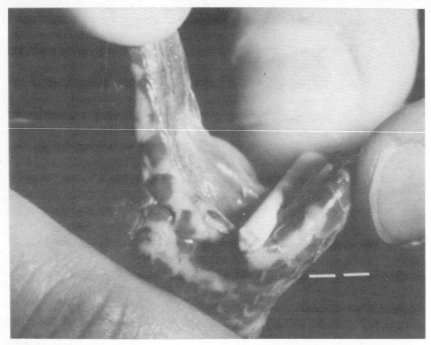

Figure 4–15.   Lateral view of the head of an anesthetized *Cylindrophis rufus* showing potential displacement of the dentary around the intramandibular joint. Dashed line shows the position of the mandible before flexion around the intra-mandibular joint.

skull kinesis in *Python*. Furthermore, in many lower henophidian species (ani-liids, uropeltids, tropidopheids, *Loxocemus,* and *Xenopeltis*), the palatine and maxilla are closely associated with both the prefrontal and the vomer (Haas, 1930; McDowell, 1975; Rieppel, 1977b). In these snakes, movements of the palatomaxillary arch may depend on equivalent movements of either the pre-frontal or the snout, or possibly both.

To summarize, if living anilioids represent the primitive condition for ale-thinophidian snakes, then structural changes during the early evolution of this group involved almost all aspects of the feeding apparatus while producing only slight increases in gape size. Further, the increase in gape size was initially achieved by mobilization of the intramandibular joint, not the mandibular tips.

Despite a wealth of anatomical information, the pattern of functional changes from this point on remains unclear. The Booidea and the Colubroidea appear to represent different solutions to the problem of feeding on prey of large diameter, although some colubroid taxa exhibit reversals and have quite limited gape sizes. Of particular importance, however, is the notion that living snakes may include most of the major structural and functional stages from a gape-limited ancestor with limited independence of the right and left jaws to the more highly derived colubroid feeding apparatus. Whether these structural-functional stages are correlated with phylogeny remains to be seen.

Venom Glands and Teeth

The evolution of venom glands (Taub, 1966, 1967; Kochva, 1978) and of their association with derivatives of either the adductor mandibulae externus superficialis (elapids and some rear-fanged colubrids: Rosenberg, 1967; Haas, 1973) or the adductor mandibulae externus profundus (viperids: Kochva, 1958, 1962, 1963; Haas, 1973) are believed to have increased prey-handling efficiency in venomous species. However, this increased efficiency may not be a simple function of envenomation. Pough and Groves (1983) have demonstrated that, for prey of equivalent size, viperid species use fewer maxillary protraction cycles than nonviperid species during prey transport. Furthermore, among the taxa examined, viperid species ingested prey of significantly greater mass relative to the mass of the snake, a function attributable to an increase in relative gape size.

Muscular control of venom injection remains poorly understood, although Rosenberg (1967) and Jansen and Foehring (1983) have showed that stimulation of selected adductor muscles associated with venom or Duvernoy's glands caused venom flow at the fangs. However, the compressor glandulae of *Agkistrodon* exhibits activity throughout prey transport, evidently serving as a mandibular adductor during this process (Cundall, 1983). Exactly what happens, both in terms of muscular contributions to compression of the venom gland and the timing of venom flow, remains unknown for natural predatory strikes in any venomous snake.

Feeding in snakes is presumed to be influenced by the form of the teeth on the various dentigerous bones. The functional properties, both of individual teeth and entire tooth rows, were examined by Frazzetta (1966). Tooth form in snakes has been reviewed by Edmund (1969), and more recent work by Savitzky (1981, 1983) has demonstrated some remarkable dental modifications, including hinged teeth in various durophagic species. The view that the teeth of snakes are simple curved or recurved cones is clearly untenable, particularly in light of recent high-resolution studies on tooth surfaces (Wright et al., 1979; Vaeth et al., 1985). Frazzetta (1966) suggested that the cutting edges on the distal ends of the teeth in many snakes may serve to enlarge the wound, facilitating extraction. If the dentigerous bones actually function as suggested by recent functional morphological analyses, teeth on the maxilla and dentary should exhibit features associated with holding, restraining, or envenomating prey, whereas the teeth of the palatopterygoid bar should be relatively conservative in form, particularly in species that usually kill their prey before ingesting them.

SUMMARY

Functional morphological studies on the musculoskeletal systems of snakes have begun to clarify how these structurally complex systems work. Patterns of muscle activity in both the trunk and head are generally more simple than the arrangement of muscles would lead one to expect. Not surprisingly, snakes retain many basic features of muscle activity patterns found in other vertebrates. However, there are differences.

During locomotion, snakes appear to be able to control the number of segments in a block of simultaneously active epaxial muscle as well as the distance between blocks and the rate of propagation of the blocks. This permits them to use irregularly spaced pivot points with maximum efficiency. The similarities between epaxial muscle activity during lateral undulation and sidewinding are indicative of the subtle relationships that exist between muscle activity, patterns of force generation, and the kinematic properties of locomotor modes. It has now become clear, however, that the apparent similarities between swimming and terrestrial lateral undulation may have concealed functional differences between these two modes of locomotion that may be critical to understanding both the structure of the axial muscular system in snakes and the basis of its coordination.

With regard to the feeding apparatus, snakes display asymmetric bilateral activity in a muscular system that produces unilateral bone movements. The retention of bilateral activity patterns during prey transport in snakes may result simply from the retention of a basic vertebrate motor pattern for jaw movements. Conversely, or additionally, it could have mechanical significance, muscle activity being modulated to maximize jaw displacement. The idea that the jaw apparatus is functionally subdivided, both in terms of muscle activity and the kinematic properties of the bones, may lead to more refined demonstrations of jaw mechanics in a variety of taxa. Hopefully, the next generation of models will incorporate empirical data on jaw mechanics during the strike.

LITERATURE CITED

Albright, R. G. and Nelson, E. M. 1959a. Cranial kinetics of the generalized colubrid snake *Elaphe obsoleta quadrivittata*. I. Descriptive morphology, *J. Morphol.* 105:193–239.

Albright, R. G. and Nelson, E. M. 1959b. Cranial kinetics of the generalized colubrid snake *Elaphe obsoleta quadrivittata*. II. Functional morphology, *J. Morphol.* 105:241–291.

Auffenberg, W. 1958. The trunk musculature of *Sanzina* and its bearing on certain aspects of the myological evolution of snakes, *Brevoria* 82:1–12.

Auffenberg, W. 1961. Additional remarks on the evolution of trunk musculature in snakes. *Am. Midl. Nat.* 65:1–16.

Auffenberg, W. 1962. A review of the trunk musculature in the limbless land vertebrates. *Am. Zool.* 2:183–190.

Bellairs, A. d'A. and Kamal, A. M. 1981. The chondrocranium and the development of the skull in recent reptiles, in: Biology of the Reptilia, vol. 11 (C. Gans and T. S. Parsons, eds.) pp. 1–263, Academic Press, New York.

Bellairs, A. d'A. and Underwood, G. 1951. The origin of snakes, *Biol. Rev. Camb. Philos. Soc.* 26:193–237.

Blight, A. R. 1977. The muscular control of vertebrate swimming movements. *Biol. Rev. Camb. Philos. Soc.* 52:181–218.

Bock, W. 1980. The definition and recognition of biological adaptation, *Am. Zool.* 20:217–227.

Bogert, C. M. 1947. Rectilinear locomotion in snakes, *Copeia* 1947:253–254.

Boltt, R. E. and Ewer, R. F. 1964. The functional anatomy of the head of the puff adder, *Bitis arietans* (Merr.), *J. Morphol.* 114:83–106.

Bourgeois, M. 1965. Contribution a la morphologie comparée due crane des ophidiens de l'Afrique Central, *Publ. Univ. Off. Congo, Lubumbashi* 18:1–293.

Brain, C. K. 1960. Observations on the locomotion of the South West African adder, *Bitis peringueyi* (Boulenger), with speculations on the origin of sidewinding, *Ann. Transvaal Mus.* 24:19–24.

Buffa, P. 1905. Richerche sulla musculatura cutanea dei serpenti e considerazioni sulla locomozione di questi animali, *Atti Acad. Ven. Trent. Ist.* 1:145–237.

Clark, B. D., Gans, C., and Rosenberg, H. I. 1978. Air flow in snake ventilation, *Respir. Physiol.* 32:207–212.

Cowles, R. B. 1956. Sidewinding locomotion in snakes, *Copeia* 1956:211–214.

Cundall, D. 1983. Activity of head muscles during feeding by snakes: A comparative study, *Am. Zool.* 23:383–396.

Cundall, D. 1986. Variations of the cephalic muscles in the colubrid snake genera *Entechinus, Opheodrys* and *Symphimus, J. Morphol.* 187:1–21.

Cundall, D. and Gans, C. 1979. Feeding in water snakes: An electromyographic study, *J. Exp. Zool.* 209:189–208.

Cundall, D. and Greene, H. 1982. Evolution of the feeding apparatus in alethinophidian snakes, *Am. Zool.* 22:924.

Dullemeijer, P. 1956. The functional morphology of the head of the common viper, *Vipera berus* (L.), *Arch. Neerl. Zool.* 11:386–497.

Dullemeijer, P. 1959. A comparative functional-anatomical study of the heads of some Viperidae, *Morphol. Jahrb.* 99:881–985.

Dullemeijer, P. 1974. Concepts and Approaches in Animal Morphology. Van Gorcum, Assen, The Netherlands.

Edmund, A. G. 1969. Dentition, in: Biology of the Reptilia, vol. 1 (C. Gans, A. d'A. Bellairs, and T. S. Parsons, eds.) pp. 117–200, Academic Press, New York.

Edwards, J. L. 1985. Terrestrial locomotion without appendages, in: Functional Vertebrate Morphology (M. Hildebrand, D. M. Bramble, K. F. Liem, and D. B. Wake, eds.) pp. 159–172, Belknap Press, Cambridge, Massachusetts.

Estes, R., Frazzetta, T. H., and Williams, E. E. 1970. Studies on the fossil snake *Dinilysia patagonica* Woodward: 1. Cranial morphology, *Bull. Mus. Comp. Zool. Harv. Univ.* 140:25–73.

Fetcho, J. R. 1986a. The organization of the motoneurons innervating the axial musculature of vertebrates. II. Florida water snakes (*Nerodia fasciata pictiventris*), *J. Comp. Neurol.* 249:551–563.

Fetcho, J. R. 1986b. The organization of the motoneurons innervating the axial musculature of vertebrates. I. Goldfish (*Carassius auratus*) and mudpuppies (*Necturus maculosus*), *J. Comp. Neurol.* 249:521–550.

Frazzetta, T. H. 1959. Studies on the morphology and function of the skull in the Boidae (Serpentes). I. Cranial differences between *Python sebae* and *Epicrates cenchris, Bull. Mus. Comp. Zool. Harv. Univ.* 119:453–472.

Frazzetta, T. H. 1966. Studies on the morphology and function of the skull in the Boidae (Serpentes). II. Morphology and function of the jaw apparatus in *Python sebae* and *Python molurus, J. Morphol.* 118:217–296.

Gans, C. 1952. The functional morphology of the egg-eating adaptations in the snake genus *Dasypeltis, Zoologica* 37:209–244.

Gans, C. 1961. The feeding mechanism of snakes and its possible evolution, *Am. Zool.* 1:217–227.

Gans, C. 1962. Terrestrial locomotion without limbs, *Am. Zool.* 2:167–182.

Gans, C. 1973. Uropeltid snakes—Survivors in a changing world. *Endeavor* 32:60–65.

Gans, C. 1974. Biomechanics: An Approach to Vertebrate Biology, J. P. Lippincott, Philadelphia.

Gans, C. 1975. Tetrapod limblessness: Evolution and functional corollaries, *Am. Zool.* 15:455–467.

Gans, C. 1976. Aspects of the biology of uropeltid snakes, in: Morphology and Biology of Reptiles (A. d'A. Bellairs and C. B. Cox, eds.) pp. 191–204, Linnean Soc. Symposium Ser., No. 3, Academic Press, London.

Gans, C. 1984. Slide-pushing—A transitional locomotor method of elongate squamates, in: The Structure, Development and Evolution of Reptiles (M. W. J. Ferguson, ed.) pp. 13–26, Symp. Zool. Soc. Lond., no. 52, Academic Press, London.

Gans, C. 1986. Locomotion of limbless vertebrates: Pattern and evolution, *Herpetologica* 42:33–46.

Gans, C. and Baic, D. 1977. Regional specialization of reptilian scale surfaces: Relation of texture and biologic role, *Science* 195:1348–1350.

Gans, C. and Mendelssohn, H. 1972. Sidewinding and jumping progression of vipers, in: Toxins of Animal and Plant Origin (A. de Vries and E. Kochva, eds.) pp. 17–38, Gordon and Breach, London.

Gans, C., Dessauer, H. C., and Baic, D. 1978. Axial differences in the musculature of uropeltid snakes: The freight-train approach to burrowing, *Science* 199:189–192.

Gasc, J.-P. 1974, L'interprétation fonctionnelle de l'appareil musculo-squelletique de l'axe vertébral chez les serpents (Reptilia), *Mem. Mus. Nat. Hist. Nat. Ser. A Zool.* 83:1–182.

Gasc, J.-P. 1981. Axial musculature, in: Biology of the Reptilia, vol. 11 (C. Gans and T. S. Parsons, eds.) pp. 355–435. Academic Press, New York.

Gray, J. 1946. The mechanism of locomotion in snakes, *J. Exp. Biol.* 23:101–120.

Gray, J. 1953. Undulatory propulsion, *Q. J. Micro. Sci.* 94:551–578.

Gray, J. and Lissmann, H. W. 1950. The kinetics of locomotion of the grass-snake, *J. Exp. Biol.* 26:354–367.

Greene, H. W. 1983. Dietary correlates of the origin and radiation of snakes, *Am. Zool.* 23:431–441.

Greene, H. W. and Burghardt, G. M. 1978. Behavior and phylogeny: Constriction in ancient and modern snakes, *Science* 200:74–77.

Grillner, S. and Kashin, S. 1976. On the generation and performance of swimming in fish, in: Neural Control of Locomotion (R. M. Herman, S. Grillner, P. S. Stein, and D. G. Stuart, eds.) pp. 181–201, Plenum Press, New York.

Groombridge, B. C. 1979. Comments on the intermandibular muscles of snakes, *J. Nat. Hist.* 13:477–498.

Haas, G. 1930. Uber die Kaumuskulatur und die Schadelmechanik einiger Wuhlschlangen, *Zool. Jahrb. Abt. Anat.* 52:95–218.

Haas, G. 1931. Uber die Morphologie der Kiefermuskulatur und die Schadel-mechanik einiger Schlangen, *Zool. Jahrb. Abt. Anat.* 54:333–416.

Haas, G. 1955. The systematic position of *Loxocemus bicolor* Cope (Ophidia), *Am. Mus. Novit.* 1748:1–8.

Haas, G. 1962. Remarques concernant les relations phylogéniques des diverses familles d'ophidiens fondées sur la differenciation de la musculature mandibulaire, *Colloq. Int. Cent. Nat. Rech. Sci.* 104:215–241.

Haas, G. 1973. Muscles of the jaws and associated structures in the Rhynchocephalia and Squamata, in: Biology of the Reptilia, vol. 4 (C. Gans and T. S. Parsons, eds.) pp. 285–490, Academic Press, New York.

Hildebrand, M., Bramble, D. M., Liem, K. F., and Wake, D. B. (eds). 1985. Functional Vertebrate Morphology, Belknap Press, Cambridge, Massachusetts.

Hoffstetter, R. and Gasc, J.-P. 1969. Vertebrae and ribs of modern reptiles, in: Biology of the Reptilia, vol. 1 (C. Gans, A. d'A Bellairs, and T. S. Parsons, eds.) pp. 201–310, Academic Press, New York.

Jansen, D. W. and Foehring, R. C. 1983. The mechanism of venom secretion from Duvernoy's gland of the snake *Thamnophis sirtalis, J. Morphol.* 175:271–277.

Jayne, B. C. 1982. Comparative morphology of the semispinalis-spinalis muscle of snakes and correlations with locomotion and constriction, *J. Morphol.* 172:83–96.

Jayne, B. C. 1985a. Mechanisms of snake locomotion: An electromyographic study, Ph.D. Dissertation, Michigan State University, East Lansing.

Jayne, B. C. 1985b. Swimming in constricting (*Elaphe g. guttata*) and non-constricting (*Nerodia fasciata pictiventris*) colubrid snakes, *Copeia* 1985:195–208.

Jayne, B. C. 1986. Kinematics of terrestrial snake locomotion, *Copeia* 1986:915–927.

Johnson, R. G. 1955. The adaptive and phylogenetic significance of vertebral form in snakes, *Evolution* 9:367–388.

Kardong, K. V. 1973. Lateral jaw and throat musculature of the cottonmouth snake. *Agkistrodon piscivorus, Gegenbaurs Morphol. Jahrb.* 119:316–335.

Kardong, K. V. 1974. Kinesis of the jaw apparatus during the strike in the cottonmouth snake, *Agkistrodon piscivorus, Forma et Functio* 7:327–354.

Kardong, K. V. 1977. Kinesis of the jaw apparatus during swallowing in the cottonmouth snake, *Agkistrodon piscivorus, Copeia* 1977:338–348.

Kardong, K. V. 1980. Jaw musculature of the West Indian snake *Alsophis cantherigerus brooksi* (Colubridae, Reptilia), *Breviora* 463:1–26.

Kochva, E. 1958. The head muscles of *Vipera palaestinae* and their relation to the venom gland, *J. Morphol.* 102:23–54.

Kochva, E. 1962. On the lateral jaw musculature of the Solenoglypha with remarks on some other snakes, *J. Morphol.* 110:227–284.

Kochva, E. 1963. Development of the venom gland and trigeminal muscles in *Vipera palaestinae, Acta Anat.* 52:49–89.

Kochva, E. 1978. Oral glands of the Reptilia, in: Biology of the Reptilia, vol. 8 (C. Gans and K. A. Gans, eds.) pp. 43–161, Academic Press, New York.

Kramer, E. 1977. Die Kopf- und Rumpfmuskulatur von *Vipera aspis* (Linnaeus, 1758), *Revue Suisse Zool.* 84:767–790.

Lauder, G. V. 1982. Introduction to E. S. Russell's Form and Function, reprinted edition, University of Chicago Press.

Lissmann, H. W. 1950. Rectilinear locomotion in a snake (*Boa occidentalis*), *J. Exp. Biol.* 26:368–379.

McDowell, S. B. 1972. The evolution of the tongue of snakes, and its bearing on snake origins, in: Evolutionary Biology, vol. 6 (T. Dobzhansky, M. K. Hecht, and W. C. Steere, eds.) pp. 191–273, Appleton-Century-Crofts, New York.

McDowell, S. B. 1975. A catalogue of the snakes of New Guinea and the Solomons, with special reference to those in the Bernice P. Bishop Museum. II. Anilioidea and Pythoninae, *J. Herpetol.* 9:1–79.

Mosauer, W. 1932a. On the locomotion of snakes, *Science* 76:583–585.

Mosauer, W. 1932b. Uber die Ortsbewegung der Schlangen, *Zool. Jahrb. Abt. Allg. Zool. Physiol. Tiere* 52:191–215.

Mosauer, W. 1935. The myology of the trunk region of snakes and its significance for ophidian taxonomy and phylogeny, *Publ. Univ. Calif. Los Angeles Biol. Sci.* 1:81–120.

Pough, F. H. and Groves, J. D. 1983. Specializations of the body form and food habits of snakes, *Am. Zool.* 23:443–454.

Pregill, G. K. 1977. Axial myology of the racer *Coluber constrictor* with emphasis on the neck region. *Trans. San Diego Soc. Nat. Hist.* 18:185–206.

Rashevsky, N. 1948. Mathematical Biophysics, 2nd ed., University of Chicago Press.

Rieppel, O. 1977a. Studies on the skull of the Henophidia (Reptilia: Serpentes), *J. Zool. (Lond.)* 181:145–173.

Rieppel, O. 1977b. The naso-frontal joint in *Anilius scytale* (Linnaeus) and *Cylindrophis rufus* (Schiegel): Serpentes, Aniliidae, *J. Nat. Hist.* 11:545–553.

Rieppel, O. 1978a. A functional and phylogenetic interpretation of the skull of the Erycinae (Reptilia, Serpentes), *J. Zool. (Lond.)* 186:185–208.

Rieppel, O. 1978b. The evolution of the naso-frontal joint in snakes and its bearing on snake origins, *Z. Zool. Syst. Evolutionforsch.* 16:14–27.

Rieppel, O. 1979. A cladistic classification of snakes based on skull structure, *Z. Zool. Syst. Evolutionforsch.* 17:140–150.

Rieppel, O. 1980a. The evolution of the ophidian feeding system, *Zool. Jahrb. Anat.* 103:551–564.

Rieppel, O. 1980b. The trigeminal jaw adductors of primitive snakes and their homologies with the lacertilian jaw adductors, *J. Zool. (Lond.)* 190:447–471.

Rosenberg, H. I. 1967. Histology, histochemistry, and emptying mechanism of the venom glands of some elapid snakes, *J. Morphol.* 123:133–156.

Rosenberg, H. I. 1973. Functional anatomy of pulmonary ventilation in the garter snake, *Thamnophis elegans, J. Morphol.* 140:171–184.

Ruben, J. A. 1977a. Some correlates of cranial and cervical myology with predatory modes in snakes, *J. Morphol.* 152:89–100.

Ruben, J. A. 1977b. Morphological correlates of predatory modes in the coachwhip (*Masticophis flagellum*) and rosy boa (*Lichanura roseofusca*), *Herpetologica* 33:1–6.

Ruben, J. A. and Geddes, C. 1983. Some morphological correlates of striking in snakes, *Copeia* 1983:221–225.

Savitzky, A. H. 1981. Hinged teeth in snakes: An adaptation for swallowing hard-bodied prey, *Science* 212:346–349.

Savitzky, A. H. 1983. Coadapted character complexes among snakes: Fossoriality, piscivory, and durophagy, *Am. Zool.* 23:397–409.

Senn, D. G. and Northcutt, R. G. 1973. The forebrain and midbrain of some squamates and their bearing on the origin of snakes. *J. Morphol.* 140:135–152.

Taub, A. M. 1966. Ophidian cephalic glands, *J. Morphol.* 118:529–542.

Taub, A. M. 1967. Comparative histological studies on Duvernoy's gland of colubrid snakes, *Bull. Am. Mus. Nat. Hist.* 138:1–50.

Vaeth, R. H., Rossman, D. A., and Shoop, W. 1985. Observations of tooth surface morphology in snakes, *J. Herpetol.* 19:20–26.

Van Riper, W. 1953. How a rattlesnake strikes, *Sci. Am.* 189:100–102.

Varkey, A. 1979. Comparative cranial myology of North American natricine snakes, *Milw. Public Mus. Publ. Biol. Geol.* 4:1–76.

Wake, D. B. 1982. Functional and evolutionary morphology, *Perspect. Biol. Med.* 25:603–620.

Walls, G. L. 1940. Ophthalmological implications for the early history of the snakes, *Copeia* 1940:1–8.

Wiedemann, E. 1932. Zur Ortsbewegung der Schlangen und Schleichen, *Zool. Jahrb. Abt. Allg. Zool. Physiol. Tiere* 50:557–596.

Willard, D. E. 1977. Constricting methods of snakes, *Copeia* 1977:379–382.

Wright, D. L., Kardong, K. V., and Bentley, D. L. 1979. The functional anatomy of the teeth of the western terrestrial garter snake, *Thamnophis elegans, Herpetologica* 35:223–228.

Techniques

CHAPTER FIVE

Collecting and Life-History Techniques

Henry S. Fitch

Perhaps more than any other animal, snakes fascinate the general public and are objects of curiosity whenever they are seen. The fact that many people are repelled or horrified by the sight of snakes makes them even more irresistible to others. Almost every herpetologist has had ego-boosting experiences early in his or her career when catching, handling, or keeping snakes has elicited awe or admiration in friends and relatives. A touch of exhibitionism often motivates the budding herpetologist's interest in these reptiles, but those with a background of biological training soon perceive the potential of snakes as material for investigations in such fields as evolution and ecology. As one gains familiarity with the literature on community ecology and related fields, one comes to realize that snakes are a neglected group much in need of investigation. Their abundance and importance in the tropics and in warm-temperature communities have not been fully appreciated.

The great diversity of snakes makes it difficult to outline procedures or formulate statements that will have general applicability in a field study. The group occurs from the subarctic to the tropics, in a variety of habitats—terrestrial, subterranean, arboreal and marine—and with a tremendous range in size, form, and life-style. Snakes are secretive and are not readily observed. Attempting to study them by direct observation in the field may be frustrating, because when they are found, snakes spend much time doing nothing and then suddenly disappear, perhaps never to be seen again. Hence the biology of snakes is still poorly known. New approaches are needed, and there are outstanding opportunities to contribute for all those who work with snakes or whose routines regularly bring them in contact with snakes in the field. Successful field study depends on the ability to make accurate and intensive observations, perseverance in keeping detailed written records filed according to a standardized system, and familiarity with the published literature.

METHODS OF OBTAINING SNAKES

Clues for Finding Snakes

Whether snakes are captured to be kept in captivity, preserved in a museum collection, or measured or observed for natural history information in a field study, some of the same methods and techniques apply. Snakes are sometimes concentrated, so that many can be taken with minimal effort if one is on hand at the right time and place. Hawken (1951) described the accidental entrapment of snakes in the San Francisco water supply system; after falling into a steep-sided aqueduct, they were carried by the swift current onto a wire screen. Elsewhere also, swift-flowing aqueducts and canals often entrap snakes, as do various man-made excavations such as wells and even natural pits. Natural concentrations occur in seasonal climates where snakes congregate at hiberna-cula, so-called dens. Raids on such dens, traditional in some regions, have supposedly been carried out on venomous snakes as a form of pest control, but more realistically have usually been a form of sport, resulting in the slaughter of large numbers of snakes, both venomous and nonvenomous. Several kinds of snakes may hibernate together at favorable sites provided by such diverse habitat features as ant burrows, rock fissures, and prairie dog "towns."

The investigator may learn to recognize visual and auditory cues by which other animals reveal the presence of a snake. In my early field study on the western rattlesnake at the San Joaquin Experimental Range in the Sierra foothills of California, a high proportion of the snakes obtained were located by observing the behavior of its favorite prey, the California ground squirrel, *Citellus beecheyi* (Fitch, 1949a). The squirrel's tail waving, cautious sidling gait, and scolding chirps revealed the presence of the snake.

On many occasions at the University of Kansas Natural History Reservation (UKNHR) I have been led to snakes, which otherwise would not have been found, by distress calls of plains leopard frogs (*Rana blairi*), usually in dense vegetation near the edge of a pond. These frogs had been caught by snakes (usually *Thamnophis sirtalis,* sometimes *Coluber constrictor*), which were in the act of swallowing them.

Climbing snakes are often scolded and mobbed by birds. On UKNHR many black rat snakes (*Elaphe obsoleta*) have been captured after birds revealed their presence. Bluejays (*Cyanocitta cristata*), because of their loud calls and con-spicuousness, most often led me to a snake. However, titmice (*Parus bicolor*), black-capped chickadees (*Parus atricapillus*), and downy woodpeckers (*Dendrocopos pubescens*) also were prominent in snake scolding, which often in-volved a mixed flock.

Domestic turkeys foraging afield are highly effective in finding snakes and revealing their presence to an investigator, as described by Smith (1946). Dogs have the ability to detect, trail, and "point" snakes, and can be used effectively in field studies if properly trained. Klauber (1956) cited several instances in which dogs had been trained to hunt rattlesnakes and showed photographs of a hound trained to find eastern diamondback rattlesnakes (*Crotalus adamanteus*) without exposing herself to their bites; in 2 yr she located about 500 of them for her owner.

Road Sampling

Road sampling has been the basis of many field studies. Detailed record keeping has been rewarding for investigators who have had to make regular trips over a stretch of road where snakes were found (Fitch, 1949b). Species previously rare in collections have been found in substantial numbers by road sampling (Klauber, 1939). The technique provides an index to the relative numbers of species comprising a local snake community and for common species can show sex ratios, age groups, seasonal changes, and the effects of temperature, sunshine or cloud cover, humidity, wind, and phases of the moon. Roads that are ungraded, little traveled, and narrow, with natural vegetation encroaching close to the wheel tracks, offer the best opportunity for finding snakes alive. Food items from stomachs (Reynolds and Scott, 1982; Seigel, 1986), stage of development of gonads, and number of eggs or embryos are data that can be obtained even from badly damaged road kills. The direction of travel may be significant as a seasonal or weather-motivated shift, especially if a snake is found alive.

Trapping

There are essentially three types of snake traps: artificial shelters placed where the animals will find and use them voluntarily; pitfall traps, into which the animals fall, and funnel traps. Each may involve considerable time and expense in installation and maintenance and may alter the habitat to varying degrees. Furthermore, in public access areas, the devices may attract the attention of meddling persons, resulting in damaging interference. Ordinarily the use of such devices is not efficient for collecting specimens, but only for life-history or population studies in which an area will be visited and checked repeatedly.

Sheet metal and boards are attractive shelters. Sun-warmed sheet metal shelters are productive in the spring when air temperatures are below the snakes' preferenda. However, after the onset of warmer weather, the metal becomes uncomfortably hot in the daytime and is avoided. Boards are more likely to be used in hot weather, providing insulation against the sun's heat. Flat rocks are better insulators than metal strips but are better heat conductors than boards and may be preferred under certain conditions.

Such artificial shelters are highly effective when they satisfy needs not already provided by the natural habitat and when they are carefully placed with respect to natural travelways and concentration points of the local snake population. Depending on the type of substrate and the species of snake desired, the shelter may be placed loosely on the soil surface or fitted snugly after the surface has been leveled or cleared of ground litter. The shelter may also be placed over a small cavity with a tunnel leading to the edge of the shelter.

Traps that restrain snakes occasionally cause mortality when weather conditions are extreme, when two or more incompatible animals happen to be caught and confined together, or when predators break into the traps.

Pitfall traps are effective for small snakes whose lengths are less than the depth of the pit (Gibbons et al., 1977; Gibbons and Semlitsch, 1982; Semlitsch and Moran, 1984). The pit consists of a smooth-walled container such as a metal can or a plastic wastebasket fitted into a vertical hole with its top flush with the ground surface. A pitfall trap may function best either with its top open, or with a flat stone or board over the opening but supported slightly above ground level so there is space for the snake to squeeze beneath the cover and into the pitfall. Pitfall traps are most effective when used in conjunction with drift fences that serve to steer snakes up to the entrance.

Funnel traps of various types have been used successfully for snakes in a variety of situations (Dargan and Stickel, 1940; Jackley, 1943, 1947; Gloyd, 1945; Imler, 1945; Fitch, 1951; Woodbury, 1951; Clark, 1966; Lohoefener and Wolfe, 1984). For example, Woodbury and his collaborators and successors effectively sampled den populations by building a barrier around the den area to prevent entry or egress of snakes except through a special opening that led them through a wire funnel from which they dropped into a spacious collecting box. The truncated apex of the funnel was covered with a transparent hinged plastic trapdoor to prevent escape of the snakes after entry, and the funnel was raised several centimeters above the floor of the box.

Relatively small portable funnel traps, consisting of wire mesh cylinders built on the plan of a commercial minnow trap, have also been used effectively for making one-at-a-time captures. They can be used in quantity and moved easily. I have had the most success with these traps when they were used with a funnel opening at each end of the cylinder and placed in habitats that presented natural barriers, serving to direct snakes into them (Figure 5–1). Success in trapping depends on placing the trap so that the bottom and sides of its funnels are tightly pressed against both the rock beside it and the substrate, with no spaces large enough for a snake to squeeze past. Double-ended funnel traps can be used effectively at bases of buildings, especially old abandoned ones isolated in forest or other natural communities, on concrete foundations of former buildings burned or torn down long before, in basements or stone walls or embankments, or along edges of streams where large boulders with vertical sides constitute barriers.

A

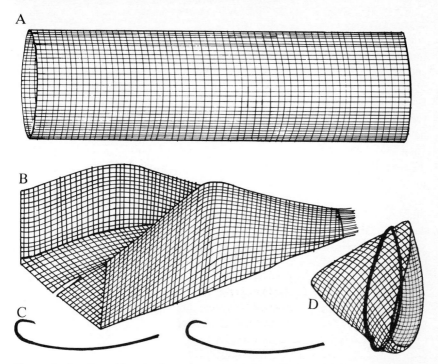

B

C

D

Figure 5–1. Portable wire funnel trap for snakes, disassembled. (A) Trap body, a cylinder with inward flange at each end. (B) Entrance funnel with inward projecting prongs and slit base to fit on end of drift fence. (C) Hooked and bowed heavy wire pins used to lock funnel and plug in place at end of trap. (D) Cone-shaped plug reinforced by heavy wire ring.

In habitats lacking any natural barriers that can be utilized for trap sites, drift fences need to be installed to direct snakes into the traps. Boards, plywood, "hardware cloth" or wire "hail screen," and sheet metal are all suitable materials, depending on availability. Wooden drift fences deteriorate rapidly and may last only one or two seasons, whereas wire or sheet metal fences may serve for many years.

The funnel traps I have used on UKNHR are mostly 15 cm in diameter and 35 cm long, with funnels about 25 cm across at the wide end and with a 3.5-cm opening at the apex. The hole is left open, and inward-projecting wire points prevent escape almost as effectively as the hinged plastic trapdoors used on earlier models. If the entrance hole is only slightly larger than the snake's diameter, and if it is raised well above the bottom of the trap, chances of accidental escape are minimized. On the other hand, too small an opening may exclude many snakes that otherwise would be caught.

Drift fences are placed to intersect diagonally the travelways that might be used by snakes, such as weedy or brushy fence lines, stone walls, dikes, or road edges. The trap bodies used in my field work have usually been made of $\frac{1}{4}$-in. wire squares. At each end of the trap's wire cylinder the edge is bent inward to produce a flange about 1 in. wide. The end of the trap pointing away from the end of the drift fence is closed with a low wire cone. A bowed piece of heavy wire with a hook at one end holds the funnel against one end of the trap cylinder, and a similar piece holds the cone-shaped plug at the opposite end. With its concave side directed inward, the wire is thrust through the trap and funnel but not far enough to engage the hooked end; it is first rotated through 180°, to pull the funnel tightly against the end of the trap, and then pushed down the remaining distance so that the hooked end is engaged, locking the funnel in place (see Figure 5–1).

On a smaller scale, funnel traps made from quart jars have been used fairly successfully for catching *Diadophis, Storeria,* and *Carphophis.* The funnels for these traps were made of window screen soldered to the inside of the jar's metal screw-top (Clark, 1966). The investigator could see through the glass to check the trap and could unscrew the funnel to remove the snakes. Funnel openings were about 1 cm in diameter.

Shading must always be considered to prevent overheating of trapped animals, and the installation should be made where there is shelter such as a thick bush. In open arid terrain, lack of dense sheltering vegetation may be remedied by digging a cavity for placement of the trap and covering it with several layers of insulating material such as old boards or flat rocks.

MARKING SNAKES

Radioactive Tags and Radiotelemetry

Spellerberg and Prestt (1978), Swingland (1978), and Ferner (1979) have reviewed methods and techniques for marking snakes and other cold-blooded vertebrates. Individual marking of snakes has made it possible to trace histories, which reveal patterns of growth, movement, reproduction, and longevity in local populations. A radioactive tag (Pendleton, 1956) or a small radiotransmitter attached to the snake permits trailing with day-to-day or hour-to-hour monitoring of activity and with more intimate glimpses of behavior than would be possible otherwise (Reinert et al., 1984). Other marking methods, including scale clipping, branding, tattooing, and attaching metal or plastic tags (Hirth, 1966) or stitching colored beads to the skin (Hudnall, 1982), have all been tried with varying degrees of success.

Radioactive tags, used successfully in several studies (e.g., Barbour et al., 1969), have the disadvantages that they may cause damage to or eventual death of the snake carrying them, that they are easily lost where they might constitute a hazard to other animals or humans, and that state or other regulations may restrict their use. Tantalum 182 and cobalt 40 have been the preferred sources of radiation among the many available radioactive substances. Cobalt 40 has more powerful gamma radiation but has a half-life of about 5 yr, whereas tantalum 182 has a half-life of approximately 6 mo. Radioactive tags are of greatest use in field studies on snakes too small to carry radiotransmitters.

Radiotelemetry has been used successfully on many species of snakes in various habitats (Fitch and Shirer, 1971; Parker and Brown, 1972; Henderson et al., 1976, 1980; Nickerson et al., 1978; Reinert, 1981; Reinert et al., 1984; Madsen, 1984). The larger the snake, the more readily it can be studied by radiotelemetry. The transmitter should be small enough not to burden the snake excessively and interfere with its normal behavior, but large enough to have a transmission range that will permit the operator to locate it consistently without undue effort. The attached battery must be large enough to provide power for several weeks so that the signal will not weaken or die unexpectedly and prematurely with resultant loss of snake and equipment at a critical stage of the investigation. The instrument is embedded in silicone rubber, which adds to its bulk but imparts a streamlined shape and insulates metal parts from the snake's body fluids. The transmitter package may be force-fed to the snake and carried in its stomach, or surgically inserted in the abdominal cavity through a small opening which is then closed by suture. Some species are inclined to disgorge the transmitter, but this may be remedied by fastening a heavy thread around the body just anterior to the transmitter's bulge, stitched through the free edge of a ventral plate, to hold it closely but not tightly against the body, preventing the transmitter from moving forward in the digestive tract. Such an object causes the snake to be less active than it would be on an empty stomach, and presumably its behavior is affected in proportion to the relative size of the transmitter and the snake.

Surgical implantation of a transmitter in the abdominal cavity involves anesthetizing the snake, opening and suturing its body wall, and squeezing in a foreign object, all ordeals which at best must cause considerable discomfort and must handicap the snake in its normal activities and alter its behavior. Healing is remarkably rapid, but depending on the life expectancy of the battery that powers the transmitter, replacement may require a repetition of the entire operation before healing is complete.

The quality of radiotransmitters and receivers has been much refined over the approximately two decades that these devices have been in use. Some commercial companies manufacture transmitters especially for use on snakes. Some field workers have learned to assemble their own instruments from the appropriate parts and have profited by greatly reducing the cost of these expensive items and by learning how to repair or replace them in the field when the necessity arises.

In open terrain such as prairie or desert, radiotelemetry allows individual snakes to be monitored quickly and effectively. With the aid of a vehicle, the investigator can cover a large area in a short time and locate the signal with minimal time and effort. Swamp or rain forest situations, however, prove less favorable. Scansorial snakes are difficult subjects because overhead signals are hard to pinpoint.

Scale Clipping

Among the multitude of marking methods, clipping ventrals or subcaudals is the oldest and perhaps the most effective (Blanchard and Finster, 1933; Fitch, 1949a, 1960a; Brown and Parker, 1976). If ventrals are marked, it is best to use those toward the rear of the series, numbering them by counting forward from the anal plate. Clipping the abdominal ventrals is probably more injurious than clipping the subcaudals. Because there are usually undersized scales, some mere granules, at the base of the subcaudal series just behind the anal plate, doubt might arise as to which scale is number 1 on each side. To resolve this problem, it is best to designate the number 1 on each side as the first scale that contacts its counterpart on the opposite side. With one scale clipped out on each side of the tail, a formula such as 2 left, 2 right, is derived, by which the individual can be recognized. To avoid confusion, the number 1 scale is never clipped.

Scales up to and including the twentieth subcaudal have been routinely clipped on each side, omitting the one at the base. Clipping beyond the twentieth is best avoided, because in short-tailed species the scales are small, in some species distal parts of the tail are liable to be lost, and counting a long series of scales is time-consuming and increases the chance of mistakes. In a common species, when all 361 left-to-right subcaudal combinations from 2 to 20 have been used, one can initiate a new series using the same combinations over again but adding to each formula a third scale identifying the series, for instance, ventral 2 left.

Conant (1948) reported that a scale-clipped rat snake regenerated its subcaudals so thoroughly that no trace of the marks remained. In all species of snakes that I have scale-clipped, regeneration occurred, and after periods of years marks became extremely faint. Persisting recognition marks may be subtle and may involve the texture of the regenerated scale's surface or its color, or the suture between it and an adjacent scale. Superficial examination of a recaptured snake has sometimes quickly revealed one or two of the scars remaining from clipped scales, but considerable further scrutiny under magnification was necessary to determine the complete formula.

Occasionally, equivocal readings of a scale formula were possible because the basal scales of the series barely contacted each other or were only slightly separated. To clarify such borderline cases, I have used formulas such as 3 left (ISB) and 5 right (NSB), indicating "including small basal" and "not small basal," respectively. Erroneous identification of an individual might be avoided by excising any small scales at the base of the subcaudal series that might cause confusion as to where the count should begin.

Natural Markings

Further assurance against mistaken identity in scale-clipped snakes is provided by recording individual variations in their natural markings. It might be possible to develop a system by which these natural variations alone would identify individuals (Carlstrom and Edelstam, 1946; Henley, 1981), but the system would be complicated, unwieldy, and much less efficient than one based on some system of serial numbering. In my studies, I have used pattern differences merely to supplement scale clipping in confirming the identity of individuals, relying on different pattern characteristics in each species of snake. Marks on the face, body, and ventral surface, especially minor departures from bilateral symmetry, provide a basis for individual recognition. For instance, in copperheads (*Agkistrodon contortrix*) I routinely recorded number and arrangement of complete and incomplete "hourglass" marks on the body, as illustrated by the following sample formula: 10 CM $+ 3\frac{1}{2} 4\frac{1}{2} 5\frac{1}{2}$ L, $8\frac{1}{2}$ R (= ten complete marks plus four half marks at numbers 3, 4 and 5 on the left side, and number 8 on the right side).

Tattooing, Tagging, Painting, and Branding

Tattooing was used successfully by Woodbury (1948) for individually marking rattlesnakes at a den and has been utilized by several later investigators. A battery-powered electric tattooing needle was used to print a large number on the snake's ventral surface. The resulting mark is large and easily read, although the system is more time-consuming than scale clipping and involves carrying burdensome equipment. There is also danger of injury to the snake if the needle penetrates too deeply and punctures the body cavity. Additionally, the method is effective only on snakes that have pale-colored venters; in darkly pigmented areas the numbers do not show up well and may, with time, become obscure. Especially in snakes marked as juveniles and recaptured after much growth, the ink spreads and blurs the number.

Colored plastic plugs (Pough, 1970), or the serially numbered metal tags used on small fish, are potentially useful for marking snakes. However, the slender, streamlined body form of the snake offers no really satisfactory site for attachment where the tag will not be liable to impede movements or be subject to excessive wear. Skin pinched by an attached tag will undergo necrosis and sloughing, with early loss of the tag. Possible sites of attachment are the free edges of anterior ventrals or of the anal plate or even the lower jaw (Hirth, 1966). The tag could be stitched to the skin by a small loop of heavy thread or fine wire, specially treated to avoid irritation or infection. In rattlesnakes the rattle provides a convenient anchor for attaching a tag with a wire or nylon thread through the proximal rattle. Colored disks in various combinations, or with numbers imprinted, identify individual snakes (Pendlebury, 1972; Stark, 1984; Brown et al., 1984).

Painting is a temporary method of marking snakes to make them easily recognizable even without recapture. However, the paint is lost with the shed exuvia. Nevertheless, the method has useful applications, as in the group markings of snakes, to obtain capture-recapture ratios that will serve for a Petersen index census. Such an operation needs to be completed shortly before ecdysis occurs in an appreciable number of the study animals. In population studies based on scale clipping or other permanent marking systems, painting provides the best method for investigating the timing of ecdysis. Recaptured marked individuals found to lack paint are known to have undergone ecdysis since their last capture. With the accumulation of many such records, the frequency of ecdysis is revealed, especially if there are many short-term recaptures. Paint can mark individual snakes for field observation, but most species of snakes are too secretive for individuals to be kept under long-term or regular observation. Paint markings that render snakes more conspicuous may increase their vulnerability to visually oriented predators, resulting in damage to the population overall and distortion of capture-recapture ratios.

Clark and Gillingham (1984), working with *Anolis,* devised a method of finding lizards at night by gluing micropipets containing a phospholuminescent liquid ("cyalume lightstick") to the dorsal surface. The method might equally well be adapted to snakes.

Weary (1969) branded snakes with a serial number on the ventral surface, using a 50-W pyrographic needle and a 110-V power source. Freeze-branding (Lewke and Stroud, 1974) is done with a copper bar dipped into a slurry of dry ice and 95% alcohol, or into Freon 12 or 22. Chromatophores are destroyed by quick-freezing the skin surface, and the brand appears as a white area.

MEASURING

Measurements provide some of the most valuable data obtained in field studies on snakes. Of many possible measurements that can be taken, snout-vent length (SVL) is the most important and also one of the most difficult to obtain. The body of a live snake is highly elastic and can stretch or contract to yield measurements over a wide range of values. Ideally, the measurement should be identical to that obtained for the same snake freshly killed or anesthetized and fully relaxed. Live measurements of SVL usually exceed by several percent measurements of the same animal after it has hardened in preservative as a museum specimen. The live animal resists stretching to full length and contracts its muscles to create a series of small lateral flexures of the spinal column, resulting in a several-percent reduction in its length, often with much different readings on successive trials. Constrictors, including boids, and colubrids such as *Pituophis, Elaphe,* and *Lampropeltis,* are especially hard to measure accurately.

One remedy is to force the snake to relax, momentarily at least, by tiring it. The front and hind ends are held in the operator's left and right hands, respectively, and pulled in opposite directions with gentle pressure, depending on the size of the snake, until it is stretched to full length with the head held against a meter stick or tape. While checking trap lines I carry a fiberglass tape dangling from my belt and, to measure a snake, pull the tape taut, holding the snake's head with the tip of the rostral at the zero mark, and take a reading at the posterior edge of the anal plate.

Handling is deleterious to a snake in many ways and should be kept to a minimum consistent with obtaining desired data. Stretching the snake to its full length for a measurement of SVL may damage delicate muscles. I found evidence that first-year *Crotalus viridis* were stunted and set back several weeks in their growth as a result of handling at the time of marking (Fitch, 1949a). Some workers have attempted to obtain length measurements without directly handling the snake, by maneuvering it into a clear plastic tube of adjustable diameter or by causing it to stretch out beside some object and marking the points opposite its ends for the measurement of SVL (W. H. Martin III, Personal communication). Other investigators have preferred to anesthetize snakes before handling and measuring. With total relaxation attained in this way, the measurements can be accurate and uniform, and the trauma of struggling and stretching is avoided. However, this method is relatively time-consuming and may cause mortality if the dosage is too large. It may also have harmful effects that are not yet evident. The snake must be protected from predation and exposure to harmful extremes of temperatures until the anesthetic wears off, and normal activities are interrupted even if there is no lasting effect.

Tail length, head length, head width, eye diameter, and maximum body circumference are all important measurements that may be taken on a live snake. Length of tail is measured from the posterior edge of the anal plate to the tip of the caudal spine. It is of course important to note whether the tail is complete. The tail should always be measured separately, and SVL is much preferred over total length. The latter measurement is misleading for comparisons, because some individuals have the terminal part of the tail missing and because the ratio of tail length to the total length differs according to age and sex (Fitch, 1960a).

SEX AND BREEDING CONDITION

A snake's sex is important to an investigator whether he or she is involved in a taxonomic investigation utilizing preserved specimens or is making a demographic study. Relative tail length is greater in males than in females (Klauber, 1943; Parker and Plummer, this volume). It should be noted that the ratio of tail to SVL is higher in preserved specimens than in their live counterparts. There is shrinkage in preservative, but the body shrinks more than the tail. After handling a large number of individuals, the investigator learns to recognize sex in adults easily without any special test, but immatures rarely show any external differences.

In live snakes, sex can be determined by inserting a blunt probe into the tail (Blanchard and Finster, 1933; Schaefer, 1934). In females, the probe cannot be inserted without encountering resistance. Biological supply houses provide metal tail probes of different sizes for sexing snakes; however, other conveniently available materials may serve just as well. In the field I use a grass stem pulled from a growing plant and having a soft, pliable tip that cannot pierce or lacerate delicate tissues. An ordinary pin with the point filed down and rounded makes a convenient probe for small to medium-sized snakes. Fine-gauge wire bent into a narrow loop also makes a good probe.

Relative length of the hemipenis is a specific trait, with important differences between species. The probe can be inserted for a distance of perhaps one-fourth the tail length before it encounters resistance against the end of the invaginated hemipenis. To insert the probe, the handler should rotate the tail base slightly and push aside the projecting edge of the anal plate covering the vent. A sharp probe could pierce the delicate wall of the cloaca in the female and could slide between muscle layers in the tail, injuring the snake and leading to an incorrect diagnosis as a male. In some newborn snakes such as copperheads, the tissues are extremely soft, and a probe can be inserted into the tail of a female with virtually no resistance. Gentle pressure on one side of the tail base may cause the hemipenis to evert or at least to show its base, permitting diagnosis as a male.

As snakes mature, various secondary sexual traits appear that facilitate recognition of sex—in males of some genera, knobbed keels on scales above the vent, and/or sensory pits on the chin (Blanchard, 1931). The vaginal portion of the female cloaca has greatly thickened walls that can be detected by palpation as a rubbery lump at the posterior end of the body in species having the male hemipenis heavily armored with spines (Fitch 1960b).

Sexual maturity in male snakes can be determined by the presence of motile sperm. Samples of sperm may be collected by pipeting a few drops of physiological saline (Ringer's solution) into the cloaca, gently massaging the rear of the abdomen, and then withdrawing the solution, which will have abundant motile sperm in a breeding male. Before attempting to collect a sample, it is best to clear the cloaca of feces and uric acid by massaging toward the vent. Female snakes also may be tested for cloacal sperm as an indication of recent copulation. Samples are examined with a dissecting microscope using a 60× magnification to detect motile sperm.

Gravid females can be recognized by their swollen abdomens, with the swelling mostly behind the mid-body, in contrast to the more anterior swelling caused by a food object in the stomach. Counts of unlaid eggs can be made by palpation. The rear end of the snake's body is held in the left hand, belly up; the right thumb, lightly pressing against the belly and moving slowly forward, can detect the eggs as they slide past. Eggs that are fully shelled and ready to be laid are most easily detected and counted. Both oviductal eggs that are not yet shelled and ovarian follicles can be counted by palpation, but less easily than shelled eggs. Lumps in the posterior part of the abdomen, consisting of loops of the intestine engorged with food residues, are of more solid consistency than ova and can be readily distinguished with a little experience. Undersized or atretic follicles also can be distinguished from others by palpation. In snakes that produce small clutches of eggs, the unlaid eggs are linearly arranged in the body cavity and sometimes can be counted by superficial inspection, even without palpation. In viviparous species that have large litters, it is difficult to obtain by palpation an accurate count of the many embryos crowded into the rear of the abdomen. In these snakes an embryo and its attached yolk may be felt through the body wall as two adjacent but separate lumps.

Even gentle palpation may be harmful to embryos. In females of *Thamnophis sirtalis* subjected to frequent palpation, the number of embryos has been noted to undergo some reduction (Fitch, 1965). Therefore palpation should be avoided if the essential data can be obtained in other ways. As an alternative, females captured near parturition or oviposition may be kept in confinement (always in separate containers) until their eggs are laid or their litters born. The hatchlings or neonates obtained from them reveal the number in the brood and possibly other important data. These young, individually marked and released at the place of the female's capture, can contribute to a population study. Especially, they provide an opportunity to trace individual careers from the outset, revealing patterns of growth, dispersal, and longevity.

CENSUSING

Because of their secretive and cryptic habits, snakes are unusually difficult subjects for field studies, and attempts at censusing them have usually been unsatisfactory. Rapid censusing using such techniques as counts from aerial photographs may be highly effective for some birds and mammals but are out of the question for snakes, and data must be accumulated from hard-won individual records. Usually it is not possible to find and count every snake in an area, and therefore it is necessary to project from capture-recapture ratios and estimate total numbers and population density from a Petersen index or one of its derivatives. However, when several sets of figures have become available for the same area at different times, they have often shown such drastic discrepancies that some workers have considered the basic method invalid (Turner, 1977).

Figures are influenced by the fact that within a species the amount and type of activity changes rapidly and progressively throughout the season (Gibbons and Semlitsch, this volume). Thus snakes are at much greater risk of capture at certain stages of the season, and ratios are distorted as a result. Adult males, breeding females, non-breeding females, and immatures may be so different from each other in their behavior and seasonal responses that further distortion occurs unless the figures for each age and sex group are dealt with separately. In most population studies on snakes, adequate sampling is time-consuming, and during the weeks or months required, immigration, emigration, reproduction, or mortality introduces bias.

Some of the best snake censuses are based on mass captures of animals concentrated at denning areas, especially when studies have been extended to times of year when the population is dispersed away from the dens, so that the size of the area served by the den can be determined (Parker and Brown, 1972; W. H. Martin, III, Personal communication).

FEEDING

From time to time snakes are found in the act of capturing or swallowing prey, and such fortuitous incidents may provide unusual insights into their trophic relationships or hunting strategy. A minority of snakes captured have undigested prey in the stomach, usually showing as a distinct bulge at somewhat less than half the distance from snout to vent. A record of the food may be one of the most valuable items of information yielded by the specimen. Therefore specimens collected for preservation should be killed promptly, before there is time for them to digest food recently eaten.

In field studies involving capture and release of snakes, each one handled should be checked by palpation for food in the stomach. If food is detected, it may be squeezed up to the mouth and identified. To obtain a sample from a medium-sized or large snake, I hold down the tail end with my foot, pull the body out straight, belly up, by gripping the anterior end with my left hand, and then with gentle pressure of the right thumb, push the ingested object forward through the stomach and gullet. When the object has reached the throat, the snake usually opens its mouth voluntarily and identification can be made at a glance. The food can then either be pushed back down to the stomach or removed to be measured, weighed, examined or its identity verified. When the needed information has been obtained, the remains can be force-fed back to the snake; foot-long metal forceps are useful for this purpose, especially when dealing with venomous snakes. Some snakes cooperate with seeming enthusiasm in reingesting a meal, whereas others tend to reject and disgorge the prey after interruption of their normal digestion. An ingested food item usually slides forward or backward easily under gentle pressure, but some cannot be removed easily. The sharp-edged projecting incisors of rodents or scales or spines of fish could cause injury by scraping or tearing the stomach wall if carelessly palpated, especially if the animal eaten is relatively large and distends the stomach. In such cases it may be better to leave the prey unidentified than to risk injury to the snake by forcing up an item that resists palpation.

When food habits are being investigated, a reference collection of local animals that are potential prey should be assembled and identified as a basis for comparison of food items or residues removed from the digestive tracts of snakes. Passing through the digestive tract, prey remains are retained considerably longer in the hindgut than in the stomach, so the incidence of snakes having fecal material is relatively high. The feces or "scats" are useful in providing residues of food items than can be identified. Snakes often void feces in struggling with a captor. After obtaining a neck grip on a captured snake with my left hand, I grasp its posterior portion with my right hand and gently massage the abdomen in the direction of the vent, squeezing onto a paper towel the fecal matter that the snake would otherwise smear over me. Essential information written on the outside of the towel in which the scat is wrapped should include the species of snake, identification formula, sex, length (SVL), and date. Identifications are made from undigested residues consisting mostly of keratinous and chitinous parts, including hair, feathers, scales, and fragments of arthropod exoskeletons, but some types of prey, notably amphibians and earthworms, may be digested without much residue to show that they have been eaten. The setae of earthworms resist digestion but are so minute that they can be detected only under magnification. Although keratinous residues such as mammal hair may permit identification, they do not reveal the number of individual prey animals. Obviously, stomach contents provide better quantitative data than scats. Residues from the digestive tract of the prey more resistant to digestion than the prey itself may contain puzzling objects. For instance, ants or small beetles in the scat of a large snake are certainly not primary food items, but instead must have come from the digestive tract of a frog or toad or other insectivorous animal that was otherwise fully digested.

HANDLING VENOMOUS SNAKES

Painful and lingering death, permanent crippling, or at best a highly traumatic experience may result from a single mistake or a momentary lapse of caution when handling a venomous snake. Therefore these snakes should never be handled without good reason, handling should be kept to a minimum, and every possible safeguard should be observed. Metal tongs 39 cm long are useful for handling venomous snakes both in the field and in the laboratory. I have relied on them regularly in removing copperheads from funnel traps and also have used them to remove snakes from cages when it is necessary to hold them firmly for such purposes as marking or force-feeding.

To handle a venomous snake I use my left hand, leaving the right hand free for writing, scale clipping, or other activities. When the snake's head has been immobilized by grasping it with tongs or holding it down with a stick, I slip my forefinger under its neck and grasp it firmly just behind the head. Its throat rests against the middle of my forefinger, with my thumb resting on its nape and holding it down in the U-shaped bend of the finger. The fourth and fifth fingers are free for other manipulations, for instance, holding the tail immobilized against the heel of my hand with the subcaudal scales exposed, to be scrutinized for previous marks or clipped. (See Figures 5–2 through 5–4 for illustrations of proper and improper handling techniques.) Although a rattlesnake or copperhead may be held securely by grasping it around the neck, I am told that this technique cannot be used safely on certain Old World snakes with relatively long fangs and muscular necks. Extreme caution should be used in handling *Azemiops,* *Causus,* and *Atractaspis.*

At the instant of release a venomous snake may strike faster than the handler can withdraw his or her hand. To bag a snake, I observe the following stages: (1) The snake is firmly held while being lowered into the bag. (2) The snake and bag are lowered to a flat surface on the ground or onto a table top. (3) The snake's head is held down against the substrate with a stick, and operator's hand is quickly withdrawn. (4) The stick is raised, releasing the snake's head, and the snake, jerking away from its restraint, snaps back inside the bag. (5) A straight stick is laid across neck of the bag, with operator's foot resting on it. (6) With the stick and the foot still in place, restricting snake to lower part of bag, the operator grasps the bag's upper edge and pulls through enough slack to tie a knot in the upper part or to tie a cord around it.

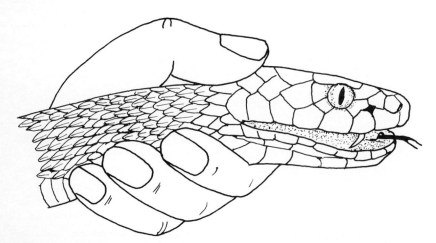

Figure 5–2. Correct handling of a venomous snake: A firm grip just behind the head, with throat in bend of handler's forefinger and thumb on snake's nape.

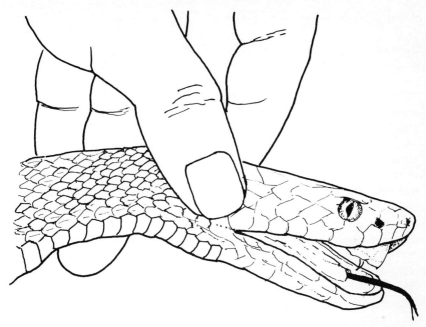

Figure 5–3. Incorrect handling of a venomous snake: Grip insecure, between tips of first two fingers and thumb; the snake may break free with sudden violent thrashing.

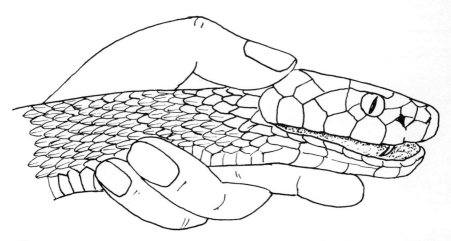

Figure 5–4. Incorrect handling of a venomous snake: Forefinger, extending too far forward beneath chin, may be pierced as the snake bites through its own lower jaw.

RESTRAINT AND ANESTHESIA

To minimize the risk in handling venomous snakes, or to measure snakes or perform surgery, various types of restraint and anesthesia have been employed. Almandarz (1978) has reviewed the subject of restraint of reptiles. Methods that have been used on snakes include taping the body to a wooden dowel for measurement (McDonald, 1964) and holding the snake down on a board with a series of transverse Velcro strips (Ward and Harrell, 1978). Various devices used on venomous snakes enclose and confine the head so that the handler is protected against bites. King and Duvall (1984) used a noose stick partly enclosed in a plastic cylinder into which the snake's head could be drawn and held. Gillingham et al. (1983) used a plastic bucket with a notch in the upper edge, and the snake's front portion was placed in the bucket, confined by the lid, while the posterior part protruded through the notch. Freed and Freed (1983) also used a plastic bucket, but with the hole to receive the snake's forebody in the center of the lid and adjustable for size. The lid was held in place with bulldog clamps. Anesthetics that have been used on snakes include ether (Brazenor and Kaye, 1953), Fluothane, a volatile liquid claimed to be five times more powerful than ether (Hackenbrock and Finster, 1963), Nembutal and Surital (Betz, 1962), Pentothal Sodium and tricaine methanesulfonate (Karlstrom and Cook, 1955), and Brevital Sodium (Wang et al., 1977). Most of these substances have disadvantages in being somewhat unpredictable in causing occasional mortality or in requiring a long recovery time. Hudnall (1982) anesthetized snakes by immersing them in ice water and chilling them to 5°C.

ENCLOSURES

Outdoor enclosures of various types can facilitate observations on snakes by restricting them to relatively small areas where they can be readily found and yet are not subjected to the highly unnatural surroundings prevailing in the laboratory. A fenced area may enclose natural habitats or hibernacula, and a count of the population enclosed may provide the best available information concerning population density (Woodbury, 1951; Gibbons and Semlitsch, 1982). Details of behavior, including interactions with conspecifics and with various other types of animals such as predators, prey, or competitors, may be observed by staging confrontations, with the expectation that reactions will be more representative than those obtained from closely confined animals in the laboratory. Individual responses to changes in weather and season may be monitored, and artificial hibernacula may be installed, monitored, and instrumented.

SUMMARY

Field studies on snakes are greatly needed, and opportunities to contribute to the knowledge of snake ecology are outstanding. Concentrations of snakes, such as those occurring at hibernation dens, facilitate study. Other wildlife, as well as trained dogs, can aid investigators in finding snakes. Road sampling is an effective field technique in some areas. Live traps with funnel entrances may utilize either natural or artificial barriers, and pitfall traps are sometimes effective in catching small snakes. Well-placed artificial shelters may also attract snakes. Individual identities of free-living snakes are recognized by equipping them with radioactive tags or small radiotransmitters, clipping scales such as subcaudals, recording details of natural markings or scars, or tagging, tattooing, painting, or branding (including freeze-branding). Snout-vent length, the most important of the various measurements, can be determined by stretching the snake until its muscles tire, or by anesthetizing it. Sex can be determined by probing into the tail or pressing on its base to reveal a hemipenis; eggs or embryos can be counted by palpation in gravid females. Food habits can be studied by palpating prey remains from the stomach or feces from the vent for identification. Censusing snakes usually involves individual marking or group marking and obtaining capture-recapture ratios for a discrete population. Various ingenious devices have been used to handle and process snakes, decreasing the stress and danger for both the animals and the operator. Anesthetics used include ether, Fluothane, Nembutal, Pentothal Sodium, tricaine methanesulfonate, Brevital Sodium, or immersion in ice water. Handling venomous snakes should be avoided as much as possible, but when they are handled, grasping the head with tongs, holding the snake firmly around the neck just behind the head, and restraining the head before withdrawing one's hand are desirable safety measures.

LITERATURE CITED

Almandarz, E. 1978. Physical restraint of reptiles, in: Zoo and Wild Animal Medicine (M. E. Fowler, ed.) W. B. Saunders, Philadelphia.

Barbour, R. W., Harvey, M. J., and Hardin, J. W. 1969. Home ranges, movements and activity of the eastern worm snake, *Carphophis amoenus amoenus, Ecology* 50:470–476.

Betz, T. W. 1962. Surgical anesthesia in reptiles, with special reference to the water snake, *Natrix rhombifera, Copeia* 1962:284–287.

Blanchard, F. N. 1931. Secondary sex characters of certain snakes, *Bull. Antivenin Inst. Am.* 4:95–104.

Blanchard, F. N. and Finster E. B. 1933. A method of marking living snakes for future recognition, with a discussion of some problems and results, *Ecology* 14:334–347.

162   FITCH

Brazenor, C. W. and Kaye, G. 1953. Anesthesia for reptiles, *Copeia* 1953:165–170.

Brown, W. S. and Parker, W. S. 1976. A ventral scale clipping system for permanently marking snakes (Reptilia, Serpentes), *J. Herpetol.* 10:247–249.

Brown, W. S., Gannon, V. P. J., and Secoy, D. M. 1984. Paint marking the rattle of rattlesnakes, *Herpetol. Rev.* 15:75–76.

Carlstrom, D. and Edelstam, C. 1946. Methods of marking reptiles for identification after recapture, *Nature* 158:748–749.

Clark, D. L. and Gillingham, J. C. 1984. A method for nocturnally locating lizards, *Herpetol. Rev.* 15:24–25.

Clark, D. R., Jr. 1966. A funnel trap for small snakes, *Trans. Kans. Acad. Sci.* 69:91–95.

Conant, R. 1948. Regeneration of clipped subcaudal scales in a pilot black snake, *Nat. Hist. Misc.* 13:1–2.

Dargan, L. M. and Stickel, W. H. 1940. An experiment with snake trapping, *Copeia* 1940:264–268.

Ferner, J. W. 1979. A review of marking techniques for amphibians and reptiles, *SSAR Herp. Circular* 9:1–41.

Fitch, H. S. 1949a. Study of snake populations in central California, *Am. Midl. Nat.* 41:513–570.

Fitch, H. S. 1949b. Road counts of snakes in western Louisiana, *Herpetologica* 5:87–90.

Fitch, H. S. 1951. A simplified type of funnel trap for reptiles, *Herpetologica* 7:77–80.

Fitch, H. S. 1960a. Autecology of the copperhead, *Univ. Kans. Publ. Mus. Nat. Hist.* 13:85–288.

Fitch, H. S. 1960b. Criteria for determining sex and breeding condition in snakes, *Herpetologica* 16:49–51.

Fitch, H. S. 1965. An ecological study of the garter snake, *Thamnophis sirtalis,* *Univ. Kans. Publ. Mus. Nat. Hist.* 15:493–564.

Fitch, H. S. and Shirer, H. W. 1971. A radiotelemetric study of spatial relationships in some common snakes, *Copeia* 1971:118–128.

Freed, P. S. and Freed, M. G. 1983. An additional restraint technique for venomous snakes, *Herpetol. Rev.* 14:114.

Gibbons, J. W. and Semlitsch, R. D. 1982. Terrestrial drift fences with pitfall traps: An effective technique for quantitative sampling of animal populations, *Brimleyana* 7:1–16.

Gibbons, J. W., Coker, J. W., and Murphy, T. M., Jr. 1977. Selected aspects of the life history of the rainbow snake (*Farancia erytrogramma*), *Herpetologica* 33:276–281.

Gillingham, J. C., Clark, D. L., and Ten Eyck, G. R. 1983. Venomous snake immobilization: A new technique, *Herpetol. Rev.* 14:40.

Gloyd, H. K. 1945. The problem of too many snakes, *Chic. Nat.* 7:87–97.

Hackenbrock, C. R. and Finster, M. 1963. Fluothane: A rapid and safe inhalation anesthetic for poisonous snakes, *Copeia* 1963:440–441.

Hawken, J. L. 1951. Water system acts as reptile and amphibian trap, *Herpetologica* 7:81–83.

Henderson, R. W., Nickerson, M. A., and Ketcham, S. 1976. Short term movements of the snakes *Chironius carinatus, Helicops angulatus* and *Bothrops atrox* in Amazonian Peru, *Herpetologica* 32:304–310.

Henderson, R. W., Binder, M. H., Sajdak, R. A., and Buday, J. A. 1980. Aggregating behavior and exploitation of subterranean habitat by gravid eastern milksnakes (*Lampropeltis t. triangulum*), *Milw. Public Mus. Contrib. Biol. Geol.* 32:1–9.

Henley, G. P. 1981. A new technique for recognition of snakes, *Herpetol. Rev.* 12:56.

Hirth, H. G. 1966. Weight changes and mortality in three species of snakes during hibernation, *Herpetologica* 22:8–12.

Hudnall, J. A. 1982. New methods for measuring and tagging snakes, *Herpetol. Rev.* 13:97–98.

Imler, R. H. 1945. Bullsnakes and their control on a Nebraska wildlife refuge, *J. Wildl. Manage.* 9:265–273.

Jackley, A. M. 1943. New snake trap and some of its strange catches, *SD. Conserv. Digest* 10:1–7.

Jackley, A. M. 1947. How to locate and trap dens of rattlesnakes, *Mont. Farmer* 34:1, 3–5.

Karlstrom, E. I. and Cook, S. F. 1955. Notes on anesthesia, *Copeia* 1955:57–58.

King, M. B. and Duvall, D. 1984. Noose tube: A lightweight, sturdy, and portable snake restraining apparatus for field and laboratory use, *Herpetol. Rev.* 15:109.

Klauber, L. M. 1939. Studies of reptile life in the arid southwest. I. Night collecting on the desert with ecological statistics, *Bull. Zool. Soc. San Diego* 14:1–100.

Klauber, L. M. 1943. Tail-length differences in snakes with notes on sexual dimorphism and the coefficient of divergence, *Bull. Zool. Soc. San Diego* 18:1–60.

Klauber, L. M. 1956. Rattlesnakes: Their Habits, Life Histories and Influence on Mankind, 2 vols., University of California Press, Berkeley.

Lewke, R. E. and Stroud, R. K. 1974. Freeze-branding as a method of marking snakes. *Copeia* 1974:997–1000.

Lohoefener, R. and Wolfe, J. 1984. A "new" live trap and comparison with a pit-fall trap, *Herpetol. Rev.* 15:25–26.

McDonald, H. S. 1964. Restraining snakes for experimental procedures, *Copeia* 1964:224–225.

Madsen, T. 1984. Movements, home range size and habitat use of radio-tracked grass snakes (*Natrix natrix*) in southern Sweden, *Copeia* 1984:707–713.

Nickerson, M. A., Sajdak, R. A., Henderson, R. W., and Ketchem, S. 1978. Notes on the movements of some neotropical snakes, *J. Herpetol.* 12:419–422.

Parker, W. S. and Brown, W. S. 1972. Telemetric study of movements and oviposition of two female *Masticophis t. taeniatus, Copeia* 1972:892–895.

Pendlebury, G. B. 1972. Tagging and remote identification of rattlesnakes, *Herpetologica* 28:349–350.

Pendleton, R. C. 1956. Uses of marking animals with radioisotopes, *Ecology* 37:686–689.

Pough, F. H. 1970. A quick method for permanently marking snakes and turtles, *Herpetologica* 26:428–430.

Reinert, H. K. 1981. Reproduction by the massasauga (*Sistrurus catenatus catenatus*), *Am. Midl. Nat.* 105:393–395.

Reinert, H. K., Cundall, D., and Bushar, L. H. 1984. Foraging behavior of the timber rattlesnake, *Crotalus horridus, Copeia* 1984:976–981.

Reynolds, R. P. and Scott, N. J., Jr. 1982. Use of a mammalian resource by a Chihuahuan snake community, in: Herpetological Communities (N. J. Scott, Jr., ed.) *U.S. Fish Wildl. Serv. Wildl. Res. Rep.* 13:99–118.

Schaefer, W. H. 1934. Diagnosis of sex in snakes, *Copeia* 1934:181.

Seigel, R. A. 1986. Ecology and conservation of an endangered rattlesnake (*Sistrurus catenatus*) in Missouri, U.S.A., *Biol. Conserv.* 35:333–346.

Semlitsch, R. D. and Moran, G. B. 1984. Ecology of the redbelly snake (*Storeria occipitomaculata*) using mesic habitats in South Carolina, *Am. Midl. Nat.* 111:33–40.

Smith, H. M. 1946. Snake detection, *Chic. Nat.* 9:63–67.

Spellerberg, I. P. and Prestt, I. 1978. Marking snakes, in: Animal Marking (B. Stonehouse, ed.) pp. 133–141, University Park Press, Baltimore, Maryland.

Stark, M. A. 1984. A quick, easy and permanent tagging technique for rattlesnakes, *Herpetol. Rev.* 15:110.

Swingland, I. R., 1978. Marking reptiles, in: Animal Marking (B. Stonehouse, ed.) pp. 119–132, University Park Press, Baltimore, Maryland.

Turner, F. B. 1977. The dynamics of populations of squamates, crocodilians and rhynchocephalians, in: Biology of the Reptilia, vol. 7 (C. Gans and D. W. Tinkle, eds.) pp. 157–264, Academic Press, New York.

Wang, R., Kubie, J. L., and Halpern, M. 1977. Brevital sodium: An effective anesthetic agent for performing surgery on small reptiles, *Copeia* 1977:738–743.

Ward, R. and Harrell, E. H. 1978. A restraining apparatus for unanesthetized snakes, *Herpetol. Rev.* 9:139–140.

Weary, G. C. 1969. An improved method of marking snakes, *Copeia* 1969:854–855.

Woodbury, A. M. 1948. Marking reptiles with an electric tattooing outfit, *Copeia* 1948:127–128.

Woodbury, A. M. 1951. A snake den in Tooele County, Utah: Introduction— A ten-year study, *Herpetologica* 7:1–14.

CHAPTER SIX

Captive Maintenance

James B. Murphy and Jonathan A. Campbell

The purpose of this chapter is to summarize reports that deal with various aspects of captive snake maintenance, especially environmental parameters, reproductive biology, and techniques. Any successful program for maintaining a colony of snakes is largely dependent on enticing them to feed, and we have devoted a disproportionate amount of space to this topic.

QUARANTINE AND MEDICAL CARE

Newly acquired captive snakes should be held in isolated quarters for a minimum of 30 days, and each group of snakes destined for quarantine should be isolated from one another. Quarantine facilities should be separate from the established collection, and sterilization procedures should be scrupulously followed using a disinfectant such as Roccal (Winthrop) or Nolvasan (Fort Dodge). Each snake should be maintained separately within quarantine facilities. Cross-contamination between cages should be avoided and, as a general procedure, diseased snakes should be serviced after healthy ones. Before a snake is introduced into an established collection, two negative fecal examinations are mandatory. As an added precaution, it is desirable that blood samples be taken for hematological values, blood chemistries, and routine analyses for etiological agents such as viruses and hemoparasites. Records should be maintained for each specimen on frequency of feeding, ecdysis, diagnoses, and treatments; these records provide the basis for individual case histories, often alert keepers that a specimen is sick or being maintained improperly, and may permit a more rapid diagnosis of possible problems. If available, records of collecting locality, date of collection, and ecological information should be maintained. These data often provide insight into the maintenance of individual snakes, are of value in comparing captive behavior with that of natural populations, and should be associated with a specimen, along with date of death, if it is ultimately deposited in a museum collection.

Epizootics of viral disease (e.g., paramyxovirus) are particularly catastrophic to snakes. If a viral infection is suspected, disinfection of contaminated enclosures with 2% Formalin, 3% sodium hypochlorite, or quaternary ammonium compounds is warranted. Division of the collection into several compartments is also recommended (Jacobson et al., 1980, 1981).

It is beyond the scope of this chapter to discuss diseases and treatments extensively; we recommend Reichenbach-Klinke and Elkan (1965), Murphy and Collins (1980), Frye (1981), Cooper and Jackson (1981), Marcus (1981), Wallach and Boever (1983), Hoff et al. (1984), and Ross and Marzec (1984).

THERMOREGULATION

Reports dealing with the thermoregulatory behavior of captive reptiles are mainly fragmentary and anecdotal in nature and are usually based on observations that may have led to reproductive success. These observations often represent the only information available, but few are based on controlled experimentation. There are comparatively few studies on thermoregulatory behavior of free-living snakes, but good general references include Cloudsley-Thompson (1971), Crews and Garrick, in Murphy and Collins (1980), Regal, in Murphy and Collins (1980), Huey (1982), Avery (1985), and Lillywhite (this volume).

Avery (1982) listed species in which activity temperatures (derived in part from radiotelemetry or laboratory observations) have been studied. Snakes are imprecise thermoregulators that employ a range of ectothermal capabilities from thermal passivity to diurnal basking (Avery, 1982); they may be active at a wide range of temperatures. Basking postures are relatively rare. Little is known about diel activity (versus inactivity), response to seasonal climate variation, social effects of circadian rhythms, regional differences in body temperature, or the requirements of various taxa that inhabit different ecological niches (Cloudsley-Thompson, 1971; Regal, in Murphy and Collins 1980; Avery, 1982, 1985).

To devise a system of thermal preferenda for captive snakes, an initial consultation with colleagues who have had field experience with the taxon in question is valuable. Literature records of the body temperatures of active snakes, such as those provided by Brattstrom (1965), give approximate ranges which can be incorporated into the thermal regimen. Always keep in mind the geographical origin of a snake and consult appropriate references to determine its native climate. Thermal gradients provide a means by which a snake's response to thermal variation may be monitored. A "hot spot," created either by use of small infrared spotlights or heat tapes, should be provided; the temperature should be high enough that the snake does not remain coiled for extended periods on the heated area. Hot spots are particularly important for gravid females. The incidence of anomalous neonates among various snake species has decreased when this regimen was initiated. (J. B. Murphy and J. A. Campbell, Personal observations). It is more difficult to determine an acceptable low-temperature point within a gradient, and we lack a ready solution for this dilemma. Firth and Turner (1982) and Huey (1982) discussed voluntary hypothermia and periodic inactivity, which might be essential for the health of captive snakes. Historically, numerous snakes have been maintained adequately (in some cases, impressive longevities have been reached) at a temperature range varying between 26 and 30°C. More recently, some boids, colubrids, and viperids have been subjected to cooling periods (22 to 24°C) before the breeding season.

Spatial complexity in the placement of cage props as outlined by Avery (1982, 1985) appears to be important for snakes. A series of ascending horizontal branches allows arboreal snakes to seek suitable sites for thermoregulation when a light is provided above the unit. Terrestrial forms, in our experience, seem to choose heated substrate areas to facilitate digestion (Regal, 1966; Marcellini and Peters, 1982).

SHEDDING

Shedding may not proceed normally when the relative humidity is less than 50%. When snakes have difficulty shedding, they should be soaked in shallow water for up to 24 h, and if shedding still does not occur, the specimen should be placed in an enclosure with a water drip system. Manual removal of the skin may be in order if the snake is still unable to shed (Frye, 1981). Before shedding, we have observed some snakes (such as *Ophiophagus*) expanding their trunks, apparently in an effort to facilitate this process. During shedding, the snake will position itself against objects to stabilize its body and attach skin to irregularities on the surface of these objects. Often a snake takes advantage of the greater radius presented by the outside curve of a loop of its body to stretch the skin. Also, the snake expands the trunk in the immediate vicinity where the sloughed skin is separating from the body. Additional information on the shedding cycle can be obtained from Maderson (1965) and Jacobson (1977).

WATER

An adult female *Bothrops asper,* observed for a few weeks in Costa Rica, on several occasions drank from beads of rainwater that formed on her body (Greene, 1986). Such observations suggest that integumentary water-holding properties may be important for some tropical snakes. We have observed arboreal and terrestrial vipers that can rarely locate a water container and often react defensively when sprayed with a fine mist of water. For these snakes a water drip system should be employed. Some species that defecate infrequently (e.g., *Cor-*

allus canina, Trimeresurus wagleri, and *Bitis nasicornis*) will do so when placed in a water drip system. Many species, however, will drink water offered in a container, but it should be changed frequently because snakes often ignore stale water.

LIGHT

At the Dallas Zoo, artificial light durations are altered to correspond to the natural photoperiod visible through skylights. However, there is a paucity of information available on the importance of photoperiod and light quality for captive reptiles (Regal, in Murphy and Collins 1980; Crews and Garrick, in Murphy and Collins 1980). The exploitation of light by captive snakes is discussed by Cloudsley-Thompson (1971), Gehrmann (1971), and Firth and Turner (1982).

Cooper, in Hoff et al. (1984), stated that there appear to be few definitive experimental studies demonstrating importance of artificial ultraviolet light. Current dogma suggests that many lizards require ultraviolet light, but snakes may not. Surprisingly, there has been little experimentation done on snakes with the use of black-light fluorescent tubes as outlined by Townsend and Cole (1985), but fruitful results might accrue if this were done.

FEEDING

During the past several decades our knowledge of the predatory behavior of snakes has increased immeasurably. This knowledge has direct application to the maintenance of snakes and forms the basis of the following account.

In order to successfully maintain a laboratory colony of snakes, it is particularly important to understand the relationship of the predator's senses to its feeding behavior and to submit prey items accordingly. If a snake refuses to feed, it is important to observe the entire attempted feeding sequence to determine at what point (pre-strike, strike, or post-strike phase) a breakdown occurs. A useful classification of feeding mechanisms, based on the role of sense organs, was described by Cock Buning (1983). His five types of hunting behavior (the *Crotalus* type, the viper type, the python type, the *Elaphe* type, and *Boa constrictor*) will be discussed in detail and specific recommendations made for submission of rodent prey in each.

Family Viperidae

Snakes of the subfamily Crotalinae (and pythons and other members of the family Boidae) possess thermal receptors (Noble and Schmidt, 1937; Newman and Hartline, 1982) that assist in the detection of prey. Furthermore, intraoral receptors sensitive to temperature and/or infrared radiation have been discovered in prairie rattlesnakes, and these receptors may have behavioral implications (Chiszar et al., 1986).

Cock Buning (1983) divided the feeding sequence of viperids into nine behaviors based on locomotor elements: rest, alertness, head turning, approach, preparation, strike, re-approach, head searching, and swallowing. We have discussed these below in three general phases: pre-strike, strike, and post-strike.

The Crotaline Type. The following remarks are based on experience with over 50 taxa of *Crotalus* and *Sistrurus,* over 15 taxa of *Bothrops,* 7 taxa of *Trimeresurus,* several *Agkistrodon,* and *Lachesis,* and involve thousands of feeding episodes at the Dallas Zoo. Most of these snakes strike, release, and trail envenomated prey by using chemical cues (Chiszar et al., 1983). In pre-strike phases for crotalines, visual and thermal cues predominate; chemosensory searching is activated after the strike. In contrast, cobras chase rodents and may deliver several strikes or hold prey in their jaws (depending on retaliatory bites from the prey) but trail prey less efficiently (Kardong, 1982; Radcliffe et al., 1983).

1. *Pre-strike phase:* The willingness of a newly obtained pit viper to feed can be judged by watching the reactions of the snake in a resting coil; alertness and head turning indicate interest. It is important to minimize human presence. If possible, the keeper should remain hidden. If this is not possible, the keeper's face should be immobile and no higher than level with the snake (Scudder and Chiszar, 1977). Next, it is necessary to determine the "focus" of the snake by ascertaining size of the prey, position of the prey relative to the snake, and acceptable distance between prey and snake. Reynolds and Scott (1982) found that *Crotalus atrox* and *C. scutulatus* selected prey on the basis of size; prey either too large or too small were not taken, nor were prey accepted that could inflict harm. Endoscopic forceps (Jackson laryngeal grasping forceps) may be used to present the lateral aspect of prey. K. V. Kardong (Personal communication), in an exhaustive study, found that rattlesnakes (*Crotalus*) struck rodents behind the head or shoulder region in over 70% of trials, and mice died faster when struck at those sites. Based on thermograms of living and dead mice (Bosch, 1983), Kardong suggested that the concentric isotherms in mice may help in directing the strike. His findings concur with our experience. In addition we have observed that striking may be inhibited in snakes when prey is approaching. That is, the "interest" mode is transformed into a defensive mode. If a rodent is dipped in water before being offered, grooming often ensues and the snake may be enticed to strike (Murphy and Armstrong, 1978).

2. *Strike phase:* Rattlesnakes discriminated between envenomated and non-envenomated mice, possibly by detecting alarm pheromones released by the mice (Duvall et al., 1978; D. Chiszar, Personal communication). For this reason, we attempt to stimulate vipers to strike defensively, even when freshly killed food is offered. We also entice snakes to strike live mice held with forceps; after a

few minutes, if the mouse has not succumbed to envenomation, it is dispatched by mechanical anesthesia and presented to the snake when all reflexive action has ceased. Chiszar et al. (1977) found that, after striking the first mouse, rattlesnakes evidenced a degree of inhibition, showing unwillingness to strike a second mouse for up to 20 min. In situations where pit vipers are reluctant to feed, we force snakes to strike at least one dozen times within a 5-min period; occasionally this has been the only successful technique to entice feeding. Two other techniques may be used for eliciting strikes from an arboreal snake: (a) touching the tail of the snake with either live or dead prey, or (b) holding the prey with endoscopic forceps directly in front of the head of the snake and then pinching the tail of the snake with another pair of forceps. This stimulates the snake to strike the prey. It is important for a snake to hold prey in its mouth, because an arboreal snake may not trail prey if it is dropped. In addition, an arboreal snake may not strike unless prey is beneath it so that the strike can be placed in the shoulder region of the prey from above. For arboreal snakes a matrix of branches of varying diameter should be provided and arranged in a horizontal plane no more than one-half of the snake's body length above the floor of the enclosure. Clusters of small-leaved plastic plants may be interspersed among the branches; arboreal vipers often seek such areas as sites from which to strike prey. For terrestrial snakes, pressing the snake in its cervical region with a freshly killed rodent held with forceps often stimulates striking. Holding a live rodent with forceps and allowing it to scratch the snake's dorsum is sometimes effective for both terrestrial and arboreal pit vipers.

3. *Post-strike phase:* During the post-strike phase, characterized by stretching of the fangs and the onset of tongue flicking for chemosensory searching (usually ranging between 5 and 15 min), the keeper should move slowly away from the enclosure; after trailing begins, snakes are easily distracted by human movement. During the post-strike phase, the tongue-flicking rate (TFR) increases, indicating a heightened level of chemosensory investigation which aids in the location of prey (Chiszar and Radcliffe, 1976). The ventral surface of the tongue makes contact with anterior processes that are the mechanisms for transferring substances to Jacobson's organ (Gillingham and Clark, 1981). Regardless of the odor present (e.g., perfume), TFR increases after the strike, which suggests that chemosensory searching is a modal action pattern (Chiszar et al., 1977). Chemosensory searching after the strike ranges between 2 and 62 min in *Crotalus adamanteus* (Brock, 1981).

Chemical cues are important during the re-approach period of the post-strike phase when the snake is trailing envenomated prey (Brock, 1981). After a strike, rattlesnakes perform a sweeping motion to locate the trail. On occasion, captive pit vipers will begin to trail for varying lengths of time but sometimes become disinterested and return to the resting coil. Various techniques can restimulate interest. The prey can be manipulated by bouncing, sliding, gliding, or moving it in any way that elicits interest. If the snake crawls aimlessly about the enclosure for extended periods (in some cases crawling directly over the prey), present the prey with the dorsal aspect of the braincase removed. Forceps should be used to hold the prey immediately in front of the snake as it crawls. Swallowing often may be induced by maintaining the position of the prey so that the snake continues to direct tongue flicks onto the exposed brain. If there is continued disinclination to swallow, allow a 30-min interval and repeat the entire prey presentation sequence.

During the head searching and swallowing period, the snake may become disoriented, directing tongue flicks toward the posterior region of the prey and attempting to orient on the hind feet or proximal portion of the tail in an effort to swallow. Prey should be placed in dorsal recumbency to allow access to the snout for swallowing. The effects of rigor mortis of the prey may be lessened by cervical disarticulation.

Low-intensity or misdirected swallowing efforts may occur that do not result in deglutition. Indications that swallowing by the snake might not occur include partially opening the mouth on the body of the prey repeatedly, recoiling when the whiskers are touched, grasping tufts of the prey's fur, or abandoning the prey. At this point, grasp the rodent with forceps, lift it several centimeters off the substrate, and present the snout to the snake in order to induce deglutition.

Wild or free-living bushmasters (*Lachesis muta*) appeared to chemosensorily pick a site at which prey might appear and then waited in ambush (Greene and Santana, 1983). Reinert et al. (1984) described the ambush posture of timber rattlesnakes (*Crotalus horridus*) coiled adjacent to fallen logs. The upper surface of a log served as a runway for small mammalian prey, and the snake maintained physical contact with the log by placing a portion of its body and lower jaw against the lateral surface, perpendicular to the longitudinal axis of the log; vibratory, visual, and thermal cues could thus be used. Observations on hunting behavior in wild eyelash pit vipers (*Bothrops schlegeli*) suggested that sites chosen (e.g., *Heliconia* flowers) were those that hummingbirds might visit (H. W. Greene, Personal communication). Prairie rattlesnakes (*Crotalus viridis*) migrated to active demes of preferred prey (deer mice) and waited near entrances of burrows to ambush rodents (Duvall et al., 1985). These observations suggest that an enriched environment with a variety of props might provide ambush sites for captive snakes that ambush prey. This represents a fertile area for future investigation.

The Viperine Type. Feeding behavior in vipers (*Vipera*) has been described by Naulleau (1967). The presentation of living rodents may stimulate feeding. True vipers appear to be as sensitive to and to as readily utilize thermal cues arising from potential prey as crotalines (D. Chiszar, Personal communication). Generally, our procedures for presenting food to snakes of the subfamily Viperinae parallel those used for pit vipers. In the highly specialized viper genus *Bitis*, three taxa (*B. arietans, B. gabonica, B. nasicornis*) observed by us released prey only rarely after striking; instead, they quickly raised it off the substrate. This behavior may be advantageous, because the struggling prey is more effectively controlled.

Family Boidae

The first locomotory components of python feeding behavior parallel those described for viperids, although the relative importance of each behavior phase differs.

1. *Pre-strike and strike phases:* Pythons possess heat-sensitive pit organs, situated along the upper and lower labials, that respond to both infrared and touch stimuli (Cock Buning et al., 1981).

In the pre-strike phase, visual, thermal, chemical, and mechanical cues in concert elicit predatory behavior. Our techniques for food presentation correspond in part to those used for viperids, although stimulating a python to strike defensively may not result in deglutition. In cases where a python is disinterested in feeding, a freshly killed mouse is gently inserted in the snake's mouth, whereupon it is often swallowed (if the snake is relatively undisturbed).

2. *Post-strike phase:* After freshly killed prey is grasped by the snake, mechanical stimulation of the prey with forceps is used and generally extends the time of constriction. It has been our experience that swallowing occurs more often with reluctant pythons if this is done.

Family Colubridae

The Colubrine Type. In the pre-strike and striking phases, rat snakes of the genus *Elaphe* are guided mainly by sight (Cock Buning, 1983). *Elaphe climacophora* directed strikes toward the heads of active mice (Diefenbach and Emslie, 1971), presumably because the heads exhibit the most noticeable movement. Strikes directed toward the side or rear of the prey's body increase the possibility of retaliatory bites. Chiszar et al. (1980a) found that *Pituophis*, when deprived of food for 1 wk, relied on visual cues, whereas food deprivation for a period of up to 1 mo resulted in increased tongue-flicking rate in response to rodent odors. Food deprivation led to changes in mode of behavior, with the initial response viewed as an ambushing strategy and, as hunger increased, viewed as a foraging strategy. Biting may activate chemosensory searching (Chiszar et al., 1980a).

Diefenbach and Emslie (1971) performed a series of experiments (direction of fur, taper of the body, and chemical stimuli of mice) suggesting that chemical and tactile cues were involved in the head searching phase in *E. climacophora*. Natricine snakes utilize chemical cues, as evidenced by increased tongue flicking, trailing, attack, and swallowing (Burghardt, 1977), but the sequence of chemical and visual or thermal stimuli in the predatory repertoire of these snakes differs from that of pit vipers (Chiszar et al., 1981). In general, more chemically oriented colubrid snakes seem to adapt well to captivity and rarely refuse to feed if appropriate prey are offered. Occasionally, live prey may be required to stimulate feeding, increasing the danger of parasitism.

Micrurus used different methods for encountering prey, typically crawling slowly and poking or probing its head beneath leaf litter with accompanying tongue-flick clusters as it searched for prey trails. Visual, tactile, and chemical cues were incorporated in the predatory sequence (Greene, 1976, 1984). Provision of leaf litter substrates for captive snakes appears to be warranted.

Feeding of Neonates

A number of studies deal with neonate feeding (see Burghardt 1977, 1978, for reviews). In our experience efficiency in handling prey improves over time in some newborn snakes, especially vipers and constricting colubrids. Newborn boids are proficient constrictors and treat prey similarly to adults, whereas constricting in young colubrids may be variable; some months may elapse before adult efficiency is attained (Burghardt, 1977; Greene and Burghardt, 1978). Czaplicki (1975) offered a discussion on behavioral habituation in relation to chemically elicited prey attack responses. Subsequent attempts to stimulate feeding are usually more successful than initial attempts (J. B. Murphy and J. A. Campbell, Personal observations). Whether this is a factor of food deprivation, adaptation to the captive environment, or prey-recognition learning (see Stimac et al., 1982) is unknown. It is important that efforts be made to stimulate neonates to accept any food object soon after their first shedding. If neonates do not feed within several weeks, assist-feeding (Radcliffe, 1975; Coote, 1985) may be necessary.

Individual variability in prey preference may occur within a litter or between populations (Burghardt, 1977; Arnold, 1981). Several techniques may be used to address widely varying preferences. Freshly killed neonatal mice should be washed with surgical soap to eliminate odor and then rinsed and rubbed with various extracts of natural prey items such as lizards, frogs, and snakes. With diffident rodent-feeding snakes, neonatal mice are frozen, thawed, heated with infrared heat lamps, and then offered with the braincase exposed. Further, placing newborn rodents in a small box with nesting material eliminates the rolling, sometimes distracting, motion made by these mammals when placed on a smooth surface. For small bird-eating green tree pythons (*Chondropython*), chick feathers are inserted in the mouth of the mouse to stimulate feeding.

Summary on Feeding

Certain generalized statements can be made about snake predatory behavior and applications to the feeding of captive ophidians.

Where to Feed. Although our inclination is to maintain snakes individually, Ananjeva and Orlov (1982) found that groups of conspecific snakes, when kept together, may stimulate each other to feed; frog-eating snakes appear to be the most responsive to these conditions. Whether kept individually or in groups, all snakes should be maintained in a quiet environment, with minimal human disturbance and no ophidian predators nearby, and should have appropriate security. Lighting should be subdued.

What to Feed. Dietary preferences of snakes have been outlined by Mushinsky (this volume). Freeze unusual food items in water for at least 3 days before thawing and offering them to snakes; this ensures availability of food and control of parasites (Stoskopf and Hudson, 1982). For rodent-feeding snakes, high-quality laboratory mice and rats are acceptable food. Neonatal mice may be used for larger snakes that are reluctant to feed on adult mice.

When to Feed. Snakes should be alert, exhibit head-turning movements, investigate new stimuli with increased tongue flicking, and usually remain in their resting coil. Both day and night feeding should be attempted. Bushmasters, for example, spend days resting under small plants but are active and alert at night (Greene and Santana, 1983).

How to Feed. The sophistication in predatory modes of snakes is impressive. Thus initial feeding attempts should begin with freshly killed prey left in the enclosure overnight. If this fails, try the same kind of prey alive a day later. If a particular type of prey is not accepted, try other types. Use endoscopic forceps to present prey. Vary the movement and constantly monitor the reaction of the snake.

How Often and How Much to Feed. Offer prey frequently to newly acquired snakes and vary the schedule. Snake feeding habits are controlled by prey availability (Fitch, 1982; Reynolds and Scott, 1982). A general rule for Temperate Zone species is to offer enough prey to ensure that two to four times the body weight of the snake is eaten during a year (Fitch, 1982). For example, *Agkistrodon contortrix* may consume an estimated twice its body weight in prey, whereas *Coluber constrictor,* an active snake, may require food biomass four times its body weight. Bushmasters (*Lachesis*) may need as few as six rats a year to maintain basal metabolism and locomoter dynamics, although more would be needed to allow for growth and reproductive behavior (Greene, 1986). In contrast, garter snakes, especially neonates, may need feeding as often as three times weekly. There are several subjective methods for evaluating the weight of a snake. An anorectic snake has lateral folds, a diminished tongue-flicking rate, a shrunken head, and impaired motor ability. Conversely, a snake is overfed if interstitial skin is visible or a tight resting coil cannot be maintained. For all snakes, food amounts should be increased immediately before the breeding season and increased feeding continued until parturition or egg deposition occurs. Keep in mind that gravid females often refuse to feed.

REPRODUCTION

During the past decade, some colubrid snakes, especially those of the genera *Lampropeltis, Elaphe, Pituophis, Thamnophis* and, to some extent *Drymarchon*, have reproduced in great numbers in captivity and have essentially assumed the status of laboratory animals. These snakes are offered food often (in some cases food is always available), sexual maturity is achieved earlier and generation time is lessened in comparison to that of wild populations, and multiple clutches or broods are commonplace.

Investigators desiring to maintain breeding colonies of snakes can find useful summaries on behavioral acts and acts systems in Carpenter and Ferguson (1978) and Carpenter, in Murphy and Collins (1980), on reproductive cycles in Fitch (1970, 1982, 1985) and Seigel and Ford (this volume), and on artificial means for inducing reproduction in Crews and Garrick, in Murphy and Collins (1980).

One of the most important aspects of a successful snake breeding program appears to be bombardment of the individual serpents with a variety of seemingly irrelevant or unrelated stimuli (Radcliffe and Murphy, 1983). Inducing ritualized male combat (Gillingham et al., 1983), trying various combinations of a large number of snakes, changing environmental parameters such as simulated rain showers, altering props, or placing snakes in a novel enclosure may be effective techniques. Snakes are maintained individually until breeding is desired. We routinely place a female in the male's enclosure during or immediately following her shedding cycle. The snakes are not disturbed for cleaning (see Chiszar et al., 1980b; Wellborn et al., 1982, on marking behavior). Should breeding not take place initially, the snakes are left together for extended periods.

With the use of these breeding techniques, over 65 ophidian taxa have reproduced at the Dallas Zoo. During the last 5 yr, the number of neonates produced has surpassed attrition significantly.

NEONATES

Captive neonates should be maintained individually in gallon jars with damp paper towels until shedding occurs. Permanent neonatal units should consist of gallon jars with water dishes, 7 to 8 cm of gravel (6 to 7 mm in diameter), and small, flat rocks or pieces of bark. Water (ca. 100 ml) is added to the gravel. Jar lids are screen mesh or have solid tops with a few small holes and are chosen according to the amount of relative humidity required. Snakes that adapt well to captivity and have a high rate of passage digestively are kept on paper towels or wood shavings.

HIBERNATION

Within the past decade, interest has increased in artificially hibernating reptiles from temperate climates to stimulate reproductive activity (Tryon, 1985) and has resulted in an impressive list of successes. In the late 1970s the Dallas Zoo began to place certain Temperate Zone snakes in hibernation, resulting in increased reproductive behavior and parturition. To utilize hibernation in order to enhance reproductive success, we recommend the following procedures. For 2 mo before the onset of hibernation, fecal examinations should be performed on the snakes. Positive helminth, trichomonad, and other protozoan parasite loads may cause ophidian deaths during hibernation. Three weeks later, feeding should be discontinued. The snake should be maintained in an individual enclosure with a hiding box containing shredded paper, and the entire enclosure should be kept in darkness. Because snakes have been observed drinking water at 11°C, a water dish should be provided. The temperature should then be decreased in 2°C increments daily until 11°C is reached. Three months later the temperature should be increased daily in 2°C increments until 26 to 30°C is reached, at which time the snake should be placed with another for breeding. After 1 to 2 wk, feeding can be initiated.

Despite careful attention in following the procedure just outlined, problems can occur. Seven snakes (*Lampropeltis, Micrurus, Crotalus, Vipera*) died during or after emerging from hibernation from December 1983 to 1 March 1984 at the Dallas Zoo. All deaths were acute or peracute, with the last four snakes dying within 4 days of each other. All snakes ($n = 57$) remaining in the hibernaculum were treated with gentocin prophylactically; however, no definitive cause of death could be ascertained. The treatment regimen consisted of 2 mg/kg body weight of gentocin intramuscularly at 72-h intervals for three treatments. No additional snakes died after the onset of therapy (B. Raphael, Personal communication). Thirteen of 22 snakes gained weight during hibernation, a phenomenon also noted by Tryon (1985). If a snake's weight begins to decline during hibernation, the animal should be moved to a warmer area (ambient temperature 26 to 30°C). Consult Gregory (1982) for additional information on reptilian hibernation in the wild.

SUMMARY AND FUTURE RESEARCH

Most individuals who maintain captive snakes have been guilty of maintaining conventional galley slave-type conditions (i.e., aquarium + water bowl +

newspaper = adequate conditions). Our knowledge of the feeding and medical care of captive snakes has advanced considerably beyond this in recent years. Many gaps in our knowledge of snake biology could be filled by observations on captive serpents, although we are often limited by small sample sizes. For example, we are woefully ignorant about the biology of most tropical snakes, owing (in part) to a lack of interest in these taxa by those actively involved in captive breeding. Still poorly known for most species are requirements for temperature, seasonal variation, photoperiod, and light quality. Attractive king snakes and albino gopher snakes are appealing, but efforts are needed to expand our horizons to include more species and to examine interesting biological phenomena currently being ignored.

ACKNOWLEDGMENTS

We are pleased to dedicate this contribution to Lyndon A. Mitchell, Supervisor of the Department of Herpetology at the Dallas Zoo, who for over twenty years has devoted his professional life to the care of living herpetofauna. His observational skills, ingenuity, and dedication are unparalleled.

For various courtesies extended to us, we thank S. J. Arnold, D. G. Barker, P. Dullemeijer, R. Hudson, W. Iliff, E. R. Jacobson, W. W. Lamar, H. R. Mushinsky, B. L. Raphael, R. Shine, F. Slavens, and B. W. Tryon. Members of the Department of Herpetology at the Dallas Zoo, D. Boyer, W. Corwin, D. Horn, and J. J. Perry, assisted us in numerous ways. Several colleagues were most helpful with stimulating discussions and reviews of early drafts of the manuscript: D. Chiszar, N. Ford, J. C. Gillingham, H. W. Greene, K. V. Kardong, and G. Toffic. Ann Bain, Linda Bigham, Susan Dalley, and Wanda Weaver typed several drafts of the manuscript.

LITERATURE CITED

Ananjeva, N. B. and Orlov, N. L. 1982. Feeding behavior of snakes, *Vertebr. Hung.* 21:25–31.
Arnold, S. J. 1981. The microevolution of feeding behavior, in: Foraging Behavior: Ecological, Ethological and Psychological Approaches (A. Kamil and T. Sargent, eds.) pp. 409–453, Garland Press, New York.
Avery, R. A. 1982. Field studies of body temperatures and thermoregulation, in: Biology of the Reptilia, vol. 12 (C. Gans and F. H. Pough, eds.) pp. 93–166, Academic Press, New York.
Avery, R. A. 1985. Thermoregulatory behaviour of reptiles in the field and in captivity, in: Reptiles, Breeding, Behaviour and Veterinary Aspects (S. Townson and K. Lawrence, eds.) pp. 45–60, British Herpetological Society, London.
Bosch, in, den, H. A. J. 1983. Snout temperatures of reptiles, with special reference to the changes during feeding behaviour in *Python molurus bivit-*

tatus (Serpentes, Boidae): A study using infrared radiation, *Amphib.-Reptilia* 4:49–61.

Brattstrom, B. H. 1965. Body temperatures of reptiles, *Am. Midl. Nat.* 73:376–422.

Brock, O. G. 1981. Predatory behavior of eastern diamondback rattlesnakes (*Crotalus adamanteus*): Field enclosure and Y-maze laboratory studies, emphasizing prey trailing behaviors, *Diss. Abstr. Int. B Sci. Eng.* 41:2510.

Burghardt, G. M. 1977. The ontogeny, evolution, and stimulus control of feeding in humans and reptiles, in: The Chemical Senses and Nutrition (M. R. Kare and O. Maller, eds.) pp. 253–275, Academic Press, New York.

Burghardt, G. M. 1978. Behavioral ontogeny in reptiles: Whence, whither, and why? in: The Development of Behavior: Comparative and Evolutionary Aspects (G. M. Burghardt and M. Berkoff, eds.) pp. 149–174, Garland STPM Press, New York.

Carpenter, C. C. and Ferguson, G. W. 1978. Variation and evolution of stereotyped behavior in reptiles, in: Biology of the Reptilia, vol. 7 (C. Gans and D. W. Tinkle, eds.) pp. 335–554, Academic Press, New York.

Chiszar, D. and Radcliffe, C. W. 1976. Rate of tongue flicking by rattlesnakes during successive stages of feeding on rodent prey. *Bull. Psychon. Soc.* 7:485–486.

Chiszar, D., Radcliffe, C. W., and Scudder, K. M. 1977. Analysis of the behavioral sequence emitted by rattlesnakes during feeding episodes. I. Striking and chemosensory searching, *Behav. Biol.* 21:418–425.

Chiszar, D., Radcliffe, C. W., and Scudder, K. M. 1980a. Use of the vomeronasal system during predatory episodes by bull snakes (*Pituophis melanoleucus*), *Bull Psychon. Soc.* 15:35–36.

Chiszar, D., Wellborn, S., Wand, M. A., Scudder, K. M., and Smith, H. M. 1980b. Investigatory behavior in snakes. II. Cage cleaning and the induction of defecation in snakes, *Anim. Learn. Behav.* 8:505–510.

Chiszar, D., Radcliffe, C. W., O'Connell, B., and Smith, H. M. 1981. Strike-induced chemosensory searching in rattlesnakes (*Crotalus viridis*) as a function of disturbance prior to presentation of rodent prey, *Psychol. Rec.* 31:57–62.

Chiszar, D., Radcliffe, C. W., and Scudder, K. M. 1983. Strike-induced chemosensory searching by rattlesnakes: The role of envenomation-related chemical cues in the post-strike environment, in: Chemical Signals in Vertebrates III (R. M. Silverstein and D. Muller-Schwarze, eds.) pp. 1–24, Plenum Press, New York.

Chiszar, D., Dickman, D., and Colton, J. 1986. Sensitivity to thermal stimulation in prairie rattlesnakes (*Crotalus viridis*) after bilateral anesthetization of the facial pits, *Behav. Neural Biol.* 45:143–149.

Cloudsley-Thompson, J. L. 1971. The Temperature and Water Relations of Reptiles, Merrow, Watford Herts, England.

Cock Buning, T. de. 1983. Thermal sensitivity as a specialization for prey capture and feeding in snakes, *Am. Zool.* 23:363–375.

Cock Buning, T. de, Terashima, S., and Goris, R. C. 1981. Python pit organs analysed as warm receptors, *Cell. Mol. Neurobiol.* 1:271–278.

Cooper, J. E. and Jackson, O. F. (eds.). 1981. Diseases of the Reptilia, 2 vols., Academic Press, New York.

Coote, J. 1985. Breeding colubrid snakes, mainly *Lampropeltis*, in: Reptiles, Breeding, Behaviour and Veterinary Aspects (S. Townson and K. Lawrence, eds.) pp. 5–17, British Herpetological Society, London.

Czaplicki, J. 1975. Habituation of the chemically elicited prey-attack response in the diamond-backed water snake, *Natrix rhombifera rhombifera, Herpetologica* 31:403–409.

Diefenbach, C. O. and Emslie, S. C. 1971. Cues influencing the direction of prey ingestion of the Japanese snake, *Elaphe climacophora* (Colubridae, Serpentes), *Herpetologica* 27:461–466.

Duvall, D., Chiszar, D., Trupiano, J., and Radcliffe, C. W. 1978. Preference for envenomated rodent prey by rattlesnakes, *Bull. Psychon. Soc.* 11:7–8.

Duvall, D., King, M. B., and Gutzwiller, K. J. 1985. Behavioral ecology and ethology of the prairie rattlesnake, *Nat. Geogr. Res.* 1:80–111.

Firth, B. T. and Turner, J. S. 1982. Sensory, neural, and hormonal aspects in thermoregulation, in: Biology of the Reptilia, vol. 12 (C. Gans and F. H. Pough, eds.), pp. 213–274, Academic Press, New York.

Fitch, H. S. 1970. Reproductive cycles in lizards and snakes, *Univ. Kans. Mus. Nat. Hist. Misc. Publ.* 52:1–247.

Fitch, H. S. 1982. Resources of a snake community in prairie-woodland habitat of northeastern Kansas, in: Herpetological Communities (N. J. Scott, Jr., ed.) *U. S. Fish Wildl. Serv. Wildl. Res. Rep.* 13:83–97.

Fitch, H.S., 1985. Variation in clutch and litter size in New World reptiles, *Univ. Kans. Mus. Nat. Hist. Misc. Publ.* 76:1–76.

Frye, F. L. 1981. Biomedical and Surgical Aspects of Captive Reptile Husbandry, Veterinary Medicine, Edwardsville, Illinois.

Gehrmann, W. H. 1971. Influence of constant illumination on thermal preference in the immature water snake, *Natrix erythrogaster transversa, Physiol. Zool.* 44:84–89.

Gillingham, J. C. and Clark, D. L. 1981. Snake tongue-flicking: Transfer mechanics to Jacobson's organ, *Can. J. Zool.* 59:1651–1657.

Gillingham, J. C., Carpenter, C. C., and Murphy, J. B. 1983. Courtship, male combat and dominance in the western diamondback rattlesnake, *Crotalus atrox. J. Herpetol.* 17:265–270.

Greene, H. W. 1976. Scale overlap, a directional sign stimulus for prey ingestion by ophiophagus snakes, *Z. Tierpsychol.* 41:113–120.

Greene, H. W. 1984. Feeding behavior and diet of the eastern coral snake *Micrurus fulvius,* in: Vertebrate Ecology and Systematics: A Tribute to Henry S. Fitch (R. A. Siegel, L. E. Hunt, J. L. Knight, L. Malaret, and N. Zuschlag, eds.) *Univ. Kans. Mus. Nat. Hist. Spec. Publ.* 10:147–162.

Greene, H. W. 1986. Natural history and evolutionary biology, in: Predator-Prey Relationships: Perspectives and Approaches from the study of Lower Vertebrates (M. Feder and G. V. Lauder, eds.) pp. 99–108. University of Chicago Press.

Greene, H. W. and Burghardt, G. M. 1978. Behavior and phylogeny: Constriction in ancient and modern snakes, *Science* 200:74–77.

Greene, H. W. and M. A. Santana. 1983. Field studies of hunting behavior by bushmasters, *Am. Zool.* 23:897.

Gregory, P. T. 1982. Reptilian hibernation, in: Biology of the Reptilia, vol. 13 (C. Gans and F. H. Pough, eds.) pp 53–154, Academic Press, New York.

Hoff, G. L., Frye, F. L., and Jacobson, E. R. (eds.). 1984. Diseases of Amphibians and Reptiles, Plenum Press, New York.

Huey, R. B. 1982. Temperature, physiology, and the ecology of reptiles, in: Biology of the Reptilia, vol. 12 (C. Gans and F. H. Pough, eds.) pp. 25–91, Academic Press, New York.

Jacobson, E. R. 1977. Histology, endocrinology, and husbandry of ecdysis in snakes (A review), *Vet. Med. Small Anim. Clin.* 72:275–280.

Jacobson, E., Gaskin, J. M., Simpson, C. F., and Terrell, T. G. 1980. Paramyxo-like virus infection in a rock rattlesnake, *J. Am. Vet. Med. Assoc.* 177:796–799.

Jacobson, E., Gaskin, J. M., Page, D., Iverson, W. O., and Johnson, J. W. 1981. Illness associated with paramyxo-like virus infection in a zoologic collection of snakes, *J. Am. Vet. Med. Assoc.* 179:1227–1230.

Kardong, K. V. 1982. Comparative study of changes in prey capture behavior of the cottonmouth (*Agkistrodon piscivorus*) and Egyptian cobra (*Naja haje*), *Copeia* 1982:337–343.

Maderson, P. F. A. 1965. Histological changes in the epidermis of snakes during the sloughing cycle, *J. Zool. (Lond.)* 146:98–113.

Marcellini, D. L. and Peters, A. 1982. Preliminary observations on endogenous heat production after feeding in *Python molurus, J. Herpetol.* 16:92–94.

Marcus, L. C. 1981. Veterinary Biology and Medicine of Captive Amphibians and Reptiles, Lea & Febiger, Philadelphia.

Murphy, J. B. and Armstrong, B. L. 1978. Maintenance of rattlesnakes in captivity, *Univ. Kans. Mus. Nat. Hist. Spec. Publ.* 3:1–40.

Murphy, J. B. and Collins, J. T. (eds.). 1980. Reproductive Biology and Diseases of Captive Reptiles, *Soc. Study Amphib. Reptiles Contr. Herpetol.* 1:1–277.

Nalleau, G. 1967. Le comportement de prédation chez *Vipera aspis, Rev. Comport. Anim.* 2:41–96.

Newman, E. A. and Hartline, P. H. 1982. The infrared "vision" of snakes, *Sci. Am.* 246:116–127.

Noble, G. K. and Schmidt, A. 1937. The structure and function of the facial and labial pits of snakes, *Proc. Am. Philos. Soc.* 77:263–288.

Radcliffe, C. W. 1975. A method for force-feeding snakes, *Herpetol. Rev.* 6:18.

Radcliffe, C. W. and Murphy, J. B. 1983. Precopulatory and related behaviours in captive crotalids and other reptiles: Suggestions for future investigation, *Int. Zoo Yearb.* 23:163–166.

Radcliffe, C. W., Poole, T., Feiler, F., Warnoch, N., Byers, T., Radcliffe, A., and Chiszar, D. 1983. Immobilization of mice following envenomation by cobras (*Naja mossambica pallida*), *Bull. Psychon. Soc.* 21:243–246.

Regal, P. J. 1966. Thermophilic response following feeding in certain reptiles, *Copeia* 1966:588–590.

Reichenbach-Klinke, H. and Elkan, E. 1965. The Principal Diseases of Lower Vertebrates, Academic Press, New York.

Reinert, H. K., Cundall, D., and Bushar, L. M. 1984. Foraging behavior of the timber rattlesnake, *Crotalus horridus, Copeia* 1984:976–981.

Reynolds, R. P. and Scott, N. J., Jr. 1982. Use of a mammalian resource by a Chihuahuan snake community, in: Herpetological Communities (N. J. Scott, Jr., ed.) *U. S. Fish Wildl. Serv. Wildl. Res. Rep.* 13:99–118.

Ross, R. A. and Marzec, G. 1984. The Bacterial Diseases of Reptiles. Their Epidemiology, Control, Diagnosis and Treatment, Institute for Herpetological Research, Stanford, California, Privately printed.

Scudder, K. M. and Chiszar, D. 1977. Effects of six visual stimulus conditions on defensive and exploratory behavior in two species of rattlesnakes, *Psychol. Rec.* 27:519–526.

Stimac, K., Radcliffe, C. W., and Chiszar, D. 1982. Prey recognition learning by red spitting cobras, *Naja mossambica pallida, Bull. Psychon. Soc.* 19:187–188.

Stoskopf, M. K. and Hudson, R. D. 1982. Commercial feed frogs as a source of trematode infection in reptile collections, *Herpetol. Rev.* 13:125.

Townsend, C. R. and Cole, C. J. 1985. Additional notes on requirements of captive whiptail lizards (*Cnemidophorus*), with emphasis on ultraviolet radiation, *Zoo Biol.* 4:49–55.

Tryon, B. W. 1985. Snake hibernation and breeding: In and out of the zoo, in: Reptiles, Breeding, Behaviour and Veterinary Aspects (S. Townson and K. Lawrence, eds.) pp. 19–31, British Herpetological Society, London.

Wallach, J. D. and Boever, W. J. 1983. Diseases of Exotic Animals. Medical and Surgical Management, W. B. Saunders, Philadelphia.

Wellborn, S., Scudder, K. M., Smith, H. M., Stimac, K. and Chiszar, D. 1982. Investigatory behavior in snakes. III. Effects of familiar odors on investigation of clean cages, *Psychol. Rec.* 32:169–177.

Life History and Ecology

CHAPTER SEVEN

Social Behavior

James C. Gillingham

THE DOMAIN OF SOCIAL BEHAVIOR

Central to an understanding of snake social behavior is the nature of what is meant by social behavior itself. Tinbergen (1966) recognized that social behavior extends beyond mere aggregation and occurs when organisms react to each other's presence. Wilson (1975) concurs that conspecific communication is a requisite for this behavior. He further believes that reproductive behavior and aggregation are properties of societies and as such can be correctly classified as social behavior. Therefore, in the ensuing discussion, social behavior in snakes is recognized as the behavioral interaction between two or more conspecific individuals regardless of their relationship to one another.

Specific social behaviors may be classified as spiteful, selfish, cooperative, or altruistic, depending on the effect of the encounter on the individual fitness of the participants (Hamilton, 1964). Spiteful behavior is difficult to record in animals other than humans. Altruistic behavior is now well documented in organisms that demonstrate parental care and are capable of kin recognition. The latter has come to be classified as kin selection (Maynard-Smith, 1964). Selfish and cooperative behaviors include the more common acts of courtship, mating, agonistic encounters, and social aggregation.

SOCIAL BEHAVIOR IN A SOLITARY REPTILE

Social behavior has been studied less frequently in reptiles than in other vertebrate classes. Numerous investigations involving territoriality, home range overlap, and courtship and mating strategies (Stamps, 1977; Jenssen, 1978; Dugan and Wiewandt, 1982; Ryan, 1982, Werner, 1982) have been devoted to lizards.

Parental care in some crocodilians has also been reported (Kushlan, 1973; Ogden and Singletary, 1973; Pooley, 1974; Pooley and Gans, 1976; Tryon, 1980). However, there are few similar studies concerning ophidian social behavior. Their solitary nature has lead some investigators to consider snakes the least social of all reptiles (Brattstrom, 1974; Wilson, 1975). Leyhausen (1965) points out that the social structure of solitary mammals may be maintained only through ongoing interindividual interaction. Snakes can therefore be recognized as social animals in light of their interindividual interactions in spacing, complex reproductive (Carpenter, 1977; Gillingham, 1979, 1980), and aggregative (Burghardt, 1983) behaviors.

It is the goal of this chapter to introduce the social biology of snakes. The mechanisms and descriptions of courtship and mating behavior, social aggregation, and aggression in snakes will be reviewed and discussed comparatively. Guidelines will be outlined for the study of snake social behavior and, finally an attempt will be made to chart the future of research on social behavior in snakes.

CONSPECIFIC INTERSEXUAL BEHAVIOR

Social behavior in snakes tends to center around their reproductive activities. Whereas unisexual or parthenogenetic reproduction has been documented in six lizard families (Cole, 1975; Darevsky et al., 1985), evidence shows that only one snake (*Ramphotyphlops braminus*) reproduces clonally (Nussbaum, 1980; Darevsky et al., 1985). This last exception notwithstanding, intersexual behavior is a requisite to successful reproduction in snakes. Consequently, social interactions related to reproduction generally include courtship and mating, but certain preliminary and subsequent behaviors are also functionally significant.

Precourtship behaviors occur before courtship and function primarily to reduce interindividual distance to a point where courtship may begin. Courtship itself may be defined as mutual communication between the sexes, generally initiated by the male, that results in interindividual distance reduction so mating can occur. Mating in snakes represents the consummation of courtship and is accompanied by transmission of seminal fluid. Postmating social behaviors in snakes are limited to intrasexual aggregating behaviors of gravid females. The combined functions of these behaviors include (1) mate attraction, (2) mate persuasion, (3) mating synchronization, (4) reproductive isolation, and (5) information exchange relative to fitness and motivation (Tinbergen, 1966; Halliday, 1983).

Precourtship Behavior

Courtship behavior and its distance-reducing function cannot commence or be realized unless the participants are within the range of one another's communication channels. No matter what courtship sensory modality is used (auditory, tactile, visual, olfactory, vomeronasal), conspecific pairs must initially be at or within some threshhold distance in order to effect signal transmission.

Snakes inhabiting higher latitudes often enter winter dormancy in conspecific aggregates and do not require precourtship intersexual distance reduction. Their proximity to one another at emergence allows them to proceed with courtship activities immediately or soon after emergence. Many species overwinter in this fashion (Aleksiuk, 1977; Parker and Brown, 1980; Gregory, 1982, 1984), and a differential emergence by sex (males earlier than females) may be exhibited. However, some of these same species may also exhibit autumnal mating (Duvall et al., 1982; Schuett, 1986), necessitating the location of and return to over-wintering sites. In species in which a seasonal state of dormancy is lacking or when individuals overwinter singly, male snakes may not find themselves in convenient proximity to females. All these instances demand that males locate females over potentially considerable distances.

Male snakes are capable of locating females by following their pheromone trails (Kubie and Halpern, 1975; Heller and Halpern, 1981; Ford 1986). The lipoprotein vitelligenin has been proposed as the species-typical pheromone establishing these trails (Garstka and Crews, 1981), but a variety of related volatile semiochemicals may be involved (Mason and Crews, 1985). During successful trailing behavior, male snakes are capable of recognizing the direction of the female's movement (Ford and Low, 1984) and whether or not she is a conspecific (Ford, 1986). Such conspecific trailing has been well documented in both invertebrates (Wilson, 1971) and mammals (Bubenik et al., 1980), but within the reptiles, snake-trailing abilities are the most spectacular. Selection pressure toward such abilities would lead to obvious adaptations with respect to efficient mate location and maintenance of the genetic integrity of the species.

Non-olfactory location of female snakes by males may also be possible. Many snakes tend to "aggregate toward movement" (Noble, 1937) and use visual cues to approach another individual (Shaw, 1951; Oliver, 1955). During foraging episodes, several colubrid snakes (*Alsophis, Coluber, Thamnophis*) use a head-raised posture from a stationary position to respond to prey movement (J. C. Gillingham, unpub. data). Such a posture may likewise be used to locate conspecifics during mating periods. Visual cues appear to provide the initial information for location of females in *Elaphe* (Gillingham, 1979) and are probably important in other genera. This reduces the individual distances so chemosensory channels can complete the specific and sexual identity of the target individual.

Courtship Behavior

In other vertebrates, sight and sound play a major role in their often conspicuous and elaborate courtship behaviors. Anuran amphibians, birds, and many mammals are notorious for their production of sound during courtship (Wells, 1977; Alcock, 1984), and intersexual communication during these episodes is undoubtedly enhanced. Among reptiles, auditory displays during courtship are less common but do occur in lizards (Marcellini, 1978), in certain crocodilians (Campbell, 1973), and in the tuatara, *Sphenodon punctatus* (Gans et al., 1984).

Behaviors communicated through visual channels are also common in vertebrates. Of the reptiles, lizards have evolved complex mechanisms for communication in this mode. The particularly well-studied iguanid lizards combine brilliant color with behavioral acts for effective displays during interindividual encounters (Carpenter and Ferguson, 1977; Cooper, 1977). Within the genus *Anolis*, color and movement are further enhanced by the protractible gular fold or dewlap (Rand and Williams, 1970). Such displays in a social context are rare in snakes.

Vision and audition are both most effective when there is minimal environmental interference (Wiley and Richards, 1978; Lythgoe, 1979). These systems best operate, therefore, in a rather open habitat. The legless proverbial "snake in the grass" is undoubtedly hampered by such constraints and may provide selection pressure toward courtship communication using other channels. Although male snakes use vision and chemoreception to initially locate females, and chemoreception is important in sexual and species identification (Gillingham and Dickinson, 1980; Ford, 1986), snake courtship proceeds primarily through tactile channels. Visual and auditory cues are essential to territorial defense in other vertebrates, but since there is currently no evidence for territoriality in snakes, there is decreased selection pressure for such modes of communication in a social context. Moreover, the tubular morphology of snakes seems to lend itself to tactile acts and permits maximal body contact between individuals. Appendages would limit this contact.

Descriptions of snake courtship are found in a scattered literature. Unfortunately, accounts of these behaviors lack consonance, and it is therefore difficult to make interspecific comparisons, particularly within the older literature. Many of the accounts are anecdotal. Observations were often made in the field without recording equipment, and subsequent descriptions were not the result of critical analyses (see following sections). Behavioral acts were often overlooked, resulting in incomplete published inventories. Furthermore, identical behaviors in different species have been given different names, and different behaviors have been similarly named. Such confusion leads to false notions about behavioral homologies and does little to advance our understanding of the evolutionary development of snake courtship behavior.

Despite the lack of consistent descriptions and terminology, certain trends are evident. In all snakes studied to date, courtship and mating behavior proceed sequentially. Three phases have been described: *tactile-chase, tactile-alignment,* and *intromission and coitus* (Gillingham et al., 1977; Gillingham, 1979) (Figure 7–1). Each aptly describes one of the sequential courtship events and has been useful in characterizing snake courtship across a wide range of taxa.

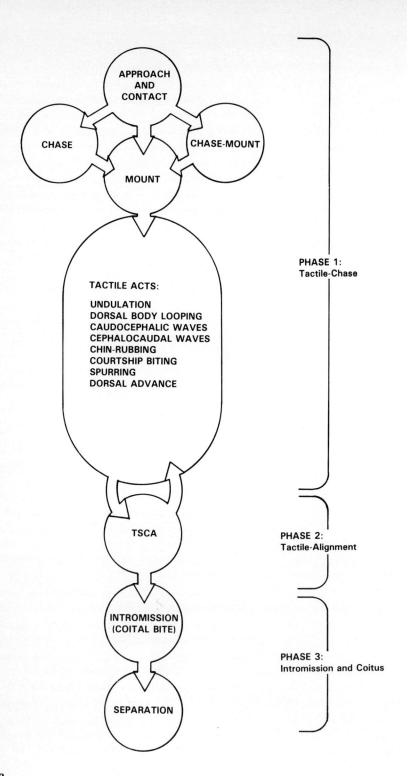

Tactile-Chase. The first phase of snake courtship includes initial contact and preliminary courtship acts. It is accompanied by much tongue flicking, and although visual cues are at least partly responsible for bringing the individuals together, tongue flicking is necessary for species recognition (Ford, 1986) and sexual recognition (Gillingham and Dickinson, 1980). Moreover, at least in garter snakes (*Thamnophis*), courtship will not occur without the transfer of the appropriate pheromone(s) to the male's vomeronasal organ (Kubie et al., 1978).

Initial contact with the female may be followed by mounting, depending on female receptivity to the male's advances. Such sexual receptivity has been shown to be under environmental and hormonal control (Crews and Garstka, 1982; Duvall et al., 1982). Often, the female will flee from the male, and he will follow with contact (*chase-mount*) or without contact (*chase*). Courtship will then commence only when she ceases fleeing and the male subsequently mounts her head-first (Figure 7–2).

Successful mounting is followed by the exhibition of one or more tactile acts (Figure 7–1). The commonest of these male behaviors are defined as follows:

Undulation: Lateral and anteroposterior sliding movements on the female's dorsum

Dorsal body looping: Pulling the body into one or more S-shaped curves on the female's dorsum

Caudocephalic waves: Muscular contractions of the integument, which are initiated in the tail region and progress toward the head; most pronounced where there is direct body contact

Cephalocaudal waves: Same as caudocephalic waves but initiated in the neck region with progression toward the tail

Chin rubbing: Adpression of the chin to the dorsum of the female while moving the head forward, backward, or laterally

Courtship biting: Biting the body of the female before phase 3

Spurring: Movement of the pelvic spurs (Boidae) while in contact with the female

Dorsal advance: Progression toward the head of the female.

The dorsal advance and chin rubbing are by far the most ubiquitous courtship acts observed in snakes. These are often accompanied by slight jerking movements of the head, particularly in the Colubridae and Viperidae. These movements are suggestive of courtship jiggles, head bobs, and head nods of iguanid lizards (Carpenter and Ferguson, 1977). Although Noble (1937) reported that chin rubbing was necessary in order to stimulate tactile receptors and elicit normal courtship behavior in the male, there is currently no evidence for such a contention (Kubie et al., 1978). However, these tactile acts undoubtedly serve to

---

Figure 7–1. Flow diagram of typical snake courtship acts (left) and the phases into which they may be partitioned (right; see text for details).

Figure 7–2. Illustration of courtship position of a male rat snake (*Elaphe obsoleta*) relative to a conspecific female.

stimulate the female. Some male snakes (*Nerodia*) possess enlarged chin tubercles (Blanchard, 1931), and there is ample evidence for integumentary touch receptors in a variety of snakes (Proske, 1969; Jackson and Sharawy, 1980).

Boas possess vestigial rear limbs or pelvic spurs (McDowell, this volume). These spurs are used actively by the male during courtship (and during intermale combat; see following section) and probably play an important role in facilitating cloacal gaping just before hemipenial intromission (Murphy et al., 1978a; Gillingham and Chambers, 1982).

Biting by the courting male snake is a behavioral act that appears to be limited to the Colubridae. Two distinctive types of bites occur. The first is a *courtship bite,* which takes place when the female is coiled up and not in the stretched-out position conducive to tail juxtaposition. The male snake responds to such coiling with biting and quick release in the neck or trunk region. This biting seldom causes tissue damage but often results in the female changing to a more tractable position (Gillingham, 1979). The more common *coital neck bite* will be discussed in the next section.

Tactile-Alignment. The second phase of snake courtship begins with the first copulatory attempt. Initially termed "tail vibrations," "tail quivering," or "tail twitching" (Davis, 1936; Noble, 1937; Shaw, 1951), this behavior has been more recently described as a *stroke-cycle* (Chiszar et al., 1976) or *tail-search copulatory attempt* (TSCA; Gillingham, 1977). The TSCA is the single most consistent courtship act exhibited by male snakes across all taxa. The result of these complex movements is a juxtaposition of the cloacal apertures so that, following female cloacal gaping, the male can introduce a single hemipenis and effect copulation. This maneuvering is not unlike that exhibited by male anoles as they achieve intromission (Greenberg and Noble, 1944; Jenssen, 1970), and in the tuatara as cloacal apposition is attempted (Gans et al., 1984).

Attendant to the TSCAs are the same tactile acts that occur during phase 1. In some species, the male snake's head and anterior body employ these acts while the tail maintains an ostensibly independent action on that portion of the female. More commonly, TSCAs are separated by periods of intense tactile stimulation (Figure 7–1). In mating aggregations of eastern garter snakes (*Thamnophis sirtalis*), it is not uncommon for a male's head to be in contact with a female other than the one with which his tail makes contact (Gillingham and Dickinson, 1980). Even if a male "mistakenly" maintains head contact with other individuals, it is ultimately the activity of his tail that determines mating success.

Intromission and Coitus. The final phase begins when hemipenial penetration of the female is effected. Although some authors have speculated that copulatory adjustment is brought about by the male through the use of hemipenial spines to lift the female's cloacal scales, with little or no female participation (Pisani, 1976; Crews and Garstka, 1982), it is now well established that female cloacal gaping is necessary for intromission (Gillingham, 1979; Schuett, 1986). Because of the proximity of the ventral surface of the juxtaposed tails just before intromission, the actual process is rarely seen. On the other hand, it is not uncommon for a receptive female to gape her cloaca before TSCA initiation or even simply in the presence of a potential mate (Gillingham et al., 1983).

Colubrid snakes such as *Elaphe* (Gillingham, 1979), *Lampropeltis* (Secor, 1985), and *Pituophis* (Shaw, 1951) exhibit coital neck biting just before intromission, and this hold is maintained throughout coitus. Such a coital posture is common in lizards (Greenberg and Noble, 1944; Jenssen, 1970; Carpenter and Ferguson, 1977) and also occurs in certain mammalian insectivores where it aids the male in positioning himself before copulation (Dewsbury, 1972). In snakes, its function is yet to be determined.

The duration of coitus in snakes varies considerably. That snakes remain joined in copulation briefly (several minutes) or for as long as 29 h (*Crotalus atrox*) is perplexing. Although it seems unlikely that such a disparity exists due to differences in the time required for successful insemination, this has yet to be tested. It is more probable that sexual selection pressures influence the duration of mating, at least in the Viperidae (Gillingham et al., 1983; Schuett, 1986). The longer a male remains coupled with a particular female, the lower the probability of her mating with another male (Trivers, 1972; Wade, 1979). Such copulatory "locking" is common in mammals (Dewsbury, 1972), and in insects undoubtedly functions to prevent male displacement by rival males (Parker, 1979). The mucoprotein copulatory plug used in the garter snakes (*Thamnophis sirtalis, T. sauritus, T. butleri:* Devine 1975, 1977) secures the same result but allows for a reduction in coition time. The advantage in this case goes to the male; he can then attempt to gain further matings without remaining with the female.

A benefit of a shortened copulatory period may be that both sexes reduce their exposure to predators (Gregory, 1977) while in this vulnerable position. Ewer (1968) proposed that, for mammals, predation pressure may be responsible for brief mounts. Realistically, copulatory duration in snakes is probably a compromise between predator pressure and competition for mates, but the details of this compromise await further study.

Postmating Behavior

Following mating there is little social behavior between the sexes. Certain post-mating activities associated with potential offspring, such as the aggregation of gravid female snakes, have been recorded in snakes. This will be treated in later sections. Captive nest-building activities in the king cobra (*Ophiophagus hannah*) have been described by Oliver (1956), and the brooding behavior of the Indian python (*Python molurus*) has not only been described but its functional significance has been ascertained (Hutchison et al., 1966). However, by definition, and because communication cannot be shown in these instances, behavioral interactions between parent and potential offspring do not constitute social behavior (Wilson, 1975).

Parental care following the birth or hatching of snakes has yet to be well documented. Neonatal snakes are quite independent and seem fully capable of an independent existence. However, newborn prairie rattlesnakes (*Crotalus viridis*) have a tendency to spend their first hours of extramaternal life quite close to their mothers (within 5 m: Duvall et al., 1985). Further, both these snakes and timber rattlesnakes (*Crotalus horridus:* Brown and MacLean, 1983) are capable of following conspecific scent trails to communal dens some distance from the birthing site. The early social interactions between mother and offspring may consequentially contribute to their trailing ability.

Intersexual Combat Behavior

In a few instances, and only under captive conditions, male and female snakes have been observed to show aggression toward one another in the form of combat or fighting behavior. Such aggression is seen in the viper *Vipera berus* and has been termed "predatory" combat (Kelleway, 1982; Kelleway and Brain, 1982). The behaviors exhibited are stimulated by food items and cannot be distinguished from intermale combat (see next section). In addition, these bouts occur not only between adults of both sexes but also between juveniles of both sexes (Kelleway, 1982).

CONSPECIFIC INTRASEXUAL BEHAVIOR

Most vertebrates compete among themselves for mating opportunities through male-male competition and female choice. This leads to a selection for characters, providing some individuals with a reproductive advantage over others of the same sex. The pressure thereby placed on intrasexual competitors is known as sexual selection (Wittenberger, 1981) and has been discussed for over a century (Darwin, 1871). Such selection is distinctive from natural selection (Arnold, 1983) and may result in aggressive behavior among males.

In snakes, aggressive interactions between males are termed "combat behavior." Historically, this very conspicuous behavior was perceived as a male-female interaction. Because the sexual identity of the participants was not verified, these behaviors were anthropomorphically mistaken as courtship dances (Davis, 1936; Carr and Carr, 1942; Lowe, 1942; Parker, 1963). Although similar behaviors may occur between males and females in captivity (Kelleway, 1982), the proximate causes are very different.

Snake combat is currently recognized as a form of social aggression (Brain, 1981), although causal factors may remain unclear. Territoriality has been repeatedly invoked as a stimulus for such aggression (Lowe, 1948; Lowe and Norris, 1950; Perry, 1978), but there is no evidence that this phenomenon exists in snakes. Currently ethologists interpret territoriality as a form of relative dominance (Kaufmann, 1983). Animals are dominant within certain spatial confines ("territories"), but they remain relatively subordinate outside these boundaries. Even in terms of dominance, we have no data to substantiate snake territoriality.

Lowe and Norris (1950) suggested that aggressive behavior in snakes might function in testing the sexual readiness of the female. They were probably referring to male-female aggression rather than to male-male combat. This was later misinterpreted by Shaw (1951). Because sex discrimination in snakes occurs rapidly and through vomeronasal channels (Gillingham and Dickinson, 1980), combat behavior probably is not involved in this process. However, because occasional "mistakes" are made and male-male courtship has been observed (Shaw, 1951; Akester, 1983), combat behavior may partially function in homosexual avoidance.

More probable causal factors resulting in male-male aggression are food (see aforementioned intersexual aggression) and competition for mates. Male animals of many taxa fight for access to females (Wittenberger, 1981), and such sexual defense during the breeding season leads to enhanced reproductive success (Alcock, 1984). Because it has now been adequately demonstrated that certain male snakes (*Agkistrodon contortrix:* Schuett, 1986) restrict their fighting to the mating season and that they also aggressively defend females, mate competition is a likely function of male-male combat behavior in snakes.

Combat Bouts

Aggressive behavior between male snakes in the form of combat bouts has been observed in the Colubridae (Shaw, 1951; Bogert and Roth, 1966; Murphy et al., 1978b; Gillingham, 1980), Viperidae (Shaw, 1948; Carpenter et al., 1976; Andren, 1981; Akester, 1983; Gillingham et al., 1983; York, 1984), Boidae (Carpenter et al., 1978; Barker et al., 1979), and Elapidae (Fleay, 1937; LeLoup, 1964; Shine et al., 1981). Usually the combat bout consists of a series of alternate attempts by one snake to depress the head and neck of its opponent. As in courtship, such fighting is dependent on the vomeronasal organ and tongue flicking for chemosensory input. Andren (1982) found that blocking the vomeronasal system in *Vipera berus* prevented the initiation of combat behavior. However, when combat does occur, the goal of each participant appears to be to maintain a superior position. It has recently been shown that the duration of time a male spends in a superior position is positively correlated with his achieving dominance as an outcome of the interaction (Clark et al., 1984). Such singular attempts to subdue another snake physically have been termed *topping* (Carpenter et al., 1976).

Colubrids such as *Elaphe* (Gillingham, 1980) and *Pituophis* (Shaw, 1951) and elapids such as *Dendroaspis* (LeLoup, 1964) and *Pseudechis* (Shine et al., 1981) exhibit topping from a relatively horizontal posture. Competing individuals enter into combat by simultaneously gliding parallel to one another while initiating head and neck movements during topping attempts. Their bodies tend to remain stretched out and parallel, while their heads exhibit various pushing, hovering, and pinning movements (Gillingham, 1980; Clark et al., 1984). The topping movements frequently lead to an entwining of the necks of the participant snakes and, as this continues, the bodies also become entwined.

Viperid combat is distinctive in that, during the aggressive interaction, the snakes elevate their heads some distance off the substrate following the initial approach, contact, and recognition (Carpenter et al., 1976; Akester, 1979; Schuett, 1986) (Figure 7–3). This vertical configuration (Figure 7–4) is maintained as the participants sway back and forth, hook necks, and attempt to top one another (Carpenter et al., 1976). After several topping attempts one individual is usually successful, and the duo topples to the substrate only to ascend and begin anew.

Aggressive behavior between male snakes in the family Boidae lacks the vertical components exhibited by the viperids. Further, and paralleling their courtship behavior, the boids use their "vestigial" pelvic spurs during combat (Carpenter et al., 1978; Barker et al., 1979). Interestingly, arboreal species such as the Madagascan boa (*Sanzinia madagascariensis*) use their anterior bodies only to maintain a purchase on limbs and branches. The actual combat interaction occurs between their entwined tails, which "wrestle with each other and at the same time the erected spurs scratch and tear vigorously. . ." (Carpenter et al., 1978). In many instances the head and remainder of the trunk can be some distance from one another.

Although the aggressiveness exhibited between males in these four families is often quite vigorous, biting during combat has been recorded only in the

————————————————————————————————⟶

Figure 7–3. Flow diagram of typical viperid snake combat acts (see text for details).

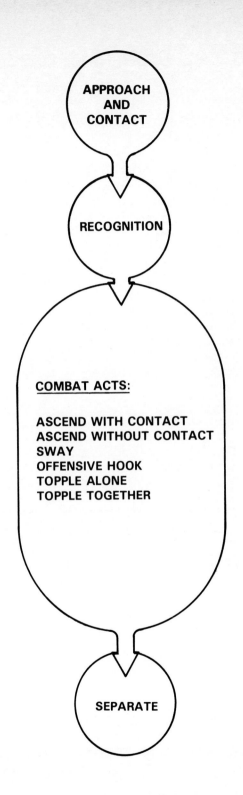

APPROACH
AND
CONTACT

RECOGNITION

COMBAT ACTS:

ASCEND WITH CONTACT
ASCEND WITHOUT CONTACT
SWAY
OFFENSIVE HOOK
TOPPLE ALONE
TOPPLE TOGETHER

SEPARATE

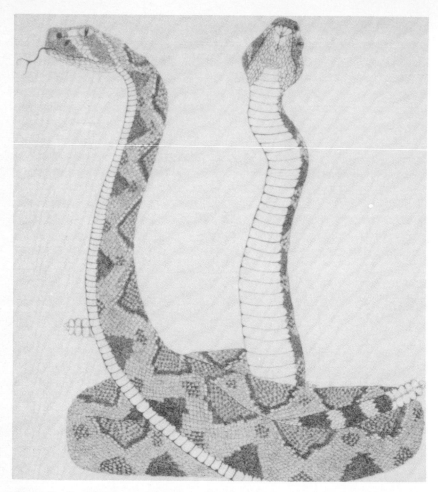

Figure 7–4. Illustration of typical combat position for two male western diamondback rattlesnakes (*Crotalus atrox*).

Colubridae. When it is exhibited it is of very short duration, often just preceding the end of an encounter.

Under captive conditions, and presumably in nature, male-male combat behavior terminates with the establishment of a dominant individual. Behaviorally the dominant individual attempts to initiate further contact, while the subordinate shows a rapid retreat with no interest in a continued behavioral exchange (Gillingham, 1980; Gillingham et al., 1983; Clark et al., 1984; Schuett, 1986). From the standpoint of mate competition, such behavioral episodes may occur as a single male courts a female. An intruder male will initiate a combat exchange and may supplant the original courting male. The complex interactions that occur when large masses of male snakes attempt to achieve coition with a single female shortly after emergence from winter dormancy (Crews and Garstka, 1982; Gregory, 1984) may also be a form of combat behavior. Such sexual interference may be a successful tactic, particularly if the intruder is larger. Sexual selection appears to favor large body size in males within species of snakes that show male-male aggression. In these instances, males are often larger than females (Shine, 1978) or have larger spurs (Stickel and Stickel, 1946). Additionally, hemipenial spines may be important in minimizing interference with a male mating with a female by preventing coital separation.

AGGREGATION

Many animals exhibit clumping or grouping behavior whereby the dispersion pattern of individuals is closer than expected by chance. Coloniality, survival groups, and asexual clones are a few examples of aggregations resulting in response to a common stimulus (Brown, 1975). Many snakes exhibit aggregations, and because there is a substantial reduction in individual distance and therefore an interaction between individuals, such grouping can be considered social behavior. Indeed, it has been considered by some to be the only social behavior exhibited by snakes (Prater, 1933).

Seasonal Aggregations

Because seasonal aggregations such as communal denning are considered in detail elsewhere in this volume by Gregory et al. and by Gibbons and Semlitsch, these social groupings will be considered only briefly here. Seasonal denning activities have a profound effect on the social behavior of the spring emergents. Snakes that enter dormancy singly, or live in regions where activity is seasonally continuous, must actively search for members of the opposite sex before mating (see previous sections). On the other hand, conspecific seasonal aggregates need not make such sojourns as a consequence of their close proximity on emergence. The resulting "snake balls" and mating aggregations have been reported for years (E.L., 1880; Gardner, 1955, 1957), but in species that mate later in the season, such aggregations at this time may be a response to optimal basking conditions (Duvall et al., 1985). Of evolutionary interest here is whether these aggregations reflect thermal adaptations for winter survival or adaptations for mate location.

In the Viperidae, gravid copperheads (*Agkistrodon contortrix:* Fitch, 1960), Japanese pit vipers (*Agkistrodon halys:* Fukuda, 1962), and gravid prairie rattlesnakes (*Crotalus viridis:* Duvall et al., 1985) aggregate in specific areas before parturition. Similar behavior has been observed in racers (*Coluber constrictor:* Swain and Smith, 1978) and milk snakes (*Lampropeltis triangulum:* Henderson et al., 1980) within the Colubridae. Although it is not clear why certain areas are selected for these *birthing rookeries* (Duvall et al. 1985), the participant females show a tolerance for reduction in interindividual distance.

Daily Aggregations

Daily non-foraging and non-sexual aggregations are common in snakes (Noble and Clausen, 1936; Dundee and Miller, 1968). The hypothetical advantages of such groupings are mate location, body surface area reduction, humidity enhancement, temperature moderation, and even "sensual satisfaction" (Dundee and Miller, 1968). Because snakes can show substantial cutaneous water loss (Bentley, 1976; Mautz, 1982) and many snakes can thermoregulate with a fair degree of precision (Stevenson et al., 1985), thermal and osmotic requirements may be important selective factors for aggregating during periods of inactivity. Gillingham and Rowe (1984) recently demonstrated that eastern garter snakes (*Thamnophis sirtalis*) showed a high degree of fidelity to specific cover items, particularly if such items were thermally optimal within their environment.

However, if such physiological factors were all that was involved in initiating such aggregations, they could not by definition be considered social behavior. This is not true in any case. Neonate brown snakes (*Storeria dekayi*) and garter snakes (*Thamnophis sirtalis*) aggregate under laboratory conditions (Burghardt, 1983). Although *Thamnophis* appeared to be more gregarious than *Storeria*, each tended to prefer aggregating with conspecifics. Such discrimination illustrates an interaction with other individuals. Further, the sensory modality used to locate conspecifics and previously used shelters is the vomeronasal organ (Halpern and Heller, 1982; Heller and Halpern, 1982).

Daily aggregations of snakes may also occur during periods of activity. When occasionally, and often seasonally, prey items are concentrated or reach high densities as a result of synchronous emergence (or other factors), it is common for snakes to locate them. This has been shown for *Nerodia* and fish prey (Brown, 1958; Gillingham and Carpenter, 1974), as well as for *Thamnophis* and amphibian prey (Arnold and Wassersug, 1978). These aggregations show that snakes will tolerate a substantial reduction in individual space while foraging. This "numerical response" is considered by Gregory et al. in more detail elsewhere in this volume.

RECORDING AND ANALYZING SNAKE SOCIAL BEHAVIOR

Field observations on sexual behavior in snakes, although rarely reported in the literature, have been made on a number of species (Prior, 1933; Gillingham, 1974; Parker and Brown, 1980; Andren, 1981). These accounts are valuable (see Crews and Moore, 1986) because they can be analyzed for correlations with environmental factors (season, temperature, humidity) and because both the antecedent and subsequent behaviors relative to courtship and mating of the participants are often known. However, there has generally been little disparity between snake courtship behaviors recorded in captivity compared with those recorded in the field (Gillingham, 1974).

Social behavior of snakes has been studied most extensively under captive conditions (Noble, 1937; Shaw, 1951; Gillingham, 1979), the only requirement being that the paired individuals be in a physiological state of sexual readiness. Snakes often court and even mate under conditions where there is human disturbance (Blanchard and Blanchard, 1942; Carpenter, 1947; Gardner, 1957). Therefore, natural conditions are not required in order for these behaviors to occur.

Analysis of specific social behaviors of snakes is greatly enhanced through the use of cinematography. Most social acts occur too rapidly to be recorded accurately without visual aid. Video and/or movie film recording equipment is therefore recommended for documenting such behavior. The former has the advantage of allowing the recording of long sequences without interruption, while the latter is superior for detailed resolution of acts. It is highly recommended that both be utilized simultaneously.

Behavioral observation chambers can be constructed from a variety of materials, and many substances make suitable substrates (paper, indoor-outdoor carpeting, pea gravel, sand, etc.). However, two important additional considerations must be made before the construction and use of such a chamber. First, one or more sides must be transparent (glass or plastic) for photographic purposes. Second, the side dimensions of the enclosure must equal or exceed the longest total length of any of the snakes to be tested. This is necessary because social behavior in snakes includes acts that involve interindividual contact while the participants are in an elongated position.

Accurately measuring male courtship behavior for snakes is more difficult than for other reptiles. In the largely quadruped lizards, courtship and territorial displays occur while the male is in a fairly well-defined and often stationary posture (Carpenter and Ferguson, 1977; Jenssen, 1978). Quantitative measurements are therefore easily made, leading to meaningful inter- and intraspecific comparisons. The snake's tubular morphology introduces an additional level of complexity. Coils, twists, and turns along the longitudinal axis during courtship tend to obscure detail and make precise measurements difficult. These problems have undoubtedly prevented workers from making estimates of degrees of stereotypy (Schleidt, 1982) within snakes as a group. Even so, the descriptions to date, comparing simple frequencies and rates (Gillingham, 1979), demonstrate that snake social behavior is fairly species-specific and may be an important isolating mechanism.

Courtship, mating, and combat behavior in snakes is composed of sequential acts. These sequences can be scrutinized statistically using a variety of methods including transition matrices (Chatfield and Lemon, 1970; Lehner, 1979) and information theory (Steinberg, 1977). Such measures were used earlier on lizard behavior (Rand and Williams, 1970; Cooper, 1977) and have recently been applied to snake social behavior (Gillingham, 1979, 1980). Even so, these statistical procedures tell us little about predicting which behavioral acts are important in transmitting specific pieces of information between the participants. This is primarily because the methods used to date represent the data in a rather coarse fashion. In setting up a typical transition matrix, one often runs into the problem of cells with no values and, to compensate, behavioral acts must be pooled. Such pooling misrepresents the behavior as it actually occurred.

Following cinematographic recording of behavioral events, the sequential order of the participants' acts must be recorded using real-time event recorders. Here behavioral events are registered as they actually occur and in their exact duration. Such data cannot be handled using ordinary statistical procedures, but new methods may provide solutions to this problem and allow investigators an opportunity to answer heretofore difficult questions regarding social behavior in snakes.

An important corollary to studies on snake social behavior is that, in addition to amassing a prodigious amount of qualitative natural historical information about these fascinating creatures, proper recording and analysis may allow us to use behavioral data to supplement current attempts to unravel squamate phylogeny. Meristic morphological measurements and electrophoretic techniques have to date been productive in this regard but are often expensive and time-consuming (see McDowell, this volume). Using behavioral information in the same way may prove a fruitful and efficient complement to these methods.

FUTURE RESEARCH

Anecdotal reports and captive studies on the social behavior of snakes, although far from taxonomically complete, provide investigators with a foundation on which to base future studies. Overall, there is a need for two significant research thrusts in this area. First, captive studies are fraught with problems related to causation, while natural anecdotal observations lack detail and follow-up information. Although the behaviors described under captive conditions may in fact be identical to those observed in the wild, their sequence may be altered as a result of the captive constraints imposed on the animals. In addition, it is as yet unknown what normally precedes and follows these behaviors and under what natural environmental conditions they occur. The outcome of a captive combat bout between two male snakes, for example, is meaningless unless it can be replicated in a natural context where an individual's subsequent mating success can be measured.

Second, regardless of how the studies were accomplished (captive or otherwise), there are substantial taxonomic gaps in our coverage of snake social behavior. Conspicuous by their absence are the Typhlopidae and Leptotyphlopidae, and there are few data for social interactions in sea snakes (but see Heatwole et al., 1978). Even within the Colubridae there is a bias toward studies on the larger, easy-to-handle species. Although studies on these species will require a greater measure of ingenuity and tapping of our rapidly expanding electronics technology, they will provide invaluable data.

Filling in the gaps across taxa represents only part of our needs. Many important questions about snakes whose behavior has been well-documented remain to be answered. More field data on snake movements relative to one another are needed. To establish whether any form of territoriality exists, snake activity must be monitored in detail on a daily basis. Because an aggressive defense of space is no longer the only criterion for territoriality, and because relative dominance in the form of mutual exclusion constitutes a type of territoriality (Kaufmann, 1983), we must take a much closer look at how these animals live. Detailed long-term field studies on snake populations are required to determine whether overlap in foraging areas leads to any fighting or even active avoidance. In temperate forms where basking before entrance into, and following emergence from, overwintering sites is an important activity, is there competition for optimal sites?

Male-male aggression must also be studied more intensively. With the exception of a few studies that attempt to relate combat outcome to mating success (Andren, 1981; Gillingham et al., 1983; Schuett, 1986), questions still remain regarding long-term reproductive success and individual recognition. It has been shown that dominance may be established as a result of male snakes fighting. Questions naturally follow regarding the duration of dominance. Is it a transient phenomenon? During secondary encounters do subordinates recognize dominant individuals and, if so, how do they respond to them? Studies on snake individual recognition lag far behind those on other vertebrates (Falls and McNichell, 1979; Snowdon and Cleveland, 1980) and are certainly necessary for the proper interpretation of our observed reproductive interactions.

Finally, although the triphasic courtship scheme for snakes (Gillingham, 1979) appears to apply to the taxa described to date, other questions relative to snake courtship and mating remain. The observed extremes in coital duration are striking, yet we currently lack an explanation for them. If coital duration is related to predation pressure, might there also be a correlation between this duration and crypsis? Certain snakes possess rather complex belly patterns that suggest a cryptic function. Are such patterns useful while their venters are exposed in other directions as a result of the various postures assumed during mating? If no correlation can be made, perhaps protracted mating duration is an aspect of sexual interference. In addition, we currently lack data on the actual duration of seminal transmission relative to overall coital duration.

Communication during courtship and mating has been demonstrated (Gillingham, 1979), but there is a need for more detailed information relative to the sensory modalities used during these encounters. The recent accumulation of information regarding the sensory mechanisms mediating snake social behavior is impressive (Burghardt, 1980; Halpern, 1983). There will undoubtedly be further progress in this area, particularly because these are laboratory studies where it is easier to maintain controls. However, there is a need for field-testing of these systems over a greater taxonomic diversity. Further, the dominant role of the snake vomeronasal organ throughout its social behavioral repertoire should not prevent our further investigating the function of vision (and other senses) in these behaviors. Although we are now aware that pheromonal production and emission play a role in snake social behavior (Garstka and Crews, 1981), we are far from identifying all the semiochemicals involved. The function of cloacal musk sacs in snakes still remains largely an enigma. These and a host of other important questions relative to the social behavior of snakes await the attention of current and future investigators.

LITERATURE CITED

Alcock, J. 1984. Animal Behavior: An Evolutionary Approach, 3rd ed., Sinauer Associates, Sunderland, England.

Akester, J. 1979. Male combat in captive gaboon vipers (Serpentes, Viperidae), *Herpetologica* 35:124–128.

Akester, J. 1983. Male combat and reproductive behavior in captive *Bitis caudalis, Br. J. Herpetol.* 6:329–333.

Aleksiuk, M. 1977. Cold-induced aggregative behavior in the red-sided garter snake (*Thamnophis sirtalis parietalis*), *Herpetologica* 33:98–101.

Andren, C. 1981. Behaviour and population dynamics in the adder, *Vipera berus* (L.). Ph.D. Dissertation, University of Göteborg, Sweden.

Andren, C. 1982. The role of the vomeronasal organs in the reproductive behavior of the adder *Vipera berus, Copeia* 1982:148–157.

Arnold, S. J. 1983. Sexual selection: The interface of theory and empiricism, in: Mate Choice (P. Bateson, ed.), pp. 67–107, Cambridge University Press.

Arnold, S. J. and Wassersug, R. J. 1978. Differential predation on metamorphic anurans by garter snakes (*Thamnophis*): Social behavior as a possible defense, *Ecology* 59:1014–1022.

Barker, D. G., Murphy, J. B., and Smith, K. W. 1979. Social behavior in a captive group of Indian pythons, *Python molurus* (Serpentes, Boidae) with formation of a linear hierarchy, *Copeia* 1979:466–477.

Bentley, P. J. 1976. Osmoregulation, in: Biology of the Reptilia, vol. 5 (C. Gans and W. R. Dawson, eds.) pp. 365–412, Academic Press, New York.

Blanchard, F. N. 1931. Secondary sex characters of certain snakes, *Bull. Antivenin Inst. Am.* 4:95–103.

Blanchard, F. N. and Blanchard, F. C. 1942. Mating of the garter snake *Thamnophis sirtalis sirtalis* (Linnaeus), *Pap. Mich. Acad. Sci. Arts Lett.* 27:215–234.

Bogert, C. M. and Roth, V. D. 1966. Ritualistic combat of male gopher snakes, *Pituophis melanoleucus affinis* (Reptilia, Colubridae). *Am. Mus. Novit.* 2245:1–27.

Brain, P. F. 1981. Differentiating types of attack and defense in rodents, in: Multidisciplinary Approaches to Aggression Research (P. F. Brain and D. Benton, eds.) pp. 53–78, Elsevier/North Holland, Amsterdam.

Brattstrom, B. H. 1974. The evolution of reptilian social behavior, Am. Zool. 14:35–49.

Brown, E. E. 1958. Feeding habits of the northern water snake, Natrix sipedon sipedon Linnaeus, Zoologica 43:55–71.

Brown, J. L. 1975. The Evolution of Behavior, W. W. Norton, New York.

Brown, W. S. and MacLean, F. M. 1983. Conspecific scent-trailing by newborn timber rattlesnakes, Crotalus horridus, Herpetologica 39:430–436.

Bubenik, A. B., Dombalagian, M., Wheeler, J. W., and Williams, O. 1980. The role of the tarsal glands in the olfactory communication of the Ontario moose, in: Chemical Signals: Vertebrates and Aquatic Invertebrates (D. Muller-Schwarze and R. M. Silverstein, eds.) p. 415, Plenum Press, New York.

Burghardt, G. M. 1980. Behavioral and stimulus correlates of vomeronasal functioning in reptiles: Feeding, grouping, sex and tongue use, in: Chemical Signals: Vertebrates and Aquatic Vertebrates (D. Muller-Schwarze and R. M. Silverstein, eds.) pp. 275–301, Plenum Press, New York.

Burghardt, G. M. 1983. Aggregation and species discrimination in newborn snakes, Z. Tierpsychol. 61:89–101.

Campbell, H. W. 1973. Observations on the acoustic behavior of crocodilians, Zoologica 58:1–11.

Carpenter, C. C. 1947. Copulation of the fox snake, Copeia 1947:275.

Carpenter, C. C. 1977. Communication and displays of snakes, Am. Zool. 17:217–223.

Carpenter, C. C. and Ferguson, G. W. 1977. Variation and evolution of stereotyped behavior in reptiles, in: Biology of the Reptilia, vol. 7 (C. Gans and D. W. Tinkle, eds.) pp. 335–554, Academic Press, New York.

Carpenter, C. C., Gillingham, J. C., and Murphy, J. B. 1976. The combat ritual of the rock rattlesnake (Crotalus lepidus), Copeia 1976:764–780.

Carpenter, C. C., Murphy, J. B., and Mitchell, L. A. 1978. Combat bouts with spur use in the Madagascan boa (Sanzinia madagascariensis), Herpetologica 34:207–212.

Carr, A. F., Jr., and Carr, M. H. 1942. Notes on the courtship of the cottonmouth moccasin, Proc. New Engl. Zool. Club 20:1–6.

Chatfield, C. and Lemon, R. E. 1970. Analysing sequences of behavioural events, J. Theor. Biol. 29:427–445.

Chiszar, D., Scudder, K., Smith, H. M., and Radcliffe, C. W. 1976. Observations of courtship behavior in the western massasauga (Sistrurus catenatus tergeminus), Herpetologica 32:337–338.

Clark, D. L., Gillingham, J. C., and Rebischke, A. 1984. Notes on the combat behavior of the California kingsnake, Lampropeltis getulus californiae, in captivity, Br. J. Herpetol. 6:380–382.

Cole, C. J. 1975. Evolution of parthenogenetic species of reptiles, in: Intersexuality in the Animal Kingdom (R. Reinboth, ed.) pp. 340–355, Springer-Verlag, New York.

Cooper, W. E. 1977. Information analysis of agonistic behavioral sequences in male iguanid lizards, *Anolis carolinensis, Copeia* 1977:721–735.

Crews, D. and Garstka, W. R. 1982. The ecological physiology of a garter snake, *Sci. Am.* 247:159–168.

Crews, D. and Moore, M. C. 1986. Evolution of mechanisms controlling mating behavior, *Science* 231:121–125.

Darevsky, I. S., Kupriyanova, L. A., and Uzzell, T. 1985. Parthenogenesis in reptiles, in: Biology of the Reptilia, vol. 15 (C. Gans and T. Billett, eds.) pp. 411–526, John Wiley, New York.

Darwin, C. 1871. The Descent of Man and Selection in Relation to Sex, Appleton, New York.

Davis, D. D. 1936. Courtship and mating behavior in snakes, *Zool. Ser. Field Mus. Nat. Hist.* 20:257–290.

Devine, M. C. 1975. Copulatory plugs in snakes: Enforced chastity, *Science* 187:844–845.

Devine, M. C. 1977. Copulatory plugs, restricted mating opportunities and reproductive competition among male garter snakes, *Nature* 267:345–346.

Dewsbury, D. A. 1972. Patterns of copulatory behavior in male mammals, *Q. Rev. Biol.* 47:1–33.

Dugan, B. and Wiewandt, T. A. 1982. Socio-ecological determinants of mating strategies in iguanine lizards, in: Iguanas of the World (G. M. Burghardt and A. S. Rand, eds.) pp. 303–319, Noyes Publications, Park Ridge, New Jersey.

Dundee, H. A. and Miller, M. C., III. 1968. Aggregative behavior and habitat conditioning by the prairie ringneck snake, *Diadophis punctatus arnyi, Tulane Stud. Zool. Bot.* 15:41–58.

Duvall, D., Guillette, L. J., Jr., and Jones, R. E. 1982. Environmental control of reptilian reproductive cycles, in: Biology of the Reptilia, vol. 13 (C. Gans and F. H. Pough, eds.) pp. 201–231, Academic Press, New York.

Duvall, D., King, M. B., and Gutzwiller, K. J. 1985. Behavioral ecology and ethology of the prairie rattlesnake, *Nat. Geogr. Res.* 1:80–111.

E. L. 1880. Bundles of snakes, *Am. Nat.* 14:206–207.

Ewer, R. F. 1968. Ethology of Mammals, Plenum Press, New York.

Falls, J. B. and McNichell, M. K. 1979. Neighbor-stranger discrimination in male blue grouse, *Can. J. Zool.* 57:457–462.

Fitch, H. S. 1960. Autecology of the copperhead, *Univ. Kans. Mus. Nat. Hist. Publ.* 13:85–288.

Fleay, D. 1937. Black snakes in combat, *Proc. Royal N.S. Wales,* August, 40–42.

Ford, N. B. 1986. The role of pheromone trails in the sociobiology of snakes, In: Chemical Signals in Vertebrates IV, (D. Duvall, D. Muller-Schwarze, and R. Silverstein, eds.), Plenum Press, New York.

Ford, N. B. and Low, J.R. 1984. Sex pheromone source location by garter snakes: A mechanism for detection of direction in nonvolatile trails, *J. Chem. Ecol.* 10:1193–1199.

Fukada, H. 1962. Biological studies on the snakes. IX. Breeding habit of *Agkistrodon halys blomhoffi* (Boie), *Bull. Kyoto Gakugei Univ. Ser. B Math. Nat. Sci.* 20:12–19.

Gans, C., Gillingham, J. C., and Clark, D. L. 1984. Courtship, mating and male combat in Tuatara, *Sphenodon punctatus, J. Herpetol.* 18:194–197.

Gardner, J. B. 1955. A ball of garter snakes, *Copeia* 1955:310.

Gardner, J. B. 1957. A garter snake "ball," *Copeia* 1957:48.

Garstka, W. R. and Crews, D. 1981. Female sex pheromones in the skin and circulation of a garter snake, *Science* 214:681–683.

Gillingham, J. C. 1974. Reproductive behavior of the western fox snake, *Elaphe vulpina* (Baird and Girard), *Herpetologica* 30:309–313.

Gillingham, J. C. 1977. Further analysis of reproductive behavior in the western fox snake, *Elaphe v. vulpina, Herpetologica* 33:349–353.

Gillingham, J. C. 1979. Reproductive behavior of the rat snakes of eastern North America, genus *Elaphe, Copeia* 1979:319–331.

Gillingham, J. C. 1980. Communication and combat behavior of the black rat snake (*Elaphe obsoleta*), *Herpetologica* 36:120–127.

Gillingham, J. C. and Carpenter, C. C. 1974. Notes on the fishing behavior of water snakes, *J. Herpetol.* 8:384–385.

Gillingham, J. C. and Chambers, J. A. 1982. Courtship and pelvic spur use in the Burmese python, *Python molurus bivittatus, Copeia* 1982:193–196.

Gillingham, J. C. and Dickinson, J. A. 1980. Postural orientation during courtship in the eastern garter snake, *Thamnophis sirtalis, Behav. Neural Biol.* 28:211–217.

Gillingham, J. C. and Rowe J. 1984. Daily foraging behavior of the eastern garter snake, *Thamnophis sirtalis, Am. Zool.* 24:17A (abstract).

Gillingham, J. C., Carpenter, C. C., Brecke, B. J., and Murphy, J. B. 1977. Courtship and copulatory behavior of the Mexican milk snake, *Lampropeltis triangulum sinaloae* (Colubridae), *Southwest. Nat.* 22:187–194.

Gillingham, J. C., Carpenter, C. C., and Murphy, J. B. 1983. Courtship, male combat and dominance in the western diamondback rattlesnake, *Crotalus atrox, J. Herpetol.* 17:265–270.

Greenberg, B. and Noble, G. K. 1944. Social behavior of the American chameleon (*Anolis carolinensis* Voigt), *Physiol. Zool.* 17:392–439.

Gregory, P. T. 1977. Life-history parameters of the red-sided garter snake (*Thamnophis sirtalis parietalis*) in an extreme environment, the Interlake region of Manitoba, *Nat. Mus. Can. Publ. Zool.* 13:1–44.

Gregory, P. T. 1982. Reptilian hibernation, in: Biology of the Reptilia, vol. 13 (C. Gans and F. H. Pough, eds.) pp. 53–154, Academic Press, New York.

Gregory, P. T. 1984. Communal denning in snakes, in: Vertebrate Ecology and Systematics: A Tribute to Henry S. Fitch (R. A. Seigel, L. E. Hunt, J. L.

Knight, L. Malaret, and N. L. Zuschlag, eds.) *Univ. Kans. Mus. Nat. Hist. Spec. Publ.* 10:57–75.

Halliday, T. R. 1983. Information and communication, in: Animal Behaviour: Communication, vol. 2 (T. R. Halliday and P. J. B. Slater, eds.) pp. 43–81, W. H. Freeman, New York.

Halpern, M. 1983. Nasal chemical senses in snakes, in: Advances in Vertebrate Neuroethology (J. Ewert, R. R. Capranica, and D. J. Ingle, eds.) NATO ASI Ser. A, 56:141–176.

Halpern, M. and Heller, S. B. 1982. Laboratory observations of aggregative behavior of garter snakes, *Thamnophis sirtalis:* Roles of the visual, olfactory and vomeronasal senses, *J. Comp. Psychol.* 96:984–999.

Hamilton, W. D. 1964. The genetical theory of social behavior, *J. Theor. Biol.* 7:1–52.

Heatwole, H., Minton, S. A., Jr., Taylor, R., and Taylor, V. 1978. Underwater observations on sea snake behavior, *Rec. Aust. Mus.* 31:737–761.

Heller, S. B. and Halpern, M. 1981. Laboratory observations on conspecific and congeneric scent trailing in garter snakes (*Thamnophis*), *Behav. Neural Biol.* 33:372–377.

Heller, S. B. and Halpern, M. 1982. Laboratory observations of aggregative behavior of garter snakes, *Thamnophis sirtalis, J. Comp. Psychol.* 96:967–983.

Henderson, R. W., Binder, M. H., Sajdak, R. A., and Buday, J. A. 1980. Aggregating behavior and exploitation of subterranean habitat by gravid Eastern milksnakes (*Lampropeltis t. triangulum*), *Milw. Publ. Mus. Contrib. Biol. Geol.* 32:1–9.

Hutchison, V. H., Dowling, H. G., and Vinegar, A. 1966. Thermoregulation in a brooding female Indian python, *Python molurus bivittatus, Science* 151:694–696.

Jackson, M. K. and Sharawy, M. 1980. Scanning electron microscopy and distribution of specialized mechanoreceptors in the Texas rat snale, *Elaphe obsoleta lindheimeri* (Baird and Girard), *J. Morphol.* 163:59–67.

Jenssen, T. A. 1970. The ethoecology of *Anolis nebulosus* (Sauria, Iguanidae), *J. Herpetol.* 4:1–38.

Jenssen, T. A. 1978. Display diversity in anoline lizards and problems of interpretation, in: Behavior and Neurology of Lizards (N. Greenberg and P. D. MacLean, eds.) pp. 269–285, National Institute of Mental Health, Washington, D.C.

Kaufmann, J. H. 1983. On the definitions and functions of dominance and territoriality, *Biol. Rev.* 58:1–20.

Kelleway, L. G. 1982. Competition for mates and food items in *Vipera berus* (L), *Br. J. Herpetol.* 5:225–230.

Kelleway, L. G. and Brain, P. F. 1982. The utilities of aggression in the viper, *Vipera verus berus* (L), *Aggressive Behav.* 8:141–143.

Kubie, J. and Halpern, M. 1975. Laboratory observations of trailing behavior in garter snakes, *J. Comp. Physiol. Psychol.* 89:667–674.

Kubie, J., Vagvolgyi, A., and Halpern, M. 1978. Roles of vomeronasal and olfactory systems in courtship behavior of male garter snakes, *J. Comp. Physiol. Psychol.* 92:627–641.

Kushlan, J. A. 1973. Observations on maternal behavior in the American alligator, *Alligator mississippiensis, Herpetologica* 29:256–257.

Lehner, P. N. 1979. Handbook of Ethological Methods, Garland STPM Press, New York.

LeLoup, P. 1964. Observations sue la reproduction du *Dendroaspis jamesoni kaimosae* (Loveridge), *Bull Soc. Roy. Zool. Anvers.* 33:13–27.

Leyhausen, P. 1965. The communal organisation of solitary mammals, *Symp. Zool. Soc. Lond.* 14:249–263.

Lowe, C. H. 1942. Notes on the mating of desert rattlesnakes, *Copeia* 1942:261–262.

Lowe, C. H. 1948. Territorial behavior in snakes and the so-called courtship dance, *Herpetologica* 4:129–135.

Lowe, C. H. and Norris, K. S. 1950. Aggressive behavior in male sidewinders, *Crotalus cerastes,* with a discussion of aggressive behavior and territoriality in snakes, *Nat. Hist. Misc. Chic. Acad. Sci.* 66:1–13.

Lythgoe, J. N. 1979. The Ecology of Vision, Clarendon Press, Oxford.

Marcellini, D. L. 1978. The acoustic behavior of lizards, in: Behavior and Neurology of Lizards (N. Greenberg and P. D. MacLean, eds.) pp. 287–300, National Institute of Mental Health, Washington, D.C.

Mason, R. T. and Crews, D. 1985. Analysis of sex attractant pheromone in garter snakes, *Am. Zool.* 25:76A (abstract).

Mautz, W. J. 1982. Patterns of evaporative water loss, in: Biology of the Reptilia, vol. 12 (C. Gans and F. H. Pough, eds.) pp. 443–481, Academic Press, New York.

Maynard-Smith, J. 1964. Group selection and kin selection, *Nature* 201:1145–1147.

Murphy, J. B., Barker, D. G., and Tryon, B. W. 1978a. Miscellaneous notes on the reproductive biology of reptiles. II. Eleven species of the family Boidae: Genera *Candoia, Corallus, Epicrates* and *Python. J. Herpetol.* 12:385–390.

Murphy, J. B., Tryon, B. W., and Brecke, B. J. 1978b. An inventory of reproduction and social behavior in captive gray-banded kingsnakes, *Lampropeltis mexicana alterna* (Brown), *Herpetologica* 34:84–93.

Noble, G. K. 1937. The sense organs involved in the courtship of *Storeria, Thamnophis* and other snakes, *Bull. Am. Mus. Nat. Hist.* 73:673–725.

Noble, G. K. and Clausen, H. J. 1936. The aggregation behavior of *Storeria dekayi* and other snakes, with especial reference to the sense organs involved, *Ecol. Monogr.* 6:269–316.

Nussbaum, R. A. 1980. The Brahmini blind snake (*Rhamphotyphlops braminus*) in the Seychelles Archipelago: Distribution, variation, and further evidence for parthenogenesis, *Herpetologica* 36:215–221.

Ogden, J. and Singletary, C. 1973. Night of the crocodile, *Audubon Mag.* 75:32–37.

Oliver, J. A. 1955. The Natural History of North American Amphibians and Reptiles, D. Van Nostrand, Princeton, New Jersey.

Oliver, J. A. 1956. Reproduction in the king cobra, *Ophiophagus hannah* Cantor, *Zoologica* 41:145–151.

Parker, G. A. 1979. Sexual selection and sexual conflict, in: Sexual Selection and Reproductive Competition in Insects (M. S. Blum and N. A. Blum, eds.) pp. 123–166, Academic Press, New York.

Parker, H. W. 1963. Snakes, Robert Hale, London.

Parker, W. S. and Brown, W. S. 1980. Comparative ecology of two colubrid snakes, *Masticophis t. taeniatus* and *Pituophis melanoleucus deserticola,* in northern Utah, *Milw. Public Mus. Publ. Biol. Geol* 7:1–104.

Perry, J. 1978. An observation of "dance" behavior in the western cottonmouth, *Agkistrodon piscivorous leucostoma* (Reptilia, Serpentes, Viperidae), *J. Herpetol.* 12:429–431.

Pisani, G. R. 1976. Comments on the courtship and mating mechanics of *Thamnophis* (Reptilia, Serpentes, Colubridae). *J. Herpetol.* 10:139–142.

Pooley, A. C. 1974. Parental care in the Nile crocodile: A preliminary report on behavior of a captive female, *Lammergeyer* 21:43–45.

Pooley, A. C. and Gans, C. 1976. The Nile crocodile, *Sci. Am.* 234:114–124.

Prater, S. H. 1933. The social life of snakes, *J. Bombay Nat. Hist. Soc.* 36:469–475.

Prior, H. T. 1933. The dance of the vipers: A remarkable example of reptilian rivalry, *Country-Side* 9:492–493.

Proske, U. 1969. An electrophysiological analysis of cutaneous mechanoreceptors in a snake, *Comp. Biochem. Physiol.* 29:1039–1046.

Rand, A. S. and Williams, E. E. 1970. An estimation of redundancy and information content of anole dewlaps, *Am. Nat.* 104:99–103.

Ryan, M. J. 1982. Variation in iguanine social organization: Mating systems in chuckwallas (*Sauromalus*), in: Iguanas of the World (G. M. Burghardt and A. S. Rand, eds.) pp. 380–390, Noyes Publications, Park Ridge, New Jersey.

Schleidt, W. M. 1982. Stereotyped feature variables are essential constituents of behavior patterns, *Behaviour* 79:230–238.

Schuett, G. W. 1986. Selected topics on reproduction of the copperhead, *Agkistrodon contortrix* (Reptilia, Serpentes, Viperidae), M.S. Thesis, Central Michigan University, Mt. Pleasant.

Secor, S. M. 1985. Courtship and mating behavior of the speckled kingsnake, *Lampropeltis getulus holbrooki,* Ph.D. Dissertation, University of Oklahoma, Norman.

Shaw, C. E. 1948. The male "combat dance" of some crotalid snakes, *Herpetologica.* 4:137–145.

Shaw, C. E. 1951. Male combat in American colubrid snakes with remarks on other colubrid and elapid snakes, *Herpetologica.* 7:149–168.

Shine, R. 1978. Sexual size dimorphism and male combat in snakes, *Oecologia (Berl.)* 33:269–277.

Shine, R., Grigg, G. C., Shine, T. G., and Harlow, P. 1981. Mating and male combat in Australian blacksnakes, *Pseudechis porphyriacus, J. Herpetol.* 15:101–107.

Snowdon, C. T. and Cleveland, J. 1980. Individual recognition of contact calls by pygmy marmosets, *Anim. Behav.* 28:717–727.

Stamps, J. A. 1977. Social behavior and spacing patterns in lizards, in: Biology of the Reptilia, vol. 7 (C. Gans and D. W. Tinkle, eds.) pp. 265–334, Academic Press, New York.

Steinberg, J. B. 1977. Information theory as an ethological tool, in: Quantitative Methods in the Study of Animal Behavior (B. A. Hazlett, ed.) pp. 47–74, Academic Press, New York.

Stevenson, R. D., Peterson, C. R., and Tsuji, J. S. 1985. The thermal dependence of locomotion, tongue-flicking, digestion, and oxygen consumption in the wandering garter snake, *Physiol. Zool.* 58:46–57.

Stickel, W. H. and Stickel, L. F. 1946. Sexual dimorphism in the pelvic spurs of *Enygrus, Copeia* 1946:10–12.

Swain, T. A. and Smith, H. M. 1978. Communal nesting in *Coluber constrictor* in Colorado (Reptilia: Serpentes), *J. Herpetol.* 34:175–177.

Tinbergen, N. 1966. Social Behaviour in Animals with Special Reference to Vertebrates, Methuen, London.

Trivers, R. L. 1972. Parental investment and sexual selection, in: Sexual Selection and the Descent of Man, 1871–1971 (B. G. Campbell, ed.) pp. 136–179, Aldine, Chicago.

Tryon, B. 1980. Observations on reproduction in the West African dwarf crocodile with a description of parental behavior, in: Reproductive Biology and Diseases of Captive Reptiles (J. B. Murphy and J. T. Collins, eds.) pp. 167–185, SSAR Contrib. Herpetol. 1.

Wade, M. J. 1979. Sexual selection and variance in reproductive success, *Am. Nat.* 114:742–746.

Wells, K. D. 1977. The social behavior of anuran amphibians, *Anim. Behav.* 25:666–693.

Werner, D. I. 1982. Social organization and ecology of land iguanas, *Conolophus subcristatus,* on Isla Fernandina, Galapagos, in: Iguanas of the World (G. M. Burghardt and A. S. Rand eds.) Noyes Publications, Park Ridge, New Jersey.

Wiley, R. H. and Richards, D. G. 1978. Physical constraints on acoustic communication in the atmosphere: Implications for the evolution of animal vocalization, *Behav. Ecol. Sociobiol.* 3:69–94.

Wilson, E. O. 1971. The Insect Societies, Belknap Press of Harvard University Press, Cambridge.

Wilson, E. O. 1975. Sociobiology. The New Synthesis, Belknap Press of Harvard University Press, Cambridge.

Wittenberger, J. F. 1981. Animal Social Behavior, Duxbury Press, Boston.

York, D. 1984. The combat ritual of the Malayan pit viper (*Calloselasma rhodostoma*), *Copeia* 1984:770–772.

CHAPTER EIGHT

Reproductive Ecology

Richard A. Seigel
Neil B. Ford

There are, arguably, more published references on the reproductive biology of snakes than on any other aspect of their biology. This is partly a reflection of the ease with which such data can be collected (Fitch, this volume) and partly because of the basic importance of reproduction to the overall ecology of the organism. This extensive literature has prompted a number of excellent reviews, although none of them deals exclusively with snakes (e.g., Fitch, 1970, 1982, 1985a; Tinkle and Gibbons, 1977; Turner, 1977; Duvall et al., 1982; Licht, 1984). Two patterns emerge from these reviews: First, despite this extensive literature, it is clear that the reproductive biology of snakes is considerably less well understood than that of any other reptilian group, with the possible exception of the crocodilians. Second, there are a number of crucial questions concerning snake reproduction that have yet to be adequately addressed (e.g., multiple clutches, tropical cycles, the relationship between hormones and behavior). It is beyond the scope of this chapter to attempt to review the entire literature on snake reproduction. Rather, our goals are to (1) review the basic patterns of snake reproductive biology, (2) synthesize the literature sufficiently to answer some of the questions noted above, and (3) draw attention to those areas of snake reproduction that we feel are badly in need of attention, or that are particularly provocative.

MALE REPRODUCTIVE CYCLES

Although early studies on reproductive cycles in snakes concentrated mainly on females, researchers have recently begun to examine the physiological and behavioral changes associated with reproduction in male snakes as well. Studies

210

on the male reproductive cycle have included examining seasonal changes in testes mass, histology, hormonal activity, and spermatogenesis, as well as changes in male behavior associated with breeding. These studies are reviewed below.

Spermatogenic Cycle

Historically, Temperate Zone snakes have been considered to have two types of seasonal reproductive patterns, *prenuptial* and *postnuptial* (Volsøe, 1944), whereas tropical snakes may show aseasonal reproduction or have seasonal cycles with several variations (Fitch, 1982) (Figure 8–1).

In postnuptial or aestival spermatogenesis (Saint Girons, 1982) (Figure 8–1), snakes exhibit a testicular weight peak in autumn, reflecting maximal spermatogenic activity in the late summer and fall. Mating activity occurs early in the following spring, utilizing sperm stored overwinter in the ductus deferens. This pattern has been termed *dissociated* (Crews, 1984), because there is a temporal separation of both reproductive behavior and androgen production from spermatogenesis (Weil and Aldridge, 1981). The sexual segment of the kidney [which functions in mating plugs and female receptivity (Nilson and Andren, 1982)] tends to exhibit only a short regression period in midsummer, with differentiation

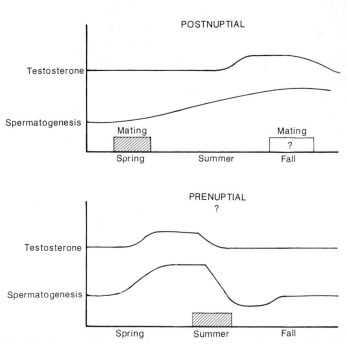

Figure 8–1. Graphical representation of the seasonal timing of male reproductive cycles in Temperate Zone snakes.

and hypertrophy from autumn through the following spring. With minor variations, this spermatogenic cycle has been reported in most colubrid snakes, several viperids, and some elapids (see reviews by Duvall et al., 1982; Saint Girons, 1982; Licht, 1984).

Snakes with postnuptial reproduction may begin spermatogenesis from as early as March or April to as late as June, ending in September or October (the reverse pattern occurs in the Southern Hemisphere). Several species show varying degrees of fall mating, from minor activity in some *Thamnophis* (Aleksiuk and Gregory, 1974) to exclusive fall mating in *Tropidoclonion lineatum* (Krohmer and Aldridge, 1985a). In addition, some species apparently mate in both spring and fall, raising the possibility of both multiple individual matings and multiple paternity (Schuett and Gillingham, 1986). This creates some difficulty in classifying these snakes according to the definitions given above. However, if the postnuptial type is considered to be characterized by an obligatory storage period for the spermatozoa (Licht, 1984), then fewer problems arise. In some species, spermatogenesis is interrupted by hibernation and is not completed until the following spring. Saint Girons (1982) classified this type as mixed. However, based on the ideas given above, these snakes could also be classified as postnuptial.

In prenuptial male cycles, maximal testis mass is achieved in the spring. The only species with the majority of spermatogenesis occurring in the spring are several elapids from Australia (Saint Girons, 1966; Shine, 1977a,b), a few colubrids from Morocco (Cheylan et al., 1981; Bons and Saint Girons, 1982), and one viperid from the Sahara (Saint Girons, 1962). The common trait of these species is a fairly late period of ovulation, apparently allowing the development of spermatozoa before mating occurs. A few vipers at northern latitudes or high altitudes do exhibit spermatogenesis in the spring just before mating, but these species overwinter with spermatids and so should be classified as postnuptial. The same is true for *Micrurus fulvius* of the southern United States, which apparently exhibits a slowing of spermatogenesis during the winter months (Quinn, 1979).

In tropical snakes, classification of male reproductive cycles is more difficult because there is evidence that reproduction can occur year-round in some species (Fitch, 1982; Vitt, 1983) and suggestions that, even in species where breeding is seasonal, spermatogenesis can occur over much of the year (Saint Girons, 1982). However, the occurrence of aseasonal spermatogenesis in individual males has not been documented. Indeed, it is likely that the completion and timing of the reproductive cycle is variable among males in a given tropical area. A number of tropical colubrid snakes show essentially a prenuptial cycle, with spermatogenesis just preceding ovulation and mating (Saint Girons and Pfeffer, 1971). Similar prenuptial cycles apparently occur in some elapids (Lofts et al., 1966; Voris and Jayne, 1979) and in some viperids (Belluomini et al., 1966; Saint Girons and Pfeffer, 1971) from tropical areas. Licht (1984) classified two colubrids as tropical postnuptial: *Elaphe taeniura* (Wong and Chiu, 1974) and *Ptyas korros* (Licht et al., unpublished data). As *E. taeniura* apparently undergoes a period of hibernation, we classify it with the temperate postnuptial species, and because no discussion of the testicular cycle of *P. korros* was given, we reserve judgment on whether a postnuptial tropical cycle actually exists. Indeed, Saint Girons (1982) suggested that avoidance of this terminology with respect to tropical snakes might be advisable.

Hormonal Cycles

The snake testis, like that of other vertebrates, produces androgens (primarily testosterone) when active. However, the relationship of testosterone to spermatogenesis and reproductive behavior is not as clear in snakes as it is in mammals (Crews, 1984). Testosterone production has been indirectly evaluated by examining cells that are presumably steroidogenic (e.g., Sertoli and Leydig cells) and directly evaluated by assays of plasma levels (Weil and Aldridge, 1981). In addition, histological examination of androgen-dependent structures such as the epididymis and renal sex segment have contributed information on male hormonal production.

The seasonal histological changes in the Sertoli cells within the seminiferous tubules have been carefully examined in reptiles (Fox, 1977), and the uptake of lipids by these cells has been documented for snakes (Marshall and Woolf, 1957; Lofts et al., 1966). It appears that the Sertoli cells are capable of producing much of the endogenous androgen of the testis (Lofts, 1972, 1977), and they likely play an important role in spermatogenic activity.

The Leydig cells have also been considered major sources of plasma androgens in snakes (Lofts, 1969, 1972; Licht, 1984). Seasonal changes in the characteristics of these cells appear to be closely related to histological and morphological changes in secondary sexual structures such as the epididymis and renal sex segment (Fox, 1977), and there is direct evidence that they can secrete testosterone in response to gonadotropins (Tsui, 1976).

The few direct assays of plasma androgen levels that have been conducted for snakes suggest that testosterone levels are maximal at the same time that spermatogenesis is occurring. *Naja naja* (Bona-Galo et al., 1980) and *Acrochordus granulatus* (Gorman et al., 1981) are known to exhibit peak androgen titers when testis mass is highest. However, testis mass peaks several months after maximal androgen levels in *Pytas korros* (Licht, 1984) and *Nerodia sipedon* (Weil and Aldridge, 1981). Although testosterone levels are high during summer spermatogenesis, they are also high in the spring when the testes are quiescent (Weil and Aldridge, 1981).

Species of snakes with aseasonal spermatogenesis presumably are acyclic in androgen production as well (Saint Girons, 1985). Examination of interstitial cells in a few tropical colubrids (Saint Girons and Pfeffer, 1971) supports this contention. However, direct assays of plasma testosterone in the tropical sea snake *Laticauda colubrina* (Gorman et al., 1981) showed a seasonal drop in androgen levels in mid-summer, even though testis mass remained constant.

Little is known concerning hypothalamic control of the male reproductive cycle except the possibility that snakes have apparently diverged from other vertebrates in having only a single pituitary gonadotropin, one that is not necessarily homologous to either follicle-stimulating hormone (FSH) or luteinizing hormone (LH) (Duvall et al., 1982; Licht, 1984). This circulating gonadotropin increases before the increase in testis mass and testosterone production in *N. naja* (Licht et al., 1979). However, until more information is available, it will be unclear how a single hormone controls the male reproductive cycle in snakes, particularly in males with postnuptial mating. In fact, because LH and FSH injections are known to have seasonally different effects on androgen levels (Weil, 1982), it may be best to reserve judgment on the number of gonadotropins in snakes.

The influence of androgens on male mating behavior is one of the most confusing aspects of snake reproduction. Although initial experiments suggested that male behavior in garter snakes (*Thamnophis*) was controlled by testosterone (Crews, 1976), later work did not confirm this (Camazine et al., 1980; Crews et al., 1984). Instead, courtship is now considered to be independent of testosterone, i.e., "dissociated" (Crews, 1984). However, testosterone levels in male Cuban boas (*Epicrates striatus*) and male water snakes (*Nerodia sipedon*) have been shown to peak during mating (V. Tuebner, personal communication; Weil and Aldridge, 1981). Clearly, additional research is needed.

Environmental Control of Male Reproduction

Although our understanding of the hormonal control of male reproductive activity is limited, there is considerable information concerning when and under what circumstances those behaviors occur. The general pattern in temperate regions is for male courtship to begin in the spring. In species that den in large aggregations, males leave hibernation earlier than females and then court females as they emerge. Most researchers suggest that temperature is the most important environmental factor stimulating mating activity, with photoperiod playing only a minor role (Aleksiuk and Gregory, 1974; Lofts, 1978; Aldridge, 1979). Nutritional status apparently plays a role in female reproduction (see FAT BODY CYCLING), but whether it does so in males is unknown. Pheromones released by the female also influence male sexual behavior, but these are short-term effects (Nilson, 1981; Garstka et al., 1982; Gillingham, this volume). Courtship activity may continue for several days to several weeks in most snakes, but male responsiveness to females decreases after a time; the physiological cause of this is unknown (Garstka et al., 1982). In several species, a second, less intense mating period occurs in the autumn (Clark, 1970; Aleksiuk and Gregory, 1974; Shine, 1977b; Schuett, 1982), and autumn mating may even predominate (Krohmer and Aldridge, 1985a). Environmental control of fall mating activity has not been examined.

Environmental control of male reproduction in tropical snakes has not been well documented. It seems likely that males should have more extended periods over which they court females (Fitch, 1982), and testicular cycles suggest that tropical snakes may have active sperm over a major portion of the year. Because female snakes are known to store viable sperm (Schuett, 1982; Schuett and Gillingham, 1986), a possible strategy for tropical snakes would be to mate with any conspecific female encountered, regardless of the time of year. Indeed, male Mexican garter snakes (*Thamnophis melanogaster*) begin courting females that have been artificially induced to become receptive, even several months after the normal mating season (Garstka and Crews, 1982). However, some tropical species are obviously seasonal breeders. Several of these species breed after the coolest part of the dry season (February–March: Neill, 1962; Lazlo, 1979), whereas other species are winter breeders, breeding during the coldest part of the dry season (Lazlo, 1979). Even aseasonal equatorial lowland rainforest species may be influenced by lowered temperatures, but photoperiod has little effect on breeding activity (Lazlo, 1979), probably reflecting the fact that natural changes in photoperiod at such locations are slight. It is obvious from even this minimal data that tropical snakes have a diversity of male reproductive patterns and that additional studies on the timing and control of mating behavior are needed.

FEMALE REPRODUCTIVE CYCLES

Most of the available data on female reproductive cycles come from Temperate Zone species, and there is a natural tendency to consider these patterns "typical" of snakes in general. This is misleading, however, because the majority of snake species are not found in the Temperate Zone but rather in tropical or sub-tropical areas. Nevertheless, because reproductive patterns in temperate areas are relatively well known, they provide a useful starting point for a consideration of female reproductive cycles.

Temperate Zone Cycles: Seasonal Reproduction

Recent reviews of reptilian reproductive cycles (Shine, 1977b; Aldridge, 1979, 1982; Licht, 1984) suggest that female cycles are relatively uniform in Temperate Zone species, and that seasonal reproduction is the rule in both the Southern and Northern hemispheres. Microscopic follicles (*oocyctes*) are apparently produced in most species in the spring, at about the same time as vitellogenesis (Licht, 1984). Aldridge (1979) divided the process of yolk deposition of these follicles into two stages: *Primary vitellogenesis* results in an increase in oocycte size up to 5 to 10 mm in length (depending on the species), where they remain until the onset of secondary vitellogenesis. In the cobra (*Naja naja*), the development time from oocyte to ovulation is about 3 yr (Lance and Lofts, 1978). The seasonal timing of primary vitellogenesis is poorly known for snakes but may occur primarily in the spring (Lance and Lofts, 1978). These follicles are transformed to ovulatory size by *secondary vitellogenesis,* which results in an increase in water, calcium, lipid, and protein levels in the follicle. At the same time as vitellogenesis, corresponding changes occur in the size and morphology of the reproductive tract, especially the oviduct and ovaries. For example, the ovarian weight of *N. naja* increases 10- to 20-fold during secondary vitellogenesis (Lance and Lofts, 1978; Bona-Galo et al., 1980). The oviduct also increases in weight at this time and becomes notably convoluted. Details of these morphological changes are reported elsewhere (Betz, 1963; Fox, 1977; Lance and Lofts, 1978). Secondary vitellogenesis is followed by ovulation, the release of follicles into the oviduct for fertilization. Ovulation in reptiles is characterized by the formation of *corpora lutea,* but there is still considerable debate over the exact role of these structures (e.g., Licht, 1984). Once follicles are released in the oviduct, fertilization may occur, but there is some evidence suggesting that it is the act of mating that stimulates vitellogenesis and ovulation, not the other way around (Bona-Galo and Licht, 1983; Licht, 1984). However, such a sequence has not been completely documented and is unlikely to occur in species such as *Carphophis vermis,* which may mate in the fall before vitellogenesis (Clark, 1970). Fertilization is, in turn, followed either by shelling and oviposition or by implantation and pregnancy in viviparous species.

Timing of Vitellogenesis

Even within temperate species, there is still considerable variation in the timing of vitellogenesis. In *prenuptial* or *type I secondary vitellogenesis* (Aldridge, 1979; Licht, 1984), the majority of follicular growth occurs immediately after emergence from hibernation, and ovarian weight and follicle size both increase very rapidly over a period of several weeks. In *postnuptial* or *type II secondary vitellogenesis,* enlargement of follicles begins in late summer, and follicles enlarge relatively slowly until the onset of hibernation. These enlarged follicles are carried through the winter and then continue to increase to ovulatory size in the spring. The two patterns are illustrated in Figure 8–2. As Aldridge (1979) has noted, these two types of vitellogenesis are apparently not correlated with reproductive mode: Prenuptial patterns have been reported in both oviparous and viviparous colubrids and in oviparous and viviparous elapids. Postnuptial patterns are likewise seen in several other oviparous colubrids and in several viviparous elapids and is especially common in the viperids.

Snakes are perhaps unique among reptiles in displaying such diversity in the timing of vitellogenesis. Most lizards are characterized by a prenuptial pattern,

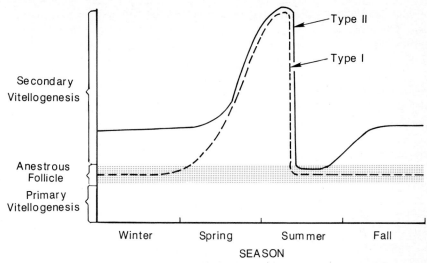

Figure 8–2.   The two major types of seasonal vitellogenesis in Temperate Zone snakes. (Reproduced with permission from *Herpetologica,* vol. 35, 1979.)

although a few high-altitude populations of iguanids and skinks (e.g., *Sceloporus jarrovi, Scincella himalayanum*) may start or even complete vitellogenesis and ovulation before winter (Goldberg, 1971; Duda and Kaul, 1977). Contrariwise, most turtles follow a postnuptial pattern, initiating or even completing vitellogenesis before entering hibernation (Moll, 1979). Unfortunately, too few detailed studies on reproduction in single populations of snakes have been conducted to quantitatively assess what proportion of snakes follow pre- or postnuptial vitellogenesis, nor has the possibility of "facultative" cycles been adequately considered, i.e., variation in the timing of vitellogenesis within a single population (but see Ford and Karges, in press). These gaps are most evident in tropical and sub-tropical populations and are discussed below.

The relative uniformity of the major aspects of female reproduction in temperate areas—fertilization and ovulation in mid- to late spring, oviposition in early summer, hatching and parturition in late summer or early fall—implies possible adaptive significance and also correlations with environmental cues. Shine (1977b) suggested that gestation should occur mainly in the spring and summer in the Temperate Zone to ensure the availability of the high and relatively constant temperatures required for normal embryonic development. Likewise, synchronous hatching and birth of neonates may be timed to coincide with periods of high food availability to maximize chances for survival before hibernation. Indeed, studies on the foraging ecology of the colubrids *Regina alleni, Thamnophis radix,* and *T. sirtalis* (Godley, 1980; Seigel, 1984) have shown that juveniles feed primarily on seasonally abundant prey. Data on environmental correlates are less clear. Although Licht (1984) showed that rainfall, photoperiod, and temperature may all have important effects on the timing of lizard reproduction, data concerning environmental control of female reproductive cycles for snakes are few. However, limited data on male reproduction (summarized in Duvall et al., 1982; Licht, 1984) indicate that temperature may be an important factor in testicular recrudescence, in turn implying that temperature may play a major role in female reproduction as well. Along these lines, Bona-Galo and Licht (1983) showed that a period of cool temperatures (and/or darkness) followed by warming temperatures and mating were necessary for vitellogenesis in garter snakes (*T. sirtalis*).

This consideration of female reproductive cycles is concerned mainly with species that produce a single annual clutch or brood. The topic of clutch or brood frequency will be discussed elsewhere in this chapter.

Tropical Zone Cycles: Seasonal and Aseasonal Reproduction

Compared with that on Temperate Zone snakes, data on tropical and sub-tropical species are limited, and data sets are often based on museum records, forcing investigators to combine information from different geographic regions and different years (e.g., Zug et al., 1979; Shine, 1980a,b; Kofron, 1983). As Vitt and Vangilder (1983) recently noted, such data, although valuable, cannot determine the magnitude of geographic or especially temporal variation in reproduction, factors that have been shown to be important in temperate species (Fitch, 1985a; Seigel and Fitch, 1985). Only a few, mostly recent, studies have been conducted in restricted localities with continuous sampling periods (Berry and Lim, 1967; Voris and Jayne, 1979; Vitt, 1980; Gorman et al., 1981; Lemen and Voris,

Table 8–1. Length of the Reproductive Season (Defined as Minimum Number of Months with Young or Enlarged Follicles) in Tropical Snakes[a]

Species	Environment	Length of season (mo)	Reference
Family Acrochordidae			
Acrochordus granulatus	Seasonal (rain)	4	Gorman et al. (1981)
A. granulatus	Seasonal?	3[+]	Lemen and Voris (1981)
Family Boidae			
Epicrates cenchria	Seasonal (rain)	4	Vitt and Vangilder (1983)
Family Colubridae			
Cerberus rhynchops	Seasonal (rain)	6–7	Gorman et al. (1981)
Clelia occipitolutea	Seasonal (rain)	2	Vitt and Vangilder (1983)
Coniophanes fissidens	Seasonal (rain)	4–5	Zug et al. (1979)
Dipsas catesbyi	Seasonal (rain)	2	Duellman (1978)
Homalopsis buccata	Aseasonal	12	Berry and Lim (1967)

(Continued)

Table 8–1. Length of the Reproductive Season (Defined as Minimum Number of Months with Young or Enlarged Follicles) in Tropical Snakes[a] (*Continued*)

Species	Environment	Length of season (mo)	Reference
Imantodes cenchoa	Seasonal (rain)	4	Duellman (1978)
I. cenchoa	Seasonal (rain)	6+	Zug et al. (1979)
Liophis lineatus	Seasonal (rain)	7	Vitt and Vangilder (1983)
L. mossoroensis	Seasonal (rain)	3	Vitt and Vangilder (1983)
L. poecilogyrus	Seasonal (rain)	7–8	Vitt and Vangilder (1983)
L. viridis	Seasonal (rain)	7	Vitt and Vangilder (1983)
Oxybelis argenteus	Seasonal (rain)	2	Duellman (1978)
Philodryas nattereri	Seasonal (rain)	4	Vitt and Vangilder (1983)
P. olfersii	Seasonal (rain)	7	Vitt and Vangilder (1983)
Sibon sanniola	Seasonal (rain)	6	Kofron (1983)
Waglerophis merremii	Seasonal (rain)	6	Vitt (1983)
Family Elapidae			
Aipysurus eydouxii	Seasonal?	4	Lemen and Voris (1981)
Cacophis harriettae	Seasonal?	6+	Shine (1980a)
Demansia atra	Seasonal?	7	Shine (1980b)
Enhydrina schistosa	Seasonal?	4	Voris and Jayne (1979)
Hydrophis brookii	Seasonal?	3	Lemen and Voris (1981)
H. caerulescens	Seasonal?	4+	Lemen and Voris (1981)
H. melanosoma	Seasonal?	4	Lemen and Voris (1981)
H. torquatus	Seasonal?	4	Lemen and Voris (1981)
Lapemis hardwickii	Seasonal?	5	Lemen and Voris (1981)
Naja naja	Seasonal (rain)	3	Lance and Lofts (1978)
Family Viperidae			
Bothrops atrox	Seasonal (rain)	2	Duellman (1978)

[a]Studies with limited sample sizes (less than five) not included.

1981; Vitt, 1983, Vitt and Vangilder, 1983). Thus broad generalizations concerning tropical or sub-tropical snake reproduction are premature, and the need for additional data on specific populations over continuous periods is critical.

Table 8–1 summarizes data on the reproductive cycle of 30 populations of tropical or sub-tropical snakes. Reproductive cycles ranged from extremely short synchronous cycles (2 to 3 mo), similar to those seen in temperate areas (e.g., *N. naja*), to extended (>6 mo) cycles that suggest continual reproduction (*Homalopsis buccata*). Although some authors have indicated that extended or aseasonal reproduction is common in the tropics (Fitch, 1982), we agree with Zug et al. (1979) that a conservative approach to these data is necessary. We find it important that, in over half the cases where local populations were studied over continuous periods, reproduction was seasonal, albeit somewhat extended (15 of 22 species in Table 8–1). However, even with this caveat, some of the species in Table 8–1 demonstrate rather elongated breeding seasons compared with those of many temperate snakes, and continuous breeding appears to be real in at least some instances (*H. buccata*). Licht (1984) suggested that such elongated reproductive cycles could be interpreted either at the individual level (implying multiple clutches) or at the population level (implying asynchronous reproduction). Multiple clutches will be discussed later in this chapter; here we consider asychronous reproduction.

As already indicated, Shine (1977b) suggested that the close synchrony of reproductive cycles in Temperate Zone snakes was necessary to ensure proper temperature availability for the female or her eggs during gestation, and to ensure hatching or birth at a time of year when resource availability for offspring is high. Because temperature varies relatively little at most tropical sites, temperature influences on females or eggs are probably minimal. However, rainfall and food availability do vary at many tropical locations, often quite dramatically (Vitt, this volume). If reproductive cycles of snakes were linked to rainfall or temperature per se, then sympatric species exposed to the same environmental conditions might be expected to show similar cycles. This, however, is not the case. In both studies where sympatric snakes were studied in tropical environments (Cambodia: Saint Girons and Pfeffer, 1971; Brazil: Vitt and Vangilder, 1983), a diversity of reproductive cycles was displayed. We concur with Vitt (1983) that foraging ecology and seasonal variation in resource availability may be crucial in determining the reproductive cycles of tropical snakes. Snakes that depend on seasonally variable prey might show seasonal reproduction. In contrast, snakes feeding on less variable prey might reproduce continuously. Clearly, this indicates the necessity for collecting as broad a data set as possible on tropical snakes (Vitt and Vangilder, 1983).

Phylogeny is another factor that may influence reproductive cycles. Moll and Legler (1971) found that the reproductive characteristics of the emydid turtle *Pseudemys scripta* (a recent tropical invader) in Panama were little different than the patterns shown by temperate conspecifics. However, the reproductive traits of more ancient tropical lineages such as *Kinosternon leucostomum* and *Rhinoclemys funerea* were quite different than those of Temperate Zone turtles. Likewise, James and Shine (1985) found that the timing of reproduction in Australian lizards was predicted best by the biogeographical history of the species. Although the fossil history and systematics of many snakes are poorly known (Rage, this volume; McDowell, this volume), such factors are important in trying to interpret tropical reproductive patterns.

Finally, we caution that there may be no true dichotomy between tropical and Temperate Zone reproductive cycles, but rather a gradient of reproductive traits. For example, Shine (1980a,b) has shown that reproduction in congeneric Australian elapids ranges from strongly seasonal cycles in temperate New South Wales to elongated or possible aseasonal cycles in tropical Queensland. Likewise, several sub-tropical North American species have elongated reproductive cycles comparable to those seen in tropical areas. *Thamnophis marcianus* in southern Texas has a reproductive cycle as long as 6 to 7 mo (Ford and Karges, in press), and South Carolina populations of ringneck snakes (*Diadophis punctatus*) may reproduce over a 4-mo period (R. Seigel, Personal observations), nearly twice as long as conspecifics in Kansas (Fitch, 1975).

Fat Body Cycling

There is considerable experimental and observational evidence that the amount of body fat (often in the form of abdominal fat bodies) is correlated with repro-duction in lizards. Female lizards with low fat reserves (either removed surgically or owing to low food availability) demonstrated delayed follicular development, follicular atresia, smaller clutch sizes, and lower clutch frequencies than females with larger amounts of fat (Hahn and Tinkle, 1965; Smith, 1968; Ballinger, 1977). Similar experimental data are lacking for snakes, but several investigators have found an inverse correlation between reproduction (vitellogenesis) and fat body size in snakes (e.g., Tinkle, 1962; Wharton, 1966; Nilson, 1981; Plummer, 1983; Diller and Wallace, 1984). In snakes with annual reproduction (e.g., *Opheodrys aestivus:* Plummer, 1983), fat bodies are large in the spring, reach a low point in early to mid-summer, and then increase gradually until hibernation. In species with apparent biennial reproduction (e.g., *Vipera berus:* Nilson, 1981), maximum fat body size occurs during the spring of the reproductive year, reaches a minimum near parturition, and then increases during autumn and during the subsequent year. This pattern is apparently absent in tropical snakes; Berry and Lim (1967) found no seasonal variation in fat body size in *Homalopsis buccata* from Malaya and suggested that foraging success in these snakes was high enough to preclude the necessity of drawing on fat reserves for reproduction. The impact of food availability and fat reserves on clutch frequency in snakes will be dis-cussed later (see FREQUENCY OF REPRODUCTION).

Endocrine Cycles

The hormonal cycles of female snakes have been recently reviewed by Licht (1984) and Saint Girons (1985). Both authors emphasized the relative lack of information on female hormonal cycles and the difficulty of making generali-zations at this time. The following brief summary is based primarily on these two reviews.

All three major female hormones (estradiol, progesterone, testosterone) appear to vary with reproductive activity, although hormonal levels often do not correlate well with each other. Because estradiol is involved in regulation of vitellogenesis, oviductal functions, and female behavior, its levels are expected to peak during reproduction and decline rapidly thereafter (Licht, 1984). This appears to be generally true in two viviparous species (*Acrochordus granulatus, Nerodia fasciata*) and two oviparous species (*Laticauda colubrina, N. naja*), but not in a third viviparous form, *Cerberus rhyncops* (summarized in Licht, 1984). Perhaps because progesterone is produced both in the adrenals and by corpora lutea (Highfill and Mead, 1975), or because of different assay techniques, progesterone levels appear to be considerably more variable than estradiol levels. In oviparous species, (e.g., *N. naja*), progestrone remains at baseline levels until after vitellogenesis, peaking immediately after ovulation (Licht, 1984; Saint Girons, 1985). In some viviparous snakes (*Nerodia*), progesterone may begin to increase during vitellogenesis, peaking during pregnancy (Licht, 1984; Saint Girons, 1985). However, in *Cerberus rhyncops*, there was only a slight rise in progesterone during pregnancy (Gorman et al., 1981). Saint Girons (1985) has suggested that testosterone cycling in female snakes is similar to estradiol levels, but specific data are often lacking and the exact function of this hormone in female reptiles is unclear (Licht, 1984).

VIVIPARITY AND PARENTAL CARE

Origins of Viviparity

The diversity of reproductive modes in reptiles—exclusively egg laying in turtles and crocodilians and both live-bearing and egg laying in squamates—has long interested biologists, and a number of authors have attempted to explain both the origin and radiation of live-bearing in reptiles (see literature review in Tinkle and Gibbons, 1977, and Shine, 1985). The following brief review summarizes some of the major findings, but space does not permit an in-depth summary of all these ideas.

Shine (1985) divided explanations for the evolution of viviparity into those based on environmental factors (cold climates or environmental uncertainty) and those based on species characteristics (e.g., defensive ability, habitat utilization). The most obvious correlate of viviparity is its association with cold temperatures, either at high altitudes or latitudes. For example, the proportion of North American squamates showing viviparity increases from 0.25 in latitudes 25 to 30 N to over 0.60 at latitudes 50 to 55 N (Tinkle and Gibbons, 1977). Because most of the apparent benefits of live-bearing involve increased offspring survival (summarized in Tinkle and Gibbons, 1977), this suggests that viviparity may have evolved as an adaptation to cold environments that might otherwise cause high mortality among eggs. Shine and Berry (1978), Shine and Bull (1979), and

Shine (1985) have strongly supported this theory based on the following scenario: (1) Because females can behaviorally regulate their body (hence offspring) temperature, even a short period of egg retention (the proposed first step toward viviparity) should decrease total incubation time, thus decreasing the probability of egg mortality; (2) Because temperature conditions are clinal, species invading colder areas might gradually increase retention time, and if retention does increase egg survivorship, the intermediate stages of viviparity can be seen as adaptive.

As an alternate to the cold environment hypothesis, Tinkle and Gibbons (1977) suggested that viviparity was primarily an adaptation to variable environments, where stochastic events (freezing temperatures, predation) jeopardize egg survivorship. Females able to retain eggs through this period of environmental uncertainty would have a considerable selective advantage. Tinkle and Gibbons (1977) further suggested that cold temperatures were a good example of such environmental uncertainty, but not exclusively so. Shine (1985) felt that this theory was too broad to generate a testable hypothesis and suggested that, in its simplest form, it was little different than the cold environment hypothesis. Except as noted below, neither Tinkle and Gibbons nor Shine found much support for the proposal that species characteristics played a major role in the evolution of viviparity.

Regardless of the specific environmental conditions favoring the evolution of live-bearing, there appears to be general agreement that egg retention is the necessary first step toward viviparity (Tinkle and Gibbons, 1977; Shine and Bull, 1979). Retaining the eggs not only allows the female to bypass periods of environmental hazard for the eggs but may also permit an enhanced thermal environment for offspring through female basking, a better choice of oviposition site, and an opportunity to add additional sustenance to the young during gestation. This latter idea has found recent physiological support (Stewart and Castillo, 1984) and may be particularly important in environments where females are unable to provide offspring with sufficient nutritional resources before oviposition (cold environments?). Once eggs are retained in the oviduct, some form of gas exchange between the developing offspring and the environment becomes necessary. The longer the period of environmental uncertainty, the longer the eggs must be retained and the more critical the need for a more sophisticated mechanism of gas exchange, such as a placenta (for details see Guillette, 1982, and PLACENTATION). Once such a mechanism has developed, the transition back to egg laying may be difficult or impossible (Tinkle and Gibbons, 1977; Shine and Bull, 1979).

Tinkle and Gibbons (1977) and Shine (1985) reviewed some of the disadvantages of viviparity, including lower clutch frequency, increased mortality risks to the parent, decreased food intake, and higher metabolic costs. Recent studies have suggested that these costs may be high: Seigel and Fitch (1984) and Seigel et al. (1986) showed that live-bearing snakes had a significantly lower relative clutch mass (RCM) than egg layers, resulting in smaller brood or offspring size (see RCM). In addition, the physiological costs of reproduction (heart rate and oxygen consumption) were found to significantly increase during pregnancy in viviparous snakes (Birchard et al., 1984). These data indicate that the "savings" in offspring survival via viviparity must be high indeed to compensate for a reduced RCM, a decreased clutch frequency (but see below), and higher female mortality associated with live-bearing. [Shine and Bull (1979) present a mathematical treatment of this idea.] Some of these costs of viviparity support the idea that live-bearing is most likely to evolve in cold climates. For example, the apparent reduction in clutch frequency associated with live-bearing would place individuals at less of a selective disadvantage at high latitudes (where multiple clutches are uncommon anyway) than in the tropics, where multiple clutches are more likely. However, because it is still debatable whether multiple clutches occur even in tropical snakes, this hypothesis may apply best to lizards (see FREQUENCY OF REPRODUCTION).

One of the distinctive ecological characteristics of snakes is their much higher proportion of viviparity compared with that of lizards. For example, the proportion of viviparous snakes in North America is two to five times higher than that of lizards at comparable latitudes (Tinkle and Gibbons, 1977). Shine (1985) showed that this did not reflect a higher rate of evolution of viviparity in snakes, but rather either a greater speciation rate or a lower extinction rate in live-bearing as compared with egg-laying snakes. The reasons for the higher proportion of viviparity among snakes is not clear. However, Shine (1985) found that the evolution of live-bearing may be favored in species with defensive capabilities such as large size or a venom apparatus. Such factors may be more common in snakes than in lizards. In addition, snakes have significantly higher RCMs than lizards (Seigel and Fitch, 1984). L. Vitt (personal communication) has suggested that limblessness may be an energetically more efficient means of locomotion than legs, indicating that snakes are better able to "afford" the increased costs of viviparity than are lizards. Confirmation of these ideas would be useful.

Placentation

Viviparity in snakes is often viewed as a simple retention of embryos until they are full-term. However, morphological specializations of the fetal and maternal tissues resembling a true placental connection have been described for reptiles (reviewed in Yaron, 1985). Most researchers suggest that true viviparity requires some structure that allows for the transfer of nutrients from the mother to the embryos. In viviparous squamates, the choriovitelline (yolk sac) placenta forms early in embryonic maturation, developing as an interlocking of the choriovitelline membrane and the oviduct (Bauchot, 1965). The structure is initially vascularized by the vitelline blood vessels, but in snakes the allantois penetrates beneath the yolk sac and fuses with this membrane and the allantoic vessels that feed into this structure (Yaron, 1985). The chorioallantoic placenta consists of a union of the chorionic and oviductal structures in which some loss of chorionic and uterine epithelia occurs (Weekes, 1935). The snake allantoplacenta appears to differ from that of lizards in having the allantoic membrane wrapped around vascular folds of the uterine wall.

Guillette (1982) suggested that the reptilian placenta evolved initially to allow for gas exchange for eggs confined to the oviduct for long periods. The passing of significant amounts of nutrition to embryos has been documented recently in *Mabuya heathi* (Blackburn et al., 1984) but has not been confirmed for snakes. Embryos of *Vipera berus* increase about 50% in mass during gestation (Jenkins and Simkiss, 1968), and *Pseudechis porphyriacus* embryos increase from 0.5 g at ovulation to 2.5 g at full term (Shine, 1977b). Some of this weight gain is water; however, the exchange of electrolytes and amino acids has been documented both histologically (Kasturirangan, 1951; Hoffman, 1970) and by radioactive tagging (Conaway and Fleming, 1960; Hoffman, 1968).

Parental Care

Care of eggs or offspring by adults (parental care) is relatively uncommon in snakes. Shine (in press) recently summarized records of parental care in squamates and found that only 47 of 1700 oviparous snakes (2.8%) showed any form of egg guarding or brooding, the major form of parental care known in snakes. Although this was a significantly higher proportion than was found for 3000 species of lizards (1.3%), parental care in snakes is still much less common than in some other ectotherms, notably teleost fish and amphibians (Shine, in press). Parental care in snakes apparently has a phylogenetic component: Only 7 of the 74 colubrids listed by Tinkle and Gibbons (1977) were known to show parental care (9.4%), whereas 9 of 19 elapids, boids, viperids, or typhlopoids showed egg guarding or brooding (47.3%). Shine (in press) independently concluded that the frequency of parental care varied phylogentically. Unfortunately, many of the reports on parental care in snakes are based on brief notes that merely describe finding females with freshly laid eggs (Shine, in press). Such accounts, even when well documented, do not allow determination of either the function of the association or how long the association might continue. The adaptive significance of many reports of parental care in snakes is therefore questionable.

Reports of parental care in snakes include the loose associations described above and a few observations of females assisting newly born offspring in freeing themselves from embryonic sacs (summarized in Shine, in press). Perhaps the best known example of parental care in snakes in the egg-brooding behavior of the genus *Python*, known to occur in as many as nine species (Shine, in press). By using rapid muscular contractions, *P. molurus* is able to maintain body temperatures up to 7°C higher than the surrounding environment and is apparently able to impart this metabolic heat to the eggs by coiling around them during incubation (Hutchison et al., 1966; Vinegar et al., 1970; Vinegar, 1973). The adaptive significance of this behavior was demonstrated by Vinegar (1973), who showed that eggs incubated at higher temperatures hatched earlier and at heavier weights than eggs incubated at lower temperatures. As discussed by Tinkle and Gibbons (1977) and Shine (in press), in order for parental care to evolve, the benefits (presumably increased offspring survival) must outweigh the costs (decreased parental survival or fecundity). Of 11 general benefits listed by Shine, only 2 (deterring potential predators and increasing incubation temperatures) apply to snakes. Conversely, all three of the major costs of parental care (increased metabolic rates, decreased food intake, and reduced fecundity) have been documented for ophidians (but see FECUNDITY). Interestingly, several authors have suggested that egg guarding or brooding may be a substitute for (or an alternative to) viviparity (Neill, 1964; Fitch, 1970; Tinkle and Gibbons, 1977). Egg guarding may provide some of the benefits of live-bearing (i.e., increased offspring survival) without many of the disadvantages associated with viviparity. For example, females that guard eggs are able to abandon them at any time and are not continuously hampered by carrying a clutch. This may enable females to continue to forage effectively even during incubation.

Shine (in press) suggested that parental care was most likely to evolve among species with some combination of the following characteristics: (1) eggs buried superficially, rather then deeply, increasing exposure to potential predators, (2) females having large body size or a defensive apparatus, allowing effective defense of the young, (3) females capable of producing only a single annual clutch, decreasing the cost in fecundity to the female, (4) eggs laid during periods of harsh environmental conditions, favoring females that remain with the eggs (Tinkle and Gibbons, 1977). The first two factors are certainly applicable to many groups of snakes that show egg guarding or brooding (pythons, elapids) and may help explain the higher proportion of parental care in this group compared with lizards. Conversely, almost all snakes are single-brooded (see FECUNDITY), and there is no empirical evidence to show that eggs are laid during periods of harsh conditions. Moreover, with the exception of *Python molurus*, data on the function and significance of egg guarding in snakes is almost entirely lacking. Such studies are critically needed.

FECUNDITY

Under the general heading of fecundity we include those reproductive characteristics of snakes normally associated with life-history strategies: clutch or brood size, offspring size, frequency of reproduction, relative clutch mass, and correlates of these traits with body size or environmental conditions [information on age and size at maturity is presented by Parker and Plummer (this volume.)] Although data on clutch or brood size are extremely common for snakes (see Fitch, 1970), efforts to synthesize this information have lagged behind those for other reptilian groups, especially lizards (Iverson, 1985). Recently, however, a number of workers have begun to critically analyze this mass of data, examining such topics as geographic variation in reproduction (Fitch, 1985a), relative clutch mass patterns (Seigel and Fitch, 1984; Seigel et al., 1986), body size–fecundity relations (Iverson, 1985), phylogenetic constraints on reproductive strategies (Dunham and Miles, 1985), and environmental influences on clutch and body size (Seigel and Fitch, 1985). In this section, we review some of these recent analyses.

Clutch and Litter Size

Reports of clutch or litter size are the most abundant source of information on reproduction in snakes (Turner, 1977). Fitch (1970, 1985a) summarized these data, and the following discussion is based primarily on his review. Reports of clutch size in oviparous snakes range from 1 egg per clutch in several species (e.g., *Coluber constrictor, Tantilla gracilis*) to over 100 eggs per clutch in some boids (*Python reticulatus*) and colubrids (*Farancia abacura*). Litter size varies from 1 in a number of species (*Charina bottae, Storeria occipitomaculata*) to a maximum of about 100 in some natricines (*Nerodia sipedon*). Obviously, these represent extreme values; Fitch (1970) noted that the modal clutch or litter size in snakes was about 7, and that most fell in the range of 2 to 16 offspring per female. Compared with lizards, snakes are considerably more prolific: The modal clutch size in lizards is only 2, with 2 to 6 offspring per female the most common range (Fitch, 1970). In addition, no snake is known to show the fixed clutch size found in geckos and some anoline lizards.

Iverson (1985) recently examined differences in relative fecundity (RF, mean clutch size/female total length in centimeters) among habitats, taxonomic groups, and reproductive modes. Iverson found that, overall, RF was significantly higher in viviparous snakes compared with oviparous forms; however, when comparisons were made by subfamily, significant differences were found only between oviparous and viviparous colubrines. Taxonomic comparisons showed that RF was significantly higher in natricines, xenodontines, and viperines when compared with boids, colubrines, lycodontines, or elapids. Finally, RF was found to be highest in aquatic and semi-fossorial snakes and lowest in terrestrial and arboreal species.

Frequency of Reproduction

Introduction. We suggest that frequency of reproduction is both the most important and the least understood aspect of snake reproductive biology. Frequency of reproduction is best determined by repeated weighing and palpation of individuals throughout the reproductive season (Vitt and Seigel, 1985). Such data have been widely collected for lizards and have produced a wealth of information on reproductive tactics in that group. Because snakes are often difficult to recapture on a regular basis (Parker and Plummer, this volume), most investigators have used a different measure of reproductive frequency, the proportion of individuals gravid at a given point in time (see references in Table 8–2). However,

Table 8–2. Summary of Data on the Proportion of Females Breeding per Year and the Relationship Between Body Size (SVL in cm) and Clutch Size in Snakes[a]

Species	Clutch size	Gravid (%)	N	Location	Regression equation				Reference
					Y-Intercept	Slope	r^2	N	
Family Boidae									
Epicrates cenchria	12.5	82.0	11	Brazil					Vitt and Vangilder (1983)
Family Acrochoridae									
Acrochordus arafurae	16.9	7.0	384	Australia			0.69*	14	Shine (1986)
A. granulatus	4.1	75.0	83?	Philippines			0.36*	20	Gorman et al. (1981)
Family Colubridae									
Arizona elegans (O)	8.4	63.0	14	New Mexico	−4.8	0.21			Aldridge (1979)
Carphophis amoenus (O)		100.0	28	Missouri					Aldridge and Metter (1973)
C. vermis (O)	2.9	78.0	116	Kansas	−6.11	0.32	0.42*	84	Clark (1970)
Cerberus rhynchops	3.6	75.0	88?	Philippines			0.11	29	Gorman et al., (1981)
Coluber constrictor (O)	11.8	64.5	31	Kansas					Fitch (1963)
Coluber constrictor (O)	5.8	80.0	26	Utah	−0.56	0.10	0.28*	18	Brown and Parker (1984)
Diadophis punctatus (O)	3.4	100.0	?	Kansas	−4.83	0.30	0.38*	389	Fitch (1975), Seigel and Fitch (1985)
Liophis lineatus (O)	6.8	83.0	23	Brazil	−4.11	0.20	0.19	19	Vitt and Vangilder (1983)
L. mossoroensis (O)	6.2	48.0	21	Brazil	−9.47	0.29	0.43*	10	Vitt and Vangilder (1983)
L. poecilogyrus (O)	7.4	44.0	29	Brazil			0.09	13	Vitt and Vangilder (1983)

Masticophis taeniatus (O)	6.6	92.0	14	Utah			0.47*	29	Parker and Brown (1980)
Nerodia cyclopion	18.4	85.0	27	Louisiana	−13.4	0.39	0.21	16	Kofron (1979a)
N. sipedon		100.0	55	Missouri	−18.4	0.49			Aldridge (1979)
N. taxispilota		100.0	41	S. Carolina			0.60*	41	Semlitsch and Gibbons (1978)
N. taxispilota	33.9	81.5	28	Virginia	−51.8	0.93	0.62*	23	White et al. (1982)
Opheodrys aestivus (O)	6.1	88.0	143	Arkansas	−4.1	0.23	0.28*	77	Plummer (1983, 1984)
Philodryas nattereri (O)	7.6	41.0	34	Brazil			0.45*	14	Vitt and Vangilder (1983)
P. olfersii (O)	6.6	87.0	47	Brazil			0.33*	39	Vitt and Vangilder (1983)
Regina grahami		93.0	14	Missouri	−11.2	0.16	0.59*	12	R. Seigel (unpubl. obs.)
R. septemvittata	11.6	95.0	20	Kentucky	0.05	0.21	0.52*	10	Branson and Baker (1974)
Sibon sanniola (O)	4	100.0	34	Yucatan	−0.10	0.13	0.18*	28	Kofron (1983)
Storeria dekayi	14.9	95.0	22	Louisiana	−12.4	0.11	0.74*	30	Kofron (1979b)
S. occipitomaculata	9.0	100.0	31?	S. Carolina	−4.96	0.86	0.33*	31	Semlitsch and Moran (1984)
Thamnophis butleri	11.0	67.0							Carpenter (1952)
T. ordinoides	8.8	80.0	55	Washington					Hebard (1951)
T. ordinoides	9.5	77.0	36	Oregon					Stewart (1968)
T. proximus	12.9	88.0	40?	Louisiana	−17.9	0.53	0.77*	10	Tinkle (1957)
T. proximus	8.4	100.0	8	Texas	−11.0	0.34	0.68*	13	Clark (1974)
T. proximus		81.0	27	Missouri	−5.2	0.09	0.68*	7	R. Seigel (unpubl. obs.)
T. radix		74.0	88	Missouri	−4.8	0.30	0.00	14	R. Seigel (unpubl. obs.)
T. sauritus		46.0	13	Michigan			0.22*	52	Burt (1928)

(Continued)

229

Table 8–2. Summary of Data on the Proportion of Females Breeding per Year and the Relationship Between Body Size (SVL in cm) and Clutch Size in Snakes[a] (*Continued*)

Species	Clutch size	Gravid (%)	N	Location	Y-Intercept	Slope	r^2	N	Reference
T. sauritus	10.0	65.0		Michigan					Carpenter (1952)
T. sirtalis	18.0	65.0		Michigan					Carpenter (1952)
T. sirtalis	14.5	64.5	181	Kansas	−15.0	0.48	0.30*	158	Fitch (1965), Seigel and Fitch (1985)
T. sirtalis	11.3	68.0	50	Oregon			0.98*	7	Stewart (1968)
T. sirtalis	16.4	78.0	121	Manitoba	−44.2	0.13	0.66*	53	Gregory (1977)
T. sirtalis		65.0	46	Missouri	−13.6	0.46	0.36*	19	R. Seigel (unpubl. obs.)
Tropidoclonion lineatum	6	98.0	45	Missouri	−10.2	0.70	0.41*	26	Krohmer and Aldridge (1985b)
Waglerophis merremii (O)	16.0	86.0	22	Brazil	−25.9	0.49	0.36*	19	Vitt and Vangilder (1983)
Family Elapidae									
Acanthophis antarcticus	7.9	59.0	22	Australia	−25.1	0.59	0.34*	14	Shine (1980c)
Austrelaps superbus	16.5	85.0	27	Australia			0.81*	19	Shine (1977b)
Cacophis harriettae (O)	5.1			Australia	−7.4	0.35	0.66*	21	Shine (1980a)
C. krefftii (O)	3.2			Australia	−1.75	0.18	0.34	11	Shine (1980a)
C. squamulosus (O)	6.2			Australia	−10.3	0.34	0.78*	17	Shine (1980a)
Drysdalia coronata	4.3	88.0	17	Australia	−2.2	0.20	0.62*	22	Shine (1981)
D. coronoides	5.0	91.0	11	Aust./NSW	1.4	0.12	0.10	25	Shine (1981)
D. coronoides	4.9	93.0	29	Aust./Victoria	−1.97	0.24	0.20*	36	Shine (1981)
D. coronoides	5.4	55.0	29	Aust./Tasmania	−0.69	0.18	0.10		Shine (1981)
D. rhodogaster	4.9	88.0	16	Australia	0.41	0.15	0.10	21	Shine (1981)

Enhydrina schistosa	13.9	100.0	26	Malaysia	−51.9	0.75	0.66*	30	Voris and Jayne (1979)
Hemiaspsis signata	10.3	92.0	15	Australia	−7.74	0.42	0.37	8	Shine (1977b)
Hoplocephalus bitorquatus	4.7	42.0	26	Australia			0.70*	17	Shine (1983)
Notechis scutatus	23.6	87.0	32	Australia	−12.3	0.44	0.28*	31	Shine (1977b)
Pseudechis porphyriacus	12.4	84.0	55	Australia	−4.75	0.16	0.20*	35	Shine (1977b)
Unechis gouldii	4.3	93.0	29	Australia	−2.18	0.21	0.31*	27	Shine (1977b)
Family Viperidae									
Agkistrodon contortrix	5.0	60.0	133	Kansas					Fitch (1960)
A. piscivorus	6.5	42.0	69	SE U.S.					Burkett (1966)
A. piscivorus	5.5	46.5	58	Florida					Wharton (1966)
A. piscivorus		87.0	15	Louisiana					Kofron (1979a)
A. piscivorus		66.0	47	Virginia					Blem (1982)
Crotalus atrox	10.0	68.0	66	Texas					Tinkle (1962)
C. horridus	12.3	52.0	31	S. Carolina	−3.19	0.13		16	Gibbons (1972)
C. horridus	8.4	64.0	42	Wisconsin	−8.39	0.16	0.37*	25	Keenlyne (1978)
C. horridus	7.0	38.0	37	Pennsylvania					Galligan and Dunson (1979)
C. viridis		57.0	47	Wyoming					Rahn (1942)
C. viridis		48.0	33	California					Fitch (1949)
C. viridis	5.5	49.0	523	Utah					Glissmeyer (1951)
C. viridis	9.5	73.0	44	New Mexico	−4.5	0.21	0.20*	23	Aldridge (1979)
C. viridis	6.1	77.0	39	Idaho	−8.36	0.22	0.53*	28	Diller and Wallace (1984)
C. viridis	5.2	58.0	40	Idaho	−8.12	0.20	0.49*	53	Diller and Wallace (1984)
C. viridis	5.4	54.0	11	Idaho	−3.94	0.14	0.32*	36	Diller and Wallace (1984)

(Continued)

231

Table 8–2. Summary of Data on the Proportion of Females Breeding per Year and the Relationship Between Body Size (SVL in cm) and Clutch Size in Snakes[a] (*Continued*)

Species	Clutch size	Gravid (%)	N	Regression equation				Location	Reference
				Y-Intercept	Slope	r^2	N		
C. viridis	9.6	55.0	97					Canada	Gannon and Secoy (1984)
C. viridis	9.7	70.0	20					Kansas	Fitch (1985b)
Sistrurus catenatus	11.7	93.0	82					Wisconsin	Keenlyne (1978)
S. catenatus	6.5	52.0	23					Pennsylvania	Reinert (1981)
S. catenatus	6.4	62.0	29	−11.0	0.30	0.61*	16	Missouri	Seigel (1986)
Trimeresurus flavoviridis (O)	8.6	100.0	17	2.80	0.04	0.04	15	Japan	Koba et al. (1970a)
T. okinavensis	6.2	100.0	29	−1.92	0.16	0.12	25	Japan	Koba et al. (1970c)
T. tokarensis (O)	3.5	100.0	10	−2.29	0.07	0.34	9	Japan	Koba et al. (1970b)
Vipera aspis		40.0	15					France	Saint Girons (1974)
V. aspis	6.7					0.30*	49	France	Naulleau and Saint Girons (1981)
V. berus		68.0	118					Sweden	Vølsoe (1944)
V. berus		59.0	49					Britain	Prestt (1971)
V. berus	8.8	58.0	45	−15.3	0.42	0.74*	19	Sweden	Nilson (1981)
V. berus		50.0						Finland	Saint Girons and Naulleau (1981)
V. berus (1974)	7.5	75.0	100			0.40*	18	Sweden	Andren and Nilson (1983)
V. berus (1981)	10.4	30.0	30			−0.09	10	Sweden	Andren and Nilson (1983)

[a] An (O) indicates an oviparous species. Proportion breeding represents mean values, if several years were averaged. * indicates $P < 0.05$.

such data are potentially misleading: Because the *rate* of follicular development is poorly known in reptiles (Licht, 1984), an investigator cannot, with complete assurance, determine whether a female with enlarged follicles will definitely reproduce that year or even whether a female with small follicles will *not* reproduce (J. Congdon, personal communication). With an adequate sample size and a thorough understanding of both the timing of reproduction and the size at maturity, this problem can be somewhat mitigated. However, although such data can tell us much about the proportion of the population reproducing (leading to speculations about biennial reproduction), this information reveals little about the number of clutches produced each year. These two topics are discussed separately.

Multiple Clutches. Using the criteria of multiple palpations of individual females, there is no conclusive evidence that snakes produce more than a single annual clutch or brood. Aldridge (1979) felt that Temperate Zone snakes were unlikely to produce multiple clutches because of the fixed timing of vitellogenesis. Most authors suggesting that snakes lay more than one clutch have based their conclusions either on captive records or on aseasonal reproductive patterns in tropical species. Tryon (1984) summarized data on multiple clutches in captive snakes, recording 20 oviparous and 3 viviparous species that had produced more than one clutch. Tryon argued that, although captivity could induce irregular and artificial reproductive patterns, snakes that produced multiple clutches under more-or-less natural conditions of light and temperature might be expected to do so in the wild as well. One major difficulty with captive breeding records is the artificially high amount of food with which snakes are provided. Because there is a direct correlation between foraging success and reproduction in snakes (see TEMPORAL VARIATION), documenting multiple clutches in captive snakes provided with much higher food resources than normally occurs in the wild may only indicate that these species have the *potential* for producing multiple clutches, not that such clutches are ever actually produced under natural conditions. Data on aseasonal or extended reproductive seasons in tropical and sub-tropical snakes also suggest the possibility of multiple clutches, but again, convincing data are lacking (see TROPICAL ZONE CYCLES). However, Ford and Karges (in press) recently suggested a possible mechanism by which some (but not all) individual *Thamnophis marcianus* from southern Texas and Mexico could produce multiple broods under certain conditions. Additional data, especially field records of females recaptured several times during the reproductive season, are urgently needed in this area.

Proportion Breeding and Biennial Reproduction. Data on the proportion of females breeding each year are summarized in Table 8–2 for 85 species or populations of snakes. The proportion breeding (defined as females with shelled eggs, developing offspring, or ovulatory-sized follicles) varied from 7% in *Acrochordus arafurae* to 100% in at least 11 species. The mean proportion gravid varied significantly among families within reproductive modes (i.e., viviparous colubrids, elapids, and viperids; arc-sine transformation, ANOVA, $F = 8.86$, df $= 2, 64, P < 0.001$), but not between reproductive modes within families (oviparous compared with viviparous colubrids, $F = 0.21$, df $= 1.37, P > 0.05$). The viperids had the lowest proportion reproducing in our comparisons, but Shine (1986) previously noted that the acrochordids had even lower proportions reproducing than viperids. These preliminary data suggest that the proportion of females breeding each year is not correlated with reproductive mode per se but rather with phylogeny. This conclusion is similar to that of Dunham and Miles (1985), who found significant family-level effects on reproductive traits of squamates, although their sample of snakes was limited to 21 species. These authors also found that body size exerted an important influence on reproductive characteristics, but our preliminary analysis has not addressed this issue.

The low proportion of reproductive females in many species of snakes (especially viperids) has led several authors to suggest that these species follow a biennial reproductive cycle, with reproduction occurring in alternate years (e.g., Fitch, 1949; Glissmeyer, 1951; Tinkle, 1962, and others). The assumption that such biennial cycles are genetically determined has been criticized in recent years by authors who suggested that reproductive frequencies are controlled primarily by local food availability and population structure (Aldridge, 1979; Blem, 1982; Diller and Wallace, 1984). This proposal is supported by several lines of evidence: First, if biennial breeding is genetically determined, then the proportion breeding should not vary from 50% (Aldridge, 1979). Instead, great variation is seen in this figure, ranging from 30 to 100% in viperids alone (Table 8–2). Second, there is apparently considerable year-to-year variation in this proportion within populations, which also should not occur if breeding is genetically controlled. For example, the proportion of female adders (*Vipera berus*) reproducing in Sweden varied from a low of 30% in a year when food availability was low to 75% in a year when resources were more abundant (Andren and Nilson, 1983). Similar temporal variation in the proportion of females breeding has been documented in *Crotalus viridis* (Glissmeyer, 1951) and *Sistrurus catenatus* (Seigel, 1986). The correlation between energy availability, fat reserves, and reproduction has already been discussed (see FAT BODY CYCLING). Third, Blem (1982) has shown that larger (older?) female *Agkistrodon piscivorus* were more likely to be gravid than smaller females within a population. Hence a primary determinant of reproductive frequency may be population size or age structure, which may also vary temporally. Finally, both Fitch (1960) and Diller and Wallace (1984) have documented that individuals of *A. contortrix* and *C. viridis* may reproduce in consecutive years, and that such occurrences may be fairly common (48% in *C. viridis*). Unless biennial reproduction is a polymorphic genetic trait, it seems more logical to conclude that fat reserves, food availability, and population structure are the primary determinants of reproductive frequency in snakes.

Discussion. As this review had indicated, multiple clutches are apparently lacking in snakes, and in many populations fewer than 100% of the females are gravid each year. These patterns contrast sharply with those of other reptilian groups (especially lizards and freshwater turtles), where most females reproduce annually and multiple clutches are common (Moll, 1979; Dunham and Miles, 1985). Bull and Shine (1979) reviewed the concept of low frequency of reproduction (LFR) and suggested that it was most common in species where the costs of reproduction were at least partially independent of fecundity (e.g., migration, brooding, or live-bearing). An LFR was likely to evolve if there was a net increase in fecundity or survivorship by deferring reproduction for some period, in comparison with reproducing in a given year. Bull and Shine found that an LFR was more common in live-bearing forms, in species that brooded their young, and in species that made long breeding migrations. The significantly higher occurrence of LFR among viperids and acrochordids could be the result of several factors: (1) If longevity among vipers and acrochordids is higher than for other snakes, these species may defer reproduction even in marginal years, in the expectation of future reproductive success. (2) The costs of reproduction may be higher among these species, although these costs have not been adequately quantified for most snakes. (3) Despite their elaborate morphological adaptations for catching and killing prey, foraging success may be lower for these groups than for other snakes. This latter idea may be more related to morphology than to phylogeny, because Shine (1980c) has offered a similar explanation for LFR in the death adder (*Acanthophis antarcticus*), a species with many morphological similarities to the viperids. The last suggestion could be tested easily using data on the foraging success of different syntopic species. Such information would be most useful in resolving this issue.

Relative Clutch Mass

The ratio of clutch mass to female mass (relative clutch mass, RCM) has been recently recognized as an important and distinctive life-history trait of lizards and snakes (Vitt and Congdon, 1978; Vitt, 1981; Vitt and Price, 1982; Cuellar, 1984; Seigel and Fitch, 1984; Seigel et al., 1986). Correlates of RCM with ecological characteristics are based on the assumption that the act of carrying offspring has an impact on female mobility and survivorship. If so, then differential mortality of gravid females should produce an RCM that is optimal for a given set of morphological and ecological characteristics, e.g., foraging or escape behavior (Vitt and Price, 1982). This assumption has been partially verified for some species. Shine (1980d) found that escape speed in scincid lizards was significantly lower in gravid females compared with male conspecifics, and that predation intensity in captivity was also higher among gravid females than among males. Recent research in our laboratory has shown that escape speed in gravid garter snakes (*Thamnophis marcianus*) is reduced significantly during gestation when compared with that in non-gravid females tested under the same conditions. Although Bauwens and Thoen (1981) found no increase in mortality associated with reproduction in the lizard *Lacerta vivipara,* Andren (1982) documented that reproductively active *Vipera berus* had significantly lower survivorship rates than non-reproductive females.

Seigel and Fitch (1984) summarized ecological correlates of RCM for snakes. Although Vitt and Congdon (1978) and Vitt and Price (1982) found that RCM in lizards varied among both foraging habits and escape behaviors, no such differences were found for snakes, probably owing to the lack of detailed information on the foraging ecology and escape strategies used by most ophidians (Fitch, this volume). Seigel and Fitch also found that RCM was stable over time in four populations studied, and that the RCM of snakes was significantly higher than that of lizards with the same reproductive mode.

The most important finding of Seigel and Fitch was the difference in RCM between live-bearing and egg-laying snakes: RCM in egg layers was about 20% higher in oviparous compared with viviparous species, and this difference occurred both among and within families. These findings suggest that the costs of reproduction (defined here as a decrease in survivorship or future fecundity) may be much higher in live-bearing species (see VIVIPARITY). Seigel and Fitch showed that the net survivorship of viviparous females at the end of the reproductive season would be much lower than that of egg layers simply because of the increased time that live-bearers carry their offspring. Seigel and Fitch suggested that the most likely way for viviparous females to increase survivorship was to reduce RCM. However, a reduced RCM would necessarily involve a reduction in either brood size or offspring size. Later work (Seigel et al., 1986) showed that, in among-species comparisons, RCM varied independently of body size in oviparous snakes. However, in viviparous snakes, RCM decreased with increasing body size. Therefore, large viviparous snakes tend to have much lower RCMs than equal-sized oviparous species.

The use of RCM as a life-history characteristic has been criticized on statistical and methodological grounds (Shine, 1980d; Cuellar, 1984). A standardized protocol for measuring RCM that includes using only fresh material, weighing eggs or hatchlings within 72 h of oviposition, avoiding data obtained from long-term captives, and calculating weight changes resulting from water loss, may help reduce some of the variation association with RCM (Seigel et al., 1986). In order to avoid statistical bias, inter- or intraspecific comparisons of RCM should be made by analysis of covariance, using female mass as the covariate (Seigel and Fitch, 1984).

Offspring Size

Once reproductive effort (the proportion of the energy budget devoted to reproduction) is set, that effort must be apportioned to the offspring. A female can produce many small or a few large young; hence clutch size is a major determinant of the energy allocated to each individual offspring (Smith and Fretwell, 1974; Pianka, 1976). However, this interaction is also influenced by female body size. Because reptiles undergo indeterminate growth, sexually mature females within a population may vary in body size (Parker and Plummer, this volume). In addition, clutch size and clutch mass are often tightly correlated with female body size in snakes (see BODY SIZE). A larger clutch may consist of more young of the same size, fewer but larger young, or some combination of the two. Therefore, three factors are involved in determining neonate size in snakes: (1) reproductive effort, (2) female body size, and (3) clutch size.

Lemen and Voris (1981) used the equation

$$\text{Birth weight} = \frac{(\text{female weight}) \, (\text{Relative reproductive effort})}{\text{clutch size}}$$

to express the relationships of factors influencing offspring size. Lemen and Voris suggested that relative reproductive effort did not vary among species of marine snakes, so they evaluated only the effects of body size and clutch size on offspring size. [These authors used relative clutch mass as a measure of relative reproductive effort; although there are difficulties with such usage (see RELATIVE CLUTCH MASS), we accept this definition for the purposes of this discussion.]

Lemen and Voris found that, in general, marine snakes produced larger young relative to terrestrial species, but that different marine snakes accomplished this in different ways (Figure 8–3). Larger species (e.g., *Lapemis hardwickii*, Figure 8–3) expended greater reproductive effort and produced the largest young, but smaller species (e.g., *Hydrophis fasciatus*) also produced relatively large young by reducing clutch size. Other small species (*H. torquatus*) reduced clutch size somewhat less, producing smaller young. Therefore, in between-species comparisons, female size was the major factor affecting offspring size, but modification of clutch size could also alter offspring size within certain limits.

Within species (at least within populations) we tend to think of offspring size as fixed through natural selection at an optimal size to forage effectively and avoid predation (Smith and Fretwell, 1974). Because both female size and clutch size can vary within species, the same equation given previously can be used and, as before, the factors controlling offspring size are female body size and clutch size. However, these two factors are intercorrelated, and their interactive effect on offspring size must be considered.

Ford and Killebrew (1983) found that, after correcting for female body size, larger clutches of *Thamnophis butleri* produced smaller young. The effect was stronger in smaller females, because larger females put less RCM into each offspring (Figure 8–4), perhaps because of the allometric effects of growth. Other workers have shown that larger females produce larger young regardless of clutch size, both in viviparous species (*T. marcianus:* Ford and Karges, 1986)

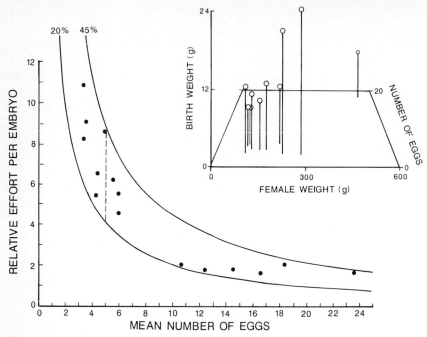

Figure 8–3. The relationship between clutch size and relative reproductive effort per embryo in marine and terrestrial snakes. The inset shows the estimated birth weight of the young of marine species relative to female weight and clutch size. (Reproduced with permission from *J. Anim. Ecol.,* vol. 50, 1981.)

and in several oviparous snakes (*Opheodrys aestivus:* Plummer, 1984; *Trimeresurus okinavensis:* Koba et al., 1970a; *T. flavoviridis:* Koba et al., 1970b). In *Trimeresurus,* larger females lay larger (wider and heavier) eggs, and within a size class, larger clutches resulted in reduced egg length.

Because the snake body is tubular, the constraint on physical space for reproduction is a simple volumetric function. As female size increases, the space available for reproduction increases 1.5 times faster than SVL. This means that a female that is twice as long as another individual can produce three times the number of the same-sized offspring. It also suggests that larger snakes can increase clutch size with less effect on offspring size. For example, an increase of four young in a 15-g *Thamnophis butleri* reduces the mass of each young by 0.2 g, but by only 0.1 g in a 45-g female (Ford and Killebrew, 1983). Increased clutch size in egg-laying snakes also has a proportionally greater effect on smaller females (Koba et al., 1970a,b).

Offspring size is an important component of female fitness (Smith and Fretwell, 1974), but it is obvious from this discussion that this aspect of snake reproductive biology needs further study. Investigators should be sure to include

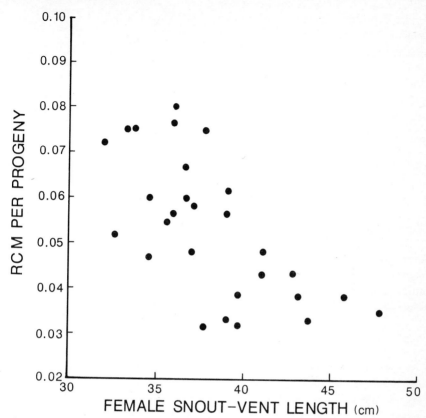

Figure 8–4. Relationship of female body size and relative clutch mass per offspring in *Thamnophis butleri*. (Reproduced with permission from *J. Herpetol.*, vol. 17, 1983.)

offspring size measurements (especially mass) in their data collection and to relate these data to female size and clutch size.

Body Size

Female body size appears to exert an important influence on the reproductive traits of snakes. As previously mentioned, female body size is significantly correlated with RCM, offspring size, and the proportion of females breeding. Many authors have also noted that female size and clutch or brood size are often positively correlated within populations (e.g., Fitch, 1970). These data are summarized in Table 8–2. Female SVL and clutch size are significantly correlated in the majority of all populations (75.4%, $N = 61$). The proportion of variation explained by the regression of clutch size on body size varied from 0.0 in *Thamnophis proximus* to 0.98 in one population of *T. sirtalis*. However, these represent extreme figures, and most values fell in the range of 0.2 to 0.6. The relatively large proportion of variance left unexplained by the regression with SVL suggests either that SVL is a poor morphological predictor of reproduction in snakes (Hedges, 1985) or that genetic or environmental factors may also exert a significant effect on fecundity. Andren and Nilson (1983) found that SVL was significantly associated with brood size in *Vipera berus* during periods of high resource availability ($r^2 = 0.40$) but not when food was limited ($r^2 = 0.09$). Data on genetic control of reproduction are almost entirely lacking for snakes and urgently need to be collected.

Temporal Variation

Although reproductive characteristics such as clutch size and offspring size are often perceived as fixed parameters, data from a variety of taxa (including lizards, turtles, and birds) indicate that these traits may fluctuate widely over time (cf. Seigel and Fitch, 1985). Because snakes generally produce only a single clutch or brood each year (see FREQUENCY OF REPRODUCTION), temporal variation in snakes involves annual, rather than seasonal, variation.

Annual variation in the proportion of snakes breeding each year has been recognized for some time (see FREQUENCY OF REPRODUCTION), but temporal variation in clutch size and related parameters has been documented in snakes only recently, possibly because relatively few populations have been studied for long enough periods to detect annual changes. Andren and Nilson (1983) compared reproduction in *Vipera berus* in Sweden for 2 years with sharply contrasting resource availability and found that the proportion of females breeding, clutch size, and offspring mass were significantly higher in the year with greater food resources. These authors also noted that female body size was significantly correlated with both clutch size and clutch mass in the year with greater resources but not when food was limited. However, RCM did not change from year to year. Seigel and Fitch (1985) showed that, even after corrections were made for annual changes in female body size, clutch size varied significantly from year to year in *Diadophis punctatus, Thamnophis sirtalis* (two populations), and *Agkistrodon contortrix* in Missouri and Kansas; only in *T. radix* were annual differences not significant. Changes in clutch size could be quite pronounced, rivaling or exceeding those in geographically distinct populations. In *D. punctatus, T. sirtalis,* and *A. contortrix,* clutch size was significantly larger in years when precipitation was higher than normal, perhaps indicating greater food availability. No annual changes in RCM were found in any of these populations, but there was some evidence that offspring size may vary from year to year.

Data from these populations suggest a strong correlation between prey availability and most reproductive parameters. The need for long-term data on reproduction is obvious: Using short-term information to characterize the reproductive strategies of snakes or to make geographic comparisons may be misleading (Seigel and Fitch, 1985). In addition, data on annual differences in resource levels and foraging success are critical. Plummer (1983) showed that reproduction in *Opheodrys aestivus* did not vary in two climatically distinct years, possibly because snakes compensated for low energy availability with increased foraging success in the spring. Additional data on long-term changes in reproductive parameters are important for understanding life-history ecology in snakes.

Geographic Variation

Geographic variation in clutch size, offspring size, and clutch frequency in snakes have been discussed by a number of authors (see review in Fitch, 1985a). Such discussions are prompted by the assumption that the reproductive traits of local populations are the outcome of selective forces acting on these traits. By comparing geographically distinct populations, we can learn much about how local demes adapt to different environmental conditions. Unfortunately, data on geographic variation in reproduction in snakes is confounded by two factors. First, the characteristics listed above are correlated with female body size and, presumably, age (see BODY SIZE). Geographic comparisons made without regard to changes in body size or age structure are apt to be misleading. Although various statistical techniques exist to correct for body size (e.g., analysis of covariance), these techniques usually require that the raw data be available for all populations, which is rarely true. Second, these reproductive traits are apparently subject to considerable temporal variation, probably as a result of changes in prey availability (see TEMPORAL VARIATION). Thus the apparent geographic differences reviewed below must be evaluated carefully.

Fitch (1985a) exhaustively reviewed geographic changes in reproduction in New World reptiles and, within the limits described previously, found that 96% of the snakes examined showed some form of geographic variation. Clutch size increased with increasing northern latitude in 60% of the species and decreased with latitude in 36%. Clutch size also apparently increased with increasing altitude in all five of the snakes for which sufficient data were available. Some geographic changes are apparently independent of body size; Semlitsch and Moran (1984) found that litter sizes in Michigan populations of *Storeria occipitomaculata* were significantly smaller than in a South Carolina population, even though body size was significantly larger in Michigan. The same authors also found evidence that neonate size was larger in Michigan, perhaps as a result of a trade-off with clutch size (see OFFSPRING SIZE). Geographic variation in clutch frequency has been suspected to occur in some species (e.g., *Sistrurus catenatus:* Reinert, 1981), but we agree with Aldridge (1979), Blem (1982), and Diller and Wallace (1984) that the main factor controlling clutch frequency is foraging success (see also FREQUENCY OF REPRODUCTION). Hence this measure cannot meaningfully be compared among populations without information on temporal changes and prey availability.

SUMMARY AND FUTURE RESEARCH

This review suggests that, although our understanding of some areas of snake reproductive biology is still limited, research is accelerating in many fields. The extensive literature on female reproductive cycles has documented both the histological changes associated with vitellogenesis and the timing of the process in temperate species. However, little is known about the reproductive cycles of tropical or subtropical snakes. Researchers have not dealt adequately with environmental control of reproduction in any tropical snake with aseasonal or even seasonal reproduction, reflecting our general lack of knowledge of the physiological control of vitellogenesis and ovulation. The hormonal regulation of reproduction, and its control by exogenous factors, is poorly understood for most snakes. Hopefully, this will change as more sophisticated enzymatic assays for hormones become widely utilized.

Our understanding of male reproductive cycles is limited to histological and physiological data concerning the development of spermatozoa and the control or reproductive behavior in temperate species. Patterns of endocrine control of reproduction in males remain poorly documented.

The evolution of viviparity in snakes has been well examined, but studies are needed to further examine the costs of live-bearing. Experimental studies on parental care in snakes are badly needed to determine the cost to the parent and the benefit to the offspring.

Data on clutch or brood sizes are abundant for many snakes, and direction is now essential. Field studies on reproductive frequency, especially in tropical and subtropical areas, are desperately needed. Recaptures of individual females to document clutch frequency are particularly important. A major problem with research on fecundity is a lack of consistency in data collection, e.g., not recording mass of females and offspring, and the use of total length rather than SVL.

Perhaps the most serious deficiency in our understanding of snake reproduction relates to temporal variation in reproductive traits. Many reviews of the literature on this subject assume no distinction between times of data collection. Although geographic variation in reproduction has been documented, it is likely that temporal variation may be equally important. Extreme care must be used when making generalizations, particularly when it is clear that prey availability, temperature, rainfall, and other environmental factors vary to some degree in even the most stable habitats. Long-term field studies designed to assess such variation are crucial.

In conclusion, the next few years should be exciting ones in the development of this field. With new techniques and carefully directed research our understanding of snake reproductive ecology should increase dramatically.

ACKNOWLEDGMENTS

We are grateful to the following colleagues for supplying us with unpublished data, unpublished manuscripts, or reprints of their papers: F. Achaval, R. Aldridge, C. Andren, C. Banks, G. Burghardt, G. Burns, D. Crews, C. Ernst, H. Fitch, J. Iverson, H. Marx, G. Nilson, T. Schwaner, H. Saint Girons, R. Shine, and B. Tryon. We thank J. Knight for helping with much of the literature search. The manuscript was improved by the comments and suggestions of R. Aldridge, J. Congdon, H. Fitch, M. Mendonca, S. Novak, N. Seigel, and R. Shine. This research was supported by Department of Energy Contract DE-AC09-76SR00819 with the University of Georgia's Institute of Ecology (SREL).

LITERATURE CITED

Aldridge, R. D. 1979. Female reproductive cycles of the snakes *Arizona elegans* and *Crotalus viridis, Herpetologica* 35:256–261.

Aldridge, R. D. 1982. The ovarian cycle of the watersnake *Nerodia sipedon,* and effects of hypophysectomy and gonadotropin administration, *Herpetologica* 38:71–79.

Aldridge, R. D. and Metter, D. E. 1973. The reproductive cycle of the worm snake, *Carphophis vermis,* in Missouri, *Copeia* 1973:472–477.

Aleksiuk, M. and Gregory, P. T. 1974. Regulation of seasonal mating behavior in *Thamnophis sirtalis parietalis, Copeia* 1974:681–689.

Andren, C. 1982. Effect of prey density on reproduction, foraging and other activities in the adder, *Vipera berus, Amphib.-Reptilia* 3:81–96.

Andren, C. and Nilson, G. 1983. Reproductive tactics in an island population of adders, *Vipera berus* (L.), with a fluctuating food resource, *Amphib.-Reptilia* 4:63–79.

Ballinger, R. D. 1977. Reproductive strategies: Food availability as a source of proximal variation in a lizard, *Ecology* 58:628–635.

Bauchot, R. 1965. La placentation chez les reptiles, *Ann. Biol.* 4:547–575.

Bauwens, D. and Thoen, C. 1981. Escape tactics and vulnerability to predation associated with reproduction in *Lacerta vivipara, J. Anim. Ecol.* 50:733–743.

Belluomini, H. E., de Mello, R. F., Penha, A. M., and Schreiber, G. 1966. Estudo citologica e ponderal de testicudo de *Crotalus durissus terrificus* durante ciclo reproductive annual, *Mem. Inst. Butantan Sao Paulo Simp. Intern.* 33:761–766.

Berry, P. Y. and Lim, G. S. 1967. The breeding pattern of the puff-faced water snake, *Homalopsis buccata* Boulenger, *Copeia* 1967:307–313.

Betz, T. W. 1963. The ovarian histology of the diamond-backed water snake, *Natrix rhombifera* during the ovarian cycle, *J. Morphol.* 113:245–260.

Birchard, G. F., Black, C. P., Schuett, G. W., and Black, V. 1984. Influence of pregnancy on oxygen consumption, heart rate and hematology in the garter snake: Implications for the "cost of reproduction" in live-bearing reptiles, *Comp. Biochem. Physiol* 77A:519–523.

Blackburn, D. G., Vitt, L. J., and Beuchat, C. A. 1984. Eutherian-like reproductive specializations in a viviparous reptile, *Proc. Natl. Acad. Sci. USA* 81:4860–4863.

Blem, C. R. 1982. Biennial reproduction in snakes: An alternative hypothesis, *Copeia* 1982:961–963.

Bona-Galo, A. and Licht, P. 1983. Effects of temperature on sexual receptivity and ovarian recrudescence in the garter snake, *Thamnophis sirtalis parietalis, Herpetologica* 39:173–182.

Bona-Galo, A., Licht, P., MacKenzie, D. S., and Lofts, B. 1980. Annual cycles in levels of pituitary and plasma gonadotropin, gonadal steroids, and thyroid activity in the Chinese cobra (*Naja naja*), *Gen. Comp. Endocrinol.* 42:477–493.

Bons, J., and Saint Girons, H. 1982. Le cycle sexuel des reptiles males au Maroc et ses rapports avec la repartition geographique et le climat, *Bull. Soc. Zool. Fr.* 107:71–86.

Branson, B. A. and Baker, E. C. 1974. An ecological study of the queen snake, *Regina septemvittata* (Say) in Kentucky, *Tulane Stud. Zool. Bot.* 18:153–171.

Brown, W. S. and Parker, W. S. 1984. Growth, reproduction and demography of the racer, *Coluber constrictor mormon,* in northern Utah, in: Vertebrate Ecology and Systematics: A Tribute to Henry S. Fitch (R. A. Seigel, L. E. Hunt, J. L. Knight, L. Malaret, and N. Zuschlag, eds.) *Univ. Kans. Mus. Nat. Hist. Spec. Publ.* 10:13–40.

Bull, J. J. and Shine, R. 1979. Iteroparous animals that skip opportunities for reproduction, *Am. Nat.* 114:296–303.

Burkett, R. D. 1966. Natural history of the cottonmouth moccasin, *Agkistrodon piscivorus* (Reptilia), *Univ. Kans. Publ. Mus. Nat. Hist.* 17:435–491.

Burt, M. D. 1928. The relation of size to maturity in the garter snakes, *Thamnophis sirtalis sirtalis* and *T. sauritus sauritus, Copeia* 1928:8–12.

Camazine, B., Garstka, W., Tokarz, R., and Crews, D. 1980. Effects of castration and androgen replacement on male courtship behavior in the red-sided garter snake (*Thamnophis sirtalis parietalis*), *Horm. Behav.* 14:358–372.

Carpenter, C. C. 1952. Comparative ecology of the common garter snake (*Thamnophis s. sirtalis*), the ribbon snake (*Thamnophis s. sauritus*), and Butler's garter snake (*Thamnophis butleri*) in mixed populations, *Ecol. Monogr.* 22:235–258.

Cheylan, M. J., Bons, J., and Saint Girons, H. 1981. Existence d'un cycle spermatogenetique vernal et prenuptial chez un serpent mediterraneen, la couleuvre de Montpellier, *Malpolon monspessulonus* (Herman) (Reptilia, Colubridae), *C. R. Acad. Sci.* 245:2416–2418.

Clark, D. R., Jr. 1970. Ecological study of the worm snake *Carphophis vermis* (Kennicott), *Univ. Kans. Publ. Mus. Nat. Hist.* 19:89–194.

Clark, D. R., Jr. 1974. The western ribbon snake (*Thamnophis proximus*): Ecology of a Texas population, *Herpetologica* 30:372–379.

Conaway, C. H. and Fleming, W. R. 1960. Placental transmission of Na^{22} and I^{131} in *Natrix, Copeia* 1960:53–55.

Crews, D. 1976. Hormonal control of male and female sexual behavior in the garter snake (*Thamnophis sirtalis sirtalis*), *Horm. Behav.* 7:451–460.

Crews, D. 1984. Gamete production, sex hormone secretion, and mating behavior uncoupled, *Horm. Behav.* 18:22–28.

Crews, D., Diamond, M., Tokarz, R., Camazine, B., and Garstka, W. 1984. Hormone independence of male sexual behavior in a garter snake, *Horm. Behav.* 18:29–41.

Cuellar, O. 1984. Reproduction in a parthenogenetic lizard: With a discussion of optimal clutch size and a critique of the clutch weight/body weight ratio, *Am. Midl. Nat.* 111:242–258.

Diller, L. V. and Wallace, R. L. 1984. Reproductive biology of the northern Pacific rattlesnake (*Crotalus viridis oreganus*) in northern Idaho, *Herpetologica* 40:182–193.

Duda, P. L. and Kaul, O. 1977. Ovarian cycle in high altitude lizards from Kashmir. II. *Scincella himalayanum* (Boulenger), *Herpetologica* 33: 427–433.

Duellman, W. E. 1978. The biology of an equatorial herpetofauna in Amazonian Ecuador, *Univ. Kans. Mus. Nat. Hist. Misc. Publ.* 65:1–352.

Dunham, A. E. and Miles, D. B. 1985. Patterns of covariation in life history traits of squamate reptiles: The effects of size and phylogeny reconsidered, *Am. Nat.* 126:231–257.

Duvall, D., Guillette, L. J., Jr., and Jones, R. E. 1982. Environmental control of reptilian reproductive cycles, in: Biology of the Reptilia, vol. 13 (C. Gans and H. Pough, eds.) pp. 201–231, Academic Press, New York.

Fitch, H. S. 1949. Study of snake populations in central California, *Am. Midl. Nat.* 41:513–579.

Fitch, H. S. 1960. Autecology of the copperhead, *Univ. Kans. Publ. Mus. Nat. Hist.* 13:85–288.

Fitch, H. S. 1963. Natural history of the racer *Coluber constrictor, Univ. Kans. Publ. Mus. Nat. Hist.* 15:351–468.

Fitch, H. S. 1965. An ecological study of the garter snake, *Thamnophis sirtalis, Univ. Kans. Publ. Mus. Nat. Hist.* 15:493–564.

Fitch, H. S. 1970. Reproductive cycles of lizards and snakes, *Univ. Kans. Mus. Nat. Hist. Misc. Publ.* 52:1–247.

Fitch, H. S. 1975. A demographic study of the ringneck snake (*Diadophis punctatus*) in Kansas, *Univ. Kans. Mus. Nat. Hist. Misc. Publ.* 62:1–53.

Fitch, H. S. 1982. Reproductive cycles in tropical reptiles, *Occas. Pap. Mus. Nat. Hist. Univ. Kans.* 96:1–53.

Fitch, H. S. 1985a. Variation in clutch and litter size in New World reptiles, *Univ. Kans. Mus. Nat. Hist. Misc. Publ.* 76:1–76.

Fitch, H. S. 1985b. Observations on rattle size and demography of prairie rattlesnakes (*Crotalus viridis*) and timber rattlesnakes (*Crotalus horridus*) in Kansas, *Occas. Pap. Mus. Nat. Hist. Univ. Kans.* 118:1–11.

Ford, N. B. and Karges, J. P. Reproduction in the checkered garter snake, *Thamnophis marcianus* from Southern Texas and Northeastern Mexico: Seasonality and evidence for multiple clutches, *Southwest. Nat.,* In press.

Ford, N. B. and Killebrew, D. W. 1983. Reproductive tactics and female body size of Butler's garter snake (*Thamnophis butleri*), *J. Herpetol.* 17:271–275.

Fox, H. 1977. The urogenital system of reptiles, in: Biology of the Reptilia, vol. 6 (C. Gans and T. S. Parsons, eds.) pp. 1–157. Academic Press, New York.

Galligan, J. H. and Dunson, W. A. 1979. Biology and status of timber rattlesnake (*Crotalus horridus*) populations in Pennsylvania, *Biol. Conserv.* 15:13–57.

Gannon, V. P. J. and Secoy, D. M. 1984. Growth and reproductive rates of a northern population of the prairie rattlesnake, *Crotalus v. viridis, J. Herpetol.* 18:13–19.

Garstka, W. R. and Crews, D. 1982. Female control of male reproductive function in a Mexican snake, *Science* 217:1159–1160.

Garstka, W. R., Camazine, B., and Crews, D. 1982. Interactions of behavior and physiology during the annual reproductive cycle of the red-sided garter snake (*Thamnophis sirtalis parietalis*), *Herpetologica* 38:104–123.

Gibbons, J. W. 1972. Reproduction, growth, and sexual dimorphism in the canebrake rattlesnake (*Crotalus horridus atricaudatus*), *Copeia* 1972:222–226.

Glissmeyer, H. R. 1951. Egg production of the Great Basin rattlesnake, *Herpetologica* 7:24–27.

Godley, J. S. 1980. Foraging ecology of the striped swamp snake, *Regina alleni,* in southern Florida, *Ecol. Monogr.* 50:411–436.

Goldberg, S. R. 1971. Reproductive cycle of the ovoviviparous iguanid lizard *Sceloporus jarrovi* Cope, *Herpetologica* 27:123–131.

Gorman, G. C., Licht, P., and McCollum, F. 1981. Annual reproductive patterns in three species of marine snakes from the central Phillippines, *J. Herpetol.* 15:335–354.

Gregory, P. T. 1977. Life-history parameters of the red-sided garter snake (*Thamnophis sirtalis parietalis*) in an extreme environment, the Interlake region of Manitoba, *Natl. Mus. Can. Publ. Zool.* 13:1–44.

Guillette, L. J., Jr. 1982. The evolution of placentation in the high elevation Mexican lizard *Sceloporus aeneus, Herpetologica* 38:94–103.

Hahn, W. E. and Tinkle, D. W. 1965. Fat body cycling and experimental evidence for its adaptive significance to ovarian follicle development in the lizard *Uta stansburiana, J. Exp. Zool.* 158:79–86.

Hebard, W. B. 1951. Notes on the life history of the Puget Sound garter snake, *Thamnophis ordinoides, Herpetologica* 7:177–179.

Hedges, S. B. 1985. The influence of size and phylogeny on life history variation in reptiles: A response to Stearns, *Am. Nat.* 126:258–260.

Highfill, D. R. and Mead, R. A. 1975. Function of corpora lutea of pregnancy in the viviparous garter snake, *Thamnophis sirtalis, Gen. Comp. Endocrinol.* 27:401–407.

Hoffman, L. H. 1968. An analysis of placentation in the garter snake, *Thamnophis s. sirtalis,* and observations of sperm storage in the oviduct, Ph.D. Dissertation, Cornell University, Ithaca, New York.

Hoffman, L. H. 1970. Placentation in the garter snake, *Thamnophis sirtalis, J. Morphol.* 131:57–87.

Hutchison, V. H., Dowling, H. G., and Vinegar, A. 1966. Thermoregulation in a brooding female Indian python, *Python molurus bivittatus, Science* 151:694–696.

Iverson, J. B. 1985. Patterns of relative fecundity in snakes, *Proc. Indiana Acad. Sci.* 94:597 (abstract).

James, C. and Shine, R. 1985. The seasonal timing of reproduction: A tropical-temperate comparison in Australian lizards, *Oecologia (Berl.)* 67:464–474.

Jenkins, N. K. and Simkiss, K. 1968. The calcium and phosphate metabolism of reproducing reptiles with particular reference to the adder (*Vipera berus*), *Comp. Biochem. Physiol.* 26:865–876.

Kasturirangan, L. R. 1951. Placentation in the sea snake, *Enhydrina schistosa* (Daudin), *Proc. Indian Acad. Sci.* 34:1–32.

Keenlyne, K. D. 1978. Reproductive cycles in two species of rattlesnakes, *Am. Midl. Nat.* 100:368–375.

Koba, K., Morimoto, H., Nakamoto, E., Yoshizaki, K., Ono, T., and Tanaka, K. 1970a. Eggs and egg-laying in the Habu, *Trimeresurus flavoviridis,* of Amami-oshima Is., *Snake* 2:22–31.

Koba, K., Tanaka, K., Nakamoto, E., and Morimoto, H. 1970b. The eggs of the Tokara-habu (*Trimeresurus tokarensis*): Condition in the oviduct, laying, and hatching, *Snake* 2:32–38.

Koba, K., Tanaka, K., Yoshizaki, K., and Nakamoto, E. 1970c. Eggs and hatching of the Hime-habu, *Trimeresurus okinavensis* Boulenger, *Snake* 2:111–121.

Kofron, C. P. 1979a. Reproduction of aquatic snakes in south-central Louisiana, *Herpetologica* 35:44–50.

Kofron, C. P. 1979b. Female reproductive biology of the brown snake, *Storeria dekayi,* in Louisiana, *Copeia* 1979:463–466.

Kofron, C. P. 1983. Female reproductive cycle of the neotropical snail-eating snake *Sibon sanniola* in northern Yucatan, Mexico, *Copeia* 1983:963–969.

Krohmer, R. W. and Aldridge, R. D. 1985a. Male reproductive cycle of the lined snake, (*Tropidoclonion lineatum*), *Herpetologica* 41:33–38.

Krohmer, R. W. and Aldridge, R. D. 1985b. Female reproductive cycle of the lined snake (*Tropidoclonion lineatum*), *Herpetologica* 41:39–44.

Lance, V. and Lofts, B. 1978. Studies on the annual reproductive cycle of the female cobra, *Naja naja, J. Morphol.* 157:161–180.

Lazlo, J. 1979. Notes on reproductive patterns of reptiles in relation to captive breeding, *Int. Zoo Yearb.* 19:22–27.

Lemen, C. A. and Voris, H. K. 1981. A comparison of reproductive strategies among marine snakes, *J. Anim. Ecol.* 50:89–101.

Licht, P. 1984. Reptiles, in: Marshall's Physiology of Reproduction, vol. 1 (G. E. Lamming, ed.) pp. 206–282, Churchill Livingston, Edinburgh.

Licht, P., Farmer, S. W., Bona-Gallo, A., and Popkoff, H. 1979. Pituitary gonadotropins in snakes, *Gen. Comp. Endocrinol.* 39:34–52.

Lofts, B. 1969. Seasonal cycles in reptilian testes, *Gen. Comp. Endocrinol Suppl.* 2:147–155.

Lofts, B. 1972. The Sertoli cell, *Gen. Comp. Endocrinol. Suppl.* 3:636–648.

Lofts, B. 1977. Patterns of spermatogenesis and steroidogenesis in male reptiles, in: Reproduction and Evolution (J. H. Calaby and C. H. Tyndale-Boscoe, eds.) pp. 127–136, Australian Academy of Science, Canberra.

Lofts, B. 1978. Reptilian reproductive cycles and environmental regulators, in: Environmental Endocrinology (I. Assenmacher and D. S. Farmer, eds.) pp. 37–43, Springer-Verlag, Berlin.

Lofts, B., Phillips, G., and Tam, W. H. 1966. Seasonal changes in the testis of the cobra, *Naja naja* (Linn), *Gen. Comp. Endocrinol. Suppl.* 6: 466–475.

Marshall, A. J. and Woolf, F. M. 1957. Seasonal lipid change in the sexual elements of a male snake, *Vipera berus, Q. J. Microsc. Sci.* 96:89–100.

Moll, E. O. 1979. Reproductive cycles and adaptations, in: Turtles: Perspectives and Research (M. Harless and H. Morlock, eds.) pp. 305–331, John Wiley, New York.

Moll, E. O. and Legler, J. M. 1971. The life history of a neotropical slider turtle, *Pseudemys scripta* (Schoepff) in Panama, *Bull. Los Angeles Co. Mus. Nat. Hist. Sci.* 11:1–102.

Naulleau, G. and Saint Girons, H. 1981. Poids des nouveau-nes et reproduction de *Vipera aspis* (Reptilia: Viperidae), dans des conditions naturelles et artificielles, *Amphib.-Reptilia* 2:51–62.

Neill, W. T. 1962. The reproductive cycles of snakes in a tropical region, British Honduras, *Q. J. Fla. Acad. Sci.* 3:234–253.

Neill, W. T. 1964. Viviparity in snakes: Some ecological and zoogeographical considerations, *Am. Nat.* 98:35–55.

Nilson, G. 1981. Ovarian cycle and reproductive dynamics in the female adder, *Vipera berus* (Reptilia, Viperidae), *Amphib.-Reptilia* 2:63–82.

Nilson, G. and Andren, C. 1982. Function of renal sex secretion and male hierarchy in the adder, *Vipera berus,* during reproduction, *Horm. Behav.* 16:404–413.

Parker, W. S. and Brown, W. S. 1980. Comparative ecology of two colubrid snakes, *Masticophis t. taeniatus* and *Pituophis malanoleucus deserticola*, in northern Utah, *Milw. Public Mus. Publ. Biol. Geol.* 7:1–104.

Pianka, E. R. 1976. Natural selection of optimal reproductive tactics, *Am. Zool.* 16:775–784.

Plummer, M. V. 1983. Annual variation in stored lipids and reproduction in green snakes (*Opheodrys aestivus*), *Copeia* 1983:741–745.

Plummer, M. V. 1984. Female reproduction in an Arkansas population of rough green snakes (*Opheodrys aestivus*), in: Vertebrate Ecology and Systematics: A Tribute to Henry S. Fitch (R. A. Seigel, L. E. Hunt, J. L. Knight, L. Malaret, and N. Zuschlag, eds.) *Univ. Kans. Mus. Nat. Hist. Spec. Publ.* 10:105–113.

Prestt, I. 1971. An ecological study of the viper *Vipera berus* in southern Britain, *J. Zool. (Lond.)* 164:373–418.

Quinn, H. R. 1979. Reproduction and growth of the Texas coral snake (*Micrurus fulvius tenere*), *Copeia* 1979:453–463.

Rahn, H. 1942. The reproductive cycle of the prairie rattler, *Copeia* 1942:233–240.

Reinert, H. K. 1981. Reproduction by the massasauga (*Sistrurus catenatus catenatus*), *Am. Midl. Nat.* 105:393–395.

Saint Girons, H. 1962. Le cycle reproductive de la vipere cornes *Cerastes cerastes* (L.) dans la nature et en captivite, *Bull. Soc. Zool. Fr.* 87:41–51.

Saint Girons, H. 1966. Le cycle sexual des serpents venimeux, *Mem. Inst. Butantan Sao Paulo Simp. Intern.* 33:105–114.

Saint Girons, H. 1974. Le cycle sexuel de *Vipera aspsis* (L.) en montagne, *Vie Milieu* 23:309–328.

Saint Girons, H. 1982. Reproductive cycles of male snakes and their relationships with climate and female reproductive cycles, *Herpetologica* 38:5–16.

Saint Girons, H. 1985. Ecophysiological characteristics of the sexual cycle of snakes from temperate regions, in: Endocrine Regulation as Adaptive Mechanisms to the Environment, Colloque International du Centre National de la Recherche Scientifique, Chize, Editions du C.N.R.S., Paris.

Saint Girons, H. and Naulleau, G. 1981. Poids des nouveau-nes et strategies reproductrices des viperes Europeennes, *Terre Vie,* 35:597–616.

Saint Girons, H. and Pfeffer, P. 1971. Le cycle sexuel de serpents du Cambodge, *Ann. Sci. Zool.* 13:543–571.

Schuett, G. W. 1982. A copperhead (*Agkistrodon contortrix*) brood produced from autumn copulations, *Copeia* 1982:700–702.

Schuett, G. W. and Gillingham, J. C. 1986. Sperm storage and multiple paternity in the copperhead (*Agkistrodon contortrix*), *Copeia.* 1986:807–811.

Seigel, R. A. 1984. The foraging ecology and resource partitioning patterns of two species of garter snakes, Ph.D. Dissertation, University of Kansas, Lawrence.

Seigel, R. A. 1986. Ecology and conservation of the massasauga (*Sistrurus catenatus*) in Missouri, *Biol. Conserv.* 35:333–346.

Seigel, R. A. and Fitch, H. S. 1984. Ecological patterns of relative clutch mass in snakes, *Oecologia (Berl.)* 61:293–301.

Seigel, R. A. and Fitch, H. S. 1985. Annual variation in reproduction in snakes in a fluctuating environment, *J. Anim. Ecol.* 54:497–505.

Seigel, R. A., Fitch, H. S., and Ford, N. B. 1986. Variation in relative clutch mass in snakes among and within species, *Herpetologica* 42:179–185.

Semlitsch, R. D. and Gibbons, J. W. 1978. Reproductive allocation in the brown water snake, *Natrix taxispilota, Copeia* 1978:721–723.

Semlitsch, R. D. and Moran, G. B. 1984. Ecology of the redbelly snake (*Storeria occiptiomaculata*) using mesic habitats in South Carolina, *Am. Midl. Nat.* 111:33–40.

Shine, R. 1977a. Reproduction in Australian elapid snakes. I. Testicular cycles and mating seasons, *Aust. J. Zool.* 25:647–653.

Shine, R. 1977b. Reproduction in Australian elapid snakes. II. Female reproductive cycles, *Aust. J. Zool.* 25:655–666.

Shine, R. 1980a. Comparative ecology of three Australian snake species of the genus *Cacophis* (Serpentes: Elapidae), *Copeia* 1980:831–838.

Shine, R. 1980b. Ecology of eastern Australian whipsnakes of the genus *Desmania, J. Herpetol.* 14:381–389.

Shine, R. 1980c. Ecology of the Australian death adder *Acanthophis antarcticus* (Elapidae): Evidence for convergence with the Viperidae, *Herpetologica* 36:281–289.

Shine, 1980d. "Costs" of reproduction in reptiles, *Oecologia (Berl.)* 46:92–100.

Shine, R. 1981. Venomous snakes in cold climates: Ecology of the Australian genus *Drysdalia* (Serpentes: Elapidae), *Copeia* 1981:14–25.

Shine, R. 1983. Arboreality in snakes: Ecology of the Australian elapid genus *Hoplocephalus, Copeia* 1983:198–205.

Shine, R. 1985. The evolution of viviparity in reptiles: An ecological analysis, in: Biology of the Reptilia, vol. 15 (C. Gans and F. Billett, eds.) pp. 606–694, John Wiley, New York.

Shine, R. 1986. Ecology of a low-energy specialist: Food habits and reproductive biology of the Arafura file snake (*Acrochordidae*), *Copeia* 1986:424–437.

Shine, R. Parental care in reptiles, in: Biology of the Reptilia (C. Gans and R. Huey, eds.) John Wiley, New York, In press.

Shine, R. and Berry, J. F. 1978. Climatic correlates of live-bearing in squamate reptiles, *Oecologia (Berl.)* 33:261:268.

Shine, R. and Bull, J. 1979. The evolution of live-bearing in lizards and snakes, *Am. Nat.* 113:905–923.

Smith, C. C. and Fretwell, S. D. 1974. The optimal balance between size and number of offspring, *Am. Nat.* 108:499–506.

Smith, R. E. 1968. Experimental evidence for a gonadal-fat body relationship in two teiid lizards (*Ameiva festiva, Ameiva quadrilineata*), *Biol. Bull.* 134:325–331.

Stewart, G. R. 1968. Some observations on the natural history of two Oregon garter snakes (genus *Thamnophis*), *J. Herpetol.* 2:71–86.

Stewart, J. R., and Castillo, R. E. 1984. Nutritional provision of the yolk of two species of viviparous reptiles, *Physiol. Zool.* 57:377–383.

Tinkle, D. W. 1957. Ecology, maturation and reproduction of *Thamnophis sauritus proximus, Ecology* 38:69–77.

Tinkle, D. W. 1962. Reproductive potential and cycles in female *Crotalus atrox* from northwestern Texas, *Copeia* 1962:306–313.

Tinkle, D. W. and Gibbons, J. W. 1977. The distribution and evolution of viviparity in reptiles, *Misc. Publ. Mus. Nat. Hist. Univ. Mich.* 154:1–55.

Tryon, B. W. 1984. Additional instances of multiple egg-clutch production in snakes, *Trans. Kans. Acad. Sci.* 87:98–104.

Tsui, H. W. 1976. Stimulation of androgen production by the lizard testis: Site of action of ovine FSH and LH, *Gen. Comp. Endocrinol.* 28:386–394.

Turner, F. B. 1977. The dynamics of populations of squamates, crocodilians and rhynchocephalians, in: Biology of the Reptilia, vol. 7 (C. Gans and D. W. Tinkle, eds.) pp. 157–264, Academic Press, New York.

Vinegar, A. 1973. The effects of temperature on the growth and development of embryos of the Indian python, *Python molurus* (Reptilia: Serpentes: Boidae), *Copeia* 1973:171–173.

Vinegar, A., Hutchison, V. H., and Dowling, H. G. 1970. Metabolism, energetics, and thermoregulation during brooding of snakes of the genus *Python* (Reptilia, Boidae), *Zoologica* 55:19–48.

Vitt, L. J. 1980. Ecological observations on sympatric *Philodryas* (Colubridae) in northeastern Brazil, *Pap. Avulsos Zool. (Sao Paulo)* 34:87–98.

Vitt, L. J. 1981. Lizard reproduction: Habitat specificity and constraints on relative clutch mass, *Am. Nat.* 117:506–514.

Vitt, L. J. 1983. Ecology of an anuran-eating guild of terrestrial tropical snakes, *Herpetologica* 39:52–66.

Vitt, L. J. and Congdon, J. D. 1978. Body shape, reproductive effort, and relative clutch mass in lizards: Resolution of a paradox, *Am. Nat.* 112: 595–608.

Vitt, L. J. and Price, H. J. 1982. Ecological and evolutionary determinants of relative clutch mass in lizards, *Herpetologica* 38:237–255.

Vitt, L. J. and Seigel, R. A. 1985. Life history traits of lizards and snakes, *Am. Nat.* 125:480–484.

Vitt, L. J. and Vangilder, L. D. 1983. Ecology of a snake community in northeastern Brazil, *Amphib.-Reptilia* 4:273–296.

Volsøe, H. 1944. Structure and seasonal variation of the male reproductive organs of *Vipera berus* (L.), *Spoila Zool. Mus. Huan.* 5:1–157.

Voris, H. K. and Jayne, B. C. 1979. Growth, reproduction and population structure of a marine snake, *Enhydrina schistosa* (Hydrophiidae), *Copeia* 1979:307–318.

Weekes, H. C. 1935. A review of placentation among reptiles with particular regard to the function and evolution of the placenta, *Proc. Zool. Soc. Lond.* 1935:625–645.

Weil, M. R. 1982. Seasonal effects of mammalian gonadotropins (bFSH and bLH) on plasma androgen levels in male water snakes, *Nerodia sipedon, Comp. Biochem. Physiol.* 73A:73–76.

Weil, M. R. and Aldridge, R. D. 1981. Seasonal androgenesis in the male water snake, *Nerodia sipedon, Gen. Comp. Endocrinol.* 44:44–53.

Wharton, C. H. 1966. Reproduction and growth in the cottonmouths, *Agkistrodon piscivorus* Lacepede, of Cedar Keys, Florida, *Copeia* 1966:149–161.

White, D. R., Mitchell, J. C., and Woolcott, W. S. 1982. Reproductive cycle and embryonic development of *Nerodia taxispilota* (Serpentes: Colubridae) at the northeastern edge of its range, *Copeia* 1982:646–652.

Wong, K. L. and Chiu, K. W. 1974. The snake thyroid gland. I. Seasonal variation in thyroidal and serum iodoamino acids, *Gen. Comp. Endocrinol.* 23:63–70.

Yaron, Z. 1985. Reptilian placentation and gestation: Structure, function, and endocrine control, in: Biology of the Reptilia, vol. 15 (C. Gans and F. Billett, eds.) pp. 527–603, John Wiley, New York.

Zug, G. R., Hedges, S. B., and Sunkel, S. 1979. Variation in reproductive parameters of three neotropical snakes, *Coniophanes fissidens, Dipsas catesbyi,* and *Imantodes cenchoa, Smithsonian Contrib. Zool.* 300:1–20.

CHAPTER NINE

Population Ecology

William S. Parker
Michael V. Plummer

The focus of this chapter is on numbers of snakes. We view population ecology as being concerned primarily with density and those population attributes such as sex ratio, age structure, reproduction, and mortality that affect density. Although we consider certain techniques, this is not a "how to" chapter. Quantitative techniques applicable to snakes are discussed by Caughley (1977), to whom we refer the reader for an exhaustive treatment.

Compared with the literature on the snakes' closest relatives, the lizards, where long-term field studies have advanced to experimental stages, studies on the dynamics of snake populations still struggle with basic descriptions. The reasons for this retardation are due largely to the less tractable nature of snakes, which can be ascribed to four chief factors: (1) Snakes are often inconspicuous and nocturnal; (2) many snakes have extended periods of inactivity; (3) apparent population densities often are low; (4) the relatively extensive and irregular movements of some snakes make it difficult to define the boundaries of a population. Such characteristics result in a comparatively poor return for an investigator's time and effort, making it difficult to dedicate the extended time and energy needed for an accurate assessment of population processes (cf. Tinkle, 1979).

Much reported "population" information in the literature is anecdotal, collected secondarily to other objectives, and frequently is based on specimens collected from widely scattered localities, over many years, or both. Because population processes function within space and time constraints, some of the available information, such as most studies based on museum collections, is not useful for our purposes. Snake populations may be differentiated among small geographic areas (Kephart, 1981; Macartney, 1985), and until we know more about the structure of populations, it seems advisable to assume that most snakes occur in relatively local populations (for an exception, see Kropach, 1975).

Information on snake populations is not distributed evenly among snake groups. Anecdotal information exists for a variety of taxa, but long-term field studies have been limited to about a dozen colubrids (mostly colubrines and natricines) and to fewer than half a dozen viperids. Except for reproduction data, there is little or no information bearing on populations of species in the families Boidae, Aniliidae, Tropidophiidae, Bolyeriidae, Uropeltidae, Leptotyphlopidae, Anomalepididae, Typhlopidae, and Elapidae (excluding hydrophines and laticaudines). Except for a few sea snakes, information on tropical snake populations is very sparse.

ABUNDANCE

Various indices of relative abundance in snakes have been reported. Examples include numbers of snakes caught per man-hour of search (Clark, 1970), numbers caught in can traps per 100 m of drift fence (Semlitsch et al., 1981), numbers seen on roads per 100 km driven (Reynolds, 1982), numbers relative to each other (Dunson and Minton, 1978), and numbers expressed as totals (including several species) per hectare (Barbault, 1970; Dunson, 1975). Although useful for specific purposes, such indices do not yield absolute population density information for a single species at a given time.

High densities of snake species sometimes occur at communal hibernacula (e.g., Woodbury, 1951; Viitanen, 1967; Gregory, 1977), at marine "slicks" (Kropach, 1971), and on certain islands (Koba, 1938; Klauber, 1972). Most such reports describe aggregations which, out of ecological necessity, could not be sustained indefinitely. Under normal long-term ecological conditions snakes occur at much lower densities (Table 9–1).

Because of their intractable nature, methods of determining population density in snakes requiring direct enumeration are feasible only in limited circumstances (e.g., aggregations). Thus most studies on population estimation in snakes have employed mark-recapture techniques (Table 9–1).

Whereas determining growth and mortality rates depends on recapturing individuals after an extended period since marking, determination of population size depends on recapturing individuals within a restricted period soon after marking (Caughley, 1977). A major problem in dealing with snakes is the difficulty in recapturing sufficient numbers over short periods. When the proportion of recaptures is plotted against time or cumulative number of snakes marked, a curve typical for snake studies (fenced den studies excepted) levels out relatively low (Figure 9–1). Because of low recapture rates, standard errors of population estimates, reported rarely, generally are large (Table 9–1). Caughley (1977) provides a method of determining the number of recaptures necessary to provide standard errors that are within 10% of Lincoln-Peterson population estimates, the index most commonly used in snake studies.

Table 9–1. Reported Population Densities and Rates of Recapture in Snakes[a]

Species	Density (no./ha)[b]	S.E. as % of Population Estimate[c]	Method[d]	No. available for recapture[e]	Recaptures (%)[e]	Reference[f]
Acrochordidae						
Acrochordus arafurae	16–97		1	32–99	3–19	1
Boidae						
Eryx tataricus	<1		2			2
Colubridae						
Carphophis amoenus	375–729		1	49–50	8–16	3
	23		4			4
Coluber constrictor	3–7		1	419–807	9–17	5
	1		2			6
	<1		1	138–244	56–78	7
Coronella austriaca	11–17		2			8
Diadophis punctatus	719–1849		1	57–386	3–11	9
			1	378	34	10
Elaphe dione	<1		2			2
Elaphe obsoleta	<1		1	38	11	11
	<1		1	9–18	31–60	12
Elaphe quadrivirgata	4–46	9–98	1	648	48	13
Elaphe vulpina	1–3	94	1,4	16	6	14
Heterodon nasicus	2–10	62–97	1			15
Heterodon platirhinos	1–7	76–109	1			15
Lampropeltis calligaster	<1		2,4	55	16	16,4
Lampropeltis triangulum	<1		1,4	58	19	17,4
			1	200	5	10
Lycodonomorphus bicolor	380	79	1	1087	1	18

Table 9–1. Reported Population Densities and Rates of Recapture in Snakes[a] (*Continued*)

256

Species	Density (no./ha)[b]	S.E. as % of Population Estimate[c]	Method[d]	No. available for recapture[e]	Recaptures (%)[e]	Reference[f]
Masticophis flagellum	<1		2			6
Masticophis taeniatus	<1	20	1	74	36	19
	<1		2			6
	<1		2			20
Natrix natrix	7		2			6
Nerodia sipedon			1			21
		9–20	1		8	22
	<1		4			4
		31–122	1			23
Natrix tessellata	<1		2			2
	<1		2			6
Opheodrys aestivus	429	5	1	210	49	24
Opheodrys vernalis	182		1	78	15	25,26
			1	170	0	10
Pituophis melanoleucus			1	54	22	27
			4			28,4
	<1		2			20
	<1		3			29
Regina alleni	1289	10	1	903	46	13
Rhabdophis tigrinus	3–25	9–99	1	7–33	6–14	14
Storeria dekayi	7–24	53–98	4			4
	16		1			10
Storeria occipitomaculata	<1		1	200	0	2
Taphrometopon lineolatum	4–9		2			30
Thamnophis butleri	13–40	26–42	1	23–69	9–39	14

Thamnophis cyrtopsis				45	18	31
Thamnophis elegans				83	27	31
Thamnophis proximus	16–61	5–133	1	5–669	14	32
Thamnophis radix	840	25–64	1	298	7	33
Thamnophis rufipunctatus			1	29		25,26
Thamnophis sauritus	10–48		1	260	5	31
Thamnophis sirtalis	16–34	9–53	1	49–173	6–25	30
	2–8		1	78–638	2–32	10
	19		1	79	8	30
		27–52	1	1100		34
		6–172	1	12–16	14	35
	3–5		1	5–501	7–33	36
			1			10
			1			14
			1			32
Virginia striatula	229–348	35–65	1			37
Elapidae						
Enhydrina schistosa		49	1	435	10	38
Hydrophis melanosoma			1	69	0	38
Hydrophis brookii			1	53	4	38
Laticauda laticauda		23	1	100	20	39
Notechis ater		10–104	1			40
Pelamis platurus			1	961	<1	41
Viperidae						
Agkistrodon contortrix	6–9		1	17–32	6–9	42
Agkistrodon halys	3		2	72	8	2
Crotalus cerastes	<1		1			43
Crotalus horridus	<1		4	679	23	4
Crotalus viridis	3	30–31	1	49–69	23	28
	1					44
	<1		2		20–41	6

(Continued)

257

Table 9–1. Reported Population Densities and Rates of Recapture in Snakes[a] *(Continued)*

Species	Density (no./ha)[b]	S.E. as % of Population Estimate[c]	Method[d]	No. available for recapture[e]	Recaptures (%)[e]	Reference[f]
	2–3	27	1			45
	3–9		1		75–95	46
Trimeresurus flavoviridis			5			47
Vipera berus	14		1	657[g]	48	48
	4		2			49
	7		1	127		50
Vipera ursinii			2			2

[a] Ranges are given when more than one census was made.

[b] Population estimates do not include hatchlings or, in most cases, juveniles.

[c] Unsymmetric standard errors were averaged.

[d] 1, mark-recapture; 2, direct count; 3, quadrat counts; 4, comparison to other syntopic species in which population density was estimated by mark-recapture; 5, removal technique.

[e] Because recapture data are presented in different ways by different authors, the number available for recapture and percentage recaptured refer either to total snakes registered only during a census or to snakes registered over the course of the study and are thus only roughly comparable among studies and do not necessarily correspond to the data used for the population estimates in the same row.

[f] 1, Shine (1986); 2, Bogdanov (1965); 3, Clark (1970); 4, Fitch (1982); 5, Fitch (1963a); 6, Turner (1977); 7, Brown and Parker (1984); 8, Spellerberg and Phelps (1977); 9, Fitch (1975); 10, Blanchard et al. (1979); 11, Fitch (1963b); 12, Stickel et al. (1980); 13, Fukada (1969); 14, Freedman and Catling (1978); 15, Platt (1969); 16, Fitch (1978); 17, Fitch and Fleet (1970); 18, Madsen and Osterkamp (1982); 19, Parker (1976); 20, Parker and Brown (1980); 21, Blanchard and Finster (1933); 22, Feaver (1977); 23, King (1986); 24, Plummer (1985a); 25, Seibert and Hagen (1947); 26, Seibert (1950); 27, Imler (1945); 28, Fitch (1949); 29, Godley (1980); 30, Carpenter (1952a); 31, Fleharty (1967); 32, Kephart (1981); 33, Clark (1974); 34, Fitch (1965); 35, Gregory (1977); 36, Blaesing (1979); 37, Clark and Fleet (1976); 38, Voris (1985); 39, Saint Girons (1964); 40, Schwaner (1985); 41, Kropach (1975); 42, Fitch (1960); 43, Brown (1970); 44, Preston (1964); 45, Duvall et al. (1985); 46, Macartney (1985); 47, Tanaka et al. (1971); 48, Viitanen (1967); 49, Prestt (1971); 50, Andrén and Nilson (1983).

[g] Composite of five populations (percentage recaptured varied from 22 to 100% among populations).

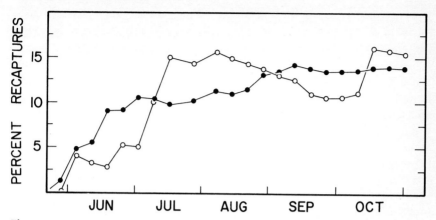

Figure 9–1. Percent recaptures in weekly samples of Illinois populations of two colubrid species (*Opheodrys vernalis,* open circles; *Thamnophis radix,* closed circles). Redrawn from Seibert and Hagen (1947).

Mark-recapture models are subject to large errors in their results if certain assumptions are not met (Caughley, 1977), and snakes have great potential for violating the assumption of equal catchability of all individuals. Despite this, the assumption of equal catchability has been tested in only a few studies (Feaver, 1977; Gregory, 1977; Macartney, 1985; Plummer, 1985a; Schwaner, 1985).

Turner (1977) constructively criticized population estimates of snakes based on mark-recapture studies. Because the quality of the data is largely a function of intractable snakes (Turner, 1977; Lillywhite, 1982), it is unlikely that the basic nature of the data in future studies will change greatly. However, this certainly does not preclude profitable population studies on snakes. We recommend several routine procedures that would permit a greater level of confidence in the results of future snake studies: (1) Determine the frequency of emigration and immigration relative to the study area (e.g., Carpenter, 1952a; Feaver, 1977; Kephart, 1981). (2) Test for equal catchability. (3) Report standard errors of population estimates. (4) Apply Bailey's correction term to Lincoln-Peterson estimates when the number of recaptures is low (Caughley, 1977; Turner, 1977). (5) Do not introduce snakes into the study area (cf. Clark, 1970; Blanchard et al., 1979) or sacrifice snakes for reproductive studies from "nearby localities" if it has not been determined that the snakes to be sacrificed actually represent a different population. Adherence to these procedures would facilitate comparisons among studies by permitting an evaluation of the reliability of population estimates, thus advancing the study of snake population dynamics.

Patterns of Abundance

If the population densities in Table 9–1 are at least reasonable estimates of actual densities, several patterns of abundance at the population level emerge.

High Density. The small, secretive, fossorial snakes *Carphophis amoenus, Diadophis punctatus,* and *Virginia striatula* are among those that occur in very high densities. All are specialists on earthworms (especially the introduced exotic *Allolobophora*), at least at the locality of study. *Diadophis punctatus* occurs in the greatest density (719 to 1849/ha) of any snake, and the small aquatic *Regina alleni* is a close second (1289/ha). Like *D. punctatus* preying on the highly successful *Allolobophora* in Kansas (Fitch, 1975), *R. alleni* specializes on an extremely abundant prey in Florida, the crayfish *Procambarus* (Godley, 1980). Other snakes with reported high densities include the small arboreal *Opheodrys aestivus* and the terrestrial *Thamnophis radix.* Higher densities of small snakes compared with large snakes should be expected (Peters and Wassenberg, 1983). However, *T. radix* is larger than any of the previously mentioned species and reportedly occurs at an order of magnitude greater than that of any other *Thamnophis* of similar size (Table 9–1).

Linear "Density." Because of the difficulty in determining the extent of habitat utilization by semiaquatic and other streamside snakes, density has been reported as the number of snakes per meter of shoreline. Values ranging from 0.02 to 0.38 snakes per meter have been reported for four species of *Nerodia, R. septemvittata, Tretanorhinus nigroluteus,* and *O. aestivus* (Branson and Baker, 1974; Hebrard and Mushinsky, 1978; Plummer, 1985a; King, 1986; J. Knight, Personal communication).

Changes in Density. Temporal changes in population density are affected by reproduction, mortality, emigration, and immigration. Migration results in drastic short-term fluctuations in density in several high-latitude communal denning species that make annual long-distance movements between their dens and summer ranges (Gregory and Stewart, 1975; Parker and Brown, 1980; Brown and Parker, 1984; Duvall et al., 1985). Similarly, the hydrophid *Laticauda colubrina* annually migrates long distances for breeding (Saint Girons, 1964). On a smaller scale, the density of *R. alleni* fluctuates 30-fold because of seasonal movements between a permanent water habitat in canals and a temporary water habitat in surrounding marshes (Godley, 1980).

Because most snakes are not migratory, short-term fluctuations in density must be attributed to reproductive success and mortality. Based on number of snakes seen, Klimstra (1958) observed large annual fluctuations in the numbers of several species and speculated that snake populations fluctuated in synchrony over extensive geographic areas. Observing seasonal fluctuations in the abundance of 38 species of snakes, Barbault (1970) stated that most of the species completed their life cycles in a year and that population turnover was very rapid. Similar apparent short-term fluctuations may be found in mark-recapture studies in which several censuses were attempted over time, with the variation between successive population estimates averaging approximately 50% (Fukada, 1969; Platt, 1969; Fitch, 1975; Feaver, 1977; Gregory, 1977).

Although large short-term reductions in population size could result from increased mortality, it is extremely difficult to reconcile large short-term increases with the typical snake life history. In comparison with early maturing short-lived lizards with a rapid population turnover (Tinkle et al., 1970), attributes such as delayed maturity, low adult mortality, and high longevity in snakes (below) are incompatible with the concept of rapid population turnover. Fitch (1982) considered snake populations to be among the most stable community components at the University of Kansas Natural History Reservation. A much more likely explanation for the numerous observations of apparent short-term population fluctuations concerns behavior. Snakes are low-energy organisms whose energy budgets permit prolonged periods of inactivity (Pough, 1983). Studies in which direct observation of snake activity by radiotelemetry (Fitch and Shirer, 1971), isotope tagging (Barbour et al., 1969), and tracking (Lillywhite, 1982) have demonstrated the tendency of snakes to be inactive and inconspicuous (and unavailable to an investigator) for prolonged periods. Apparent short-term fluctuations in snake numbers probably result mostly from changes in availability due to behavior (which greatly affects recapture indices). Therefore, many reports of short-term numerical changes should be considered similar to "seasonal incidence" studies on snakes (e.g., Henderson and Hoevers, 1977; Reynolds, 1982) that attempt to relate snake activity to some environmental variable.

Apparent uniform population decreases were found over the course of several years in studies on the small snakes *C. amoenus* (Clark, 1970), *T. proximus* (Clark, 1974), and *V. striatula* (Clark and Fleet, 1976). In each case, the authors correlated population decreases with decreases in annual precipitation. Soil moisture is important in the ecology of small fossorial snakes (Elick and Sealander, 1972), but other factors may have been involved. If in fact the populations decreased over the course of the studies, the possibility exists that the decreases were augmented by increased mortality due to processing. Handling (forced elongation, measuring, marking) may result in subsequent retardation of growth (Fitch, 1949, 1975, this volume; Clark, 1970). Handling retarded growth in first-year *Pituophis melanoleucus* but did not affect older (and larger) snakes (Platt, 1984). Carpenter (1952a) did not find a handling effect on growth in three species of *Thamnophis* but later analysis (Willis et al., 1982) revealed that injured (loss of tail) first-year snakes suffered higher mortality than non-injured snakes. These data suggest that handling effects (unnatural injuries) are greater on small snakes than on larger snakes, and that such effects can increase mortality. Perhaps measuring length with a "squeeze box" (Quinn and Jones, 1974), or a similar device, would diminish the undesirable effects of stretching on small snakes.

Long-term changes in density have been related to successional community changes (Clark, 1970; Fitch, 1982), catastrophic environmental events, and human predation. Statements pertaining to long-term declines in snake populations abound, but few quantitative studies exist (but see Klauber, 1972; King, 1986). Substantially fewer indications of long-term increases exist. The abundances of *P. melanoleucus* and *Masticophis flagellum* increased greatly after the advent of irrigation in the Imperial Valley of California (Klauber, 1972). The best documentation of both long-term population decreases (*Crotalus viridis, M. taeniatus*) and increases (*Coluber constrictor, P. melanoleucus*) is found in a series of studies on a major communal den in northern Utah covering 34 yr (Woodbury, 1951; Hirth and King, 1968; Parker and Brown, 1973, 1974; Brown and Parker, 1982).

Geographic Variation in Density. Macrogeographic and microgeographic variation in density in such wide-ranging species as *C. constrictor* and *T. sirtalis* can be great (Table 9–1) (Kephart, 1981). The relative extent to which phenotypic and genetic responses contribute to such variation is unknown. Comparative demographic studies (e.g., Kephart, 1981; Brown and Parker, 1984) can provide interesting information on responses of snakes to different environments and are sorely needed. Variation in density on offshore islands may offer an opportunity in this regard (e.g., Schwaner, 1985; King, 1986).

Brown's (1984) model of the relationship between geographic distribution and abundance suggests that population density generally should be greatest near the center of the geographic range and decline toward the margins. Brown found it difficult to obtain quantitative data for any vertebrates other than birds. Pendlebury's (1977) map of *Crotalus viridis* in Canada is suggestive of reduced abundance at range margins in a snake but, in general, sufficient quantitative data to test Brown's hypothesis for snakes are lacking.

Density and Biomass. Maximum population biomass (4.6 kg/ha) among 38 species of snakes surveyed by Iverson (1982) is exceeded by the biomass of *R. alleni* (30.8 kg/ha: Godley, 1980) and *O. aestivus* (7.1 kg/ha: calculated from Plummer, 1985a,b). These three values are greater than the maximum values for birds and carnivorous mammals (Table 2 in Iverson, 1982). High biomass values result from either a high standing crop or high productivity. Assuming that biomass lost to mortality is a good approximation of production in a stable population, Iverson (1982) calculated annual biomass production of *D. punctatus* (1.3 kg/ha/yr) based on Fitch (1975), and we did the same for *O. aestivus* (4.0 kg/ha/yr) based on Plummer (1985a,b). After converting to calories (Vitt, 1978), values of 2569 and 7902 kcal/ha/yr were obtained, respectively. The production value for *D. punctatus* is well within the range of values for birds and mammals, and that of *O. aestivus* is greater than the maximum values (Ricklefs, 1979; Iverson, 1982). Although preliminary, these biomass and production calculations suggest that at least some snakes may have a greater role in community function than formerly recognized.

AGE AND GROWTH

Aging Techniques

Assigning accurate ages to animals in natural populations is critical to understanding any age-specific population process, including individual growth rates, age structure, fecundity, maturity, and survivorship. Caughley (1977) discussed the consequences of errors in aging for population analyses.

Gibbons (1976) summarized the four most common approaches to aging individuals in natural populations of reptiles. Three of these are applicable to snakes: (1) histological examinations of one or more bones of the skeleton, presuming that "growth" rings indicate periods of cessation of growth (i.e., winter); (2) utilizing size groups discernible in samples taken at the same or numerous localities, often in different seasons over periods sometimes as long as decades; and (3) utilizing mark-recapture techniques with local populations, whereby young individuals of known age, preferably in their first year of life, can be marked individually (see Fitch, this volume) and followed over several years under natural conditions. This is demonstrably the most accurate method of aging.

Introduction to Growth

Studies on growth rates are important in detecting differences in resource levels, occurrences of food limitation, and genetic differences between populations. Andrew's (1982) review is the best source of information on growth in reptiles, including an analysis of growth in 17 species of snakes from four families. The two most important points she emphasizes about growth in reptiles were that maximal growth rates are constrained by mass-specific metabolic rates and that high variability in intraspecific growth rates is an important adaptation reflecting the energy-conservative nature of reptilian life (Pough, 1983).

Post-natal Growth

Seasonal Size Groups. Table 9–2 summarizes growth and maturity characteristics based on 39 species of colubrids, 8 species of viperids, and 36 species of elapids. About 33% of the colubrid, 50% of the viperid, and over 90% of the elapid studies on growth were based on seasonal size frequencies in samples usually taken from many local populations over broad geographical areas and in many different years. Vitt (1983) criticized the arbitrary drawing of lines through seasonal size frequency data that have not been correlated with growth rates measured independently and recommended using more sophisticated analyses (e.g., Harding, 1949). Nevertheless, the approximate nature of first-year growth may be described in seasonally reproducing temperate snakes by using the size frequency method. Growth beyond the first year, however, is usually difficult to discern because of the merging of size groups. At later ages, the degree of sheer guesswork continues to increase.

Types of Growth in Snakes. Until recently, most studies on growth in snakes reported descriptive rather than quantitative analyses of growth patterns, preventing valid comparative analyses. Only a few recent studies have quantitatively analyzed growth in local populations (e.g., Plummer, 1985b).

The only extensive and comprehensive attempt to generalize about growth in snakes and its relation to other aspects of their ecology and behavior was made by Feaver (1977). The results of his analyses and comparisons are shown in Table 9–3, representing two large groups of species distinguished primarily by the sex that attains the larger size and the resultant presence or absence of male combat, and one small group with intermediate characteristics. Examples of growth in representatives of each of the larger groups are shown in Figure 9–2.

First-year Growth. Andrews (1982) compared the maximum rate of length growth with hatchling length in 17 species of snakes and found that the growth rate was significantly higher in species with larger hatchlings. Platt (1984) compared absolute length increases during the first year with normal adult size in 21 populations of 17 colubrid species. The growth rate was highest in species with larger hatchlings and species with a larger adult size and was influenced by geography, taxonomic differences, and age at maturity. Interspecific comparisons are hindered by a lack of quantitative analysis in most earlier studies.

The first-year growth of females of a wide variety of snake taxa are compared in relative and absolute terms in Table 9–2. As demonstrated by Andrews (1982) and Platt (1984), small oviparous colubrids and small to medium-sized elapids have low relative first-year length increases, as do viperids. Groups of species with substantially higher relative first-year growth are small viviparous and medium-sized oviparous colubrids and most medium-sized and large elapids. On this basis relative growth rates are low in most of the smallest snakes (Colubridae and Elapidae), viviparous colubrids being an exception, and low in viperids. Other size or taxonomic patterns are not as obvious. Andrews (1982) pointed out the difficulty of separating intrinsic and extrinsic factors in explaining existing patterns, suggesting possible relations between growth and niche adaptations and/or between growth and availability or utilization of extrinsic energy resources allotted to growth (see also Mushinsky, this volume).

Growth to Maturity in Females. Relative growth from hatchling to minimum mature length (approximate length at first ovulation) in female snakes is shown in Table 9–2. Small oviparous colubrids and small to medium-sized elapids

Table 9–2. Comparison of Mean Sizes at Hatching and at Maturity, Mean Minimum Ages at Maturity, and Mean Growth Characteristics in Snake Species Grouped by Size, Family, and Reproductive Mode[a]

Species group	No. Studies	No. species	HFL (cm)	MiFL (cm)	MiF age (yr)	MiML (cm)	MiM age (yr)	MaFL (cm)	MiFL/MaFL	F PIM	F PI-1	F AI-1 (cm)	Ref.[b]
Small oviparous colubrids	9	7	9.9 (6)	21.9 (9)	2.3 (8)	17.4 (5)	2.0 (6)	29.6 (6)	0.74 (6)	1.2 (6)	0.70 (5)	6.5 (5)	1
Small viviparous colubrids	6	4	7.9 (4)	22.5 (6)	1.9 (5)	14.4 (3)	1.6 (4)	28.3 (4)	0.69 (4)	1.6 (4)	1.40 (3)	10.3 (3)	2
Medium oviparous colubrids	8	7	16.1 (8)	47.5 (8)	3.2 (8)	41.0 (8)	2.2 (8)	72.3 (8)	0.65 (8)	1.9 (8)	1.29 (6)	21.8 (6)	3
Medium viviparous colubrids	19	10	17.1 (16)	44.4 (18)	2.7 (16)	38.5 (13)	1.8 (14)	73.7 (18)	0.61 (18)	1.6 (16)	0.85 (14)	15.3 (14)	4
Large oviparous colubrids	11	8	28.0 (11)	75.1 (10)	3.3 (10)	60.1 (8)	2.4 (8)	119.3 (11)	0.64 (10)	1.8 (10)	1.04 (11)	28.1 (11)	5
Large viviparous colubrids	3	3	23.7 (2)	75.4 (3)	3.0 (1)			107.3 (2)	0.61 (2)	1.7 (2)	0.90 (2)	21.3 (2)	6
Medium viviparous viperids	4	2	16.3 (4)	45.0 (4)	4.6 (3)	40.0 (3)	3.7 (3)	63.8 (4)	0.71 (4)	1.8 (4)	0.51 (3)	7.8 (3)	7
Large viviparous viperids	17	6	27.1 (16)	68.6 (17)	4.2 (13)	65.0 (9)	2.8 (5)	96.1 (13)	0.72 (13)	1.5 (16)	0.77 (12)	21.5 (12)	8

(Continued)

Table 9–2. Comparison of Mean Sizes at Hatching and at Maturity, Mean Minimum Ages at Maturity, and Mean Growth Characteristics in Snake Species Grouped by Size, Family, and Reproductive Mode[a] (*Continued*)

Species group	No. Studies	No. species	HFL (cm)	MiFL (cm)	MiF age (yr)	MiML (cm)	MiM age (yr)	MaFL (cm)	MiFL/MaFL	F PIM	F PI-1	F AI-1 (cm)	Ref.[b]
Small oviparous elapids	8	8	10.7 (8)	21.0 (8)	2.0 (5)	19.9 (8)	1.5 (5)	33.9 (8)	0.62 (8)	1.0 (8)	0.85 (3)	10.4 (3)	9
Small viviparous elapids	9	9	10.4 (9)	25.1 (9)	2.4 (2)	24.3 (9)	1.9 (2)	40.8 (9)	0.64 (9)	1.2 (9)	0.46 (2)	5.3 (2)	10
Medium oviparous elapids	8	7	16.7 (6)	41.3 (8)	2.4 (5)	35.6 (8)	1.6 (5)	77.6 (6)	0.51 (6)	1.2 (6)	0.71 (3)	11.9 (3)	11
Medium viviparous elapids	7	7	16.9 (7)	45.3 (7)	2.7 (4)	45.6 (6)	1.8 (3)	82.6 (7)	0.55 (7)	1.7 (7)	1.33 (4)	21.7 (4)	12
Large oviparous elapids	3	3	31.7 (3)	99.8 (3)	2.2 (2)	73.4 (3)	1.4 (2)	159.3 (3)	0.62 (3)	2.2 (3)	1.94 (1)	66.0 (1)	13
Large viviparous elapids	2	2	23.4 (2)	80.5 (2)	2.3 (2)	72.0 (2)	1.8 (2)	122.0 (2)	0.66 (2)	2.5 (2)	1.95 (2)	45.6 (2)	14
Acrochordidae	1	1	36	113		85		163	0.69	2.1			15

[a] Figures are those given or best estimates from cited studies, in some cases requiring approximation from graphs or conversion of total length (TL) to snout-vent length (SVL) based on data in cited reference or from Klauber (1943) or Clark (1966). Numbers in parentheses are number of studies on which mean value is based. First-year growth is to 10 to 14 mo of age. HFL, hatchling female SVL; MiFL, minimum female SVL at maturity; MiML, minimum male SVL at maturity; MaFL, maximum female SVL; PIM, proportionate addition to SVL from H to Mi (amount of increase divided by original SVL); PI-1, proportional addition to SVL from H to age 1 yr; AI-1, absolute increase from H to age 1.

[b] Asterisk indicates that T-to-SVL conversion is required. P, Population study in field; SG, Size group study usually from >1 local population.

1. Blanchard et al. (1979), P; Brattstrom (1953), SG; Clark (1970), P; Fitch (1975), P; Force (1934), *SG; Kassing (1961), *SG; Kofron (1983), SG; Myers (1965), *SG; Semlitsch et al. (1981), SG.

2. Blanchard (1937), *SG; Blanchard and Force (1930), *SG; Clark and Fleet (1976), P; Krohmer and Aldridge (1985a,b), SG; Pisani and Bothner (1970), SG; Semlitsch and Moran (1984), SG.

3. Duguy and Saint Girons (1966), *SG; Fitch and Fleet (1970), P; Fukada (1959), *P; Madsen (1983), *P; Petter-Rousseaux (1953), SG; Platt (1969), P; Plummer (1985b), P.

4. Bauman and Metter (1977), SG; Branson and Baker (1974), *P; Brown (1940), SG; Carpenter (1952b), P; Clark (1974), P; Feaver (1977), P; Fitch (1965), P; Ford and Killebrew (1983), SG; Gregory (1977), P; Hall (1969), SG; Kephart (1981), P; King (1986), P; Spellerberg and Phelps (1977), P; Stewart (1968), SG; Tinkle (1957), P.

5. Brown and Parker (1984), P; Fitch (1963a, b, 1978), P; Fukada (1960, 1978), P; Gibbons et al. (1977), *SG; Parker and Brown (1980), P; Platt (1984), P; Stickel et al. (1980), P.

6. Betz (1963), SG; Preston (1970), SG.

7. Andrén and Nilson (1983), P; Prestt (1971), P; Saint Girons (1957), SG; Volsøe (1944), SG.

8. Blem (1981), *SG; Burkett (1966), SG; Diller and Wallace (1984), P; Fitch (1949, 1960), P, (1985), SG; Gannon and Secoy (1984), P; Gibbons (1972), SG; Glissmeyer (1951), P; Keenlyne (1978), *SG; Klauber (1972), SG; Macartney (1985), P; Preston (1964), P; Tinkle (1962), SG; Wharton (1966), *P; Woodbury (1951), P.

9. Shine (1977, 1980a, 1981a, 1984a), all SG.

10. Shine (1981b, 1982, 1983a), all SG.

11. Jackson and Franz (1981); Quinn (1979); Shine (1980a–c); all SG.

12. Shine (1977, 1980d, 1983b, 1984b); Shine and Charles (1982); all SG.

13. Saint Girons (1964), SG; Shine and Covacevich (1983), SG.

14. Shine (1977), SG; Voris and Jayne (1979), P.

15. Shine, (1986), SG.

267

Table 9–3. Characteristics of Each of Three Groups of Snake Species Based on Growth Patterns as Described by Feaver (1977)

Characteristic	Group I	Group II	Group III
Growth			
Males	Rapid	Slower	Slower
Slope of post-maturity growth regression	0.315	0.163	
Females	Slower	Rapid	Faster
Slope of post-maturity growth regression	0.164	0.260	
Larger sex	Male	Female	Female
Male combat	Present	Absent	Present
Fecundity			
Relation to female SVL	1.3 eggs/ 10 cm F SVL	3.4 eggs/ 10 cm F SVL	5.4 eggs/10 cm F SVL
Maturity	Later	Earlier	Later
Adult survivorship	High	Low	High
Examples	Large viperids, colubrids, and elapids	Most colubrids and elapids	*Vipera berus*

slightly more than double their hatchling length in reaching maturity, while most other size groups in each family increase by about 2.5 to 2.9 times hatchling length (except the largest elapids, which more than triple their length to maturity).

Table 9–2 also compares minimum mature and maximum mature lengths of females, thereby giving an indication of how much of the total possible growth in length the minimum represents (Mi/Ma). Most snakes mature at 60 to 75% of maximum length. Exceptions are the medium-sized elapids, which generally mature at about half the maximum length.

POPULATION STRUCTURE

Sex Ratio

Sex ratio theory (Fisher, 1930) predicts that, if male and female young are equally expensive to produce, natural selection will favor equal production of each sex. Fisher's concept serves as a useful null hypothesis, and deviations from an equal sex ratio are of interest.

As expected, sex ratios of snakes at birth (primary sex ratios) generally are not statistically different from 1:1. Four known exceptions are male-biased (*Agkistrodon contortrix:* Fitch, 1960; *Elaphe quadrivirgata:* Fukada, 1960; *Notechis scutatus:* Shine and Bull, 1977; *P. melanoleucus:* Gutzke et al., 1985). According to theory, such an imbalance could evolve if the production of females required greater parental expenditure of energy than production of males. However, no

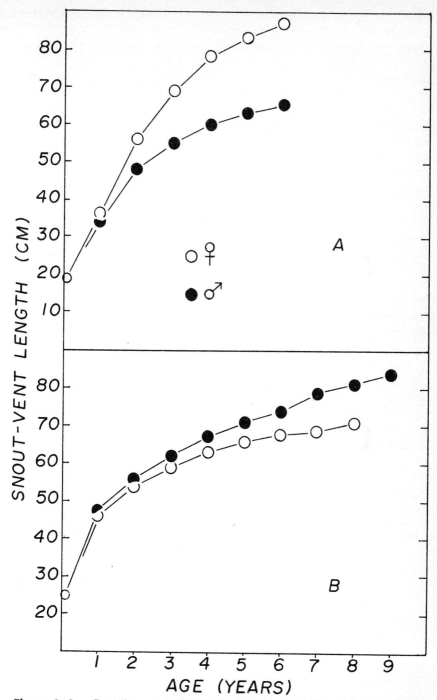

Figure 9–2. Growth curves (SVL) of sexually dimorphic snake species exemplifying one species with female larger (A) (*Nerodia sipedon* redrawn from Feaver, 1977) and one species with male larger (B) (*Crotalus viridis* from Heyrend and Call, 1951, and redrawn from Fukada, 1961). **269**

evidence of unequal energy expenditure exists in any of the four species. Shine and Bull (1977) offered two alternatives to Fisher's model to explain the imbalance in *N. scutatus*, but the data were insufficient to test either model. Gutzke et al. (1985) explained the male bias in *P. melanoleucus* on the basis of a report attributed to Parker and Brown (1980) that males dispersed farther than females after spring emergence from hibernacula. However, we can find no indication of sexual differences in dispersal in Parker and Brown's paper.

The primary sex ratio of *E. climacophora* is unique among ratios so far known for snakes in that it statistically favors females, at least in one out of three years (Fukada, 1956). In huge field samples of *D. punctatus*, Fitch (1975) found a heavy male bias in both first-year snakes and adults. Perhaps significantly, females are larger than males at birth (Fitch, 1975). These observations suggest the possibility of a biased primary sex ratio in *D. punctatus*, and only large samples of newborn young can answer this question.

Contrary to what might be expected based on generally unbiased primary sex ratios in snakes, observed sex ratios in later age groups (secondary sex ratios) often deviate from equality. The basic question is whether the deviations are real, reflecting actual population structure, or are apparent, reflecting different behavioral traits of males and females.

Male snakes often predominate in spring samples because of high sexual activity (Fitch, 1949, 1975; Saint Girons, 1957; Viitanen, 1967; Clark and Fleet, 1976; Gregory, 1977; Voris and Jayne, 1979). However, the direction of the sex ratio bias may favor females depending on where collections are made. Male *T. sirtalis* emerge quickly from communal dens in large numbers and remain at the den for long periods to mate, whereas females emerge slowly over a longer period but disperse soon after mating (Gregory, 1974). This behavioral difference enhances male bias at the den and leaves road-collected samples in the surrounding areas heavily female-biased (Gregory, 1974). A similar sex ratio bias may result when sexual differences in habitat preference (Viitanen, 1967; Macartney, 1985) or foraging behavior (Feaver, 1977) occur in a species.

As in males, the reproductive status of females can alter behavior and thus bias field samples. Gravid females are known to become more reclusive or sedentary (Fitch, 1961; Shine, 1979), to bask more frequently (Saint Girons, 1957; Fitch, 1961; Gregory, 1977), to migrate (Gorman et al., 1981), and to feed less frequently (Fitch and Shirer, 1971, Gregory and Stewart, 1975) as compared with males.

Subtle sexual differences in habitat selection or activity patterns may explain such results as differences in sex ratios between hand-collected versus trawl-collected *Acrochordus granulatus* (Gorman et al., 1981; Lemen and Voris, 1981), hand-collected versus drift fence-collected *Crotalus viridus* (Diller and Wallace, 1984), and apparently random variations in observed sex ratios in 14 species of marine snakes sampled at four sites (Lemen and Voris, 1981).

When sexual differences in mortality occur, the result is an actual unbalanced secondary sex ratio and an altered population structure. However, before a bias in an observed sex ratio can be attributed to sexual differences in mortality, one must be familiar with the species' biology so that sampling biases can be eliminated or at least minimized. The best data come from long-term studies on the same population using the same tested methods over several years. In such cases sex ratios have been found to be equal in some years and unequal in other years (e.g., Gregory, 1977; Plummer, 1985a).

If it is assumed that significant deviations from an equal sex ratio reflect the actual population structure, 19 colubrid and viperid species have populations with unequal secondary sex ratios. Males are favored in populations of 9 species (*Coluber constrictor:* Brown and Parker, 1984; *D. punctatus:* Fitch, 1975; *Heterodon platirhinos:* Platt, 1969; *Phyllorhynchus decurtatus:* Brattstrom, 1953; *Pituophis melanoleucus:* Fitch, 1949; Gutzke et al., 1985; *Tantilla coronata:* Semlitsch et al., 1981; *A. contortrix:* Fitch, 1960; *C. viridis:* Fitch, 1949; Julian, 1951; Klauber, 1972; *Vipera berus:* Viitanen, 1967). Females are favored in populations of 9 species (*Lycodonomorphus bicolor:* Madsen and Osterkamp, 1982; *Nerodia cyclopion, N. fasciata:* Mushinsky et al., 1980; *N. sipedon:* Fitch, 1982; *Opheodrys aestivus:* Plummer, 1985a; *Storeria dekayi:* Freedman and Catling, 1978; *T. elegans:* Fitch, 1965; Fleharty, 1967; *T. radix:* Seibert and Hagen, 1947; *T. sauritus:* Carpenter, 1952a). In *M. taeniatus,* males are favored in one population and females in another (Julian, 1951; Hirth and King, 1968). The direction of the sex ratio deviation is related to two groups of snakes identified by Feaver (1977), based on whether males or females grow larger. Feaver argued that the faster growing sex would feed more, which would expose it to greater risk of predation. Thus the larger sex should be underrepresented in field samples because of greater mortality. Based on the sexual dimorphism data of Parker and Brown (1980), Fitch (1981), and Semlitsch et al. (1981), females are larger in 9 of the 10 species with populations favoring females. In 6 of the 10 species with sex ratios favoring males, males are larger than or equal in size to females. Male-male combat (which also increases exposure to predation) is known in at least 5 of these 6 species (Feaver, 1977). Thus greater mortality in the larger sex is not supported by sex ratio data; in fact, it appears that the opposite is true. Perhaps being larger, although possibly increasing exposure to predation, also increases survivorship.

Observed sex ratios can be misleading without a thorough knowledge of a species' biology and the conditions under which the samples were taken. Deviations from equal sex ratios in samples can be a clue to interesting or overlooked facets of a life history. For example, finding no males in his samples of *Ramphotyphlops braminus,* Nussbaum (1980) suggested that the species was all-female and parthenogenetic, a condition previously unknown in snakes. Whether observed deviations indicate actual sexual differences in mortality or a sampling bias can be determined only by long-term population studies that provide an interpretation of the sex ratio in light of the biology of the animal.

Size and Age Structure

The size structure of populations may depend on numerous factors (see AGE AND GROWTH). Age structure, however, is a reflection of age-specific population parameters. Among these, age at first reproduction, fecundity, and survivorship are crucial. Neither size nor age structures of snake populations are easy to compare among or within species because of various sampling biases (see ABUNDANCE and SEX RATIO). The most severe bias in most studies is a lack of adequate sampling of juveniles.

We compare some aspects of size and age structure in local populations of snakes in Table 9–4. Species are arranged taxonomically and are divided into early-maturing (females mature in <3 yr) and late-maturing (>3 yr) groups, based on characteristics described in MATURITY AND FECUNDITY.

Intergroup Comparisons of Size and Age

Little can be discerned about population age structure from size, primarily because of the high variability of individual growth rates. The early-maturing colubrids in Table 9–4 are mostly moderate-sized species with an adult SVL of 40 to 70 cm, although there are several much smaller early-maturing species (Table 9–2). Females are larger than males in all early-maturing species except *Elaphe quadrivirgata*. Late-maturing colubrids include large species with male combat and males as large as or larger than females (*Elaphe, Masticophis, Pituophis*), but also some small (*Carphophis, Diadophis*) and moderate-sized species (*Coluber, Coronella*) in which females are the larger sex.

Differences in age structure between the three major groups of species in Table 9–4 are more clear-cut. Maximum longevity, one indicator of age structure, is consistently lower (<10 yr) in the early-maturing group and higher (>10 yr) in species with delayed maturity. In early-maturing species, the proportion of a population older than 4 yr is low ($\bar{x} = 0.09$ for seven species), but is much higher in both late-maturing colubrids ($\bar{x} = 0.42$ in eight species) and viperids ($\bar{x} = 0.35$ in five species).

Ratios of mature to immature individuals show much less consistency among populations because of sampling problems and seasonal changes, but the basic pattern is the same as previously noted. The ratio of mature to immature individuals averages 2.3:1 in early-maturing colubrids (14 populations), whereas late-maturing colubrids average 4.2:1 (11 populations). This variation in age structure results from differences in survivorship schedules of the two groups: Juvenile survivorship is low in both groups, but adult survivorship is higher in the late-maturing group (see MORTALITY AND SURVIVORSHIP and LIFE TABLES).

Late-maturing viperids are like late-maturing colubrids in longevity, proportion of older individuals, and high adult survivorship but differ from both

Table 9–4. Size and Age Structure in Various Populations of Snakes[a]

Species	SVL Mean (Range) Median	Modal SVL/ (cm) and age	Mature/ Immature Ratio	Prop. > 4 yr	EL (yr)	Reference and Location
Early maturing temperate colubrids						
Elaphe quadrivirgata	M (66.6–111.5) F (54.9–94.1) 74.5 89.1			<0.02	8	Fukada (1960), Japan
Heterodon nasicus	M (30.9–54) 42.5 F 51.5 (35–70)	30–44 35–45	5.3:1	0.23	8	Platt (1969), Kansas
H. platirhinos	M (48.8–67) 57.9 F (56–72.5) 64.3		0.45:1	0.06	5	Platt (1969), Kansas
Nerodia sipedon	M (37.5–57) 47.3 F 64.5 (47–97)	45–55 48–75	1.5:1	<0.04	7	Feaver (1977), Michigan
N. sipedon	M 62.5 (44–85) F 82.1 (60–110)	50–72 75–90	1.3:1 1.5:1		7	King (1986), Lake Erie Islands
Opheodrys aestivus	M 39.0 (28–50) F 44.7 (35–55)	2 yr	0.56:1 3.9:1	0.11	8	Plummer (1985a,b), Arkansas
Regina septemvittata	M (35.2–64.2) 49.7 F (45.9–69.5) 57.7		3.6:1			Branson and Baker (1974) Kentucky
Rhabdophis tigrinus	M (55.6–69) 62.3 F (54.8–86.1) 70.5		3.8:1	0	4–6	Fukada (1959), Japan
Thamnophis butleri	M (32.1–41) 36.6 F (34.5–48) 41.3	30–39	0.88:1			Carpenter (1952a), Michigan
T. elegans	M (30–55) 42.5 F (40–65) 52.5	40–50 40–55	2.4:1		10	Kephart (1981), California
T. sauritus	M (max. 57) F (42.1–67) 54.6	40–49 40–59	1.6:1			Carpenter (1952a), Michigan

(Continued)

Table 9–4. Size and Age Structure in Various Populations of Snakes[a] (*Continued*)

Species	SVL Mean (Range) Median	Modal SVL (cm) and age	Mature/ Immature Ratio	Prop. > 4 yr	EL (yr)	Reference and Location
T. sirtalis	M (37.2–60) 48.6 F (50.4–81.5) 65.9	74.7%, 2–3 yr		0.10	8	Fitch (1965), Kansas
T. sirtalis	M (32–69) 50.5 F (50–85) 67.5	40–52 50–54				Gregory (1977), Canada
T. sirtalis	M (39–60) 49.5 F (42.6–72) 57.3	40–49 50–59	1.5:1			Carpenter (1952a), Michigan
T. sirtalis	M (30–71) 50.5 F (45–80) 62.5	40–50 40–55	3.5:1		10–20	Kephart (1981), California
Late-maturing temperate colubrids						
Carphophis vermis	M (21.6–29.7) 25.7 F 28 (25–29)	63%, 1–3 yr 58%, 1–3 yr	1.9:1	0.24 0.26	10	Clark (1970), Kansas
Coluber constrictor	M (42–90) 66 F 83.4 (59–108.8)	59.3%, 2–3 yr	6.1:1 to 2.7:1	0.28	10	Fitch (1963a), Kansas
C. constrictor	M (39–65) 52 F 63.3 (57–88)	>5 yr >5 yr	6.6:1	0.33	15	Brown and Parker (1984), Utah
Coronella austriaca	M (42–60) 51 F 58 (42–102)		4.3:1			Spellerberg and Phelps (1977), England
Diadophis punctatus	M (16.6–28) 22.3 F (23.5–34) 28.8		1.4:1	0.30	15	Fitch (1975), Kansas
D. punctatus	M (min. 22) F (25.6–40) 32.8		2.5:1		16	Blanchard et al. (1979), Michigan
Elaphe climacophora	M (86–164.4) 125.2 F (85–145.6) 115.3	102–125 94–125			>10	Fukada (1978), Japan

274

Species	SVL	Size/age at maturity	Sex ratio		Longevity (yr)	Reference
E. obsoleta	M (90–153) 121.5 F 125.8 (90–140)			0.42	>20	Fitch (1963b), Kansas
E. obsoleta	M (max. 177.4) F117.4 (110–151.6)	110–160 100–150	5.0:1	0.75	30	Stickel et al. (1980), Maryland
Masticophis taeniatus	M (53–108) 80.5 F 88.9 (74–103)	81–100	G2.8:1[b] LR8.1:1	G0.44 LR0.43	20	Parker and Brown (1980); Parker (1976), Utah
Pituophis melanoleucus	M (67–125) 96 F 98.5 (78–114)	81–95	5.3:1	0.59	16	Parker and Brown (1980), Utah
Late-maturing temperate viperids						
Agkistrodon contortrix	M (55–93.6) 74.3 F 60.8 (42–75)	21.4%, 2 yr	0.73:1	0.22	13	Fitch (1960), Kansas
Crotalus horridus	M 109.2 (98–127) F 98.7 (max. 103.8)	43% 2–4yr	0.54:1	0.20		Fitch (1985), Kansas
C. viridis	M 93.2 (81–104) F 87.3 (78.3–95)	24.7%, 3rd yr	2.1:1	0.21	8	Fitch (1985), Kansas
C. viridis	M (75–130) 102.5 F 79.9 (75–102)	90–110 75–90	1.2:1	0.29– 0.43	16–20	Fitch (1949), California
C. viridis	M (max. 99) F (56.4–69.3) 62.9	68–84 63–71			15	Woodbury (1951), Utah
C. viridis	M (max. 89) F 74.7 (66–81)	>7 yr >7 yr	1.8:1	0.59– 0.92		Parker and Brown (1974), Utah
C. viridis	M (77–86) 81.5 F (65–78.4) 71.7		4.9:1			Preston (1964), Canada
C. viridis	M (54–110) 82 F (65–95) 80	65–95 65–85	1.1:1		21	Macartney (1985), Canada
C. viridis	M (79–112.6) 95.8 F 97 (70–125)	105–110 105–110	1.5:1			Gannon and Secoy (1984), Canada
C. viridis	M 70.6 (52–93) F 65.9 (55–78)	71–80 59–70	2.2:1			Diller and Wallace (1984), Idaho

Table 9–4. Size and Age Structure in Various Populations of Snakes[a] (*Continued*)

Species	SVL Mean (Range) Median	Modal SVL/ (cm) and age	Mature/ Immature Ratio	Prop. > 4 yr	EL (yr)	Reference and Location
Vipera aspis	M (45.4–60) 52.7 F 49.5 (46.3–54)	40% of mature at 6–7 yr	4.1:1		>20	Saint Girons (1957, 1975), France
V. berus			2.7:1			Saint Girons (1975), France
V. berus			1.8:1			Viitanen (1967), Finland
Tropical elapids						
Laticauda colubrina	M (50–89) 69.5 F (65–115) 90	55–80	1.7:1			Saint Girons (1964), New Caledonia
Enhydrina schistosa	M (66–97) 81.5 F (73–112) 92.5	55–105	0.96:1	<0.01		Voris (1985), Voris and Jayne (1979), Malaysia

[a]SVL, Snout-vent length; EL, estimated longevity; M, adult male; F, adult female. Median SVLs estimated if mean was not given.
[b]G = Grantsville; LR = Lone Rock.

groups of colubrids in having higher juvenile survivorship. This results in a ratio of mature to immature individuals (2.2:1 for 11 populations) similar to that of the early-maturing colubrid group.

Population structure in tropical species is poorly known, and there are few detailed studies. In two marine species, growth is rapid and age structure appears similar to that in early-maturing temperate colubrids (Table 9–4).

Intraspecific Comparisons

Geographic variation in the size structure of populations occurs in some species but not in others. Despite variations in growth rate, age at maturity, and fecundity, various populations of *Thamnophis sirtalis* have remarkably similar adult mean body sizes (Fitch, 1965), although a population in northern Canada has a much larger average size (P. T. Gregory and K. W. Larsen, Personal communication). In contrast, body sizes of other species in Table 9–4 show considerable inter-populational variation. Island populations of *Nerodia sipedon* in Lake Erie have larger individuals of both sexes than other populations have. Racers (*Coluber constrictor*) studied in mesic habitats in Kansas are larger and have higher growth rates than those in more arid, less productive habitats in Utah. Rattlesnakes (*Crotalus viridis*) range from populations with small adults in Idaho, Utah, and British Columbia to populations with much larger than average adults in California, Kansas, and Saskatchewan. Selective agents leading to these extremes are poorly known but are doubtless related to the growth process and food resources. For example, Schwaner (1985) found that the size structure of island populations of the elapid *Notechis ater* was closely correlated with the size of available prey.

MATURITY AND FECUNDITY

Maturity

Definition. Age at maturity may be a life-history trait acted on by natural selection and is dependent on a species' demographic environment. Correlates of age at maturity may drive it toward a minimum or a maximum; individuals in growing populations may tend toward earlier maturity, whereas members of declining populations mature later (Stearns, 1976).

Age at maturity needs to be clearly defined for comparisons between different studies. Different workers have unfortunately used different criteria, so the accuracy of comparisons suffers. Age at first mating is the most acceptable and appropriate definition (Feaver, 1977), although this is difficult to detect or observe in the field. However, in male snakes, physiological maturity may precede the breeding season by several months, especially in Temperate Zone species that mature in autumn but do not mate until the following spring. In females, ovulation and mating may be chronologically close, but viviparous species carry embryos much longer than oviparous species carry eggs. Defining maturity as age at oviposition or parturition is thus inappropriate.

Sexual Differences in Snakes. In about 66% of the 58 temperate species with available data on minimum size and age at maturity for both sexes, males mature earlier than females (Table 9–2). In the remaining species, males and females mature at similar ages. Costs to males for early maturity are lower than those for females, whose fecundity is proportional to body size (Seigel and Ford, this volume) and whose reproduction may involve greater energy expenditure (Shine, 1978a). The average difference in age at maturity between the sexes for all Temperate Zone species is about 1 yr. In temperate colubrids, smaller species tend to mature earlier and larger species later in both sexes; temperate viperids have overall later maturity in both sexes, especially in European *Vipera* species; Australian elapids show earlier maturity in all size groups as compared with corresponding groups of temperate colubrids.

Species with Delayed Maturity. Sixteen temperate species in Table 9–2 have their maturity delayed beyond 3 yr in one or both sexes. Among males, 5 of 53 species (9.4%) have their maturity delayed this long, and all five are species with male combat (but not necessarily larger males: Shine, 1978b). Among females, 27.1% (16 of 59 species) mature after 3 yr. In general, these are moderate-sized species found at high latitudes (North American *Nerodia* and European *Coronella* and *Natrix*) or high altitudes (western North American *Thamnophis*), or colubrids in genera with a typically large size (*Elaphe, Lampropeltis, Masticophis, Pituophis*). Six of the 16 species have a low frequency of female reproduction (5 viperids in the genera *Agkistrodon, Crotalus,* and *Vipera,* and 1 elapid, *Hoplocephalus*) (see Bull and Shine, 1979).

Tropical Species. Little is known about age at maturity in tropical snakes. Several species of colubrids probably mature in less than 1 yr, such as the Mexican *Sibon sanniola* (Kofron, 1983), Brazilian *Liophis* (Vitt, 1983), and several Cambodian species (Saint Girons and Pfeffer, 1971). Female colubrids of the genera *Coniophanes, Dipsas,* and *Imantodes* from Central and South America may mature later, at 2 to 3.5 yr (Zug et al., 1979). Some marine snakes also mature later, at 1.5 yr (male) to 2.5 yr (female) (Saint Girons, 1964; Voris and Jayne, 1979).

Maturity Groups. Tinkle et al. (1970) divided lizards into two groups based on age at maturity: (1) early-maturing species that first reproduce at or before 1 yr of age, have small clutches, are small in size at maturity, have multiple broods per year, are usually oviparous, and are found in both temperate and tropical regions; (2) late-maturing species that mature later than 1 yr, have large clutches, are large in size, are usually viviparous, and are found in temperate regions.

Feaver (1977) analyzed similar traits for 20 populations of 17 species of Temperate Zone snakes. His early-maturing group included species with female maturity at or before 2 yr, small size, large annual clutches, females larger than males, and low adult survivorship. His late-maturing group included species with female maturity after 2 yr, large size, small annual or biennial clutches, males larger than females, and high adult survivorship. Oviparity and viviparity occurred in both groups.

We attempted a similar dichotomous arrangement for 47 populations of 34 species of colubrids, 24 populations of 8 species of viperids, and 20 species of elapids. Because there were so few obvious patterns, we conclude (as did Vitt, 1983) that it is probably a mistake at this stage of our knowledge to try to dichotomize snakes when size and fecundity traits correlate so poorly with a particular maturity group. The only trait with a consistent relationship is high adult survivorship among late-maturing colubrids and viperids. Better data, other criteria, and more extensive analyses of relationships between species possessing particular suites of these and other traits (such as foraging mode) will be required before further generalizations concerning maturity patterns can be developed.

Fecundity

The aspects of female reproduction most important in understanding population ecology are (1) measuring fecundity in particular species and taking follicular atresia, infertility, and embryo mortality into account, (2) relating fecundity to female size and age, and (3) estimating the periodicity at which females reproduce (see Seigel and Ford, this volume).

MORTALITY AND SURVIVORSHIP

Identifying Sources of Mortality

Few studies have identified or quantified sources of mortality in snake populations. Low temperatures in cold climates may kill hibernating snakes (Gregory, 1982), but little is known of proportions of populations killed in this way (see also Lillywhite, this volume). In Canadian garter snakes (*Thamnophis sirtalis*), winter losses may be substantial, up to 34 to 48.8% (Gregory, 1977). Feaver (1977) estimated a combined autumn-winter mortality of 25 to 40% in various age and sex groups of Michigan *Nerodia sipedon*. Extremely hot summers may accentuate winter mortality in *Vipera* species, especially among females that had reproduced during the previous summer (Saint Girons, 1981). Especially severe winters may have a decimating effect on northern populations, but few workers have closely monitored marked individuals entering and emerging from hibernation. Viitanen (1967) found a total mortality of 18.1% over three winters among adult *Vipera berus* entering hibernation in Finland, and 47.2% among juveniles. In a frequently cited study, Hirth (1966) purportedly found a 34 to 50% winter mortality among three species, including juveniles, in a hibernaculum in Utah during one winter. Unfortunately, these figures continue to be cited as valid despite being strongly contested by more extensive studies over several years at the same hibernaculum, which showed much lower winter mortality (Parker and Brown, 1974, 1980; Brown and Parker, 1984).

Humans are an increasingly important cause of mortality in snake populations (Dodd, this volume). Species that aggregate for hibernation are especially vulnerable. Aleksiuk (1977) stated that over 63,000 garter snakes were removed for commercial purposes in 1 yr from a 2500 km^2 area in Canada. Rattlesnake populations have been particularly decimated in many areas (Klauber, 1972; Parker and Brown, 1973, 1974).

Seasonal and Annual Differences in Mortality

Studies in two geographic areas have measured seasonal components of annual mortality for five species. In Michigan, *Nerodia sipedon* male and female adults had similar annual mortalities (65.5%), but 47% of the total male mortality occurred during the spring mating season, whereas 50% of the female deaths occurred in the summer, during periods of increased feeding (Feaver, 1977). Among four species studied at hibernacula in Utah, the annual mortality of adults was divided between winter and spring-summer combined, as follows: *Coluber constrictor* averaged 21% annual mortality, with 33.3% of the total in winter and 66.7% in spring-summer (Brown and Parker, 1984); *Masticophis taeniatus* averaged 20% annual mortality, with 20% in winter and 80% in spring-summer; *Pituophis melanoleucus* averaged 25% annual mortality, with 45% in winter and 55% in spring-summer (Parker and Brown, 1980); and *Crotalus viridis* averaged 17.7% annual mortality, with 4.5% in winter and 95.5% in spring-summer (Parker and Brown, 1974).

The annual variation in adult mortality in these same species over three consecutive years was substantial. In *C. constrictor,* male mortality was 31.2, 10.0, and 38.0%, and for females, 21.0, 21.8, and 44.7%. In *M. taeniatus* adults, mortality (both sexes) was 7.7, 21.1, and 12.5%; *P. melanoleucus* adults (both sexes) showed mortalities of 27.3, 17.7, and 29.7%; and in male *C. viridis,* mortalities were 25.0, 33.3, and 12.5%. Correlates of annual variations in mortality rates with environmental factors are difficult to identify (Brown and Parker, 1984).

Differential Mortality

Camin and Ehrlich (1958) studied the frequency of color patterns in polymorphic *Nerodia sipedon* on islands in Lake Erie, where unbanded individuals better matched the limestone rocks and banded snakes were more conspicuous to predators. Frequencies of the plain pattern increased from a range of 8 to 28% in litters on the islands to a range of 38 to 63% in the adults themselves. Because there was no evidence for an ontogenetic pattern change in individuals, selection pressure presumably eliminated banded snakes, but banded frequencies were maintained by the immigration of banded individuals from the mainland.

Melanistic individuals in some snake populations such as *Thamnophis sirtalis* (Gibson and Falls, 1979; R. Gibson and J. B. Falls, Personal communication) and *Vipera berus* (Andrén and Nilson, 1981) may exhibit a balance between positive and negative selective pressures. Melanistic garter snakes stayed warmer during cool periods and cooler during summer, perhaps giving them a thermal advantage over striped individuals (Gibson and Falls, 1979), but melanistic animals had higher injury frequencies and were more conspicuous to predators (R. Gibson, Personal communication). Andrén and Nilson (1981) reported a positive correlation between melanism and male weight in *V. berus*. Heavier males had an advantage in winning male combats and had reduced basking times as well. These advantages were countered by higher predation pressure on melanistics. Experiments with melanistic and patterned models in the field showed almost twice as many attacks by predatory birds on the melanistic forms. Experiments to identify physiological, behavioral, and reproductive trade-offs in melanistic variants should be pursued in other polymorphic species.

Problems of Pre-natal and Juvenile Survivorship

Probably the most glaring deficiency in population studies on snakes is the lack of quantitative data on survival from fertilization to hatching, from hatching to entering hibernation (in temperate species), and from hibernation to the 1-yr mark. Overall first-year survivorship has been crudely estimated by most authors by calculating the total number of offspring likely to be produced by females in the population and comparing this figure with the number of 1-yr-olds present the next year. Brown and Parker (1984) broke down first-year survivorship into the appropriate components: Survivorship of *Coluber constrictor* in Utah was 92% at hatching, 72% from hatching to hibernation (45 days later), and 17% at 1 yr. Clearly, more data are needed on component rates of early survivorship.

Hatchling snakes may be produced in large numbers, but their activity may be considerably reduced (Lillywhite, 1982) because of limited physiological endurance for locomotion (Pough, 1977) or because of other factors; thus they are underrepresented in almost all studies on snake populations (see POPU-

Table 9–5. Life Table Characteristics of Various Snake Populations.[a]

Species	S-1	FA-1R	S-A	EL	R_0	AMax	PR_0	CGT	RM	RF	Reference
Early-maturing temperate colubrids											
Elaphe quadrivirgata	17.7	2	60	7	1.035	2,3	79.8	2.83	o	An	Fukada (1965, 1969), Japan[c]
Heterodon nasicus	38 (to 2 yr)	2	63	8	0.904	3,4	50.5	3.84	o	Bi	Platt (1969), Kansas[b]
H. platirhinos	15 (to 2 yr)	2	47	5	1.065	2,3	72.3	2.87	o	An	Platt (1969), Kansas[b]
Nerodia sipedon	19	2	35	7	0.619	2,3	80.6	2.43	v	An	Feaver (1977), Michigan
Opheodrys aestivus	21.2	2	49	8	0.836	1,2	60.6	2.49	o	An	Plummer (1985a,b) Arkansas
Rhabdophis tigrinus	19.9	2	41	4	0.793	2,3	93.7	2.43	o	An	Fukada (1965, 1969), Japan[c]
Thamnophis sirtalis	36	2	50	8	1.054	2,3	54.4	3.32	v	An	Fitch (1965), Kansas[b]
Late-maturing temperate colubrids											
Carphophis vermis	55	3	65	10	0.52	3,4	53.1	4.82	o	An	Clark (1970), Kansas[b]
Coluber constrictor	31.3	3	62	10	0.46	3,4	35.1	5.1	o	An	Fitch (1963a) Kansas[b]
C. constrictor	17	3	79	15	1.19	3,4	30.8	6.89	o	An	Brown and Parker (1984), Utah
Diadophis punctatus	34	3	74	15	1.123	3,4	36.6	6.24	o	An	Fitch (1975), Kansas[c]
Masticophis taeniatus	14.5	3	80	20	1.097	4,5	27.3	7.4	o	An	Parker and Brown (1980) Utah

Species	S-1	FA-1R	S-A	EL	R_0	AMax	PR_0	CGT	RM	RF	Reference
Pituophis melanoleucus	20	3	63	16	0.899	5,6	39.6	6.4	o	An	Parker and Brown (1980), Utah
Late-maturing temperate viperids											
Agkistrodon contortrix	30 (to SM)	3	71	13	0.818	3,5	75.8	4.83	v	Bi	Fitch (1960), Kansas[b]
Crotalus viridis	67	3	69	15	1.377	3,5	54.4	5.14	v	Bi	Fitch (1960), Kansas[d]
	40	3	75	15	0.947	3,5	57.2	6.27	v	Bi	Woodbury (1951), Utah[c]
C. viridis	46	7	85	21	0.496	7,10	66.1	10.5	v	Bi/Tr	Macartney (1985), Canada
Vipera aspis	20 (to SM)	5	80	23	1.018	5,8	69.4	8.6	v	Tr	Saint Girons (1957), France[c]
V. aspis	13.8 (to SM)	5	75	19	0.939	5,7	69.0	7.4	v	Bi	Saint Girons (1957), France[c]
V. berus	12 (to SM)	3	77	13	1.113	3,5	67.8	5.37	v	Bi	Prestt (1971), England[b]

[a]S-1, First-year survivorship; FA-1R, female age at first reproduction (years); S-A, mean adult survivorship; EL, estimated longevity (years); R_0, net reproductive rate; AMax, ages L_xM_x maximum; PR_0, maximum L_xM_x as proportion of R_0; CGT, cohort generation time; RM, reproductive mode (o, oviparous; v, viviparous); RF, reproductive frequency (An, annual; Bi, biennial; Tr, triennial); SM, sexual maturity.

[b]Calculated by F. B. Turner (Personal communication). *Carphophis vermis*: 100% reproductive at age 3 and older; 33% egg mortality. *Coluber constrictor*: 50% egg mortality. *Heterodon nasicus*: 50% reproductive at age 2 up to 100% at age 4; 60% egg mortality. *Heterodon platirhinos*: 100% reproductive at age 3 and older; 62% egg mortality. *Thamnophis sirtalis*: 42% reproductive at age 2 up to 100% at age 6; fecundity reduced 19% for female mortality, infertile eggs, and fetal mortality. *Agkistrodon contortrix*: Fecundity reduced for male-biased primary sex ratio. *Vipera berus*: Survival to maturity estimated.

[c]Calculated by present authors from original data in cited references. *Elaphe quadrivirgata*: Fecundity 3.5 at age 2, 4.2 at 3, 4.5 at 4, 5 at 5, 5.2 at 6, 5.4 at 7. *Diadophis punctatus*: Fecundity reduced by 15%; 1.15 at 3, 1.38 at 4, 1.56 at 5 and 6, 1.67 at 7 and 8, 1.81 at 9, 2.15 at 10, 2.24 at 11 to 15. *Rhabdophis tigrinus*: Fecundity 4.8 at 2, 7.7 at 3, 8.3 at 4. *Crotalus viridis*: Survivorship 0 to 1 estimated from Fitch (1985); 50% reproductive at 3, 100% at 5 and older; fecundity 2 at age 3, 2.5 at 5 and 7, 2.75 at 9 to 15. *Vipera aspis*: Fecundity 2 at 5 yr, 3 at all older.

[d]Calculated by Vial et al. (1977).

LATION STRUCTURE). One approach is to release hatchlings into the field from laboratory clutches or litters in large numbers. Fukada (1969) achieved encouraging results with this approach in two oviparous Japanese colubrids, releasing 880 hatchling *Rhabdophis tigrinus* and 493 *Elaphe quadrivirgata* over 13 yr and measuring first-year and subsequent survivorship. Similarly, Blanchard et al. (1979) released 38 hatchling *Diadophis punctatus* in Michigan, with 10 surviving for at least 1 yr and 2 for at least 8 yr.

Effect of Hatchling Size on Survivorship

Hatchling body size may determine prey size (Mushinsky, this volume), thus affecting first-year survival. The effect of variation in hatchling size on subsequent survival has been most closely studied in sceloporine lizards that reduce clutch size but increase egg and hatchling size as the reproductive season progresses (Ferguson and Fox, 1984). There are no comparable studies on juvenile snakes, but Saint Girons and Naulleau (1981) followed the survival of 236 newborn *Vipera* (six species) in outdoor enclosures and found that the original weight of young surviving >10 months was significantly higher than that of those that died. Female *V. berus* in Sweden produced heavier young in a year with high food availability for adults, and lighter young in a year with low resources, but subsequent survival of the young was not described (Andrén and Nilson, 1983).

Considerable variation in hatchling length and weight occurs both between and within species of snakes, and within litters. Quantitative studies on geographic variation and intra-clutch variation, and their effect on survival are sorely needed.

Age-Specific Survivorship

Most studies on age-specific survivorship in snakes (Table 9–5) have involved methods that assume a stable age distribution and use as survivorship estimates the proportion of individuals in each age class at time n that are still present at time $n + 1$. This approach avoids the problem of infrequent recapture of marked individuals but requires a stable age distribution and some measure of emigration and immigration rates. Most workers have used a combination of this procedure and following survivorship (or loss rates) within cohorts of known-age individuals. This may be done by releasing large cohorts of hatchlings (Fukada, 1969) or by estimating ages in the more distinct younger age groups and measuring the subsequent age-specific survivorship of each group (Prestt, 1971; Feaver, 1977; Parker and Brown, 1980; Brown and Parker, 1984). Rates of immigration and especially of emigration must be estimated for this technique to be successful.

Comparative Survivorship Patterns

Survivorship figures for 13 populations of colubrids and 6 populations of viperids are shown in Table 9–5 with the species grouped by age at first reproduction. Despite deficiencies in some aspects of the data or interpretations of these studies, tentative generalizations are possible.

First-year survivorship is low in most colubrids, with little substantial difference between the two maturity groups. Only 2 of 12 species have >40% first-year survivorship. Although data are less reliable in viperids, juvenile survivorship is generally much higher than in colubrids, except apparently for *Vipera berus*. Problems involved in capturing and estimating numbers of juveniles were discussed in earlier sections. Whether annual variation in juvenile survivorship occurs is unknown.

Survivorship after the first year (post-juvenile survivorship) is higher in all species than first-year survivorship, as the number of potential predators and other sources of mortality decreases. Early-maturing colubrids average about 50% survivorship, late-maturing colubrids about 70%, and viperids about 75% annual post-juvenile survivorship. Apparently, only minor variations in age-specific post-juvenile survivorship occur among snake species. Juvenile survivorship is much lower than adult survivorship in most late-maturing colubrids (42% difference) but is closer to that of adults in early-maturing colubrids and viperids. Annual variation in post-juvenile survivorship may occur within species (see SEASONAL AND ANNUAL DIFFERENCES IN MORTALITY), but it is not clear whether juvenile or adult survivorship is more "predictable" (Brown and Parker, 1984).

Survivorship curves for snakes appear to conform to a type II pattern, showing age-constant mortality after age 1. This pattern is typical of other vertebrates such as some lizards, birds, and turtles (Gibbons and Semlitsch, 1982; Pianka, 1983).

LIFE TABLES

An important objective of gathering data on age, growth, population structure, maturity, fecundity, reproductive rate, and survivorship in local populations is to develop a life table or schedule of age-specific survivorship and fecundity. A life table can be used to calculate parameters such as net reproductive rate, cohort generation time, age-specific life expectancy, and reproductive value. Accurate life tables for diverse taxa permit an understanding of life-history evolution through the degree of correlation of demographic traits with environmental constraints. In this section, we compare life-table attributes of 16 snake species (Table 9–5) to contrast our knowledge of snake demography and its heuristic potential to demographic analyses of other selected vertebrates. The shortcomings of the data for snakes noted in previous sections should be emphasized. Variations in interpretation of the same data set are illustrated by the two different analyses of Fitch's (1960) work on *Agkistrodon contortrix* (cf. Table 9–5).

A net reproductive rate of 1.0 indicates a stable population with a stable age distribution. Most of the analyses in Table 9–5 assumed a stable age distribution and deliberately attempted to adjust survivorship and fecundity figures within the constraints of the data to yield an R_0 value as close as possible to 1 unless populations were demonstrably declining (e.g., *Carphophis, Coluber* in Kansas) or increasing (*Coluber* in Utah).

An outline summary contrasting the three groups in Table 9–5 will most clearly emphasize the rather substantial differences between the groups (first-year survivorship is ignored here because of its high potential for inaccuracy):

Early-maturing colubrids (seven species):
1. Low adult survivorship, $\bar{x}$ = 49.3% annually
2. Two young age groups (2- and 3-yr-olds) contribute most to the next generation (70.3% of R_0).
3. Short cohort generation time, $\bar{x}$ = 2.9 yr
4. Low longevity, $\bar{x}$ = 6.7 yr
5. High fecundity, $\bar{x}$ = 12.2 offspring per year (range 6.1 to 22.3).
6. Reproduction usually annual

Late-maturing colubrids (six populations of five species)
1. High adult survivorship, $\bar{x}$ = 70.3% annually
2. Two older age groups contribute most to R_0 (3- and 4-, 4- and 5-, or 5- and 6-yr-olds), averaging only 37.1% of R_0; thus contribution to the next generation is spread over several ages
3. Long cohort generation time, $\bar{x}$ = 6.1 yr
4. High longevity, $\bar{x}$ = 14.3 yr
5. Low fecundity, $\bar{x}$ = 6.4 offspring per year (range 3–11.7).
6. Annual reproduction

Late-maturing viperids (six populations of four species)
1. High adult survivorship, $\bar{x}$ = 77% annually
2. Two older age groups contribute most to R_0 (3- and 5-yr-olds), $\bar{x}$ = 65.8% of R_0, but this is an artifact of the mechanism of life-table construction that restricts reproduction to alternate years or every third year. In reality, some females of each age reproduce each year, so the contribution to R_0 is similar to that of late-maturing colubrids.
3. Long cohort generation time, $\bar{x}$ = 7.2 yr
4. High longevity, $\bar{x}$ = 17.5 yr
5. Low fecundity, $\bar{x}$ = 6.0 offspring per year (range 4.6 to 7.9)
6. Reproductive frequency biennial or triennial.

Exceptions to these general patterns in regard to one or more life-table parameters are *Elaphe quadrivirgata*, a large species with high adult survivorship; *Heterodon nasicus*, a species with several traits like those of viperids, including high juvenile and adult survivorship and biennial reproduction; *Opheodrys aestivus*, with lower than average fecundity for its group; and *Carphophis vermis*, with very high juvenile survivorship.

Two questions can be raised concerning the value of comparative demographic studies on snakes: (1) Do these studies contribute to a better understanding of snake evolution and adaptive responses to particular sets of environmental conditions? (2) Are they likely to be an empirical source for testing general theories of the evolution of life-history traits?

The answer to the first question is undoubtedly yes. Snakes radiated widely and successfully during the Cenozoic era through the evolution of unique locomotory and feeding adaptations, allowing the utilization of niches largely unoccupied by other vertebrates (Rabb and Marx, 1973; Kardong, 1980; Greene, 1983; Pough and Groves, 1983). Parallel studies on population ecology have revealed (and will continue to reveal) unusual sets of ecological adaptations in snakes, allowing a more thorough understanding of this widespread but comparatively little known group of vertebrates.

The second question is not so easily answered. Turner (1977), Lillywhite (1982), and Plummer (1985a) have all commented on the difficulties encountered in sampling snake populations and on our current inability to measure demographic traits for adequate population analysis, even when maximum time and effort are expended by dedicated and competent workers. If one examines corresponding studies on other vertebrates with more extensive and thorough population analyses and their potential contribution to testing theory, these comments seem justified. In quality of field data no single study on snake populations measures up to numerous studies on lizards (e.g., Ferguson et al., 1980) or mammals (Millar and Zammuto, 1983), and even the best studies have had difficulty in either supporting current theories of life-history evolution or in generating new ones. Certainly, snakes with their unique constellation of adaptive traits could contribute more than they have to date.

FUTURE RESEARCH

Criteria for the Selection of Populations

Here we identify some of the most obviously important criteria on which future population studies on snakes should be based.

Population Densities. Most snake species occur at intractably low population densities. Therefore, for snakes to contribute to our knowledge of evolutionary ecology, accessible species found at locally high population densities and capable of yielding extensive basic data should be selected for study. Certainly such species and populations exist, as demonstrated in previous sections. This includes species with high densities much of the year (e.g., *Diadophis punctatus, Regina alleni*) and those that aggregate for some portion of the year, allowing annual mass sampling (e.g., *Thamnophis sirtalis* and *Crotalus viridis* at hibernacula, *Enhydrina schistosa* in estuaries, and *Acrochordus arafurae* as a result of seasonal drought).

Geographic Distribution and Phylogeny. Studies on common species with broad geographic distributions seem likely to contribute the most to an understanding of snake population ecology. More detailed studies on such species as *Coluber constrictor, Diadophis punctatus, Nerodia sipedon, Pituophis melanoleucus, Thamnophis sirtalis, Agkistrodon piscivorus, Crotalus horridus, C. viridis, Vipera aspis,* and *V. berus* are needed. In addition, the vast majority of population studies to date have focused on temperate colubrids or viperids. Detailed work on populations of elapids and boids is lacking, as are studies on most tropical species.

Convergent Species. Hedges (1985) suggested detailed studies on convergent species as a mechanism for separating out the effects of phylogeny on life-history traits. Several common body forms and/or patterns have evolved independently in different genera or families of snakes: diurnal whip snakes (Shine, 1980b; Vitt, 1980), viperid body forms in colubrids and elapids (Shine, 1980d; Pough and Groves, 1983), banded snakes (Shine, 1980c), taipans and mambas (Shine and Covacevich, 1983), and arboreal vine snakes (Henderson and Binder, 1980.)

Late-Maturing Species. Little is known of population properties of large snake species such as tropical boas and pythons. Age at maturity may be much higher in such species than in smaller snakes (Holstrom, 1980). Careful recording of length (SVL) and weight in hatchlings of known sex at regular intervals (at least annually) during maturation, along with records of initial sexual activity and clutch or litter size, even in captivity, might contribute more knowledge than is likely to be forthcoming from field studies.

Island Populations. Substantial microgeographic variation in intraspecific population parameters on islands of different sizes (e.g., Schwaner, 1985; King, 1986) suggests that studies on such populations may yield an understanding of population ecology more rapidly than traditional studies.

Experimental Population Biology

Snakes are poorly represented in experimental population studies on vertebrates in laboratory or field situations. Are snakes appropriate experimental animals? If so, new and imaginative techniques will be required. Examples follow (see also chapters in this volume by Fitch, Murphy and Campbell, and Mushinsky).

Supplemental Feeding. Lizards have proven amenable to supplemental feeding under natural conditions for observations on the degree of food limitation on reproduction (e.g., Andrews, 1982). Although it would probably be difficult to provide food supplementation to wild populations of snakes, laboratory studies (e.g., Malaret and Fitch, 1984) seem to be a feasible alternative.

Fencing Populations. Elaborate techniques have been devised for fencing terrestrial and arboreal lizard populations (Pacala et al., 1983) and other terrestrial and semi-aquatic vertebrates (Gibbons and Semlitsch, 1981; Vogt and Hine, 1982). Certainly these techniques or modifications of them could be used to conduct long-term manipulatory studies on terrestrial snake species (e.g., *Diadophis punctatus*) or to make seasonal studies on aquatic species (e.g., *Regina alleni*). Fencing would facilitate an evaluation of the effects of density on various population processes such as emigration, reproduction, growth, survivorship, and age at maturity.

Transplantation Experiments. A separation of the genetic and environmental contributions to life-history traits can be approached through reciprocal transplants of juveniles between populations of species found in radically different environments, such as at different altitudes or latitudes. Successful transplant studies have been done on frogs (Berven, 1982) and lizards (Ballinger, 1979). Ecologically widely distributed species of snakes seem to be ideal for such experiments; Kephart's (1981) populations of California garter snakes are an example.

Laboratory Populations. Certain population parameters of many snake species may be identifiable only through organized laboratory studies such as those made by Zweifel (1980). See Murphy and Campbell (this volume) for more detail.

SUMMARY

This chapter describes and summarizes the diverse literature on abundance, age and growth, population structure, maturity, mortality and survivorship, and demographic studies on snakes. Most studies are taxonomically and regionally biased toward Temperate Zone colubrids, elapids, and viperids. Generally, the data base is meager compared with that of other abundant vertebrates.

Patterns of abundance ranged from densities as high as 1849/ha in small terrestrial colubrids to <1/ha in many terrestrial species. Linear densities of snakes in streamside habitats range from 0.02 to 0.38/m of shoreline.

Snakes are divisible into two large groups based on sexual dimorphism: one with males larger than females, where larger males have an advantage in intrasexual combat, and the other with females larger than males, where larger females are favored because of higher fecundity. First-year growth and growth to maturity are compared in colubrid, viperid, elapid, and acrochordid females grouped according to size and family. Small viviparous colubrids and large colubrids and elapids have higher relative growth rates than small oviparous colubrids, elapids, or temperate viperids. Data on primary and secondary sex ratios in various snake populations show few consistent deviations from an expected 1:1.

Early-maturing Temperate Zone colubrids have a relatively young age structure, with 0 to 23% older than 4 yr, whereas later-maturing colubrids and viperids have an older age structure with 20 to 75% older than 4 yr. Among Temperate Zone species, most colubrids and elapids mature at younger ages than viperids. Maturity is delayed beyond 3 yr in males of larger species with male combat, in females of species found at high latitudes or altitudes, in species with a large body size, and in species found in habitats with low productivity. In general, early-maturing colubrids have low juvenile and adult survivorship, low longevity, short generation times, and high fecundity, with the youngest mature females contributing most to future generations. Late-maturing colubrids have low juvenile survivorship, high adult survivorship, high longevity, long generation time, and low fecundity, with females of different ages contributing to future generations. Late-maturing viperids differ from the latter only in having high juvenile survivorship. Wide extremes in these characters may occur, however, between nearby populations of the same species.

ACKNOWLEDGMENTS

We are grateful to the following individuals for supplying copies of hard-to-locate materials, manuscripts that were in preparation, or works in press: W. S. Brown, J. T. Collins, D. G. Cook, L. V. Diller, H. S. Fitch, H. Fukada, J. W. Gibbons, A. R. Gibson, P. T. Gregory, W. H. Gutzke, R. A. King, J. L. Knight, H. B. Lillywhite, J. C. Mitchell, T. D. Schwaner, R. Scudder-Davis, R. Shine, F. Turner, H. K. Voris, and G. R. Zug. Special thanks go to W. S. Brown, other reviewers, and the editors and editorial staff. Parker's participation was supported by a Faculty Summer Research Grant from Mississippi University for Women in 1985. Release time for Plummer was provided by Dean D. B. Priest of Harding University. Thanks also go to our wives and families.

LITERATURE CITED

Aleksiuk, M. 1977. Sources of mortality in concentrated garter snake populations, *Can. Field Nat.* 91:70–72.

Andrén, C. and Nilson, G. 1981. Reproductive success and risk of predation in normal and melanistic colour morphs of the adder, *Vipera berus, Biol. J. Linn. Soc.* 15:235–246.

Andrén, C. and Nilson, G. 1983. Reproductive tactics in an island population of adders, *Vipera berus* (L.), with a fluctuating food resource, *Amphib.-Reptilia* 4:63–79.

Andrews, R. M. 1982. Patterns of growth in reptiles, in: Biology of the Reptilia, vol. 13 (C. Gans and F. H. Pough, eds.) pp. 273–320, Academic Press, New York.

Ballinger, R. E. 1979. Intraspecific variation in demography and life history of the lizard, *Sceloporus jarrovi*, along an altitudinal gradient in southeastern Arizona, *Ecology* 60:901–909.

Barbault, R. 1970. Recherches ecologiques dans la savane de Lamto (Cote d'Ivoire): Les traits quantitatif du peuplement des ophidiens, *Terre Vie* 24:94–107.

Barbour, R. W., Harvey, M. J., and Hardin, J. W. 1969. Home range, movements, and activity of the eastern worm snake, *Carphophis amoenus*, *Ecology* 50:470–476.

Bauman, M. A. and Metter, D. E. 1977. Reproductive cycle of the northern watersnake, *Natrix s. sipedon* (Reptilia, Serpentes, Colubridae), *J. Herpetol.* 11:51–59.

Berven, K. A. 1982. The genetic basis of altitudinal variation in the wood frog *Rana sylvatica*. I. An experimental analysis of life history traits, *Evolution* 36:962–983.

Betz, T. W. 1963. The gross ovarian morphology of the diamond-backed water snake, *Natrix rhombifera*, during the reproductive cycle, *Copeia* 1963: 692–697.

Blaesing, M. E. 1979. Some aspects of the ecology of the eastern garter snake (*Thamnophis sirtalis sirtalis*) in a semi-disturbed habitat in west-central Illinois, *J. Herpetol.* 13:177–181.

Blanchard, F. N. 1937. Data on the natural history of the red-bellied snake, *Storeria occipito-maculata* (Storer), in northern Michigan, *Copeia* 1937:151–162.

Blanchard, F. N. and Finster, E. B. 1933. A method of marking living snakes for future recognition, with a discussion of some problems and results, *Ecology* 14:334–347.

Blanchard, F. N. and Force, E. R. 1930. The age of attainment of sexual maturity in the lined snake, *Tropidoclonion lineatum* (Hallowell), *Bull. Antivenin Inst. Amer.* 3:96–98.

Blanchard, F. N., Gilreath, M. R., and Blanchard, F. C. 1979. The eastern ringneck snake (*Diadophis punctatus edwardsii*) in northern Michigan (Reptilia, Serpentes, Colubridae), *J. Herpetol.* 13:377–402.

Blem, C. R. 1981. Reproduction of the eastern cottonmouth *Agkistrodon piscivorus piscivorus* (Serpentes: Viperidae) at the northern edge of its range, *Brimleyana* 5:117–128.

Bogdanov, O. P. 1965. Ecology of the Reptiles of Central Asia, "Nauka" Uzbekistan SSR, Tashkent.

Branson, B. A. and Baker, E. C. 1974. An ecological study of the queen snake, *Regina septemvittata* (Say) in Kentucky, *Tulane Stud. Zool. Bot.* 18:153–171.

Brattstrom, B. H. 1953. Notes on a population of leaf-nosed snakes *Phyllorhynchus decurtatus perkinsi, Herpetologica* 9:57–64.

Brown, E. E. 1940. Life history and habits of the northern water snake, *Natrix sipedon sipedon* Linne, Ph.D. Dissertation, Cornell University, Ithaca, New York.

Brown, J. H. 1984. On the relationship between abundance and distribution of species, *Am. Nat.* 124:255–279.

Brown, T. W. 1970. Autecology of the sidewinder (*Crotalus cerastes*) at Kelso Dunes, Mojave Desert, California, Ph.D. Dissertation, University of California, Los Angeles.

Brown, W. S. and Parker, W. S. 1982. Niche dimensions and resource partitioning in a Great Basin desert snake community, in: Herpetological Communities (N. J. Scott, Jr., ed.) *U.S. Fish Wildl. Serv. Wildl. Res. Rep.* 13:59–81.

Brown, W. S. and Parker, W. S. 1984. Growth, reproduction and demography of the racer, *Coluber constrictor mormon,* in northern Utah, in: Vertebrate Ecology and Systematics: A Tribute to Henry S. Fitch (R. A. Seigel, L. E. Hunt, J. L. Knight, L. Malaret, and N. L. Zuschlag, eds.) *Univ. Kans. Mus. Nat. Hist. Spec. Publ.* 10:13–40.

Bull, J. J. and Shine, R. 1979. Iteroparous animals that skip opportunities for reproduction, *Am. Nat.* 114:296–303.

Burkett, R. D. 1966. Natural history of cottonmouth moccasin, *Agkistrodon piscivorus* (Reptilia), *Univ. Kans. Publ. Mus. Nat. Hist.* 17:435–491.

Camin, J. H. and Ehrlich, P. R. 1958. Natural selection in water snakes (*Natrix sipedon*) on islands in Lake Erie, *Evolution* 12:504–511.

Carpenter, C. C. 1952a. Comparative ecology of the common garter snake (*Thamnophis s. sirtalis*), the ribbon snake (*Thamnophis s. sauritus*) and Butler's garter snake (*Thamnophis butleri*) in mixed populations, *Ecol. Mongr.* 22:235–258.

Carpenter, C. C. 1952b. Growth and maturity of three species of *Thamnophis* in Michigan, *Copeia* 1952:237–243.

Caughley, G. 1977. Analysis of Vertebrate Populations, John Wiley, New York.

Clark, D. R., Jr. 1966. Notes on sexual dimorphism in tail-length in American snakes, *Trans. Kans. Acad. Sci.* 69:226–232.

Clark, D. R., Jr. 1970. Ecological study of the worm snake, *Carphophis vermis* (Kennicott), *Univ. Kans. Publ. Mus. Nat. Hist.* 19:85–194.

Clark, D. R., Jr. 1974. The western ribbon snake (*Thamnophis proximus*): Ecology of a Texas population, *Herpetologica* 30:372–379.

Clark, D. R., Jr., and Fleet, R. R. 1976. The rough earth snake (*Virginia striatula*): Ecology of a Texas population, *Southwest. Nat.* 20:467–478.

Diller, L. V. and Wallace, R. L. 1984. Reproductive biology of the northern Pacific rattlesnake (*Crotalus viridis oreganus*) in northern Idaho, *Herpetologica* 40:182–193.

Duguy, R. and Saint Girons, H. 1966. Cycle annuel d'activite et reproduction de la coulevre viperine *Natrix maura* L., d'apres les notes manuscrites de Rollinat et des observations personnelles, *Terre Vie* 20:423–457.

Dunson, W. A. 1975. Sea snakes of tropical Queensland between 18 and 20 degrees south latitude, in: The Biology of Sea Snakes (W. A. Dunson, ed.) pp. 151–162, University Park Press, Baltimore, Maryland.

Dunson, W. A. and Minton, S. A. 1978. Diversity, distribution, and ecology of Philippine marine snakes (Reptilia, Serpentes), *J. Herpetol.* 12:281–286.

Duvall, D., King, M. B., and Gutzwiller, K. J. 1985. Behavioral ecology and ethology of the prairie rattlesnake, *Nat. Geogr. Res.* 1:80–111.

Elick, G. E. and Sealander, J. A. 1972. Comparative water loss in relation to habitat selection in small colubrid snakes, *Am. Midl. Nat.* 88:429–439.

Feaver, P. E. 1977. The demography of a Michigan population of *Natrix sipedon* with discussions of ophidian growth and reproduction, Ph.D. Dissertation, University of Michigan, Ann Arbor.

Ferguson, G. W. and Fox, S. F. 1984. Annual variation of survival advantage of large juvenile side-blotched lizards, *Uta stansburiana:* Its causes and evolutionary significance, *Evolution* 38:342–349.

Ferguson, G. W., Bohlen, C. H., and Woolley, H. P. 1980. *Sceloporus undulatus:* Comparative life history and regulation of a Kansas population, *Ecology* 61:313–322.

Fisher, R. A. 1930. The Genetical Theory of Natural Selection, Clarendon Press, Oxford.

Fitch, H. S. 1949. Study of snake populations in central California, *Am. Midl. Nat.* 41:513–579.

Fitch, H. S. 1960. Autecology of the copperhead, *Univ. Kans. Publ. Mus. Nat. Hist.* 13:85–288.

Fitch, H. S. 1961. Longevity and age-size groups in some common snakes, in: Vertebrate Speciation (W. F. Blair, ed.) pp. 396–414, University of Texas Press, Austin.

Fitch, H. S. 1963a. Natural history of the racer, *Coluber constrictor, Univ. Kans. Publ. Mus. Nat. Hist.* 15:351–468.

Fitch, H. S. 1963b. Natural history of the black rat snake (*Elaphe o. obsoleta*) in Kansas, *Copeia* 1963:649–658.

Fitch, H. S. 1965. An ecological study of the garter snake, *Thamnophis sirtalis, Univ. Kans. Publ. Mus. Nat. Hist.* 15:493–564.

Fitch, H. S. 1975. A demographic study of the ringneck snake (*Diadophis punctatus*) in Kansas, *Univ. Kans. Mus. Nat. Hist. Misc. Publ.* 62:1–53.

Fitch, H. S. 1978. A field study of the prairie kingsnake (*Lampropeltis calligaster*), *Trans. Kans. Acad. Sci.* 81:353–363.

Fitch, H. S. 1981. Sexual size differences in reptiles, *Univ. Kans. Mus. Nat. Hist. Misc. Publ.* 70:1–72.

Fitch, H. S. 1982. Resources of a snake community in prairie-woodland habitat of northeastern Kansas, in: Herpetological Communities (N. J. Scott, Jr., ed.) *U.S. Fish Wildl Serv. Wildl. Res. Rep.* 13:83–97.

Fitch, H. S. 1985. Observations on rattle size and demography of prairie rattlesnakes (*Crotalus viridis*) and timber rattlesnakes (*Crotalus horridus*) in Kansas, *Occas. Pap. Mus. Nat. Hist. Univ. Kans.* 119:1–11.

Fitch, H. S. and Fleet, R. R. 1970. Natural history of the milk snake (*Lampropeltis triangulum*) in northeastern Kansas, *Herpetologica* 26:387–396.

Fitch, H. S. and Shirer, H. W. 1971. A radiotelemetric study of spatial relationships in some common snakes, *Copeia* 1971:118–128.

Fleharty, E. D. 1967. Comparative ecology of *Thamnophis elegans, T. cyrtopsis,* and *T. rufipunctatus* in New Mexico, *Southwest. Nat.* 12:207–229.

Force, E. R. 1934. A local study of the opisthoglyph snake, *Tantilla gracilis* Baird and Girard, *Pap. Mich. Acad. Sci. Arts Lett.* 20:645–659.

Ford, N. B. and Killebrew, D. W. 1983. Reproductive tactics and female body size in Butler's garter snake, *Thamnophis butleri, J. Herpetol.* 17:271–275.

Freedman, W. and Catling, P. M. 1978. Population size and structure of four sympatric species of snakes at Amherstburg, Ontario, *Can. Field Nat.* 92:167–173.

Fukada, H. 1956. Biological studies on the snakes. III. Observations on hatching of *Elaphe climacophora, E. conspicillata,* and *Natrix vibakari, Bull. Kyoto Gakugei Univ. Ser. B Math. Nat. Sci.* 9:21–29.

Fukada, H. 1959. Biological studies on the snakes. VI. Growth and maturity of *Natrix tigrina, Bull. Kyoto Gakugei Univ. Ser. B Math. Nat. Sci.* 15:25–41.

Fukada, H. 1960. Biological studies on the snakes. VII. Growth and maturity of *Elaphe quadrivirgata, Bull. Kyoto Gakugei Univ. Ser. B Math. Nat. Sci.* 16:6–21.

Fukada, H. 1961. Biological studies on the snakes. VIII. On the growth formulae of snakes and their applications to other reptiles, *Bull. Kyoto Gakugei Univ. Ser. B Math. Nat. Sci.* 17:16–40.

Fukada, H. 1965. Breeding habits of some Japanese reptiles (critical review), *Bull. Kyoto Gakugei Univ. Ser. B Math. Nat. Sci.* 27:65–82.

Fukada, H. 1969. Biological studies on the snakes. XIII. Preliminary estimate of population size in Tambabashi study area, *Bull. Kyoto Univ. Educ. Ser. B Math. Nat. Sci.* 36:3–9.

Fukada, H. 1978. Growth and maturity of the Japanese rat snake, *Elaphe climacophora* (Reptilia, Serpentes, Colubridae), *J. Herpetol.* 12:269–274.

Gannon, V. P. J. and Secoy, D. M. 1984. Growth and reproductive rates of a northern population of the prairie rattlesnake, *Crotalus v. viridis, J. Herpetol.* 18:13–19.

Gibbons, J. W. 1972. Reproduction, growth, and sexual dimorphism in the canebrake rattlesnake (*Crotalus horridus atricaudatus*), *Copeia* 1972:222–226.

Gibbons, J. W. 1976. Aging phenomena in reptiles, in: Special Review of Experimental Aging Research (M. F. Elias, B. E. Eleftheriou, and P. K. Elias, eds.) pp. 454–475, EAR, Bar Harbor, Maine.

Gibbons, J. W. and Semlitsch, R. D. 1981. Terrestrial drift fences with pitfall traps: An effective technique for quantitative sampling of animal populations, *Brimleyana* 7:1–16.

Gibbons, J. W. and Semlitsch, R. D. 1982. Survivorship and longevity of a long-lived vertebrate species: How long do turtles live? *J. Anim. Ecol.* 51:523–527.

Gibbons, J. W., Coker, J. W., and Murphy, T. M., Jr. 1977. Selected aspects of the life history of the rainbow snake (*Farancia erytrogramma*), *Herpetologica* 33:276–281.

Gibson, A. R. and Falls, J. B. 1979. Thermal biology of the common garter snake *Thamnophis sirtalis* (L.) II. The effects of melanism, *Oecologia (Berl.)* 43:99–109.

Glissmeyer, H. R. 1951. Egg production of the Great Basin rattlesnake, *Herpetologica* 7:24–27.

Godley, J. S. 1980. Foraging ecology of the striped swamp snake, *Regina alleni,* in southern Florida, *Ecol. Monogr.* 50:411–436.

Gorman, G. C., Licht, P., and McCollum, F. 1981. Annual reproductive patterns in three species of marine snakes from the central Philippines, *J. Herpetol.* 15:335–354.

Greene, H. W. 1983. Dietary correlates of the origin and radiation of snakes, *Am. Zool.* 23:431–441.

Gregory, P. T. 1974. Patterns of spring emergence of the red-sided garter snake (*Thamnophis sirtalis parietalis*) in the Interlake region of Manitoba, *Can. J. Zool.* 52:1063–1069.

Gregory, P. T. 1977. Life-history parameters of the red-sided garter snake (*Thamnophis sirtalis parietalis*) in an extreme environment, the Interlake region of Manitoba, *Nat. Mus. Can. Publ. Zool.* 13:1–44.

Gregory, P. T. 1982. Reptilian hibernation, in: Biology of the Reptilia, vol. 13 (C. Gans and F. H. Pough, eds.) pp. 53–154, Academic Press, New York.

Gregory, P. T. and Stewart, K. W. 1975. Long-distance dispersal and feeding strategy of the red-sided garter snake (*Thamnophis sirtalis parietalis*) in the Interlake of Manitoba, *Can. J. Zool.* 53:238–245.

Gutzke, W. H. N., Paukstis, G. L., and McDaniel, L. L. 1985. Skewed sex ratios for adult and hatchling bullsnakes, *Pituophis melanoleucus,* in Nebraska, *Copeia* 1985:649–652.

Hall, R. J. 1969. Ecological observations on Graham's watersnake, *Regina grahami* Baird and Girard, *Am. Midl. Nat.* 81:156–163.

Harding, J. P. 1949. The use of probability paper for the graphical analysis of polymodal frequency distributions, *J. Mar. Biol. Assoc. U. K.* 28:141–153.

Hebrard, J. J. and Mushinsky, H. R. 1978. Habitat use by five sympatric water snakes in a Louisiana swamp, *Herpetologica* 34:306–311.

Hedges, S. B. 1985. The influence of size and phylogeny on life history variation in reptiles: A response to Stearns, *Am. Nat.* 126:258–260.

Henderson, R. W. and Binder, M. H. 1980. The ecology and behavior of vine snakes (*Ahaetulla, Oxybelis, Thelotornis, Uromacer*): A review, *Milw. Public Mus. Contrib. Biol. Geol.* 37:1–38.

Henderson, R. W. and Hoevers, L. G. 1977. The seasonal incidence of snakes at a locality in northern Belize, *Copeia* 1977:349–355.

Heyrend, F. L. and Call, A. 1951. Growth and age in western striped racer and Great Basin rattlesnake, *Herpetologica* 7:28–40.

Hirth, H. F. 1966. Weight changes and mortality of three species of snakes during hibernation, *Herpetologica* 22:8–12.

Hirth, H. F. and King, A. C. 1968. Biomass densities of snakes in the cold desert of Utah, *Herpetologica* 24:333–335.

Holstrom, W. F., Jr. 1980. Observations on the reproduction of the common anaconda, *Eunectes murinus,* at the New York Zoological Park, *Herpetol. Rev.* 11:32–33.

Imler, R. H. 1945. Bullsnakes and their control on a Nebraska wildlife refuge, *J. Wildl. Manage.* 9:265–273.

Iverson, J. B. 1982. Biomass in turtle populations: A neglected subject, *Oecologia (Berl.)* 55:69–76.

Jackson, D. R. and Franz, R. 1981. Ecology of the eastern coral snake (*Micrurus fulvius*) in northern peninsular Florida, *Herpetologica* 37:213–228.

Julian, G. 1951. Sex ratios of the winter populations, *Herpetologica* 7:21–24.

Kardong, K. V. 1980. Evolutionary patterns in advanced snakes, *Am. Zool.* 20:269–282.

Kassing, E. F. 1961. A life history study of the Great Plains ground snake, *Sonora episcopa episcopa* (Kennicott), *Tex. J. Sci.* 13:185–203.

Keenlyne, K. D. 1978. Reproductive cycles in two species of rattlesnakes, *Am. Midl. Nat.* 100:368–375.

Kephart, D. G. 1981. Population ecology and population structure of *Thamnophis elegans* and *Thamnophis sirtalis,* Ph.D. Dissertation, University of Chicago.

King, R. B., 1986. Population ecology of Lake Erie water snakes, *Nerodia sipedon insularum, Copeia* 1986:757–772.

Klauber, L. M. 1943. Tail-length differences in snakes with notes on sexual dimorphism and the coefficient of divergence, *Bull. Zool. Soc. San Diego* 18:1–60.

Klauber, L. M. 1972. Rattlesnakes: Their Habits, Life Histories, and Influence on Mankind, 2nd ed., 2 vols., University of California Press, Berkeley.

Klimstra, W. D. 1958. Some observations on snake activities and populations, *Ecology* 39:232–239.

Koba, K. 1938. Some notes on *Agkistrodon halys* (Pallas) from Syoryuzan Island, Kwangtung, South Manchuria (I), *Zool. Mag. (Japan)* 50:245–264.

Kofron, C. P. 1983. Female reproductive cycle of the neotropical snail-eating snake *Sibon sanniola* in northern Yucatan, Mexico, *Copeia* 1983:963–969.

Krohmer, R. W. and Aldridge, R. D. 1985a. Male reproductive cycle of the lined snake (*Tropidoclonion lineatum*), *Herpetologica* 41:33–38.

Krohmer, R. W. and Aldridge, R. D. 1985b. Female reproductive cycle of the lined snake (*Tropidoclonion lineatum*), *Herpetologica* 41:39–44.

Kropach, C. 1971. Sea snake (*Pelamis platurus*) aggregations on slicks in Panama, *Herpetologica* 27:131–135.

Kropach, C. 1975. The yellow-bellied sea snake, *Pelamis,* in the eastern Pacific, in: The Biology of Sea Snakes (W. A. Dunson, ed.) pp. 185–216, University Park Press, Baltimore, Maryland.

Lemen, C. A. and Voris, H. K. 1981. A comparison of reproductive strategies among marine snakes, *J. Anim. Ecol.* 50:89–101.

Lillywhite, H. B. 1982. Tracking as an aid in ecological studies of snakes, in: Herpetological Communities (N. J. Scott, Jr., ed.) *U.S. Fish Wildl. Serv. Wildl. Res. Rep.* 13:181–191.

Macartney, J. M. 1985. The ecology of the northern Pacific rattlesnake, *Crotalus viridis oreganus,* in British Columbia, M.S. Thesis, University of Victoria, British Columbia.

Madsen, T. 1983. Growth rates, maturation and sexual size dimorphism in a population of grass snakes, *Natrix natrix,* in southern Sweden, *Oikos* 40:277–282.

Madsen, T. and Osterkamp, M. 1982. Notes on the biology of the fish-eating snake *Lycodonomorphus bicolor* in Lake Tanganyika, *J. Herpetol.* 16:185–188.

Malaret, L. and Fitch, H. S. 1984. Effects of overfeeding and underfeeding on reproduction in four species of reptiles, *Acta Zool. Pathol. Antverp.* 78: 77–84.

Millar, J. S. and Zammuto, R. M. 1983. Life histories of mammals: An analysis of life tables, *Ecology* 64:631–635.

Mushinsky, H. R., Hebrard, J. H., and Walley, M. G. 1980. The role of temperature on the behavioral and ecological associations of sympatric water snakes, *Copeia* 1980:744–754.

Myers, C. W. 1965. Biology of the ringneck snake, *Diadophis punctatus,* in Florida, *Bull. Fla. State Mus. Biol. Sci.* 10:43–90.

Nussbaum, R. A. 1980. The Brahminy blind snake (*Ramphotyphlops braminus*) in the Seychelles Archipelago: Distribution, variation, and further evidence for parthenogenesis, *Herpetologica* 36:215–221.

Pacala, S., Rummel, J., and Roughgarden, J. 1983. A technique for enclosing *Anolis* lizard populations under field conditions, *J. Herpetol.* 17:94–97.

Parker, W. S. 1976. Population estimates, age structure, and denning habits of whipsnakes, *Masticophis t. taeniatus,* in a northern Utah *Atriplex-Sarcobatus* community, *Herpetologica* 32:53–57.

Parker, W. S. and Brown, W. S. 1973. Species composition and population changes in two complexes of snake hibernacula in northern Utah, *Herpetologica* 28:319–326.

Parker, W. S. and Brown, W. S. 1974. Weight changes and mortality of Great Basin rattlesnakes (*Crotalus viridis*) at a hibernaculum in northern Utah, *Herpetologica* 30:234–239.

Parker, W. S. and Brown, W. S. 1980. Comparative ecology of two colubrid snakes, *Masticophis t. taeniatus* and *Pituophis melanoleucus deserticola,* in northern Utah, *Milw. Public Mus. Publ. Biol. Geol.* 7:1–104.

Pendlebury, G. B. 1977. Distribution and abundance of the prairie rattlesnake, *Crotalus viridis viridis,* in Canada, *Can. Field Nat.* 91:122–129.

Peters, R. H. and Wassenberg, K. 1983. The effect of body size on animal abundance, *Oecologia (Berl.)* 60:89–96.

Petter-Rousseaux, A. 1953. Recherches sur la croissance et le cycle d'activite testiculaire de *Natrix natrix helvetica, Terre Vie* 15:175–223.

Pianka, E. R. 1983. Evolutionary Ecology, 3rd ed., Harper and Row, New York.

Pisani, R. G. and Bothner, R. C. 1970. The annual reproductive cycle of *Thamnophis brachystoma, Sci. Stud. St. Bonaventure Univ.* 26:15–34.

Platt, D. R. 1969. Natural history of the hognose snakes, *Heterodon platyrhinos* and *Heterodon nasicus, Univ. Kans. Publ. Mus. Nat. Hist.* 18:253–420.

Platt, D. R. 1984. Growth of bullsnakes (*Pituophis melanoleucus sayi*) on a sand prairie in south central Kansas, in: Vertebrate Ecology and Systematics: A Tribute to Henry S. Fitch (R. A. Seigel, L. E. Hunt, J. L. Knight, L. Malaret, and N. L. Zuschlag, eds.) *Univ. Kans. Mus. Nat. Hist. Spec. Publ.* 10:41–55.

Plummer, M. V. 1985a. Demography of green snakes (*Opheodrys aestivus*), *Herpetologica* 41:373–381.

Plummer, M. V. 1985b. Growth and maturity in green snakes (*Opheodrys aestivus*), *Herpetologica* 41:28–33.

Pough, F. H. 1977. Ontogenetic change in blood oxygen capacity and maximum activity in garter snakes (*Thamnophis sirtalis*), *J. Comp. Physiol.* 116:337–345.

Pough, F. H. 1983. Amphibians and reptiles as low-energy systems, in: Behavioral Energetics: The Cost of Survival in Vertebrates (W. P. Aspey and S. I. Lustick, eds.) pp. 141–188, Ohio State University Press, Columbus.

Pough, F. H. and Groves, J. D. 1983. Specializations of the body form and food habits of snakes, *Am. Zool.* 23:443–454.

Preston, W. B. 1964. The importance of the facial pit of the northern Pacific rattlesnake, *Crotalus viridis oreganus,* under natural conditions in southern British Columbia, M.S. Thesis, University of British Columbia.

Preston, W. B. 1970. The comparative ecology of two water snakes, *Natrix rhombifera* and *Natrix erythrogaster* in Oklahoma, Ph.D. Dissertation, University of Oklahoma., Norman.

Prestt, I. 1971. An ecological study of the viper *Vipera berus* in southern Britain, *J. Zool.* 164:373–418.

Quinn, H. R. 1979. Reproduction and growth of the Texas coral snake (*Micrurus fulvius tenere*), *Copeia* 1979:453–463.

Quinn, H. and Jones, J. P. 1974. Squeeze box technique for measuring snakes, *Herpetol. Rev.* 5:35.

Rabb, G. B. and Marx, H. 1973. Major ecological and geographic patterns in the evolution of colubroid snakes, *Evolution* 27:69–83.

Reynolds, R. P. 1982. Seasonal incidence of snakes in northeastern Chihuahua, Mexico, *Southwest. Nat.* 27:161–166.

Ricklefs, R. E. 1979. Ecology, 2nd ed., Chiron Press, New York.

Saint Girons, H. 1957. Croissance et fecondite de *Vipera aspis* (L.), *Vie Milieu* 8:265–286.

Saint Girons, H. 1964. Notes sur l'ecologie et la structure des populations des Laticaudinae (Serpentes, Hydrophidae) en Nouvelle Caledonie, *Terre Vie* 111:185–214.

Saint Girons, H. 1975. Coexistence de *Vipera aspis* et de *Vipera berus* en Loire-Atlantique: Un probleme de competition interspecifique, *Terre Vie* 29:590–613.

Saint Girons, H. 1981. Cycle annuel et survie de quelques viperes d'Europe: Influence des temperatures exceptionellement elevees de l'annee 1976, *Vie Milieu* 31:59–64.

Saint Girons, H. and Naulleau, G. 1981. Poids des nouveau-nes et strategies reproductrices des viperes Europeennes, *Terre Vie* 35:579–616.

Saint Girons, H. and Pfeffer, P. 1971. Le cycle sexual de serpents du Cambodge, *Ann. Sci. Zool.* 13:543–571.

Schwaner, T. D. 1985. Population structure of black tiger snakes, *Notechis ater niger,* on offshore islands of South Australia, in: Biology of Australasian Frogs and Reptiles (G. Grigg, R. Shine and H. Ehmann, eds.) pp. 35–46, Surrey Beatty and Sons, Chipping Norton, New South Wales, Australia.

Seibert, H. C. 1950. Population density of snakes in an area near Chicago, *Copeia* 1950:229–230.

Seibert, H. C. and Hagen, C. W., Jr. 1947. Studies on a population of snakes in Illinois, *Copeia* 1947:6–22.

Semlitsch, R. D. and Moran, G. B. 1984. Ecology of the redbelly snake (*Storeria occipitomaculata*) using mesic habitats in South Carolina, *Am. Midl. Nat.* 111:33–40.

Semlitsch, R. D., Brown, K. L., and Caldwell, J. P. 1981. Habitat utilization, seasonal activity, and population size structure of the southeastern crowned snake *Tantilla coronata, Herpetologica* 37:40–46.

Shine, R. 1977. Reproduction in Australian elapid snakes. II. Female reproductive cycles, *Aust. J. Zool.* 25:655–666.

Shine, R. 1978a. Growth rates and sexual maturation in six species of Australian elapid snakes, *Herpetologica* 34:73–79.

Shine, R. 1978b. Sexual size dimorphism and male combat in snakes, *Oecologia* (*Berl.*) 33:269–277.

Shine, R. 1979. Activity patterns in Australian elapid snakes (Squamata: Serpentes: Elapidae), *Herpetologica* 35:1–11.

Shine, R. 1980a. Comparative ecology of three Australian snake species of the genus *Cacophis* (Serpentes: Elapidae), *Copeia* 1980:831–838.

Shine, R. 1980b. Ecology of eastern Australian whipsnakes of the genus *Demansia, J. Herpetol.* 14:381–389.

Shine, R. 1980c. Reproduction, feeding and growth in the Australian burrowing snake *Vermicella annulata, J. Herpetol.* 14:71–77.

Shine, R. 1980d. Ecology of the Australian death adder *Acanthophis antarcticus*

(Elapidae): Evidence for convergence with the Viperidae, *Herpetologica* 36:281–289.

Shine, R. 1981a. Ecology of Australian elapid snakes of the genera *Furina* and *Glyphodon*, *J. Herpetol.* 15:219–224.

Shine, R. 1981b. Venomous snakes in cold climates: Ecology of the Australian genus *Drysdalia* (Serpentes: Elapidae), *Copeia* 1981:14–25.

Shine, R. 1982. Ecology of the Australian elapid snake *Echiopsis curta*, *J. Herpetol.* 16:388–393.

Shine, R. 1983a. Food habits and reproductive biology of Australian elapid snakes of the genus *Denisonia*, *J. Herpetol.* 17:171–175.

Shine, R. 1983b. Arboreality in snakes: Ecology of the Australian elapid genus *Hoplocephalus*, *Copeia* 1983:198–205.

Shine, R. 1984a. Ecology of small fossorial Australian snakes of the genera *Neelaps* and *Simoselaps* (Serpentes, Elapidae), in: Vertebrate Ecology and Systematics: A Tribute to Henry S. Fitch (R. A. Seigel, L. E. Hunt, J. L. Knight, L. Malaret, and N. L. Zuschlag, eds.) *Univ. Kans. Mus. Nat. Hist. Spec. Publ.* 10:173–183.

Shine, R. 1984b. Reproductive biology and food habits of the Australian elapid snakes of the genus *Cryptophis*, *J. Herpetol.* 18:33–39.

Shine, R. 1986. Ecology of a low-energy specialist: Food habits and reproductive biology of the arafura filesnake (Acrochordidae), *Copeia* 1986:424–437.

Shine, R. and Bull, J. J. 1977. Skewed sex ratios in snakes, *Copeia* 1977:228–234.

Shine, R. and Charles, N. 1982. Ecology of the Australian elapid snake *Tropidechis carinatus*, *J. Herpetol.* 16:383–387.

Shine, R. and Covacevich, J. 1983. Ecology of highly venomous snakes: The Australian genus *Oxyuranus* (Elapidae), *J. Herpetol.* 17:60–69.

Spellerberg, I. F. and Phelps, T. E. 1977. Biology, general ecology and behavior of the snake, *Coronella austriaca* Laurenti, *Biol. J. Linn. Soc.* 9:133–164.

Stearns, S. C. 1976. Life-history tactics: A review of the ideas, *Q. Rev. Biol.* 51:3–47.

Stewart, G. R. 1968. Some observations on the natural history of two Oregon garter snakes (genus *Thamnophis*), *J. Herpetol.* 2:71–86.

Stickel, L. F., Stickel, W. H., and Schmid, F. C. 1980. Ecology of a Maryland population of black rat snakes (*Elaphe o. obsoleta*), *Am. Midl. Nat.* 103:1–14.

Tanaka, H., Wada, Y., Oguma, Y., Sasa, M., Noboru, Y., Ono, T., and Matsuschita, N. 1971. A method of population estimation for the habu, *Trimeresurus flavoviridis*, *Snake* 3:9–13.

Tinkle, D. W. 1957. Ecology, maturation and reproduction of *Thamnophis sauritus proximus*, *Ecology* 38:69–77.

Tinkle, D. W. 1962. Reproductive potential and cycles in female *Crotalus atrox* from northwestern Texas, *Copeia* 1962:306–313.

Tinkle, D. W. 1979. Long-term field studies, *BioScience* 20:717.

Tinkle, D. W., Wilbur, H. M., and Tilley, S. G. 1970. Evolutionary strategies in lizard reproduction, *Evolution* 24:55–74.

Turner, F. B. 1977. The dynamics of populations of squamates and crocodilians, in: Biology of the Reptilia, vol. 7 (C. Gans and D. W. Tinkle, eds.) pp. 157–264, Academic Press, New York.

Vial, J. L., Berger, T. J., and McWilliams, W. T., Jr. 1977. Quantitative demography of copperheads, *Agkistrodon contortrix* (Serpentes: Viperidae), *Res. Popul. Ecol. (Kyoto)* 18:223–234.

Viitanen, P. 1967. Hibernation and seasonal movements of the viper, *Vipera berus berus* (L.), in southern Finland, *Ann. Zool. Fennici* 4:472–546.

Vitt, L. J. 1978. Caloric content of lizard and snake (Reptilia) eggs and bodies and the conversion of weight to caloric data, *J. Herpetol.* 12:65–72.

Vitt, L. J. 1980. Ecological observations on sympatric *Philodryas* (Colubridae) in northeastern Brazil, *Pap. Avulsos Zool. (Sao Paulo)* 34:87–98.

Vitt, L. J. 1983. Ecology of an anuran-eating guild of terrestrial tropical snakes, *Herpetologica* 39:52–66.

Vogt, R. C. and Hine, R. L. 1982. Evaluation of techniques for assessment of amphibian and reptile populations in Wisconsin, in: Herpetological Communities (N. J. Scott, Jr., ed.) *U.S. Fish Wild. Serv. Wildl. Res. Rep.* 13:210–217.

Volsøe, H. 1944. Structure and seasonal variation of the male reproductive organ of *Vipera berus* (L.), *Spolia Zool. Mus. Haun.* 5:1–157.

Voris, H. K. 1985. Population size estimates for a marine snake (*Enhydrina schistosa*) in Malaysia, *Copeia* 1985:955–961.

Voris, H. K. and Jayne, B. C. 1979. Growth, reproduction and population structure of a marine snake, *Enhydrina schistosa* (Hydrophiidae), *Copeia* 1979: 307–318.

Wharton, C. H. 1966. Reproduction and growth in the cottonmouths, *Agkistrodon piscivorus* Lacepede, of Cedar Keys, Florida, *Copeia* 1966:149–161.

Willis, L., Threlkeld, S. T., and Carpenter, C. C. 1982. Tail loss patterns in *Thamnophis* (Reptilia: Colubridae) and the probable fate of injured individuals, *Copeia* 1982:98–101.

Woodbury, A. M. 1951. A snake den in Tooele County, Utah: Introduction— A ten year study, *Herpetologica* 7:4–14.

Zug, G. R., Hedges, S. B., and Sunkel, S. 1979. Variation in reproductive parameters of three neotropical snakes, *Coniophanes fissidens, Dipsas catesbyi,* and *Imantodes cenchoa, Smithson. Contrib. Zool.* 300:1–20.

Zweifel, R. G. 1980. Aspects of the biology of a laboratory population of kingsnakes, in: Reproductive Biology and Diseases of Captive Reptiles (J. B. Murphy and J. T. Collins, eds.) *SSAR Contrib. Herpetol.* 1:141–152.

CHAPTER TEN

Foraging Ecology

Henry R. Mushinsky

The trophodynamics of the elongate legless creatures we call snakes has attracted the attention of many herpetologists over the years. Hundreds of papers published on this topic document a kernel conviction that foraging and predator-prey relations are prime ecological and evolutionary forces in snake ontogeny and phylogeny. In fact, most life-history or ecological studies on snakes are built around an understanding of the trophic relations of the serpents under investigation (see Fitch, this volume). Unfortunately, much of the literature on the diet and food habits of snakes consists of little more than anecdotal lists of prey taken from the stomachs of dead snakes. This literature is used to provide much of the information for the summary of snake prey in Table 10-1. Generally, Table 10-1 should not be considered an all-inclusive summary of the prey of individual snake species but rather a preliminary listing of snake food habits awaiting verification and testing. Most of this chapter is devoted to addressing specific aspects of foraging ecology, beginning with some unusual morphological and behavioral adaptations associated with feeding and ending with community studies that address resource partitioning among sympatric species. Foraging of venomous snakes and foraging of aquatic snakes are treated separately because both involve unique suites of morphological or behavioral characteristics. At the end of the chapter, I indicate some directions for future research, but there are numerous comments throughout the chapter aimed at stimulating discussion and additional research. Finally, I would be remiss if I failed to point out (see Duellman, 1984) that much of what we know about the foraging ecology of North American Colubridae and Viperidae stems from the pioneering efforts of Henry S. Fitch (1940b, 1949).

Table 10–1. Summary of Literature Records for the Primary Prey of Snakes

Snake Taxon	Primary Prey	Reference
Family Acrochordidae		
Acrochordus arafurae	Fish	Shine (1986)
Family Boidae		
Boa constrictor	Bats	Thomas (1974)
Calabaria reinhardii	Rodents	Lehmann (1971)
Charina bottae	Rodents, snakes	Linder (1963)
Corallus enydris	Lizards, rodents	Wehekind (1955), Pendlebury (1974)
Epicrates angulifer	Bats	Hardy (1957)
Eunectes murinus	Rodents, birds	Wehekind (1955)
Family Colubridae		
Antillophis parvifrons	Lizards, rodents	Franz and Gicca (1982)
Boiga dendrophila	Rodents	Minton and Dunson (1978)
Carphophis amoenus	Earthworms, salamanders	Clark (1970)
C. vermis	Earthworms	Clark (1970)
Cemophora coccinea	Reptile eggs	Dickson (1948), Minton and Bechtel (1958), Palmer and Tregembo (1970)
Chionactis occipitalis	Scorpions, crickets	Glass (1972)
Coluber constrictor	Birds, rodents, insects, amphibians, reptiles	Klimstra (1959a), Brown and Parker (1982)
Dasypeltis sp.	Eggs	Gans (1974)
Diadophis punctatus	Earthworms	Fitch (1975)
	Reptiles	Gehlbach (1974)
	Amphibians	Barbour (1950)
Dipsas sp.	Snails	Gans (1975)
Drymarchon corais	Reptiles, birds, mammals	Babis, (1949), Dilley (1954), Wehekind (1955)
Drymobius chloroticus	Anurans	Seib (1984)
D. margaritiferus	Anurans, reptiles	Seib (1984)
Elaphe obsoleta	Birds, mammals	Fitch (1963)
E. quatuorlineata	Birds, eggs	Cattaneo (1979)
E. situla	Birds, eggs	Steward (1971)
E. subocularis	Rodents	Reynolds and Scott (1982)
Farancia abacura	Amphibians	Tinkle (1959)
F. erytrogramma	Fish, amphibians	Richmond (1945), Metrolis (1971)
Hypsiglena torquata	Lizards	Cowles (1941)
Lampropeltis calligaster	Rodents, reptiles	Fitch (1978)
L. getulus	Birds, reptiles, eggs	Howell (1954), Knight and Loraine (1986)
L. triangulum	Reptiles, mammals	Fitch and Fleet (1970)
Leptodeira sp.	Anurans	Duellman (1958)

(Continued)

Table 10–1. Summary of Literature Records for the Primary Prey of Snakes (*Continued*)

Snake Taxon	Primary Prey	Reference
Leptophis mexicanus	Anurans	Henderson et al. (1977)
Liophis spp.	Anurans	Vitt (1983)
Masticophis taeniatus	Snakes, mammals	Brown and Parker (1982)
Mastigodryas melanolomus	Lizards	Seib (1984)
Natrix maura	Fish, anurans	Steward (1971)
N. natrix	Lizards, mammals	Kratzer (1974)
N. tessellata	Amphibians	Lanka (1975–1976)
	Rodents, mammals	Steward (1958)
Nerodia erythrogaster	Anurans	Diener (1957), Brown (1979)
N. rhombifera	Fish	Sisk and McCoy (1964), Bowers (1966), Mushinsky and Hebrard (1977)
N. sipedon	Fish, amphibians	Brown (1958)
N. taxispilota	Fish	Camp et al. (1980)
Opheodrys aestivus	Insects, spiders	Plummer (1981)
Philodryas chamissonis	Amphibians, reptiles	Jaksic et al. (1981)
P. nattereri	Lizards, mammals	Vitt (1980)
P. olfersii	Mammals, anurans	Vitt (1980)
Pituophis melanoleucus	Rodents, lizards	Brown and Parker (1982), Reynolds and Scott (1982)
Regina alleni	Crayfish	Kofron (1978), Godley (1980)
R. grahami	Crayfish	Hall (1969), Branson and Baker (1974)
R. rigida	Crayfish	Kofron (1978), Godley (1980)
R. septemvittata	Crayfish	Hall (1969), Branson and Baker (1974)
Rhabdophis tigrinus	Anurans, fish	Fukada (1959)
Rhadinaea flavilata	Anurans	Allen (1939)
Stilosoma extenuatum	Snakes	Carr (1934), Mushinsky (1984)
Storeria dekayi	Earthworms	Judd (1954)
Tantilla relicta	Beetle larvae	Smith (1982)
Thamnophis elegans	Slugs, fish, frogs, birds	Fitch (1940a), Fox (1952), Arnold (1977, 1981a, b), James et al. (1983)
T. ordinoides	Slugs	Gregory (1978)
T. sirtalis	Anurans	Fitch (1965)
	Earthworms, birds, fish	Lagler and Salyer (1945), Gregory and Stewart (1975), Arnold (1978), Gregory (1978), Kephart (1982), Greenwell et al. (1984)

(*Continued*)

Table 10–1. Summary of Literature Records for the Primary Prey of Snakes (*Continued*)

Snake Taxon	Primary Prey	Reference
Uromacer frenatus	Lizards	Horn (1969)
Waglerophis merremii	Anurans	Vitt (1983)
Family Elapidae		
Acanthophis antarcticus	Lizards, mammals	Shine (1980a)
Cacophis (three species)	Lizards	Shine (1980b)
Demansia sp.	Lizards	Shine (1980c)
Denisonia fasciata	Lizards	Shine (1983)
D. punctata	Lizards	Shine (1983)
D. devisi	Frogs	Shine (1983)
D. maculata	Frogs	Shine (1983)
Drysdalia (three species)	Lizards	Shine (1981a)
D. coronata	Lizards, frogs	Shine (1981a)
Echiopsis carata	Lizards, frogs	Shine (1982)
Furina (one species)	Lizards	Shine (1981b)
Glyphodon (three species)	Lizards	Shine (1981b)
Micruroides euryxanthus	Reptiles	Gates (1960), Vitt and Hulse (1973)
Micrurus fulvius	Reptiles, fish	Schmidt (1932), Greene (1984)
Naja haje	Anurans, reptiles	Rasmussen (1974)
N. mossambica	Rodents, lizards, anurans	Rasmussen (1974)
N. naja	Insects, rodents, reptiles, birds	Mao (1970), Agrawal (1979)
Neelaps sp.	Lizards	Shine (1984)
Notechis scutatus	Anurans	Shine (1977)
Ophiophagus hannah	Reptiles	Greene (1976)
Oxyuranus scutellatus	Mammals	Shine and Covacevich (1983)
O. microlepidotus	Mammals	Shine and Covacevich (1983)
Pseudonaja textilis	Lizards	Shine (1977)
Simoselaps bertholdi	Lizards	Shine (1984)
S. semifasciatus	Squamate eggs	Shine (1984)
Tropidechis carinatus	Mammals	Shine and Charles (1982)
Unechis gouldii	Lizards	Shine (1977)
Vermicella annulata	Snakes	Shine (1980d)
Walterinnesia aegyptia	Lizards	Zinner (1971)
Family Leptotyphlopidae		
Leptotyphlops dulcis	Termites, ants	Punzo (1974)
L. humilis	Ants, termites	Punzo (1974)
Family Typhlopidae		
Typhlops sp.	Insects, termites, ants	Wehekind (1955), Steward (1971)
Family Viperidae		
Agkistrodon acutus	Rodents, lizards	Mao (1970)
A. contortrix	Birds, mammals, snakes	Fitch (1960)

(*Continued*)

Table 10–1. Summary of Literature Records for the Primary Prey of Snakes (*Continued*)

Snake Taxon	Primary Prey	Reference
A. piscivorous	Fish, anurans, reptiles, birds, mammals	Schmidt and Davis (1941), Clark (1949), Klimstra (1959b), Burkett (1966), Kofron (1978)
Bothrops atrox	Lizards, birds, mammals	Sexton (1956–1957)
Bungarus multicinctus	Fish, reptiles	Mao (1970)
Crotalus adamanteus	Mammals	Funderburg (1968)
C. atrox	Birds, mammals	Beevers (1976), Best and James (1984), Reynolds and Scott (1982)
C. horridus	Mammals	Fitch (1982), Reinert et al. (1984)
C. molossus	Rodents	Reynolds and Scott (1982)
C. scutulatus	Rodents	Reynolds and Scott (1982)
C. willardi	Birds, mammals, lizards	Klauber (1972), Parker and Stotz (1977)
C. viridis	Mammals, conspecifics	Gloyd (1933), Fitch and Twining (1946), Powers (1972), Lillywhite (1982), Gannon and Secoy (1984)
Dendroaspis angusticeps	Rodents	Lloyd (1974)
Lacheis muta	Mammals	Greene (1983a)
Sistrurus catenatus	Mammals, birds	Keenlyne and Beer (1973)
Trimeresurus mucrosquamatus	Rodents, anurans, reptiles	Mao (1970)
T. stejnegeri	Anurans	Mao (1970)
Vipera berus	Amphibians, lizards, mammals	Prokopev et. al. (1978), Kjaergaard (1981)
V. russelli	Lizards	Vit, 1977

MORPHOLOGICAL ADAPTATIONS OF THE FEEDING APPARATUS

The general morphology of the snake skull and jaw apparatus is described by Cundall (this volume). Adaptations for handling different prey types are illustrated by specialized foragers. Piscivorous snakes such as the Acrochordidae have long quadrate bones to increase gape during feeding, and numerous long, highly curved or recurved, sharp teeth to increase purchase on their scaled prey (Savitzky, 1983). Extreme dietary specialization is exemplified by members of the colubrid genus *Regina* (Rossman, 1963). *Regina grahami* and *R. septemvittata* eat recently molted crayfish (Hall, 1969; Branson and Baker, 1974; Mushinsky and Hebrard, 1977), while *R. alleni* and *R. rigida* eat crayfish in all stages of their molt cycle (Kofron, 1978; Godley, 1980; Godley et al., 1984).

Ingestion of these hard-shelled arthropods necessitates behavioral feeding adaptations (Franz, 1977) and morphological modifications manifest in hinged teeth (Savitsky, 1981; Godley et al., 1984). Other examples of morphological feeding adaptations include those of *Dasypeltis* (Colubridae), which extracts the liquid contents of an ingested egg by passing it over the enlarged hypapophyses of cervical vertebrae protruding into the esophagus. The eggshells are slit open, emptied, and regurgitated (Gans, 1952, 1974). The storage capacity of the esophagus of *Dasypeltis* also is quite large (Billing and Zisweller, 1981). Members of the genus *Dipsas* (Colubridae) ingest snails by attacking the exposed snail and drawing out the soft anatomy using mandibular manipulation (Mertens, 1952; Gans, 1975). Kofron (1982) described a pivot joint on the lower jaw that permitted rotation of the dentary bone and teeth outward to a nearly horizontal position.

BEHAVIORAL TRAITS ASSOCIATED WITH FEEDING

Comparative studies on snake feeding have provided insight into phylogenetic relations. Greene and Burghardt (1978) compared action patterns used for constricting prey by 75 species from 5 snake families. They found intergeneric, interspecific, and occasionally individual variability in coil application to prey. According to Greene and Burghardt, constriction can be viewed as a key ethological innovation in the early evolution of snakes. They proposed that constriction was a behavioral protoadaptation that permitted and favored evolutionary loss of the mandibular symphysis and development of a streptostylic (movable) quadrate bone. Generally, constriction is thought to be most effective on endothermic birds and mammals. Observations of non-venomous snakes killing ectotherms by constriction often involve lengthy time- or energy-consuming battles (Carr, 1934; Tinkle, 1959; Mushinsky, 1984). Hence ophiophagous snakes often ingest living prey or kill their prey by crushing them with powerful jaws.

Among the most primitive of the living snakes are the members of the family Aniliidae, which feed on relatively large elongate vertebrates. Large aniliids ingest small as well as large prey, a situation that is paralleled in the advanced snakes. Greene (1983b) suggested that very early snakes used constriction and powerful jaws to eat elongate heavy prey. The dietary habits of modern snakes include ingestion of large prey by venomous elapids and viperids, and somewhat more frequent foraging for small prey by other advanced snakes. Detailed comparative studies on the relationship between prey size and snake size are needed to test these proposed ideas (see Pough and Groves, 1983).

There appears to be a dichotomy in the strategies employed by snakes to capture prey. Schoener (1971) described foraging behavior as either sit-and-wait or active foraging. As regards snakes, the term "ambush hunter" often is used to replace "sit-and-wait." Reinert et al. (1984) described the sit-and-wait tactics of *Crotalus horridus* (Viperidae) which, coiled near fallen logs, sometimes rest their chins on a log while waiting for the next mammal to pass within striking distance. Typically, members of the Elapidae are active foragers, a fact that led Shine (1980a) to recognize the atypical ambush hunting behavior of *Acanthophis antarcticus* (Elapidae) as convergent with that of the Viperidae. Many species of the Colubridae have been described as active foragers and as such have served as the focal point of much of the ecological research on serpents. Understandably, we know more about the feeding habits of visibly active foragers than about those of ambush hunters who often spend long periods of time inactive. For example, Greene (1983a) radiotagged bushmasters, *Lachesis muta* (Viperidae), and followed a female who used three sites for 3, 6, and 25 days and moved a total of 50 m. She was alert for 40% of 35 days and spent 1% of her alert time moving about. The snake ate a meal on the twenty-fourth night of observation. In contrast, Carpenter (1952) reported that searching for mates, a hibernating den, shelter, and food constituted the major activity of three species of *Thamnophis* (Colubridae). Likewise, Mushinsky and Hebrard (1977) reported frequent observations on four species of *Nerodia* (Colubridae) swimming actively in pursuit of prey, as well as the capture of actively foraging snakes that regurgitated living prey.

ONTOGENY, BODY SIZE, AND ENERGETIC CONSTRAINTS ON SNAKE FORAGING

Ecologically, snakes are very different from the closely related lizards. Herbivory and the elongate legless snake body appear incompatible. Snakes eat few large meals relative to the frequent ingestion of small meals seen in most lizards (Greene, 1982, 1983b). Elongation of the body, serpentine locomotion, and reduction of trunk diameter allow many predatory snakes to enter the burrows of their prey (Gans, 1961, 1975). Research on feeding specializations of stout-bodied snakes that appear to be exceptions to some generalizations on snake morphology (Pough and Groves, 1983) has revealed a suite of characters associated with swallowing large prey. In addition, the proteolytic venom of vipers facilitates the ingestion of large prey (Thomas and Pough, 1979) by increasing the rate of prey decomposition and preventing putrefaction.

Juvenile snakes quickly become exhausted physiologically (Pough, 1977, 1978), but we do not know how morphology and physiology interact to constrain the size of prey ingested. Several recent studies have considered ontogenetic restrictions on snake foraging ecology and have found prey size discrimination. Voris and Moffett (1981) observed that large sea snakes (*Enhydrina shistosa*) ingested absolutely larger prey than smaller individuals did. They also found that the lower limit of prey size increased during ontogeny such that snakes in their second year or older did not feed on the smaller prey eaten by first-year snakes. Within the genus *Nerodia* (Colubridae), Mushinsky et al. (1982) found that the prey of *N. erythrogaster* and *N. fasciata* changed from fish to amphibians as the snakes matured. Sympatric *N. rhombifera* and *N. cyclopion* had similar diets as young snakes, but each species ingested a different array of prey as they grew older and larger. The sexual dimorphism in body size of the two species allowed the larger females to feed on prey not consumed by conspecific males. *Nerodia rhombifera* captured at a fish hatchery, where prey availability was very high, were found to exhibit a parallel ontogenetic dietary shift (Plummer and Goy, 1984).

In Denmark, *Vipera berus* (Viperidae) showed an ontogenetic shift in diet (Kjaergaard, 1981). Young vipers preyed primarily on ectotherms (lizards), and adults preyed on endotherms (mammals). These results were similar to those of Saint Girons (1980), who studied the feeding patterns of 10 taxa of vipers. Species that grew to a large size as adults exclusively ate lizards as juveniles (up to about 40 cm) and then switched to small mammals as adults. Two vipers that matured at a relatively small body length preyed on both lizards and mammals as adults. The fer-de-lance (*Bothrops atrox*) was reported by Sexton (1956–1957) to show an ontogenetic shift in prey; frogs and lizards were ingested by young snakes, whereas birds and mammals were taken by adults. The rather ubiquitous pattern of juvenile snakes feeding on species of prey different from that consumed by adults was also found in *Acanthophis antarcticus,* the Australian death adder (Shine, 1980a). Young of this species preyed on lizards, while adults were more likely to ingest small mammals. Fitch (1982) also found that first-year copperheads (*Agkistrodon contortrix*) preyed on a different array of species than adults did.

Young *Regina alleni* (Colubridae) feed primarily on odonate naiads (Libellulidae) and (when available) shrimp (Palaemonidae) or crayfish (Astacidae). As the snakes mature, there is a reorganization of their feeding behavior (Franz, 1977) to accommodate the crayfish preyed on by adults. The diet of young *R. alleni* provides a greater energetic intake (per gram body mass) than that of the crayfish-eating adults (Godley, 1980). Findings such as these are invaluable to proper understanding of snake biology. Ecologists are beginning to recognize that ontogenetic shifts in diet can cause an animal to move from one trophic unit (Livingston, 1980) as a juvenile to a different trophic unit as an adult. For example, Godley (1980) found that adult *R. alleni* consumed about 10% of the local crayfish population. However, juveniles removed over 90% of the available odonate population during the same time interval. Conclusions regarding trophodynamics and energetic factors that control the population dynamics of *R. alleni* would have been erroneous if based exclusively on the adult segment of the population.

Snakes can and do ingest spectacularly large prey. The larger the snake, the larger the individual prey that can be manipulated and swallowed. However, the literature indicates that snakes rarely ingest prey of the size that would be limited by the snake's own morphology. There is obvious survival value in "knowing" when prey exceed the size limit that can be handled successfully, and there are anecdotal reports of snakes found dead with large prey lodged in their mouths

(Barton, 1949; Howard, 1949; H. R. Mushinsky, unpublished observations), indicating that snakes occasionally attempt to take prey that exceed their ingestive capacity. The probability of a snake attempting to ingest large prey is much greater in young (small) than in old (large) snakes. The prey available to a newborn snake represents a small fraction of what is available to mature conspecifics, yet the energetic demands on a young snake are great. The ubiquitous tendency of adult snakes to ingest an array of prey types and sizes completely different from those taken by smaller conspecifics is an area of snake foraging ecology begging for further research. As well, the morphological and physiological capacities of young snakes put severe restrictions on prey size, and the brief latency to exhaustion (Pough, 1977, 1978) further may constrain the size and type of prey that can be taken. A metabolism equation from Bennett and Dawson (1976) indicates that the per-gram metabolism of a small snake is higher than that of a large conspecific. Small snakes likely require more food per gram body mass than large snakes.

The vast majority of our understanding of the trophic relations of snakes is based on the diets of adults. As predators, the underlying supposition of many ecological studies on sympatric snake species has been that snakes are prime subjects for the wrath of competitive exclusion and have partitioned resources (especially food) to reduce interspecific competition (see Toft, 1985). Furthermore, the assumptions implicit in resource partitioning await verification. Are the prey of snakes sufficiently limiting so as to provide the evolutionary force needed to drive the documented partitioning of resources? Or are we documenting the results of historical stochastic events (see Vitt, this volume)?

Shine (1986) summarized data from 66 taxa to address the related topic of frequency of snake feeding. The percentage of snakes that had food in their stomachs ranged from 5 to 100% and can be summarized as follows: In 18 taxa, from 5 to 29% of the individual snakes had food in their stomachs, 30 taxa had from 30 to 69% of the individuals with food, and over 70% of the stomachs contained prey in the final 18 taxa. One can argue that the low number of taxa that had a high proportion of individuals with food in their stomachs is evidence that snakes are prey (food)-limited. However, the results of studies that have assessed prey availability do not indicate that prey limit these populations (see Kephart and Arnold, 1982; Mushinsky et al., 1982; Reynolds and Scott, 1982). Alternatively, the same data (from Shine, 1986) could be used to support the argument that foraging frequency is low because of the low energetic requirements (Bennett and Dawson, 1976) and low rates of energy flow (Pough, 1980, 1983; Gans and Pough, 1982) in snakes. Schoener (1977) reported that *Diadophis punctatus* ate 27 meals, totaling 3 times body mass per active season (214 days), and *Agkistrodon contortrix* ate 8 meals, totaling 1.25 times body mass during its active period. Fitch (1982) reported that *Agkistrodon contortrix* ate prey averaging 18.5% of their body mass and consumed about 8 meals per growing season, totaling no more than 200% of the body mass. Saint Girons (1979) reported that the average ration of 115% body mass per growing season increased to 140 to 150% during hot years for captive vipers. Young growing males ingested 190% of their body mass, and females ate 276% of their body mass as they recovered from being gravid. When reproductive, females consumed 55% of their mass during that season. If we compare foraging frequency of snakes to that of lizards, we find that lizards forage much more frequently than snakes. Johnson (1966), Whitford and Bryant (1979), and Best and Gennaro (1984) found that lizards foraged frequently. Because lizards and snakes are known to have similar resting metabolic rates, this suggests that lizards are more active than snakes (Schoener, 1977). Detailed field and laboratory studies are necessary to resolve these issues regarding snake energetic requirements, foraging frequency, and prey availability. Future studies should address these issues experimentally and should be designed to answer specific questions. Do young individuals of a species forage more frequently than adults? How does the morphology and physiology of a young snake limit its capacity to ingest prey? Are the energetic requirements of males and females different? Do prey (types and sizes) limit the abundance of snakes?

OPTIMAL FORAGING AND PREY SIZE

Tests of optimal foraging theories (Schoener, 1971; Pyke et al., 1977), as they may apply to snakes, must await further refinement of our knowledge of the morphological constraints of the snake feeding apparatus. An understanding of the relationship between prey size and snake size is beginning to emerge from the literature. This understanding is prerequisite to specific tests of theories regarding foraging time and frequency, handling time for prey, energetic costs of foraging, and energy gain from prey. Knowledge of the relationship between prey size and snake size is the first step in evaluating hypotheses about snake foraging that assume ecological factors such as competition and/or resource availability limit population density or community composition. Arnold (1983) argued that selection and morphological adaptations can be studied directly by characterizing the relationships between morphology, performance, and fitness and outlined both the procedures for studying these relationships and statistical methods for interpretation of the results.

Pough and Groves (1983) used seven morphological measurements from 15 species of non-vipers and 17 species of vipers to test specific hypotheses about body stoutness and skull characteristics. They found that the suite of morphological characteristics that facilitate prey swallowing were best expressed among the vipers, but there was some convergence by elapids and colubrids. Movement of the jaw in swallowing prey was linearly related to prey size, and very small or very large prey were not disproportionately difficult to ingest. Finally, vipers swallowed prey with fewer jaw movements than colubrids or boids and were capable of ingesting prey three times larger in relation to their body size. The ecological implications of this research are profound. For example, the largest prey taken by a viper was 2.6 times the relative size of the largest prey of a non-viper. Using a variety of reasonable assumptions, Pough and Groves calculated that the viper's meal (up to 36% of the snake's mass) could sustain a 2-kg snake for 285 days. Vipers are able to ingest these large prey without sacrificing their capacity to swallow small prey. Comparative ecological field studies that address foraging frequency, prey size, and related topics will provide us with an understanding of manifestations of the morphological adaptation of snakes.

Some recent field studies indicate prey size discrimination by snakes. Mushinsky et al. (1982) analyzed the relationship between prey mass and snake mass and concluded that large water snakes eat absolutely larger prey than small snakes do. Voris and Moffett (1981) used several morphometric prey characteristics and reached the same conclusion. Voris and Voris (1983) used an index of snake gape (ratio of length of quadrate bone to width of parietal bone) to evaluate gape and prey size in 14 species of sea snakes. They found pronounced differences in gape between snakes of similar girth (at the neck) that ingest different prey species. Additional work is needed before we can begin to address ecological trends in diverse groups of snakes.

TONGUE FLICKING AND SNAKE FORAGING ECOLOGY

Much of a snake's behavioral repertoire is exhibited in response to information gained from Jacobson's organ or the vomeronasal organ. A systematic quantitative study on serpents' chemoreceptive responses was initiated by Gordon M. Burghardt who showed that, in the absence of chemical cues, visual stimuli from live prey did not elicit attack by newborn snakes (Burghardt, 1966). He concluded that Jacobson's organ was the receptor most involved in initiating attack behavior by newborn garter snakes (Burghardt, 1968). This research and the studies spawned by it have created a paradigm regarding the relationship between a snake's tongue flick attack score, chemoreception in the vomeronasal organ, and foraging ecology. The central assumption is that a snake tongue-flicks and/or attacks extracts of its prey at a rate commensurate with the likelihood of pursuing that prey. There is much interest also in genetic ancestry and ontogenetic development of prey preference. Generally, the nature-nurture question is of secondary interest, and most of the research has focused on proximal questions aimed at ecological events. This research assumes an unambiguous link between tongue flicking and the motivation to forage (see Burghardt, 1980, for additional considerations).

Operating within this paradigm has allowed investigators to delve into the genetics, sensory physiology, ecology, and evolutionary aspects of foraging ecology. The literature is too vast to be reviewed completely in this chapter; however, a few recent studies will be used to illustrate the approach of researchers in the field. Chiszar and Radcliffe (1976) found that three species of rattlesnakes (*Crotalus*) exhibited no tongue flicking before striking live mice at regular feeding sessions, although after striking and releasing a mouse, the snakes flicked their tongues at high rates. Kubie and Halpern (1979) established the role of the vomeronasal organ in trailing prey, and Chiszar et al. (1976) found that general exploratory behavior was under the control of the same sensory systems that mediate food-related activity. Czaplicki and Porter (1974), Burghardt and Pruitt (1975), and Drummond (1979) investigated the role of vision in snake foraging behavior, and all concluded that vision plays some role in snake foraging.

Arnold (1981a,b) summarized the results of numerous field studies on the feeding ecology of *Thamnophis elegans* and used the data as a basis for laboratory assessment of geographic variation in feeding behavior. The slug-eating habit of *T. elegans* is an adaptation that evolved in the mollusc-rich environment of coastal California (Fitch, 1940a; Fox, 1952; Arnold, 1977, 1981a). Where available, slugs constituted more than 90% of the snake's diet, whereas outside the range of slugs, *T. elegans* ingested frogs and fish. Arnold analyzed the feeding responses of three parental populations and their F_1 progeny. Garter snakes that were sympatric with slugs showed the highest incidence of slug eating (68 to 85%), while in an allopatric population the incidence was 17%. Studies on the microevolution of feeding behaviors can provide valuable insight into evolutionary relations of predators and their prey. The phenotypic plasticity of food preferred by *T. sirtalis* was recently studied by Greenwell et al. (1984). An insular population of snakes was found frequently to ingest birds. They tested the prey preferences of neonates and adults of the insular population and a nearby mainland population and found no difference in responses to prey species.

Burghardt (1975) found individual variation in the tongue-flick responses of garter snakes to various prey. Arnold (1978) reported that the effects of early experience were dependent on the type of prey. However, Henderson et al. (1983) found a close correlation between the responses of newborn vine snakes (*Uromacer*) and the saurophagous diets of adults in the field. Naive king snakes (*Lampropeltis*) were able to distinguish between the odors of crotalid and colubrid snakes, and they attacked the crotalid extracts more often, implicating chemoreceptive responses in their feeding behavior (Weldon and Schell, 1984). Tongue-flick studies have provided (1) a fine-grained look at predator-prey relations (Mushinsky and Lotz, 1980) and (2) through systematic research in the laboratory, a detailed appreciation of the variation and genetics of foraging ecology (see Arnold, 1978, 1981a,b). Much of the research on chemoreception in snakes has focused on the two closely related genera *Nerodia* and *Thamnophis;* interpretation of laboratory tests of a snake's responses to extracts is facilitated by a thorough understanding of the snake's natural history.

FORAGING ECOLOGY OF VENOMOUS SNAKES

The evolution of teeth modifications and the associated venom delivery systems have been summarized by Marx and Rabb (1972), Gans (1978), Kardong (1980), Savitzky (1980), and Cundall (1983, and this volume). Kardong (1979) argued that these modifications facilitated prey manipulation and swallowing; elongation of the teeth permitted deeper penetration into tissue, hence increased purchase of the jaws on the prey. In viperids, the highly evolved fangs have little to do with prey handling and swallowing but are specialized for venom delivery.

Members of the genus *Agkistrodon* (Viperidae) illustrate the behavioral and morphological adaptations that increase their predatory prowess. Young *Agkistrodon* exhibit tail luring behavior. During this display they expose the brightly colored tip of their tail as potential prey to attract anurans (Allen, 1949; Wharton, 1960). Other vipers are known to exhibit similar behavior patterns as juveniles (Neill, 1960; Henderson, 1970). Greene and Campbell (1972) observed an arboreal green pit viper, *Bothrops bilineatus,* luring a lizard, and Heatwole and Davison (1976) noted that the Saharan sand viper, *Cerastes vipera,* exhibited this behavior as an adult in order to lure lizards.

Prey search, approach, strike, bite, release, and post-release behaviors were analyzed in *Agkistrodon piscivorus* by Kardong (1975), as was the kinesis of the jaw apparatus during prey swallowing (Kardong, 1977). Field observations of *A. piscivorus* indicated that they search for prey with their head either above (Barbour, 1950) or below the surface of the water (Bothner, 1974) and either eat the prey in the water on capture or take it to the shore before ingestion. The copperhead, *A. contortrix,* is the upland ecological counterpart of the lowland and riverine cottonmouth. Copperheads were reported to eat a wide variety of prey ranging from hawk moth larvae (Orth, 1939) to box turtles (Murphy, 1964). Fitch (1960, 1982) listed over 30 prey categories (mostly species) taken from over 600 copperheads. Using radiotelemetry, Fitch and Shirer (1971) tracked *A. contortrix* and reported that gravid females did not eat while carrying young.

North American crotalids (*Crotalus, Sistrurus*) primarily feed on endotherms, especially birds and small mammals (Table 10-1). However, juveniles of these genera may be ophiophagous. In Wisconsin, Keenlyne and Beer (1973) found 85% of the prey of *S. catenatus* to be *Microtus pennsylvanicus*. Likewise, Seigel (1986) found voles, *Microtus ochrogaster,* to be the most common prey of massasaugas in Missouri. However, both studies found newborn massasaugas to feed mainly on other snakes. Ophiophagy was considered aberrant behavior (Fox, 1975), i.e., a behavior released by an inappropriate stimulus. However, Polis and Myers (1985) surveyed oophagy and cannibalism in reptiles and listed 20 species of serpents as cannibalistic. The list will likely grow as the foraging ecology of more species is studied.

In contrast to the New World vipers, some members of the Old World genus *Vipera* feed heavily on ectotherms, especially lizards and amphibians (Vit, 1977), although some rodents are taken (Table 10-1). Saint Girons and Naulleau (1981) reported that the reproductive effort of adult vipers reflected the food habits of very young snakes; species that fed on invertebrates and lizards as juveniles had many small young, while species that ate mammals had fewer, larger offspring. Observations such as these can provide the necessary framework for testing specific hypotheses regarding evolutionary trends in the relationship between life-history characteristics and foraging ecology (see Seigel and Ford, this volume).

Compared with colubrids and viperids, less is known about the foraging ecology of elapids. In a detailed analysis of the feeding behavior and diet of the eastern coral snake, *Micrurus fulvius,* Greene (1984) found that they used stereotyped head-poking movements and chemical cues to search for and follow prey trails. Both visual and chemical stimuli elicited attack by these snakes, which hold their prey until it is immobolized by venom. *Micrurus fulvius* was reported to feed almost exclusively on small terrestrial snakes, elongate lizards (especially of the family Scincidae), and amphisbaenians (Jackson and Franz, 1981). Greene reported that large coral snakes ingested larger prey than did juveniles but also continued to feed on relatively small prey. There was no apparent ontogenetic dietary shift in prey. Greene (1976) reported that king cobras (*Ophiophagus hannah*) and several species of *Micrurus* used ventral scale overlap patterns as directional sign stimuli for the head-first ingestion of prey snakes. Vitt and Hulse (1973) found that the Sonoran coral snake, *Micruroides euryxanthus,* ate *Leptotyphlops humilis* (family Leptotyphlopidae), a small, burrowing blind snake.

Shine (1980c) remarked on the convergence of the Australian whip snakes of the genus *Demansia* with colubrid whip snakes from other continents. He interpreted the slender body, long tail, large eyes, rapid movement, diurnality, terrestriality, and oviparity of whip snakes as adaptations that facilitate the chase and capture of fast-moving diurnal prey, especially lizards. The diets of each of the four members of *Demansia* consisted primarily of lizards of the genera *Lampropholis, Carlia,* and *Leiolopisma.* However, *D. atra* was also reported to eat frogs as well. Zinner (1971) reported that the nocturnal African desert elapid *Walterinnesia aegyptia* foraged in a manner similar to that described by Shine for *Demansia.* Zinner wrote that the shining black coloration of *Walterinnesia* contrasted sharply with the light-colored soil of the desert floor. This poor-sighted snake foraged at night in cool temperatures (10°C) on sleeping, diurnally active lizards.

FORAGING IN WATER

Members of the family Acrochordidae are entirely aquatic. The file snake, *Acrochordus granulatus,* fed primarily on fish (McDowell, 1979), and Voris and Glodek (1980) thought it was likely that they feed by exploring the sea bottom. This foraging habitat differs from that reported by Cogger (1975), who observed that they foraged in the intertidal zone on crabs and fish. Working under the hypothesis that a low metabolic rate is an adaptation to a low energy input, Shine (1986) studied the rates of foraging, growth, and reproduction of *Acrochordus arafurae* in tropical Australia. This species feeds on fish exclusively, including carrion. Live prey are subdued by constriction. Shine reported that 5% of the freshly captured snakes contained food, a figure lower than that for most other snakes. He suggested that either foraging frequency could be very low or digestive efficiency could be high.

The ecology of sea snakes (including foraging ecology) was summarized by Dunson (1975). Voris and Voris (1983) published additional data on sea snake diets and focused on the interrelationships of morphology, behavior, and ecology in 39 snake species and their prey. Eels and gobies are consumed by the greatest number of snake species. Most sea snakes take their prey head-first, and most prey species are relatively sedentary, dwelling on the sea bottom or within burrows and reef crevices. Several modes of feeding were used by sea snakes: Feeding occurred both in nooks and crannies at reef bottoms and in drift lines. The prey of eight marine snake species (including *Acrochordus granulatus;* see above) was analyzed and indicated very little dietary overlap. As concluding remarks, they noted, "We have yet to understand at even a single locality, the factors that determine sea snake community composition and the relative importance of feeding roles" (see Vitt, this volume).

Heatwole et al. (1978) observed the underwater feeding behavior of the sea snakes *Aipysurus laevis, A duboisii,* and *Astrotia stokesii* to be virtually identical, although they differed in their primary place of foraging. These authors indicated that sea snakes could subdue large prey, even rivaling land snakes in terms of prey size taken. Prey swallowing is not restricted to the surface. Fish are manipulated before ingestion and, if of suitable size, prey are ingested head-first.

Ecological studies on North American water snakes (family Colubridae) have focused on diet and partitioning of resources among sympatric species. Early ecological studies on water snakes (King, 1939; Uhler et al., 1939; Lagler and Salyer, 1947; Raney and Roecker, 1947) revealed that fish were the primary prey of water snakes and amphibians were secondary. The abundant and diverse assemblages of water snakes in the southeastern states have been well-studied. Mushinsky and co-workers (1977, 1982) and Kofron (1978) have detailed the diets of sympatric species of *Nerodia* and the closely related crayfish-eating snakes of the genus *Regina* (previously discussed). Partitioning of food resources occurred among *Nerodia,* with *N. erythrogaster* feeding primarily on anurans, *N. cyclopion* and *N. rhombifera* being piscivorous, and the smallest species (*N. fasciata*) preying on frogs and fish. The largest individuals of the two fish-eating species (*N. rhombifera* and *N. cyclopion*) ate catfish and centrarchids, respectively. The anuran-eating *N. erythrogaster* underwent distinct changes in prey preference as they matured. The strong preference of young snakes for fish was replaced by an equally strong preference for frogs (Mushinsky and Lotz, 1980). The diets of some water snake species seem to be quite predictable. For example, Sisk and McCoy (1964) reported that *N. rhombifera* in Oklahoma ate ictalurid catfish; Bowers (1966) found the same prey in Texas populations of this species. The frog-eating tendencies of *N. erythrogaster* also appear widespread (Diener, 1957; Brown, 1979). The literature suggests that in the Coastal Plain and Florida, where *N. rhombifera* is replaced by *N. taxispilota,* the brown water snake also feeds on relatively abundant ictalurid catfish (Camp et al., 1980).

One species of water snake has attracted attention because of its ecological and phenotypic plasticity. Most studies on inland populations have found *Nerodia fasciata* to prey on a combination of amphibians and fish (Clark, 1949; Mushinsky and Hebrard, 1977; Kofron, 1978; Brown, 1979). Several dimunitive subspecies have invaded the saltwater marshes and mangrove swamps along the Gulf of Mexico and coastal Florida. These docile, colorful snakes appear to be exclusively piscivorous (Hebrard and Lee, 1981).

Abbott (1884) commented on the haphazard foraging technique of *Nerodia sipedon,* and Cope (1869) described a water snake striking below the surface as minnows (*Notropis*) passed within the snake's striking range, although the strikes often fell short. Evans (1942) expanded the description to include the term "fishing," which he defined as swimming with the head submerged and the mouth kept open wide while sweeping through the water from one side to another in a continuous series of figure eights. These snakes use their bodies to entrap small fish in very shallow water and use side-to-side sweeping motions of the head to find prey (Mushinsky and Hebrard, 1977). Prey are not necessarily brought to shore or out of the water for swallowing; Brown (1958) reported that a northern water snake swallowed a large frog underwater. The adaptability of snake foraging behavior to prevailing conditions was illustrated by Gillingham and Rush (1974), who observed snakes sitting near moving water with their mouths open, eating *Cyprinus carpio* that were swept in by the current.

The fish-eating snake, *Lycodonomorphus bicolor,* from Lake Tanganyika, Africa, was studied by Madsen and Osterkamp (1982), who found a monthly peak in feeding activity that corresponded to the period of the new moon. As they point out, no other study has reported a distinct effect of moonlight on the feeding ecology of a nocturnal snake. The exclusive prey of *L. bicolor* are fish of the family Cichlidae. Madsen and Osterkamp speculated that the moonlight-dependent feeding cycle of *L. bicolor* might be indicative of the effect of moonlight on the perceived distance of the cichlids, thus reducing the hunting efficiency of the snakes.

FOOD AS A PARTITIONED RESOURCE

Toft (1985) reviewed over 250 published papers dealing with resource partitioning among sympatric groups of reptiles or amphibians. The central hypothesis was that closely related (or at least ecologically similar) species can avoid competitive exclusion by partitioning available resources, hence reducing the assumed competitive interactions. The results of her literature search indicated that snakes were a notable exception to the general finding that habitat was the resource most likely to be partitioned. The most important niche dimension partitioned by snakes was food, specifically prey type (see Henderson, 1974, for similar results). The underlying assumption of the competitive exclusion principle has always been that resources limit the co-existence of the species in question. However, to date, no one has demonstrated that food availability limits the population growth of snakes [see Platt (1984) for an additional discussion of food availability and snake growth]. There is no doubt that some snake communities partition the available food resources. However, at this time, the evolutionary forces that guide the partitioning are not known. Previously, I have dealt with food partitioning in water snakes, sea snakes, and venomous snakes, and Vitt (this volume) discusses the relationships between prey species richness and snake community composition (especially in tropical habitats). Below are some selected examples of food partitioning studies.

Sympatric *Thamnophis* in North America were among the first congeners to be studied synecologically. Carpenter (1952) concluded that differences in the selection of size and type of prey decreased food competition between *T. sirtalis, T. sauritus,* and *T. butleri.* He found that garter snakes did not feed extensively when they first emerged from hibernation. Rather, feeding peaked in early summer, and snakes continued to feed until autumn. The data showed little food preference. Using museum specimens and field observations on four *Thamnophis* species in Texas, Fouquette (1954) determined that there was some overlap in the diets of selected species pairs. Food habits reflected differences in the habitats occupied by each species.

Gregory (1978) studied the ecology of *T. sirtalis, T. ordinoides,* and *T. elegans* on Vancouver Island, Canada. Overall, amphibians and slugs were the major prey of *T. sirtalis,* earthworms and slugs were taken by *T. ordinoides,* and *T. elegans* ingested slugs, fish, and mammals. These three species occurred in varying local abundance at the eight study sites selected by Gregory (1984). Generally, the diets showed less overlap at sites that had nearly equal representation of the three species. His data suggested that part of the pattern of diet variation was due to subtle diet shifts, and Gregory expressed reservations about concluding that these results were shaped by competitive interactions. The work of Lagler and Salyer (1945, 1947), White and Kolb (1974), Hart (1979), Catling and Freedman (1980a,b), Kephart (1982), and Kephart and Arnold (1982), as well as the studies discussed previously, suggest an opportunistic foraging strategy for most species of *Thamnophis.* Kephart (1982) used the terminology of Fox and Morrow (1981) to describe members of the genus *Thamnophis* as examples of species that exhibit local specialization. Without a rigorous experimental approach that produces repeatable results, it does not seem possible to determine the cause of present-day species assemblages, species diversity, or patterns of resource use. Connell (1980) has cautioned ecologists about the problems associated with the ghost of competition past.

Three sympatric colubrid snakes from the Great Basin cold desert shrub habitat were studied extensively by Brown and Parker (1982). *Coluber constrictor* was insectivorous and was found to have the narrowest food niche. *Pituophis melanoleucus* ate primarily lizards (*Uta stansburiana*), and the rodent-eating *Masticophis taeniatus* had the broadest diet, which included members of the other two snake species. The authors were cautious about invoking competition as the cause for the apparent partitioning of the food resource and stated that the fluctuating environment (rainfall) likely had a strong influence on the population structure of *Coluber* and *Pituophis* [see Weins (1977) for additional comments on the role of fluctuating environments and competitive interactions of sympatric species].

The use of a mammalian resource by sympatric snakes in Chihuahua, Mexico, was reported by Reynolds and Scott (1982). They examined snake capture sites for biotic and abiotic factors, including the plant species present, vegetation, structure, topographic features, and local rodent species. The vipers *Crotalus atrox, C. molossus,* and *C. scutulatus* and the colubrids *Elaphe subocularis* and *Pituophis melanoleucus* were the five species considered major rodent predators. Reynolds and Scott concluded that the use of food and habitat dimensions clearly was complementary in this snake community, and that more food and habitat types were available to the snakes than were used. Hence a snake species exhibited a choice of the habitat it occupied or the prey it ingested. This research may well serve as a model for other community-level studies; it is one of a very few that attempts to assess the role of habitat structure, prey availability, and prey use in relation to snake abundance. (Herpetologists often tend to ignore the fact that vegetation structure can influence foraging patterns of snakes.)

Studies on the foraging ecology of the diverse fauna of northeastern Brazil revealed complex relationships of sympatric snakes (Vitt and Vangilder, 1983). Among these sympatric snakes were species that preyed on mammals, birds, bird and reptile eggs, lizards, snakes, frogs, and toads. Only the genera *Clelia, Philodryas* (Colubridae), and *Epicrates* (Boidae) fed on prey from several categories. The remainder had diets restricted to one prey category, including 7 species that were anuran specialists. Surprisingly, none of the 19 species preyed on invertebrates. Vitt (1983) found varying degrees of feeding specializations for an anuran-eating guild of terrestrial tropical snakes (Colubridae) from Brazil. *Waglerophis merremii* was reported to attack *Bufo* with its head twisted to puncture the air sacs and so facilitate ingestion of the toad. Four sympatric members of the genus *Liophis* were found to eat different sets of anuran species. Vitt concluded that differences in body length, mass, and head size were associated with differences in foraging ecology (see Vitt, this volume).

Henderson and Hoevers (1977) found a positive correlation between the number of snakes collected in northern Belize and the amount of precipitation. They observed that, of the 22 species, 38% had food in their stomachs during the wet season and 22% had food during the dry season. Prey were mostly anurans that showed increased activity during rainfall. Prey use by three syntopic neotropical racers (Colubridae) was reported by Seib (1984). *Drymobius chloroticus* ate mostly *Eleutherodactylus* frogs, *D. margaritiferus* ingested a broad array of vertebrates, and *Mastigodryas melanolomus* ate mostly lizards.

Henderson et al. (1977) reported that the diurnal predator *Leptophis mexicanus* fed on nocturnally active frogs, *Hyla* and *Smilisca,* in Belize. *Leptophis* were reported to eat *Anolis* (Henderson, 1976) and the snake *Ninia sebae.* Sympatric arboreal snakes tended to be either ambush hunters or active foragers; snakes that were active at the same time as their prey were ambush hunters, while those that occupied a temporal niche different from that of their prey were active foragers. Henderson et al. (1979) analyzed the trophic relationships of congeneric and heterogeneric species occupying the tropical rain forests of Peru. They found four genera that had from four to seven species represented at a single locality. In *Bothrops* (Viperidae) and *Micrurus* (Elapidae), increasing numbers of species per genus resulted in fewer individuals per species. *Chironius* and *Atractus* (Colubridae) did not show this trend. Henderson et al. (1979) found most species to be stenophagous, feeding primarily on one prey class (fish, anurans). Snakes studies in the upper Amazon Basin indicated rain forest snakes also to be stenophagous, with 19 of 22 species eating only one class of prey (Duellman, 1978).

The colubrid snake genus *Uromacer* is endemic to Hispaniola and the surrounding islands. Three of these four diurnal species have slender bodies and long, attenuated snouts. Horn (1969) found that one of the apparently arboreal (slender) species preyed on terrestrial lizards. Henderson and Horn (1983) further investigated the diet of *U. frenatus* and found that especially those larger than 700 mm preyed on ground-dwelling lizards. The shift in diet was not an abrupt ontogenetic event, and arboreal lizards were not completely abandoned as a food source once a snake reached a certain size. Rather, terrestrial lizards were added gradually to the diet as arboreal lizards diminished in importance.

Beshkov and Gerasimov (1980) reported that small mammals were the primary prey of the genera *Elaphe, Coluber, Coronella, Malpolon,* and *Vipera* in the Maleshino Mountains of Bulgaria. Based on an examination of 621 individuals (12 species), *Natrix natrix* and *N. tessellata* were batrachophagous and *Coluber jugularis, C. najadum, Coronella austriaca, Malpolon monspessulanus, Telescopus fallax, Vipera ammodytes,* and *V. berus* were herpetophagous, according to Beshkov and Dushkov (1981). Two species, *Elaphe situla* and *E. quatuorlineata,* ate no amphibians or reptiles, and *Vipera ammodytes* contained lizards.

Among the Elapidae from Australia, Shine (1984) summarized what was known about the food habits (based on museum specimens) of two small fossorial genera consisting of five distinct species groups. He found a clear dichotomy in food habits; scincid and pygopodid lizards were the exclusive prey of *Neelaps* and the *Simoselaps bertholdi* species group, whereas the *Simoselaps semifasciatus* species group ingested only squamate eggs. Oophagy was common in *S. australis* and recorded in *S. fasciolatus.* Shine (1980d) reported that oophagous snakes had flat, bladelike posterior maxillary teeth for slitting eggshells. Another Australian burrowing snake, *Vermicella annulata* (Elapidae) ingested only *Ramphotyphlops* (Typhlopidae).

FUTURE RESEARCH

The area of snake foraging ecology is prime for creative detailed studies on snake trophodynamics. Studies such as those by Feaver (1977), Godley (1980), Parker and Brown (1980), Arnold (1981b), Reynolds and Scott (1982), and Brown and Parker (1984) provide the kinds of data and approaches necessary to address the role of snakes in biological systems. We can evaluate energy availability, assimilation through the food chain, and allocation within these carnivorous reptiles. As well, we gain insight into and understanding of the details of ontogeny and the dynamics of foraging ecology (Mushinsky et al., 1982). Few could argue that young snakes are under the same selective pressures as mature conspecifics, yet little is known about the constraints governing juvenile serpents. Evidence that mature snakes prey on a different array of species than young conspecifics is widespread among ophidians and especially evident in large species. This can be viewed as an adaptation of large snakes in order to forage for the most profitable prey, as a manifestation of constraints on young snakes that force them to forage on prey sizes and types that permit them to grow rapidly to a mature status, or both. Carefully designed tests are needed to clarify these issues.

How does predation affect snakes? As carnivorous predators, snakes are often placed in the category of species that are resource-limited and subject only to the rules of competition (Hairston et al., 1960). Food often has been considered the resource in limited supply, yet the set of morphological characters that limits the size of prey an individual can ingest has not been identified for any snake. Analysis of the allometric growth of structures associated with the feeding apparatus (Rossman, 1980) of specialized foragers would allow assessment of the evolutionary costs (because of dietary restrictions) of the associated modifications. If predation is a driving force in snake evolution, how does it affect an individual's foraging ecology? Do young snakes forage more efficiently than mature conspecifics? Do known physiological constraints on snake energy levels restrict the size of prey and/or foraging frequency? The field is ready for rigorous testing of hypotheses that will answer these and other questions regarding foraging ecology.

LITERATURE CITED

Abbott, C. C. 1884. A Naturalist Rambles About Home, Appleton, New York.

Agrawal, H. P. 1979. Food and feeding habits of *Naja naja naja*, *J. Anim. Morphol. Physiol.* 26:272–275.

Allen, E. R. 1939. Habits of *Rhadinaea flavilata*, *Copeia* 1939:175.

Allen, E. R. 1949. Observations of the feeding habits of the juvenile cantil, *Copeia* 1949:225–226.

Arnold, S. J. 1977. Polymorphism and geographic variation in the feeding behavior of the garter snake *Thamnophis elegans, Science* 197:676–678.

Arnold, S. J. 1978. Some effects of early experience on feeding responses in the common garter snake, *Thamnophis sirtalis. Anim. Behav.* 26:455–462.

Arnold, S. J. 1981a. The microevolution of feeding behavior, in: Foraging Behavior: Ecological, Ethological and Psychological Approaches (A. Kamil and T. Sargent, eds.) pp. 409–453, Garland Press, New York.

Arnold, S. J. 1981b. Behavioral variation in natural populations. II. The inheritance of a feeding response in crosses between geographic races of the garter snake *Thamnophis elegans, Evolution* 35:510–515.

Arnold, S. J. 1983. Morphology, performance and fitness, *Am. Zool.* 23:347–361.

Babis, W. A. 1949. Notes on the food of the indigo snake, *Copeia* 1949:147.

Barbour, R. W. 1950. The reptiles of Big Black Mountain, Harlan County, Kentucky, *Copeia* 1950:100–107.

Barton, A. J. 1949. Ophiophagy by a juvenile copperhead, *Copeia* 1949:232.

Beavers, R. A. 1976. Food habits of the western diamondback rattlesnake, *Crotalus atrox,* in Texas (Viperidae), *Southwest. Nat.* 20:503–515.

Bennett, A. F. and Dawson, W. R. 1976. Metabolism, in: Biology of the Reptilia, vol 5 (C. Gans and W. R. Dawson, eds.) pp. 127–211, Academic Press, New York.

Beshkov, V. A. and Dushkov, D. T. 1981. Materials on the batrachophagy and herpetophagy of snakes in Bulgaria, *Ekologiya* 9:43–50.

Beshkov, V. A. and S. Gerasimov. 1980. Small mammals as food components of snakes in the Maleshevo Mountain, southwestern Bulgaria, *Ekologiya* 6:51–61.

Best, T. L. and Gennaro, A. L. 1984. Feeding ecology of the lizard, *Uta stansburiana,* in southeastern New Mexico, *J. Herpetol.* 18:291–301.

Best, T. L. and James, H. C. 1984. Rattlesnakes (genus *Crotalus*) of the Pedro Armendariz lava field, New Mexico, *Copeia* 1984:213–215.

Billing, H. and Ziswiler, V. 1981. Adaptations in the alimentary tract in some species of colubrid snakes with exclusive food preferences, *Rev. Suisse Zool.* 88:835–846.

Bothner, R. C. 1974. Some observations on the feeding habits of the cottonmouth in southeastern Georgia, *J. Herpetol.* 8:257–258.

Bowers, J. H. 1966. Food habits of the diamond-backed water snake, *Natrix rhombifera rhombifera,* in Bowie and Red River counties, Texas, *Herpetologica* 22:225–229.

Branson, B. A. and Baker, E. C. 1974. An ecological study of the queen snake, *Regina septemvittata* (Say) in Kentucky, *Tulane Stud. Zool. Bot.* 18:153–171.

Brown, E. E. 1958. Feeding habits of the northern water snake, *Natrix sipedon sipedon* Linnaeus, *Zoologica* 43:55–71.

Brown, E. E. 1979. Some snake food records from the Carolinas, *Brimleyana* 1:113–124.

Brown, W. S. and Parker, W. S. 1982. Niche dimensions and resource partitioning in a great basin desert snake community, in: Herpetological communities, (N. J. Scott, Jr., ed.) *U.S. Fish Wildl. Serv. Wildl. Res. Rep.* 13:59–81.

Brown, W. S. and Parker, W. S. 1984. Growth, reproduction and demography of the racer, *Coluber constrictor mormon,* in northern Utah, in: Vertebrate Ecology and Systematics: A Tribute to Henry S. Fitch (R. A. Seigel, L. E. Hunt, J. L. Knight, L. Malaret, and N. L. Zuschlag, eds.) *Univ. Kans. Mus. Nat. Hist. Spec. Publ.* 10:13–40.

Burghardt, G. M. 1966. Stimulus control of the prey attack response in naive garter snakes, *Psychon. Sci.* 4:37–38.

Burghardt, G. M. 1968. Factors influencing the chemical release of prey-attack on newborn snakes, *J. Comp. Pyschol.* 66:289–295.

Burghardt, G. M. 1975. Chemical prey preference polymorphism in newborn garter snakes, *Thamnophis sirtalis, Behaviour* 52:202–225.

Burghardt, G. M. 1980. Behavioral and stimulus correlates of vomeronasal functioning in reptiles: Feeding, grouping, sex and tongue use, in: Chemical Signals, Vertebrate and Aquatic Invertebrates (N. Muller-Schwartz and R. M. Silverstein, eds.) pp. 275–301, Plenum Press, New York.

Burghardt, G. M. and Pruitt, C. H. 1975. Role of the tongue and senses in feeding of naive and experienced garter snakes, *Physiol. Behav.* 14: 185–194.

Burkett, R. D. 1966. Natural history of cottonmouth moccasin, *Agkistrodon piscivorus* (Reptilia), *Univ. Kans. Publ. Mus. Nat. Hist.* 17:435–491.

Camp, C. D., Sprewell, W. D., and Powders, V. N. 1980. Feeding habits of *Nerodia taxispilota* with comparative notes on the foods of sympatric congeners in Georgia, *J. Herpetol.* 14:301–304.

Carpenter, C. C. 1952. Comparative ecology of the common garter snake (*Thamnophis s. sirtalis*), the ribbon snake (*Thamnophis s. sauritus*), and Butler's garter snake (*Thamnophis butleri*) in mixed populations, *Ecol. Monogr.* 22:235–258.

Carr, A. F. 1934. Notes on the habits of the short-tailed snake, *Stilosoma extenuatum* Brown, *Copeia* 1934:138–139.

Catling, P. M. and Freedman, B. 1980a. Variation in distribution and abundance of four sympatric species of snakes at Amherstburg, Ontario, Canada, *Can. Field Nat.* 94:19–27.

Catling, P. M. and Freedman, B. 1980b. Food and feeding behavior of sympatric snakes at Amherstburg, Ontario, Canada, *Can. Field Nat.* 94:28–33.

Cattaneo, A. 1979. Observations on the nutrition of *Elaphe quatuorlineata* at Castelporziano Rome, Italy (Reptilia, Squamata, Colubridae), *Atti Soc. Ital. Sci. Nat. Mus. Civ. Stor. Nat. Milano.* 120:203–218.

Chiszar, D. and Radcliffe, C. W. 1976. Rate of tongue flicking by rattlesnakes during successive stages of feeding on rodent prey, *Bull. Psychon. Soc.* 7:485–486.

Chiszar, D., Carter, T., Knight, L., Monsen, S., and Taylor, S. 1976. Investigatory behavior in the plains garter snake (*Thamnophis radix*) and several additional species, *Anim. Learn Behav.* 4:273–278.

Clark, D. R. 1970. Ecological study of the worm snake *Carphophis vermis* (Kennicott), *Univ. Kans. Publ. Mus. Nat. Hist.* 19:85–194.

Clark, R. F. 1949. Snakes of the hill parishes of Louisiana, *J. Tenn. Acad. Sci.* 24:244–261.

Cogger, H. G. 1975. Reptiles and Amphibians of Australia, A. H. and A. W. Reed, London.

Connell, J. H. 1980. Diversity and the coevolution of competitors, or the ghost of competition past, *Oikos* 35:131–138.

Cope, E. D. 1869. Synopsis of the Cyprinidae of Pennsylvania, *Trans. Am. Philos. Soc.* 13:351–410.

Cowles, R. B. 1941. Evidence of venom in *Hypsiglena ochrorhynchus, Copeia* 1941:4–6.

Cundall, D. 1983. Activity of head muscles during feeding by snakes: A comparative study, *Am. Zool.* 23:383–396.

Czaplicki, J. A. and Porter, R. H. 1974. Visual cues mediating the selection of goldfish (*Carassius auratus*) by two species of *Natrix, J. Herpetol.* 8:129–134.

Dickson, J. D., III. 1948. Observations on the feeding habits of the scarlet snake, *Copeia* 1948:216–217.

Diener, R. A. 1957. An ecological study of the plain-bellied water snake, *Herpetologica* 13:203–211.

Dilley, W. E. 1954. Indigo snake versus flat-tailed water snake, *Everglades Nat. Hist.* 2:48.

Drummond, H. M. 1979. Stimulus control of amphibious predation in the northern water snake (*Nerodia s. sipedon*), *Z. Tierpsychol.* 50:18–44.

Duellman, W. E. 1958. A monographic study of the colubrid snake genus *Leptodeira, Bull. Am. Mus. Nat. Hist.* 114:1–52.

Duellman, W. E. 1978. The biology of an equatorial herpetofauna in Amazonian Ecuador, *Univ. Kans. Mus. Nat. Hist. Misc. Publ.* 65:1–352.

Duellman, W. E. 1984. Henry S. Fitch in perspective, in: Vertebrate Ecology and Systematics: A Tribute to Henry S. Fitch (R. A. Seigel, L. E. Hunt, J. L. Knight, L. Malaret, and N. L. Zuschlag, eds.) *Univ. Kans. Mus. Nat. Hist. Spec. Publ.* 10:3–9.

Dunson, W. A. 1975. The Biology of Sea Snakes, University Park Press, Baltimore, Maryland.

Evans, P. D. 1942. A method of fishing used by water snakes, *Chic. Nat.* 5:53–55.

Feaver, P. E. 1977. The demography of a Michigan population of *Natrix sipedon* with discussions of ophidian growth and reproduction, Ph.D. Dissertation, University of Michigan, Ann Arbor.

Fitch, H. S. 1940a. A biogeographical study of the ordinoides artenkreis of garter snakes (genus *Thamnophis*), *Univ. Calif. Publ. Zool.* 44:1–150.

Fitch, H. S. 1940b. Outline for ecological life history studies of reptiles, *Ecology* 30:520–532.

Fitch, H. S. 1949. Study of snake populations in central California, *Am. Midl. Nat.* 41:513–579.

Fitch, H. S. 1960. Autecology of the copperhead, *Univ. Kans. Publ. Mus. Nat. Hist.* 13:85–288.

Fitch, H. S. 1963. Natural history of the black rat snake (*Elaphe o. obsoleta*) in Kansas, *Copeia* 1963:649–658.

Fitch, H. S. 1965. An ecological study of the garter snake, *Thamnophis sirtalis, Univ. Kans. Publ. Mus. Nat. Hist.* 15:493–564.

Fitch, H. S. 1975. A demographic study of the ringneck snake (*Diadophis punctatus*) in Kansas, *Univ. Kans. Mus. Nat. Hist. Misc. Publ.* 62: 1–53.

Fitch, H. S. 1978. A field study of the prairie king snake, *Lampropeltis calligaster, Trans. Kans. Acad. Sci.* 81:353–364.

Fitch, H. S. 1982. Resources of a snake community in prairie-woodland habitat of northeastern Kansas, in: Herpetological Communities (N. J. Scott, Jr., ed.) *U.S. Fish Wildl. Serv. Wild. Res. Rep.* 13:83–97.

Fitch, H. S. and Fleet, R. R. 1970. Natural history of the milk snake (*Lampropeltis triangulum*) in northeastern Kansas, *Herpetologica* 26:387–396.

Fitch, H. S. and Shirer, H. W. 1971. A radio-telemetric study of spatial relationships in some common snakes, *Copeia* 1971:118–128.

Fitch, H. S. and Twining, H. 1946. Feeding habits of the Pacific rattlesnake, *Copeia* 1946:64–71.

Fouquette, M. J., Jr. 1954. Food competition among four sympatric species of the genus *Thamnophis, Tex. J. Sci.* 2:172–188.

Fox, L. R., 1975. Cannibalism in natural populations, *Annu. Rev. Ecol. Syst.* 6:87–106.

Fox, L. R. and Morrow, P. A. 1981. Specialization: Species property or local phenomenon? *Science* 211:887–893.

Fox, W. 1952. Notes on feeding habits of Pacific Coast garter snakes, *Herpetologica* 8:4–8.

Franz, R. 1977. Observations on the food, feeding behavior, and parasites of the striped swamp snake, *Regina alleni, Herpetologica* 33:91–94.

Franz, R. and Gicca, D. F. 1982. Observations on the Haitian snake, *Antillophis parvifrons alleni, J. Herpetol.* 16:419–421.

Fukada, H. 1959. Biological studies on the snakes. V. Food habits in the fields, *Bull. Kyoto Gakugei Univ. Ser. B Math. Nat. Sci.* 14:25–41.

Funderburg, J. B. 1968. Eastern diamondback rattlesnake feeding on carrion, *J. Herpetol.* 2:161–162.

Gannon, V. P. J. and Secoy, D. M. 1984. Growth and reproductive rates of a northern population of the prairie rattlesnake, *Crotalus v. viridis, J. Herpetol.* 18:13–19.

Gans, C. 1952. The functional morphology of the egg-eating adaptations in the snake genus *Dasypeltis, Zoologica* 37:209–244.

Gans, C. 1961. The feeding mechanism of snakes and its possible evolution, *Am. Zool.* 1:217–227.

Gans, C. 1974. Biomechanics: An Approach to Vertebrate Biology, J. P. Lippincott, Philadelphia.

Gans, C., 1975. Tetrapod limblessness: Evolution and functional corollaries, *Am. Zool.* 15:455–467.

Gans, C. 1978. Reptilian venoms: Some evolutionary considerations, in: Biology of the Reptilia, Vol. 8 (C. Gans and K. A. Gans, eds.) pp. 1–42, Academic Press, New York.

Gans, C. and Pough, F. H. 1982. Physiological ecology: Its debt to reptilian studies, its value to students of reptiles, in: Biology of the Reptilia, vol. 12 (C. Gans and F. H. Pough eds.) pp. 1–16, Academic Press, New York.

Gates, G. O. 1960. A study of the herpetofauna in the vicinity of Wickenburg, Maricopa County, Arizona, *Trans. Kans. Acad. Sci.* 60:403–418.

Gehlbach, F. R. 1974. Evolutionary relations of southwestern ringneck snakes (*Diadophis punctatus*), *Herpetologica* 30:140–148.

Gillingham, J. C. and Rush, T. 1974. Notes on the fishing behavior of water snakes, *J. Herpetol.* 8:384–385.

Glass, J. K. 1972. Feeding behavior of the western shovel-nosed snake *Chionactis occipitalis klauberi* with special reference to scorpions, *Southwest. Nat.* 16:445–447.

Gloyd, H. K. 1933. An unusual feeding record for the prairie rattlesnake, *Copeia* 1933:98.

Godley, J. S. 1980. Foraging ecology of the striped swamp snake, *Regina alleni,* in southern Florida, *Ecol. Monogr.* 50:411–436.

Godley, J. S., McDiarmid, R. W., and Rojas, N. N. 1984. Estimating prey size and number in crayfish-eating snakes, genus *Regina, Herpetologica* 40:82–88.

Greene, H. W. 1976. Scale overlap as a directional sign stimulus for prey ingestion by ophiophagus snakes, *Z. Tierpsychol.* 41:113–120.

Greene, H. W. 1982. Dietary and phenotypic diversity in lizards: Why are some organisms specialized? in: Environmental Adaptation and Evolution: A Theoretical and Empirical Approach (D. Mossakowski and G. Roth, eds.) G. Fisher-Verlag, Stuttgart.

Greene, H. W. 1983a. Field studies of hunting behavior by bushmasters, *Am. Zool.* 23:897.

Greene, H. W. 1983b. Dietary correlates of the origin and radiation of snakes, *Am. Zool.* 23:431–441.

Greene, H. W. 1984. Feeding behavior and diet of the eastern coral snake, *Micrurus fulvius,* in: Vertebrate Ecology and Systematics: A Tribute to Henry S. Fitch (R. A. Seigel, L. E. Hunt, J. L. Knight, L. Malaret, and N. L. Zuschlag, eds.) *Univ. Kans. Mus. Nat. Hist. Spec. Publ.* 10:147–162.

Greene, H. W. and Burghardt, G. M. 1978. Behavior and phylogeny: Constriction in ancient and modern snakes, *Science* 200:74–77.

Greene, H. W. and Campbell, J. A. 1972. Notes on the use of caudal lures by arboreal green pit vipers, *Herpetologica* 28:32–34.

Greenwell, M.G., Hall, M., and Sexton, O. J. 1984. Phenotypic basis for a feeding change in an insular population of garter snakes *Thamnophis sirtalis*, *Dev. Psychobiol.* 17:457–464.

Gregory, P.T. 1978. Feeding habits and diet overlap of three species of garter snakes (*Thamnophis*) on Vancouver Island, *Can. J. Zool.* 56:1967–1974.

Gregory, P. T. 1984. Habitat, diet, and composition of assemblages of garter snakes (*Thamnophis*) at eight sites on Vancouver Island, *Can. J. Zool.* 62:2013–2022.

Gregory, P. T. and Stewart, K. W. 1975. Long distance dispersal and feeding strategy of the red-sided garter snake *Thamnophis sirtalis parietalis* in the Interlake of Manitoba, Canada, *Can. J. Zool.* 53:238–245.

Hairston, N. G., Smith, F. E., and Slobodkin, L. B. 1960. Community structure, population control and competition, *Am. Nat.* 94:421–425.

Hall, R. J. 1969 Ecological observations on Graham's water snake, *Regina grahami* (Baird and Girard), *Am. Midl. Nat.* 18:156–163.

Hardy, J. D. 1957. Bat predation by the Cuban tree boa, *Epicrates angulifer* Bibron, *Copeia* 1957:151–152.

Hart, D. R. 1979. Niche relationships of *Thamnophis radix haydeni* and *Thamnophis sirtalis parietalis* in the Interlake district of Manitoba, Canada, *Tulane Stud. Zool. Bot.* 21:125–140.

Heatwole, H. and Davison, E. 1976. A review of caudal luring in snakes with notes on its occurrence in the Saharan sand viper, *Cerastes vipera*, *Herpetologica* 32:332–336.

Heatwole, H., Minton, S. A., Jr., Taylor, R., and Taylor, V. 1978. Underwater observations on sea snake behavior, *Rec. Aust. Mus.* 31:737–762.

Hebrard, J. J. and Lee, R. C. 1981. A large collection of brackish water snakes from the central Atlantic coast of Florida, *Copeia* 1981:886–889.

Henderson, R. W. 1970. Caudal luring in a juvenile Russell's viper, *Herpetologica* 26:276–277.

Henderson, R. W. 1974. Resource partitioning among the snakes of the University of Kansas Natural History Reservation, a preliminary analysis, *Milw. Publ. Mus. Contrib. Biol. Geol.* 1:1–11.

Henderson, R. W. 1976. A new insular subspecies of the colubrid snake *Leptophis mexicanus* from Belize, *J. Herpetol.* 10:329–331.

Henderson, R. W. and Hoevers, L. G. 1977. The seasonal incidence of snakes at a locality in northern Belize, *Copeia* 1977:349–355.

Henderson, R. W. and Horn, H. S. 1983. The diet of the snake *Uromacer frenatus dorsalis* on Ile de la Gonave, Haiti, *J. Herpetol.* 17:409–412.

Henderson, R. W., Nickerson, M. A., and Hoevers, L. G. 1977. Observations and comments on the feeding behavior of *Leptophis* (Reptilia, Serpentes, Colubridae), *J. Herpetol.* 11:231–232.

Henderson, R. W., Dixon, J. R. and Soini P. 1979. Resource partitioning in Amazonian Peru snake communities, *Milw. Public Mus. Contrib. Biol. Geol.* 22:1–12.

Henderson, R. W., Binder, M. H., and Burghardt, G. M. 1983. Responses of neonate Hispaniolan vine snakes (*Uramacer frenatus*) to prey extracts, *Herpetologica* 39:75–77.

Horn, H. S. 1969. Polymorphism and evolution of the Hispaniolan snake genus *Uromacer* (Colubridae), *Breviora* 324:1–23.

Howard, W. E. 1949. Gopher snake killed trying to swallow cottontail, *Copeia* 1949:289.

Howell, T. R. 1954. The kingsnake, *Lampropeltis getulus holbrooki* preying on the cardinal, *Copeia* 1954:224.

Jackson, D. R. and Franz R. 1981. Ecology of the eastern coral snake (*Micrurus fulvius*) in northern peninsular Florida, *Herpetologica* 37:213–228.

Jaksic, F. M., Greene, H. W., and Yanez, J. L. 1981. The guild structure of a community of predatory vertebrates in central Chile, *Oecologia (Berl.)* 49:21–28.

James, D. K., Petrinovich, L., and Patterson, T. L. 1983. Predation of white-crowned sparrow nestlings by the western terrestrial garter snake in San Francisco, California, *Copeia* 1983:511–513.

Johnson, D. R. 1966. Diet and estimated energy assimilation of three Colorado lizards, *Am. Midl. Nat.* 76:504–509.

Judd, W. W. 1954. Observation on the food of the little brownsnake, *Storeria dekayi* at London, Ontario, *Copeia* 1954:62–64.

Kardong, K. V. 1975. Prey capture in the cottonmouth snake (*Agkistrodon piscivorus*), *J. Herpetol.* 9:169–176.

Kardong, K. V. 1977. Kinesis of the jaw apparatus during swallowing in the cottonmouth snake, *Agkistrodon piscivous, Copeia* 1977:338–348.

Kardong, K. V. 1979. "Protovipers" and the evolution of snake fangs, *Evolution* 33:433–443.

Kardong, K. V. 1980. Evolutionary patterns in advanced snakes, *Am. Zool.* 20:269–282.

Keenlyne, K. D. and Beer, J. R. 1973. Food habits of *Sistrurus catenatus catenatus, J. Herpetol.* 7:382–384.

Kephart, D. G. 1982. Microgeographic variation in the diets of garter snakes, *Oecologia (Berl.)* 52:287–291.

Kephart, D. G. and Arnold, S. J. 1982. Garter snake diets in a fluctuating environment: A seven year study, *Ecology* 63:1232–1236.

King, W. 1939. A survey of the herpetology of the Great Smokey Mountains National Park, *Am. Midl. Nat.* 21:531–582.

Kjaergaard, J. 1981. A method for examination of stomach content in live snakes and some information on feeding habits in common viper (*Vipera berus*) in Denmark, *Nat. Jutl.* 19:45–48.

Klauber, L. M. 1972. Rattlesnakes: Their Habits, Life Histories, and Influence on Mankind, University of California Press, Berkeley.

Klimstra, W. D. 1959a. Foods of the racer, *Coluber constrictor,* in Southern Illinois, *Copeia* 1959:210–214.

Klimstra, W. D. 1959b. Food habits of the cottonmouth in southern Illinois, *Chic. Acad. Sci. Nat. Hist. Misc.* 168:1–8.

Knight, J. L. and Loraine, R. K. 1986. Notes on turtle egg predation by *Lampropeltis getulus getulus* (Reptilia: Colubridae) on the Savannah River Plant, South Carolina. *Brimleyana* 12:1–4.

Kofron, C. P. 1978. Foods and habits of aquatic snakes (Reptilia, Serpentes) in a Louisiana swamp, *J. Herpetol.* 12:543–554.

Kofron, C. P. 1982. A review of the Mexican snail-eating snakes, *Dipsas brevifacies* and *Dipsas gaigeae, J. Herpetol.* 16:270–286.

Kratzer, H. 1974. Observations on the feeding of the milos ring snake *Natrix natrix schweigeri, Salamandra* 10:49–54.

Kubie, J. L. and Halpern, M. 1979. Chemical senses involved in garter snake prey trailing, *J. Comp. Physiol. Psychol.* 93:648–667.

Lagler, K. F. and Salyer, J. C., II. 1945. Influence of availability on the feeding habits of the common garter snake, *Copeia* 1945:159–162.

Lagler, K. F. and Salyer, J. C., II. 1947. Food and habits of the common water snake, *Natrix s. sipedon,* in Michigan, *Pap. Mich. Acad. Sci. Arts Lett.* 31:169–180.

Lanka, V. 1975-76. Variability and biology of the tessellated snake, *Natrix tessellata, Acta Univ. Carol. Biol.* 5–6:167–208.

Lehmann, H. D. 1971. Notes on feeding and defense behavior of *Calabaria reinhardii* (Serpentes, Boidae), *Salamandra* 7:55–60.

Lillywhite, H. B. 1982. Cannibalistic carrion ingestion by the rattlesnake, *Crotalus viridis, J. Herpetol.* 16:95.

Linder, A. D. 1963. Ophiophagy by the rubber boa, *Herpetologica* 19:143.

Livingston, R. J. 1980. Ontogenetic trophic relationships and stress in a coastal seagrass system in Florida, in: Estuarine Perspectives (V. S. Kennedy, ed.) pp. 423–435, Academic Press, New York.

Lloyd, C. N. V. 1974. Feeding behavior in the green mamba *Dendroaspis angusticeps, J. Herpetol. Assoc. Afr.* 12:12–17.

McDowell, S. B. 1979. A catologue of the snakes of New Guinea and the Solomons, with special reference to those in the Bernice P. Bishop Museum. III. Boinae and Acrochordoidea (Reptilia, Serpentes), *J. Herpetol.* 13: 1–92.

Madsen, T. and Osterkamp, M. 1982. Notes on the biology of the fish-eating snake *Lycodonomorphus bicolor* in Lake Tanganyika, *J. Herpetol.* 16:185–188.

Mao, S. 1970. Food of the common venomous snakes of Taiwan, *Herpetologica* 26:45–48.

Marx, H. and Rabb, G. B. 1972. Phyletic analysis of fifty characters of advanced snakes, *Fieldiana Zool.* 63:1–321.

Mertens, R. 1952. On snail-eating snakes, *Copeia* 1952:279.

Metrolis, A. P. 1971. A feeding observation on the rainbow snake, *Farancia erytrogramma erytrogramma, Bull. Md. Herpetol. Soc.* 7:41.

Minton, S. A., Jr. and Bechtel, H. B. 1958. Another Indiana record of *Cemophora coccinea* and a note on egg-eating, *Copeia* 1958:47.

Minton, S. A. and Dunson, W. A. 1978. Observations on the Palawan mangrove snake. *Boiga dendrophila multicincta* (Reptilia, Serpentes, Colubridae), *J. Herpetol.* 12:107–108.

Murphy, T. D. 1964. Box turtle, *Terrapene carolina,* in stomach of copperhead, *Agkistrodon contortrix, Copeia* 1964:221.

Mushinsky, H. R. 1984. Observations of the feeding habits of the short-tailed snake, *Stilosoma extenuatum* in captivity, *Herpetol. Rev.* 15:67–68.

Mushinsky, H. R. and Hebrard, J. J. 1977. Food partitioning by five species of water snakes in Louisiana, *Herpetologica* 33:162–166.

Mushinsky, H. R. and Lotz, K. H. 1980. Chemoreceptive responses of two sympatric water snakes to extracts of commonly ingested prey species: Ontogenetic and ecological considerations, *J. Chem. Ecol.* 6:523–535.

Mushinsky, H. R., Hebrard, J. J., and Vodopich, D. S. 1982. Ontogeny of water snake foraging ecology, *Ecology* 63:1624–1629.

Neill, W. T. 1960. The caudal lure of various juvenile snakes, *Q. J. Fla. Acad. Sci.* 23:173–200.

Orth, J. C. 1939. Moth larvae in a copperhead's stomach, *Copeia* 1939:54–55

Palmer, W. M. and Tregembo, G. 1970. Notes on the natural history of the scarlet snake, *Cemophora coccinea copei* in North Carolina, *Herpetologica* 26:300–302.

Parker, S. A. and Stotz, D. 1977. An observation on the foraging behavior of the Arizona ridge-nosed rattlesnake, *Crotalus willardi willardi* (Serpentes: Crotalidae), *Bull. Md. Herpetol. Soc.* 13:123.

Parker, W. S. and Brown, W. S. 1980. Comparative ecology of two colubrid snakes, *Masticophis t. taeniatus* and *Pituophis melanoleucus deserticola, Milw. Public Mus. Publ. Biol. Geol.* 7:1–104.

Pendlebury, G. B. 1974. Stomach and intestine contents of *Corallus enydris:* A comparison of island and mainland specimens, *J. Herpetol.* 8: 241–244.

Platt, D. R. 1984. Growth of bullsnakes (*Pituophis melanoleucus sayi*) on a sand prairie in south central Kansas, in: Vertebrate Ecology and Systematics: A Tribute to Henry S. Fitch (R. A. Seigel, L. E. Hunt, J. L. Knight, L. Malaret, and N. L. Zuschlag, eds.) *Univ. Kans. Mus. Nat. Hist. Spec. Publ.* 10:41–56.

Plummer, M. V. 1981. Habitat utilization, diet and movements of a temperate arboreal snake (*Opheodrys aestivus*), *J. Herpetol.* 15:425–432.

Plummer, M. V. and Goy, J. M. 1984. Ontogenetic dietary shift of water snakes (*Nerodia rhombifera*) in a fish hatchery, *Copeia* 1984:550–552.

Polis, G. A. and Myers, C. A. 1985. A survey of intraspecific predation among reptiles and amphibians, *J. Herpetol.* 19:99–107.

Pough, F. H. 1977. Ontogenetic change in blood oxygen capacity and maximum activity in garter snakes, *Thamnophis sirtalis, J. Comp. Physiol. B Metab. Transp. Funct.* 116:337–345.

Pough, F. H. 1978. Ontogenetic changes in endurance in water snakes (*Natrix sipedon*): Physiological correlates and ecological consequences, *Copeia* 1978:69–75.

Pough, F. H. 1980. The advantages of ectothermy for tetrapods, *Am. Nat.* 115:92–112.

Pough, F. H. 1983. Amphibians and reptiles as low-energy systems, in: Behavioral Energetics: Vertebrate Costs of Survival (W. P. Aspey and S. Lustic, eds.) pp. 141–188, Ohio State University Press, Columbus.

Pough, F. H. and Groves, J. D. 1983. Specialization of the body form and food habits of snakes, *Am. Zool.* 23:443–454.

Powers, A. 1972. An instance of cannibalism in captive *Crotalus viridis helleri* with a brief review of cannibalism in rattlesnakes, *Bull. Md. Herpetol. Soc.* 8:60–61.

Prokopev, L. V., Pshennikov, A. E., Belimov, G. T., and Sedalishchev, V. T. 1978. Ecology of the common adder *Vipera berus* inhabiting the Yakutsk-ASSR USSR, *Vestn. Zool.* 1:83–84.

Punzo, F. 1974. Comparative analysis of the feeding habits of 2 species of Arizona blind snakes *Leptotyphlops humilis humilis* and *Leptotyphlops dulcis dulcis, J. Herpetol.* 8:153–156.

Pyke, G. H., Pulliam, H. R., and Charnov, E. L. 1977. Optimal foraging: A selective review of theory and tests, *Q. Rev. Biol.* 52:137–154.

Raney, E. C. and Roecker, R. M. 1947. Food and growth of two species of water snakes from western New York, *Copeia* 1947:171–174.

Rasmussen, G. 1974. Observations on snakes feeding, *J. Herpetol. Assoc. Afr.* 12:18–20.

Reinert, H. K., Cundall, D., and Bushar, L. M. 1984. Foraging behavior of the timber rattlesnake. *Crotalus horridus, Copeia* 1984:976–981.

Reynolds, R. P. and Scott, N. J., Jr. 1982. Use of a mammalian resource by a Chihuahuan snake community, in: Herpetological Communities (N. J. Scott, Jr., ed.) *U.S. Fish Wildl. Serv. Wildl. Res. Rep.* 13:99–118.

Richmond, N. D. 1945. The habits of the rainbow snake in Virginia, *Copeia* 1945: 28–30.

Rossman, C. E. 1980. Ontogenetic changes in skull proportions of the diamondback water snake, *Nerodia rhombifera, Herpetologica* 36:43–46.

Rossman, D. A. 1963. Relationships and taxonomic status of the North American natricine snake genera *Liodytes, Regina,* and *Clonophis, Occas. Pap. Mus. Zool. La. State Univ.* 29:1–29.

Saint Girons, H. 1979. Feeding cycles of European vipers maintained in seminatural conditions, *Ann. Biol. Anim. Biochem. Biophys.* 19:125–134.

Saint Girons, H. 1980. Selective modifications in the diet of vipers (Reptilia: Viperidae) during growth, *Amphib.-Reptilia* 1:127–136.

Saint Girons, H. and Naulleau, G. 1981. Poids des nouveau—nes et strategies reproductrices des vipères Européennes, *Terre Vie* 35:597–616.

Savitzky, A. H. 1980. The role of venom delivery strategies in snake evolution, *Evolution* 34:1194–1204.

Savitzky, A. H. 1981. Hinged teeth in snakes: An adaptation for swallowing hard-bodied prey, *Science* 212:346–349.

Savitzky, A. H. 1983. Coadapted character complexes among snakes: Fossoriality, piscivory, and durophagy, *Am. Zool.* 23:397–409.

Schmidt, K. P. 1932. Stomach contents of some American coral snakes, with the description of a new species of *Geophis*, *Copeia* 1932:6–9.

Schmidt, K. P. and Davis, D. D. 1941. Field Book of Snakes of the United States and Canada, G. P. Putnam, New York.

Schoener, T. W. 1971. Theory of feeding strategies, *Annu. Rev. Ecol. Syst.* 11:369–404.

Schoener, T. W. 1977. Competition and the niche, in: Biology of the Reptilia vol. 7 (C. Gans and D. W. Tinkle, eds.) pp. 35–136, Academic Press, New York.

Seib, R. L. 1984. Prey use in three syntopic neotropical racers. *J. Herpetol.* 18:412–420.

Seigel, R. A. 1986. Ecology and conservation of an endangered rattlesnake *Sistrurus catenatus,* in Missouri, USA, *Biol. Conserv.* 35:333–346.

Sexton, O. J. 1956–1957. The distribution of *Bothrops atrox* in relation to food supply, *Bol. Mus. Cienc. Nat.* 2–3:47–54.

Shine, R. 1977. Habitats, diets and sympatry in snakes: A study from Australia, *Can. J. Zool.* 55:1118–1128.

Shine, R. 1980a. Ecology of the Australian death adder *Acanthophis antarcticus* (Elapidae): Evidence for convergence with the Viperidae, *Herpetologica* 36:281–289.

Shine, R. 1980b. Comparative ecology of three Australian snake species of the genus *Cacophis* (Serpentes: Elapidae), *Copeia* 1980:831–838.

Shine, R. 1980c. Ecology of eastern Australian whipsnakes of the genus *Demansia, J. Herpetol.* 14:381–389.

Shine, R. 1980d. Reproduction, feeding and growth in the Australian burrowing snake *Vermicella annulata, J. Herpetol.* 14:71–77.

Shine, R. 1981a. Venomous snakes in cold climates: Ecology of the Australian genus *Drysdalia* (Serpentes: Elapidae), *Copeia* 1981:14–25.

Shine, R. 1981b. Ecology of the Australian elapid snakes of the genera *Furina* and *Glyphodon, J. Herpetol.* 15:219–224.

Shine, R. 1982. Ecology of the Australian elapid snake *Echiopsis curta, J. Herpetol.* 16:388–393.

Shine, R. 1983. Food habits and reproductive biology of Australian elapid snakes of the genus *Denisonia, J. Herpetol.* 17:171–175.

Shine, R. 1984. Ecology of small fossorial Australian snakes of the genera *Neelaps* and *Simoselaps* (Serpentes, Elapidae), in: Vertebrate Ecology and

Systematics: A Tribute to Henry S. Fitch (R. A. Seigel, L. E. Hunt, J. L. Knight, L. Malaret, and N. L. Zuschlag, eds.) *Univ. Kans. Mus. Nat. Hist. Spec. Publ.* 10:173–184.

Shine, R. 1986. Ecology of a low-energy specialist: Food habits and reproductive biology of the Arafura file snake (Acrochordidae), *Copeia* 1986:424–437.

Shine, R. and Charles, N. 1982. Ecology of the Australian elapid snake *Tropidechis carinatus, J. Herpetol.* 16:383–387.

Shine, R. and Covacevich, J. 1983. Ecology of highly venomous snakes: The Australian genus *Oxyuranus* (Elapidae), *J. Herpetol.* 17:60–69.

Sisk, M. E. and McCoy, C. J. 1964. Stomach contents of *Natrix r. rhombifera* (Reptilia: Serpentes) from an Oklahoma lake, *Proc. Okla. Acad. Sci.* 44:68–71.

Smith, C. R. 1982. Food resource partitioning of fossorial Florida reptiles, in: Herpetological Communities (N. J. Scott, Jr., ed.) *U.S. Fish Wildl. Serv. Wildl. Res. Rep.* 13:173–178.

Steward, J. W. 1958. The dice snake (*Natrix tessellata*) in captivity, *Br. J. Herpetol.* 2:7.

Steward, J. W. 1971. The Snakes of Europe, David and Charles, Ltd., Newton Abbot, England.

Thomas, M. E. 1974. Bats as a food source for *Boa constrictor, J. Herpetol.* 8:188.

Thomas, R. G. and Pough, F. H. 1979. The effect of rattlesnake, *Crotalus atrox,* venom on digestion of prey, *Toxicon* 17:221–228.

Tinkle, D. W. 1959. Observations of reptiles and amphibians in a Louisiana swamp, *Am. Midl. Nat.* 62:189–205.

Toft, C. A. 1985. Resource partitioning in amphibians and reptiles, *Copeia* 1985:1–21.

Uhler, F. M., Cottam, C., and Clarke, T. E. 1939. Food of snakes of the George Washington National Forest, Virginia, *Trans. N. Am. Wildl. Conf.* 4:605–622.

Vit, Z. 1977. The Russell's viper *Vipera russelli, Prezgl. Zoo.* 21:185–188.

Vitt, L. J. 1980. Ecological observations on sympatric *Philodryas* (Colubridae) in northeastern Brazil, *Pap. Avulsos Zool.* (*Sao Paulo*) 34:87–98.

Vitt, L. J. 1983. Ecology of an anuran-eating guild of terrestrial tropical snakes, *Herpetologica* 39:52–66.

Vitt, L. J. and Hulse, A. C. 1973. Observations on feeding habits and tail display of the Sonoran coral snake *Micruroides euryxanthus, Herpetologica* 29:302–304.

Vitt, L. J. and Vangilder, L. D. 1983. Ecology of a snake community in northeastern Brazil, *Amphib.-Reptilia* 4:273–296.

Voris, H. K. and Glodek, G. S. 1980. Habitat, diet and reproduction of the file snake, *Acrochordus granulatus,* in the Straits of Malacca, *J. Herpetol.* 14:108–111.

Voris, H. K. and Moffett, M. W. 1981. Size and proportion relationship between the beaked sea snake and its prey, *Biotropica* 13:15–19.

Voris, H. K. and Voris, H. H. 1983. Feeding strategies in marine snakes: An analyses of evolutionary, morphological, behavioral and ecological relationships, *Am. Zool.* 23:411–425.

Wehekind, L. 1955. Notes on the foods of the Trinidad snakes, *Br. J. Herpetol.* 2:9–13.

Wiens, J. A. 1977. On competition and variable environments, *Am. Sci.* 65:590–597.

Weldon, P. J. and Schell, F. M. 1984. Responses by king snakes *Lampropeltis getulus* to chemicals from colubrid and crotaline snakes. *J. Chem. Ecol.* 10:1509–1520.

Wharton, C. H. 1960. Birth and behavior of a brood of cottonmouths, *Agkistrodon piscivorus piscivorus* with notes on tail-luring, *Herpetologica* 16:125–129.

White, M. and Kolb, J. A. 1974. A preliminary study of *Thamnophis* near Sagehen Creek, California, *Copeia* 1974:126–136.

Whitford, W. G. and Bryant, M. 1979. Behavior of a predator and its prey: The horned lizard (*Phynosoma cornutum*) and harvester ants (*Pegonomyrmex* sp.), *Ecology* 60:686–694.

Zinner, H. 1971. On ecology and the significance of semantic coloration in the nocturnal desert elapid *Walterinnesia aegyptia* (Reptilia: Ophidia), *Oecologia* (*Berl.*) 7:257–275.

CHAPTER ELEVEN

Communities

Laurie J. Vitt

Like many fields of biology, community ecology has progressed a great deal during the past two decades. Seminal papers by the late Robert MacArthur set the stage for much of the development that has taken place, and his students and colleagues have continued to make many of the major contributions to the field. In a broad sense, community ecology can include such diverse research areas as competition, predator-prey relationships, symbiosis, and patterns of species richness and diversity. Underlying most community studies is the notion that natural selection results in differential survival of the individual organisms best adapted to existing biotic and abiotic conditions. Community studies could include all organisms existing and consequently interacting in a given place at a given time. However, the term has been used most frequently in reference to specific higher taxa. For example, there are community studies on fishes (Kushlan, 1976; Matthews and Hill, 1980; Quinn, 1980; Ross et al., 1985; and others), lizards (Schoener, 1967; Pianka, 1969, 1973; Vitt et al., 1981; Huey et al., 1983; and others), birds (Orians, 1969; Diamond, 1973, 1975; Cody, 1974, 1975; Karr and James, 1975; and others), and mammals (Rosenzweig and Winakur, 1969; McNab, 1971; Brown, 1973, 1975; Brown and Lieberman, 1973).

The contemporary view of animal and plant communities champions the notion that competition among coexisting species has played some prior role in effecting observed differences, *or* that competition has functioned to maintain existing historically based differences, but may also include such agents as predation and various types of symbiosis.

Few studies on snakes have involved more than one species studied simultaneously in the same location. These studies fall into several rather broad categories: (1) communities, (2) guilds, (3) patterns of seasonal abundance, (4) populations, (5) large collections for taxonomic or survey purposes, and (6) topical or taxonomic subsets of these, chosen for a variety of logistic reasons. In this review, I consider studies involving two or more species but focus on those involving the entire snake fauna of a particular locality [for patterns of seasonal abundance see Gibbons and Semlitsch (this volume), although here I consider data in those studies as they relate to this treatment]. I will also not emphasize life histories or diets of sympatric snakes, except in a general way, for the same reason (Seigel and Ford, this volume; Mushinsky, this volume; respectively). I use the term "community" with reference to one taxon, the Serpentes.

My primary emphases are (1) patterns of species richness and their correlates, (2) patterns of species diversity, (3) niche relationships, (4) morphological correlates of community structure, and (5) local patterns of life-history diversity. I will, however, comment on other aspects of snake biology as they pertain to community ecology.

Before considering these questions, it is necessary to comment on four aspects of the biology of snakes that render them particularly unusual for investigating questions of community ecology. First, snakes as a group are top-order carnivores. Not a single species is known to eat vegetation or plant products (fruits, seeds). Consequently the potential prey fauna of a given area would be expected to play a major role in determining the local snake community. Second, because snakes swallow their prey whole, prey size becomes an important limiting factor. This is less true for predatory mammals and certain large predatory lizards (e.g., *Varanus:* Auffenberg, 1981). Third, because of their unique limbless morphology, snakes as a group are considerably more limited than other vertebrate groups in terms of prey capture and handling. This last topic has been recently reviewed (Arnold, 1983; Greene, 1983; Pough, 1983; Savitzky, 1983; Pough and Groves, 1983; Voris and Voris, 1983). Fourth, because snakes eat particularly large prey items and are capable of fasting for long periods of time, they may be buffered from the sorts of energy acquisition problems that face most predatory vertebrates, particularly homeotherms. Each of these aspects of snake biology will be discussed where pertinent.

Because this is a review, most data have been taken directly from published papers. In some instances, it has been necessary to extrapolate from data presented in papers in order to summarize categories I have chosen. Hopefully, each author's intent is reflected accurately. For clarity, I define terms as follows: *tropics*—that portion of the world lying between the Tropic of Capricorn (23°S) and the Tropic of Cancer (23°N); *Temperate Zones*—the remainder of the planet, excluding the Antarctic and Arctic regions; *wet regions*—areas receiving more than 1000 mm rainfall per year; *dry regions*—areas receiving less than 1000 mm rainfall per year; *resource partitioning*—the apparent division of resources by sympatric species with no specific cause identified; *niche*—the multidimensional set of characteristics describing the position of an organism with respect to variables in its environment (Hutchinson, 1959); *species richness* or *species density*—the number of species in the area being considered (comparable to α

diversity; see following); *species diversity*—some measure of the relationship of number of species to the relative abundance of those species. In addition, I will occasionally refer to α, β, and γ diversity as proposed by Cody (1975): α *diversity* refers to the number of species in a defined area, β *diversity* to species turnover rates relative to differences among habitat types, and γ *diversity* to geographic species turnover, i.e., differences in species composition between similar habitats in different zoogeograhic areas.

SPECIES RICHNESS

Latitudinal Patterns of Species Richness

Although there is considerable variation, particularly at lower latitudes (see following discussion), the number of snake species tends to increase with decreasing latitude. Using data on the number of species of snakes in each of four countries situated from north to south, Dobzhansky (1950) showed that snake species richness increased substantially with decreasing latitude. Unfortunately, because he included all species occurring across longitudes for each country, his latitudinal estimates at times grossly overestimated the number of snake species occurring in any one locality by nearly an order of magnitude. Nevertheless, later studies have substantiated, to varying degrees, the negative correlation between number of snake species and latitude. In the Northern Hemisphere alone, Arnold (1972), using data from 45 mainland localities (Figure 11–1) showed clearly that the number of snake species decreased with increasing latitude. A plot of data taken from the literature reveals the same overall trend (Figure 11–2). The latitudinal trends are fairly clear-cut, even though the east-west axis varies considerably, particularly at lower latitudes. Because this variation is most often associated with major habitat differences, it will be considered in more detail in the next section.

A clear pattern of increasing species richness with decreasing latitude is also evident in other groups of animals (Schall and Pianka, 1978). With respect to snakes, Schall and Pianka (1978) found that Australian and U.S. snake species density correlated best with temperature (r^2 = 0.43 and 0.78, respectively) but correlated negatively with bird species density. A general trend of increasing snake species density is also evident when considering only North American species, as demonstrated by Keister (1971), using reptiles as a group. A perusal of distribution maps in North American field guides (Stebbins, 1954; Conant, 1975) reveals that much of the correlation that Keister (1971) found can be attributed to snakes. Biases in Keister's treatment are difficult to assess even though the general patterns do appear to hold for snakes. I would not expect, for example, to find that lizard, snake, and turtle faunas were correlated with the same biotic factors. Snakes as a group feed primarily on vertebrate or subsoil invertebrate prey (with exceptions), lizards feed primarily on surface invertebrate

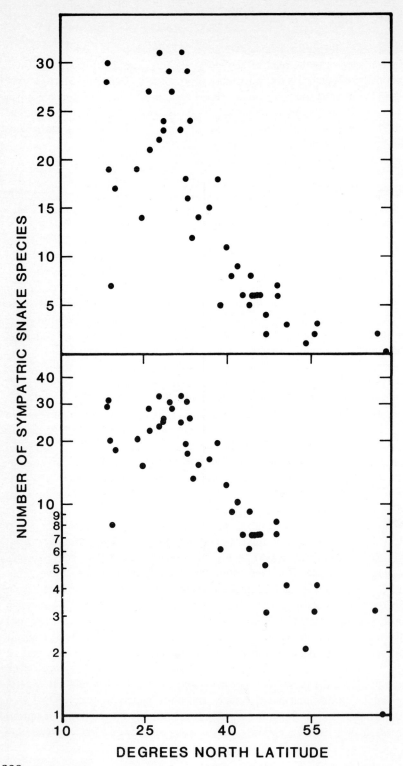

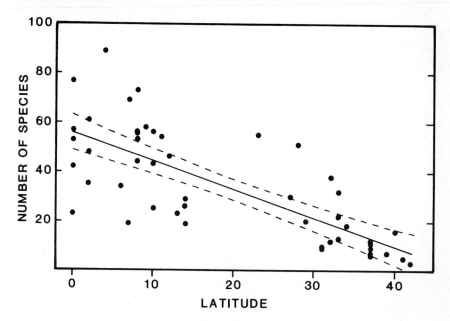

Figure 11–2.   Relationship between number of snake species and latitude based on data in unpublished appendix (available with expanded reference list from the author by request). Fifty-seven percent of the variance in species number is explained by latitude, and the slope of the regression line is significantly different from zero ($t = 7.94$, $p < 0.05$, $n = 50$). The 95% confidence intervals of the regression are indicated by the dotted lines.

prey and/or plants, and most turtle species are aquatic and thus their distributional patterns are subject to the constraints of the distribution of aquatic systems.

Elevational Patterns of Species Richness

There have been few studies that specifically address the question, are there more species of snakes at low elevations than at high elevations, all else being equal? Several studies from different parts of the world show a trend toward decreasing species density with increasing elevation.

Scott (1976) found a distinct decrease in the number of tropical snake species in Costa Rica with increasing elevation (Figure 11–3). In a study of the amphibians and reptiles of Texas, Rogers (1976) divided the state according to county boundaries and correlated the county herpetofaunas with standard cli-

←————————————————————————————————

Figure 11–1.   Linear and semilog plots of species densities of sympatric snakes as a function of latitude for 45 Northern Hemisphere localities. Redrawn from Arnold (1972).

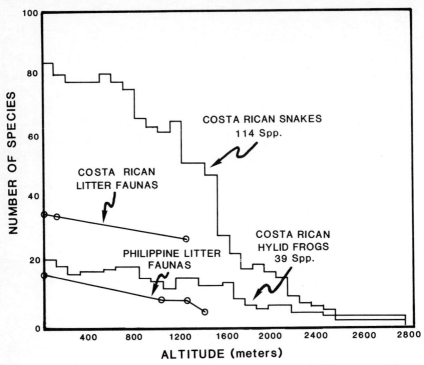

Figure 11–3. Number of species of Costa Rican snake, hylid frog, and litter herpetofaunas at different elevations. Redrawn from Scott (1976).

matological data (10-yr averages, with standard deviations as a measure of variability), while correcting for the differences in area among counties. Multiple regression and partial correlation analyses with all environmental data and the number of small terrestrial mammal species revealed that the number of snake species (1) increased with topographic relief (see following discussion), (2) decreased with elevation, (3) increased with precipitation (see following discussion), and (4) increased with the number of small mammals (see following discussion).

In an analysis of African snake faunas, Hughes (1983) pointed out that few snakes are limited to montane (high-elevation) forests and that the montane snake fauna consists generally of a relatively small subsample of the species occurring in the surrounding lowland forest or savanna. Montane snake faunas in tropical Africa therefore also appear depauperate compared with faunas at lower elevations.

Data on snake species occurring on mountaintops in southeastern Arizona compared with the species occurring in nearby low-elevation habitats (Pough, 1966; L. J. Vitt, unpublished observations) also suggest that there are fewer species of snakes at higher elevations (elevation per se is most likely not the causative agent). The mountaintop fauna of the Chiricahua Mountains (elevation 2400 to 3000 m) in southeastern Arizona consists of 6 species of snakes (3 colubrids, 3 viperids). About 15 km away at Portal, Arizona, at an elevation of approximately 1447 m, 21 species of snakes coexist, including 2 leptotyphlopids, 14 colubrids, 1 elapid, and 4 viperids (based on my own field observations; there may be more species near Portal, but I have not observed them personally). Thus species richness is reduced from 21 to 6 in fewer than 15 km and with an elevational increase of about 1200 m. Similar differences would be apparent in comparisons of montane faunas from the Graham (Pinaleño), Huachuca, or Santa Rita Mountains of southeastern Arizona. There is a bias in this comparison, however, because the bases of each of these mountain ranges consist of transition habitats between two and in some cases three (Portal) major southwest habitats. The high snake species richness at Portal therefore is not associated solely with elevation. An examination of the flatland desert snake fauna just north of the Chiricahua Mountains does indicate a higher number of species than in the montane fauna, but a lower number than in Portal. Thirteen species (1 leptotyphlopid, 9 colubrids, 1 elapid, and 2 viperids) occur in the flatland desert between Bowie, Arizona, and the base of the Chiricahuas. As with the Portal data, this is a minimal estimate.

An examination of distribution maps in field guides of North American snakes reveals similar patterns associated with elevation. Gaps exist in the distribution of many species associated with the Sierra Nevada of California and Nevada and the Rocky Mountains of the western United States. Likewise, the aforementioned examples from Arizona (Pough, 1966; L. J. Vitt, unpublished data) and Costa Rica (Scott, 1976) show that many species drop out with elevation, even on a microgeographic scale. The greatest numbers of snake species in the United States occur in low-elevation deserts of the Southwest and low-elevation wetlands of the southeastern Coastal Plain.

Habitat Patterns of Species Richness

Although it was not apparent in the previous discussion, there are distinct differences in species richness and composition among habitats at approximately the same elevation at the same or nearly the same latitude. Depending on the degree of separation of the habitats, these species turnover rates could be considered β diversity (due to habitat gradients) or γ diversity (geographic). Rogers' (1976) study on Texas reptiles and amphibians reveals that snake species densities are correlated with several habitat characteristics (topographic relief and precipitation). Additional data for Texas reptiles is provided by Fouquette and Lindsay (1955). On a finer geographic scale, Sullivan (1981) found considerable differences in the snake faunas of three habitat types in central California. In an oak woodland habitat, 6 species were recorded, compared with 7 species in a grassland habitat. Only 3 species were common to the two habitats, and an ecotonal habitat contained 11 species consisting of all snakes reported from either of the first two habitats.

Two strikingly different habitats in North America (the Sonoran Desert and the southeastern Coastal Plain) at nearly the same latitude and elevation exemplify the effect of habitat on snake species density. In the Sonoran Desert of central Arizona, the number of snake species co-existing varies, depending on locality, from as few as 13 at South Mountain near Phoenix (Brown and Parker, 1982) to as many as 22 at the Verde River, also near Phoenix (L. J. Vitt et al., unpublished data). Eighteen species co-exist at approximately the same latitude on the lower Colorado River (Vitt and Ohmart, 1978). Much of the variation in the number of snake species among Sonoran Desert localities can be attributed to habitat differences on a microgeographic scale. For example, the Verde River locality (Vitt et al., unpublished data) and the Colorado River site (Vitt and Ohmart, 1978) contain mixtures of a variety of habitats including relatively species-rich mesquite woodlands. The South Mountain site in the Sonoran Desert lacks the mesquite woodland and consists of relatively low-density xerophytic vegetation (Brown and Parker, 1982). At the Savannah River Plant near Aiken, South Carolina, 32 species of snakes occur within a 24-km radius (Gibbons and Patterson, 1978; J. W. Gibbons et al., unpublished data). The latter habitat is complex in that it contains pine and hardwood forests, streams, a river, swamps, and a variety of soil types. Only three species (*Masticophis flagellum, Pituophis melanoleucus,* and *Lampropeltis getulus*) are common to the Sonoran Desert and the southeastern Coastal Plain, and these are considered different at the subspecific level.

Large differences in snake species richness are also apparent between habitats in the tropics. Lowland tropical forests appear to support large numbers of snake species, whereas relatively dry tropical habitats contain relatively depauperate faunas. The lowland tropical forests generally experience high annual rainfall [Duellman's (1978) Santa Cecilia, Ecuador site, for example, received 4289.5-mm rainfall in one year] and exhibit high plant species diversity. Typically these habitats also contain large numbers of species of other animal groups. This is illustrated by comparisons of neotropical snake faunas occurring within 10° of the equator. Duellman (1978) reported 53 species of snakes at Santa Cecilia, while Dixon and Soini (1977) reported 89 co-existing snake species at a relatively similar lowland tropical forest site near Iquitos, Peru. In the state of Pernambuco in northeastern Brazil, only 19 species of snakes co-occur in a caatinga habitat (Vitt and Vangilder, 1983). Although the Pernambuco locality is at 7°S latitude, the region is considered semi-arid (Reis, 1976), receiving less than 1000 mm rainfall annually.

Hughes (1983) analyzed snake faunas within and among major habitat types at various latitudes and longitudes in Africa (see also Leston and Hughes, 1968). Initially, he examined species composition by African territories, producing a matrix giving the number of species in each, the number of species shared by various territory pairs, and the percentage of the total species numbers shared by territory pairs (Table 11–1). This analysis revealed that high proportions of the snake faunas are shared by territories, particularly those that are adjacent. Hughes then made a similar comparison by dividing Africa on the basis of localities with differing habitat types. These results revealed much less similarity in snake faunas (see Table 2 in Hughes, 1983). Species of African snakes appear to occur either in forests or savannas, but generally not both habitat types. Large proportions of the snake faunas in each habitat type are wide-ranging in Africa within that habitat type. Hughes provided an enlightening discussion of African snake faunas incorporating general habitat information with biogeographical information on the snakes. Of particular importance in determining African snake faunas is the distribution of forest versus savannah, and the boundary of the savannah between Guinea and Sudan.

Considerable variations in snake species density among habitats have been reported in studies from other localities. In the Yucatan Peninsula of Mexico, Lee (1980) found differences in the number of snakes in seven localities differing in climatological and vegetational structure. Sixty-six percent of the variation in snake species density among habitats was attributable to plant height diversity alone, and when considered with three additional variables (percentage of mean annual rainfall occurring from May to October, species volume diversity, and plant volume diversity) accounted for 99% of the variation. Barbault (1971) found similar differences in snake species density among habitats in tropical Africa.

Perhaps the most thorough analysis of snake faunas in different habitats on a microgeographic scale is that of Inger and Colwell (1977), who divided contiguous habitats of Thailand into three types (evergreen forest, deciduous forest, and agricultural land) and examined the structure of the herpetofauna of each, including resource utilization (states) of the species. Of 47 possible snake species,

Table 11–1. Number of Snake Species Occurring in Various African Territories[a]. Entries below the italicized numbers in boldface represent numbers of species in common; entries above indicate species in common as a percentage of the smaller total compared.

Territory	Liberia	Ghana	Nigeria	Cameroon	Gabon	Zaire	Uganda	Kenya
Liberia	*44*	93	91	82	70	75	57	57
Ghana	41	*56*	91	82	70	71	52	70
Nigeria	40	51	*56*	89	73	77	71	70
Cameroon	36	46	50	*73*	98	79	81	78
Gabon	31	39	41	56	*57*	93	78	74
Zaire	33	40	43	58	53	*77*	100	100
Uganda	25	29	30	34	33	42	*42*	100
Kenya	13	16	16	18	18	23	23	*23*

[a]Restructured from Hughes (1983). Italicized numbers in boldface represent the total possible species for the given territory.

Table 11–2. Summary of Factors Potentially Affecting the Structure of Snake Communities.[a]

Factor	Presumed Effect
Historical	
Age or recency of geographic area	Relatively old areas should have more species than relatively young areas.
Source of snake fauna	Areas distant from a potential source (e.g., Hawaii) may have depauperate or no snake fauna.
Biogeographical	
Nearness to taxon distribution center	Number of species should be higher near the center of distribution than far from the center of distribution.
Nearness to areas in flux	Number of species could be high near areas that fluctuate drastically in evolutionary time (e.g., tropical Amazonia; see "Climatic stability" below)
Abiotic	
Latitude	Increasing species number with decreasing latitude (accounts partially for season-length effects).
Elevation	Increasing species number with decreasing elevation (accounts partially for season-length effects).
Temperature	Increasing number of species with increasing temperature.
Moisture	Increasing number of species with increasing moisture.
Habitat structure	Increasing number of species with increasing habitat diversity
Climatic stability	More stable habitat will support more species (MacArthur, 1972), but exactly the opposite is proposed to account for the high diversity of tropical Amazonian species (Haffer, 1969; Vanzolini and Williams, 1970).
Biotic	
Prey species richness	Increasing number of species or diversity with increasing number of prey species.
Prey species diversity	Increasing number of species or diversity with increasing prey species diversity.
Prey abundance	Increasing number of species or diversity with increasing prey species abundance, particularly if predation controls population densities of snakes.
Potential predators	Affect could be variable, depending on the type and efficiency of predators.
Habitat productivity	Increasing number of species or diversity with increasing habitat productivity.

[a]Even though snake species richness and/or diversity may respond to the factors listed above, the response in most cases may be indirect, resulting from the effect of the identified factor on prey species richness and diversity.

29 occurred in evergreen forest, 27 in deciduous forest, and 19 on agricultural land. Of a possible 64 resource states (all areas combined), 44 were utilized by evergreen forest snakes, 28 by deciduous forest snakes, and only 14 by snakes occurring on agricultural land. These examples indicate that the structure of snake faunas, including the absolute number of species, can vary significantly on a micro- and macrographic scale.

Determinants of Snake Species Richness

Patterns of snake species richness clearly are complex and are influenced by latitude, elevation, moisture, and habitat complexity (Table 11–2). The effects of these variables may be indirect with respect to snake faunas, acting on the patterns of species richness in potential prey types for snakes. Historical factors such as patterns of speciation may also influence patterns of snake species richness. For example, why do so many species of *Crotalus* occur in sympatry in the deserts of the southwestern United States while most other snake genera are represented by but a single species in the same general habitat? In Amazonian Ecuador and Peru, why do so many genera of snakes represented by two, three, and sometimes more species appear ecologically similar?

The underlying cause of the apparent latitudinal, elevational, and/or habitat patterns in snake species density appears best explained on the basis of the number and abundance of prey types available. Significant correlations exist between the numbers of species of lizards, anurans, and various snake guilds. Arnold (1972) explored this idea by correlating snake species density with latitude (including climatological variables) and possible prey types. He argued that snakes generally consume prey types, not prey species, and categorized prey types as (1) lizards, (2) frogs and lizards, (3) frogs only, (4) mammals, and (5) invertebrates. Although he found that snake species increased with decreasing latitude, removal of the effect of latitude showed that prey species accounted for most of the variation in snake species density. Specifically, he found that (1) the density of lizard-eating and mammal-eating snake species correlated with the density of lizard species and (2) the density of anuran-eating and anuran- and lizard-eating snake species correlated with anuran species density (summarized in Figure 11–4). Unfortunately, Arnold did not have similar data on the numbers of species of mammals, birds, and invertebrates to compare with the numbers of snakes eating these items. Such data would have presumably added support to his findings. Arnold concluded that strong relationships between numbers of predators and their prey are not due to a common correlation with latitude but rather to predator-prey relationships and competition.

The results of most of the other cited studies indicated that snake species density and/or diversity is best explained on the basis of prey species density. For example, Rogers (1976) found that one of the correlates of snake species density in Texas was the number of species of small mammals. Scott (1976), Duellman (1978), Vitt and Vangilder (1983), Inger and Colwell (1977), and Lee (1980) have presented data that concur, and several examples follow.

The extreme difference in snake species richness between lowland tropical forest and semi-arid caatinga appears best explained relative to prey species richness. Because the best data on the species composition of non-ophidian vertebrate groups are from Santa Cecilia, Ecuador, I compare the caatinga snake fauna with this alone. Unfortunately, only the amphibians and reptiles of Santa Cecilia are well known. The herpetofauna of Santa Cecilia, in addition to in-

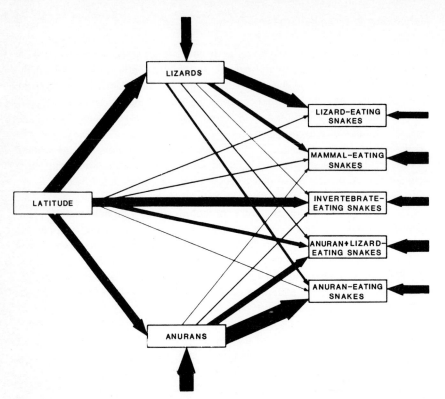

Figure 11–4. Coefficients of determination for path coefficients (assuming *a priori* directionality) relating categorical trophic groupings of snakes with potential prey and latitude. The greater the absolute value of the path coefficient, the greater the relationship between the trophic group and the other variable. The arrow widths indicate relative proportional coefficients of determination. Arrows and associated path coefficients entering from outside the figure indicate effects that are unaccounted for. Redrawn from Arnold (1972).

cluding 53 known snake species, contains 30 lizard, 87 anuran, 5 caecilian, 2 salamander, 6 turtle, and 2 crocodilian species (Duellman, 1978). The caatinga herpetofauna at Exu, Pernambuco, in addition to including 19 known snake species, contains 17 lizard, at least 22 anuran, no caecilian, salamander, or crocodilian species, and two turtle species. Presumably there are similar differences between Santa Cecilia and the caatinga in the number of species of other vertebrate groups. Notably, there were no species of snakes in caatinga at Exu that fed on invertebrates, whereas there were several at Santa Cecilia. Many species of snakes at Santa Cecilia fed on frogs, whereas only a few caatinga snakes did. The comparative data on these tropical habitats support the notion that the richness of prey species determines the number of snake species.

Examination of other species lists from around the world reveals a similar pattern. In Thailand, Inger and Colwell (1977) reported 47 snake, 31 lizard, and 24 frog species (all areas combined). At Iquitos, Peru, Dixon and Soini (1975, 1977), reported 87 snake and 42 lizard species (amphibians were not studied); at Cuatro Cienegas in Coahila, Mexico, McCoy (1984) reported 30 snake, 24 lizard, and 9 frog species; in South Carolina, Gibbons and Patterson (1978) reported 31 snake, 9 lizard, 26 frog, and 17 salamander species. Even though data are lacking or difficult to assemble for birds, mammals, and invertebrates at these localities, snake species density appears to increase with increasing density of potential prey species.

I have not yet considered sea snakes in this discussion. Because they occur in marine environments, primarily in connection with the Pacific Ocean, comparisons with terrestrial faunas and the temperate-tropical dichotomy are of little applicability. One of the overriding problems in dealing with species densities of sea snakes on a global level is a universal lack of data. In addition, their absence from the Atlantic Ocean reduces the possibility of making certain comparisons. Nevertheless, some patterns are evident.

The center of distribution for sea snakes [which may have three independent origins (Voris, 1977)] appears to be in the shore areas of the Straits of Malacca (27 species are known to co-exist), the Gulf of Siam (16 species), and the southern end of the China Sea (22 species) (Voris, 1972, 1977). Moving away from these areas results in a decrease in the number of co-occurring species, and presently it is difficult to associate species density with any biotic or abiotic feature of the environment. Most are restricted to relatively shallow coastal areas where prey abundance is high, but one genus, *Pelamis,* is pelagic and very widespread. The determinants of the structure of sea snake faunas remains unclear (but see NICHE RELATIONSHIPS).

A number of hypotheses are presented by Voris (1977) to account for the lack of a worldwide distribution of sea snakes. Pertinent to this review, it is possible that the group is relatively young and still in the process of speciating and increasing in distribution. This is consistent with the lack of a fossil record for the family, the absence of any species in the Atlantic Ocean or the Mediterranean Sea, and the decreased number of species associated with increased distance from the presumed center of distribution. This fits well Voris' (1977) first hypothesis, that the group is young, indeed dating only to the Miocene. An alternate hypothesis is that sea snakes do not occur in the Atlantic or Mediterranean for ecological reasons. I comment on this later in this chapter.

SPECIES DIVERSITY

Accurate estimates of species diversity in snake assemblages are rare, partially because, unlike birds, lizards, and small mammals, which can usually be easily trapped and/or counted, all the snakes at a given locality can rarely be censused accurately. In many tropical localities, even the actual number of species of snakes remains ill-defined. The best estimates of the number of individuals and species of snakes are from temperate regions where the faunas contain relatively low numbers of species and where communal aggregations occur for overwintering (Gregory et al., this volume).

Brown and Parker (1982) found an apparent relationship between the log of the number of species of snakes and species diversity (the Shannon-Weiner measure, H), based on data from 10 Temperate Zone studies. I have added data from 20 additional temperate and tropical studies and, although there is an overall pattern of increasing species diversity with the log of the number of species (Figure 11–5), the relationship is not impressive ($r^2 = 0.185$) and shows considerable scatter. The same data set shows a weak decrease in species diversity with increasing latitude (Figure 11–6) and a pattern similar to that for species richness. Taken together, the data on species diversity are also consistent with the notion that prey species richness and diversity affect predator species richness and diversity.

The relationships between the number of snake species and the relative abundance of each have not been well studied. The data I have examined were collected in a variety of ways, each of which introduced its own biases. In some

Figure 11–5. Relationship between the log (base 10) of the number of snake species and species diversity (H, the Shannon-Weiner measure) for studies listed in unpublished appendix containing appropriate data. In calculating species diversity values, it is assumed that regardless of how the numbers of snakes were determined in each study, they represent actual relative abundances of the snakes where studied. In some cases this assumption is valid, in others it is questionable.

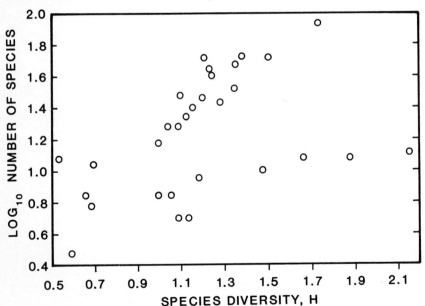

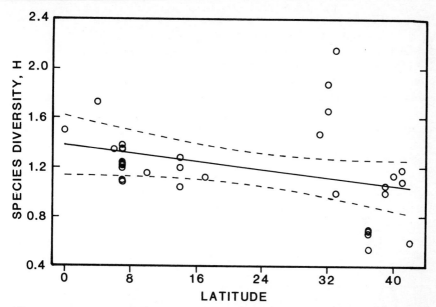

Figure 11–6. Relationship between species diversity and latitude for the same snake community data as represented in Figure 11–5. Only 11.1% of the variance in species density is accounted for by latitude. The 95% confidence intervals of the regression are indicated by the dotted lines.

of the better examples, the estimates of relative abundances are probably relatively good [e.g., Fitch's (1982) Kansas data]. Estimates at many tropical localities (Santa Cecelia: Duellman, 1978; Iquitos: Dixon and Soini, 1977; Pernambuco: Vitt and Vangilder, 1983; northern Venezuela: Silva et al., 1985) are based on the relative number of each snake species collected by any means possible and are biased toward species that are terrestrial and easy to collect.

NICHE RELATIONSHIPS

Temperate Zone Snakes

Examinations of niche relationships among sympatric Temperate Zone snakes have been descriptive, providing data on diet, habitat utilization, and occasionally activity periods. This research has generally followed protocol similar to that used by lizard ecologists (Pianka, 1973), breaking the niche into three major categories: food, place, and time (or various deviations of these) and occasionally examining overlaps in resource utilization.

Several studies on the same populations of sympatric water snakes (five species; *Nerodia,* with some data on *Regina*) reveal differences in prey utilization

(Mushinsky and Hebrard, 1977a), activity periods (Mushinsky and Hebrard, 1977b), and habitat (Hebrard and Mushinsky, 1978). Spatial overlap was high for three of the species (*N. cyclopion, N. rhombifera,* and *N. erythrogaster*), but there were differences in microhabitat utilization. Certain species pairs had similar diets or activity times. Overall, the data indicate that a complex interaction of differences in prey use, time use, and habitat or occasionally microhabitat use account for sympatry in these aquatic snakes. The issue is somewhat complicated by the observation that ontogenetic changes may occur in diets of at least four species (Mushinsky et al., 1982). This ontogenetic effect has two major components: prey type and prey size (which are not entirely independent). This presents a major complication in analysis and interpretation of snake diets when compared with those of insectivorous lizards, particularly when the snake fauna contains species reaching extremely large body sizes (see Mushinsky, this volume).

Brown and Parker (1982) examined niche relationships among three common species of snakes (*Coluber constrictor, Masticophis taeniatus,* and *Pituophis melanoleucus*) in northern Utah. Their approach was similar to that discussed previously and revealed relatively low dietary overlap. Examination of the place niche of these species was somewhat complicated by seasonal variation in microhabitat. Like many other studies on snakes (Carpenter, 1952; Arnold, 1972; Toft, 1985), this suggests that separation along a food axis is most important.

Tropical Snakes

Few attempts have been made to examine niche relationships of tropical snakes, presumably because of a lack of habitat and prey type data. In some studies, snake data are combined with data on other vertebrates in community analyses and thus cannot be extracted separately. Duellman (1978) coded habitat (four categories), microhabitat (six categories), activity period (four categories), activity when captured (six categories), food (two categories), and size (snout-vent length, SVL) data and used a phenetic analysis to examine similarities among sympatric species of Amazonian reptiles and amphibians. He restricted the snake analysis to data on habitat, vertical distribution, diel activity, and food and produced a phenogram of relationships (Figure 11–7). As in most studies on snake communities, patterns of differential resource utilization are apparent, even withstanding sample size limitations.

Henderson et al. (1979) attempted to examine resource partitioning among snakes from three localities in the Peruvian Amazon region. Although the data set was not adequate for a community analysis, a comparison of the species of

——————————————————————————————————→

Figure 11–7. Modal resource utilization by snakes and amphisbaenians based on four parameters: habitat, vertical distribution, diel activity, and food. From Duellman (1978).

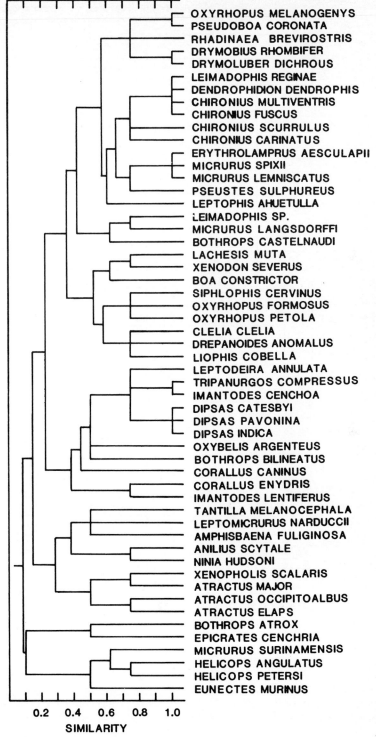

OXYRHOPUS MELANOGENYS
PSEUDOBOA CORONATA
RHADINAEA BREVIROSTRIS
DRYMOBIUS RHOMBIFER
DRYMOLUBER DICHROUS
LEIMADOPHIS REGINAE
DENDROPHIDION DENDROPHIS
CHIRONIUS MULTIVENTRIS
CHIRONIUS FUSCUS
CHIRONIUS SCURRULUS
CHIRONIUS CARINATUS
ERYTHROLAMPRUS AESCULAPII
MICRURUS SPIXII
MICRURUS LEMNISCATUS
PSEUSTES SULPHUREUS
LEPTOPHIS AHUETULLA
LEIMADOPHIS SP.
MICRURUS LANGSDORFFI
BOTHROPS CASTELNAUDI
LACHESIS MUTA
XENODON SEVERUS
BOA CONSTRICTOR
SIPHLOPHIS CERVINUS
OXYRHOPUS FORMOSUS
OXYRHOPUS PETOLA
CLELIA CLELIA
DREPANOIDES ANOMALUS
LIOPHIS COBELLA
LEPTODEIRA ANNULATA
TRIPANURGOS COMPRESSUS
IMANTODES CENCHOA
DIPSAS CATESBYI
DIPSAS PAVONINA
DIPSAS INDICA
OXYBELIS ARGENTEUS
BOTHROPS BILINEATUS
CORALLUS CANINUS
CORALLUS ENYDRIS
IMANTODES LENTIFERUS
TANTILLA MELANOCEPHALA
LEPTOMICRURUS NARDUCCII
AMPHISBAENA FULIGINOSA
ANILIUS SCYTALE
NINIA HUDSONI
XENOPHOLIS SCALARIS
ATRACTUS MAJOR
ATRACTUS OCCIPITOALBUS
ATRACTUS ELAPS
BOTHROPS ATROX
EPICRATES CENCHRIA
MICRURUS SURINAMENSIS
HELICOPS ANGULATUS
HELICOPS PETERSI
EUNECTES MURINUS

0.2 0.4 0.6 0.8 1.0
SIMILARITY

351

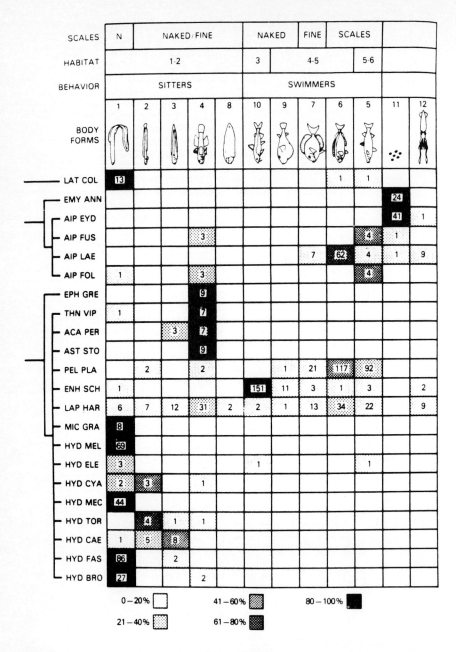

Figure 11–8. Sea snake relationships and diets (from Voris and Voris, 1983). The phylogenetic relationships of 22 sea snake species for which there are at least five identifiable stomach contents each are given on the vertical axes. The 12 body form categories and associated characteristics of sea snake prey are given on the horizontal axis. For each sea snake species, the number and proportion of stomach contents in each body form category is given in the body of

Micrurus along three axes (size, food, and habitat) revealed species separation in ecological space. Even though the small sample sizes render the analysis of questionable value, some of the differences among species appear well supported.

In a study on five sympatric anuran-eating tropical snakes, relatively clear differences were apparent in prey utilization, with percentage overlaps in diet ranging from as low as 14.1% to as high as 60% based on reasonably large samples (Vitt, 1983). Morphological differences among snake species corresponded well with prey utilization differences. Unfortunately I did not collect accurate data on either microhabitat utilization or activity periods, and thus only a portion of niche differentiation among these species was examined.

Sea snakes provide a particularly interesting group for examination of niche relationships. Large numbers of species may co-exist (up to 27 species), and nearly all of the species are restricted to relatively shallow shore regions of tropical seas. In an analysis of the diets of 22 species, Voris and Voris (1983) showed that there were clear differences among species in the prey generally taken, that categorical types of prey were taken (as opposed to species of prey) apparently based on the shape of the prey and the snake species, and that there appeared to be no particular prey preferences based on the taxonomic relationships of the sea snakes (Figure 11–8). Considering only eight sea snake species from the Straits of Malacca for which extensive diet data exist, there appears to be very little similarity in prey utilization between species pairs, the highest overlap being 26.8%, with 15 pairwise combinations showing no overlap (Glodek and Voris, 1982).

However, diversity in feeding roles and the relatively large number of potential (160 fish families) and actual (56 fish families, fish eggs, and invertebrates) prey suggest that number of prey types should not be limiting for sea snakes (Voris and Voris, 1983). If sea snakes represent a relatively recent group, it is possible that they are only beginning to utilize an incredibly diverse resource. This could explain both a lack of large numbers of specialist species and the utilization of general prey types. In addition, if indeed sea snakes are undergoing relatively rapid radiation and expansion of distribution, a competition hypothesis may not be necessary to explain any aspect of their biology because they may have never experienced limited resources during their evolutionary history. The apparent prey partitioning and associated morphological correlates of sea snakes may represent diversification in a relatively unlimited environment (temporally). Clearly, this area of snake research has a potential for some exciting results.

It is clear from the above that much remains to be learned about niche

---

the table. Species are, from top to bottom: *Laticauda colubrina, Emydocephalus annulatus, Aipysurus eydouxii, A. fuscus, A. laevis, A. foliosquama, Ephalophis greyi, Thalassophina viperina, Acalyptophis peronii, Astrotia stokesii, Pelamis platurus, Enhydrina schistosa, Lapemis hardwickii, Microcephalophus gracilis, Hydrophis melanosoma, H. elegans, H. cyanocinctus, H. melanocephalus, H. torquatus, H. caerulescens, H. fasciatus,* and *H. brookii.*

relationships and resource partitioning in snake communities. A majority of the studies and data again suggest that prey types may be the important determinant of the structure of snake communities.

MORPHOLOGICAL ANALYSES

The morphology of snakes has seldom been correlated with their ecological attributes, at least at the community level. Most often, body size as snout-vent length or mass is compared among species (e.g., Fitch, 1982). Realistic comparisons should reflect the snake's life-style. For example, knowing that one species of snake averages 300 mm SVL and another averages 600 mm SVL tells us little about the life-style of each. The first might be aquatic and stout-bodied, and the second might be arboreal and thin-bodied, but from length data alone we cannot conclude this. Additional morphological measurements such as head, body, tail, or length-weight relationships can provide much more information about what a snake species might do in its environment. One problem in dealing with such data is that morphological characters are not independent of body size within a species, and it is often unknown whether ontogenetic changes occur in the relationship of morphological characters to body size. I suggest the following data set as minimal for interpreting snake morphology in an ecological context: SVL, mass, tail length, head width, head length, head height, body width, and body height [exact details are given in Vitt and Vangilder (1983)]. Additional variables such as eye diameter and position of the eyes are also useful. Allometric problems (if they exist) can generally be resolved with regression analyses, and comparisons between sexes and species can be made with analysis of covariance using body size as the independent variable. These data can then be analyzed with a variety of multivariate techniques. I comment on a few of the attempts to examine the morphology of snakes in an ecological context.

Four genera of vine snakes (*Ahaetulla, Oxybelis, Thelotornis, Uromacer*) have very similar ecologies. All are arboreal and feed on active prey, usually lizards (Henderson and Binder, 1980) (although some vine snakes in other genera feed on frogs). Species in these four genera are diurnal, have acute vision with wide binocular fields, and orient on prey movement. In addition, they are strikingly similar in morphology. Henderson and Binder (1980) used measurements of head length, eye diameter, snout length, snout base width, and snout anterior width to compare vine snakes as a group with other arboreal and terrestrial snakes. They selected a small size range of large individuals, to avoid allometric effects, and divided each variable by the SVL to correct for body size. The analysis showed that vine snakes differed from every other group (arboreal snakes, blunt-nosed arboreal snakes, diurnal snakes, nocturnal snakes, terrestrial snakes, frog predators, lizard predators) in head length and snout base width. In some of the comparisons, vine snakes differed from various other groups in three or more characters. Additional body measurements could improve the comparison (the non-herpetologist, for example, would still not know whether *Oxybelis* was thin-bodied with a narrow head and *Ahaetulla* was stout-bodied with a narrow head), as could analysis of covariance. Nevertheless, the vine snakes appear to be one of the most distinctive groupings, ecologically and morphologically, among the snakes that have been studied.

The two tree snakes, *Uromacer catesbyi* and *U. oxyrhynchus,* occur in sympatry in Hispaniola. They are both diurnal and arboreal (Henderson et al., 1981). *Uromacer catesbyi* uses relatively thin perches during the day and feeds exclusively on *Anolis* and *Ameiva* lizards, whereas *U. oxyrhynchus* uses relatively low perches and feeds on relatively more sedentary hylid frogs in addition to *Anolis*. Differences in perch diameter corresponding to patterns of prey availability are also evident. A morphological comparison [using methods similar to those of Henderson and Binder (1980)] reveals that *U. catesbyi* is thinner-bodied and more narrow-headed than *U. oxyrhynchus,* a result expected on the basis of the ecological differences described above. This situation holds promise for an experimental study on competitive interactions in snakes. Removal of *U. catesbyi* might result in a habitat and dietary shift in *U. oxyrhynchus,* and vice versa, if

Figure 11–9. Plot of scores for each of 19 species of snakes from tropical caatinga of northeastern Brazil on the first two principal component axes derived from morphological data. Factor 1 is an axis representing increasing body size, whereas factor 2 is an axis representing increasing tail length and decreasing head and body width. Numbers on the figure refer to individual species (see Vitt and Vangilder, 1983, for details).

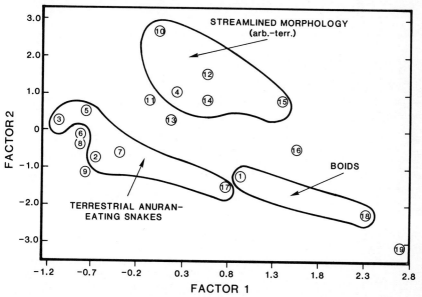

indeed competition plays a role in maintaining the observed differences between these snakes.

Vitt and Vangilder (1983) attempted an analysis relating morphology to ecological groupings for a relatively well-studied tropical snake assemblage where diets, activity periods, and habitat associations were known for each species. Principal component analysis was performed on eight morphological variables (SVL, tail length, total mass, head length, head width, gape, body width, and body height) transformed to their logarithms (base 10). This produced approximate scores on two axes as shown in Figure 11–9. The results were, for the most part, disappointing. On the basis of morphology alone, we could not distinguish streamlined terrestrial snakes from streamlined arboreal species. This problem may, however, be solved by comparisons of head shape independent of body size, particularly with the addition of the variables used by Henderson and Binder (1980). Moreover, the relatively slow-moving arboreal species behave quite differently from the very fast-moving terrestrial species. An entire guild of anuran-eating snakes (see also Vitt, 1983) was spread across half of the factor-1 axis and one-third of the factor-2 axis. Many of the differences in actual body

Figure 11–10. Mean values of snout-vent length, relative girth (girth at neck/girth at two-thirds of snout-vent length), and gape index (quadrate bone length/parietal bone width) for 14 sea snake species. Redrawn from Voris and Voris (1983).

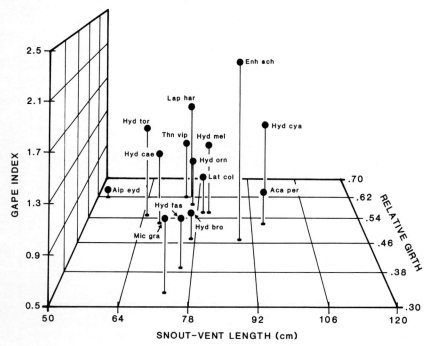

and head size among the anuran-eating species correlated well with the differences in prey type among species (Vitt, 1983).

Voris and Voris (1983) have provided a particularly useful analysis of the morphology of sea snakes relative to dietary differences. First, they have shown that sea snakes do not select prey on the basis of prey species, but rather on the basis of general shape (see Figure 11–8). Characteristics of sea snakes associated with prey acquisition and handling [snout-vent length, relative girth, and a gape index (ratio of length of the quadrate to the width of the parietal bones)] were used to show the separation of these species in morphological space (Figure 11–10). Because the diets were known for the species examined, it was possible to link sea snake morphology with prey types eaten.

I strongly encourage researchers to couple morphological data in studies on snake communities with ecological and behavioral data. The vine snake (Henderson and Binder, 1980) and sea snake analyses (Voris and Voris, 1983) illustrate the utility of such analyses. At the same time, I caution against using morphological data alone for predicting ecological attributes of snakes. Overall, in the absence of ecological data and field observations on the species in question, morphological results could not have been interpreted adequately in any of the studies discussed above.

LIFE-HISTORY DIVERSITY

This discussion will be limited to one specific question related to snake communities: Do all snakes at a given locality (and thus under the same general set of environmental conditions) exhibit the same life-history characteristics?

Temperate Zones

I know of no attempts to examine the diversity of life histories exhibited by any one Temperate Zone snake fauna. However, sufficient studies conducted at a given locality have at least begun to examine this question. Over many years, Henry Fitch and his students have undertaken various studies on snakes at the University of Kansas Natural History Reservation and have shown that (1) oviparous and viviparous species do co-exist, and (2) most species of sympatric snakes at the site produce one litter or clutch per year. The notable differences are in clutch size, and at least some of these differences can be attributed to history (phylogenetic effects) or body size differences among and within species (Dunham and Miles, 1985).

Any generalizations about the diversity of life-history patterns of sympatric snakes in Temperate Zones must be made with caution, particularly at higher latitudes and elevations where the available season for activity and reproduction is short. An overall similarity in reproductive characteristics among these sympatric species may reflect only the overriding effect of a season-length constraint. Differences in life histories associated with lineage, foraging mode, or any other variable may be obscured by the effect of season length.

Tropics

In many tropical habitats, temperature varies relatively little throughout the year, providing a 12-mo thermal season for reproduction and activity. Where seasonality does occur, it is reflected primarily in rainfall. Thus the effects of rainfall and its correlates [presumed higher resource levels associated with wet periods (Janzen and Schoener, 1968)] on the reproductive patterns of sympatric snakes can be evaluated. Unfortunately, few tropical snake communities have been sufficiently studied to critically examine this question. By selecting some of the more complete studies, however, it is possible to show that (1) a diversity of life-history patterns may exist at a given locality, and (2) the primary differences among species in seasonality or reproductive mode appear to be associated with lineage, whereas the primary differences in clutch or brood size appear to be associated with the body size. In a study on two sympatric species of *Philodryas* in northeastern Brazil (Vitt, 1980), it was shown that females produced eggs during a relatively short time period near the end of the tropical dry season. Four species of *Liophis* studied during the same time period at the same locality produced eggs over an extended time period. Three of the species (*L. lineatus, L. poecilogyrus, L. viridis*) produced eggs nearly year-round. Another sympatric genus, *Waglerophis*, produced eggs during 7 mo of the year (Vitt, 1983). Taken together, these data show that a diversity of reproductive strategies exists at one locality. Similar results are apparent in Duellman's (1978) analysis of reproductive data from Santa Cecilia (see also Seigel and Ford, this volume).

SUMMARY AND FUTURE RESEARCH

In reviewing and selecting papers and data for this chapter, it has become clear to me that our current understanding of various aspects of snake communities lags considerably behind that for other groups of vertebrates. In particular, community studies on fishes, small mammals, birds, and lizards have contributed greatly to understanding ecological phenomena of interest to community ecologists, including resource partitioning, patterns of species density and diversity, and trophic structure within and between communities. Snake studies have contributed little to these general areas. This is not to imply that people working with snakes have lagged behind in terms of their ability and insight, but rather that snakes represent a difficult group from which to extract the kinds of data necessary for community analyses. If we take into consideration the difficulty in acquiring data, some snake studies rank comparably with the best lizard, bird, or small-mammal studies (comparative). Among the difficulties I perceive in working with snakes is that, first, the observational data that are easy to collect for birds and lizards are nearly impossible to collect for most snakes. Consequently, accurate information on habitat utilization by snakes is lacking, and categorical data often reflect "gut" feelings based on experience or types of prey found in the snakes (in the latter case, this means that habitat and diet data were not independently gathered). Second, for analyses that require sampling of snakes, it is often difficult to collect large enough samples for adequate statistical treatment. Third, with respect to diet studies, because some snakes feed infrequently on large items, it is sometimes difficult to obtain the necessary samples to ensure that the portion of the samples containing prey are large enough for analyses (but see Mushinsky, this volume). These, of course, are logistical problems, but they are formidable nonetheless. In some cases, particularly in respect to tropical studies, they may be insurmountable. A careful choice of snake communities should be a top priority for those interested in contributing to the testing of extant theory with snake data.

Like most ecologically oriented herpetologists, I would like to believe that competition, past or present, has played at least a partial role in structuring snake communities. Indeed, in most of the studies concerned with resource partitioning, the very basis of these studies is the notion that some sort of competitive interaction has resulted in the observed differences. As in much comparative ecology, we are often faced with data consistent with a competition hypothesis (low overlaps on at least one niche axis), but we have in no way shown that the presence of one species depresses the abundance of another (or ever has), nor have we demonstrated that a resource is limiting.

There is no doubt that we have progressed significantly in attempts to understand what determines the structure of snake communities. The consensus, based on discussions in the reviewed literature and data in most of the literature, is that prey community structure is a major determinant of the structure of snake communities. If certain prey types are unavailable, then the categories of snakes feeding on that prey type will be absent. Unfortunately, I have not found a single study that adequately addresses the question of whether prey abundance is limiting to snake populations. This is a difficult question to approach with snakes for a variety of logistical reasons. Often the prey types eaten by snakes cannot be sampled in any quantitative manner—indeed, new species of small reptiles have been described from the stomachs of snakes. Consequently, we cannot estimate the carrying capacity at any one time. To complicate such an attempt, snakes are capable of fasting for considerable periods of time. Any accurate measure of current prey abundance might have little bearing on the size of a snake population. Populations regulated to seasonal highs in terms of prey density would be entirely overlooked even with intense spot-sampling. The problems in determining the potential role of competition in snake communities have been summarized by Reichenbach and Dalrymple (1980). They indicated that, of the three important parameters necessary for an adequate examination of the potential role of competition (niche overlap, a limiting resource, and reduced reproductive success due to common use of the limited resource), most snake studies include data on two of these at best.

There are several areas of snake community research that I believe could produce significant contributions to our understanding of community ecology in general. First, careful surveys across habitat gradients would allow examination of the determinants of species turnover rates (β diversity). If these surveys were coordinated such that potential prey types for snakes could be determined, even qualitatively, we could then determine whether snake distributions are tracking prey or whether some other factor determines these distributions. If the latter is true, we should see some distinct dietary shifts associated with turnover of prey species along the gradient. Likewise, using the same kinds of data, an examination of snake faunas on different continents would allow an assessment of similarity between faunas in community structure (γ diversity). For example, are snake faunas of the African tropical forest similar to those of the Amazonian tropical forest in terms of guild structure? If so, are there corresponding similarities in the prey spectra?

Capture-recapture studies using effective trapping techniques could provide adequate data for examining the relationships between species number and relative abundance. This approach has met with varying success in the past, partly because the trapping methods often work better on some species than on others. Simultaneous monitoring of resource levels might provide clues as to the determinants of diversity patterns. If such studies were long-term in nature, it might be possible to determine whether snakes cue in to average resource levels, seasonal peaks, or both. It is possible that snake populations are always below carrying capacity because of predation, and consequently, competition may affect snake communities only sporadically. From the point of view of an individual snake, in this situation, resources would always be unlimited. These are important questions to address, and the simple observation of dietary differences among species provides few clues to the underlying mechanisms.

It is difficult to predict whether the necessary data will be forthcoming, at least for very many snake communities. The logistical problems may be solved by experienced field herpetologists and by the use of new and innovative techniques. Unfortunately, many of the prime habitats for exciting field studies on snakes are disappearing rapidly. The needed long-term studies will most likely never be feasible in the tropics because the opening of any road leading to a potentially good field site provides a pathway for hoards of migrating slash-and-burn farmers who have no interest in snakes.

On the more positive side, certain areas in the southwestern desert of the United States provide potential opportunities for long-term studies on snake communities because (1) the communities are relatively simple, (2) most potential prey types can be monitored, (3) because of relatively low habitat diversity, the animals can potentially be located, and (4) carefully chosen sites may remain undisturbed for the duration of the study. Some of the protected reserves, such as the University of Kansas Natural History Reservation and the Savannah River Plant in South Carolina (through the Savannah River Ecology Laboratory), also have the potential for long-term community studies, although the habitat structure is complex enough to increase the logistical problems. Each of the latter localities is advantageous in that there is an existing data base spanning many years.

Finally, there may be some snake communities where experimental manipulations are possible. In desert snake communities where prey can be increased or decreased or snake species removed and populations monitored over long time periods, it might be possible to determine whether resource availability regulates snake populations or whether niche expansion or contraction can occur. This experimental approach provides an opportunity to attempt to determine whether snakes, given their peculiar set of adaptations, respond to the same ecological pressures shown to be important for many other organisms.

ACKNOWLEDGMENTS

A number of people have allowed me to use data, provided literature, or discussed snake ecology with me over the years. The following have been particularly helpful in one way or another: J. Whitfield Gibbons, Raymond D. Semlitsch, Paulo E. Vanzolini, Larry D. Vangilder, Justin D. Congdon, William S. Brown, Richard Shine, Paul Feaver, Donald W. Tinkle, William E. Duellman, and Harry W. Greene. I apologize to anyone I have overlooked. Constructive criticism was provided by Henry Mushinsky and an anonymous reviewer. Financial support for portions of this review were provided by research grants from the UCLA Faculty Senate.

LITERATURE CITED

Arnold, S. J. 1972. Species densities of predators and their prey, *Am. Nat.* 106:220–236.

Arnold, S. J. 1983. Morphology, performance and fitness, *Am. Zool.* 23:347–361.

Auffenberg, W. 1981. The Behavioral Ecology of the Komodo Monitor, University Presses of Florida, Gainesville.

Barbault, R. 1971. Les peuplements d'ophidiens des savanes de Lamto (Cote d'Ivoire), *Ann. Univ. Abidjan Ser. E. Ecol.* IV:133–194.

Brown, J. H. 1973. Species diversity of seed-eating rodents in sand dune habitats, *Ecology* 54:775–787.

Brown, J. H. 1975. Geographical ecology of desert rodents, in: Ecology and Evolution of Communities (M. L. Cody and J. M. Diamond, eds.) pp. 315–341, Belknap Press of Harvard University Press, Cambridge.

Brown, J. H. and Lieberman, G. A. 1973. Resource utilization and coexistence of seed-eating desert rodents in sand dune habitats, *Ecology* 54:788–797.

Brown, W. S. and Parker, W. S. 1982. Niche dimensions and resource partitioning in a Great Basin desert snake community, in: Herpetological Communities (N. J. Scott, Jr., ed.) *U.S. Fish Wildl. Serv. Wildl. Res. Rep.* 13:59–81.

Carpenter, C. C. 1952. Comparative ecology of the common garter snake (*Thamnophis s. sirtalis*), the ribbon snake (*Thamnophis s. sauritus*), and Butler's garter snake (*Thamnophis butleri*) in mixed populations, *Ecol. Monogr.* 22:235–258.

Cody, M. L. 1974. Competition and the Structure of Bird Communities, Princeton University Press, Princeton.

Cody, M. L. 1975. Towards a theory of continental species diversities: Bird distributions over Mediterranean habitat gradients, in: Ecology and Evolution of Communities (M. L. Cody and J. M. Diamond, eds.) pp. 214–257, Belknap Press of Harvard University Press, Cambridge.

Conant, R. 1975. A Field Guide to Reptiles and Amphibians of Eastern and Central North America, 2nd ed., Houghton-Mifflin, Boston.

Diamond, J. M. 1973. Distributional ecology of some New Guinea birds, *Science* 179:759–769.

Diamond, J. M. 1975. Assembly of species communities, in: Ecology and Evolution of Communities, (M. L. Cody and J. M. Diamond, eds.) pp. 342–444, Belknap Press of Harvard University Press, Cambridge.

Dixon, J. R. and Soini, P. 1975. The reptiles of the upper Amazon Basin, Iquitos region, Peru. I. Lizards and amphisbaenians, *Milw. Public Mus. Contrib. Biol. Geol.* 4:1–58.

Dixon, J. R. and Soini, P. 1977. The reptiles of the upper Amazon Basin, Iquitos region, Peru. II. Crocodilians, turtles and snakes, *Milw. Public Mus. Contrib. Biol. Geol.* 12:1–91.

Dobzhansky, T. 1950. Evolution in the tropics. *Am. Sci.* 38:209–221.

Duellman, W. E. 1978. The biology of an equatorial herpetofauna in Amazonian Ecuador, *Univ. Kans. Mus. Nat. Hist. Misc. Publ.* 65:1–352.

Dunham, A. E. and Miles, D. B. 1985. Patterns of covariation in life history traits of squamate reptiles: The effects of size and phylogeny reconsidered, *Am. Nat.* 126:231–257.

Fitch, H. S. 1982. Resources of a snake community in prairie-woodland habitat of northeastern Kansas, in: Herpetological Communities (N. J. Scott, Jr., ed.) *U.S. Fish Wildl. Serv. Wildl. Res. Rep.* 13:83–97.

Fouquette, M. J., Jr. and Lindsay, H. L., Jr. 1955. An ecological survey of reptiles in parts of northwestern Texas, *Tex. J. Sci.* 7:402–421.

Gibbons, J. W. and Patterson, K. K. 1978. The Reptiles and Amphibians of the Savannah River Plant, Dept. of Energy, SRO-NERP-2, Aiken, South Carolina.

Glodek, G. S. and Voris, H. K. 1982. Marine snake diets: Prey composition, diversity and overlap, *Copeia* 1982:661–666.

Greene, H. W. 1983. Dietary correlates of the origin and radiation of snakes, *Am. Zool.* 23:431–441.

Haffer, J. 1969. Speciation in Amazonian forest birds, *Science* 165:131–137.

Hebrard, J. J. and Mushinsky, H. R. 1978. Habitat use by five sympatric snakes in a Louisiana swamp, *Herpetologica* 34:306–311.

Henderson, R. W. and Binder, M. H. 1980. The ecology and behavior of vine snakes: A review, *Milw. Public Mus. Contrib. Biol. Geol.* 37:1–38.

Henderson, R. W., Dixon, J. R., and Soini, P. 1979. Resource partitioning in Amazonian snake communities, *Milw. Public Mus. Contrib. Biol. Geol.* 22:1–11.

Henderson, R. W., Binder, M. H., and Sajdak, R. A. 1981. Ecological relationships of the tree snakes *Uromacer catesbyi* and *U. oxyrhynchus* (Colubridae) on Isla Saona, Republica Dominicana, *Amphib.-Reptilia* 2:153–163.

Huey, R. B., Pianka, E. R., and Schoener, T. W. 1983. Lizard Ecology: Studies of a Model Organism, Harvard University Press, Cambridge.

Hughes, B. 1983. African snake faunas, *Bonn. Zool. Beitr.* 34:311–356.

Hutchinson, G. E. 1959. Homage to Santa Rosalia, or why are there so many kinds of animals?, *Am. Nat.* 93:145–159.

Inger, R. F. and Colwell, R. F. 1977. Organization of contiguous communities of amphibians and reptiles in Thailand, *Ecol. Monogr.* 47:229–253.

Janzen, D. H. and Schoener, T. W. 1968. Differences in insect abundance and diversity between wetter and drier sites during a tropical dry season, *Ecology* 49:96–110.

Karr, J. R. and James, F. C. 1975. Eco-morphological configurations and convergent evolution in species and communities, in: Ecology and Evolution of Communities (M. L. Cody and J. M. Diamond, eds.) pp. 258–291, Belknap Press of Harvard University Press, Cambridge.

Keister, A. R. 1971. Species density of North American amphibians and reptiles, *Syst. Zool.* 20:127–137.

Kushlan, J. A. 1976. Environmental stability and fish community diversity, *Ecology* 57:821–825.

Lee, J. C. 1980. An ecological analysis of the herpetofauna of the Yucatan Peninsula, *Univ. Kans. Mus. Nat. Hist. Misc. Publ.* 67:1–75.

Leston, D. and Hughes, B. 1968. The snakes of Tafo, a forest cocoa-farm locality in Ghana, *Bull. Inst. Fr. Afr. Noire Ser. A Sci. Nat.* 2:737–770.

MacArthur, R. H. 1972. Geographical Ecology, Harper and Row, New York.

McCoy, C. J. 1984. Ecological and zoogeographic relationships of amphibians and reptiles of the Cuatro Cienegas basin, *J. Ariz.-Nev. Acad. Sci.* 19:49–59.

McNab, B. K. 1971. The structure of tropical bat faunas, *Ecology* 52:352–358.

Matthews, W. J. and Hill, L. J. 1980. Habitat partitioning in the fish community of a southwestern river, *Southwest. Nat.* 25:51–66.

Mushinsky, H. R. and Hebrard, J. J. 1977a. Food partitioning by five species of water snakes in Louisiana, *Herpetologica* 33:162–166.

Mushinsky, H. R. and Hebrard, J. J. 1977b. The use of time by sympatric water snakes, *Can. J. Zool.* 55:1545–1550.

Mushinsky, H. R., Hebrard, J. J., and Vodopich, D. S. 1982. Ontogeny of water snake foraging ecology, *Ecology* 63:1624–1629.

Orians, G. H. 1969. The number of bird species in some tropical forests, *Ecology* 50:783–801.

Pianka, E. R. 1969. Sympatry of desert lizards (*Ctenotus*) in western Australia. *Ecology* 50:1012–1030.

Pianka, E. R. 1973. The structure of lizard communities, *Annu. Rev. Ecol. Syst.* 4:53–74.

Pough, F. H. 1966. Ecological relationships of rattlesnakes in southeastern Arizona with notes on other species, *Copeia* 1966:676–683.

Pough, F. H. 1983. Feeding mechanisms, body size, and the ecology and evolution of snakes: Introduction to the symposium, *Am. Zool.* 23:339–342.

Pough, F. H. and Grooves, J. D. 1983. Specializations of the body form and food habits of snakes, *Am. Zool.* 23:443–454.

Quinn, N. J. 1980. Analysis of temporal changes in fish assemblages in Serpentine Creek, Queensland, *Environ. Biol. Fishes* 5:133–177.

Reichenbach, N. G. and Dalrymple, G. H. 1980. On the criteria and evidence for interspecific competition in snakes, *J. Herpetol.* 14:409–412.

Reis, A. C. de S. 1976. Clima da caatinga, *An. Acad. Bras. Cienc.* 48:325–335.

Rogers, J. S. 1976. Species density and taxonomic diversity of Texas amphibians and reptiles, *Syst. Zool* 25:26–40.

Rosenzweig, M. L. and Winakur, J. 1969. Population ecology of desert rodent communities: Habitats and environmental complexity, *Ecology* 50:558–572.

Ross, S. T., Matthews, W. J., and Echelle, A. A. 1985. Persistence of stream fish assemblages: Effects of environmental change, *Am. Nat.* 126:24–40.

Savitzky, A. H. 1983. Coadapted character complexes among snakes: Fossoriality, piscivory, and durophagy, *Am. Zool.* 23:397–409.

Schall, J. J. and Pianka, E. R. 1978. Geographical trends in numbers of species, *Science* 201:679–686.

Schoener, T. W. 1967. The ecological significance of sexual dimorphism in size in the lizard *Anolis conspersus, Science* 155:474–477.

Scott, N. J. 1976. The abundance and diversity of the herpetofaunas of tropical forest litter. *Biotropica* 8:41–58.

Silva, J. L., Valdez, J., and Ojasti, J. 1985. Algunos aspectos de una comunidad de ofidios del norte de Venezuela, *Biotropica* 17:112–115.

Stebbins, R. C. 1954. Amphibians and Reptiles of Western North America, McGraw-Hill, New York.

Sullivan, B. K. 1981. Distribution and relative abundance of snakes along a transect in California. *J. Herpetol.* 15:247–248.

Toft, C. A. 1985. Resource partitioning in amphibians and reptiles, *Copeia* 1985:1–21.

Vanzolini, P. E. and Williams, E. E. 1970. South American Anoles: The geographic differentiation and evolution of the *Anolis chrysolepis* species group (Sauria, Iguanidae), *Arq. Zool. São Paulo* 19:1–298.

Vitt, L. J. 1980. Ecological observations on sympatric *Philodryas* (Colubridae) in northeastern Brazil, *Pap. Avulsos Zool. (São Paulo).* 34:87–98.

Vitt, L. J. 1983. Ecology of an anuran-eating guild of terrestrial tropical snakes, *Herpetologica* 39:52–66.

Vitt, L. J. and Ohmart, R. D. 1978. Herpetofauna of the lower Colorado River: Davis Dam to the Mexican border, *Proc. West. Found. Vertebr. Zool.* 2:33–72.

Vitt, L. J. and Vangilder, L. D. 1983. Ecology of a snake community in northeastern Brazil, *Amphib.-Reptilia* 4:273–296.

Vitt, L. J., Van Loben Sels, R. C., and Ohmart, R. D. 1981. Ecological relationships among arboreal desert lizards, *Ecology* 62:398–410.

Voris, H. K. 1972. The role of sea snakes (Hydrophiidae) in the trophic structure of coastal ocean communities, *J. Mar. Biol. Assoc. India* 14:429–442.

Voris, H. K. 1977. A phylogeny of sea snakes (Hydrophiidae), *Fieldiana Zool.* 70:79–169.

Voris, H. K. and Voris, H. H. 1983. Feeding strategies in marine snakes: An analysis of evolutionary, morphological, behavioral and ecological relationships, *Am. Zool.* 23:411–425.

CHAPTER TWELVE

Spatial Patterns and Movements

Patrick T. Gregory
J. Malcolm Macartney
Karl W. Larsen

Spatial pattern, or dispersion, reflects many aspects of a species' ecology and has important consequences of its own. For example, the spacing pattern of a population of animals may reflect behavioral interactions among individuals (Brown and Orians, 1970; Waser and Wiley, 1979) or the physicochemical heterogeneity of the environment (Allee, 1931). Spatial arrangements of both predators and prey are important components of predator-prey interactions (e.g., Hamilton, 1971; Wood, 1985). A major role for dispersion is implicit in Wilson's (1980) concept of structured demes, in relation to group selection. Dispersion also has clear implications for population dynamics; the effects of spatial variation in density (and therefore in density-dependent effects) may be profound (Gill, 1978), and territoriality plays a role, even if indirect, in population density limitation in some species (Wynne-Edwards, 1962; Brown and Orians, 1970). Lloyd (1967) suggests that the way the "patchiness" of a population changes with variations in population density allows us to make inferences about the kinds of factors that affect population size (density-independent versus density-dependent). Spatial variation in abundance also affects the precision with which population parameters such as overall density can be estimated (Pielou, 1974).

For mobile animals, any treatment of dispersion also must include consideration of movement patterns and the factors that affect them, because movements of individuals are the means by which specific dispersion patterns are achieved or change with time (Pielou, 1977).

The objectives of this chapter are to review what is known about dispersion and movements in snakes, to elucidate general patterns, and to suggest directions for further research. A review of these phenomena in snakes is opportune for two reasons. First, such information has never been brought together for snakes, so that such an exercise should increase our knowledge of snakes per se. Migratory movements of snakes have been summarized by Gregory (1982, 1984), but these do not represent the full spectrum of movements undertaken by snakes, and a solid theoretical foundation is lacking. Second, and in a broader context, any general, comprehensive theory about spatial patterns and movements requires empirical information from a wide range of taxa. Without this, one's perception of general phenomena is very much colored by the peculiarities of a few well-studied groups. Snakes are interesting because they are ectotherms, and much of their ecology and behavior is therefore controlled by the physical environment, and because they are widely regarded as relatively asocial animals (Brattstrom, 1974; see SNAKE BEHAVIOR AND COMMUNICATION). Thus they are quite different animals from, say, birds, on which many of our ideas about spacing patterns are based (e.g., Brown and Orians, 1970; Waser and Wiley, 1979).

SPATIAL PATTERNS

Kinds of Patterns and Their Measurement

Patterns of arrangement of individuals in space may be classified into one of three general categories (Hutchinson, 1953; Pielou, 1977): random, overdispersed, or aggregated. Such categories may be combined in complex hierarchies of pattern (Pielou, 1977). In a random arrangement, each individual acts independently of all others and its position in space is therefore not influenced by the positions of other individuals. On the other hand, overdispersed animals are more evenly spaced than would be expected by chance; the position of any individual is affected by the positions of others. Animals arranged in an aggregated pattern show the opposite effect in that individuals are more closely spaced than would be expected by chance (i.e., they form "clumps"); again, at least in a statistical sense, individuals affect each other's positions.

Measurement of the spatial pattern of animals, especially mobile animals such as snakes, inevitably presents problems. There is no universal index of pattern (Pielou, 1977), but two useful ones are the variance/mean ratio (Pielou, 1977), and Lloyd's (1967) index of patchiness, both derived from counts per sampling unit. In any statistical study of dispersion, special consideration must be given to choice of index, size of sampling unit, and spatial scale on which dispersion is being measured (Pielou, 1977). Of additional importance is the related question of population density, which may confound the interpretation of pattern (Lloyd, 1967; Pielou, 1977). If, for example, density is low, the measured dispersion of the population might be statistically indistinguishable from random, even though the animals would not occupy the environment in a random fashion if they were abundant enough to interact with each other.

Designing field studies to measure spatial arrangements of snakes, their relationships to factors such as population density, and their variation in time and space will be a challenge for ecologists. So far as we can determine, the dispersion of snakes has never been studied explicitly in the field. Such lack of study is hardly surprising, as snakes are difficult subjects in this respect. Much of this difficulty is attributable to their generally secretive nature. In addition, many species are small or are small when young, making random sampling an elusive ideal in most cases. Nevertheless, there are many published observations germane to a discussion of spatial arrangements of snakes.

Snake Behavior and Communication

Social mechanisms obviously are involved both in the spacing behavior of territorial animals (Waser and Wiley, 1979) and in the aggregative behavior of animals that live in groups (Wilson, 1975). It is in fact difficult to imagine a spatial arrangement in vertebrates that does not have some component of social behavior. Animals that aggregate simply because they are attracted to the same physical conditions rather than to each other must still be able to tolerate one another's presence and may maintain minimum inter- individual distances within aggregations (Conder, 1949; Wilson, 1975).

Snakes may well be less social than most other vertebrates (Brattstrom, 1974), but recent reviews reveal a diversity of snake behavior (Gillingham, this volume). Chemosensory organs, especially the vomeronasal organ, play a leading role in conspecific recognition among snakes (e.g., Halpern and Kubie, 1984; Ford, 1986) and therefore in social interactions. Snakes also have the ability to recognize individuals of other species in some cases (Froese, 1980), especially potentially predatory species (e.g., Weldon and Schell, 1984); clearly, such an ability can influence spatial patterns.

Spatial Patterns in Snakes

Should Snakes Be Dispersed at Random? It is worth considering, at the outset, the extent to which we can expect random patterns of dispersion to occur in nature in general and among snakes in particular. A truly random pattern requires that the animals be completely asocial and that the environment be completely homogeneous with respect to critical resources. Few, if any, mobile animals meet the former criterion, and most environments cannot be considered homogeneous over any significant expanse of space. *A priori,* then, one would predict that snakes will not show random patterns of spatial arrangement except on a temporary basis or at very low population densities.

Evidence for Spacing in Snakes. Spacing patterns of animals depend on the spatial and temporal distribution of resources; dispersion is therefore related to the problem of optimal foraging, whether the resource in question is food, a mate, or a basking site. However, as Waser and Wiley (1979) point out, several factors other than the spatiotemporal distribution of resources are important in determining spatial patterns of animals, and there is no simple relationship between the dispersion of animals and that of their resources.

A central concept in any consideration of spacing patterns is territory. Territoriality has been well reviewed by Brown and Orians (1970), Wilson (1975), and Waser and Wiley (1979). We adopt here Noble's (1939) definition of territory as "any defended area." Thus territory need not be fixed in space but can move if the resource being defended also moves. Defense can involve agonistic behavior or signals of various types (Waser and Wiley, 1979). Obviously, the resource, besides being in limited supply, must be economically defendable (Brown and Orians, 1970).

There is little evidence of territorial behavior in snakes. There is no known case of snakes defending a food supply, although Sutherland (1958) describes "combat dances" in male *Crotalus horridus* in the presence of individual food items. Most suspected cases of territorial behavior in snakes involve defense of either a mate or a nest. Carpenter (1984) identified several apparent cases of temporary territorial defense of mates, with the retreat of "losers" and the mating of "winners." Females of some Asiatic elapid species are known to brood their eggs or to stay in the general vicinity of their nest and act aggressively toward intruders (Lowe and Norris, 1950; Oliver, 1956). Whether this can be extended easily to territorial defense against intruding conspecifics is doubtful (Lowe and Norris, 1950). There are two isolated references in the literature to territorial-like behavior of colubrid snakes without any obvious resource being contested (McCauley, 1945, cited in Fitch, 1963a; Kennedy, 1965). In both cases, one snake chased another away when the latter approached the former's site. Space per se might be a valuable resource (for basking or shelter) and might be defendable against conspecifics. There are no definite instances of snakes defending space for such a purpose, but *Vipera berus* maintain spacing without obvious aggression during the non-feeding basking period shortly after emergence from hibernation (Viitanen, 1967; Prestt, 1971).

If snakes do hold territories, they apparently do so for a specific purpose and only for a short time. Furthermore, such territories are probably often not fixed in location and involve a very small area. It therefore seems more useful, in most cases, to consider snakes as merely maintaining an individual distance (Conder, 1949; Wilson, 1975) that changes with circumstances. At times, such as during hibernation, individual distance may collapse to zero.

Maintenance of individual distance might play a role in the foraging behavior of snakes. One prediction is that a foraging snake will avoid an area being used, or one recently used, by a conspecific because that conspecific has caused a "resource depression" in the area (Charnov et al., 1976). Solitary foraging by snakes would therefore be achieved by mutual avoidance without the risk and expenditure of energy involved in territorial defense, provided that appropriate signals could be transmitted and received. Such signals well might be olfactory, because they could then operate, despite their limitations (Waser and Wiley, 1979), in the absence of the signaling animal. However, the evidence for avoidance of conspecific odors by snakes is scant (Porter and Czaplicki, 1974; King et al., 1983). Other senses could be involved. Lawson (1985) showed that *Thamnophis radix* avoided food trails where both visual and olfactory stimuli (but not either alone) of conspecifics were also present and chose food trails alone. However, a foraging snake needs to avoid conspecifics (and heterospecifics) only when those other individuals will cause its foraging success to be lowered significantly. Thus snakes should assess prey availability as well as the presence or absence of other snakes.

We suspect that, for most snakes, spatiotemporal variation in food availability is significant. If so, snakes should have activity ranges that overlap considerably, with individuals forming temporary aggregations where food is highly concentrated (Waser and Wiley, 1979; see SNAKE AGGREGATIONS). There is little evidence of mutually exclusive activity ranges of conspecific snakes in either space or time (see MOVEMENTS AND HOME RANGES), although recent work on *Pituophis melanoleucus* in Nebraska suggests that individuals occupy non-overlapping ranges when active (J. Fox, personal observation). Spacing of snakes in general probably occurs on such a small spatial scale that it is ordinarily undetectable except at locally high levels of snake density.

Snake Aggregations. Aggregations of snakes often have been noted in the field and laboratory. The term "aggregation," as used here, is subjective, because it is usually not based on any statistical measure. However, aggregations of snakes are so obvious that there is no reason to doubt their reality. An aggregation is any concentration of snakes in a relatively small area such that the density of snakes in the aggregation contrasts sharply with that in the surrounding area. There is no necessary implication of physical contact among the snakes in the aggregation, but this may occur.

Aggregations of animals (usually conspecific, although not always) may occur for two reasons. The most parsimonious explanation is that the individuals involved are simply attracted to a common site that offers conditions favorable for a particular function (e.g., basking). Presumably, such sites must be in limited supply, or be particularly favorable compared with other sites, for aggregation to occur. Thus aggregation formation is a result of habitat selection.

An alternative to habitat selection hypotheses of aggregation formation is that animals aggregate because they are attracted to one another; i.e., animals in groups derive individual benefits that they would not have if isolated. This may not be obvious in the field if suitable aggregating sites are limited or vary in some important quality; thus the two hypotheses are not mutually exclusive. Lloyd (1967) distinguished between aggregations as accumulations (resulting from a common response to environmental conditions) and as congregations (resulting from mutual attraction). However, we agree with Burghardt (1983) that "aggregation" should be used as a descriptive term to cover a wide range of phenomena seen in snakes, at least for the time being.

Nevertheless, snake aggregations fall into a number of major categories; most are of a seasonal or short-term nature. Foraging snakes may be concentrated at sites where prey abundance or availability is high (e.g., Prater, 1933; Wharton, 1969; Arnold and Wassersug, 1978; P. T. Gregory, unpublished observations). Many species of snakes aggregate in winter at communal hibernacula (see review by Gregory, 1984). Snakes also often aggregate when mating (e.g., Finneran, 1949; Tinkle and Liner, 1955; Aleksiuk and Gregory, 1974). The gravid females of many species of snakes aggregate (Matheson, 1962; Hibbard, 1964; Gordon and Cook, 1980; Henderson et al., 1980; Plummer, 1981a; Reichenbach, 1983; Duvall et al., 1985), sometimes leading to communal oviposition in oviparous species. Myers (1945) speculated that a large concentration of young sea snakes, *Pelamis platurus,* might have resulted from communal birth. In contrast, Noble and Clausen (1936) singled out gravid *Storeria dekayi* as being non-gregarious, despite the fact that this species is highly gregarious otherwise. However, Noble and Clausen apparently considered snakes to be aggregated only if they were in physical contact (as did Burghardt, 1983); physical contact does not necessarily occur in reported aggregations of gravid snakes of other species. Physical contact (or huddling) is usually a component of an aggregation of snakes under stressful physical conditions (Noble and Clausen, 1936; Myers and Eells, 1968; Aleksiuk, 1977). Some isolated reports of snake concentrations in the field seem to have no features in common with any of these examples and no obvious explanation (Slevin, 1950; McCoy, 1960).

There is evidence in some species of an "aggregative drive" (e.g., Noble and Clausen, 1936; Dundee and Miller, 1968; Heller and Halpern, 1982a; Burghardt, 1983). Although vision is involved in some cases (Noble and Clausen, 1936; Heller and Halpern, 1982a; Burghardt, 1983), the chemical senses appear to play the leading role in the formation of aggregations in these species. Noble and Clausen (1936) maintained that olfaction is the major chemoreceptive sense involved in aggregative behavior, but Heller and Halpern (1982a) justifiably criticized their sensory deprivation techniques and showed that the vomeronasal organ played the major chemosensory role, at least in *Thamnophis sirtalis*.

Communal oviposition and aggregation of female snakes may be chemically mediated (Plummer, 1981a; Ford, 1986). Such phenomena occur even where apparently identical sites are found throughout the habitat (Fitch, 1958; Plummer, 1981a). If so, they are not merely a consequence of habitat heterogeneity. However, critical evaluation of alternative site availability has not been made in most reports of aggregative behavior in snakes. One must beware of assessing site suitability on the basis of a superficial examination. For example, winter temperature data collected by K. W. Larsen (unpublished data) indicate that suitable snake hibernacula in northern Canada may be very limited despite the superficial impression of an abundance of sites. Thus we need careful studies to separate the effects of habitat heterogeneity from those of aggregative behavior.

Burghardt (1983) suggested that the response to a site where another snake has been ("habitat conditioning") is a component of aggregation separate from the response to another individual snake. The former might explain perennial use of particular sites even when alternative sites apparently are available (e.g., Magnusson and Lima, 1984). Perennial nesting (e.g., Foley, 1971; Covacevich and Limpus, 1972; Parker and Brown, 1972) and denning (Gregory, 1984) sites are known in snakes but have not been examined from this point of view. Temporary aggregation and perennial use of a site are related but not necessarily equivalent.

What do individual animals gain by aggregating with others? This is an interesting question because aggregating might be expected to increase the risk of predation. Not only might a large group be more conspicuous to a predator, but an individual in the group would have a heightened chance of being detected once any other individual is detected. Often, however, there must be a low risk that the predator will take all the individuals in a group; while the predator is handling one prey, the remainder can escape. Thus, in a sense, aggregation is merely cover-seeking behavior, even when actual physical cover is not involved (the "selfish herd," Hamilton, 1971). Perhaps gravid female snakes gain such anti-predator advantages (Shine, 1979). Their reduced mobility would make them, as individuals, easy targets for most predators. Consequently, they often are found where there is a combination of suitable basking sites and shelter (Gregory, 1975). A predator that comes upon a large group of such animals is likely to catch one or two of them, but the remainder have a good chance of escaping. Similar considerations might apply to aggregations of moulting snakes (*Crotalus viridis:* J. M. Macartney, unpublished observations); if vision is impaired by this process, individuals may gain by being in a group. However, this advantage does not accrue to eggs in communal nests, especially if nest sites are used perennially, making the location of eggs predictable to predators. There is no obvious advantage to communal nesting in homogeneous habitats (Plummer, 1981a).

Aggregations in which the individuals huddle in close physical contact occur for different reasons. Noble and Clausen (1936) showed that *Storeria dekayi* and *Thamnophis butleri* had a lower weight loss (probably mainly water) at high temperatures when huddled than when isolated. Other authors have hypothesized that snakes cluster together to reduce water loss (Thomas, 1965; Duvall et al.,

1985). Thus tight aggregations should be expected under desiccating conditions because of the reduced surface area/mass ratio of the aggregation compared with that of a single individual. Similarly, snakes should form clusters under cold conditions to retain heat (Myers and Eells, 1968; Aleksiuk, 1977). White and Lasiewski (1971) suggested that communally hibernating snakes huddle when underground to maintain a high body temperature. However, although huddled snakes lose heat less quickly than isolated ones (Myers and Eells, 1968), they do so much too quickly for this to be of any value in hibernation. It is more likely a means of escaping short-term cool conditions (e.g., overnight). Furthermore, the need to conserve energy over a long period suggests that snakes should not hibernate at too high a body temperature (Gregory, 1982). Communally hibernating snakes are sometimes known to form tight clusters (Gregory, 1982), but it seems more likely that they do so to conserve moisture. The huddling behavior of *Thamnophis* and *Storeria* in the laboratory experiments of Heller and Halpern (1982a,b) and Burghardt (1983) remains without functional explanation.

Predators often aggregate temporarily at sites of high prey availability (e.g., Wood, 1985). This is called the "aggregative numerical response" (Readshaw, 1973). For such feeding aggregations to occur, predators need not forage in groups nor be attracted to other feeding individuals. If the discovery of a prey item causes an individual predator to change its search pattern and spend more time in a particular area, then aggregation of predators is simply a consequence of all of them doing so independently (Readshaw, 1973); as prey become less abundant, the stimulus to stay decreases, and the predators disperse. If snakes behave as "ideal free" individuals (i.e., make independent assessments of the profitability of a given patch of food), then individuals should distribute themselves among patches of food in the ratio of the profitabilities of the patches and therefore equalize the payoff per individual (Harper, 1982). It is unlikely that snakes are perfectly ideal free animals, but they are minimally social, so that this model might be reasonably descriptive if alternative patches are within easy cruising range of individual snakes. A variant of the feeding aggregation phenomenon is shown by the sea snake, *Pelamis platurus*. This species is often seen aggregated in "slicks" with flotsam (Dunson and Ehlert, 1971; Kropach, 1971; Tu, 1976). Apparently the snakes arrive in these aggregations through passive drifting. Fish, on which *Pelamis* feeds, are attracted to slicks; Kropach (1971) found that most snakes in slicks were full of food, while those away from slicks contained no food.

Interesting questions abound. *Diadophis punctatus* is a highly gregarious species, but the only significant study of aggregation in this species failed to suggest any clear advantage to such behavior (Dundee and Miller, 1968). The numerous aggregation phenomena observed in snakes and the well-developed body of theory relating to spacing and aggregation make this a fertile area for future studies on snake ecology.

MOVEMENTS AND HOME RANGES

Introductory Comments

Movements are presumably costly—either energetically or in terms of risk of predation. Animals should therefore move only when necessary. The extent of an animal's movements is dependent on the availability of resources and their distribution in space, as well as the animal's needs at a particular time. Although we can observe movements of animals, we usually have little more than a rudimentary understanding of what motivates animals to move where they do when they do. This is because: (1) we have an incomplete understanding of an animal's needs; (2) we seldom measure the availability of required resources; and (3) given that we could measure resource availability, our perception of availability may not be the same as that of the animal.

In this section we have attempted to summarize the current state of knowledge concerning movement patterns and home range in snakes. Information on these phenomena in snakes ranges from anecdotal observations to detailed studies aimed at addressing specific questions about habitat use; hence the quality of information varies widely among studies. For many taxa we know nothing at all about these subjects. Most of the literature deals with Temperate Zone snakes.

Patterns of Movements in Snakes

Guibé and Saint Girons (1955) recognized two categories of reptiles based on the use of space: (1) erratics, which wander randomly, sometimes over large and poorly delineated areas; and (2) sedentary forms, whose activities are restricted to small areas within which there may or may not be centers of activity. Both types occur in snakes, and the distinction between them may depend on resource availability. For example, erratic movements are expected where resources are patchy and unpredictable (e.g., desert forms: Brown, 1971). Sedentary behavior should occur where resources are abundant and predictable (e.g., Naulleau, 1966; Barbour et al., 1969; Goddard, 1980).

Clearly, however, these categories are inadequate to describe the full spectrum of snake movement patterns. When different resources are required at different times and when these resources are widely separated in space, snakes must move between them. A good example of such a situation is that of communally denning snakes, which often move long distances from a hibernaculum to summer habitat and then back (Gregory, 1984), but other examples exist (see Gregory, 1982). The area between the two seasonal habitats may be used only for travel (e.g., Duvall et al., 1985), or animals may localize their activities at particular sites as the season progresses (e.g., Brown and Parker, 1976; *Crotalus viridis:* P. Dumas, personal communication). In some cases, snakes make a loop-like migration, eventually returning to their starting point (e.g., the hibernaculum) with little backtracking (e.g., Madsen, 1984; Macartney, 1985; *Thamnophis sirtalis:* K. W. Larsen, unpublished data).

"Migration," as used here, refers exclusively to seasonal movements of snakes between different habitats. In the literature, "migration" is often used synonymously with "dispersal" (e.g., Gregory, 1984), but the two terms actually have different meanings. Dispersal is any act that increases the mean distance between individual members of the population, while migration, in its simplest form, refers to movements of an individual or group from one spatial unit to another (Baker, 1978). Migration is therefore not equivalent to dispersal if all animals travel as a unit. However, in communally denning snakes, spring migrations lead to increased dispersion on the summer range relative to the winter habitat and can thus be regarded as dispersals; the return autumn migration, on the other hand, results in convergence on the den. Parker and Brown (1980) used the term "remigration" for these regularly repeated seasonal movements. Pielou (1977) used "dispersal" (or "diffusion"), in a more restricted way, to describe the spreading movement of animals away from a central point. Diffusion models may be useful in describing the movement of young animals away from a birthplace (Murray, 1967), about which nothing is known in snakes.

Non-migratory interpopulation movements have been recorded only occasionally for adult snakes. Kephart (1981) found little evidence of movements of garter snakes among populations; instances of individuals switching communal dens, which may or may not function as demes, are also relatively uncommon (Gregory, 1984). In both cases, exchanges seem most frequent between nearby populations.

These various patterns of movements probably are not discrete categories, but points along a continuum. Combinations of the various types also exist. It also would be prudent to avoid labeling particular species as exhibiting particular kinds of movements. Different populations of the same species (and different sexes, ages, etc., within a population) exhibit different kinds of movement behavior under different circumstances.

Methods and Concepts

Various techniques have been used to study snake movements. Track following has limited application but has been used for a few species (Mermod, 1970; Michael, 1971; see review by Lillywhite, 1982). Mark-recapture records frequently have been used (e.g., Blanchard and Finster, 1933; Gregory and Stewart, 1975) and are well suited to describing general movement patterns of a population, but they yield little information on the details of individual movements. Radioisotope tagging has been used in a few studies (Naulleau and Courtois, 1965; Barbour et al., 1969; Hirth et al., 1969; Smith, 1971) but, because snakes cannot be distinguished individually, this technique merely facilitates locating snakes. It may be especially useful for studying small or juvenile snakes (e.g.,

Smith, 1971), which are more difficult to find by other means. Individual movements of larger snakes probably can be studied best by radiotelemetry (e.g., Fitch and Shirer, 1971; Reinert and Kodrich, 1982). These methods are reviewed elsewhere in this volume by Fitch.

Movements are difficult to summarize because of their multidimensional nature. At least five measurements can be recorded for any movement: (1) distance, (2) direction, (3) elevational change, (4) time elapsed since last location, and (5) actual path or route. From these variables, additional descriptors of movements may be calculated (e.g., rates of movements, angular dispersion, and areas or volumes of home ranges). These variables in turn may be summarized in any number of biologically relevant or arbitrarily chosen ways, such as on a temporal basis (daily, weekly, seasonal), in some behavioral or functional context (e.g., oviposition, mating, foraging), in relation to an attribute of the individual (sex, size or age, reproductive condition), or combinations of these. Thus in any given study we not only may recognize several types of movements, but a spectrum of variables that can be used to describe them. Analyses and presentation of data also differ widely between studies. Mean displacement, for example, has been summarized in studies of snakes in at least four ways: (1) distance between captures, (2) distance per move, (3) distance from a particular site, and (4) distance between first and last capture. Movements are usually presented as arithmetic means, but geometric means also have been reported (Clark, 1974). Distances are usually measured as straight lines between location points, but the longer the interval between captures, the greater the possibility for underestimation of the true extent or rate of movement.

There is no standardized way to summarize movement data to help reduce this multidimensionality or make the results of individual studies more comparable. It is not our aim to suggest a standardized method for collection or presentation of such data, because different methods are required to suit various needs. However, a useful measure that has come largely from radiotelemetry studies is distance per move. Because a move has a start and an end, it may be a useful common currency for movement studies. The relative sizes of distance per move (excluding intervals lacking movement) and distance moved per day or other time unit (including time units when no movements are made) may provide a valuable index of the vagility of an individual. These measures are directly comparable across season, sex, species, etc. (e.g., Parker and Brown, 1980).

Home Range

What Is a Home Range? A home range is an integrated expression of an animal's location and movements over a specific time interval. However, the lack of a unified approach to defining a home range has led to some confusion. For example, in the snake literature alone, we noted six different terms that have been used to describe various forms of home range (activity range: Carpenter, 1952; Reinert and Kodrich, 1982; total range: Hirth et al., 1969; home range: Stickel and Cope, 1947; Brown and Parker, 1976; limited movement area: Goddard, 1980; total home range and combined home range: Madsen, 1984). Some of these labels refer to different patterns of movement within a home range (e.g., with or without a center of activity: Fitch, 1958), while others have specific quantitative meanings.

The term "home range" is often taken to imply familiarity with or repeated use of a particular area, suggesting an inherent ability to home (return) to such sites if displaced. These connotations may not have been intentional in Burt's (1943) original selection of the term "home range," but they clearly have become infused into the concept of home range in snakes (e.g., Carpenter, 1952; Barbour et al., 1969; Fraker, 1970). However, the absence of homing ability does not mean that specific home ranges are not occupied. A distinction should be made, therefore, between the ability to home and the existence of a home range.

One's view of a home range is influenced strongly by the method of data collection. Hirth et al. (1969) recorded movements of a large number of *Coluber constrictor* using radioisotope tagging, observed that these snakes wandered extensively, and concluded that they did not possess home ranges, using the criterion of Stickel and Cope (1947) that snakes with home ranges are sedentary or tend to return to previous capture points. They advocated the use of the term "total range," which encompasses the area used for all seasonal movements, including those involved in travel to and from a hibernaculum. In a more thorough study of the same population, Brown and Parker (1976) recognized small, discrete areas of summer use by intensive tracking of a few individuals with radiotelemetry. Furthermore, they showed that some snakes returned to the same general area in successive summers. Consequently, they considered Brown and Orian's (1970) more restrictive definition of home range (which excludes seasonal migrations and erratic wanderings) the most appropriate description of home range in that species.

We feel that "home range" and other such terms should be viewed only as convenient labels to describe the area covered by an animal in the course of its normal daily activities during a specified time period. We recognize that this area may change in location, size, or shape over time and that the use of particular sites within the area also may vary over time, but applying different names to each category only obscures the main purpose of collecting such data, namely, to determine objectively the spatiotemporal dispersion of an individual in its environment.

Home Range Measurements. The two principal methods used to calculate home range size in snakes are the circle method (Fitch, 1958) and the convex polygon method (Jennrich and Turner, 1969). The circle method uses the mean distance between captures of an individual as an estimate of the diameter of an average circular home range. This method has been shown to overestimate substantially home range size as calculated by convex polygon procedures (Jennrich and Turner, 1969; Rose, 1982) and has largely been abandoned in favor of the latter. The convex polygon method yields a more satisfactory description of the area used by an individual because it is based only on actual sightings; however, it is extremely sensitive to sample size bias and tends to underestimate home range size if only a few locations are known. Jennrich and Turner (1969) developed a correction factor to adjust for sample size bias, but use of this factor requires that particular assumptions about the distributions of movements and locations within the home range be made. Correction factors applied to data that do not meet these assumptions produce inflated home range estimates (Rose, 1982). Adjusted home ranges are commonly reported for snakes, but we could find no studies in which the assumptions were tested before the corrections were applied, and in some studies only adjusted home ranges were reported (e.g., Reinert and Kodrich, 1982). Some authors appear to use the correction factor to compensate for different sample sizes for individuals within a study before performing statistical tests (Goddard, 1980; Reinert and Kodrich, 1982). In other cases, the recurrent inappropriate use of correction factors may not reflect ignorance of the problem so much as a desire to make measurements comparable to previous work (Shine and Lambeck, 1985). We stress that future workers should avoid inappropriate use of the correction factor; otherwise, this problem will be perpetuated. Excellent critiques of methods of home range measurements are provided by Schoener (1981) and Rose (1982), and the reader is referred to their articles for a detailed discussion. Rose (1982) also discussed empirical methods for determining the number of sample points needed to describe home ranges adequately.

Although home range area is an attractively simple index of the two-dimensional space traversed by an animal, it conveys no information about an animal's actual use of space (Waser and Wiley, 1979). Attempts have been made to make home ranges reflect such use more accurately. For example, Nickerson et al. (1978) calculated the three-dimensional home range (volume) for an arboreal neotropical snake. Other workers have noted that home ranges calculated by convex polygons often include areas never used by snakes (Naulleau, 1966; Fitch and Shirer, 1971; Madsen, 1984). Madsen (1984) computed a "combined home range" for *Natrix natrix* by summing the areas of smaller parcels of the home range, which corresponded to monthly uses of a larger area. A similar approach was taken by Brown and Parker (1976).

Shape and intensity of use are also important properties of a home range and may provide more biologically relevant information about an individual's use of space than area alone. Waser and Wiley (1979) proposed the term "activity field," defined as an individual's time as a function of location, as a more informative means of describing spatial distribution of an individual. The value of an individual's activity field at any point is the proportion of time spent there in all activities. The end result is a home range map showing spatial distribution and intensity of use.

Such utilization distribution maps are not unlike the illustrations of locations determining home ranges that have been reported by some snake researchers (Barbour et al., 1969; Fitch and Shirer, 1971; Brown and Parker, 1976; Madsen, 1984). The latter actually may impart more information about use of space because they preserve sequential information. For example, showing location sequence may convey information on seasonal habitat selection or enable one to determine whether individual home ranges overlap in both time and space. Many recent researchers have studied movements in order to obtain an understanding of seasonal patterns of habitat use (Reinert and Kodrich, 1982; Madsen, 1984; Shine and Lambeck, 1985; Weatherhead and Charland, 1985); this is a step beyond simply reporting movements and home range sizes.

Factors Influencing Movements and Home Ranges

General Comments. Space prohibits inclusion of a detailed tabular summary of available information on home range and movements of snakes and their relationship to various factors. A survey of such data for nearly 50 snake populations (J. M. Macartney et al., unpublished observations) shows that home range estimates for various snakes vary between 0.0009 and 34.5 ha. Migratory movements of snakes are summarized by Gregory (1982, 1984).

Comparisons among studies (inter- or intraspecific, e.g., Parker and Brown, 1980; Plummer, 1981b; Reinert and Kodrich, 1982; Shine and Lambeck, 1985) are plagued by dissimilar methodologies and variable quality of information, making it difficult to interpret differences or discern general patterns. Information on movements and home range may be very useful in understanding the biology of a species at a particular site, but caution clearly should be exercised when attempting to infer trends from a wide variety of studies. Here we consider mainly factors that influence movements and home range within a study, because at least the methodology is consistent, and make only modest comparison among studies.

Effects of Sex and Reproductive Activities. There is no definite trend for snakes of one sex to make more extensive movements or have larger home range areas than those of the other in general, although there are intersexual differences associated with reproductive activities. In some studies data are available for only one sex, while in others either no distinction is made between sexes (or between gravid and nongravid females) or differences are not tested statistically. Where data for both sexes have been collected and differences tested, most studies have not found significant differences in movements or home range size (Clark, 1970, 1974; Freedman and Catling, 1979; Goddard, 1980; Plummer, 1981b; Michot, 1981; Reinert and Kodrich, 1982). Many studies suggesting greater home range size in males lack credibility because they either used the circle method or did not test differences (Fitch, 1958, 1960, 1963a,b, 1965; Naulleau, 1968). There apparently has been only one study in which females were shown to have significantly larger home range areas than males (Madsen, 1984).

Reproductive activities strongly influence movements during part or all of the active season. Extensive and frequent movements by males, relative to females, during the breeding period have been related to mate-searching activity (Viitanen, 1967; Prestt, 1971; Parker and Brown, 1980; Madsen, 1984; Duvall et al., 1985). Females have been reported to travel rapidly over long distances to reach oviposition sites (Parker and Brown, 1972; Madsen, 1984). However, females often reduce their movements when gravid and remain in restricted areas (Viitanen, 1967; Keenlyne, 1972; Shine, 1979; Brown et al., 1982; Reinert and Kodrich, 1982; see SNAKE AGGREGATIONS), occupying home ranges different from those used when non-gravid (Goddard, 1980; Macartney, 1985). Gravid female rattlesnakes sometimes move short distances between basking sites (Sehman, 1977; Brown et al., 1982; Macartney, 1985), perhaps thereby making their location less predictable to predators.

Effects of Age and Size. Too little is known about the movements of neonate or juvenile snakes to reach any general conclusions at this time. Some authors believe that juveniles wander haphazardly without occupying any form of home range (Fitch, 1949; P. Dumas, Personal communication). Studies of newborn snakes have shown that movements are variable but not particularly extensive (Smith, 1971; Saint Girons, 1981). The first major movements of some neonate snakes occur between the birth site and a hibernaculum (e.g., Duvall et al., 1985; Macartney, 1985).

One might expect that, within species, the size of a snake would affect the extent of its average daily movements, because vagility should increase with size, as noted by Clark (1970, 1974). However, dispersal distances or distances between captures for juveniles have been shown to be as variable and as great as those for adults (Fitch, 1960; Clark, 1974; Macartney, 1985). Viitanen (1967) suggested that the range of movements from the hibernaculum increases with size and age in *Vipera berus,* but his data are not very convincing. For other species no correlation has been found between body length (or weight) and distance moved (Fraker, 1970) or home range size (Barbour et al., 1969; Goddard, 1980; Michot, 1981). Certainly, one area where we need more research is in the movements of young snakes.

Habitat Structure and Resource Availability. Perhaps the most obvious and most important factors that affect movement patterns and home ranges are extrinsic: habitat structure and resource availability. Spectacular long-distance seasonal migrations in Temperate Zone snakes result when two required resources, overwintering sites and feeding areas, occur in widely separated habitats. Small-scale migrations may occur when habitats (resources) change seasonally. Aquatic and semi-aquatic snakes are known to move to more favorable areas when ponds dry up (Holman and Hill, 1961; Godley, 1980; Kephart, 1981) or when new habitats become available, such as following wet season flooding (Fukada, 1958; Shine and Lambeck, 1985). Platt (1969) believed that the variation in movements between two populations of *Heterodon nasicus* was related to resource distribution. Movement patterns of well-studied species may range along a continuum from relatively sedentary to migratory (e.g., *Thamnophis sirtalis:* Gregory, 1984; *Crotalus viridis:* Macartney, 1985), and differences among populations are likely due to differences in habitat structure and resource availability.

The size and shape of home ranges may be influenced by physical features of the environment. Most visible examples include home ranges delineated by natural or man-made edge habitats (Naulleau, 1966; Fitch, 1963a; Fraker, 1970; Freedman and Catling, 1979; Plummer, 1981b; Madsen, 1984). In other cases, topographical features may impose physical or ecological barriers to movements and modify their extent or direction (Carpenter, 1952; Brown et al., 1982). There are a myriad of other possible influences that habitat structure and resource availability might have on movements and home range size, shape, and overlap.

Other Factors. Changes in population density may be correlated with mean dispersal distances from hibernacula in *Coluber constrictor* (Brown and Parker, 1976), a competition hypothesis. Whether competition leads to spacing in snakes is not known (see EVIDENCE FOR SPACING IN SNAKES). Activity areas of individuals overlap considerably in some species (Fitch, 1949, 1963a; Naulleau, 1966, 1968; Goddard, 1980; Reinert and Kodrich, 1982; Madsen, 1984; M. Stark, personal communication), but this tells us little. Overlaps provide evidence only against exclusivity of an area in snakes. For example, male *Vipera berus* basking in early spring maintain spacing, even though their small activity ranges at this time overlap one another (Viitanen, 1967). On the other hand, activity ranges of *Pituophis melanoleucus* in Nebraska apparently do not overlap at all (J. Fox, Personal communication), strongly suggesting spacing behavior.

Another factor that affects movements of individuals is ecdysis. Snakes generally restrict movements for a short period until ecdysis is completed (Galligan and Dunson, 1979; Brown et al., 1982; Madsen, 1984; Macartney, 1985).

ORIENTATION AND NAVIGATION

Introductory Comments

Any animal that moves must be able to direct its movements toward its destination. Of particular interest are movements over great distances, but the same general principles apply to shorter movements. Most investigations aimed at determining how vertebrates direct their movements over relatively long distances have been conducted on birds (see reviews by Keeton, 1974; Emlen, 1975) and fish (McKeown, 1984). Among reptiles, the best studied species are sea turtles (e.g., Carr, 1972). Snakes are relatively unstudied in this respect. Our objective here is to summarize relevant information for snakes, but interpretation and speculation rely heavily on work done on other animals.

Terminology

There is not yet complete consensus on terminology in studies of how animal movements are directed. "Orientation" and "navigation," for example, are often used synonymously, but they actually have distinct meanings. Rather than becoming embroiled in semantic arguments here, we adopt a simple heuristic approach to terminology.

Any directed movement by an animal requires orientation ability. Orientation is the process whereby the animal positions itself in relation to local landmarks, environmental cues (Adler, 1970), or a given compass direction (McKeown, 1984). An animal moving to a particular location must continually orient itself as the movement, however long, progresses. Griffin (1952) showed that displaced pigeons fell into three categories with respect to homing ability. These categories seem to have general utility. In type I homing, or piloting, the animal uses familiar landmarks or sensory cues to negotiate a route home, presumably over relatively short distances. Exploratory wandering may be an element of piloting (Griffin, 1952). Animals that exhibit type II homing, on the other hand, orient themselves strictly with respect to compass direction. Thus, if displaced, their ability to home depends on the direction of displacement. In type III homing, or navigation, animals are able to move in the correct direction toward home, no matter what the direction and distance of displacement, without using local landmarks. We hypothesize that animals showing different patterns of natural migratory behavior will have different degrees of orientation ability corresponding to the three categories of homing ability. Animals exhibiting the migratory equivalent of type II homing have only a compass (e.g., celestial co-ordinates), while those with the equivalent of type III homing ability need both a compass and an internal map of some sort (Keeton, 1974; Rodda, 1984). Rodda (1984) discusses major hypotheses about the nature of internal maps.

Evidence for Orientation and Navigation in Snakes

Evidence that snakes have long-distance orientational ability comes principally from two sources: (1) Long-distance migration between seasonal habitats (Gregory, 1984; see MOVEMENTS AND HOME RANGES), and (2) successful return to a capture site following displacement.

In some ways displacement studies provide the most convincing evidence of orientation and navigation, but they also have a number of significant weaknesses, not the least of which is that they are very unnatural experiments. One difficulty is that the displaced animal may be disinclined to return "home." This might depend on the kind of habitat to which the animal is displaced. A low percentage of returns of marked snakes to the home site also may be a better indicator of capture success, or mortality suffered en route, than of poor homing ability. Knowledge of natural movement patterns in general is indispensable to understanding the results of displacement studies. For example, unknowingly displacing a snake in the direction of its normal migratory route may lead to results that will be interpreted erroneously (cf. Brown and Parker, 1976; Parker and Brown, 1980).

The distances by which snakes have been displaced have varied considerably depending on species and site, but have ranged up to 5.6 km (e.g., Imler, 1945). Brown and Parker (1976) found that the return time of displaced *Coluber constrictor* was not correlated with displacement distance. Homing success was inversely correlated with displacement distance in two studies (Fraker, 1970; Parker and Brown, 1980). In both cases, some displaced individuals remained near the release point. Fraker (1970) also found that large snakes had higher homing success than small ones, at least for relatively small displacements. Some authors have found significant ability of displaced snakes to home over fairly long distances (>1 km, e.g., Noble and Clausen, 1936), while others have found little or no evidence of such homing ability (Imler, 1945; Fitch, 1949; Platt, 1969; Fitch and Shirer, 1971; Reinert and Kodrich, 1982).

The main conclusion to be derived from simple displacement studies is that snakes are sometimes capable of homing, especially over short distances. Displacement studies that incorporate other experimental techniques (e.g., sensory deprivation) are discussed in the next section.

Possible Mechanisms and Sensory Cues

General Comments. Studies on migration and on simple displacement can provide us with clues about modes of orientation, but the elucidation of these mechanisms requires more sophisticated experimental techniques, often using controlled laboratory conditions.

Displacement studies are sometimes performed in conjunction with some form of sensory deprivation. Caution must be exercised in interpreting the results of such manipulations. An animal that is successful in returning home, following displacement and deprivation of one or more senses, may tell the researcher only that it is capable of compensating for the loss of these senses by using others; successful homing in this case does not necessarily mean that the eliminated senses would not be used if available. A similar caution applies to laboratory studies using sensory deprivation. An additional risk is that sensory deprivation may cause an animal to behave in an abnormal manner having nothing to do with the absence of the particular sense per se. Appropriate use of control animals, or eliminating the sensory cues from the environment, rather than interfering with the animal, are possible alternatives.

Visual Landmark Recognition. Recognition of visual landmarks is possibly important in short movements of snakes, but it seems unlikely that it is important in long-distance travel because of the low vantage point of snakes. If such cues are employed in long-distance orientation, it is likely that they are mainly used by species inhabiting open areas with largely unobstructed views.

In one study on snakes, individual *Vipera aspis* were able to home when their home area, or a slope adjacent to it, was within view (Saint Girons, 1953). However, homing did not occur when the snake's view of the home area was obstructed either by fluid accumulation under the ocular scute (before ecdysis) or by displacement out of sight of the home range. Parker and Brown (1980) found that homing *Masticophis taeniatus* changed direction when approaching the base of a ridge, suggesting a role for visual cues, but a "blinded" male successfully homed over 200 m. Thus physical landmarks are not the only source of environmental cues for these snakes.

Celestial Cues. The use of visual celestial cues as an orienting mechanism has been demonstrated in a wide range of animals. See Able (1980) for a comprehensive review.

Relatively little evidence for celestial orientation in snakes has been found, although it is suggested by the directional movement shown by some snakes following displacement (Landreth, 1973; Galligan and Dunson, 1979; Lawson, 1985). Results of orientation tests led Landreth (1973) to conclude that *Crotalus atrox* used solar cues in making directional choices. A similar study on celestial orientation of *Nerodia sipedon* and *Regina septemvittata* showed that both species used the sun for compass orientation (Newcomer et al., 1974). *Nerodia* demonstrated "y-axis" orientation, whereby an animal moves along an axis perpendicular to a "learned component" (e.g., a body of water). Y-axis orientation also requires a celestial cue (in this case the sun) and an internal clock to compensate for the daily movement of the sun. Newcomer et al. (1967) corroborated the latter using phase-shift experiments. Seasonally migrating snakes also might have to account for seasonal changes in the sun's position if they use solar cues.

In addition to its azimuthal position, the sun provides a celestial cue in the form of polarized light. Ability to use polarized light in orientation also requires an internal clock. A recent study on the lizard *Uma notata* has provided the first demonstration of sensitivity to polarized light in a reptile and its use as a time-compensated sky compass (Adler and Phillips, 1985). The site of polarization sensitivity in *Uma* was not isolated. Whether snakes use polarized light is unknown, but Lawson (1985) suspected a role for it in the time-compensated solar orientation of *Thamnophis radix*. The possibility that stellar or lunar cues are used by nocturnal snakes has not been investigated.

Olfactory Cues (Pheromones). The importance of chemical perception, especially via the vomeronasal system, to snake behavior is well established (Halpern and Kubie, 1984). Chemosensory cues play a major role in the trailing behavior of conspecific snakes (see Ford, 1986 for a review), especially trailing of females by males during the mating season. However, the role of chemical cues in orienting in other circumstances or over long distances is not clear.

Hirth (1966) and Klauber (1972) suggested that immature rattlesnakes might trail adults to hibernacula in autumn, as suggested by the later arrival of immature rattlesnakes (Hirth, 1966). Presumably, the first adults to arrive at the den use other cues gained from past experience. However, Macartney (1985), in a more detailed study, found no such pattern of arrival of *Crotalus viridis* at dens in autumn. Brown and MacLean (1983) showed that juvenile *Crotalus horridus* followed adult scent trails in autumn, but they did not test the possibility that adults might trail juveniles (or other adults) equally well. It is not clear what advantage a snake gains by leaving a trail for others in general to follow, although a postpartum female might leave a trail for her own young to follow.

Inherent in this sort of study is the need to establish how long scent trails last, and under what conditions. Can a "well-worn" trail last over the course of a season? Migrating snakes may move across bodies of water (K. W. Larsen, unpublished observations), making us skeptical of the importance of continuous scent trails, if such exist, in long-distance movements. On the other hand, snakes might orient with respect to airborne odors of other features of their environment (Fraker, 1970). In fact, an area might be identifiable by a combination of odors emanating from conspecifics, prey, other species, and inanimate objects. Such a combination would provide a unique chemical "fingerprint" of an area.

Chemical cues almost certainly are not the sole means by which snakes orient, but they must play a major role. Lawson (1985) found that conspecific pheromone trails influenced the ability of *Thamnophis radix* to orient toward a home site in the presence of solar cues, although not in any clear way. Revealing the full spectrum of chemical cues to which snakes respond and their interaction with other factors remains a fruitful area for snake orientation research.

Other Possible Cues. It has long been suggested that the earth's magnetic field functions as a non-visual cue for migrating birds, but its role is equivocal (Lednor and Walcott, 1983). Among reptiles, the orientation ability of alligators (Rodda, 1984) and box turtles (F. Moore, personal communication) appears to be affected by geomagnetism. Although nothing is known of geomagnetic sensitivity in snakes, it might be best developed in long-distance migrators, and this is an area that could repay critical attention.

Various more esoteric orientation and navigation mechanisms have been suggested from time to time for animals, especially birds. These include sensitivity to mechanical forces resulting from the earth's rotation (Griffin, 1952) or to infrasounds (Griffin, 1969), kinesthetic memory (Twitty, 1959), and inertial navigation systems (Barlow, 1964). Given the primitive state of knowledge of snake orientation mechanisms, it seems premature to speculate on these now.

FUTURE RESEARCH

We have attempted to point out fruitful areas for further research in various parts of this section. Clearly, two of the most important will be the ontogenetic development of orientation and navigation mechanisms and the use of multiple cues and orientation mechanisms. For example, we need to know the degree to which orienting mechanisms of snakes are innate or are the result of developmental or learning processes. The use of multiple cues seems highly probable given the wide range of information potentially available to a snake. An animal that utilizes as much information as possible should have advantages over one relying exclusively on one source or type of cue. Redundant information systems (Emlen, 1975) also ensure that the snake is still able to orient even in the absence of cues normally used. The combination of cues used probably varies with the circumstances; for instance, a snake migrating to a hibernaculum in the autumn might rely on celestial cues at the beginning of its movement but make increasing use of olfactory cues as it approaches the den (Lawson, 1985). The information from different cues presumably must match for successful orientation. Able (1980) discussed the integration of orientation cues in other animal taxa, and the reader is advised to consult his review for this information, as well as for a more general, comprehensive treatment of what is known about orientation and related phenomena in animals.

SUMMARY

A knowledge of spatial arrangement and movements is critical to any complete understanding of the ecology of a species. Movements of snakes have been studied fairly frequently, but the spatial pattern of snakes in the field has never been studied explicitly. However, the significant body of literature on spacing patterns in general and numerous relevant observations on snakes allow us to make some speculations and reach a few conclusions.

A truly random dispersion of a population of animals is to be expected only in the absence of social interactions among individuals and in a completely homogeneous environment, neither of which is likely to occur. Although there is evidence of spacing and aggression among snakes of many species in connection with mating, there is little indication of territorial defense of fixed areas. It may be more appropriate to regard snakes as maintaining individual distances that vary with the circumstances. Aggregations of snakes are more common than examples of spacing. Aggregations associated with various activities simply may be a consequence of habitat heterogeneity or may represent some advantage to the individuals involved.

The major patterns of movements exhibited by snakes seem to be related to variation in abundance and dispersion of critical resources. Thus movements may vary as much within populations and species as among them. Movements are multidimensional in nature and not easily summarized by a single number. However, the relative sizes of distance per move and distance moved per time unit may be a useful index of vagility. No general correlations of home range properties with attributes of individuals, populations, species, or local environments are apparent in studies of snakes done so far. However, most of this may have to do with differences in methodology, much of which is inadequate.

All animals need to be able to orient themselves within their environment. The problem of orientation is particularly great for animals, including some snakes, that make regular migrations between seasonal habitats over long distances. Displacement studies suggest that some snakes have a homing ability. The sensory cues used in migration or homing remain enigmatic, but there is reasonable evidence that snakes can use chemical and solar cues effectively. Snakes presumably use combinations of available cues, rather than just one kind of cue, but whether snakes possess true navigational ability is unknown.

ACKNOWLEDGMENTS

We thank Brent Charland, Dan Farr, and Peggy Lawson (all of the University of Victoria), Bill Brown (Skidmore College), and two anonymous reviewers for their critical comments. Bill Reed (University of Victoria) gave us useful suggestions about a statistical analysis in an earlier version of the manuscript. Frank Moore (University of Southern Mississippi), Malcolm Stark (Lethbridge Community College), and Philip Dumas (Central Washington University), and Jules Fox (Omaha) all provided us with valuable information from their unpublished work. Neil Ford (University of Texas at Tyler) allowed us access to one of his manuscripts scheduled for publication. Barbara Waito typed the manuscript. The Natural Sciences and Engineering Research Council of Canada supplied the funds (to PTG) for this undertaking.

LITERATURE CITED

Able, K. P. 1980. Mechanisms of orientation, navigation, and homing, in: Animal Migration, Orientation and Navigation (S. A. Gauthreaux, Jr., ed.), pp. 283–373, Academic Press, New York.

Adler, H. E. 1970. Ontogeny and phylogeny of orientation, in: Development and Evolution of Behavior (L. R. Aronson, E. Tobach, D. S. Lehrman, and J. S. Rosenblatt, eds.), pp. 303–336, W. H. Freeman, San Francisco.

Adler, K. and Phillips, J. B. 1985. Orientation in a desert lizard (*Uma notata*): Time-compensated compass movement and polarotaxis, *J. Comp. Physiol. A* 156:547–552.

Aleksiuk, M. 1977. Cold-induced aggregative behavior in the red-sided garter snake (*Thamnophis sirtalis parietalis*), *Herpetologica* 33:98–101.

Aleksiuk, M. and Gregory, P. T. 1974. Regulation of seasonal mating behavior in *Thamnophis sirtalis parietalis, Copeia* 1974:681–689.

Allee, W. C. 1931. Animal Aggregations: A Study in General Sociology, University of Chicago Press.

Arnold, S. J. and Wassersug, R. J. 1978. Differential predation on metamorphic anurans by garter snakes (*Thamnophis*): Social behavior as a possible defense, *Ecology* 59:1014–1022.

Baker, R. R. 1978. The Evolutionary Ecology of Animal Migration, Hodder and Stoughton, London.

Barbour, R. W., Harvey, M. J., and Hardin, J. W. 1969. Home range, movements, and activity of the eastern worm snake, *Carphophis amoenus amoenus, Ecology* 50:470–476.

Barlow, J. S. 1964. Inertial navigation as a basis for animal navigation, *J. Theor. Biol.* 6:76–117.

Blanchard, F. N. and Finster, E. B. 1933. A method of marking living snakes for future recognition, with a discussion of some problems and results, *Ecology* 14:334–347.

Brattstrom, B. H. 1974. The evolution of reptilian social behavior, *Am. Zool.* 14:35–49.

Brown, J. L. and Orians, G. H. 1970. Spacing patterns in mobile animals, *Ann. Rev. Ecol. Syst.* 1:239–262.

Brown, T. W. 1971. Autecology of the sidewinder (*Crotalus cerastes*) at Kelso Dunes, Mojave Desert, California, *Diss. Abstr. Int. B. Sci. Eng.* 31:6336–6337.

Brown, W. S. and MacLean, F. M. 1983. Conspecific scent-trailing by newborn timber rattlesnakes, *Crotalus horridus, Herpetologica* 39:430–436.

Brown, W. S. and Parker, W. S. 1976. Movement ecology of *Coluber constrictor* near communal hibernacula, *Copeia* 1976:225–242.

Brown, W. S., Pyle, D. W., Greene, K. R., and Friedlaender, J. B. 1982. Movements and temperature relationships of timber rattlesnakes (*Crotalus horridus*) in northeastern New York, *J. Herpetol.* 16:151–161.

Burghardt, G. M. 1983. Aggregation and species discrimination in newborn snakes, *Z. Tierpsychol.* 61:89–101.

Burt, W. H. 1943. Territoriality and home range concepts as applied to mammals, *J. Mammal.* 24:346–352.

Carpenter, C. C. 1952. Comparative ecology of the common garter snake (*Thamnophis s. sirtalis*), the ribbon snake (*Thamnophis s. sauritus*), and Butler's garter snake (*Thamnophis butleri*) in mixed populations, *Ecol. Monogr.* 22:235–258.

Carpenter, C. C. 1984. Dominance in snakes, in: Vertebrate Ecology and Systematics: A Tribute to Henry S. Fitch (R. A. Seigel, L. E. Hunt, J. L. Knight, L. Malaret, and N. L. Zuschlag, eds.), *Univ. Kans. Mus. Nat. Hist. Spec. Publ.* 10:195–202.

Carr, A. 1972. The case for long-range chemoreceptive piloting in *Chelonia,* in: Animal Orientation and Navigation (S. R. Galler, K. Schmidt-Koenig,

G. J. Jacobs, and R. E. Belleville, eds.), pp. 469–483, National Aeronautics and Space Administration, Washington.

Charnov, E. L., Orians, G. H., and Hyatt, K. 1976. Ecological implications of resource depression, *Am. Nat.* 110:247–259.

Clark, D. R., Jr., 1970. Ecological study of the worm snake, *Carphophis vermis* (Kennicott), *Univ. Kans. Publ. Mus. Nat. Hist.* 19:85–194.

Clark, D. R., Jr., 1974. The western ribbon snake (*Thamnophis proximus*): Ecology of a Texas population, *Herpetologica* 30:372–379.

Conder, P. J. 1949. Individual distance, *Ibis* 91:649–655.

Covacevich, J. and Limpus, C. 1972. Observations on community egg-laying by the yellow-faced whip snake, *Demansia psammophis* (Schlegel) 1837 (Squamata: Elapidae), *Herpetologica* 28:208–210.

Dundee, H. A. and Miller, M. C., III. 1968. Aggregative behavior and habitat conditioning by the prairie ringneck snake, *Diadophis punctatus arnyi*, *Tulane Stud. Zool. Bot.* 15:41–58.

Dunson, W. A. and Ehlert, G. W. 1971. Effects of temperature, salinity, and surface water flow on distribution of the sea snake *Pelamis*, *Limn. Ocean.* 16:845–853.

Duvall, D., King, M. B., and Gutzwiller, M. J. 1985. Behavioral ecology and ethology of the prairie rattlesnake, *Nat. Geogr. Res.* 1:80–111.

Emlen, S. T. 1975. Migration: Orientation and navigation, in: Avian Biology, vol. V (D. S. Farner and J. R. King, eds.), pp. 129–219, Academic Press, New York.

Finneran, L. C. 1949. A sexual aggregation of the garter snake, *Thamnophis butleri* (Cope), *Copeia* 1949:141–144.

Fitch, H. S. 1949. Study of snake populations in central California, *Am. Midl. Nat.* 41:513–579.

Fitch, H. S. 1958. Home ranges, territories, and seasonal movements of vertebrates of the Natural History Reservation, *Univ. Kans. Publ. Mus. Nat. Hist.* 11:63–326.

Fitch, H. S. 1960. Autecology of the copperhead, *Univ. Kans. Publ. Mus. Nat. Hist.* 13:85–288.

Fitch, H. S. 1963a. Natural history of the racer, *Coluber constrictor*, *Univ. Kans. Publ. Mus. Nat. Hist.* 15:351–468.

Fitch, H. S. 1963b. Natural history of the black rat snake (*Elaphe o. obsoleta*) in Kansas, *Copeia* 1963:649–658.

Fitch, H. S. 1965. An ecological study of the garter snake, *Thamnophis sirtalis*, *Univ. Kans. Publ. Mus. Nat. Hist.* 15:493–564.

Fitch, H. S. and Shirer, H. W. 1971. A radiotelemetric study of spatial relationships in some common snakes, *Copeia* 1971:118–128.

Foley, G. W. 1971. Perennial communal nesting in the black racer (*Coluber constrictor*), *Herpetol. Rev.* 3:41.

Ford, N.B. 1986. The role of pheromone trails in the sociobiology of snakes, in: Advances in Vertebrate Chemoreception, vol. 4 (R. M. Silverstein,

D. Müller-Schwarze, and D. Duvall, eds.), Plenum Press, New York. In press.

Fraker, M. A. 1970. Home range and homing in the watersnake, *Natrix sipedon sipedon, Copeia* 1970:665–673.

Freedman, B. and Catling, P. M. 1979. Movements of sympatric species of snakes at Amherstburg, Ontario, *Can. Field-Nat.* 93:399–404.

Froese, A. D. 1980. Reptiles, in: Species Identity and Attachment: A Phylogenetic Evaluation (M. A. Roy, ed.), pp. 39–68, Garland STPM Press, New York.

Fukada, H. 1958. Biological studies on the snakes. IV. Seasonal prevalence in the fields, *Bull. Kyoto Gakugei Univ. Ser. B. Math. Nat. Sci.* 13:22–35.

Galligan, J. H. and Dunson, W. A. 1979. Biology and status of timber rattlesnake (*Crotalus horridus*) populations in Pennsylvania, *Biol. Conserv.* 15:13–58.

Gill, D. E. 1978. The metapopulation ecology of the red-spotted newt, *Notophthalmus viridescens* (Rafinesque), *Ecol. Monogr.* 48:145–166.

Goddard, P. 1980. Limited movement areas and spatial behaviour in the smooth-snake *Coronella austriaca* in southern England, in: Proceedings of the European Herpetological Symposium (J. Coborn, ed.), pp. 25–40, Cotswold Wild Life Park, Oxford.

Godley, J. S. 1980. Foraging ecology of the striped swamp snake, *Regina alleni,* in southern Florida, *Ecol. Monogr.* 50:411–436.

Gordon, D. M. and Cook, F. R. 1980. An aggregation of gravid snakes in the Quebec Laurentians, *Can. Field-Nat.* 94:456–457.

Gregory, P. T. 1975. Aggregations of gravid snakes in Manitoba, Canada, *Copeia* 1975:185–186.

Gregory, P. T. 1982. Reptilian hibernation, in: Biology of the Reptilia, vol. 13 (C. Gans and F. H. Pough, eds.), pp. 53–154, Academic Press, London.

Gregory, P. T. 1984. Communal denning in snakes, in: Vertebrate Ecology and Systematics: A Tribute to Henry S. Fitch (R. A. Seigel, L. E. Hunt, J. L. Knight, L. Malaret, and N. L. Zuschlag, eds.), *Univ. Kans. Mus. Nat. Hist. Spec. Publ.* 10:57–75.

Gregory, P. T. and Stewart, K. W. 1975. Long-distance dispersal and feeding strategy of the red-sided garter snake (*Thamnophis sirtalis parietalis*) in the Interlake of Manitoba, *Can. J. Zool.* 53:238–245.

Griffin, D. R. 1952. Bird navigation, *Biol. Rev.* 27:359–393.

Griffin, D. R. 1969. The physiology and geophysics of bird navigation. *Q. Rev. Biol.* 44:255–276.

Guibé, J. and Saint Girons, H. 1955. Espace vitale et territoire chez les reptiles, *La Nature* 3245:358–362.

Halpern, M. and Kubie, J. L. 1984. The role of the ophidian vomeronasal system in species-typical behavior, *Trends Neurosci.* 7:472–477.

Hamilton, W. D. 1971. Geometry for the selfish herd, *J. Theor. Biol.* 31:295–311.

Harper, D. G. C. 1982. Competitive foraging in mallards: "Ideal free" ducks, *Anim. Behav.* 30:575–584.

Heller, S. B. and Halpern, M. 1982a. Laboratory observations of aggregative behavior of garter snakes, *Thamnophis sirtalis:* Roles of the visual, olfactory, and vomeronasal senses, *J. Comp. Physiol. Psychol.* 96:984–999.

Heller, S. B. and Halpern, M. 1982b. Laboratory observations of aggregative behavior of garter snakes, *Thamnophis sirtalis, J. Comp. Physiol. Psychol.* 96:967–983.

Henderson, R. W., Binder, M. H., Sajdak, R. A., and Buday, J. A. 1980. Aggregating behavior and exploitation of subterranean habitat by gravid eastern milksnakes (*Lampropeltis t. triangulum*), *Milw. Publ. Mus., Contr. Biol. Geol.* 32.

Hibbard, C. W. 1964. A brooding colony of the blind snake, *Leptotyphlops dulcis dissecta* Cope, *Copeia* 1964:222.

Hirth, H. F. 1966. The ability of two species of snakes to return to a hibernaculum after displacement, *Southwest. Nat.* 11:49–53.

Hirth, H. F., Pendleton, R. C., King, A. C., and Downard, T. R. 1969. Dispersal of snakes from a hibernaculum in northwestern Utah, *Ecology* 50:332–339.

Holman, J. A. and Hill, W. H. 1961. A mass unidirectional movement of *Natrix sipedon pictiventris, Copeia* 1961:498–499.

Hutchinson, G. E. 1953. The concept of pattern in ecology, *Proc. Nat. Acad. Sci.* 105:1–12.

Imler, R. H. 1945. Bullsnakes and their control on a Nebraska wildlife refuge, *J. Wildl. Manage.* 9:265–273.

Jennrich, R. I. and Turner, F. B. 1969. Measurement of non-circular home range, *J. Theor. Biol.* 22:227–237.

Keenlyne, K. D. 1972. Sexual differences in feeding habits of *Crotalus horridus horridus, J. Herpetol.* 6:234–237.

Keeton, W. 1974. The orientational and navigational basis of homing in birds, in: Advances in the Study of Behavior, vol. 5 (D. S. Lehrman, J. S. Rosenblatt, R. A. Hinde, and E. Shaw, eds.), pp. 47–132, Academic Press, New York.

Kennedy, J. P. 1965. Territorial behavior in the eastern coachwhip, *Masticophis flagellum, Anat. Rec.* 151:499 (abstract).

Kephart, D. G. 1981. Population ecology and population structure of *Thamnophis elegans* and *Thamnophis sirtalis,* Ph.D. Dissertation, University of Chicago.

King, M., McCarron, D., Duvall, D., Baxter, G., and Gern, W. 1983. Group avoidance of conspecific but not interspecific chemical cues by prairie rattlesnakes (*Crotalus viridis*), *J. Herpetol.* 17:196–198.

Klauber, L. M. 1972. Rattlesnakes, 2nd ed., 2 vols., University of California Press, Berkeley.

Kropach, C. 1971. Sea snake (*Pelamis platurus*) aggregations on slicks in Panama, *Herpetologica* 27:131–135.

Landreth, H. F. 1973. Orientation and behavior of the rattlesnake, *Crotalus atrox, Copeia* 1973:26–31.

Lawson, M. A. 1985. Preliminary investigations into the roles of visual and pheromonal stimuli on aspects of the behaviour of the western plains garter snake, *Thamnophis radix haydeni*, M.S. Thesis, University of Regina, Saskatchewan.

Lednor, A. J. and Walcott, C. 1983. Homing pigeon navigation: The effects of in-flight exposure to a varying magnetic field, *Comp. Biochem. Physiol.* 76A:665–671.

Lillywhite, H. B. 1982. Tracking as an aid in ecological studies of snakes, in: Herpetological Communities (N. J. Scott, Jr., ed.), *U.S. Fish Wildl. Serv. Wildl. Res. Rep.* 13:181–191.

Lloyd, M. 1967. "Mean crowding," *J. Anim. Ecol.* 36:1–30.

Lowe, C. H., Jr. and Norris, K. S. 1950. Aggressive behavior in male sidewinders, *Crotalus cerastes,* with a discussion of aggressive behavior and territoriality in snakes, *Chic. Acad. Sci. Nat. Hist. Misc.* 66:1–13.

Macartney, J. M. 1985. The ecology of the northern pacific rattlesnake, *Crotalus viridis oreganus,* in British Columbia, M.S. Thesis, University of Victoria, British Columbia.

McCoy, C. J., Jr. 1960. An unusually large aggregation of *Leptotyphlops, Copeia* 1960:368.

McKeown, B. A. 1984. Fish Migration, Croom Helm, London.

Madsen, T. 1984. Movements, home range size and habitat use of radio-tracked grass snakes (*Natrix natrix*) in southern Sweden, *Copeia* 1984:707–713.

Magnusson, W. E. and Lima, A. P. 1984. Perennial communal nesting by *Kentropyx calcaratus, J. Herpetol.* 18:73–75.

Matheson, C. 1962. An infestation of grass snakes near Swansea, *Brit. J. Herpetol.* 3:33–34.

Mermod, C. 1970. Domaine vital et déplacements chez *Cerastes vipera* (L.) et *Cerastes cerastes* (L.) (Reptilia, Viperidae), *Rev. Suisse Zool.* 77:555–562.

Michael, E. D. 1971. Snake visits to an earthen tank in south Texas, *J. Herpetol.* 5:195–196.

Michot, T. C. 1981. Thermal and spatial ecology of three species of water snakes (*Nerodia*) in a Louisiana swamp, *Diss. Abstr. Int. B Sci. Eng.* 42:4292 (abstract).

Murray, B. G., Jr. 1967. Dispersal in vertebrates, *Ecology* 48:975–978.

Myers, B. C. and Eells, M. M. 1968. Thermal aggregation in *Boa constrictor, Herpetologica* 24:61–66.

Myers, G. S. 1945. Nocturnal observations on sea-snakes in Bahia Honda, Panama, *Herpetologica* 3:22–23.

Naulleau, G. 1966. Etude complémentaire de l'activité de *Vipera aspis* dans la nature, *Vie Milieu* 17:461–509.

Naulleau, G. 1968. Espace vital et territoire chez *Vipera aspis, Ecoethologie* 1:55–77.

Naulleau, G. and Courtois, G. 1965. Utilisation du cobalt 60 pour le marquage des serpents, *C.R. Acad. Sci. Paris* 260:6219–6222.

Newcomer, R. T., Taylor, D. H., and Guttman, S. I. 1974. Celestial orientation in two species of water snakes (*Natrix sipedon* and *Regina septemvittata*), *Herpetologica* 30:194–200.

Nickerson, M. A., Sajdak, R. A., Henderson, R. W., and Ketcham, S. 1978. Notes on the movements of some neotropical snakes (Reptilia, Serpentes), *J. Herpetol.* 12:419–422.

Noble, G. K. 1939. The role of dominance in the social life of birds, *Auk* 56:263–273.

Noble, G. K. and Clausen, H. J. 1936. The aggregation behavior of *Storeria dekayi* and other snakes, with especial reference to the sense organs involved, *Ecol. Monogr.* 6:269–316.

Oliver, J. A. 1956. Reproduction in the king cobra, *Ophiophagus hannah,* Cantor, *Zoologica* 41:145–152.

Parker, W. S. and Brown, W. S. 1972. Telemetric study of movements and oviposition of two female *Masticophis t. taeniatus, Copeia* 1972:892–895.

Parker, W. S. and Brown, W. S. 1980. Comparative ecology of two colubrid snakes, *Masticophis t. taeniatus* and *Pituophis melanoleucus deserticola,* in northern Utah, *Milw. Public Mus. Publ. Biol. Geol.* 7:1–104.

Pielou, E. C. 1974. Population and Community Ecology: Principles and Methods, Gordon and Breach, New York.

Pielou, E. C. 1977. Mathematical Ecology, John Wiley, New York.

Platt, D. R. 1969. Natural history of the hognose snakes *Heterodon platyrhinos* and *Heterodon nasicus, Univ. Kans. Publ. Mus. Nat. Hist.* 18:235–420.

Plummer, M. V. 1981a. Communal nesting of *Opheodrys aestivus* in the laboratory, *Copeia* 1981:243–246.

Plummer, M. V. 1981b. Habitat utilization, diet and movements of a temperate arboreal snake (*Opheodrys aestivus*), *J. Herpetol.* 15:425–432.

Porter, H. and Czaplicki, J. A. 1974. Responses of water snakes (*Natrix r. rhombifera*) and garter snakes (*Thamnophis sirtalis*) to chemical cues, *Anim. Learn. Behav.* 2:129–132.

Prater, S. H. 1933. The social life of snakes, *J. Bombay Nat. Hist. Soc.* 36:469–476.

Prestt, I. 1971. An ecological study of the viper *Vipera berus* in southern Britain, *J. Zool. (Lond.)* 164:373–418.

Readshaw, J. L. 1973. The numerical response of predators to prey density, *J. Appl. Ecol.* 10:342–351.

Reichenbach, N. G. 1983. An aggregation of female garter snakes under corrugated metal sheets, *J. Herpetol.* 17:412–413.

Reinert, H. R. and Kodrich, W. R. 1982. Movements and habitat utilization by the massasauga, *Sistrurus catenatus catenatus, J. Herpetol.* 16:162–171.

Rodda, G. H. 1984. The orientation and navigation of juvenile alligators: Evidence of magnetic sensitivity, *J. Comp. Physiol. A* 154:649–658.

Rose, B. 1982. Lizard home ranges: Methodology and function, *J. Herpetol.* 16:253–269.

Saint Girons, H. 1953. Ecologie et éthologie des vipères de France, *Ann. Sci. Nat. (Zool.)* 11 Ser. 14:263–343.

Saint Girons, H. 1981. Quelques observations sur la dispersion des nouveaunés chez *Vipera berus* et *Vipera aspis* dans le bocage atlantique (Reptilia: Viperidae), *Amphib.-Reptilia* 2:269–272.

Schoener, T. W. 1981. An empirically based estimate of home range, *Theor. Pop. Biol.* 20:281–325.

Sehman, R. W. 1977. Hibernaculum dynamics of the Great Basin rattlesnake (*Crotalus viridis lutosus*), M.S. Thesis, Idaho State University, Pocatello.

Shine, R. 1979. Activity patterns in Australian elapid snakes (Squamata: Serpentes: Elapidae), *Herpetologica* 35:1–11.

Shine, R. and Lambeck, R. 1985. A radiotelemetric study of movements, thermoregulation and habitat utilization of Arafura filesnakes (Serpentes: Acrochordidae), *Herpetologica* 41:351–361.

Slevin, J. B. 1950. A remarkable concentration of desert snakes, *Herpetologica* 6:177–178.

Smith, D. L. 1971. Movements of eastern garter snakes (*Thamnophis sirtalis sirtalis*) tagged with radioactive cobalt, *Diss. Abstr. Int. B. Sci. Eng.* 32:

Stickel, W. H. and Cope, J. B. 1947. The home ranges and wanderings of snakes, *Copeia* 1947:127–136.

Sutherland, I. D. W. 1958. The "combat dance" of the timber rattlesnakes, *Herpetologica* 14:23–24.

Thomas, R. 1965. A congregation of the blind snake, *Typhlops richardi*, *Herpetologica* 21:309.

Tinkle, D. W. and Liner, E. A. 1955. Behavior of *Natrix* in aggregations, *Field Lab.* 23:84–87.

Tu, A. T. 1976. Investigation of the sea snake, *Pelamis platurus* (Reptilia, Serpentes, Hydrophiidae), on the Pacific coast of Costa Rica, Central America, *J. Herpetol.* 10:13–18.

Twitty, V. C. 1959. Migration and speciation in newts, *Science* 130:1735–1743.

Viitanen, P. 1967. Hibernation and seasonal movements of the viper, *Vipera berus berus* (L.) in southern Finland, *Ann. Zool. Fenn.* 4:472–546.

Waser, P. M. and Wiley, R. H. 1979. Mechanisms and evolution of spacing in animals, in: Handbook of Behavioral Neurobiology, vol. 3, Social Behavior and Communication (P. Marler and J. G. Vandenbergh, eds.), pp. 159–223, Plenum Press, New York.

Weatherhead, P. J. and Charland, M. B. 1985. Habitat selection in an Ontario population of the snake, *Elaphe obsoleta*, *J. Herpetol.* 19:12–19.

Weldon, P. J. and Schell, F. M. 1984. Responses by king snakes (*Lampropeltis getulus*) to chemicals from colubrid and crotaline snakes, *J. Chem. Ecol.* 10:1509–1520.

Wharton, C. H. 1969. The cottonmouth moccasin on Sea Horse Key, Florida, *Bull. Fla. St. Mus. Biol. Sci.* 14:227–272.

White, F. N. and Lasiewski, R. C. 1971. Rattlesnake denning: Theoretical considerations on winter temperatures, *J. Theor. Biol.* 30:553–557.

Wilson, D. S. 1980. The Natural Selection of Populations and Communities, Benjamin/Cummings, Menlo Park, California.

Wilson, E. O. 1975. Sociobiology: The New Synthesis, Belknap Press, Cambridge, Massachusetts.

Wood, C. C. 1985. Aggregative response of common mergansers (*Mergus merganser*): Predicting flock size and abundance on Vancouver Island salmon streams, *Can. J. Fish. Aquat. Sci.* 42:1259–1271.

Wynne-Edwards, V. C. 1962. Animal Dispersion in Relation to Social Behaviour, Oliver and Boyd, Edinburgh.

CHAPTER THIRTEEN

Activity Patterns

J. Whitfield Gibbons
Raymond D. Semlitsch

Our objective in this chapter is to address the question, why do snakes move from one location to another? Or, what are the benefits of activity? In a consideration of the activity patterns of snakes, the fundamental question is why do individuals of a species move at particular times and to particular places? A snake that moves from one place to another presumably incurs a risk of mortality and expends more energy than one that is immobile (Huey and Pianka, 1981). Presumably, then, a snake is active only when the potential benefits of being at another point in space and time outweigh the costs of remaining in the same place. An ultimate research goal is to provide evolutionary explanations for the activity patterns observed among snakes, with the premise that natural selection has governed the activities of individuals and resulted in the activity patterns we observe in each species. An opposing view is that some or all snake activities are stochastic events not under any consistent influence of natural selection.

We define the term "activity" as any movement of an individual snake from one location to another. An "activity pattern" is the identifiable, consistent, generally predictable activity of the individuals in a population or species. Our emphasis throughout the chapter will be on the temporal aspect of activity rather than the spatial (see Gregory et al., this volume). However, because the time involved in travel by snakes relates directly to the distance traveled in many instances, some consideration must also be given to spatial aspects.

The initial step in approaching the problem is to identify and categorize activity patterns. To do this we have examined empirical evidence both in the literature and from our own studies on the activity patterns of particular species. The presence or absence of phylogenetic relationships, geographic trends, ontogenetic changes, and variation between sexes and among seasons, years, and

396

populations should reveal information about the natural selection processes involved in the evolution of activity and movement patterns of snakes.

Establishing general patterns is a difficult task because of the limited number of thorough studies that lend themselves to appropriate geographic comparisons of the same species, or local comparisons of species in the same habitat. However, certain trends among the data have emerged that we hope will help future researchers suitably frame questions about activity patterns.

The literature is replete with observations of snake activity and movement. Most field studies on snakes are based on specimens that were at least temporarily active, although the majority of observations have been anecdotal. The first challenge in organizing and understanding activity patterns is to properly categorize them. We have attempted to do this by organizing the literature on activity patterns into two categories: seasonal and daily. An additional objective has been to establish trends and identify differences among and within species, which will be useful in understanding the evolutionary significance of the observed activity patterns.

SEASONAL ACTIVITY PATTERNS

Conducting intensive and extensive research on snake populations is difficult because of their secretive habits and patchy distribution. Several detailed studies conducted throughout the year, however, have provided valuable information on annual activity patterns. A few studies have defined year-round activity patterns of species and reported detailed observations of when and where individuals differing in sex and reproductive condition moved seasonally. These studies have been among the most valuable in establishing possible causes for the activity patterns observed.

A challenge to us in addressing seasonal activity patterns was to identify meaningful subcategories for use in understanding why snakes are active at particular times of the year. The following four subcategories were ones of convenience that were established partially as a function of the manner in which they have been presented in the literature. They are not intended as biologically functional categories but as a mechanism for grouping similar studies. The biological categorization of seasonal activity patterns is considered in DISCUSSION AND CONCLUSIONS.

Seasonal Activity Peaks

Several studies have revealed peaks of relatively high seasonal activity for particular species of snakes. Based on highway mortality records in Nebraska, Oliver (1955) noted that *Coluber constrictor, Heterodon nasicus,* and *Thamnophis radix* each showed bimodal peaks of activity in spring and autumn and reduced activity during summer, in contrast to *Pituophis melanoleucus* which appeared to be equally abundant from early summer into autumn. Jackson and Franz (1981) reported year-round surface activity of *Micrurus fulvius* in Florida but noted spring and autumn peaks and periods of lower activity during summer and winter. They attributed much of the bimodal pattern to greater activity by males during spring and autumn. Fukada (1958) compared the seasonal activity patterns of *Natrix tigrina* and *Elaphe quadrivirgata* in Japan. Two activity peaks occurred in each species each year. The exact dates of the peaks were not consistent from year to year, but one occurred during spring or early summer and the other occurred in autumn.

Landreth (1973) used radiotelemetry to demonstrate that the level of activity by individuals of *Crotalus atrox* in Oklahoma varied seasonally. During winter and early spring, daily movements were short and irregular, increasing as the days became warmer. Directional movement toward foraging areas (up to 3.5 km) occurred during early summer. Daily movements during summer were short until late summer, when snakes returned to the dens. Autumn movements around the den were similar to those observed in early spring. The overall pattern of activity was presumably bimodal, with the greatest activity occurring during early summer and autumn. Seigel (1986) also observed a bimodal seasonal activity pattern in *Sistrurus catenatus* in Missouri. Although Seigel noted that the lower number of snakes found in summer could be indicative of reduced activity, he indicated that sampling bias was also a possible explanation.

A field enclosure experiment with southwestern speckled rattlesnakes (*Crotalus mitchelli*) and desert sidewinders (*C. cerastes*) in California revealed two different patterns of seasonal activity (Moore, 1978). *Crotalus mitchelli* showed a unimodal pattern, initially becoming active above ground in April. The number of hours of activity increased in each successive month through September. Activity was greatly reduced in October and November and ceased between December and March. *Crotalus cerastes* were also inactive from December through March but showed greater activity during May and October when compared with June through September. Activity during April and November was slightly below that of the summer months.

Crowned snakes (*Tantilla coronata*) in South Carolina showed a strongly unimodal seasonal activity cycle, being most commonly captured in pitfall traps during the hottest months, July and August. Few or no individuals were seen each month from November through March (Semlitsch et al., 1981). Stewart (1965) provided a comparison of annual activity patterns of the garter snakes

→

Figure 13–1. Seasonal activity patterns of 11 species of terrestrial snakes from the Savannah River Plant near Aiken, South Carolina. All species are susceptible to capture by drift fences and pitfall traps with minimal bias (Gibbons and Semlitsch, 1982), and the capture levels are indicative of terrestrial aboveground activity. A three-point moving average (dashed line) was used as a smoothing function. The only species for which the pattern was appreciably changed was *Virginia valeriae*.

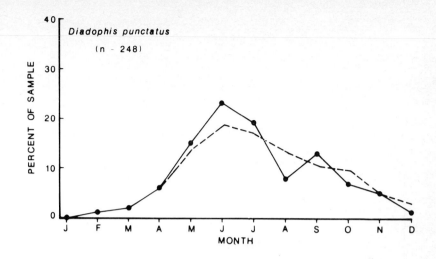

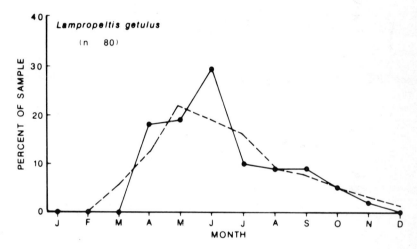

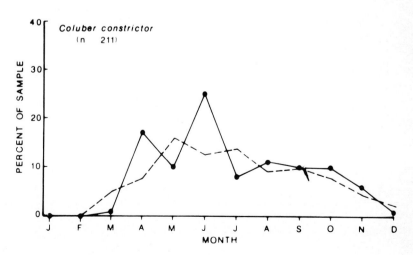

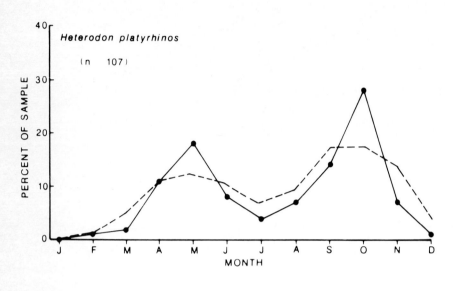

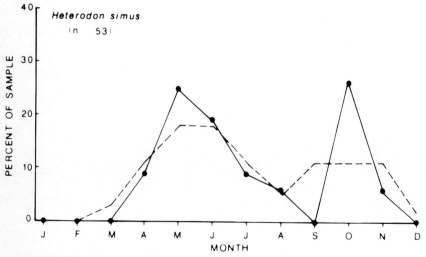

Figure 13–1 (*Cont.*).

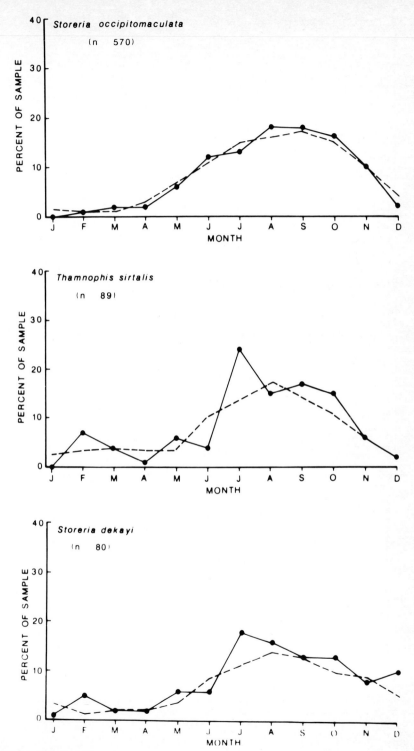

Figure 13–1 (*Cont.*).

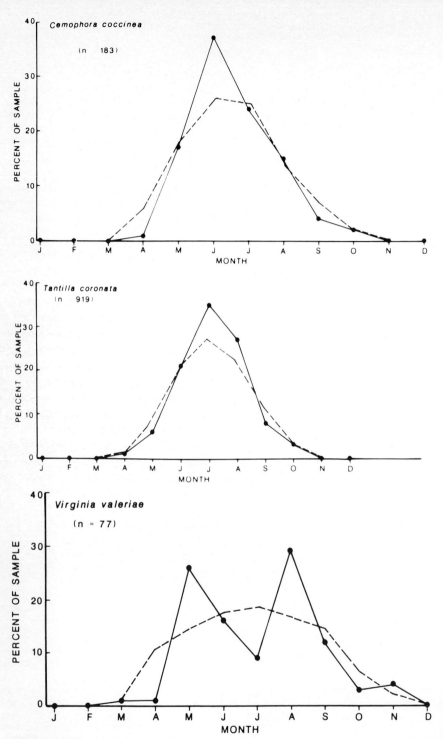

Figure 13–1 (*Cont.*).

Thamnophis sirtalis and *T. ordinoides*, with the former species commonly emerging from hibernacula to bask on warm winter days but the latter seldom being seen during winter.

Our research in South Carolina revealed different patterns of seasonal activity among 11 terrestrial species (Figure 13–1). Drift fences are an effective means of estimating aboveground activity in each of these species in the habitats being sampled, although certain sampling considerations are important in using such data (Gibbons and Semlitsch, 1982). *Virginia* and the two species of *Heterodon* had bimodal peaks of activity (spring and late summer or autumn). *Cemophora* and *Tantilla* displayed sharp peaks of activity in mid-summer with sharply reduced activity during the months before and after. Duever (1967) observed a similar phenomenon with *Cemophora* using systematic road collecting. Each of the other species had a single peak of activity between early spring and autumn. However, the period of the initial peak varied among species (Figure 13–1). The data reveal that some species are seldom active from late autumn until spring (e.g., *Cemophora coccinea*), whereas others become active during any month when environmental temperatures are warm (e.g., *Thamnophis sirtalis*). Such data can be extremely valuable in identifying general trends and generating hypotheses as to why a particular pattern has evolved and is maintained, particularly if sex, size, and reproductive mode and condition are considered.

The seasonal activity patterns of tropical snakes have been difficult to characterize, partly because of the apparent rarity of most species. Studies using samples of all snakes in a region to discern seasonal peaks of activity or inactivity can lead to conflicting interpretations (Kopstein, 1938; De Haas, 1941; Leston and Hughes, 1968; Henderson and Hoevers, 1977; Henderson et al., 1978). The diversity of seasonal patterns observed in Temperate Zone species, even among closely related sympatric species, indicates that in the tropics a clear understanding can only come through detailed observations of each species, rather than of snakes as a group, if the pattern is to have evolutionary significance. Presumably, each will have adapted to the seasonal vagaries in a species-specific manner.

Summary. Two distinct patterns of species-specific annual activity can be identified in Temperate Zone snakes.

1. *Unimodal:* A single peak of activity sometime between late spring and late summer (e.g., *Cemophora coccinea*).
2. *Bimodal:* A peak of activity in the spring and another in autumn (e.g., *Heterodon platirhinos*). Although polymodal activity patterns have not been documented for any species of snake, it seems likely that some tropical species may have more than two peaks of activity in response to wet-dry cycles.

Most thoroughly studied species of Temperate Zone snakes fall into one of the above categories, and in some instances an explanation for the pattern of activity has been suggested. An additional categorization is that some species are active throughout the year (continuous) when temperatures are warm enough (e.g., *T. sirtalis*), whereas other species appear to be endogenously inactive during the cooler months, even during warm spells (e.g., *C. coccinea*). No information is available to determine whether the seasonal activity peaks of snakes in the former category shift in response to differences in the temperature regime from year to year.

Activity Associated with Hibernacula

Among the most obvious and well-documented snake activity patterns are long-range movements to and from hibernacula where large numbers of individuals can be observed or captured. Activities associated with hibernation have been reported in a wide variety of species and geographic regions (Gregory, 1982; Gregory et al., this volume). It is useful to examine some of the findings of individual studies to establish trends and general patterns and to assess the proximal cues that cause the timing of movement.

Den site fidelity has been reported in several Temperate Zone snakes that hibernate in aggregations, including *Crotalus viridis* (Woodbury, 1951), *Agkistrodon contortrix* (Fitch, 1960), *Coluber constrictor* (Fitch, 1963), *Thamnophis sirtalis* (Fitch, 1965), and *Vipera berus* (Viitanen, 1967; Prestt, 1971). Lang (1969) reported that more than 90% of the *Storeria occipitomaculata* leaving hibernacula in Minnesota returned the following winter. Brown and Parker (1976) found that a similarly high proportion of *Coluber constrictor* returned to the same den in Utah. However, fidelity of individual snakes to a particular hibernaculum is not universal (Fitch, 1963; Viitanen, 1967).

Galligan and Dunson (1979) found that the date of emergence of *Crotalus horridus* from a den in Pennsylvania varied for 3 yr only between April 23 and 30. They did not measure temperatures within the den itself (so cannot be certain what temperatures the snakes were experiencing), but they could detect no relationship between air and ground temperatures and the dates of emergence. Gregory and Stewart (1975) reported that garter snakes (*T. sirtalis*) in Manitoba, Canada, left wintering den areas in May, moving in a directional manner toward summer feeding areas and returning in September.

Hirth et al. (1969) reported that individuals of three species of snakes at a hibernaculum in Utah moved more than 1 km from the den site in April and returned mostly in September. *Masticophis taeniatus, Coluber constrictor,* and *Crotalus viridis* dispersed intermediate distances. Although numerous recoveries were made during the 4 mo of activity, they concluded that summer movements were unpredictable.

The several-year study by Viitanen (1967) on *Vipera berus* in Finland gave insight into when and for what purpose this species may be active on a seasonal basis. Both sexes of adults and juveniles in some areas congregated at identifiable denning sites from mid-September until early November. Between late March and early May males emerged from the wintering dens. Females emerged about 2 wks after males, and juveniles shortly afterward. Initial emergence was apparently dependent on temperature conditions, although the precise environmental cues were not identified.

Jacob and Painter (1980) used temperature-sensitive radiotransmitters in six *Crotalus viridis* in New Mexico to determine relationships between body temperature and winter activity. Snakes were active within the dens when body temperatures were about 10°C and emerged to bask on sunny days during November and December. After early January, temperatures were too cold, and the snakes did not emerge again until April. The authors suggested that winter basking behavior stimulated gonadal activity in both sexes. Prestt (1971) observed that both sexes and all size classes of *V. berus* hibernated together in populations in southern England. Individuals at different dens initiated emergence from hibernation from February 20 to early March, whereupon they exhibited local dispersal to "lying-out" areas. Individuals basked during the day and returned to nearby surface dens at night until about mid-April. Return to the wintering dens was initiated by some individuals in August and lasted into November. Prestt observed no *V. berus* above ground at the hibernacula during December or January.

Gannon and Secoy (1985) observed *C. viridis* emerging from dens in Saskatchewan, Canada, from late April into early May during a year of observation. Emergence of adults preceded that of juveniles by several days. Dispersal from the den area occurred over a 2-day period during the second week of May. Some gravid females basked throughout the summer near the dens. Phelps (1978) recorded the dates of emergence of three species (*Coronella austriaca, V. berus, Natrix natrix*) in southern England for 2 yr at two denning sites. The dates of initial emergence of a species varied by as much as 3 wk from year to year at the same den, and by 1 to 2 wk at different dens in the same year. However, the three species varied consistently in their dates of first emergence, *V. berus* usually being first, *N. natrix* second, and *C. austriaca* always last. Based on experiments in which *Vipera aspis* were allowed to choose winter dormancy or remain active at room temperature, Naulleau (1975) concluded that a period of winter dormancy is part of an endogenous annual cycle in some species. Therefore, movement to winter denning areas presumably occurs during the late summer or autumn in response to photoperiod regardless of environmental temperatures, a presumed proximal cue for the initiation of denning activity in Temperate Zone snakes.

For some species, emergence from, or entry into, a hibernaculum is apparently a function of environmental temperatures persistent enough to create a change in the thermal gradient within the hibernaculum. Sexton and Hunt (1980) found that *Coluber constrictor* and *Elaphe obsoleta* that hibernated in a cave in Missouri responded to the thermal gradient from the entrance to the rear of the cave, moving from the cooler to the warmer end. By reversing the thermal gradient with heating devices during winter in an experimental den, Sexton and

Marion (1981) induced *Crotalus viridis* in Colorado to move from the rear of the den (normally the warmest section) to the front. The underground shift in thermal gradients may be the most important factor determining when snakes emerge from hibernation and may explain why emergence times are not always well correlated with short-term local temperature conditions on the surface.

One of the most thorough studies on activity patterns of colubrid snakes in relationship to hibernacula was that of Parker and Brown (1972, 1973, 1980) who observed *Masticophis taeniatus* and *Pituophis melanoleucus* in Utah. They observed that spring emergence from hibernacula varied considerably from year to year, presumably as a function of springtime temperatures. *Pituophis melanoleucus* initiated emergence later than *M. taeniatus* did in 2 of 4 yr and completed emergence later in all years. Return to the hibernacula in autumn began in September for both species but ranged from the first to the last week in different years. Juveniles of both species arrived later in autumn than did adults, but arrival times did not vary between adult males and females. Parker and Brown (1980) reported that early autumn arrival at the den was positively correlated with an early emergence the previous spring.

Summary. Movement to and away from hibernation sites is clearly a common phenomenon among Temperate Zone snakes, particularly in colder regions (Gregory, 1982). Winter cold has obviously been a powerful selective force in the life cycle of temperate snakes and in some instances has resulted in long-range movements by individuals between foraging sites and hibernacula. This overland movement (and its associated risks and energetic costs) is sometimes extensive, bespeaking the critical nature of finding a suitable site to survive winter temperatures. The greatest perceived activity of snakes inhabiting cold temperate regions should therefore be highest in spring and autumn during migrations between hibernacula and foraging sites.

Activity Associated with Habitat Selection

Identifying habitat shifts by snakes, particularly during the warmer parts of the year in Temperate Zones, and determining the potential causes of such shifts are important in understanding snake ecology and evolution. Fitch (1960) identified three types of movements by *Agkistrodon contortrix* in Kansas: (1) movement within a home range, (2) abandonment of a home range and occupancy of another, (3) movement to and from hibernacula. He noted that males moved more often between home ranges than females did and that gravid females and young of the year tended to remain closer to a hibernaculum than older animals did.

Habitat choice has been demonstrated in *Crotalus horridus* and *A. contortrix* by Reinert (1984), who used radiotelemetry to track individuals in Pennsylvania. Gravid females of both species preferred open habitats with higher temperatures.

Copperheads selected primarily open sites. Melanistic *C. horridus* were most often associated with mature forest areas, whereas the lighter color phases preferred early successional forest sites with abundant leaf litter. Advantages to the individuals are apparently related to thermoregulatory requirements and camouflage potential for concealment from both predators and prey.

Shine and Lambeck (1985) used radiotelemetry to document a seasonal shift in habitat in file snakes (*Acrochordus arafurae*) in Australia, presumably in response to prey availability. Because wet season activity occurred in newly flooded areas, they concluded that seasonal shifts occurred in response to foraging opportunities. Distinct habitat shifts of generally less than 300 m between April and October were observed in *Sistrurus catenatus* by Reinert and Kodrich (1982) in Pennsylvania. *Sistrurus catenatus* in Missouri shifted from a prairie habitat in the spring to upland areas of old fields and deciduous woods for the summer, returning to the prairie during autumn (Seigel, 1986). Prestt (1971) observed that, in early June, *Vipera berus* traveled 500 to 1200 m from hibernacula to summer feeding areas and began to return to the wintering dens in August. Godley (1980) observed significant changes in population densities of *Regina alleni* in water hyacinth communities of southern Florida. The changes in density were probably a result of habitat shifts by the snakes in response to changing water levels and foraging opportunities during a wet-dry seasonal cycle. A shift in habitat by *Storeria occipitomaculata* was observed by Semlitsch and Moran (1984) who used drift fences around natural wetlands (Carolina bays) in South Carolina. They observed that individuals increased overland movement concomitant with the drying of the wetlands in spring and summer and their refilling in autumn. They suggested that the snakes were following a food resource (slugs) that moved in relation to the moisture gradient.

An unusual opportunity to observe intrapopulational variability in the seasonal timing of a habitat shift was reported by Andren (1982), who described the pattern of movement from hibernacula for an island population of *V. berus* in Sweden. In 1974 adult males and females remained in the vicinity of the wintering area during spring and moved to foraging areas in early summer. The previous summer had been characterized by high densities of mammal prey. The following year, prey densities dropped considerably, and the snakes appeared to have an inadequate food supply during the summer of 1974. During the spring of 1975, most adults did not remain in the hibernation area but proceeded immediately to foraging sites. Reproduction was limited or absent entirely. Thus the same habitat shift was observed as during the previous year, but activity was instituted several weeks earlier because of the change in the nutritional status of the population.

Summary. Activity of snakes as a consequence of habitat selection should be a universal phenomenon. However, the level of activity within a species will probably be a function of environmental patchiness, prey abundance, density and availability, and population density of predators, competitors, and the species itself.

Sexual Differences in Activity Patterns

Although few studies have addressed the question of sexual differences in activity patterns, differential patterns between the sexes have been revealed. Naulleau (1965, 1966) found that male *Vipera aspis* moved further and were more active during reproductive periods than were females. Hammerson (1978) observed that male *Masticophis lateralis* kept in an outdoor enclosure were more active than females during the spring period of sexual activity. Males of both *M. taeniatus* and *Pituophis melanoleucus* tended to emerge from wintering dens several days earlier than females, and male *Masticophis* appeared to move about more than females in the general vicinity of the den for several days following emergence (Parker and Brown, 1972, 1973, 1980). In a study on *Coronella austriaca, V. berus,* and *Natrix natrix* in southern England, males emerged from denning areas several days before females of their species in every instance (Phelps, 1978).

After leaving the wintering dens, male *V. berus* moved several meters away to "basking spots," whereas females and juveniles remained in the vicinity of the dens (Viitanen, 1967). In early May, adult males and reproductive females moved to prescribed mating areas where they remained for about a month, with the males moving around in the mating area more than the females. Adult males then moved to summer feeding grounds, while gravid females remained in the wintering area. Non-reproductive females left the wintering dens and traveled from 0.3 to 1.2 km away during May. Juveniles traveled away from the wintering dens also, but did not move as far. Garstka et al. (1982) observed that male *Thamnophis sirtalis* at a denning site in Canada generally emerged earlier in the day than females and that both sexes returned to the den at night. Males were active around the den site earlier in the spring than were females and remained in the vicinity of the den for about a month, whereas females left the den area immediately following mating.

No differences in movement patterns were noted between the sexes of *Sistrurus catenatus,* but gravid females were judged to be more sedentary than non-gravid individuals, because the maximum distances moved within a particular habitat were shorter (Reinert and Kodrich, 1982). Parker and Brown (1980) observed that, during the summer, gravid females of *M. taeniatus* and *P. melanoleucus* moved more frequently, suggesting that some activity by gravid females was directed toward locating a nesting site. Madsen (1984) radio-tracked *N. natrix* in Sweden and observed that males were more active than females during the breeding season (May to early June). Males were relatively less active for the remainder of the summer. Females were most active in July a few days before and after the egg laying period but were relatively quiescent before and after this time. In southern England, Phelps (1978) observed that adult males and non-reproductive females of *V. berus* dispersed at about the same time from denning sites during early summer. Gravid females at one denning site left 2 to 3 wk later than the males, and some gravid females at the other denning site apparently remained in the vicinity of the den. Gravid females that had left the denning area were the first to return in early September, at which time parturition occurred in the vicinity of the den.

Prestt (1971) reported differences in activity patterns between the sexes, between adults and juveniles, and between gravid and non-gravid females of *V. berus* around hibernacula in southern England. Adult males characteristically emerged from hibernation earlier than adult females, and juveniles emerged later than adults. In late summer gravid females were the first to return to the hibernaculum sites, where parturition occurred.

Shine (1979) observed that gravid females of two Australian elapids (*Pseudechis porphyriacus, Notechis scutatus*) were more likely to bask and less likely to have fed recently than were non-gravid individuals. In field enclosure experiments, Gannon and Secoy (1985) observed female *Crotalus viridis* to be significantly more active than males in each season and found gravid females to be more active than non-gravid ones. Gannon and Secoy (1985) did not give a definition of activity, but they apparently used it to include any time a snake was above ground.

Females of some viviparous snake species apparently become inactive and cease foraging during gestation. Fitch and Twining (1946) concluded that gravid *C. viridis* in California fed in the spring but were sedentary during the later stages of gestation. Krohmer and Aldridge (1985) reported that gravid *Tropidoclonion lineatum* in Missouri did not feed during the later stages of pregnancy, although some of the specimens taken during early gestation and after parturition had recently fed. Shine (1980) showed that food intake was reduced in gravid females in 18 of 20 species.

Communal egg laying sites or aggregations of gravid females have been documented for several species of snakes from different regions (e.g., Cook, 1964; Hibbard, 1964; Lynch, 1966; Brodie et al., 1969; Covacevich and Limpus, 1972; Gregory, 1975; Palmer and Braswell, 1976; Swain and Smith, 1978; Gordon and Cook, 1980; Henderson et al., 1980). Whether female snakes select communal oviposition (and presumably parturition) sites because of certain habitat characteristics or whether there is a social component is unknown. Females may congregate in an area for the purpose of attaining optimal temperatures during gestation or because they select a thermally suitable location for egg deposition. Presumably, gravid females of species that aggregate in this manner could be more active than other individuals during the search period and would be more sedentary once a suitable site had been located (see Gillingham, this volume; Gregory et al., this volume).

Summary. Sex, reproductive condition, and stage of maturity are critical determinants of activity within a species. Males are consistently active earlier and more often during the spring, presumably because a direct fitness advantage accrues to the male encountering and mating with the most females. Gravid females presumably seek sites on the basis of suitability for gestation, oviposition, or parturition and not on the basis of foraging opportunities. Although less is known about juvenile activities, some studies suggest that they are the last to emerge from hibernation, presumably because there is no benefit to a juvenile to become active before the initiation of foraging.

DAILY ACTIVITY PATTERNS

We categorized our review of daily activity patterns into those emphasizing the time of day when activity occurs (diel patterns) and those focusing on thermoregulation and temperature relationships. In many instances the two categories were not mutually exclusive. A disappointing feature of much of the research on daily movement patterns of snakes is that many investigators have satisfied themselves with proximal or superficial answers as to why the activity occurs and have not addressed the evolutionary question involving the selective advantage of the activity. Numerous studies have documented that many snakes will attempt to increase their body temperature when given certain opportunities, through "temperature regulation" (Pough and Gans, 1982). The questions that should be more thoroughly addressed are why a particular body temperature is favored at a particular time and why a snake will undergo risk to attain it. Maintaining body temperatures at certain levels is apparently critical to many species of snakes. The optimal body temperature may vary as a function of season, feeding condition, body size, and reproductive condition of the individual. In addition, the optimal body temperature may vary considerably among species and may dictate the level of activity during different periods of the year, thus explaining in part the differential activity patterns observed among species. Explaining the differences in activity patterns in terms of thermoregulation is useful in a predictive sense but serves only as a proximal and mechanistic explanation for the cause of the activity. Thermoregulatory considerations are thoroughly covered by Lillywhite elsewhere in this volume; therefore we have concentrated only on diel activity patterns and not on thermoregulation per se.

Studies that establish the diurnal-nocturnal pattern of activity are useful in determining whether snakes have daily activity patterns and why such patterns are characteristic of particular species. Many studies document only the timing of activity, although some have identified suspected reasons for the pattern.

Heckrotte (1962) reported that *Thamnophis radix* adjusted its diel activity pattern in response to temperature. At low temperatures snakes were diurnal, at intermediate temperatures they showed a bimodal pattern in being crepuscular, and at the highest temperatures they were nocturnal. Landreth (1973) established that the diel activity pattern of adult *Crotalus atrox* in Oklahoma is temperature-dependent. He found that, in the colder months of winter and early spring, the snakes showed a unimodal daily activity pattern by moving to basking sites during mid-day. In late spring and early autumn, activity was bimodal, the snakes being most active during early morning and late evening. During the hottest part of the summer they were nocturnal, their activity being unimodal with a peak at about midnight. His nearly 10,000 observations give credence to the data and allow interpretations that can seldom be made with the small sample sizes of most radiotelemetry studies on snakes. Sanders and Jacob (1980) reported that *Agkistrodon contortrix* were nocturnal during the summer and diurnal during the spring and autumn. They attributed the change in activity patterns to thermoregulation requirements that permitted nighttime activity on warm summer nights but necessitated basking on cooler days. Seasonal shifts between nocturnal and diurnal activity have been documented for a variety of other species (Clark, 1970; Moore, 1978; Robinson and Hughes, 1978; Hudnall, 1979; Mushinsky et al., 1980; Seigel, 1986).

Platt (1969) found two species (*Heterodon nasicus* and *H. platirhinos*) to be diurnal, although the diel activity pattern in *H. nasicus* was influenced by daily temperatures. On hot days the snakes were active in early morning and late afternoon. On cooler days they were active primarily in late morning. Shine and Lambeck (1985) found that *Acrochordus arafurae* in Australia moved more extensively at night than during the day, during both wet and dry seasons. They provided evidence that file snakes are a major prey item of a diurnal predator, the white-breasted sea eagle, and suggested that this may be a driving force for file snakes to be nocturnal. Stewart (1965) reported that *Thamnophis sirtalis* and *T. ordinoides* in Oregon are strictly diurnal. Their diel activity pattern varied as a function of daytime temperature and degree of cloudiness, the snakes apparently using the conditions of the day to adjust their body temperatures within a preferred range. The implication is that a snake with a higher body temperature can more effectively search for or capture prey, thus giving a reason for their inclination to actively seek a basking site that might expose the snake to predation.

Shine (1979) reported that *Austrelaps superbus, Notechis scutatus, Pseudechis porphyriacus,* and *Pseudonaja textilis* in Australia were diurnal. Captive individuals of *Unechis gouldii* were strictly nocturnal. Shine (1979) stated that the diurnal nature of the majority of elapids studied was in contrast to the behavior of most large colubrids, crotalids, and viperids, which "are usually nocturnal or crepuscular. . . ." This is probably a misstatement of the situation for colubrids and viperids, many of which are strictly diurnal (see below). We currently see no compelling reason for a generalization that Australian elapids exhibit diel activity patterns that differ from those of other families of snakes.

McAlpine (1981) observed daily activity patterns in captive *Casarea dussumieri* and found them to be primarily nocturnal. The light-dark regime used was similar to that of their native island of Mauritius and averaged about 13 h of light and 11 h of dark. Despite small sample sizes, Thomas and Thomas (1978) provided convincing evidence in laboratory experiments that *Typhlops pusilla* and *T. biminiensis* are active nocturnally, even though they are primarily a burrowing species. They suggested that predator avoidance may be a factor.

Other species of snakes have also been reported to be primarily or exclusively diurnal (*Vipera berus:* Prestt, 1971; *Micrurus fulvius:* Jackson and Franz, 1981;

Crotalus viridis: Gannon and Secoy, 1985; *Opheodrys aestivus:* Plummer, 1981; *Uromacer catesbyi* and *U. oxyrhynchus:* Henderson et al., 1981) or nocturnal (*Cemophora coccinea:* Duever, 1967; Palmer and Tregembo, 1970; Nelson and Gibbons, 1972; *Eryx conicus:* Griffiths, 1984) in certain geographic regions, whereas some species have been observed to be active throughout most of the 24-h cycle (*Carphophis amoenus:* Barbour et al., 1969). Many of the investigators noted that activity was closely related to environmental temperatures. It is also notable that *Thamnophis sirtalis* and *Crotalus viridis* are sometimes nocturnal in other parts of their ranges (J. W. Gibbons, unpublished observations).

Yamagishi (1974) reported that the nocturnal activity observed in captive *Trimeresurus flavoviridis* was influenced by the level of light, including that of the moon. Snakes did not emerge until illumination levels were less than 10^{-3} lux and became inactive again when levels reached as high as 10^{-2} lux. Madsen and Osterkamp (1982) concluded that *Lycodonomorphus bicolor,* a nocturnal fish-eating snake from Africa, was less active on nights of the full moon than during the dark phases of the moon. Duellman (1978) reported that the activity of nocturnal species of snakes in the Ecuadoran tropics was negatively correlated with the amount of moonlight. He did not provide specific data but indicated that snake activity was considerably reduced on nights when the moon was three-quarters to full. A significant aspect of his observations is that activity was low even when there was a cloud cover, suggesting an endogenous lunar rhythm.

Summary. Some species of snakes appear to have a strong endogenous rhythm for a specific diel activity pattern despite seasonal changes in temperature. Some species are active both diurnally and nocturnally whenever temperatures are suitable. Others appear to respond to environmental temperatures in a seasonal manner, being diurnal during cool periods and shifting to a nocturnal activity pattern during the hottest part of the year. Light intensity has been poorly studied but may be a factor in the activity of some nocturnal species. In any species, the relative benefit of remaining nocturnal for predator avoidance or foraging activities must be weighed against the costs of reduced body temperature. Identifying the relative costs and benefits of light-dark conditions and of environmental and body temperatures is a first step in addressing the ultimate reason for the diel activity pattern of a species.

DISCUSSION AND CONCLUSIONS

Snakes show a variety of activity patterns. One of our objectives was to determine when snakes were active, both seasonally and daily, and to focus on both the proximal and ultimate reasons. The most obvious proximal explanations for overland activity are those related to movement from hibernacula to foraging habitats or to areas important for reproductive functions (Figure 13–2). Once a snake is at a site, daily activity may be a function of several factors, including

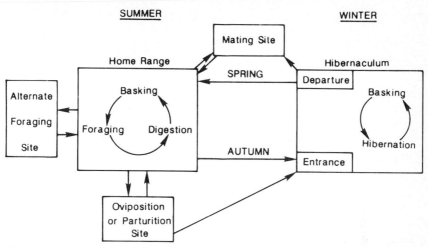

Figure 13–2. Activity by snakes incurs energetic costs and mortality risks; therefore, snakes move for specific reasons. Movements can be classed as seasonal or daily, long or short, directional or searching. Activity levels are a function of the combination of the various causes of movement. The chart indicates the basic annual movement patterns of a Temperate Zone snake and the points to which questions about the causes of activity should be directed.

searching for mates or food, avoiding predators, or thermoregulation. Many other factors, of unknown importance, may also influence the actual and perceived activity patterns of snakes. We recognize three basic reasons why snakes move from one place to another (Table 13–1).

The following may also explain some of the specific patterns observed by investigators:

1. *Sit-and-wait predators versus wide-ranging foragers:* Two foraging categories have been recognized in lizards (Huey and Pianka, 1981) and may be useful in considering the activity patterns of snakes. Except during periods related to reproductive activity or movement to and from hibernation sites, the warm months of the year presumably are used by most species for foraging. After a sit-and-wait forager has reached a summer foraging habitat, its level of activity (as measured in movement from one place to another) decreases considerably, which may explain why certain species (e.g., rattlesnakes) have a perceived reduction in activity during the warmer months. Conversely, wide-ranging foragers maintain their level of activity during the warmer months of the year.

2. *Burrowing species:* Species that forage primarily underground appear to be less active during the summer months because of a tendency to remain underground and out of sight. Burrowing species could be perceived as more active during the spring and autumn if migration to denning sites occurs, or if aboveground movement is associated with reproductive activity such as mating or searching for oviposition sites.

Table 13–1. Three Major Categories of Snake Activity That Can Be Directly Acted on by Natural Selection[a]

Survival
   Dispersal of recently hatched or newborn young from nests
   Diel activity with propensity for being nocturnal, diurnal, or both
   Movement to and from hibernacula
   Movement to and from aestivation sites or other sanctuaries
   Predator avoidance
   Daily thermoregulation to maintain body temperature to avoid predation and increase
      digestive rates
Reproduction
   Movement to and from breeding congregations
   Mate seeking by males
   Maintenance of elevated body temperatures by gravid females
   Seeking of egg-laying and parturition sites
Feeding
   Foraging activity in general
   Temporal or spatial shifts in feeding areas in response to prey availability
   Selection of digestion sites

[a]Processes affecting these categories of activity should be viewed in an evolutionary framework.

3. *Intermittent versus continual foraging:* Individuals of some species of snakes (e.g., water snakes, racers) may eat continually throughout the warmer months, whereas individuals of other species (e.g., rattlesnakes) feed less frequently and more sporadically (Mushinsky, this volume). In addition, some species (e.g., rat snakes) concentrate on seasonally abundant prey (bird eggs), so that their foraging activity may be limited to, or altered during, certain seasons. Although data are not available at this time to establish how such differential feeding patterns affect warm weather activity, they could presumably be influential in this regard.

4. *Prey availability:* Some prey may have seasonal or daily patterns that determine their availability. As a result, the foraging activity of most snake species is influenced by the density and availability of prey species.

5. *Predator density:* The activity patterns of some species of snakes may be governed during certain years, seasons, or times of day by the presence of particular predators. Understanding the relationships between predators and snakes (as prey) in terms of the costs and benefits associated with predator avoidance could be instructive in explaining some activity patterns.

6. *Perceived activity and collecting bias:* Certain generalizations can be made about activity patterns of snakes based on current information in the literature. However, a major problem in developing models of activity patterns in snakes is that most thorough studies have been conducted on large, easily observed species in which the measure of activity is their being visible to the collector. Collecting bias must always be a consideration when interpreting activity patterns of snakes.

The following conclusions can be made about activity patterns in snakes based on the current literature: (1) No phylogenetic trends in seasonal or daily activity patterns are apparent. Even species in the same genus can display different activity patterns in the same or different geographic regions. Activity patterns within species have not been shown to vary in any consistent manner, but this may be a function of insufficient data for comparing activity in species across broad geographic ranges. (2) The tendency toward nocturnal activity in some species may be related to avoidance of diurnal predators, avoidance of high temperatures, availability of prey, or some combination of these factors. (3) Sexual differences in activity patterns have been demonstrated in all species that have been thoroughly studied. Males of some species are more active than females during the mating season, whereas egg-laying females seeking nesting sites have been observed to be more active than males. The generality of this pattern has not been documented, but should be tested. Gravid viviparous females of some species will seek areas for purposes of thermoregulation and for hiding when male activity during the same period is directed toward foraging. (4) Half a century ago, Blanchard and Finster (1933) declared that the "wanderings . . . [of snakes] . . . are not predictable." Today's evidence suggests that movement by snakes is highly deterministic and that the potential exists to predict the conditions under which individuals will be active. Today's challenge is to identify these conditions and understand their evolutionary significance.

FUTURE RESEARCH

A review of the literature on activity patterns of snakes has revealed certain areas where data are incomplete, missing, or inconclusive. New or more intense research efforts are needed in many areas: in particular, geographic intraspecific comparisons, measurements of annual variation, and experimental manipulation of environmental variables (e.g., density, food level, sex ratios, predation level) to establish cause-and-effect relationships. Research designed to investigate these areas in regard to activity patterns would add significantly to our understanding of the ecology and evolution of snakes. The following warrant special attention:

1. *Activity patterns of juveniles:* Presumably, juvenile snakes are not involved in activities associated with reproduction. Such activities have been a major component of the different patterns of movement of adult snakes (see SEXUAL DIFFERENCES IN ACTIVITY PATTERNS). Therefore, juvenile snakes might have different activity schedules than adults, but few studies have made a distinction between juvenile and adult patterns. We assume that different patterns are possibly a consequence of juveniles having different selective pressures (e.g., diets, predators), as has been demonstrated for a variety of taxa (e.g., Mushinsky, this volume).

2. *Diel patterns of activity:* Intensive investigations of daily patterns of activity have been determined for surprisingly few snake species. Some of the

studies referenced in this paper have clearly documented that some species are exclusively diurnal, whereas others are exclusively nocturnal. Some species modify their diel pattern of activity depending on the season. Some appear to be active as a function of temperature conditions, so that their activity patterns shift seasonally. It appears that the diel activity pattern may be genetically determined in some species to the extent that their response to the light-dark cycle is endogenous and invariable, whereas in other species a variable response occurs, depending on the environmental temperature. Enclosure and manipulative experiments conducted on particular species on an annual basis would add greatly to our understanding of the variability among and within species in regard to daily activity patterns.

3. *Site selection by gravid females:* During gestation, gravid females of viviparous species (and possibly oviparous ones) apparently seek out sites different from those selected by non-gravid individuals. There is also an indication that the search for oviposition or parturition sites is a directed activity. Research designed to examine the differential activity of gravid females would be worthwhile, particularly for species that have not yet been examined, in order to test the generality of the phenomenon and to determine whether shorter gestation periods, larger offspring, or increased survival of offspring are consequences of such movements.

4. *Activity in the tropics:* The level of activity of some Temperate Zone snakes is known to be related to the distance traveled between habitats during different seasons. Practically nothing is known about whether any species of tropical snake (other than sea snakes) migrates long distances to adjust to shifts in spatial or temporal resource availability. Seasonal shifts in the activity of tropical species is also virtually unknown, although natural selection has presumably operated to cause seasonal patterns in regions with definable and predictable wet-dry seasons. Species-specific research on the year-round activity patterns of tropical species could reveal useful information about the observed scarcity of most tropical snakes.

ACKNOWLEDGMENTS

We thank the numerous individuals at SREL who have contributed to the knowledge of snake activity patterns through the collection of specimens. D. H. Bennett, J. P. Caldwell, J. L. Greene, G. B. Moran, D. H. Nelson, J. H. K. Pechmann, D. E. Scott, M. H. Smith, L. J. Vitt, and others provided drift fence data that were useful in our examination of activity patterns of snakes on the SRP. The manuscript benefited from comments by J. D. Congdon, J. L. Knight, S. S. Novak, D. E. Scott, and R. A. Seigel. Manuscript preparation was aided by Contract DE-AC0976SROO-819 between the U.S. Department of Energy and the University of Georgia's Institute of Ecology.

LITERATURE CITED

Andren, C. 1982. Effect of prey density on reproduction, foraging and other activities in the adder, *Vipera berus, Amphib.-Reptilia* 3:81–96.

Barbour R. W., Harvey, M. J., and Hardin, J. W. 1969. Home range, movements, and activity of the eastern worm snake, *Carphophis amoenus amoenus, Ecology* 50:470–476.

Blanchard, F. N. and Finster, E. B. 1933. A method of marking living snakes for future recognition, with a discussion of some problems and results, *Ecology* 14:334–347.

Brodie, E. D., Nussbaum, R. A., and Storm, R. M. 1969. An egg-laying aggregration of five species of Oregon reptiles, *Herpetologica* 25:223–227.

Brown, W. S. and Parker, W. S. 1976. Movement ecology of *Coluber constrictor* near communal hibernacula, *Copeia* 1976:225–242.

Clark, D. R., Jr. 1970. Ecological study of the worm snake *Carphophis vermis (Kennicott), Univ. Kans. Publ. Mus. Nat. Hist.* 19:85–194.

Cook, F. R. 1964. Communal egg laying in the smooth green snake, *Herpetologica* 20:206.

Covacevich, J. and Limpus, C. 1972. Observations of community egg-laying by the yellow-faced whip snake, *Demansia psammophis* (Schlegel) 1837 (Squamata: Elapidae), *Herpetologica* 28:208–210.

De Haas, C. P. J. 1941. Some notes on the biology of snakes and on their distribution in two districts of West Java, *Truebia* 18:327–375.

Duellman, W. E. 1978. The biology of an equatorial herpetofauna in Amazonian Ecuador, *Univ. Kans. Mus. Nat. Hist. Misc. Publ.* 65:1–352.

Duever, M. J. 1967. Distributions in Space and Time of Reptiles on the Savannah River Plant in South Carolina, M. S. Thesis, University of Georgia, Athens.

Fitch, H. S. 1960. Autecology of the copperhead, *Univ. Kans. Publ. Mus. Nat. Hist.* 13:85–288.

Fitch, H. S. 1963. Natural history of the racer, *Coluber constrictor, Univ. Kans. Publ. Mus. Nat. Hist.* 15:351–468.

Fitch, H. S. 1965. An ecological study of the garter snake, *Thamnophis sirtalis, Univ. Kans. Publ. Mus. Nat. Hist.* 15:493–564.

Fitch, H. S. and Twining, H. 1946. Feeding habits of the Pacific rattlesnake, *Copeia* 1946:64–71.

Fukada, H. 1958. Biological studies on the snake. IV. Seasonal prevalence in the fields, *Bull. Kyoto Gakugei Univ. Ser. B Math. Nat. Sci.* 13:22–35.

Galligan, J. H. and Dunson, W. A. 1979. Biology and status of timber rattlesnake (*Crotalus horridus*) populations in Pennsylvania, *Biol. Conserv.* 15:13–58.

Gannon, V. P. J. and Secoy, D. M. 1985. Seasonal and daily activity patterns in a Canadian population of the prairie rattlesnake, *Crotalus viridus viridis, Can. J. Zool.* 63:86–91.

Garstka, W. R., Camazine, B., and Crews, D. 1982. Interactions of behavior and physiology during the annual reproductive cycle of the red-sided garter snake (*Thamnophis sirtalis parietalis*), *Herpetologica* 38:104–123.

Gibbons, J. W. and Semlitsch, R. D. 1982. Terrestrial drift fences with pitfall traps: An effective technique for quantitative sampling of animal populations, *Brimleyana* 1982:1–16.

Godley, J. S. 1980. Foraging ecology of the striped swamp snake, *Regina alleni*, in southern Florida, *Ecol. Monogr.* 50:411–436.

Gordon, D. M. and Cook, F. R. 1980. An aggregation of gravid snakes in the Quebec Laurentians, *Can. Field-Nat.* 94:456–457.

Gregory, P. T. 1975. Aggregation of gravid snakes in Manitoba, Canada, *Copeia* 1975:185–186.

Gregory, P. T. 1982. Reptilian hibernation, in: Biology of the Reptilia, vol. 13 (C. Gans and F. H. Pough, eds.) pp. 53–154, Academic Press, New York.

Gregory, P. T. and Stewart, K. W. 1975. Long-distance dispersal and feeding strategy of the red-sided garter snake (*Thamnophis sirtalis parietalis*) in the Interlake of Manitoba, *Can. J. Zool.* 53:238–245.

Griffiths, R. A. 1984. The influence of light and temperature on diel activity rhythms in the sand boa, *Eryx conicus, J. Herpetol.* 18:374–380.

Hammerson, G. A. 1978. Observations on the reproduction, courtship, and aggressive behavior of the striped racer, *Masticophis lateralis euryxanthus* (Reptilia, Serpentes, Colubridae), *J. Herpetol.* 12:253–255.

Heckrotte, C. 1962. The effect of the environmental factors in the locomotory activity of the plains garter snake (*Thamnophis radix radix*), *Anim. Behav.* 10:193–207.

Henderson, R. W. and Hoevers, L. G. 1977. The seasonal incidence of snakes at a locality in northern Belize, *Copeia* 1977:349–355.

Henderson, R. W., Dixon, J. R., and Soini, P. 1978. On the seasonal incidence of tropical snakes, *Milw. Public Mus. Contrib. Biol. Geol.* 17:1–15.

Henderson, R. W., Binder, M. H., Sajdak, R. A., and Buday, J. A. 1980. Aggregating behavior and exploitation of subterranean habitat by gravid eastern milksnakes (*Lampropeltis t. triangulum*), *Milw. Public Mus. Contrib. Biol. Geol.* 32:1–9.

Henderson, R. W., Binder, M. H., and Sajdak, R. A. 1981. Ecological relationships of the tree snakes *Uromacer catesbyi* and *U. oxyrhynchus* (Colubridae) on Isla Saona, Republica Dominicana, *Amphib.-Reptilia* 2:153–163.

Hibbard, C. W. 1964. A brooding colony of the blind snake, *Leptotyphlops dulcis dissecta* Cope, *Copeia* 1964:222.

Hirth, H. F., Pendleton, R. C., King, A. C., and Downard, T. R. 1969. Dispersal of snakes from a hibernaculum in northwestern Utah, *Ecology* 50:332–339.

Hudnall, J. A. 1979. Surface activity and horizontal movements in a marked population of *Sistrurus miliarius barbouri, Bull. Md. Herpetol. Soc.* 15:134–138.

Huey, R.B. and Pianka, E. R. 1981. Ecological consequences of foraging mode, *Ecology* 62:991–999.

Jackson, D. R. and Franz, R. 1981. Ecology of the eastern coral snake (*Micrurus fulvius*) in northern peninsular Florida, *Herpetologica* 37:213–228.

Jacob, J. S. and Painter, C. W. 1980. Overwinter thermal ecology of *Crotalus viridis* in the north-central plains of New Mexico, *Copeia* 1980:799–805.

Kopstein, F. 1938. Beitrag zur Eierkunde und zur Fort pflanzung der *Malaiischen* Reptilien, *Bull. Rafles Mus.* 14:81–167.

Krohmer, R. W. and Aldridge, R. D. 1985. Female reproductive cycle of the lined snake (*Tropidoclonion lineatum*), *Herpetologica* 41:39–44.

Landreth, H. F. 1973. Orientation and behavior of the rattlesnake *Crotalus atrox*, *Copeia* 1973:26–31.

Lang, J. W. 1969. Hibernation and movements of *Storeria occipitomaculata* in northern Minnesota, *J. Herpetol.* 3:196–197.

Leston, P. and Hughes, B. 1968. The snakes of Tafo, a forest cocoa-farm locality in Ghana, *Bull. Inst. Fr. Afr. Noire Ser. A Sci. Nat.* 30:737–770.

Lynch, J. D. 1966. Communal egg laying in the pilot blacksnake, *Elaphe obsoleta obsoleta*, *Herpetologica* 22:305.

McAlpine, D. F. 1981. Activity patterns of the keel-scaled boa *Casarea dussumieri* at the Jersey Wildlife Preservation Trust, *Dodo: J. Jersey Wildl. Preserv. Trust* 18:74–78.

Madsen, T. 1984. Movements, home range size and habitat use of radio-tracked grass snakes (*Natrix natrix*) in southern Sweden, *Copeia* 1984:707–713.

Madsen, T. and Osterkamp, M. 1982. Notes on the biology of the fish-eating snake *Lycodonomorphus bicolor* in Lake Tanganyika, *J. Herpetol.* 16: 185–188.

Moore, R. G. 1978. Seasonal and daily activity patterns and thermoregulation in the southwestern speckled rattlesnake (*Crotalus mitchelli pyrrhus*) and the Colorado desert sidewinder (*Crotalus cerates laterorepens*), *Copeia* 1978:439–442.

Mushinsky, H. R., Hebrard, J. J., and Walley, M. G. 1980. The role of temperature on the behavioral and ecological associations of sympatric water snakes, *Copeia* 1980:744–754.

Naulleau, G. 1965. Etude préliminaire de l'activité de *Vipera aspis* dans la nature, *Union Int. Sci. Biol. Sér.* pp. 147–154.

Naulleau, G. 1966. Etude complementaire de l'activite de *Vipera aspis* dans la nature, *Vie Milieu* 17:461–509.

Naulleau, G. 1975. Cycle d'activite de *Vipera aspis* (L.) et choix entre des conditions climatiques naturelles et artificielles, *Vie Milieu* 25:119–136.

Nelson, D. H. and Gibbons, J. W. 1972. Ecology, abundance, and seasonal activity of the scarlet snake, *Cemophora coccinea*, *Copeia* 1972:582–584.

Oliver, J. A. 1955. The Natural History of North American Amphibians and Reptiles, Van Nostrand, New York.

Palmer, W. M. and Braswell, A. L. 1976. Communal egg laying and hatchlings of the rough green snake, *Opheodrys aestivus* (Linnaeus) (Reptilia, Serpentes, Colubridae), *J. Herpetol.* 10:257–259.

Palmer, W. M. and Tregembo, G. 1970. Notes on the natural history of the scarlet snake *Cemophora coccinea copei* in North Carolina, *Herpetologica* 26:300–302.

Parker, W. S. and Brown, W. S. 1972. Telemetric study of movements and oviposition of two female *Masticophis t. taeniatus, Copeia* 1972:892–895.

Parker, W. S. and Brown, W. S. 1973. Species composition and population changes in two complexes of snake hibernacula in northern Utah, *Herpetologica* 29:319–326.

Parker, W. S. and Brown, W. S. 1980. Comparative ecology of two colubrid snakes in northern Utah, *Milw. Public Mus. Publ. Biol. Geol.* 7:1–104.

Phelps, T. W. 1978. Seasonal movement of the snakes *Coronella austriaca, Vipera berus* and *Natrix natrix* in southern England, *Br. J. Herpetol.* 5:775–761.

Platt, D. R. 1969. Natural history of hognose snakes *Heterodon platyrhinos* and *Heterodon nasicus, Univ. Kans. Publ. Mus. Nat. Hist.* 18:253–420.

Plummer, M. V. 1981. Habitat utilization, diet and movements of a temperate arboreal snake (*Opheodrys aestivus*), *J. Herpetol.* 15:425–432.

Pough, F. H. and Gans, C. 1982. The vocabulary of reptilian thermoregulation, in: Biology of the Reptilia, vol. 12 (C. Gans and F. H. Pough, eds.) pp. 17–23, Academic Press, New York.

Prestt, I. 1971. An ecological study of the viper, *Vipera berus,* in southern Britain, *J. Zool.* (*Lond.*) 164:373–418.

Reinert, H. K. 1984. Habitat variation within sympatric snake populations, *Ecology* 65:1673–1682.

Reinert, H. K. and Kodrich, W. R. 1982. Movements and habitat utilization by the massasauga, *Sistrurus catenatus catenatus, J. Herpetol.* 16:162–171.

Robinson, M. D. and Hughes, D. A. 1978. Observations on the natural history of Peringuey's adder, *Bitis peringueyi* (Boulenger) (Reptilia: Viperidae), *Ann. Transvaal Mus.* 31:189–193.

Sanders, J. S. and Jacob, J. S. 1980. Thermal ecology of the copperhead (*Agkistrodon contortrix*), *Herpetologica* 37:264–270.

Seigel, R. A. 1986. Ecology and conservation of an endangered rattlesnake (*Sistrurus catenatus*), in Missouri, USA, *Biol. Conserv.* 35:333–346

Semlitsch, R. D. and Moran, G. B. 1984. Ecology of the redbelly snake (*Storeria occipitomaculata*) using mesic habitats in South Carolina, *Am. Midl. Nat.* 111:33–40.

Semlitsch, R. D., Brown, K. L., and Caldwell, J. P. 1981. Habitat utilization, seasonal activity, and population size structure of the southeastern crowned snake *Tantilla coronata, Herpetologica* 37:40–46.

Sexton, O. J. and Hunt, S. R. 1980. Temperature relationships and movements of snakes (*Elaphe obsoleta, Coluber constrictor*) in a cave hibernaculum, *Herpetologica* 36:20–26.

Sexton, O. J. and Marion, K. R. 1981. Experimental analysis of movements by prairie rattlesnakes, *Crotalus viridis,* during hibernation, *Oecologia (Berl.)* 51:37–41.

Shine, R. 1979. Activity patterns in Australian elapid snakes (Squamata: Serpentes: Elapidae), *Herpetologica* 35:1–11.

Shine, R. 1980. "Costs" of reproduction in reptiles, *Oecologia (Berl.)* 46:92–100.

Shine, R. and Lambeck, R. 1985. A radiotelemetric study of movements, thermoregulation and habitat utilization of arafura filesnakes (Serpentes: Acrochordidae), *Herpetologica* 41:351–361.

Stewart, G. R. 1965. Thermal ecology of the garter snakes *Thamnophis sirtalis concinnus* (Hallowell) and *Thamnophis ordinoides* (Baird and Girard), *Herpetologica* 21:81–102.

Swain, T. A. and Smith, H. M. 1978. Communal nesting in *Coluber constrictor* in Colorado (Reptilia: Serpentes), *Herpetologica* 34:175–177.

Thomas, K. R. and Thomas, R. 1978. Locomotor activity responses to photoperiod in four West Indian fossorial squamates of the genera *Amphisbaena* and *Typhlops* (Reptilia, Lacertilia), *J. Herpetol.* 12:35–41.

Viitanen, P. 1967. Hibernation and seasonal movements of the viper, *Vipera berus berus* (L.), in southern Finland, *Ann. Zool. Fennici* 4:472–546.

Woodbury, A. M., ed. 1951. Symposium: A snake den in Tooele County, Utah, *Herpetologica* 7:1–52.

Yamagishi, M. 1974. Observations on the nocturnal activity of the habu with special reference to the intensity of illumination, *Snake* 6:37–43.

CHAPTER FOURTEEN

Temperature, Energetics, and Physiological Ecology

Harvey B. Lillywhite

Physiological research is of primary importance in understanding the ecology and behavior of snakes. Publications reflecting scientific interest in the physiology of snakes predate the present century, and snakes figured prominently in the inception of the diffuse discipline called vertebrate physiological ecology. Yet snakes are not always frequent subjects of physiological investigation, nor are they generally regarded as representative models for depicting "reptilian" grades of physiological adaptation. Consequently, knowledge of the physiological attributes of snakes often lags behind investigations of other reptiles, especially lizards and turtles. This dearth of research emphasis on snakes is no doubt largely attributable to the conspicuousness and availability of animals such as lizards and the predisposition of most investigators to utilize subjects that are safely and easily handled.

Because of their long body shape, range of size, taxonomic diversity, and breadth of ecological adaptation, snakes offer unique and challenging opportunities for investigating the interactions of physiology with the environment. Since their origin in the Cretaceous, snakes have undergone an impressive adaptive radiation while retaining the specialized morphology of an elongated and limbless body. The attenuated and (usually) slender form of snakes is a feature that necessitates special solutions to fundamental physiological problems (Gans, 1983). Larger surface-to-mass ratios simultaneously demand and constrain specializations for maintaining body temperature, fluid volumes, or the concentration of osmotically active solutes. Transport functions of the elongated circulation require adaptations to resist the stresses of hydrostatic gradients imposed by gravity in aerial environments (Lillywhite, 1987). Elongation also requires specialization of feeding and digestive systems to allow the extraction of energy from prey that are ingested whole (Gans, 1975). These features of physiology are basic to the ability of individuals to perform essential activities that influence growth, reproduction, and survival.

An elongated body has important consequences for energetics. In reference to behavior, the length and shape of snakes determine their mode of locomotion, set limits for predation tactics, and allow access to crevices and other spaces used for short- or long-term reclusion. Like other reptiles, snakes are ectothermic and rely on external sources of heat to elevate their body temperature to the levels required for various activities. The source of energy used to control body temperature distinguishes snakes from endothermic birds and mammals, which generate heat from metabolic reactions in tissues. This is a fundamentally important distinction, for it enables snakes (and other reptiles) to exist on a fraction of the energy required for the maintenance of endotherms. Thus ecologists have determined that reptiles may produce as much new biomass annually as birds and mammals in the same community, despite the fact that they consume a much smaller fraction of the net primary production in their environment (Pough, 1983).

Clearly, snakes possess the intrinsic machinery for increasing metabolic heat production in special limited circumstances (see below). But continuous endothermy is theoretically not feasible because of the rapid heat loss that would result from the large surface-to-mass ratio and thermal conductance of active or uncoiled animals. Norwithstanding the mechanical difficulties associated with insulating the elongated body without sacrificing behavioral performance, the shape factor sets biophysical limits by itself (Brown and Lasiewski, 1972). Undoubtedly, other selection forces have acted to preclude endothermy in modern reptiles. The point here is that the specialized morphology of snakes provides a clear illustration of the constraints of physiological characteristics.

These fundamental biological distinctions suggest that studies on snakes can contribute important insights concerning the mechanisms, effectiveness, and evolution of physiological adaptations. This chapter is concerned with an ecological perspective of physiology and the opportunities for contributing new information from research with snakes. Clearly, it is not possible to provide a thorough review of what is presently known about the physiological ecology of snakes in the limited space available. Instead, I will emphasize certain major themes and attempt to illustrate the relevance of physiology to the behavior and ecology of snakes, utilizing a selected set of case studies and, where appropriate, generalizations. This chapter will focus on the subjects of thermal adaptations and energetics, because of the breadth of interest in these topics and their historical importance.

THERMAL RELATIONS OF SNAKES

Historical Aspects

The behavior and physiology of snakes are dependent on body temperature, which is determined largely by external sources of heat. Thus, like other reptiles and ectotherms, snakes are tightly coupled to their physical environment. To address questions relating to aspects of the distribution, abundance, activity, and reproduction of snakes requires detailed information about the animals' thermal relationships.

A half-century ago it was generally assumed that the body temperature of reptiles passively followed that of the environment. Thus snakes were regarded as obligatorily ectothermic and poikilothermic. Scientific interest in the thermal physiology of squamate reptiles grew primarily from the influence of Walter Mosauer and Raymond Cowles. Both Mosauer and Cowles were influenced by Laurence Klauber, who recognized that temperature limited the activity of snakes (Klauber, 1939). Mosauer conducted crude laboratory tests and successfully demonstrated that desert snakes were not especially tolerant of high body temperatures (Mosauer and Lazier, 1933). Studies by Raymond Cowles reaffirmed the findings of Mosauer and further established that squamate reptiles have rather specific preferences for body temperature (Bogert, 1939; Cowles, 1939; Sergeyev, 1939; Cowles and Bogert, 1944). The works of these men stimulated what was to be a long-lasting interest in behavioral temperature regulation and the significance of temperature in the ecological relations of reptiles. It is widely known that such studies on lizards have advanced more rapidly than those on other reptiles. There is, however, a substantive and growing literature relating to the body temperatures of snakes (reviews in Fitch, 1956; Brattstrom, 1965; Cloudsley-Thompson, 1971; Heatwole, 1976; Avery, 1982; Peterson, 1982).

During the past several decades body temperatures have been reported for roughly 100 species of snakes representing at least 10 families. Many of the earlier measurements were obtained opportunistically with the use of mercury or thermistor thermometers and without knowledge of a snake's previous behavior or the thermal structure of its habitat. Consequently, the use of such data for interpretive purposes is strictly limited. Much of the available field data is based on nonrepetitive measurements from different animals and thus does not allow adequate evaluaton of thermoregulation, nor does it provide information about individual differences in temperature selection. As in lizards, temperature measurements in snakes are biased to a large extent by the time budgets of investigators and the difficulty of observing snakes when they are inactive or inconspicuous. Recognition of these limitations can contribute a great deal toward implementing a meaningful research design. Studies employing various temperature-recording methods have correlated body temperature with behavioral activities or physiology in the laboratory. Field studies on thermoregulation in free-living snakes have been made possible through the use of biotelemetry, and this technology will no doubt continue to be useful in future behavioral and ecological research (Fitch, this volume).

Behavioral Thermoregulation

The body temperature (BT) of a snake is tightly coupled to a combination of physical, behavioral, and physiological factors. Behavior is overridingly important because it modulates the physical factors to influence rates and direction of temperature change, which are dependent on the net flux of heat. Thermoregulation is achieved by shuttling between contrasting thermal environments and by flattening, tilting, coiling, or extending the body (Dmi'el and Borut, 1972; Johnson, 1972; Saint Girons, 1975; Hammerson, 1977; Heatwole and Johnson, 1979; Lillywhite, 1980; and references therein). Such behaviors alter the exposure and contour of body surfaces, thereby modifying the regional exchanges of heat between the snake and its environment. Careful observations of an elapid, *Pseudechis porphyriacus,* implanted with thermocouples, have shown that postural adjustments associated with a rather narrow range of BT abruptly alter thermal gradients within the bodies of thermoregulating snakes (Heatwole and Johnson, 1979). Retreat to subterranean shelters or under leaf mounds can retard heat loss in snakes and is of obvious importance in limiting nocturnal cooling (Johnson, 1972; Johnson et al., 1975; Ruben, 1976a; Peterson, 1987). Conversely, boa constrictors in tropical climates maintain their BT as much as 7°C below shaded ground temperature by seeking out subterranean retreats that are cooler (McGinnis and Moore, 1969).

Opportunities for thermoregulation are restricted in aquatic snakes, and the use of thermoregulatory postures is ineffective because of the high thermal conductivity and heat capacity of the surrounding medium. The black dorsal surface of the pelagic sea snake *Pelamis platurus* absorbs solar radiation and consistently elevates its BT slightly above ambient when snakes are in calm water (Graham, 1974). Several authors have suggested that *Pelamis* thermoregulates either by basking at the water surface or by alternating basking with diving (see references in Graham, 1974; Kropach, 1975). There is no compelling evidence that movements of sea snakes up or down water columns are thermoregulatory, however, and laboratory tests indicate that *Pelamis* neither seeks nor avoids heat when presented with thermal choices (Graham, 1974).

There is evidence that aquatic file snakes (*Acrochordus arafurae*) thermoregulate by selecting appropriate microhabitats such that variance of BT is significantly less than that of the ambient water temperature (Shine and Lambeck, 1985). The behavior of the snakes reduces the variability of BT to the extent that for much of the year file snakes are effectively homeothermic (BT varies no more than a few degrees Celsius).

Behaviors of terrestrial snakes confer thermoregulatory precision comparable

Table 14–1. Tolerance, Activity, and Preferred Body Temperatures of Snakes[a]

Species	CTMin (°C)	CTMax (°C)	Activity Range and Preferred Range (°C)[a,b]	Preferred Body Temperature (°C)[b]	Reference
Acrochordidae					
Acrochordus arafurae			(24–35)		Shine and Lambeck (1985)
Boidae					
Aspidites melanocephalus			(?–35) (H) / (?–37) (B)		Johnson (1973), Johnson et al. (1975)
Boa constrictor			21–38		McGinnis and Moore (1969), Montgomery and Rand (1978)
Candoia aspera			(?–35) (H) / (?–36) (B)	34 (H) / 34 (B)	Johnson (1975b)
C. carinata			(?–37) (H) / (?–37) (B)	34 (H) / 35 (B)	Johnson (1975b)
Charina bottae			20–31		Vitt (1974)
Liasis amethystinus				34	Johnson (1973)
L. childreni				29	Johnson (1973)
L. fuscus			(?–33) (H) / (?–37) (B)	33 (H) / 36 (B)	Johnson (1973)
Python (= *Morelia*) *spilotes*			(25–36)	30–32	Cogger and Holmes (1960), Webb and Heatwole (1971), Johnson (1972)
Colubridae					
Arizona elegans[c]		42	19–?	27	Cowles and Bogert, 1944
Boiga irregularis			(?–35) (H) / (?–37) (B)	35 (H) / 36 (B)	Johnson (1975b)
Carphophis amoenus[c]			(14–31)	23	Clark (1967)
Chionactis occipitalis[c]		37	20–?		Cowles and Bogert (1944)
Coluber constrictor		>41?	20–34 / (22–37)	32–34	Fitch (1963), Hirth and King (1969), Vitt (1974)

Species					References
Coronella austriaca[c]			17–31	26–28	Spellerberg and Phelps (1975)
Diadophis punctatus[c]	6–9		(10–36)	26	Clark (1967)
Elaphe obsoleta		>41	(21–31)		Jacob and McDonald (1975)
Heterodon nasicus	≈7		(18–30)	30	Platt (1969)
Heterodon platirhinos			21–36		Platt (1969)
			22–34		
			(23–37)		
Masticophis flagellum			(26–40) (H)	29–32	Cowles and Bogert (1944), Hammerson (1977)
			(24–36) (B)	34 (H)	
				32 (B)	
M. lateralis			(28–35)	33	Hammerson (1979)
M. taeniatus			(18–37)		Hirth and King (1969)
Nerodia cyclopion			(24–34)	28–29	Mushinsky et al. (1980)
N. erythrogaster				27–29	Gehrmann (1971), Mushinsky et al. (1980)
N. fasciata	6	40 (15)		26–29	Mushinsky et al. (1980)
N. rhombifera	9	41 (30)		26–29	Jacobson and Whitford (1970), Mushinsky et al. (1980)
N. sipedon			(21–35)	28	Kitchell (1969)
Phyllorhynchus decurtatus[c]		38	24–?		Cowles and Bogert (1944)
Pituophis melanoleucus			16–33		Cunningham (1966), Dill (1972)
			(25–33)		
Regina grahamii			(30–35)	30	Mushinsky et al. (1980)
Salvadora hexalepis	7	44	(20–35)	33	Jacobson and Whitford (1971)
Spalerosophis cliffordi			(20–30)	30	Dmi'el and Borut (1972)
Tantilla gracilis[c]				25	Clark (1967)
Thamnophis brachystoma				30	Asplund (1963)
T. cyrtopsis			22–32?	31 (4)	Fleharty (1967)
T. elegans hammondi			19–32	25 (21–23)	Cunningham (1966)
T. elegans vagrans		43	20–36	30	Fleharty (1967), Scott and Pettus (1979), Scott et al (1982), Peterson (1987)
T. ordinoides	4	39	17–34	27	Stewart (1965)
			(20–34)		

(Continued)

Table 14–1. Tolerance, Activity, and Preferred Body Temperatures of Snakes[a] (*Continued*)

Species	CTMin (°C)	CTMax (°C)	Activity Range and Preferred Range (°C)[a,b]	Preferred Body Temperature (°C)[b]	Reference
T. proximus	4	39 (15)			Jacobson and Whitford (1970)
	8	42 (30)			
T. radix			21–36		Hart (1979)
T. rufipunctatus			20–29?		Fleharty (1967)
T. sirtalis concinnus	4	39	10–36 (20–35)	28	Stewart (1965)
T. sirtalis spp.			19–35 (20–35)	26–30	Fitch (1965), Kitchell (1969), Gibson and Falls (1979), Hart (1979), Lysenko and Gillis (1980)
Tropidoclonion lineatum[c]			(19–33)	27	Clark (1967)
Uromacer catesbyi			(28–32)	29	Henderson (1982)
U. oxyrhynchus			(28–30)	30	Henderson (1982)
Elapidae					
Acanthophis antarcticus			(27–39)	33	Lillywhite (1980)
Austrelaps superbus	1–3	41	(26–37)	31–33	Heatwole (1976), Shine (1979), Lillywhite (1980)
Cryptophis nigrescens[c]		40			Heatwole (1976)
Demansia psammophis				31	Heatwole (1976)
Denisonia signata[c]				31	Heatwole (1976)
Notechis scutatus	1–2	38	25–34 (23–36)	30–32	Heatwole (1976), Shine (1979), Lillywhite (1980)
Oxyuranus scutellatus			(39) (H) (41) (B)	35 (H) 38 (B)	Johnson (1975a)
Pseudechis porphyriacus	3	42	(26–36)	30–34	Heatwole and Johnson (1979), Shine (1979), Lillywhite (1980)
Pseudonaja nuchalis	7		(30–37)	32–34	Lillywhite (1980)
P. textilis	4–7	40	(29–38)	35	Heatwole (1976), Lillywhite (1980)

Species					Reference
Suta flagellum	3				Heatwole (1976)
Unechis flagellum[c]			(24–36)	30	Lillywhite (1980)
Leptotyphlopidae					
Leptotyphlops dulcis[c]			(16–28)	21	Clark (1967)
Viperidae					
Agkistrodon contortrix	4–9	41	23–31	26–29(?)	Fitch (1960), Sanders and Jacob (1981)
Cerastes cerastes				32–34	Saint Girons and Saint Girons (1956)
Crotalus atrox		39	18–?		Cowles and Bogert (1944)
C. cerastes[c]		42	14–41	26–32	Mosauer (1936), Cowles and Bogert (1944), Moore (1978)
Crotalus mitchelli			19–39	31	Moore (1978)
C. viridis lutosus			(15–35)		Hirth and King (1969)
Vipera aspis	5–6?		16?–35	29–32	Saint Girons (1975, 1978), Naulleau (1979)
V. ammodytes			16?–35	30–32	Saint Girons (1975, 1978)
V. berus	4–5?		14?–34	31–32	Saint Girons and Saint Girons (1956), Saint Girons (1975, 1978)
V. latastei			16?–34	31–32	Saint Girons (1978)
V. seoanei			16?–34	30–32	Saint Girons (1975, 1978)
V. ursinii	4–5?		16?–35	30–33	Saint Girons and Saint Girons (1956), Saint Girons (1975, 1978)

[a] Data do not include temperatures published in Fitch (1956) and Brattstrom (1965) and are based on measurements from animals that are active in environments where heat sources are sufficient to allow thermoregulation (except for tolerance limits). In some cases this condition was assumed by considering data only from warm seasons. The activity range refers to the range of body temperatures between the voluntary minimum and voluntary maximum as determined from field measurements. The preferred range (in parentheses) is similar but is based on measurements from snakes in a laboratory thermal gradient. To simplify the table, individual differences attributable to sex, age, feeding condition and (sometimes) acclimation are incorporated within the ranges listed. The references may be consulted for further details. Numbers in parentheses, other than preferred ranges, refer to acclimation temperatures.

[b] H, head temperature; B, body temperature.

[c] Fossorial, secretive, or nocturnal habits.

to that of heliothermic lizards. This conclusion is contrary to earlier suggestions that snakes are imprecise thermoregulators, based on the variability of body temperatures reported from field measurements (Avery, 1982). Careful study of individual snakes, however, demonstrates that standard errors of thermal preferenda are rather consistently less than 1°C (Hammerson, 1979; Heatwole and Johnson, 1979; Lillywhite, 1980; Peterson, 1987).

In the majority of snakes for which data are sufficient to define a thermal preferendum, preferred body temperatures (PBTs) are within the range 28 to 34°C and are frequently very near 30°C, irrespective of taxonomic affiliation (Table 14–1). Surprisingly, the uniformity of PBT appears to be more consistent among snakes than among lizards. Several points of information, not previously emphasized, bear on this conclusion. First, the suggestion that snakes maintain lower BTs than lizards (Saint Girons and Saint Girons, 1956; Brattstrom, 1965) does not seem generally valid. For example, the occurrence of low PBTs (<28°C) in snakes having nocturnal habits or inhabiting fossorial and shaded habitats has its counterpart in lizards (Avery, 1982). A second point is that garter snakes (*Thamnophis* spp.) appear to be more thermophilic than was previously assumed. Recent studies indicate that even northern and high-altitude species of *Thamnophis* regulate BT near 30°C (or even warmer) when heat sources are accessible (Vincent, 1975; Gibson and Falls, 1979; Scott and Pettus, 1979; Peterson, 1987). Third, diurnal and heliothermic species of snakes inhabiting open environments tend to regulate BT at levels that exceed 30°C but are generally not higher than 35°C (Jacobson and Whitford, 1971; Hammerson, 1977, 1979; Lillywhite, 1980). The taipan, *Oxyuranus scutellatus,* may be an exception, because it appears to voluntarily tolerate somewhat higher temperatures (Johnson, 1975a). Generally, however, these open-habitat thermophilic species provide a contrast with lizards, for many saurian counterparts adapted to arid environments maintain activity BTs above 38°C (Avery, 1982). The limited thermophily of snakes is likely a result of their limbless morphology, which couples body temperatures more closely to that of the substratum than is true in the case of thermophilic lizards. Thus, in hot, sunlit environments, snakes that are active with high BTs are at greater risk of overheating because locomotion involves contact with a hot substratum. Selection for more moderate PBTs reduces the risk of overheating. In any event, the apparent absence of higher PBTs in snakes contributes to the homogeneity of PBT that characterizes the group.

It is important to recognize that the occurrence, level, and precision of thermoregulation depends on the motivational state of the snake and on the availability of an appropriate physical environment. Behavioral studies using laboratory thermal gradients permit assessment of the capabilities of animals to control body temperature and evaluation of the mechanisms of the process. Variability of thermal preferenda may also be evaluated in relation to genetic or physiological variables (see below). In the field, however, numerous factors potentially influence the temperatures that are either selected or passively assumed by reptiles (Huey, 1982). Therefore, investigations must be carefully designed to discriminate whether BT variation in the field is attributable to biophysical constraints, to the behavior of individual snakes, or to both.

Telemetry techniques were employed recently to evaluate the daily variation in BT in garter snakes (*Thamnophis elegans*) at a site in eastern Washington (Peterson, 1987). Body temperatures of free-ranging snakes were monitored and compared with simultaneously measured temperatures of painted copper models (so-called operative temperatures, T_e, see Bakken and Gates, 1975). The model

Figure 14–1. Patterns of body temperature variaton in garter snakes, *Thamnophis elegans vagrans*. Body temperatures (T_b) were telemetered from free-ranging snakes and are plotted as a function of time of day (local solar time). T_m indicates the "operative" or equilibrium temperature of a painted copper model positioned in the open, aboveground environment, and T_g indicates deep ground temperatures at 20 cm depth. Sunrise and sunset times are indicated by arrows. The upper panel (A) illustrates the plateau pattern of T_b where the snake has access to warm temperatures during the day. The lower panel (B) illustrates the oscillating pattern where the daylight period is characterized by availability of moderate and oscillating temperatures. Reprinted with permission from Peterson (1987). Copyright © 1987 by Ecological Society of America.

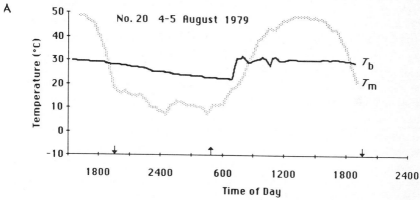

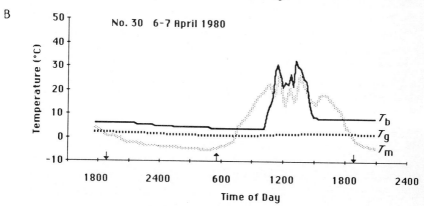

temperatures were used to describe the range of BT potentially available to the snakes during the periods that were monitored. During the night and on cool days (max. T_e at ground surface $\leqslant 15°C$), snakes remained underground and BT changed gradually or not at all. On moderate days ($15°C <$ max. $T_e < 30°C$), snakes usually emerged but were unable to maintain preferred temperatures consistently. Body temperatures on these days showed oscillations and variability (Figure 14–1). On warm days ($T_e \geqslant 30°C$), active snakes selected a BT within their preferred range, and the variation in BT was small (Figure 14–1). Body temperatures were constrained by the physical environment to some extent on all of the days that were monitored. The duration of periods during which snakes were unable to attain their PBT correlated with weather conditions and ranged from entire days during cold periods in the spring and fall to approximately 7 h during the night on warm, sunny days. Thus the biophysical characteristics of the available microenvironments were shown to limit where and when snakes could be active and the level and precision of thermoregulation that was possible.

The importance of the PBT to garter snakes is suggested from Peterson's data by the "plateau" pattern of BT that was predominant on warm days (Figure 14–1). During the morning, snakes warmed quickly (0.22°C/min) from the minimum daily BT and soon achieved the PBT of approximately 30°C. The initial rapid heating corresponded to the snake's emergence and exposure to the sun. During the plateau phase BTs were relatively stable for periods varying from 4 to 12 h. Snakes were often active during this phase and utilized a variety of microhabitats. A cooling phase began in the afternoon and ended the following morning. Rates of cooling were considerably less than the prior heating rates, averaging 0.03°C/min, and corresponded to snakes retreating to subterranean sites that remained warmer than the aboveground T_e when insolation was reduced or absent. The behavior of snakes in relation to the diel cycle of heat availability results in a frequency distribution of body temperatures that is bimodal, corresponding to the plateau and cooling phases, respectively (Figure 14–2). Note that this distribution of BT is quite different from the unimodal distributions that usually result from opportunistic measurements of BT from snakes that are accessible to capture.

The use of continuously monitored BT and T_e data can improve the estimates of thermal selection and the interpretations of their significance. For example, in Peterson's study, wild garter snakes selected a narrow range of BT during the plateau phase, corresponding to preferred temperatures that snakes maintained in laboratory gradients (ca. 30°C). In contrast, field measurements of activity temperatures in this same species averaged several degrees lower in other studies in which records were taken when T_e was below the preferred temperature and when snakes were still heating to preferred levels (see Peterson, 1987). It seems likely that field data from various sources may have underrepresented or misrepresented preferred levels of activity temperature simply because animals that are exposed and immobile during heating are likely to be readily captured.

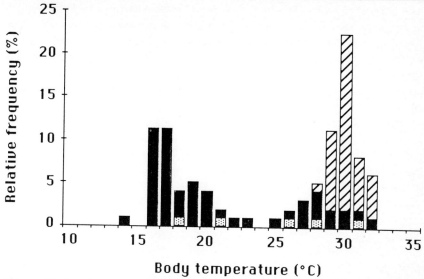

Figure 14–2. Frequency distribution of body temperatures based on 97 telemetry readings taken from a free-ranging *Thamnophis elegans vagrans* that produced a plateau pattern record (see Figure 14–1) during 22–23 June 1979. Temperature readings from cooling, heating, and plateau phases are indicated by solid, stippled, and cross-hatched areas, respectively. Reprinted with permission from Peterson, (1987). Copyright © 1987 by Ecological Society of America.

Plasticity of Thermal Preferenda

Thermal preferences of snakes can be altered significantly by changes in physiological factors or physical environment. Preferred body temperatures of garter snakes are inversely related to acclimation temperature and undergo a seasonal decrease from spring to summer (Scott, 1978; Scott and Pettus, 1979). Acclimatization-caused shifts in thermoregulatory set points might explain seasonal patterns of BT reported in field studies, although changing constraints of the physical environment in relation to time of capture are likely contributing causes (Carpenter, 1956; Hirth and King, 1969; Clark, 1970; Gibson and Falls, 1979).

   If it is assumed that temperature preference acclimatizes inversely with temperature, a higher PBT following emergence from overwinter temperatures in the spring might effectively enhance physiological performance and reproductive processes. More generally, an inverse relationship between PBT and acclimation temperature (also seen in other vertebrate ectotherms) might be important in driving BT in a direction opposite to prolonged exposure to constant extremes. For hibernating snakes, an upward resetting of the thermoregulatory set point would increase the error signal generated by a lowered BT. The snake might then experience increased ability to seek out subtle changes in thermal profile in its winter environment, where a few degrees of temperature difference could potentially influence survival. It must be remembered that the measured increase in PBT that presumably influences thermal behavior during emergence in the spring is an *acute response*. It seems likely that the effect lasts for only brief periods when snakes are acclimatizing to warming temperatures, probably while still at the den site.

Further research into these subjects would benefit from at least three considerations. First, a distinction between *acute* thermal preferenda and *final* preferenda would facilitate species comparisons and the testing of hypotheses relating the behavioral aspects of PBT to ecology. The term "final preferendum" refers to the temperature at which preference and acclimation are equal and which is ultimately selected in a thermal gradient regardless of prior thermal history (Fry, 1947). This concept has advanced studies on thermoregulation in fishes (Reynolds and Casterlin, 1979) but has been ignored by herpetologists. A second point concerning thermal acclimation of PBT is that some information about the mechanism(s) inducing the shift in the thermoregulatory set point would also contribute insight regarding its significance. Finally, acclimation effects of constant temperatures may not be strictly relevant to situations where snakes experience daily variations in BT.

Reports are mixed concerning the extent to which food ingestion alters PBT and causes heat-seeking behavior in snakes. Several studies have demonstrated that a pronounced thermophilic response is induced by feeding and digestion (Regal, 1966; Naulleau and Marques, 1973; Saint Girons, 1975, 1978; Greenwald and Kanter, 1979; Lysenko and Gillis, 1980), whereas others have found that such responses are absent (Kitchell, 1969; Hammerson, 1979; Lysenko and Gillis, 1980). Digestive hyperthermia enhances energy assimilation but also entails risks if basking behaviors increase the exposure of snakes to predators. Intensive field investigations will be required before we will know unequivocally whether digestive hyperthermia is important in natural circumstances (see Peterson, 1987). Feeding curtails the mobility of snakes and results in seclusion rather than activity on the part of most animals. Depending on the environment, it is conceivable that seclusion could result in a lowering of BT rather than in hyperthermia, even though the laboratory-determined PBT of a species shifts upward in response to feeding. Differential predation risks have been advanced as possible selective causes of species differences in the effects of ingestion on PBT (Lysenko and Gillis, 1980). Digestive hyperthermia in vipers appears to be proportional to the mass or volume of the ingested prey (Saint Girons, 1975), suggesting that gastrointestinal mechanoreceptors play a role in the response. However, a mechanistic analysis of these thermophilic behaviors remains to be undertaken.

A variety of other factors potentially alter thermal preferences, including illumination, reproductive condition, skin shedding, age, and sex (Kitchell, 1969; Gehrmann, 1971; Gibson and Falls, 1979; Lillywhite, 1980; Sanders and Jacob,

1981). Endogenous seasonal or circadian rhythms also conceivably influence thermoregulatory behavior directly or indirectly (Licht, 1972; Gratz and Hutchison, 1977). Some snakes apparently do not exhibit inherent circadian rhythms of body temperature when given continuous access to heat (Lueth, 1941; Lysenko and Gillis, 1980). However, seasonal changes in thermoregulatory behavior that are well documented in snakes and in other reptiles may well have underlying causal components related to endogenous rhythmicity. Obviously, multivariate investigations are required to further our understanding of the causes and significance of thermoregulatory plasticity.

In snakes, as in other ectothermic vertebrates, there are ample data illustrating intrageneric variability of PBT (Table 14–1). On the other hand, little attention has been paid to intraspecific variability of preferred temperatures existing among individuals or populations. Assuming that PBTs are subjected to selection, it is desirable to determine the range of variation in individual PBTs and their genetic components relative to interactions with selective forces in the species' environment. Evidently, preferred temperatures do not change with altitude in *Vipera aspis* (Duguy, 1972) and *Thamnophis elegans* (C. R. Peterson, unpublished data).

Physiological Thermoregulation

The elongate body form of snakes is physiologically disadvantageous in specific circumstances, but the ability to coil allows remarkable control over the body surface area-to-mass ratio. The extended body of a snake may present a large mass–relative surface to the environment, especially when flattened, and very rapid rates of heat exchange are possible. When the body is tightly coiled, however, the surface-to-mass ratio is greatly reduced and in some species may approach the minimum possible ratio exemplified by a sphere. This latter circumstance minimizes heat exchange with the environment and increases the feasibility of controlling body temperature by means of endothermy and cardiovascular adjustments. The social behavior of aggregating may modify surface-environment interactions even further.

Aggregative behavior has been reported in a number of snakes, including terrestrial and aquatic species (see Gregory et al., this volume), and there is increasing evidence that some aggregations are thermoregulatory. Aggregations of large snakes, such as pythons and boas, are known only from the northern part of the species' range (Myers and Eells, 1968). This tends to be generally true for north temperate colubrids as well, and only northern species of rattlesnakes den in large numbers (Klauber, 1956). Within the den, the tendency of snakes to form tight aggregations, both intra- and interspecifically, is temperature-dependent (Gillingham and Carpenter, 1978). Elapid snakes inhabiting latitudes with a moderate climate tend to overwinter singly (Shine, 1979).

Heat retention is increased in both coiled and aggregated snakes under laboratory conditions (Cogger and Holmes, 1960; Myers and Eells, 1968; Johnson, 1972). In large constrictors such as boas and pythons, cooling rates are approximately halved if the animal assumes a coiled position, although this factor varies with the microclimate and the level of activity. Estimates of fat consumption have been used to predict heat production relative to the effective surface area of a hypothetical aggregate of 150 denning rattlesnakes (White and Lasiewski, 1971). The analysis predicts a mean BT for the winter season that is about 15°C above the ambient den site temperature. The level of aggregate endothermy is attributable to the metabolic heat production relative to an aggregate effective surface area that is 40% of the summed surface areas of individual animals in isolation. While this calculation is subject to criticism (Brown et al., 1974), it is possible that mean body temperatures of snakes in winter aggregations may be higher than indicated by the ambient climate. Clearly, these "aggregate" temperatures are important for annual energy budgets and might well accelerate annual reproductive cycles. In addition to thermal effects, aggregation could substantially reduce integumentary water exchange and modify the den microclimate.

Endothermic enhancement of BT in individual snakes is suggested by reports that pythons can maintain temperatures 5 to 12°C above ambient throughout clear nights in an aviary (Cogger and Holmes, 1960) and raise body temperature by coiling more tightly after feeding (Marcellini and Peters, 1982). In these situations, the snakes appear to actively control thermal conductance by their coiling behavior, but there is no direct evidence that metabolic heat production is regulated for thermoregulation. However, facultative endothermy by shivering has been well documented in brooding female pythons (Vinegar et al., 1970; Van Mierop and Barnard, 1976, 1978; Harlow and Grigg, 1984). Other pythons have been observed shivering while brooding eggs but have not been shown conclusively to regulate temperature by this mechanism (references in Harlow and Grigg, 1984).

Thermogenesis during brooding results from intermittent spasmodic contractions of body musculature, the frequency of which varies inversely with ambient temperature and directly with metabolism (Figure 14–3). This has become a textbook example of facultative endothermy and parallels physiological thermoregulation in birds and mammals. It has been pointed out that under tropical climatic conditions the increase in metabolism required to maintain brooding temperatures may be relatively modest compared with the maximum rates of metabolism that are possible (Bartholomew, 1982). Furthermore, some species are known to supplement metabolic heat production with heat gained from opportunistic sun basking. Harlow and Grigg (1984) have suggested that shivering thermogenesis may be important as a mechanism for allowing geographic range extension into areas where ambient temperatures would otherwise not permit embryonic development. Further investigations of ophidian reproductive behavior and the thermal requirements of embryonic development will be of great interest.

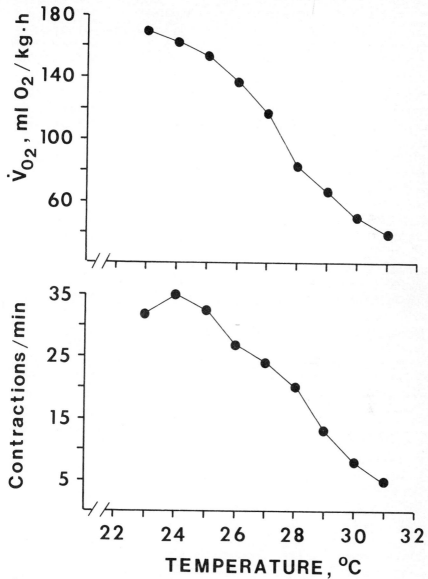

Figure 14–3. Oxygen consumption and rate of body muscle contractions measured in a brooding female *Python molurus bivittatus,* plotted as functions of ambient temperature. Data from Van Mierop and Barnard (1978).

Studies on a variety of reptiles—principally lizards, turtles, and crocodilians—have demonstrated the ability of these animals to control heating and cooling rates by physiological changes in thermal conductance. Evidence for the control of thermal conductance comes primarily from experiments demonstrating differences in thermal time constants during heating and cooling in response to step changes in the ambient temperature. The thermal time constant is a useful comparative measure derived from the slope of the exponential rate of heating or cooling, independent of the magnitude of the step temperature (Bakken, 1976; Smith, 1976).

The mechanisms by which thermal conductance is altered in various species involve physiological modifications of metabolic heat production and blood circulation rates (reviewed in Bartholomew, 1982). In general, the more important variable appears to be circulatory. Physiological contributions to control of heat exchange have been evaluated in the desert colubrid *Spalerosophis cliffordi* (Dmi'el and Borut, 1972). Under experimental conditions, live snakes heat more rapidly than they cool by a factor of about 20%, and their heart rate exhibits a parallel pattern. Simultaneous measurements of oxygen consumption showed that during heating the metabolism at a given BT was near the minimal level found in resting snakes, whereas the heart rate was maximal. This is in contrast to the cooling cycle, in which the metabolic rate was maximal and the heart rate minimal. In addition to these physiological and presumably regulatory responses, local blood flow variation may be attributable to changes in blood viscosity, which varies inversely with temperature and alters vascular resistance in a parallel manner. Thus heating reduces viscosity locally, thereby reducing resistance to flow and allowing greater passage of blood through the vascular bed. Further research is required to resolve the extant issue of how the component of flow resistance attributable to blood viscosity compares with that arising from active vasomotor adjustments (discussed in Firth and Turner, 1982).

The usual significance attached to reptilian control of thermal conductance is that it extends the time an animal can maintain a favorable body temperature. The rapid heating and metabolic responses of *S. cliffordi* conceivably enable this snake to achieve its PBT rapidly and to be active for a relatively long time even when the ambient conditions are less than optimal. Studies on other snakes may reveal similarly interesting physiological responses, but these will be best exemplified in relatively large species. Analysis indicates that control of thermal conductance is likely to be ineffective in modifying rates of heat exchange in small reptiles (<20 g: Fraser and Grigg, 1984), especially if the animal lacks limbs (Turner, 1986).

There is considerable circumstantial evidence suggesting that the cardiovascular system contributes to the local distribution of heat and temperature in snakes. The length of a snake may simultaneously occupy different microclimates, and the animal may expose different segments of its trunk so that there are regional differences in the rate of heat exchange. The most thoroughly documented example of this phenomenon, and presumably the most important, is that persistent and significant differences exist between head and body temperature in several species of snakes (Table 14–1).

Data suggest that in some snake species the brain may be preferentially warmed (by radiation) before morning exposure or activity (Johnson, 1975a,b; Hammerson, 1977) and that the unexposed body may be warmed by the distribution of heat from the head (Webb and Heatwole, 1971). In warming pythons, however, the body may heat more rapidly than the head (Johnson, 1973), and the postural behaviors of several elapid species in a photothermal gradient suggest that all parts of the body are heated such as to minimize the regional heterogeneity of body temperature (Lillywhite, 1980). In any case, the most consistent and significant finding in a number of studies is that head temperatures are regulated with much greater precision than posterior body temperatures. Within preferred limits, head temperatures are usually lower than body temperatures and show lower tolerance maxima (Table 14–1). Presumably, the maintenance of a head-body temperature difference involves venomotor control of blood flow in the internal jugular vein and orbital sinuses, but this remains to be investigated directly (Webb and Heatwole, 1971; Johnson, 1973). Head temperatures in various snakes are also controlled by gaping, hiding the head (usually inside or beneath a coil, as in balling pythons), elevating the head above the substrate, or burying the head in the substrate. Temperature differences between head and body can also result from physical factors independent of the animal's control (Pough and McFarland, 1976).

Tolerance Limits and the Distribution of Species

While much of the research concerning reptilian thermal relations has emphasized thermoregulation during warm periods, snakes can be active over very broad ranges of environmental and body temperature. When the environment permits, snakes are able to maintain high rates of physiological processes as a result of precise thermoregulation within the preferred temperature range (see next section). Near-optimal temperatures for many vital processes, however, extend over a somewhat broader range of activity temperatures bounded by voluntary minima and maxima. This range may extend 15°C or more in terrestrial eurythermal species. Movement and limited activity are possible within a still broader range of BT extending between ecological tolerance limits defined by critical thermal minima (CTMin) and critical thermal maxima (CTMax). Survival below the voluntary and critical minima is possible for limited periods, whereas exposure to temperatures above the CTMax is imminently lethal because of possible cardiorespiratory stress, acid-base imbalance, and disruption of protein and enzyme function.

The range of thermal tolerance within which locomotor activity is possible can be relatively broad, extending more than 35°C in many species. Ultimately the survival and fitness of snakes depends on the "optimal" level or range of

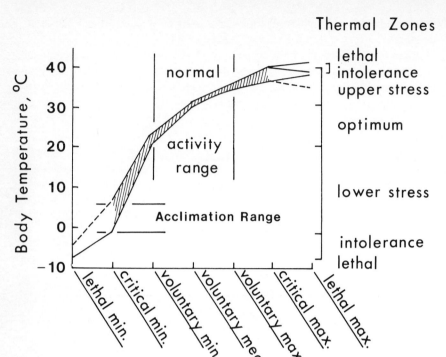

Figure 14–4. Graphic representation of the ranges of possible body temperatures of snakes. Adapted from Spellerberg (1972), with permission.

temperature, just as there is such a temperature range for endotherms. However, variation in BT during cool or inactive periods should receive greater attention from investigators because the majority of the animals' time may be spent at these temperatures. A graphic depiction of thermal zones describing ophidian thermal relations is shown in Figure 14–4, while representative data for tolerance and activity temperatures are listed in Table 14–1.

Temperatures exceeding the lethal limits for snakes occur in many species' environments. Colder temperatures generally persist longer than hotter temperatures, but they are easier to accommodate physiologically. Acclimation and acclimatization of tolerance limits to temperature are commonly demonstrated in snakes and probably underlie the observation that resistance to cold in garter snakes (*Thamnophis sirtalis*) varies with the severity of the cold season in different years, colder seasons producing increased resistance (Vincent and Secoy, 1978). A snake is also able to escape the lethal effects of freezing by supercooling its entire body to as low as −7.4°C, several degrees below the freezing point of body tissues (ca. −0.6°C) (Lowe et al., 1971). This is probably important to individuals that successfully occupy shallow subsurface soil and rock crevice retreats where they may be subjected to temperatures well below freezing (Cowles, 1941). The mechanisms and possible physiological adjustment of these supercooling points are in need of further investigation.

Species differences in tolerance limits are related to geographical range and features of the habitat, suggesting that thermal tolerances are adaptively determined (Stewart, 1965; Spellerberg, 1972; Lillywhite, 1980; and others). Although the distributional limits of snakes sometimes appear to be determined by temperature, particularly in sea snakes and in species inhabiting extreme habitats, it is not clear how natural selection interacts with the biology of snakes to result in a specific set of thermal adaptations. Cause and effect are difficult to separate. Investigators should be encouraged to study the variance as well as the mean tolerance temperatures in populations and to expand investigations of topics such as heat and energy budgets, viviparity, and the thermal tolerance of eggs and embryos.

THERMAL DEPENDENCE OF PHYSIOLOGY AND BEHAVIOR

Enzymatic reaction rates are highly dependent on temperature, as are physico-chemical processes such as molecular diffusion. Therefore, cellular biochemistry, tissue metabolism and, ultimately, whole-animal functions depend on the maintenance of a suitable body temperature. Within limits, an increasing temperature accelerates most processes. Biological temperature coefficients (Q_{10}) typically vary between 2 and 3 but diminish at higher temperatures. Thus the behavioral and physiological capacities of snakes can be limited or optimized by temperature. Considerable information is now available concerning the effects of temperature on cellular and whole-animal level processes of reptiles (Dawson, 1975; Huey, 1982). Most of this information is based on studies on lizards, however, and investigations on snakes are still relatively limited.

Metabolic Rates

Resting oxygen consumption varies considerably in snakes subjected to different temperatures, as judged from R-T curves and Q_{10} values reported for various species (see references in Bennett and Dawson, 1976). Generally, Q_{10} values range between 1.5 and 3.0 at temperatures between 15 and 35°C. Higher Q_{10} values may occur at temperatures both below and above this range, although sometimes they may be attributable to increased activity. In some species there is a rather constant thermal dependence of oxygen consumption over a broad thermal range (Benedict, 1932). More commonly, perhaps, there is a pattern of reduced Q_{10} at moderately higher temperatures, or a pattern of a "metabolic plateau" where oxygen consumption is essentially stable over a limited (and intermediate) BT range (Buikema and Armitage, 1969; Jacobson and Whitford, 1970; Aleksiuk, 1971a; Abe and Mendes, 1980). Fundamental questions involve whether and how these departures of metabolism from strict thermal dependence are adaptive. While there is compelling evidence attaching ecological significance to metabolic plateaus, the functional bases and selective advantages of thermal patterns of metabolism merit further intensive investigation.

Metabolic adjustments to temperature have been studied in some detail in red-sided garter snakes, *Thamnophis sirtalis parietalis* (Aleksiuk, 1971a,b, 1976). This species occurs throughout most of North America and is abundant at northern latitudes where snakes are subjected to long, cold winters and summers of variable temperature. Rates of standard metabolism decrease with temperature from 30 to 15°C, increase between 15 and 11°C, and then continue to decrease with temperature (Figure 14–5). Aleksiuk interpreted the elevated lower portion of the *R-T* curve as indicating an instantaneous temperature-dependent mechanism of temperature compensation. When physical conditions permit, individuals maintain their BT near 30°C. When BT decreases, a low Q_{10} for metabolic rates maintains metabolism near optimal levels from 30 to about 17°C. If BT continues to decrease below 17°C, appetite is depressed and individuals seek shelter, although the increasing metabolic rate may function to sustain neuromuscular capabilities and bodily processes during periods of reduced activity to temperatures as low as 12°C. If BT decreases further, extraordinarily high Q_{10} values below 10°C depress rates of oxygen consumption, accelerating the transition from an active to an inactive state (torpor?) and conserving energy during periods of low temperature (see also Johansen and Lykkeboe, 1979). Then, with the return of high temperatures, the high Q_{10} promotes a rapid increase in metabolic rate toward levels maintained by a lower Q_{10} at higher temperatures. Acclimation to temperature or photoperiod does not alter the shape or position of the *R-T* curve, suggesting that the responses of metabolism are inherently stable. The *R-T* curves are consistently repeatable for a given individual, although the precise temperature range comprising the compensatory shift varies among individuals. These metabolic responses to immediate temperature changes are considered to be adaptive in cold climates where temperature fluctuations are frequent and unpredictable.

Metabolic compensation for temperature is both time- and temperature-dependent in many other ectothermic vertebrates, so the "instantaneous" nature of cold-compensated metabolism in *Thamnophis s. parietalis* represents an unusual ability to resist cold. The underlying basis appears to be biochemical (rather than behavioral), as cardiac activity exhibits temperature-dependent shifts *in vitro* similar (but not parallel) to those seen for metabolism (Figure 14–5). Studies on enzyme kinetics in *T. sirtalis* indicate the presence in muscle and liver of various LDH and MDH isoenzymes exhibiting different velocity-temperature

──➤

Figure 14–5. The relationship of *in vitro* heart rates (A) and standard metabolism (B) to temperature in cool temperate (solid circles) and subtropical (open circles) representatives of *Thamnophis sirtalis*. Note that the shift or plateau of metabolism that characterizes snakes from Manitoba does not occur in subtropical (Miami) representatives of the species. Adapted with permission from Aleksiuk (1971a) (Pergamon Press, Ltd.).

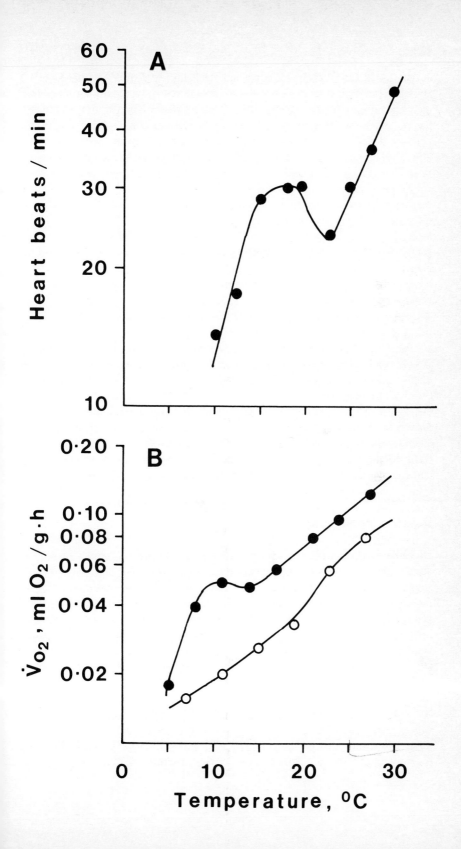

curves (Aleksiuk, 1971b; Hoskins and Aleksiuk, 1973). Maintenance of the activity of certain isoenzymes at low temperatures is apparently attributable to their high affinity for the substrate at such temperatures. Temperature acclimation has no effect on the number of LDH or MDH isoenzymes, suggesting a temperature-dependent but time-independent transition from one isoenzyme to another. Synthesis of new enzymes is expected to be induced by thermal acclimation in species possessing time-dependent mechanisms of metabolic adjustment.

Maximal rates of oxygen consumption incurred by activity show strong thermal dependence and continue to increase up to the highest body temperatures measured in *Pituophis melanoleucus* (Greenwald, 1971) and *Spalerosophis cliffordi* (Dmi'el and Borut, 1972). In *Nerodia rhombifera,* however, aerobic capacity shows a high thermal dependence between 15 and 25°C ($Q_{10} = 3.46$) but not between 25 and 35°C ($Q_{10} = 1.13$) (Gratz and Hutchison, 1977). Maximal aerobic scopes occur at body temperatures higher than preferred levels but generally do not change markedly over the range of activity temperatures. Further discussion of activity metabolism may be found in the section on energetics (see below).

Future studies on thermal patterns of reptilian metabolism will likely focus largely on the mechanisms of adjustments and their significance to natural populations. Descriptive data will continue to be valuable in contexts related to estimating energy budgets in the field. Caution should always be exercised to distinguish whether patterns of resting metabolism reflect truly biochemical adjustments of standard rates or changes in activity levels of animals in metabolic chambers. A major challenge will be to demonstrate whether adjustments of Q_{10} from strictly linear R-T curves actually are expressed as improvements in animal performance or meaningful economy of energy.

Digestive Functions and Growth

Digestive hyperthermia confers the important advantage on reptiles of accelerating digestive processes and preventing the putrefaction of ingested food (first suggested by Cowles and Bogert, 1944). Secretory processes, enzymatic reaction rates, and gut motility are all functions having well-documented thermal dependencies (Dandrifosse, 1974). Digestive rates in snakes have been quantified indirectly by observing passage time or gut evacuation (Henderson, 1970; Greenwald and Kanter, 1979; Naulleau, 1983) or have been assessed by means of x-ray analysis (Skoczylas, 1970a; Stevenson et al., 1985). Generally, digestion is completely inhibited and snakes regurgitate food at low temperatures (<10°C). Increasing the temperature above 10°C accelerates digestion, with peak rates occurring within a range of 30 ± several °C (Figure 14–6). In grass snakes, *Natrix natrix,* both the rate of gastric secretion and its composition vary with temperature such that proteolytic activity is little different at 25 and 35°C, but is inhibited at lower temperatures (Skoczylas, 1970b).

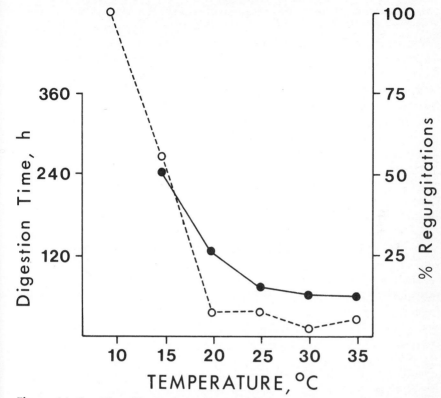

Figure 14–6. The effects of constant ambient temperature on digestion time and meal regurgitations in *Vipera aspis*. Data are means for pooled sexes (*N* varies from 17 to 40). Modified from Naulleau (1983) with permission of Society for the Study of Amphibians and Reptiles.

While the digestive rate is highly dependent on BT, digestive efficiency (DE, or percentage of energy extracted from food) is relatively insensitive to temperature changes in corn snakes, *Elaphe guttata* (Greenwald and Kanter, 1979). This appears to be generally true for other reptiles, although a pronounced thermal dependency of DE was reported for the desert lizard *Dipsosaurus dorsalis* (Harlow et al., 1976). Generally, the digestive efficiencies of most lizards and snakes that have been studied approach or exceed 90%. Thus thermoregulation at a high BT increases energy gain primarily by speeding up the passage rate. In a behavioral context, it is important to note that food acceptance also is dependent on a high temperature (Naulleau, 1983).

The net energy gain from feeding is a function of the ingested energy less the sum of fecal and urinary energy losses, metabolic costs of digestion, and the metabolic cost of maintenance (which increases with thermoregulation at high temperatures). In strictly energetic terms, thermoregulation for the sake of growth or reproduction should entail set-point temperatures at which both fecal passage time and metabolic costs are minimized, assuming that food is not limited and that ecological costs are ignored. Preliminary calculations based on the thermal dependence of the digestive and metabolic rates of garter snakes (*Thamnophis elegans*) indicate that net energy gains are maximized at 29°C, which closely approximates the preferred body temperature (Stevenson et al., 1985). Calculations further indicate that, as the food ration decreases, the BT that is optimal for energy acquisition also decreases. Thus metabolic expenditure of energy must be reduced to compensate for reduced energy input attributable to the decreased availability of food (see also Brett, 1971).

It is not clear how the energetic picture is affected by prey or meal size. Meal size has been shown to affect the digestive rate in *Natrix natrix* (Skoczylas, 1970a) and in the lizard *Anolis carolinensis* (Kitchell and Windell, 1972). Moreover, in *Anolis* the proportion of ingested energy that is converted to biomass varies inversely with the meal size, presumably because an increased meal size incurs a disproportionate increase in metabolic costs associated with digestion (a specific dynamic effect). In other snakes (*Thamnophis elegans, Vipera aspis*) digestive rates are found to be unaffected by prey size (Naulleau, 1983; Stevenson et al., 1985).

Knowledge of the nutritional and digestive physiology of snakes and other reptiles is sparse, and many research questions related to these topics are relatively unexploited. Because snakes consume relatively large unmasticated meals at variable and sometimes long intervals, they may provide especially useful models for studies on digestive controls related to periodic feeding. Starved water snakes (*Natrix tessellata*) do not possess high levels of pancreatic enzymes, but these levels increase sevenfold within 24 h of feeding (Alcon and Bdolah, 1975). Detailed studies on the subcellular modulating mechanisms affecting these and other phenomena would contribute new and important data, particularly if thermal dependencies of processes were evaluated. In a more ecological context, multivariate studies on digestive parameters are especially needed to advance a more thorough understanding of the energetic implications of thermoregulation in relation to microclimatic and prey resources, growth, and reproduction.

Neuromuscular Performance

The influence of temperature on motor functions is one of the more pervasive and important thermal effects on living systems and one that limits the behavioral capacities of animals. Terrestrial ectotherms, in particular, experience large changes in body temperature with daily or seasonal periodicity, and such effects acting vis-á-vis the neuromuscular system determine the duration and qualitative nature of activity periods. In ecological and behavioral contexts, knowledge of the thermal dependency of behaviors (e.g., locomotory performance) and the underlying physiological limitations are both exceedingly important.

Temperature can alter significantly the rates of contraction and power output of muscle (reviewed by Bennett, 1984). Contractile forces generated by muscles of both endothermic and ectothermic vertebrates are largely independent of temperature, although anuran muscle can develop maximum force at lower temperatures than mammalian muscle. Prolonged tension (tetany) is maximal at normal activity temperatures in a variety of animals, but this is seldom true for twitch tension. In contrast to the low thermal dependence of force generation, the rate of development of tension (or shortening velocity) is markedly sensitive to temperature (Q_{10} values of 2 to 2.5). Consequently, the possible power output of muscle also varies with body temperature. High body temperatures permit rapid rates of muscle contraction, whereas low body temperatures limit the performance that is possible.

Based on these considerations, rate-dependent performance parameters of snakes are predicted to improve as the temperature increases over a broad, but limited, dynamic range. This expectation is borne out by data from investigations examining the thermal relationships of motor functions in several snake species. The frequency of rattling in the tail of rattlesnakes (*Crotalus atrox* and *C. viridis*) increases with BT through a range of 3 to 40°C (Chadwick and Rahn, 1954; Martin and Bagby, 1972), presumably reflecting the thermal dependence of shortening velocity and/or activation of the shaker muscle. The rate of contraction varies from 15 to 20 Hz at 10°C to 70 to 90 Hz at 40°C. Velocity during the strike of gopher snakes (*Pituophis melanoleucus*) and the percentage of strikes that result in successful prey capture increase with temperature from 18 to 27°C, remaining near maximal at 33°C (Greenwald, 1974). These performance optima for prey capture correspond favorably to activity and preferred temperatures in this species. Further, several investigators have demonstrated thermal dependence of tongue flicking (Burghardt and Pruitt, 1975; Arnold, 1978; Stevenson et al., 1985). In *Thamnophis elegans* the rate of tongue flicking increases markedly from 20 to 35°C, with peak rates at 30°C (again, the approximate PBT).

The thermal dependence of locomotion has been studied in two species of garter snakes (Heckrotte, 1967; Stevenson et al., 1985). Maximum crawling speed in *Thamnophis elegans* increases with BT from 5 to 35°C, while speed of swimming increases from 5 to 30°C and then diminishes slightly at 35°C. In *T. sirtalis*, maximum crawling speed increases with temperature, whereas cruising speed is nearly temperature-independent from 15 to 33°C. These data indicate that garter snakes perform similarly to most diurnal lizards that have been studied (Bennett, 1980a; Huey, 1982), such that field activity temperatures closely match those at which neuromuscular performance is maximal.

Although diurnal activity cycles of snakes show thermal correlations, temperature effects can interact with other factors. Thus temperature and humidity act jointly to influence the activity cycles of garter snakes (Heckrotte, 1962). Activity and oxygen consumption patterns of water snakes (*Nerodia rhombifera*) suggest that the photoperiod interacts to alter activity and may regulate activity alone at extreme temperatures of 15 and 35°C (Gratz and Hutchison, 1977). For these reasons, it is not always possible to predict the activity patterns of snakes

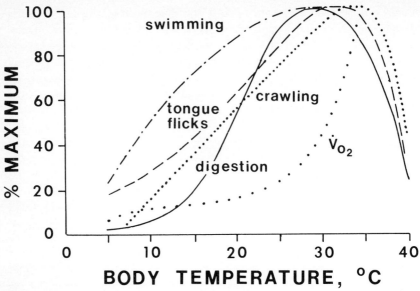

Figure 14–7. The effects of body temperature on various performance functions, determined from statistical models for the snake *Thamnophis elegans.* Adapted with permission from Stevenson et al. (1985), (University of Chicago Press).

by the expedient of matching modeled *possibilities* of BT (from biophysical data) with data for thermoregulatory parameters or thermal performance optima. Field studies indicate that the activity of snakes can be markedly depressed during dry conditions that are otherwise associated with the availability of thermal resources favorable for thermoregulation (Lillywhite, 1982).

If we consider the various parameters of performance and physiological function studied in relation to temperature in *Thamnophis elegans,* the thermal sensitivities and performance maxima are generally similar, although small, consistent differences exist (Figure 14–7). While certain optima correspond closely to the PBT determined in laboratory studies, it is also true that others do not. Thus different functions may vary in terms of their thermal maxima, reflecting different mechanistic causes and conceivably differences in thermal adaptation. For example, the association of swimming performance over a breadth of temperatures might be an advantage for feeding in cold water. Body temperatures as cold as 13°C have been recorded for *T. elegans* while it was foraging for aquatic prey (Scott, 1978). Generally, however, the breadth of temperatures at which snakes achieve, for example, 80% of maximum performance in all measured parameters, matches very well the range of activity BTs of this species. The data suggest that such high performances achievable during normal activity will be greatly reduced during periodic bouts of low-temperature exposure.

Cardiorespiratory Function

Because of the pronounced influence of temperature on metabolism, ventilatory and circulatory adjustments are expected to provide for changes in respiratory gas exchange rates and the acid-base status of the body fluids and intracellular environment. In addition, passive thermal effects modify the hydraulic properties of blood and also influence the contractile activity of cardiac muscle. A knowledge of the functional properties of cardiorespiratory parameters is therefore important in understanding the interactive forces influencing the thermal tolerances and behavioral capacities of snakes.

Cardiac muscle responds directly to temperature such that heart rate increases *in vivo* and *in vitro* with temperature coefficients (Q_{10}) usually in the range 2 to 2.5 (e.g., Aleksiuk, 1971a; Jacobson and Whitford, 1971; Dmi'el and Borut, 1972; Landreth, 1972; Lillywhite and Seymour, 1978). In garter snakes (*Thamnophis sirtalis*), there is a pronounced downward shift in the mid-range of the *R-T* curve for heart rates measured *in vitro,* resembling the *R-T* pattern for metabolism described in this species (Aleksiuk, 1971a) (Figure 14–5). In most snakes examined, however, the response of the cardiac rate to temperature is uniformly linear in logarithmic *R-T* plots. Judging from the magnitude of the changes in heart rate, ventricular output increases at higher temperatures to meet the increased demand of tissues for oxygen. Measurements of the oxygen pulse, which is the amount of oxygen consumed per unit mass of tissue per heartbeat, indicate that (at least for temperature ranges of 15°C or more) increases in heart rate are sufficient to meet the increasing oxygen demands of elevated BT in some species (Vinegar et al., 1970; Dmi'el and Borut, 1972).

In spite of several-fold changes in heart rate during heating or cooling in tiger snakes (*Notechis scutatus*), arterial blood pressure remains comparatively stable, particularly within a thermal range encompassing normal activity temperatures (Lillywhite and Seymour, 1978). These data imply that peripheral vascular resistance decreases inversely with heart rate during heating, thus mediating increased blood flow to warming tissues. A major part of the change in vascular resistance is likely to be attributable to a local, direct influence of heat on vascular smooth muscle (Baker et al., 1972). Resistance attributable to blood viscosity also decreases as the temperature increases, although the viscosity of reptilian blood may have inherently lower thermal sensitivity than mammalian blood (Snyder, 1971).

The ability of tiger snakes to reflexly control arterial pressure is maximal within a range of temperatures (28 to 38°C) that includes the PBT (33°C) (Figure 14–8). Control of pressure diminishes markedly at 10°C (below normal activity temperatures), and this change is correlated with a reduced ability to control the heart rate (Figure 14–8). Thus the ability to maximize cardiovascular performance is coupled with opportunities for thermoregulation, although utility of function is maintained over a broad thermal range.

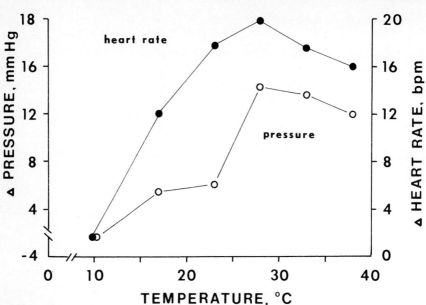

Figure 14–8. Changes in heart rate and mean aortic blood pressure at mid-body during 60° head-up tilt of tiger snakes (*Notechis scutatus*) at different body temperatures. The magnitude of positive change in blood pressure at the body center indicates the extent to which the cardiovascular system compensates for the passive hydrostatic reduction in pressure at the head due to gravity. Data from Lillywhite and Seymour (1978).

The volume of oxygen carried to tissues depends on blood flow and on a number of factors that influence the oxygen capacity and binding characteristics of the circulating hemoglobin. Values of parameters reflecting the oxygen transport characteristics of blood from 52 species of snakes were summarized by Pough (1979). Hematocrit averaged 28.5%, hemoglobin concentration 8.8 g/100 ml blood, and oxygen capacity 8.4 ml/100 ml blood. These numbers are higher in some species of sea snakes (Pough and Lillywhite, 1984), and exceptionally high hematocrit values (>50%) and blood oxygen capacity (up to 20 ml/100 ml blood) occur in the file snake (*Acrochordus granulatus*) (Feder, 1980; Lillywhite and Smits, 1985). The unusually high oxygen capacity of *Acrochordus* blood is interpreted as being an adaptation to increase the blood oxygen store and thereby extend the duration of dives.

With the exception of *Acrochordus* (which has an unusually low metabolic rate), it is conceivable that erythrocyte numbers are related to whole-blood viscosity at activity or preferred body temperatures so as to optimize oxygen transport. There is no evidence that erythrocyte numbers change on a daily or short-term basis when snakes experience changes in temperature, but this topic invites investigation. It is quite possible that acute changes in hematocrit might result from thermally dependent changes in the distribution of body fluids and plasma volume. Temperature might also affect hematocrit values indirectly by its influence on locomotor activity, which increases the filtration of plasma from capillaries (Lillywhite and Smits, 1984). Prolonged exposure to low temperatures can alter erythrocyte concentration, but the significance and consistency of the response are not understood (Pough, 1980).

Aside from the possibility of *in vivo* hematocrit adjustments, a direct effect of temperature on blood oxygen capacity can be demonstrated *in vitro*. Whole blood from a variety of squamates shows a reversible reduction in oxygen capacity of as much as 40% when exposed *in vitro* to ranges of temperature normally experienced by the animals (Pough, 1976). For most species the temperatures at which the oxygen capacity is maximal correspond to activity or preferred ranges. The mechanism responsible for altering oxygen capacity is not known but conceivably relates to aspects of the hemoglobin molecule that regulate its oxygen-binding functions (affinity) in the face of changing temperature and blood pH (Pough, 1980). The blood oxygen capacity of several species of sea snakes that do not experience abrupt or extreme temperature changes exhibits little thermal sensitivity (Pough and Lillywhite, 1984). However, the oxygen capacity of blood from the sea krait, *Laticauda colubrina*, which spends periods on land and experiences temperature changes exceeding 15°C, has a thermal sensitivity comparable to that of terrestrial snakes. The correspondence of thermal sensitivity of blood oxygen capacity with thermal heterogeneity of the environment in reptiles of diverse phylogenetic and ecological assemblages suggests that the phenomenon has adaptive, albeit unknown, significance.

In snakes, as in other animals, oxygen dissociation curves of whole blood are sensitive to temperature. An increase in temperature normally shifts the dissociation curve to the right, thereby reducing the affinity of blood for oxygen and reducing the oxygen content at constant Po_2. The effect is reversible, and low temperatures increase the affinity of blood for oxygen. In addition to the direct action of temperature on oxygenation, there is an indirect effect caused by the temperature-induced changes in blood pH. This dual effect of temperature can easily shift the position of the oxygen dissociation curve to the extent that oxygen delivery is impaired if both the temperature and proton sensitivity of hemoglobin have high values. Generally, the thermal sensitivity of ophidian (and reptilian) blood is less than that of mammals (Pough, 1980; Wood, 1980).

The respiratory properties of blood can be altered by thermal acclimation, but these phenomena have been little studied in snakes. Cold acclimation of *Vipera berus* from northern temperate latitudes increases both the oxygen capacity and oxygen affinity of the blood, whereas oxygen consumption decreases relative to that in warm-acclimated snakes (5 versus 25°C: Johansen and Lykkeboe, 1979). The increase in blood oxygen affinity is correlated with a marked reduction in red cell organic phosphate concentration. The acclimation effects on oxygen uptake and hemoglobin oxygen affinity are opposite those generally obtained for reptiles at lower latitudes. Presumably, the high affinity in winter is adaptive with respect to low oxygen availability that may occur in the underground winter microhabitat, while the elevated oxygen capacity (and hematocrit) might merely reflect a readjustment of fluid compartment volumes in response to the lowered temperature.

Intracardiac shunts provide for an admixture of systemic and pulmonary blood flows and have predictable consequences for gas transport and control of body temperature in most reptiles (see Burggren, 1987; Wood et al., 1987). Right-to-left (R-L) shunts reduce arterial oxygen saturation and either R-L or L-R shunts produce unequal pulmonary and systemic flows. Several adaptive consequences are thought to result from controlled variability of the magnitude and direction of such intracardiac blood shunts. R-L shunts function to increase the rate of heating by augmenting perfusion of the skin (Baker and White, 1970) and to provide pulmonary bypass during diving (Seymour, 1978; White, 1978).

A less obvious but important consequence of R-L cardiovascular shunts is the partial uncoupling of "mixed" arterial P_{O_2} from ventilation and P_{O_2} of the lung (Wood et al., 1987). The P_{O_2} of mixed arterial blood varies with body temperature and blood pH as these factors induce shifts in the oxygen dissociation curve (Wood, 1982). The degree of variation in arterial P_{O_2} with BT depends on the shunt fraction and its variability, as well as on the extent of the temperature- and/or pH-induced shift in the oxygen dissociation curve. These effects may have important consequences for metabolism and temperature regulation. In the racer, *Coluber constrictor,* lung ventilation increases with rising BT but does not keep pace with the increment in resting oxygen consumption. Consequently, the air convection requirement (ventilation/oxygen uptake) decreases, particularly at BTs $> 27°C$ and causes lung P_{O_2} to fall while lung P_{CO_2} increases (Stinner, 1987). Despite the inverse relationship between temperature and pulmonary P_{O_2} systemic arterial P_{O_2} is about 80 mm Hg higher at 35°C than at 15°C (Figure 14–9). This increase in arterial P_{O_2} as the snake warms is explained by right-shifting of the oxygen dissociation curve in the presence of a constant R-L intracardiac shunt. As predicted by Wood (1982), arterial P_{O_2} at 40°C exceeds calculated lung P_{O_2} because the dissociation curve of arterial blood is to the right of the curve for pulmonary venous blood. Systemic venous blood is relatively rich in CO_2, and mixing with pulmonary venous blood in the heart shifts the oxygen dissociation curve to the right owing to the Bohr effect. This also occurs at lower temperatures but, because of the leftward position of the curve and the relative proportional increase in ventilation, the resultant arterial P_{O_2} is lower than the end-capillary P_{O_2} at the lung. The elevated arterial P_{O_2} that accompanies higher BTs may be important in maintaining tissue P_{O_2} above critical oxygen tensions, which also increase with temperature (Wood, 1982). It is of interest that the activity temperatures of *Coluber* extend to 36°C (Fitch, 1963), but that the snake avoids temperatures at which the arterial P_{O_2} might fall below the critical tensions of tissues.

The magnitude of cardiovascular shunts measured in snakes varies considerably, but few studies have involved direct assessment of the shunt fractions

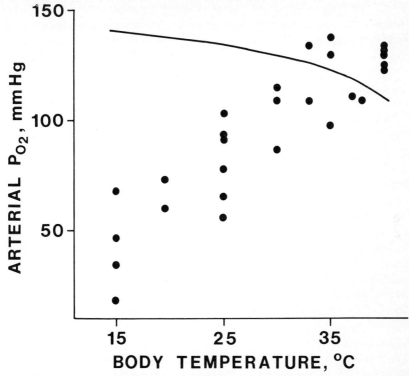

Figure 14–9.   Effects of body temperature on expired faveolar and arterial P_{O_2} in *Coluber constrictor*. Circles denote arterial P_{O_2} measured in six snakes. The line represents faveolar P_{O_2} calculated from alveolar gas equations. Note that, as the temperature increases, the faveolar-arterial P_{O_2} difference decreases and, at 40°C, arterial P_{O_2} exceeds calculated faveolar P_{O_2} by about 20 mm Hg. Adapted from Stinner (1987) with permission. Copyright by American Society of Zoologists.

(Seymour and Webster, 1975; Seymour, 1978; Seymour et al., 1981a; Lillywhite and Gallagher, 1985). The thermal dependence of intracardiac shunts and their interdependence on respiratory and hemodynamic variables remain to be evaluated.

Acid-Base Regulation

Current concepts of acid-base regulation in ectothermic animals emphasize the maintenance of a constant OH^-/H^+ ratio (relative alkalinity) in the blood or a constant net charge on proteins (reviewed in Reeves, 1977; Jackson, 1982). In both cases it is necessary that the pH of the blood vary inversely with the temperature such that when the temperature rises, the pH declines by about 0.017

units/°C and remains about 0.6 pH units above the neutral pH of water. For blood *in vitro* this temperature dependence of pH (the Rosenthal effect) is attributable to changes in the solubility of CO_2 and the dissociation constants of imidazole and the CO_2–$NaHCO_3$ system. In the case of pH determinants *in vivo*, the ratio of metabolic CO_2 production to ventilation at different temperatures must control arterial PO_2 so as to mimic the Rosenthal relation of pH to temperature. Air-breathing ectotherms increase PO_2 and reduce pH by lowering the air convection requirement as body temperature increases. Thus precise regulation of ventilation is necessary for achieving the acid-base status appropriate for a given temperature.

The dissociation constants of weak acids (CO_2, protein, and phosphate) all change with temperature according to their thermodynamic properties. Of particular significance is the observation that the pK of the imidazole groups of histidine moieties in tissue proteins changes in parallel with the blood pH such that thermally induced ionization of imidazole groups is prevented by the common ion effect. The imidazole groups are thought to be especially important in determining the net protein charge over the physiological pH range. Hence pH regulation in ectotherms may be directed toward preserving net protein charge (termed "alpha"), which stabilizes enzyme activity and the Donnan equilibrium across cell membranes. The concept that acid-base regulation in animals can be viewed as preserving the imidazole charge is referred to as the imidazole-alphastat hypothesis (Reeves, 1972, 1977).

Alphastat pH regulation has been demonstrated in the snake *Coluber constrictor* at BTs above about 27°C. At cooler temperatures, however, plasma pH changes little and the pH status of the blood does not preserve the protein charge as required by the imidazole-alphastat hypothesis (Stinner, 1987). A departure from alphastat control of pH is reported to occur in other vertebrates and reptiles, but more studies are required to determine whether or not this is a common pattern for snakes. It is important to emphasize that intracellular pH may have a different thermal dependence than that of blood. Clearly, more attention will have to be focused on the question of how temperature changes affect acid-base parameters in snakes before a unifying understanding of physiological and biochemical adaptations can emerge.

Water Relations

Space does not permit an in-depth treatment of the water relations of snakes in this chapter. However, some comment seems appropriate concerning the thermal dependencies of water exchange processes. Several areas of interest are briefly summarized in the next paragraph, while further discussion may be found in Gans and Pough (1982).

Temperature increases rates of water exchange because of its physical influence on vapor pressure and the activity of water molecules, compounded by the indirect influence on behavioral activity. Total water loss from snakes thus increases with temperature, and the majority of the loss occurs through the skin (e.g., Dmi'el, 1972). Because the principal barrier to water exchange across the integument is attributable to lipids within the epidermis (Lillywhite and Maderson, 1982), it is possible that both acute changes in temperature and prolonged thermal acclimation alter the lipid profiles and thus permeability properties of the integument, especially at extreme temperatures. This subject is in need of further investigation. The thermal increment of metabolism attributable to increased temperature might also elevate pulmonary water losses if ventilation increases. However, any increase in ventilatory losses is roughly offset by the increased production of metabolic water. Gaping or panting is employed by some colubrids and pythons as a response to heat stress and presumably facilitates evaporative cooling of the head (e.g., Jacobson and Whitford, 1971). Whether or not panting behavior is actually effective in mitigating the rise in body temperature has not been evaluated. With respect to urinary losses of water, temperature may exert a profound influence by reducing blood pressure and glomerular filtration at very low temperatures. This topic has not received attention, either. Finally, it should be mentioned that temperature can have significant effects on water exchanges of eggs buried in soil or in cavities (Ackerman et al., 1985).

Reproduction

Courtship and mating behavior, gonadotropic responses, testicular recrudescence, and spermatogenesis have all been shown to be thermally dependent in snakes (Tsui and Licht, 1974; Weil and Aldridge, 1979; Andrén, 1981; and others). Therefore, temperature is a principal forcing function of reproductive cycles, especially in temperate climates. Indeed, comparative data for ophidian reproductive cycles suggest a trend toward a shorter and more synchronized reproductive period in climatically extreme environments (Nilson, 1980). With respect to embryos, it is well established that normal development is temperature-dependent, as are the metabolism and water exchange processes of developing eggs (e.g., Ackerman et al., 1985). It has not been demonstrated that the sex of embryos is environmentally determined by temperature, as in representatives of other reptilian taxa. However, only a single species of snake has been studied in detail (reviewed in Bull, 1983). There appear to be rich opportunities for studying the effects of temperature in the endocrine and ecological interrelationships of ophidian reproduction. Further discussion of the reproductive biology of snakes may be found in Seigel and Ford (this volume).

ENERGETICS

The exchange of heat energy by ectothermic animals determines body temperature and thereby modulates the interplay of biochemical, physiological, and behavioral processes. Food is ingested, and chemical energy is released by metabolic processes so that energy is available for maintenance, growth, and movement or can be stored for use in reproduction or in meeting future energy demands. Thus energetic considerations have provided a fundamental unifying perspective for understanding diverse adaptations in ecology, behavior, and physiology. Reptiles have been a particularly important group with respect to energetics because of interest in reconstructing the evolutionary steps leading to the development of endothermy. Equally important, however, is an appreciation for the phylogenetic, geographical, and behavioral diversity that reptiles exhibit, and for contemporary interest in exploring systematically the functional correlates of this diversity (Pough, 1983). Snakes are of key interest in this context because of their evolutionary success at diversification while retaining an extremely specialized morphology.

Resting Metabolism

Investigators have amassed numerous metabolic measurements of squamate reptiles, snakes contributing approximately 45% of the represented species. Several reviews have provided summary listings of these metabolic determinations and discussions of their variability (Bennett and Dawson, 1976; Andrews and Pough, 1985). Measurement of standard metabolic rates has generally been regarded as the most reproducible and meaningful comparison of inherent metabolic levels among different animals, although many studies have entailed conditions that are not truly standard.

Compared with endothermic birds and mammals, the standardized resting metabolic rates of reptiles are generally 80 to 90% lower if body temperature and mass are comparable. Under natural conditions, however, a free-living lizard (*Sceloporus occidentalis*) uses only 3 to 4% as much energy per day as a bird or mammal because its body temperature decreases when it is inactive (Bennett and Nagy, 1977). Therefore, low energy expenditure characterizes reptilian maintenance metabolism and represents a fundamental advantage of the ectothermic condition.

Equations describing the allometry of metabolism in snakes at temperatures of 20 and 30°C have been calculated by Bennett and Dawson (1976). The least-squares regression of metabolic rate on body mass at 20°C is

$$\text{Milliliters } O_2/h = 0.120 M^{0.77}$$

where mass M is in grams. The equation for 30°C is

$$\text{Milliliters } O_2/h = 0.280 M^{0.76}$$

Considerable controversy has been directed toward the value of the mass regression exponent (b), which is reported to vary in intraspecific comparisons from about 0.67 (surface area proportionality) to 1.0 (mass proportionality). Recently,

226 metabolic measurements from 107 species of squamates were analyzed to describe the multivariate relationships among metabolic rate, temperature, and body mass (Andrews and Pough, 1985). In this analysis, metabolic rate was shown to scale with body mass by a power of 0.80, so there is good agreement between the univariate (Bennett and Dawson, 1976) and multivariate (Andrews and Pough, 1985) assessments of the global mass exponent. Moreover, field metabolic rates of free-living iguanid lizards also scale to the 0.80 power (Nagy, 1982). It should be stated, however, that global mass exponents computed from interspecific data sets largely compare adults of the different species. Intraspecific comparisons yield mass exponents that are variable and are very often lower than 0.80, so that a common mass exponent cannot be assumed for intraspecific comparisons. Therefore, metabolic rates of juvenile animals cannot necessarily be predicted from data based on adults (Andrews and Pough, 1985). There are relatively few published metabolic measurements for snakes that include a good ontogenetic series within a species.

At present there are insufficient data from snakes to encourage generalizations regarding the coupling of metabolism levels to phylogeny or ecology. With respect to lizards, variation in metabolism is explained more by ecological groupings than by familial taxonomic groupings (Andrews and Pough, 1985). In general, metabolic rates of snakes are statistically indistinguishable in taxonomic comparisons within the Ophidia or with those of other squamates. There are, however, two noteworthy exceptions. Both boids (Andrews and Pough, 1985; unpublished data) and acrochordids (Standaert and Johansen, 1974; Heatwole and Seymour, 1975; Glass and Johansen, 1976; Seymour et al., 1981b; Lillywhite and Smits, 1985) have metabolic rates about one-half those of other snakes that have been studied. Both groups exhibit comparatively sluggish behavior and are relatively more primitive than derived, possibly through evolutionary ties (see McDowell, this volume). The unusually low metabolism of the aquatic acrochordids is considered one of a suite of adaptations that allow prolonged submergence. The higher levels of resting (or standard) metabolism measured in snakes are generally associated with diurnal heliothermic colubrids capable of rapid locomotion. More species need to be studied, however, before hypotheses can be tested concerning the coupling of metabolic levels to behavioral ecology. Measurements of metabolism in elapids would be particularly instructive in this context.

Activity Energetics

Activity and locomotion increase energy expenditure of animals at rates that are usually proportional to the intensity of activity. Physiological ecologists are particularly interested in these energetic costs because they help to define the behavioral capacities of animals and their feasible interactions with the biotic and abiotic environment (Bennett, 1980b). During the past few decades there has been a great deal of interest in the energetic performance of ectothermic vertebrates with regard to locomotory costs, speed and endurance capacity, foraging modes, prey capture, vulnerability to predation, territory defense, courtship, and other activities. Snakes are particularly interesting in these contexts because of their specializations for locomotion and feeding.

Judging from a large number of studies on lizards and a more limited sampling of snakes, the energetic requirements of maintenance and activity are fundamentally similar in all squamates (Bennett, 1982). Activity involving slow to moderate speed of movement is powered by aerobic metabolism that requires the transport of oxygen through a cascade of resistances from the lung to muscle tissue. Such activity is sustainable and can be continued for long periods as long as the flow of oxygen and energy substrates are not interrupted. As the intensity of activity increases, however, the demands for oxygen transport eventually exceed the oxygen transport capability, and anaerobically generated energy must contribute to the metabolic effort in order to sustain the activity.

In snakes (as in all vertebrates), the principal form of anaerobic energy production is the catabolism of glycogen or glucose to lactic acid, usually accompanied by a relative depletion of cellular ATP and creatine phosphate stores. This mode of energy production involves readily accessible substrates without the lags or limitations inherent in the cardiovascular convective and diffusive transport of oxygen. On the other hand, anaerobic glycolysis depletes metabolic substrates and high-energy phosphate stores while accumulating high levels of lactic acid in the blood and tissues, thus causing physiological disturbances related to pH imbalance and disruptions in blood chemistry. The net result is that behavioral performance becomes increasingly curtailed. Intensive anaerobic metabolism results in rapid exhaustion and termination of activity, although the causal factors in fatigue are not entirely understood. The greatest lactate production occurs during the initial burst of activity (0.5 to 2 min), so that debilitation of the maximal movement capability begins rather immediately.

Anaerobic metabolism is roughly 10% as efficient as aerobic pathways on the basis of energy yield per unit of fuel substrate catabolized. Thus the rate of fuel depletion is 10 times as great in sustaining an equivalent rate of ATP production. This inefficiency could constitute an important limitation of activity if the substrate fuel is in limited or depleted supply. Muscle glycogen is decreased significantly during activity in diamondback water snakes (*Nerodia rhombifera;* Gratz and Hutchison, 1977). The lactate produced may eventually be oxidized or reconverted to glycogen, but the gluconeogenic resynthesis entails a net loss of 4 ATP equivalents per lactate cycle. Significant gluconeogenesis occurs in snakes during recovery from activity that may require several hours (Gratz and Hutchison, 1977). Therefore, the cost of relieving the metabolic acidosis incurred by lactic acid and of restoring depleted glycogen is a significant added energy cost to recovery. Notwithstanding these energetic "inefficiencies," reptilian anaerobic glycolysis is much more effective in generating ATP per unit time than aerobic metabolism. Thus anaerobic power is more appropriate than aerobic power during intense activity such as rapid escape, pursuit, or struggling.

Snakes are well known for their sedentary behavior and long periods of seclusion. Moreover, many routine activities are perceived as slow and deliberate, although snakes may locomote for considerable distances during active periods. Sidewinder rattlesnakes (*Crotalus cerastes*) can move well over 1 km in a single evening (Brown, 1970), and aquatic file snakes (*Acrochordus arafurae*), otherwise known for their "sluggish" behavior, can move nightly distances approaching 1 km (Shine and Lambeck, 1985). Presumably, these behaviors employ aerobiosis as their major energy source. Thus factorial increments in oxygen consumption above minimum vary from about 1.5 to 2.5 and are closely correlated with peaks of routine activity (Dmi'el and Borut, 1972; Gratz and Hutchison, 1977).

The role of anaerobiosis in the normal activity of sea snakes has been assessed by sampling blood from snakes swimming and diving in Philippine seas (Seymour, 1979). The data indicate that in most snakes, lactate concentrations are near resting levels, while an occasional dive is associated with severe anaerobiosis. The circumstances of these dives and whether the anaerobic component is related to anoxia or strenuous activity are not known. It has been suggested that some water snakes (*Nerodia rhombifera*) employ anaerobic metabolism during escape activity but not during normal feeding behavior, which does not appear to be very strenuous (Gratz and Hutchison, 1977). On the other hand, garter snakes (*Thamnophis elegans*) may accumulate significant quantities of lactic acid during attack and capture of salamander prey (Feder and Arnold, 1982).

Energy contributions to maximal activity have been studied by measuring oxygen consumption and whole-body lactate concentration in snakes that are prodded or stimulated electrically to induce bouts of intense movement. Such data are available for several species of snakes including colubrids, a crotalid, a boid, and an acrochordid (Greenwald, 1971; Ruben, 1976b; Gratz and Hutchison, 1977; Pough, 1977, 1978; Seymour et al., 1981b). Increments in oxygen consumption above resting levels (factorial aerobic scope) vary from about 2- to more than 10-fold in active snakes at close to preferred body temperatures. However, it appears that in all squamates examined anaerobic glycolysis is the primary source of energy for activity, accounting for more than half of the energy mobilized. In comparison with oxygen consumption, the anaerobic component of energy production is relatively independent of body mass and is less sensitive to temperature. Therefore, the contribution of anaerobiosis is proportionally greater at low temperatures (Gratz and Hutchison, 1977).

Comparatively high levels of oxygen consumption and lactate production (aerobic and anaerobic capacities, respectively) are found in species that are heliothermic, highly active, and characterized by rapid locomotory capabilities (e.g., *Coluber constrictor*, *Masticophis flagellum*). Indeed, the maximal metabolic rates of these active snakes are among the highest measured in reptiles and exceed the resting metabolic rates of many endothermic mammals. These aerobic capacities are correlated with a complex lung structure and relatively high levels of muscle myoglobin, features likely to enhance the delivery of oxygen to tissues (Ruben, 1976c). The high anaerobic capacities are correlated with high activity levels of presumed rate-controlling glycolytic enzymes (Ruben, 1976c).

On the other hand, species of snakes that possess low aerobic or anaerobic capabilities are relatively sluggish (*Lichanura trivirgata roseofusca, Acrochordus arafurae*) and may show inverse correlations with respect to the parameters discussed above. *Crotalus viridis* is characterized by an intermediate level of aerobic and anaerobic capabilities, while *Nerodia rhombifera* exhibits yet another pattern with a high anaerobic capacity but a low aerobic capacity (Table 14–2). *Acrochordus arafurae* appears incapable of high energy utilization during activity and can become exhausted before its arterial oxygen stores are significantly depleted (Seymour et al., 1981b). In this species, the major resistance to oxygen delivery lies not at the pulmonary or cardiovascular level but at the tissue level (as appears to be true for reptiles generally: Pough, 1980). In spite of the variability and limited number of species measurements, there is a clear suggestion that levels of maximal energy production in snakes are related adaptively to modes of predation and defense.

Particularly insightful examples of how physiology can limit behavioral performance may be taken from case studies examining ontogenetic changes in these parameters in garter snakes (*Thamnophis sirtalis*) and in water snakes (*Nerodia sipedon*) (Pough, 1977, 1978). Newborn snakes are exhausted after 3 to 5 min of activity, while adults can sustain activity for 20 to 50 min. The increased endurance of adult snakes is attributed to ontogenetic increases in both aerobic and anerobic capacity. Among the mechanisms thought to enhance aerobic capabilities are more effective ventilation of the lung, a decrease in blood oxygen affinity (favoring the delivery of oxygen to tissues), and a three-fold increase in blood oxygen capacity. The rapid exhaustion of small snakes limits their prey

Table 14–2. Quantities of Energy Attributable to Aerobic and Anaerobic Metabolism During Forced Activity at 32 to 35°C in Different Snake Species[a]

| Species[b] | Activity duration (min) | Micromoles ATP per gram body mass | | |
		Aerobic	Anaerobic	Total
Crotalus viridis (4)	5	10.59	16.20	26.79
Coluber constrictor (2) *Masticophis flagellum* (4)	5	23.03	29.06	52.09
Lichanura trivirgata roseofusca (6)	5	4.64	5.00	9.64
Nerodia rhombifera (15)	10	10.30	28.89	39.19

[a]Data are from Ruben (1976b) and Gratz and Hutchison (1977).
[b]Number of snakes is given in parentheses.

selection and accounts for differences in defensive behavior, which is passive in juvenile water snakes and active in adults. Moreover, maximum crawling speed in garter snakes is size-dependent, larger animals having greater speeds (Heckrotte, 1967). Because of these physiological differences, juvenile snakes are ecologically quite different from adults (see also Mushinsky, this volume).

Muscle and Locomotory Energetics

Perhaps the most fascinating aspect of ophidian energetics is the ability of muscle to convert chemical energy into the mechanical work of locomotion. The subject of muscle has attracted the wide attention of many physiologists, biochemists, and functional morphologists working with various animal taxa, and there is now considerable knowledge concerning the mechanisms of force generation and its application in various modes of animal movement. Little is known about the muscle physiology of ophidians, however—an unfortunate omission considering the success of the group and their diverse specializations for limbless locomotion.

The requirements of muscle vary according to circumstance and determine its molecular and cellular structure. The types of fibers in reptilian muscle are basically quite similar to those found in mammals, except that tonic-type fibers are far more common (reviewed in Guthe, 1981). The slower tonic fibers play important roles in effecting slow movements and maintaining prolonged tension with energetic efficiency. Economic isometric contraction is important, for example, with respect to posture and certain aspects of locomotion such as tensioning tendons. Trunk muscles contain up to 30 or 40% tonic fibers in *Nerodia, Coronella,* and *Vipera,* whereas head, neck, and tail muscles have smaller proportions. The majority of fibers in body musculature are large-diameter fast-twitch fibers that are important for quicker movements and for shortening to do work. They generally have a low resistance to fatigue and are utilized for short bursts of activity requiring strength and speed. Such fibers must be important even in sluggish snakes such as boids and acrochordids, which nonetheless are capable of very rapid movements used in capturing prey.

The so-called shaker muscle of rattlesnakes deserves some mention because of its extreme specialization (Clark and Schultz, 1980; Schultz et al., 1980). Over 90% of the fibers are of one major type that is unlike any fiber present in the body musculature. The myofibers of the shaker muscle contract extremely fast, yet are highly resistant to fatigue, containing large deposits of glycogen and possessing a capacity for both oxidative and glycolytic metabolism. The deep red muscle contains high concentrations of myoglobin and an unusually dense capillary network. Rarely are all of these characteristics combined into a single functional unit. Direct measurements have demonstrated that oxygen consumption by the shaker muscle is greater than that of mammalian (rat and dog) red and cardiac muscle. One *Crotalus atrox* is reported to have rattled continuously for 3 h while sustaining contractions at frequencies of 43 to 50 Hz (Martin and Bagby, 1972). The percentage of fiber volume devoted to myofibrils is small, suggesting that the muscle is weak. Presumably, it is specialized for the sole function of moving the rattles in short but rapid excursions.

The few locomotory muscles of snakes that have been examined exhibit five different fiber types, including twitch and tonic contracting fibers and fibers of both high and low oxidative capacity. However, patterns of fiber composition have not been studied in relation to locomotor parameters, and there are too few studies to detect any trends within taxa. Thus further research on ophidian muscles and their adaptations to behavior and ecology, such as that being gathered for lizards (e.g., Gleeson, 1983; Bennett, 1984; Gleeson et al., 1984; and others), will be most welcome. It remains to be learned whether the diversity of fiber types in various squamates enables muscles to contract efficiently over wide ranges of shortening velocities by progressively recruiting different fiber populations, as occurs in fishes.

The mechanics of ophidian locomotion are reasonably well understood and are discussed by Cundall (this volume). Theoretical considerations and a few direct measurements suggest that the energy cost of ophidian locomotion is less than that in quadrupedal reptiles and many other vertebrates with limbs. The cost of locomotion in a garter snake (*Thamnophis sirtalis*) is reported to be only 31% of that in a lizard of similar body size (Chodrow and Taylor, 1973), reflecting economy, probably because of less effort needed to support the body and the lack of vertical displacement of its center of mass. Much of the work inherent in quadrupedal locomotion involves lifting and lowering the center of gravity, in addition to accelerating and decelerating the limbs. Although snakes are expected to have low energy costs of locomotion, the data of Chodrow and Taylor require confirmation because it is not clear whether their measurements of oxygen consumption represent truly minimal energetic costs unsupported by unmeasured anaerobic input.

Locomotion in water is energetically less demanding than that on land because less effort is required to support the body and to negotiate irregularities in the terrain. Thus calculated locomotory costs in swimming sea snakes are roughly one order of magnitude less than the costs measured in terrestrial *Thamnophis* (Seymour, 1982). The cost of swimming in sea snakes is similar to that in eels but considerably less than that in marine turtles or iguanas, suggesting that streamlining and shape are important determinants of power expenditure. Movements such as sidewinding and partial gliding among branches are presumably energetically economical, but this has not yet been tested. Clearly, comparative analyses of the mechanics and energetics of ophidian locomotion offer exciting and important opportunities for research.

Brief mention should be made regarding the importance of locomotor capacity in natural populations, which is the focus of ongoing investigations of garter snakes, *Thamnophis* spp. (Garland and Arnold, 1983; S. J. Arnold and A. F. Bennett, unpublished data). An important finding is that locomotor capabilities of newborn snakes are highly and consistently variable. Parameters such as burst speed, distance capacity, and endurance vary significantly among individuals, reflecting inherent variability that is prerequisite for differential selection in natural populations. Larger animals perform better and have fewer morphological abnormalities when a series of morphological and locomotor performance variables are measured. An interesting question concerns whether ontogenetic differences are due to developmental changes during the life of an individual or whether such differences result from "pruning" through time by natural selection. Ongoing studies by Arnold and Bennett on newborn garter snakes released into the field have been designed with these questions in mind. Their investigations should provide important information regarding the heritability of performance parameters and address the question whether superior performance capacities do indeed result in improved survivorship and fitness. The project is exemplary of new directions seeking to couple physiological investigation with meaningful field ecology using snakes as the model organism.

Energy Budgets

Energetic analysis provides a unifying focus for ecological studies on snakes and facilitates understanding their adaptation to different environments. In recent years, methodological advances have enabled physiological ecologists to better evaluate energetic adaptations manifest in ecological processes such as foraging behavior, competition, predation, reproductive success, and population dynamics (Spotila and Standora, 1985). Analysis of heat energy budgets can be used to predict BTs of snakes in addition to evaluating microclimatic requirements and patterns of daily or seasonal activity. Food energy budgets and metabolic rate measurements are used to assess limitations on the energy available for growth, reproduction, and other life-history phenomena. Heat and food energy budgets interact through their effects on BT and metabolism, which in turn modify behavior.

Energy budget analysis has been applied to studies on snakes to a lesser extent than in other reptiles, especially lizards. However, the few analyses that have been published serve to emphasize several major features of ophidian ecology and natural history. First, energy balance simulations have been employed to predict the prey consumption required for maintenance, growth, and reproduction of garter snakes, *Thamnophis sirtalis* (Porter and Tracy, 1974). These data emphasize the low energy requirements of snakes compared with those of endotherms. For example, a 50-g mink would require roughly 16 times more prey than a 50-g snake in South Carolina and 26 times more prey than a 50-g snake in Michigan, just considering maintenance.

A second important feature of these simulations is that the total biomass of prey needed by ophidian predators requires only occasional predation, and most of the biomass requirement is coupled to growth and reproduction. Therefore, the predatory impact of snake populations seems limited by their reproductive capacity and survivorship. If only maintenance is considered, one must assume (Porter and Tracy, 1974) that snakes will have a significant impact on prey populations only when biomass levels approach those of the prey. It therefore seems that the major effects of predation should be attributable to endotherms and that snakes probably are not involved in intraspecific competition for food unless they are present at unusually high densities (see Vitt, this volume). These considerations no doubt impact importantly on the behavior of snakes as predators. For example, many snakes do not appear to forage intensely (sit-and-wait strategy), and others do not forage actively except at certain times or seasons (e.g., Feaver, 1977). Snakes are obviously ideal subjects for assessments of foraging strategies as they relate to thermoregulation, energetics, and ecological costs (Huey, 1982).

Energy balance equations may be used to construct the "climate space" of a snake, which specifies the limits of the microclimatic conditions under which a particular species can survive. The utilization of climate space and estimates of its limits have been described for montane garter snakes (*Thamnophis elegans*) occupying habitats at 2600 m in Colorado (Scott et al., 1982). The analysis emphasizes the harshness of such habitats for ectothermic snakes compared with endotherms. For example, on cool or cloudy days in May and September, a snake could barely attain the minimum activity temperature in any microhabitat above ground. On the other hand, during July the maximum voluntary BT (35°C) was exceeded in open areas for about 6 h on each clear day. Activity temperatures and preferred BTs could be attained for only 1.5 to 2.5 h daily, and the CTMax was exceeded for at least 3 h in areas of rock or bare ground. The choice of subterranean environments is undoubtedly very important to the ecology of this montane species.

These analyses are useful for examining constraints but cannot necessarily or consistently predict variation in BT or activity, especially in less extreme climates, because unknown variability in factors such as water or food availability may alter thermal preferences and behavior. These factors and acclimatization also influence metabolic rates, so that estimates of energy expenditure based on simulations of "expected" BT variation may not be reliable. The problem of estimating energy expenditure can be circumvented by direct measurements of field metabolic rates using radioisotope turnover in isotope-labeled free-ranging animals (Nagy, 1975). This valuable technique has not yet been used to evaluate the energetics of any snake.

Energy budgets have been constructed for overwintering snakes based on observed changes in body composition (see Gregory, 1982). Such analysis indicates that the energy expenditure for hibernating garter snakes (*Thamnophis sirtalis*) is about 1.9 J/g per day (Costanzo, 1985). This low cost reflects the low energy level characteristic of ectothermy, compounded by the high-Q_{10} depression of metabolism at low body temperatures. The energy required for the maintenance of ophidian torpor is impressively small when compared to that needed by mammalian hibernators, which expend more than two orders of magnitude more energy while at their lowest metabolic level. Body lipids, proteins, and glycogen in liver and muscle may all contribute as energy sources during winter dormancy in snakes. However, the timing and extent of the use of different energy substrates varies with species and with circumstance. For example, snakes that hibernate at warmer temperatures appear to use more body lipids than snakes hibernating at colder temperatures. The maintenance of winter fat stores by some snakes may be important with respect to the requirement of lipids for reproduction in the ensuing spring.

SUMMARY AND FUTURE RESEARCH

Many aspects of the biology of snakes reflect physiological specializations related to ectothermy and limbless morphology. As research animals, snakes have contributed significantly to the growth of physiological ecology as a recognized discipline and provide unparalleled opportunities as model organisms for investigating questions related to adaptation and the interdependence of physiology, ecology, and behavior. This is largely attributable to the diverse specializations of snakes related to feeding, locomotion, and energetic requirements.

Generally, snakes rely on ambient heat sources to regulate body temperature within preferred activity ranges that usually center near 30°C. Contrary to earlier opinions, snakes employ behavioral and physiological mechanisms to regulate temperature very precisely when sources of heat energy are available.

Physiological and behavioral capabilities of snakes are thermally dependent such that maximum or optimum function and performance usually require higher temperatures at or near the preferred body temperature of a species. Consequently, the survival and reproductive success of snakes are ultimately dependent on opportunities and capacities for thermoregulation.

Resting or standard metabolic rates of snakes are far lower than those of endotherms and are generally indistinguishable from those of other squamates. The low metabolic rates are coupled to a limited capacity for aerobic power output during activity and reliance on anaerobic glycolysis in muscle for short bursts of intense activity. The aerobic and anaerobic capacities of species appear to underlie ecological differences in predatory and escape behavior. Aerobic capacities may increase during ontogeny in parallel with the changes in cardiovascular parameters that improve oxygen transport.

The limbless morphology of snakes allows locomotion at comparatively low energy costs. There are relatively few studies on muscle function in snakes, although gross morphology and fiber composition of muscle clearly determine the nature and rapidity of the movements that characterize different species.

Energy budget analysis of snakes emphasizes their ectothermy and low food requirements, which allow sedentary behavior, periodic or casual predation, efficient conversion of food to biomass, low energy flow, and the occupation of niche dimensions that are not possible for endotherms. In spite of methodological advances and interest in these topics, it remains for herpetological physiologists and ecologists to evaluate energetic adaptations manifest in ecological processes such as foraging behavior, competition, predation, reproductive success, and population dynamics.

Knowledge of physiological adaptation is essential in understanding the behavior and ecology of snakes. Insofar as new directions will occupy the future goals of physiological ecologists, research will likely focus on an analysis of selection that acts on physiological variation within a population and the contribution of physiological variation to performance and fitness, utilizing multivariate approaches. This will require combined field and laboratory investigations. There is clearly a potential for snakes to serve as model subjects as these research directions get underway.

REFERENCES

Abe, A. S. and Mendes, E. G. 1980. Effect of body size and temperature on oxygen uptake in the water snakes *Helicops modestus* and *Liophis miliaris* (Colubridae), *Comp. Biochem. Physiol.* 65A:367–370.

Ackerman, R. A., Seagrave, R. C., Dmi'el, R., and Ar, A. 1985. Water and heat exchange between parchment-shelled reptile eggs and their surroundings, *Copeia* 1985:703–711.

Alcon, E. and Bdolah, A. 1975. Increase of proteolytic activity and synthetic capacity of the pancreas in snakes after feeding, *Comp. Biochem. Physiol.* 50A:627–631.

Aleksiuk, M. 1971a. Temperature dependent shifts in the metabolism of a cool temperate reptile, *Thamnophis sirtalis parietalis, Comp. Biochem. Physiol.* 39A:495–503.

Aleksiuk, M. 1971b. An isoenzymic basis for instantaneous cold compensation in reptiles: Lactate dehydrogenase kinetics in *Thamnophis sirtalis, Comp. Biochem. Physiol.* 40B:671–681.

Aleksiuk, M. 1976. Metabolic and behavioral adjustments to temperature in the red-sided garter snake (*Thamnophis sirtalis parietalis*): An integrated approach, *J. Thermal Biol.* 1:153–156.

Andrén, C. 1981. Behaviour and population dynamics in the adder, *Vipera berus* (L.), Ph.D. Dissertation, University of Göteborg, Sweden.

Andrews, R. M. and Pough, F. H. 1985. Metabolism of squamate reptiles: Allometric and ecological relationships, *Physiol. Zool.* 58:214–231.

Arnold, S. J. 1978. Some effects of early experience on feeding responses in the common garter snake *Thamnophis sirtalis, Anim. Behav.* 26:455–462.

Asplund, K. K. 1963. Ecological factors in the distribution of *Thamnophis brachystoma* (Cope), *Herpetologica* 19:128–132.

Avery, R. A. 1982. Field studies of body temperatures and thermoregulation, in: Biology of the Reptilia, vol. 12 (C. Gans and F. H. Pough, eds.) pp. 93–166, Academic Press, New York.

Baker, L. A. and White, F. N. 1970. Redistribution of cardiac output in response to heating in *Iguana iguana, Comp. Biochem. Physiol.* 35:253–262.

Baker, L. A., Weathers, W. W., and White, F. N. 1972. Temperature induced peripheral blood flow changes in lizards, *J. Comp. Physiol.* 80:313–323.

Bakken, G. S. 1976. An improved method for determining thermal conductance and equilibrium body temperature with cooling curve experiments, *J. Thermal Biol.* 1:169–175.

Bakken, G. S. and Gates, D. M. 1975. Heat transfer analysis of animals: Some implications for field ecology, physiology, and evolution, in: Perspectives of Biophysical Ecology (D. M. Gates and R. B. Schmerl, eds.) pp. 255–290, Springer-Verlag, New York.

Bartholomew, G. A. 1982. Physiological control of body temperature, in: Biology of the Reptilia, vol. 12 (C. Gans and F. H. Pough, eds.) pp. 167–211, Academic Press, New York.

Benedict, F. G. 1932. The physiology of large reptiles, with special reference to the heat production of snakes, tortoises, lizards and alligators, Publ. 425, Carnegie Institution, Washington, D.C.

Bennett, A. F. 1980a. The thermal dependence of lizard behavior, *Anim. Behav.* 28:752–762.

Bennett, A. F. 1980b. The metabolic foundations of vertebrate behavior, *BioScience* 30:452–456.

Bennett, A. F. 1982. The energetics of reptilian activity, in: Biology of the Reptilia, vol. 13 (C. Gans and F. H. Pough, eds.) pp. 155–199, Academic Press, New York.

Bennett, A. F. 1984. Thermal dependence of muscle function, *Am. J. Physiol.* 247:217–229.

Bennett, A. F. and Dawson, W. R. 1976. Metabolism, in: Biology of the Reptilia, vol. 5 (C. Gans and W. R. Dawson, eds.) pp. 127–223, Academic Press, New York.

Bennett, A. F. and Nagy, K. A. 1977. Energy expenditure of free-ranging lizards, *Ecology* 58:697–700.

Bogert, C. M. 1939. Reptiles under the sun, *Nat. Hist.* 44:26–37.

Brattstrom, B. H. 1965. Body temperatures of reptiles, *Am. Midl. Nat.* 73:376–422.

Brett, J. R. 1971. Energetic responses of salmon to temperature: A study of some thermal relations in the physiology and freshwater ecology of sockeye salmon (*Oncorhynchus nerka*), *Am. Zool.* 11:99–113.

Brown, J. H. and Lasiewski, R. C. 1972. Metabolism of weasels: The cost of being long and thin, *Ecology* 53:939–943.

Brown, T. W. 1970. Autecology of the sidewinder (*Crotalus cerastes*) at Kelso Dunes, Mojave Desert, California, Ph.D. Dissertation, University of California, Los Angeles.

Brown, W. S., Parker, W. S., and Elder, J. A. 1974. Thermal and spatial relationships of two species of colubrid snakes during hibernation, *Herpetologica* 30:32–38.

Buikema, A. L. and Armitage, K. B. 1969. The effect of temperature on the metabolism of the prairie ringneck snake, *Diadophis punctatus arnyi* Kennicott, *Herpetologica* 25:194–206.

Bull, J. J. 1983. Evolution of Sex Determining Mechanisms, Benjamin/ Cummings, Menlo Park, California.

Burggren, W. 1987. Form and function in reptilian circulation, *Am. Zool.* 27:5–19.

Burghardt, G. M. and Pruitt, C. H. 1975. Role of the tongue and senses in feeding of naive and experienced garter snakes, *Physiol. Behav.* 14:185–194.

Carpenter, C. C. 1956. Body temperatures of three species of *Thamnophis*, *Ecology* 37:732–735.

Chadwick, L. E. and Rahn, H. 1954. Temperature dependence of rattling frequency in the rattlesnake, *Crotalus v. viridis, Science* 119:442–443.

Chodrow, R. E. and Taylor, C. R. 1973. Energetic cost of limbless locomotion in snakes, *Fed. Proc. Fed. Am. Socs. Exp. Biol.* 32:422.

Clark, A. W. and Schultz, E. 1980. Rattlesnake shaker muscle. II. Fine structure, *Tissue Cell* 12:335–351.

Clark, D. R. 1967. Experiments into selection of soil type, soil moisture level, and temperature by five species of small snakes, *Trans. Kans. Acad. Sci.* 70:490–496.

Clark, D. R., Jr. 1970. Ecological study of the worm snake *Carphophis vermis* (Kennicott), *Univ. Kans. Publ. Mus. Nat. Hist.* 19:85–194.

Cloudsley-Thompson, J. L. 1971. The Temperature and Water Relations of Reptiles, Merrow, Watford Herts, England.

Cogger, H. G. and Holmes A. 1960. Thermoregulatory behavior in a specimen of *Morelia spilotes variegata* Gray (Serpentes: Boidae), *Proc. Linn. Soc. N. S. W.* 85:328–333.

Costanzo, J. P. 1985. The bioenergetics of hibernation in the eastern garter snake *Thamnophis sirtalis sirtalis, Physiol. Zool.* 58:682–692.

Cowles, R. B. 1939. Possible implications of reptilian thermal tolerance, *Science* 90:465–466.

Cowles, R. B. 1941. Observations on the winter activities of desert reptiles, *Ecology* 22:125–140.

Cowles, R. B. and Bogert, C. M. 1944. A preliminary study of the thermal requirements of desert reptiles, *Bull. Am. Mus. Nat. Hist.* 83:261–296.

Cunningham, J. D. 1966. Additional observations on the body temperatures of reptiles, *Herpetologica* 22:184–189.

Dandrifosse, G. 1974. Digestion in reptiles, in: Amphibia and Reptilia, vol. 9 (M. Florkin and B. Scheer, eds.) pp. 249–276, Academic Press, New York.

Dawson, W. R. 1975. On the physiological significance of the preferred body temperatures of reptiles, in: Perspectives of Biophysical Ecology (D. M. Gates and R. B. Schmerl, eds.) pp. 443–473, Springer-Verlag, New York.

Dill, C. D. 1972. Reptilian core temperatures: Variation within individuals, *Copeia* 1972:577–579.

Dmi'el, R. 1972. Effect of activity and temperature on metabolism and water loss in snakes, *Am. J. Physiol.* 223:510–516.

Dmi'el, R. and Borut, A. 1972. Thermal behavior, heat exchange and metabolism in the desert snake *Spalerosophis cliffordi, Physiol. Zool.* 45:78–94.

Duguy, R. 1972. Notes sur la biologie de *Vipera aspis* L. dans les Pyrenees, *Terre Vie* 26:98–117.

Feaver, P. A. 1977. The demography of the Michigan population of *Natrix sipedon* with discussions of ophidian growth and reproduction, Ph.D. Dissertation, University of Michigan, Ann Arbor.

Feder, M. E. 1980. Blood oxygen stores in the file snake, *Acrochordus granulatus,* and in other marine snakes, *Physiol. Zool.* 53:394–401.

Feder, M. E. and Arnold, S. J. 1982. Anaerobic metabolism and behavior during predatory encounters between snakes (*Thamnophis elegans*) and salamanders (*Plethodon jordani*), *Oecologia (Berl.)* 53:93–97.

Firth, B. T. and Turner, J. S. 1982. Sensory, neural, and hormonal aspects of thermoregulation, in: Biology of the Reptilia, vol. 12 (C. Gans and F. H. Pough, eds.) pp. 213–274, Academic Press, New York.

Fitch, H. S. 1956. Temperature responses in free-living amphibians and reptiles of northeastern Kansas, *Univ. Kans. Publ. Mus. Nat. Hist.* 8:417–476.

Fitch, H. S. 1960. Autecology of the copperhead, *Univ. Kans. Publ. Mus. Nat. Hist.* 13:85–288.

Fitch, H. S. 1963. Natural history of the racer, *Coluber constrictor, Univ. Kans. Publ. Mus. Nat. Hist.* 15:351–468.

Fitch, H. S. 1965. An ecological study of the garter snake, *Thamnophis sirtalis, Univ. Kans. Publ. Mus. Nat. Hist.* 15:493–564.

Fleharty, E. D. 1967. Comparative ecology of *Thamnophis elegans, T. cyrtopsis,* and *T. rufipunctatus* in New Mexico, *Southwest. Nat.* 12:207–230.

Fraser, S. and Grigg G. C. 1984. Control of thermal conductance is insignificant to thermoregulation in small reptiles, *Physiol. Zool.* 57:392–400.

Fry, F. E. J. 1947. Effects of the environment on animal activity, *Univ. Toronto Stud. Biol. Ser. 55, Publ. Ontario Fish. Res. Lab.* 68:1–62.

Gans, C. 1975. Tetrapod limblessness: Evolution and functional corollaries, *Am. Zool.* 15:455–467.

Gans, C. 1983. Snake feeding strategies and adaptations—Conclusion and prognosis, *Am. Zool.* 23:455–460.

Gans, C. and Pough, F. H. (eds.) 1982. Biology of the Reptilia, vol. 12, Academic Press, New York.

Garland, T., Jr., and Arnold, S. J. 1983. Effects of a full stomach on locomotory performance of juvenile garter snakes (*Thamnophis elegans*), *Copeia* 1983:1092–1096.

Gehrmann, W. H. 1971. Influence of constant illumination on thermal preference in the immature water snake, *Natrix erthrogaster transversa, Physiol. Zool.* 44:84–89.

Gibson, A. R. and Falls, J. B. 1979. Thermal biology of the common garter snake *Thamnophis sirtalis.* I. Temporal variation, environmental effects and sex differences, *Oecologia (Berl.)* 43:79–97.

Gillingham, J. C. and Carpenter, C. C. 1978. Snake hibernation: Construction of and observations on a man-made hibernaculum (Reptilia, Serpentes), *J. Herpetol.* 12:495–498.

Glass, M. and Johansen, K. 1976. Control of breathing in *Acrochordus javanicus,* an aquatic snake, *Physiol. Zool.* 49:329–340.

Gleeson, T. T. 1983. A histochemical and enzymatic study of the muscle fiber types in the water monitor, *Varanus salvator, J. Exp. Zool.* 227:191–201.

Gleeson, T. T., Nicol, C. J. M., and Johnston, I. A. 1984. Capillarization, mitochondrial densities, oxygen diffusion distances and innervation of red and white muscle of the lizard *Dipsosaurus dorsalis, Cell Tissue Res.* 237:253–258.

Graham, J. B. 1974. Body temperatures of the sea snake *Pelamis platurus, Copeia* 1974:531–533.

Gratz, R. K. and Hutchison, V. H. 1977. Energetics for activity in the diamondback water snake, *Natrix rhombifera, Physiol. Zool.* 50:99–114.

Greenwald, O. E. 1971. The effect of body temperature on oxygen consumption and heart rate in the Sonora gopher snake, *Pituophis catenifer affinis* Hallowell, *Copeia* 1971:98–106.

Greenwald, O. E. 1974. Thermal dependence of striking and prey capture by gopher snakes, *Copeia* 1974:141–148.

Greenwald, O. E. and Kanter, M. E. 1979. The effects of temperature and behavioral thermoregulation on digestive efficiency and rate in corn snakes (*Elaphe guttata guttata*), *Physiol. Zool.* 52:398–408.

Gregory, P. T. 1982. Reptilian hibernation, in: Biology of the Reptilia, vol. 13 (C. Gans and F. H. Pough, eds.) pp. 53–154, Academic Press, New York.

Guthe, K. F. 1981. Reptilian muscle: Fine structure and physiological parameters, in: Biology of the Reptilia, vol. 11 (C. Gans and T. S. Parsons, eds.) pp. 265–354, Academic Press, New York.

Hammerson, G. A. 1977. Head-body temperature differences monitored by telemetry in the snake *Masticophis flagellum piceus, Comp. Biochem. Physiol.* 57A:399–402.

Hammerson, G. A. 1979. Thermal ecology of the striped racer, *Masticophis lateralis, Herpetologica* 35:267–273.

Harlow, H. J., Hillman, S. S., and Hoffman, J. 1976. The effect of temperature on digestive efficiency in the herbivorous lizard, *Dipsosaurus dorsalis, J. Comp. Physiol.* 111:1–6.

Harlow, P. and Grigg, G. 1984. Shivering thermogenesis in a brooding diamond python, *Python spilotes spilotes, Copeia* 1984:959–965.

Hart, D. R. 1979. Niche relationships of *Thamnophis radix haydeni* and *Tham-*

nophis sirtalis parietalis in the Interlake district of Manitoba, *Tulane Studies Zool. Bot.* 21:125–140.

Heatwole, H. 1976. Reptile Ecology, University of Queensland Press, St. Lucia.

Heatwole, H. and Johnson, C. R. 1979. Thermoregulation in the red-bellied blacksnake, *Pseudechis porphyriacus* (Elapidae), *Zool. J. Linn. Soc.* 65: 83–101.

Heatwole, H. and Seymour, R. 1975. Pulmonary and cutaneous oxygen uptake in sea snakes and a file snake, *Comp. Biochem. Physiol.* 51A:399–405.

Heckrotte, C. 1962. The effect of the environmental factors in the locomotory activity of the plains garter snake (*Thamnophis radix radix*), *Anim. Behav.* 10:193–207.

Heckrotte, C. 1967. Relations of body temperature, size, and crawling speed of the common garter snake, *Thamnophis s. sirtalis, Copeia* 1967:759–763.

Henderson, R. W. 1970. Feeding behavior, digestion, and water requirements of *Diadophis punctatus arnyi* Kennicott, *Herpetologica* 26:520–26.

Henderson, R. W. 1982. Thermoregulation in an Hispaniolan tree snake, *Uromacer catesbyi, J. Herpetol.* 16:89–91.

Hirth, H. F. and King, A. Ç. 1969. Body temperatures of snakes in different seasons, *J. Herpetol.* 3:101–102.

Hoskins, M. A. H. and Aleksiuk, M. 1973. Effects of temperature on the kinetics of malate dehydrogenase from a cold climate reptile, *Thamnophis sirtalis parietalis, Comp. Biochem. Physiol.* 45B:343–353.

Huey, R. B. 1982. Temperature, physiology, and the ecology of reptiles, in: Biology of the Reptilia, vol. 12 (C. Gans and F. H. Pough, eds.) pp. 25–91, Academic Press, New York.

Jackson, D. C. 1982. Strategies of acid-base control in ectothermic vertebrates, in: A Companion to Animal Physiology (C. R. Taylor, K. Johansen and L. Bolis, eds.) pp. 73–90, Cambridge University Press, Cambridge.

Jacob, J. S. and McDonald, H. S. 1975. Temperature preferences and electrocardiography of *Elaphe obsoleta* (Serpentes), *Comp. Biochem. Physiol.* 52A:591–594.

Jacobson, E. R. and Whitford, W. G. 1970. The effect of acclimation on physiological responses to temperature in the snakes, *Thamnophis proximus* and *Natrix rhombifera, Comp. Biochem. Physiol.* 35:439–449.

Jacobson, E. R. and Whitford, W. G. 1971. Physiological responses to temperature in the patch-nosed snake. *Salvadora hexalepis, Herpetologica* 27:289–295.

Johansen, K. and Lykkeboe, G. 1979. Thermal acclimation of aerobic metabolism and O_2-Hb binding in the snake, *Vipera berus, J. Comp. Physiol.* 130:293–300.

Johnson, C. R. 1972. Thermoregulation in pythons. I. Effect of shelter, substrate type and posture on body temperature of the Australian carpet python, *Morelia spilotes variegata, Comp. Biochem. Physiol.* 43A:271–278.

Johnson, C. R. 1973. Thermoregulation in pythons. II. Head-body temperature differences and thermal preferenda in Australian pythons, *Comp. Biochem. Physiol.* 45A:1065–1087.

Johnson, C. R. 1975a. Head-body thermal control, thermal preferenda, and voluntary maxima in the taipan, *Oxyuranus scutellatus* (Serpentes: Elapidae), *Zool. J. Linn. Soc.* 56:1–12.

Johnson, C. R. 1975b. Thermoregulation in the Papuan-New Guinean boid and colubrid snakes, *Candoia carinata, Candoia aspera,* and *Boiga irregularis, Zool. J. Linn. Soc.* 56:283–290.

Johnson, C. R., Welsh, G. J. W., and Johnson, C. 1975. Thermoregulation in pythons. III. Thermal ecology and behavior of the black-headed rock python, *Aspidites melanocephalus, Herpetologica* 31:326–332.

Kitchell, J. F. 1969. Thermophilic and thermophobic responses of snakes in a thermal gradient, *Copeia* 1969:189–191.

Kitchell, J. F. and Windell, J. T. 1972. Energy budget for the lizard, *Anolis carolinensis, Physiol. Zool.* 45:178–187.

Klauber, L. M. 1939. Studies of reptile life in the arid Southwest, *Bull. Zool. Soc. San Diego* 14:1–100.

Klauber, L. M. 1956. Rattlesnakes: Their Habits, Life Histories, and Influence on Mankind, 2 vols., University of California Press, Berkeley.

Kropach, C. 1975. *Pelamis,* in: The Biology of Sea Snakes (W. A. Dunson, ed.) pp. 185–213, University Park Press, Baltimore, Maryland.

Landreth, H. F. 1972. Physiological responses of *Elaphe obsoleta* and *Pituophis melanoleucus* to lowered ambient temperatures, *Herpetologica* 28:376–380.

Licht, P. 1972. Problems in experimentation in timing mechanisms for annual physiological cycles in reptiles, in: Hibernation and Hypothermia, Perspectives and Challenges (F. E. South, ed.) pp. 681–711, Elsevier, New York.

Lillywhite, H. B. 1980. Behavioral thermoregulation in Australian elapid snakes, *Copeia* 1980:452–458.

Lillywhite, H. B. 1982. Tracking as an aid in ecological studies of snakes, in: Herpetological Communities (N. J. Scott, Jr., ed.) *U.S. Fish Wildl. Serv. Wildl. Res. Rep.* 13:181–191.

Lillywhite, H. B. 1987. Circulatory adaptations of snakes to gravity, *Am. Zool.* 27:81–95.

Lillywhite, H. B. and Gallagher, K. P. 1985. Hemodynamic adjustments to head-up posture in the partly arboreal snake, *Elaphe obsoleta, J. Exp. Zool.* 235:325–334.

Lillywhite, H. B. and Maderson, P. F. A. 1982. Skin structure and permeability, in: Biology of the Reptilia, vol. 12 (C. Gans and F. H. Pough, eds.) pp. 397–442, Academic Press, New York.

Lillywhite, H. B. and Seymour, R. S. 1978. Regulation of arterial pressure in Australian tiger snakes, *J. Exp. Biol.* 75:65–79.

Lillywhite, H. B. and Smits, A. W. 1984. Lability of blood volume in snakes and its relation to activity and hypertension, *J. Exp. Biol.* 110:267–274.

Lillywhite, H. B. and Smits, A. W. 1985. Diving adaptations in the aquatic file snake, *Acrochordus granulatus, Physiologist* 28:283.

Lowe, C. H., Lardner, P. J., and Halpern, E. A. 1971. Supercooling in reptiles and other vertebrates, *Comp. Biochem. Physiol.* 39A:125–135.

Lueth, F. X. 1941. Effects of temperature on snakes, *Copeia* 1941:125–132.

Lysenko, S. and Gillis, J. E. 1980. The effect of ingestive status on the thermoregulatory behavior of *Thamnophis sirtalis sirtalis* and *Thamnophis sirtalis parietalis, J. Herpetol.* 14:155–159.

McGinnis, S. M. and Moore, R. G. 1969. Thermoregulation in the boa constrictor *Boa constrictor, Herpetologica* 25:38–45.

Marcellini, D. L. and Peters, A. 1982. Preliminary observations on endogenous heat production after feeding in *Python molurus, J. Herpetol* 16:92–94.

Martin, J. H. and Bagby, R. M. 1972. Temperature-frequency relationship of the rattlesnake rattle, *Copeia* 1972:482–485.

Montgomery, G. G. and Rand, A. S. 1978. Movements, body temperature and hunting strategy of a *Boa constrictor, Copeia* 1978:532–533.

Moore, R. G. 1978. Seasonal and daily activity patterns and thermoregulation in the southwestern speckled rattlesnake (*Crotalus mitchelli pyrrhus*) and the Colorado desert sidewinder (*Crotalus cerastes laterorepens*), *Copeia* 1978:439–442.

Mosauer, W. 1936. The toleration of solar heat in desert reptiles, *Ecology* 17:56–66.

Mosauer, W. and Lazier, E. L. 1933. Death from insolation in desert snakes, *Copeia* 1933:149.

Mushinsky, H. R., Hebrard, J. J., and Walley, M. G. 1980. The role of temperature on the behavioral and ecological associations of sympatric water snakes, *Copeia* 1980:744–754.

Myers, B. C. and Eells, M. M. 1968. Thermal aggregation in *Boa constrictor, Herpetologica* 24:61–66.

Nagy, K. A. 1975. Water and energy budgets of free-living reptiles: Measurement using isotopically labeled water, in: Environmental Physiology of Desert Organisms (N. F. Hadley, ed.) pp. 227–245, Dowden and Ross, Stroudsburg, Pennsylvania.

Nagy, K. A. 1982. Energy requirements of free-living iguanid lizards, in: Iguanas of the World (G. M. Burghardt and A. S. Rand, eds.) pp. 49–59, Noyes, Park Ridge, New Jersey.

Naulleau, G. 1979. Etude biotélémétrique de la thermorégulation chez *Vipera aspis* (L.) elevée on conditions artificielles, *J. Herpetol.* 13:203–208.

Naulleau, G. 1983. The effects of temperature on digestion in *Vipera aspis, J. Herpetol.* 17:166–170.

Naulleau, G. and Marques, M. 1973. Etude biotélémétrique préliminaire de la thérmoregulation de la digestion chez *Vipera aspis, C. R. Hebd. Seances Acad. Sci. Paris* 276D:3433–3436.

Nilson, G. 1980. Male reproductive cycle of the European adder, *Vipera berus,* and its relation to annual activity periods, *Copeia* 1980:729–737.

Peterson, C. R. 1982. Body temperature variation in free-living garter snakes (*Thamnophis elegans vagrans*), Ph.D. Dissertation, Washington State University, Pullman.

Peterson, C. R. 1987. Daily body temperature variation in free-ranging garter snakes (*Thamnophis elegans vagrans*) *Ecology,* In press.

Platt, D. R. 1969. Natural history of the hognose snakes *Heterodon platyrhinos* and *Heterodon nasicus, Univ. Kans. Publ. Mus. Nat. Hist.* 18:253–420.

Porter, W. P. and Tracy, C. R. 1974. Modeling the effects of temperature changes on the ecology of the garter snake and leopard frog, in: Thermal Ecology AEC Conference 730505 (J. W. Gibbons and R. R. Sharitz, eds.) pp. 595–609, Oak Ridge, Tennessee.

Pough, F. H. 1976. The effect of temperature on oxygen capacity of reptile blood, *Physiol. Zool.* 49:141–151.

Pough, F. H. 1977. Ontogenetic change in blood oxygen capacity and maximum activity in garter snakes (*Thamnophis sirtalis*), *J. Comp. Physiol.* 116:337–345.

Pough, F. H. 1978. Ontogenetic changes in endurance in water snakes (*Natrix sipedon*): Physiological correlates and ecological consequences, *Copeia* 1978:69–75.

Pough, F. H. 1979. Summary of oxygen transport characteristics of reptilian blood, Smith. Herpetol. Inform. Serv. 45:1–18.

Pough, F. H. 1980. Blood oxygen transport and delivery in reptiles, *Am. Zool.* 20:173–185.

Pough, F. H. 1983. Amphibians and reptiles as low-energy systems, in: Behavioral Energetics: The Cost of Survival in Vertebrates (W. P. Aspey and S. I. Lustick, eds.) pp. 141–188, Ohio State University Press, Columbus.

Pough, F. H. and Lillywhite, H. B. 1984. Blood volume and blood oxygen capacity of sea snakes, *Physiol. Zool.* 57:32–39.

Pough, F. H. and McFarland, W. N. 1976. A physical basis for head-body temperature differences in reptiles, *Comp. Biochem. Physiol.* 53A:301–303.

Reeves, R. B. 1972. An imidazole alphastat hypothesis for vertebrate acid-base regulation: Tissue carbon dioxide content and body temperature in bullfrogs. Respir. Physiol. 14:219–236.

Reeves, R. B. 1977. The interaction of body temperature and acid-base balance in ectothermic vertebrates, *Annu. Rev. Physiol.* 39:559–586.

Regal, P. J. 1966. Thermophilic response following feeding in certain reptiles, *Copeia* 1966:588–590.

Reynolds, W. W. and Casterlin, M. E. 1979. Behavioral thermoregulation and the "final preferendum" paradigm, *Am. Zool.* 19:211–224.

Ruben, J. A. 1976a. Reduced nocturnal heat loss associated with ground litter burrowing by the California red-sided garter snake, *Thamnophis siralis infernalis, Herpetologica* 32:323–325.

Ruben, J. A. 1976b. Aerobic and anaerobic metabolism during activity in snakes, *J. Comp. Physiol.* 109:147–157.

Ruben, J. A. 1976c. Correlation of enzymatic activity, muscle myoglobin and lung morphology with activity metabolism in snakes, *J. Exp. Zool.* 197:313–320.

Saint Girons, H. 1975. Observations préliminaries sur la thermorégulation des vipéres d'Europe, *Vie Millieu* 25:137–168.

Saint Girons, H. 1978. Thermorégulation comparée des vipéres d'Europe. Etude biotélémétrique, *Terre Vie* 32:417–440.

Saint Girons, H. and Saints Girons, M. C. 1956. Cycle d'activité et thermorégulation chez les reptiles (Lézards et Serpents), *Vie Milieu* 7:133–226.

Sanders, J. S. and Jacob, J. S. 1981. Thermal ecology of the copperhead (*Agkistrodon contortrix*), *Herpetologica* 37:264–270.

Schultz, E., Clark, A. W., Suzuki, A., and Cassens, R. G. 1980. Rattlesnake shaker muscle. 1. A light microscopic and histochemical study, *Tissue Cell* 12:323–334.

Scott, J. R. 1978. Thermal biology of the wandering garter snake, Ph.D. Dissertation, Colorado State University, Fort Collins.

Scott, J. R. and Pettus, D. 1979. Effects of seasonal acclimation on the preferred body temperature of *Thamnophis elegans vagrans*, *J. Thermal Biol.* 4:307–309.

Scott J. R., Tracy, C. R., and Pettus, D. 1982. A biophysical analysis of daily and seasonal utilization of climate space by a montane snake, *Ecology* 63:482–493.

Sergeyev, A. 1939. The body temperature of reptiles in natural surroundings, *Dokl. Akad. Nauk SSSR* 22:49–52.

Seymour, R. S. 1978. Gas tensions and blood distribution in sea snakes at surface pressure and at simulated depth, *Physiol. Zool.* 51:388–407.

Seymour, R. S. 1979. Blood lactate in free-diving sea snakes, *Copeia* 1979:494–497.

Seymour, R. S. 1982. Physiological adaptations to aquatic life, in: Biology of the Reptilia, vol. 13 (C. Gans and F. H. Pough, eds.) pp. 1–51, Academic Press, New York.

Seymour, R. S. and Webster, M. E. D. 1975. Gas transport and blood acid-base balance in diving sea snakes, *J. Exp. Zool.* 191:169–182.

Seymour, R. S., Spragg, R. G., and Hartman, M. T. 1981a. Distribution of ventilation and perfusion in the sea snake, *Pelamis platurus*, *J. Comp. Physiol.* 145:109–115.

Seymour, R. S., Dobson, G. P., and Baldwin, J. 1981b. Respiratory and cardiovascular physiology of the aquatic snake, *Acrochordus arafurae*, *J. Comp. Physiol.* 144:215–227.

Shine, R. 1979. Activity patterns in Australian elapid snakes (Squamata: Serpentes: Elapidae), *Herpetologica* 35:1–11.

Shine, R. and Lambeck, R. 1985. A radiotelemetric study of movements, thermoregulation and habitat utilization of Arafura filesnakes (Serpentes: Acrochorchidae), *Herpetologica* 41:351–361.

Skoczylas, R. 1970a. Influence of temperature on gastric digestion in the grass snake *Natrix natrix* L., *Comp. Biochem. Physiol.* 33:793–804.

Skoczylas, R. 1970b. Salivary and gastric juice secretion in the grass snake *Natrix natrix* L., *Comp. Biochem. Physiol.* 35:885–903.

Smith, E. N. 1976. Heating and cooling rates of the American alligator, *Alligator mississippiensis, Physiol. Zool.* 49:37–48.

Snyder, G. K. 1971. Influence of temperature and hematocrit on blood viscosity, *Am. J. Physiol.* 220:1667–1672.

Spellerberg, I. F. 1972. Temperature tolerances of southeast Australian reptiles examined in relation to reptile thermoregulatory behavior and distribution, *Oecologia (Berl.)* 9:23–46.

Spellerberg, I. F. and Phelps, T. E. 1975. Voluntary temperatures of the snake, *Coronella austriaca, Copeia* 1975:183–185.

Spotila, J. R. and Standora, E. A. 1985. Energy budgets of ectothermic vertebrates, *Am. Zool.* 25:973–986.

Standaert, T. and Johansen, K. 1974. Cutaneous gas exchange in snakes, *J. Comp. Physiol.* 89:313–320.

Stevenson, R. D., Peterson, C. R., and Tsuji, J. S. 1985. The thermal dependence of locomotion, tongue flicking, digestion and oxygen consumption in the wandering garter snake, *Physiol. Zool.* 58:46–57.

Stewart, G. R. 1965. Thermal ecology of the garter snakes *Thamnophis sirtalis concinnus* (Hallowell) and *Thamnophis ordinoides* (Baird and Girard), *Herpetologica* 21:81–102.

Stinner, J. N. 1987. Thermal dependence of air convection requirement and blood gases in the snake *Coluber constrictor, Am. Zool.* 27:41–47.

Tsui, H. W. and Licht, P. 1974. Pituitary independence of sperm storage in male snakes, *Gen. Comp. Endocrinol.* 22:277–279.

Turner, J. S. 1987. The cardiovascular control of heat exchange: Consequences of body size, *Am. Zool.* 27:69–79.

Van Mierop, L. H. S. and Barnard, S. M. 1976. Thermoregulation in a brooding female *Python molurus bivittatus, Copeia* 1976:398–401.

Van Mierop, L. H. S. and Barnard, S. M. 1978. Further observations on thermoregulation in the brooding female *Python molurus bivittatus* (Serpentes: Boidae), *Copeia* 1978:615–621.

Vincent, T. 1975. Body temperatures of *Thamnophis sirtalis parietalis* at the den site, *J. Herpetol.* 9:252–254.

Vincent, T. K. and Secoy, D. M. 1978. The effects of annual variation in temperature on cold resistance in a northern population of the red-sided garter snake. *Thamnophis sirtalis parietalis* (Reptilia, Serpentes, Colubridae), *J. Herpetol.* 12:291–294.

Vinegar, A., Hutchison, V. H., and Dowling, H. G. 1970. Metabolism, energetics, and thermoregulation during brooding of snakes of the genus *Python* (Reptilia, Boidae). *Zoologica* 55:19–48.

Vitt, L. J. 1974. Body temperatures of high latitude reptiles, *Copeia* 1974:255–256.

Webb, G. and Heatwole, H. 1971. Patterns of heat distribution within the bodies of some Australian pythons, *Copeia* 1971:209–220.

Weil, M. R. and Aldridge, R. D. 1979. The effect of temperature on the male reproductive system of the common water snake (*Nerodia sipedon*), *J. Exp. Zool.* 210:327–332.

White, F. N. 1978. Circulation: A comparison of mammals, reptiles, and birds, in: Respiratory Function of Birds, Adult and Embryonic (J. Piiper, ed.) pp. 51–60, Springer-Verlag, Berlin.

White, F. N. and Lasiewski, R. C. 1971. Rattlesnake denning: Theoretical considerations on winter temperatures, *J. Theor. Biol.* 30:553–557.

Wood, S. C. 1980. Adaptation of red blood cell function to hypoxia and temperature in ectothermic vertebrates, *Am. Zool.* 20:163–172.

Wood, S. C. 1982. Effect of O_2 affinity on arterial Po_2 in animals with central vascular shunts, *J. Appl. Physiol. Respir. Environ. Exercise Physiol.* 53:1360–1364.

Wood, S. C., Hicks, J. W., and Dupré, R. K. 1987. Hypoxic reptiles: Blood gases, body temperatures and control of breathing, *Am. Zool.* 27:21–29.

CHAPTER FIFTEEN

Status, Conservation, and Management

C. Kenneth Dodd, Jr.

Snakes have held a curious fascination for humans from the beginnings of recorded history, both as objects of fear and as subjects of worship. This may be due to the selective advantage of recognizing a potentially dangerous animal, particularly in regions with dense human populations and highly venomous snakes. One might think, however, that the need for recognition of dangerous species would lead to acute species discrimination, or at least to the discrimination of particular color patterns, rather than to a generalized fear of all species. Wilson (1984) and others (see Steinhart, 1984) have speculated that ophidophobia may be a product of human evolution. Whatever the reason, prejudice against snakes can prove an impediment in conserving them.

While the general public has debated whether to conserve snakes, biologists and conservationists have generally agreed that conservation efforts should be provided, at least since 1916 when Ruthling first noted the need to conserve gopher snakes (*Pituophis*) in California. However, the lack of basic information on the life history of most species and the lack of agreement on terminology, the goals of conservation, or even whether particular species should be protected and managed constitute major impediments in conserving species and the ecosystems on which they depend.

LITERATURE ON THE STATUS OF SNAKES

Whereas a review of the literature (Table 15–1) may not provide a biologically rigorous assessment of the status of snakes of the world, it provides a starting

478

Table 15–1. The Causes of Problems for Snakes Identified in the Literature as in Need of Conservation and Management

Species	Continent	Threats[a]	Reference
Agkistrodon contortrix contortrix	N. America	4,5	Roosa (1977), Fogarty (1978)
A. himalayanus	Asia	5	Sharma (1982)
Ahaetulla dispar	Asia	5	Murthy (1982)
A. nasuta	Asia	5	Murthy (1982)
A. perroteti	Asia	5	Murthy (1982)
A. prasina	Asia	5	Khan (1982)
Argyrogena fasciolatus	Asia	5	Khan (1982)
Bitis gabonica	Africa	1,3,5	McLachlan (1978)
B. schneideri	Africa	5	McLachlan (1978)
B. xeropaga	Africa	5	McLachlan (1978)
Boiga cynodon	Asia	5	Khan (1982)
B. dighotoni	Asia	5	Murthy (1982)
B. multimaculata	Asia	5	Khan (1982)
Bolyeria multocarinata	Island	1	Bullock (1977), Temple (1977)
Bungarus caeruleus	Asia	5	Khan (1982), Saha (1982), Sharma (1982)
B. fasciatus	Asia	2,5	Khan (1982)
Calliophis beddomei	Asia	5	Murthy (1982)
C. nigrescens	Asia	5	Murthy (1982)
Casarea dussumieri	Island	1	Bullock (1977), Temple (1977)
Cemophora coccinea	N. America	5	Nordstrom et al. (1977)
Cerastes cerastes cerastes	Asia	1	Tuck (1977)
Charina bottae umbratica	N. America	1	California Fish and Game (1980), Honegger (1975)
Chersydrus granulatus	Asia	5	Murthy (1982)
Chondropython viridis	Australia	3	Cogger (1982), Covacevich et al. (1982)
Chrysopelea ornata	Asia	2,3,4,5	Biswas (1982), Khan (1982), Murthy (1982)
Clonophis kirtlandii	N. America	5	Tinkle et al. (1979)
Coluber constrictor constrictor	N. America	5	Stewart (1974)
C. c. flaviventris	N. America	5	Stewart (1974)
C. c. foxi	N. America	5	Stewart (1974)
C. hippocrepis	Europe	1,3,5	Honegger (1978b, 1981b)
C. viridiflavus	Europe	1,4,5	Anonymous (1979), Hotz and Broggi (1982)
Contia tenuis	N. America	5	Stewart (1974)

(*Continued*)

479

Table 15–1. The Causes of Problems for Snakes Identified in the Literature as in Need of Conservation and Management (*Continued*)

Species	Continent	Threats[a]	Reference
Coronella austriaca	Europe	1,3,4,5	Anonymous (1979), Honegger (1978b, 1981b), Hotz and Broggi (1982), Spellerberg (1975a), Terhivuo (1981), Groombridge (1982)
Crotalus adamanteus	N. America	4	Lawler and Lee-Fulgham (1977), Palmer (1977a)
C. horridus	N. America	3,4,5	Steward (1974), Nordstrom et al. (1977), Betts (1979), Galligan and Dunson (1979), Williamson (1979), Brown (1984)
C. unicolor	Island	1,3	Honegger (1975)
C. viridis	N. America	3,4	Roosa (1977)
C. willardi obscurus	N. America	3	Harris (1974), Shaw (1978)
Dasypeltis medici	Africa	5	McLachlan (1978)
Dendrelaphis tristis	Asia	5	Sharma (1982)
Diadophis punctatus acricus	Island	5	Weaver and Christman (1978)
Dromicus cerastes	Island	5	Leveque (1963)
Drymarchon corais couperi	N. America	1,3,4,5	Speake and Mount (1973), Speake et al. (1978), Landers and Speake (1980), Bender (1981), Diemer and Speake (1981), Speake and McGlincy (1981), Speake et al. (1981)
Dryocalamus gracilis	Asia	5	Murthy (1982)
D. nympha	Asia	5	Murthy (1982)
Echiopsis atriceps	Australia	1	Cogger (1982)

(*Continued*)

Table 15–1. The Causes of Problems for Snakes Identified in the Literature as in Need of Conservation and Management (*Continued*)

Species	Continent	Threats[a]	Reference
Elachistodon westermanni	Asia	5	Khan (1982)
Elaphe guttata	N. America	1,3,5	Morris and Smith (1981)
E. hodgsonii	Asia	5	Sharma (1982)
E. longissima	Europe	1,3,4,5	Bannikov et al. (1978), Honegger (1978b, 1981b), Anonymous (1979), Groombridge (1982), Hotz and Broggi (1982)
E. obsoleta	N. America	1,4,5	Steward (1974), Roosa (1977), Tinkle et al. (1979)
E. quatuorlineata	Europe	1,3,4,5	Honegger (1978b, 1981b), Groombridge (1982)
E. radiata	Asia	1,2,3	Khan (1982)
E. situla	Europe	1,3,4,5	Bannikov et al. (1978), Honegger (1978b, 1981b), Groombridge (1982)
E. vulpina gloydi	N. America	1,4,5	Stewart (1974), Tinkle et al. (1979)
Elapognathus minor	Australia	5	Cogger (1982)
Epicrates angulifer angulifer	Island	1,4	Honegger (1975)
E. inornatus	Island	3,4,5	Anonymous (1973a)
E. monensis granti	Island	1,5	Nellis et al. (1983)
E. m. monensis	Island	3,5	Grant (1932), Perez-Rivera and Velez (1978)
E. striatus fosteri	Island	1,3	Honegger (1978a)
E. subflavus	Island	5	Mittermeier (1972)
Eristicophis macmahonii	Asia	5	Tuck (1977)
Eryx conicus	Asia	2,5	Biswas (1982), Sharma (1982)
E. jaculus turcicus	Europe	5	Honegger (1978b)
E. jayakari	Asia	1	Tuck (1977)
E. johni johni	Asia	2	Biswas (1982)
Farancia erytrogramma	N. America	1,3	Anonymous (1973b)

(Continued)

Table 15–1. The Causes of Problems for Snakes Identified in the Literature as in Need of Conservation and Management (*Continued*)

Species	Continent	Threats[a]	Reference
Fordonia leucobalia	Asia	5	Khan (1982)
Heterodon nasicus	N. America	1,4	Nordstrom et al. (1977), Morris and Smith (1981), Stewart (1974)
H. platirhinos	N. America	4	Stewart (1974)
Hoplocephalus bungaroides	Australia	1,3	Jenkins (1978), Cogger (1982)
Lampropeltis calligaster rhombomaculata	N. America	5	Means (1978a)
L. getulus goini	N. America	3	Means (1978b)
L. g. holbrooki	N. America	1,4	Roosa (1977)
L. g. sticticeps	N. America	3,4,5	Stephan (1977)
Lamprophis fiskii	Africa	5	McLachlan (1978)
L. swazicus	Africa	5	McLachlan (1978)
Leptotyphlops occidentalis	Africa	5	McLachlan (1978)
Liopeltis calamaria	Asia	5	Murthy (1982)
L. nicobarensis	Island	5	Murthy (1982)
L. rappi	Asia	5	Murthy (1982)
Lycophidion semiannule	Africa	5	McLachlan (1978)
Masticophis flagellum	N. America	1,3,5	Morris and Smith (1981)
M. f. ruddocki	N. America	1	Honegger (1975)
M. lateralis euryxanthus	N. America	1	Honegger (1975), California Fish and Game (1980)
Melanophidium bilineatum	Asia	5	Murthy (1982)
M. wynaudense	Asia	5	Murthy (1982)
Micrurus fulvius fulvius	N. America	1	Palmer (1977b)
M. nigrocinctus babaspul	Island	5	Roze (1982), Villa (1984)
Morelia spilotes spilotes	Australia	1,3,5	Cogger (1982)
Naja naja naja	Asia	3,4,5	Khan (1982), Saha (1982), Sharma (1982)
N. n. kaouthia	Asia	2,3,4	Khan (1982), Saha (1982)
N. oxiana	Asia	5	Bannikov et al. (1978), Sharma (1982)
Natriciteres variegata	Africa	5	McLachlan (1978)
Natrix maura	Europe	1,4,5	Anonymous (1979), Hotz and Broggi (1982)
N. natrix cetti	Europe	1,5	Honegger (1978b, 1981b)

(*Continued*)

Table 15–1. The Causes of Problems for Snakes Identified in the Literature as in Need of Conservation and Management (*Continued*)

Species	Continent	Threats[a]	Reference
N. n. helvetica	Europe	1,4,5	Anonymous (1979), Hotz and Broggi (1982)
N. n. natrix	Europe	1,3,5	Spellerberg (1975b), Hotz and Broggi (1982)
N. tessellata	Europe	1,3	Anonymous (1979), Hotz and Broggi (1982)
Neelaps calonotus	Australia	1,3,5	Cogger (1982), Jenkins (1978)
Nerodia cyclopion	N. America	1	Nordstrom et al. (1977)
N. erythrogaster flavigaster	N. America	1	Roosa (1977)
N. e. neglecta	N. America	1,4,5	Tinkle et al. (1979)
N. fasciata clarki	N. America	1,5	Kochman and Christman (1978a)
N. f. compressicauda	Island	5	Jaume (1974)
N. f. confluens	N. America	1	Morris and Smith (1981)
N. f. taeniata	N. America	1,5	Kochman and Christman (1978b)
N. harteri harteri	N. America	1	Maxwell (1982)
N. h. paucimaculata	N. America	1	Flury and Maxwell (1981)
N. rhombifera	N. America	1	Roosa (1977)
N. sipedon insularum	N. America	4	Stewart (1974)
Notechis scutatus	Australia	1,3,5	Softly (1971)
Ogmodon vitianus	Island	5	Honegger (1978a)
Oligodon cinereus	Asia	5	Khan (1982)
O. dorsalis	Asia	5	Khan (1982)
O. taeniolatus	Asia	?	Bannikov et al. (1978)
O. theobaldi	Asia	5	Khan (1982)
Opheodrys vernalis	N. America	5	Nordstrom et al. (1977)
Ophiophagus hannah	Asia	2,5	Biswas (1982), Murthy (1982)
Pareas macularia	Asia	5	Khan (1982)
P. monticola	Asia	5	Khan (1982)
Pituophis melanoleucus catenifer	N. America	5	Stewart (1974)
P. m. lodingi	N. America	1,3,5	Mount (1976), Jennings and Fritts (1983)
P. m. mugitus	N. America	4	Mount (1976)

(*Continued*)

Table 15–1. The Causes of Problems for Snakes Identified in the Literature as in Need of Conservation and Management (*Continued*)

Species	Continent	Threats[a]	Reference
P. m. ruthveni	N. America	5	Jennings and Fritts (1983)
Plectrurus aureus	Asia	5	Murthy (1982)
Prosymna frontalis	Africa	5	McLachlan (1978)
Psammophis leithi	Asia	5	Sharma (1982)
Pseudechis australis	Australia	5	Cogger (1982)
P. porphyriacus	Australia	5	Cogger (1982)
Ptyas mucosus	Asia	2,3,4,5	Bannikov et al. (1978), Biswas (1982), Khan (1982), Murthy (1982)
Python amethistinus	Australia	1,3,5	Cogger (1982)
P. molurus molurus	Asia	1,2,5	Biswas (1982), Khan (1982), Saha (1982), Sharma (1982)
P. reticulatus	Asia	1,2	Biswas (1982), Khan (1982)
P. sebae	Africa	2,5	McLachlan (1978)
Ramphotyhlops andamanensis	Island	5	Murthy (1982)
R. braminus	Asia	5	Sharma (1982)
R. leucoproctus	Australia	5	Covacevich et al. (1982)
R. oatesi	Island	5	Murthy (1982)
R. tindalli	Asia	5	Murthy (1982)
Regina grahami	N. America	1,4	Roosa (1977)
R. septemvittata	N. America	1	Stewart (1974), Nordstrom et al. (1977)
Rhabdophis tigrinus	Asia	1	Fukada (1969)
Rhabdops olivaceus	Asia	5	Murthy (1982)
Rhinophis fergusonianus	Asia	5	Murthy (1982)
Rhynchocalamus melanocephalus satunini	Asia	?	Bannikov et al. (1978)
Sibynophis bistrigatus	Island	5	Murthy (1982)
S. sagittarius	Asia	5	Khan (1982)
S. subpunctatus	Asia	5	Khan (1982), Murthy (1982)
Simoselaps warro	Australia	5	Covacevich et al. (1982)
S. woodjonesi	Australia	5	Covecevich et al. (1982)
Sistrurus catenatus	N. America	1,4,5	Stewart (1974), Nordstrom et al. (1977), Roosa (1977), Seigel (1986)

(Continued)

Table 15-1. The Causes of Problems for Snakes Identified in the Literature as in Need of Conservation and Management (*Continued*)

Species	Continent	Threats[a]	Reference
Spalerosophis diadema diadema	Asia	5	Murthy (1982)
Stilosoma extenuatum	N. America	1	Campbell (1978a)
Tantilla oolitica	N. America	1	Campbell (1978b), Porras and Wilson (1979)
Telescopus beetzii	Africa	5	McLachlan (1978)
Thamnophis brachystoma	N. America	5	Bothner (1976)
T. butleri	N. America	5	Stewart (1974)
T. couchi gigas	N. America	1,3	Honneger (1975), California Fish and Game (1980), Hanson and Brode (1980)
T. radix radix	N. America	1	Dalrymple and Reichenbach (1984)
T. sauritus septentrionalis	N. America	1	Morris and Smith (1981), Stewart (1974)
T. sirtalis tetrataenia	N. America	1,3	Anonymous (1973a), Medders (1976), Barry (1978), California Fish and Game (1980)
Typhlops porrectus	Asia	5	Sharma (1982)
T. tenuicollis	Asia	5	Sharma (1982)
Uropeltis dindigalensis	Asia	5	Murthy (1982)
U. nitidus	Asia	5	Murthy (1982)
Vipera ammodytes montandoni	Europe	1,4,5	Honegger (1978b, 1981b)
V. a. transcaucasiana	Asia	1,3	Bannikov et al. (1978), Honegger (1978a)
V. aspis	Europe	1,3,4,5	Honegger (1978b, 1981b), Anonymous (1979), Hotz and Broggi (1982)
V. berus	Europe	1,3,4,5	Honneger (1978b, 1981b), Anonymous (1979), Terhivuo (1981), Hotz and Broggi (1982)

(*Continued*)

Table 15–1. The Causes of Problems for Snakes Identified in the Literature as in Need of Conservation and Management (*Continued*)

Species	Continent	Threats[a]	Reference
V. kaznakovi	Asia	2	Bannikov et al. (1978), Honegger (1978b)
V. latifii	Asia	1,3	Tuck (1977), Andren and Nilson (1979)
V. lebetina	Asia	3,4,5	Groombridge (1982), Murthy (1982), Sharma (1982)
V. l. schweizeri	Europe	3,4,5	Honegger (1978b, 1981b)
V. russelli	Asia	2,5	Khan (1982), Murthy (1982), Saha (1982), Sharma (1982)
V. ursinii anatolica	Europe	5	Honegger (1978b)
V. u. rakosiensis	Europe	1,4,5	Honegger (1978b, 1981b)
V. u. renardi	Europe	1	Honegger (1978b, 1981b)
V. u. ursinii	Europe	1,3,4,5	Honegger (1978b, 1981b), Groombridge (1982)
V. u. wettsteini	Europe	1,3,4,5	Honegger (1978b)
V. xanthina raddei	Asia	1,3,5	Bannikov et al. (1978), Tuck (1977), Honegger (1978a)
Virginia valeriae elegans	N. America	1	Roosa (1977)
V. v. pulchra	N. America	1	Anonymous (1973b)
Xenocalamus transvaalensis	Africa	5	McLachlan (1978)
Zacoys nigromarginatus	Asia	5	Khan (1982)

[a]1, Habitat alteration or destruction; 2, collection for use as leather or meat; 3, collection for use as pets; 4, malicious killing; 5, rare, obscure, or specific threat undetermined.

point for assessing our rudimentary knowledge of snake status and biology. Many of these papers and reports have not been subject to critical peer review, and nearly all reflect the biases, experiences, and opinions of the authors. I have not attempted to standardize terminology, and authors may use the same words with different connotations. Because the quality of these references varies considerably, readers are advised to use Table 15–1 with caution and to consult the

Table 15–2. Distribution of Snakes Considered in Need of Conservation, Management, and/or an Assessment of Status Based on Literature Records

Continent	N	%	Comments on Data
North America	56	30.1	Many species listed by Canada and various U.S. states are not endangered throughout their range. More survey work is required to assess overall status.
South America	0	0	Nothing reported on status of snakes, especially effects of trade.
Africa	13	7.0	All data from South Africa; little known about the rest of the continent.
Asia	66	35.5	Most information from Indian subcontinent; data largely subjective with few scientific studies; much interest.
Australia	13	7.0	Most species in need of conservation are narrow endemics affected by habitat loss and collection.
Europe	21	11.3	Generally best data base; declines occurring in northern part of ranges, and many vipers are endangered.
Caribbean and other island species	17	9.1	Endemics particularly vulnerable; the group most in need of conservation as a whole.
Total	186		In general, the data are too incomplete at present to provide an accurate overall assessment of the status of the world's snakes.

original paper. This review revealed 186 species and subspecies considered by the authors to be declining, rare, endangered, or in some other manner in need of conservation and management (Table 15–1). Most of the assessments were not supported by studies actually documenting declines or particular threats but were meant to call attention to a perceived problem in need of further study. "Unknown cause" or "unsure of status" caveats frequently appeared, especially in the Red Data Book formats popularized by the International Union for the Conservation of Nature and Natural Resources (IUCN).

In a few noteworthy instances, particularly those dealing with the Indian subcontinent, summaries were in the form of species lists that tended to bias the totals of species by geographic region (Table 15–2). Even in North America, the majority of species listed as endangered or threatened (36 of 56) occurred in a geographic region peripheral to their entire range and would not be so considered if assessed throughout their range. In Canada, for example, Stewart (1974) listed 15 species as endangered, all of which, except *Nerodia sipedon insularum,* have extensive ranges further south and 12 of which are not considered in trouble throughout their range. This is not to imply criticism of those who made assessments within particular areas and included peripheral species; biologists recognize the need to conserve genetic variability. However, if assessed throughout their range, relatively few species and subspecies would appear to be declining. It is likely that this reflects a lack of knowledge concerning the life history of many species, particularly in developed nations and nations with large human populations, rather than an accurate assessment of the status of the world's snakes.

Europe

In general, assessment of the status of European snakes has advanced further than that of any other region, possibly because of the large number of persons interested in snakes and the small number of species (27: Arnold and Burton, 1978). Considering full species, 19 of 27 (70%) were identified as needing conservation and management (Table 15–1). Most species in northern Europe were in this category because they are on the periphery of geographic ranges where local snake populations inhabit areas of dense human populations, and are subject to fluctuations because of climatic extremes. Thus species such as *Natrix tessellata* and *Elaphe longissima* are considered endangered in West Germany, although southern populations are not declining (Groombridge, 1982).

Europe presented a mosaic of statuses, although nearly all species were suspected of local population declines, principally due to habitat alteration (20 of 21 species); *Vipera schweizeri* was the exception. The other factors in Table 15–1 affected species about equally: other or unspecified (18), malicious killing (14), collecting for the pet trade (13).

While some species and subspecies were considered rare, in no instance was rarity per se identified as the reason for listing a species as endangered or threatened. Other factors thought to affect status included the use of biocides and the introduction of exotic species. Spellerberg (1975a) and Moser et al. (in press) speculated that declining populations might be related to climatic cooling at northern latitudes or high elevations.

North America

In North America, I identified 56 species and subspecies in the literature warranting endangered or threatened status at least in parts of their range; 15 occurred in Canada (Stewart, 1974). No references to the status of mainland snakes could be found for Mexico or Central America.

In the United States and Canada, few species were reported to definitely warrant endangered or threatened classification throughout their range. Several snakes in the United States were listed as endangered or threatened primarily because of rarity, although often with concern expressed for loss of habitat. For instance, fewer than 50 specimens are known for the Louisiana pine snake (*Pituophis melanoleucus ruthveni*), which would make this one of the rarest North American snakes. Yet it has always seemed rare (Conant, 1956), and there is disagreement about the point at which a rare species, though perhaps not declining in numbers, should be termed endangered and afforded statutory protection (Jennings and Fritts, 1983). Because of their elusive and/or secretive nature, some species suspected of being endangered or threatened may prove exceedingly difficult to survey (e.g., *Diadophis punctatus acricus, Tantilla oolitica, Stilosoma extenuatum, P. m. ruthveni, Clonophis kirtlandi*).

The principal cause of decline in North American snakes was identified as habitat destruction (33 of 56 species), followed by rare, unspecified, or other factors (24), malicious killing (16), and collecting by hobbyists (11). Concern for commercial collecting either for pets or for the leather trade rarely has been raised with regard to individual species, at least since the eastern indigo snake (*Drymarchon corais couperi*), San Francisco garter snake (*Thamnophis sirtalis tetrataenia*), and New Mexico ridgenose rattlesnake (*Crotalus willardi obscurus*) received federal protection.

Geographically, most snakes identified as in need of conservation in the United States are found in the South (18), followed by the Midwest (17), West (6), and East (3). The South is now the fastest growing section of the United States and contains localized endemic species likely to be adversely affected by human population growth (Mount, 1976; Cooper et al., 1977; McDiarmid, 1978; Wilson and Porras, 1983). The Midwest is a largely agricultural area whose fauna probably has undergone massive depletion and whose snake populations have declined (Roosa, 1977; Tinkle et al., 1979; Christiansen, 1981; Morris and Smith, 1981). While no baseline data are available, there are a few anecdotal accounts. For instance, Fitch (1963) related the story of a farmer who told him that racers (*Coluber constrictor*) had decreased by a factor of 5, a decline he attributed to mechanized agricultural equipment. In the West, most of the affected snakes are found in restricted areas in California and are subject to increased human population pressures.

Asia

Interest in the status of snakes has been greatest on the Indian subcontinent where snakes are feared for their venom, eaten, prepared as medicines and potions, used as leather and, for some tribes such as the Irula (Whitaker, 1979), have formed a major part of tribal life. Unfortunately, nearly all information on Asian snakes was based on the impressions of individual biologists, with little emphasis on published surveys.

Assessment of the status of Asian snakes is complicated by rarity, or at least by the lack of specimens available for study. For instance, in Sri Lanka (de

Silva, 1980), each of the following are known from only one specimen: *Typhlops ceylonicus, Uropeltis ruhunae, Rhinophis porrectus, Platyplectrurus madurensis ruhunae,* and *Dendrelaphis oliveri.* There are systematic or locality problems with some of these species, and whether they should be considered valid species must await further study. The problem of rarity was also emphasized by Biswas (1982), who listed 33 species of Indian snakes known from fewer than four specimens and stated, "Most of these species may appear rare because proper surveys have not been made in their ecological niches or habitats."

Elsewhere in Asia, few reviews have appeared. Bannikov et al. (1978) noted that habitat loss or collecting was causing the decline of several species in southern Russia. In Iran, Tuck (1977) listed *Eryx jayakari* and *Cerastes cerastes cerastes* as endangered because of threats from dune stabilization programs even though both species occur widely outside Iran; *Eristicophis macmahonii* because it is known from only a single specimen; and *Vipera xanthina raddei* because of limited distribution. Both Tuck (1977) and Andren and Nilson (1979) proposed endangered status for *V. latifii* because of the collection of over 8000 specimens from its only known locality and threats from a proposed dam construction, respectively. In Japan, Fukada (1969) reported a marked decline in a single population of *Rhabdophis tigrinus* due to road construction, pollution, and the destruction of a wall used as shelter; elsewhere the species is considered common.

The primary reasons for calling for conservation measures in Asia were either that a particular snake was rare or that the apparent cause of decline was not known or specified (48 species and subspecies). Threats from the leather trade (10 species, particularly *Python, Ptyas,* and *Ophiophagus*), habitat destruction (8), miscellaneous collecting (7), and malicious killing (5) were less often identified. Rather than concentrate on a particular species, a few authors (for instance, Rajendran, 1982, for uropeltids) emphasized the need for conserving particular groups.

Australia

Australia has a diverse snake fauna, but few people and much open habitat; consequently, relatively few species have been identified as requiring management or conservation, and Cogger (1982) stated that no species was in danger of extinction. The only species consistently identified in Australian literature as threatened was *Hoplocephalus bungaroides,* restricted to a sandstone habitat near Sydney and subject to habitat loss and collecting (Jenkins, 1978; Cogger, 1982). A few species, such as *Neelaps calonotus,* seemed to be listed because of the potential for collection rather than a demonstrated threat. For the 13 species in Table 15–1, unidentified causes or lack of information was singled out for 10, followed by habitat destruction (6) and collecting (6).

In a thoughtful paper on reptile conservation, Rawlinson (1981) emphasized the need for more information and focused on the effects of habitat alteration and biocides on herpetological communities rather than on restrictive regulations on the collection of specimens. He pointed to a number of instances where chemicals had been used with serious though unquantified side effects on reptile populations, such as the use of malathion in Victoria in 1969 after which "reptiles were virtually nonexistent." Longmore and Lee (1981) believed that no snakes were captured after a prescribed burn in Sturt National Park because all had either migrated or been killed, although they presented no data to support a population decrease.

Australia is the only region in which the potentially serious consequences of an exotic nonmammalian introduction for a snake fauna has been documented. The giant toad (*Bufo marinus*) was introduced in Queensland to control sugarcane beetles. Suspecting adverse impacts from the introduction, Covacevich and Archer (1975) showed that the toad was toxic to elapids and some colubrids. At the same time that frog-eating elapids were declining, based on collection records, mammal-eating elapids such as *Oxyuranus* seemed to increase. While noting the difficulty in attributing these trends to a single cause, Shine and Covacevich (1983) believed the toad was at least partly responsible.

Caribbean and Other Islands

As a number of authors have noted (reviewed by Diamond, 1984), the risk of extinction decreases with increasing habitat size and population density. Therefore, island species with a spatially limited habitat should be more vulnerable than mainland species to extinction (Soule, 1983), especially if affected by human activities. The literature showed 17 island species in need of immediate conservation and management. One, *Nerodia fasciata compressicauda* on Cuba (Jaume, 1974), is not really an island endemic because it is found extensively in the southeastern United States. The reason for its rarity was unknown, but may be influenced by its peripheral distribution.

Other island snakes have been adversely affected primarily by habitat destruction and the introduction of non-native animals. Parker (1936) first called attention to several species in the Caribbean that he thought were extinct, though all have subsequently been found extant. All snakes listed by Honegger (1980–1981) as extinct were island species: *Alsophis ater* (Jamaica), *A. sancticrucis* (St. Croix), *Dromicus cursor* (Martinique, Rocher de Diamont), and *D. ornatus* (St. Lucia). However, *D. cursor* was collected in 1962 on Rocher de Diamont (Lazell, 1967) and *D. ornatus* in 1973 on Maria Island off eastern St. Lucia (Schwartz and Thomas, 1975; A. Schwartz, Personal communication). To a potential extinct list might be added *Bolyeria multocarinata,* a boa from Round Island in the Indian Ocean, which has not been reported since a single specimen was observed in 1975 (Temple, 1977; S. Tonge, Personal communication), the coral snake *Micrurus nigrocinctus babaspul* from the Corn Islands of Nicaragua, not reliably reported since 1976 (Villa, 1984; Roze, 1982), and *Chironius vincenti* from the island of St. Vincent in the Caribbean (A. Schwartz, Personal communication).

The most common reason for declines in island populations was the introduction of animals such as the mongoose *Herpestes auropunctatus* (Mittermeier, 1972; Honegger, 1980–1981), which preys on snakes, or domestic livestock, particularly sheep and goats, that alter vegetation to the extent that cover is lost (Bullock, 1977; Temple, 1977). This factor apparently affected the survival of the two endemic boas, *Casarea dussumieri* and *Bolyeria multocarinata,* on Round Island.

Other species, such as *Crotalus unicolor,* live on relatively small islands whose habitat is desired by humans (Honegger, 1975); this species now survives on about 10% of Aruba, and snakes are rare and seldom seen (K. Peterson, Personal communication). Habitat loss, coupled with adverse impacts created by introduced animals, also caused *Dromicus cerastes* to decline on the Galapagos (Leveque, 1963).

A number of island species appear to be rare. The boas *Epicrates monensis monensis* and *E. m. granti* inhabit islands on the Puerto Rico Bank, and until recently when a substantial population of *E. m. granti* was discovered on a small cay off Puerto Rico (P. Tolson, Personal communication), fewer than 15 specimens of each subspecies were known. Rivero et al. (1982) argued that this rarity was an artifact of inadequate sampling. For *E. m. monensis,* however, Grant (1932) noted that long-time residents of Mona (now uninhabited) were not familiar with the species, and scientists who have spent considerable time on the island have not seen it (T. Wiewandt and S. Peck, Personal communication). The reported rarity of other *Epicrates* on larger islands may indeed be an artifact of inadequate sampling. Grant (1932) and anonymous (1973a) reported *E. inornatus* to be rare on Puerto Rico, and Mittermeier (1972) did likewise for *E. subflavus* on Jamaica. While both species are affected by malicious killing, habitat loss, and killing for their oil, they are probably more abundant than reported in the literature (Oliver, 1982; R. Crombie, G. Drewry, and A. Schwartz, Personal communication). There are other snakes that seem rare in the Caribbean, such as certain *Alsophis* on particular islands, but it is likely that these species are more abundant than collections indicate because their fossorial or arboreal habits make them difficult to find (A. Schwartz, Personal communication).

Africa and South America

The literature on snake conservation from these two continents is nearly nonexistent. While some data exist on trade in South American species (see TRADE), no publication discusses the status of any of these snakes. Skinner (1973) mentioned the need to conserve African snakes without discussing any particular species. In Africa, the only publication that discussed individual species was McLachlan (1978) concerning South African snakes. Of the 13 species, 8 were listed as rare because their ranges are peripheral to South Africa, and 5 as rare even though their ranges are primarily within the borders of the country. Habitat destruction and collecting for the leather and pet trades each affected one species.

THREATS TO SNAKE POPULATIONS

Habitat Destruction

The greatest threat to snakes as a group is habitat destruction, which results in the physical elimination of both animals and their ecosystems and the fragmentation of remaining populations which are then subject to reduced population size and the resulting potential loss of genetic diversity (Wilcox and Murphy, 1985). Habitat loss is difficult to quantify, however, because few or no baseline data exist to document either the extent of loss of habitat in many areas or the resulting effects on snake populations.

As is true for nearly all factors affecting a species' status, loss of habitat may be only one of a series of factors simultaneously threatening a population and can set in motion other detrimental effects, such as disruption of social behavior or genetic problems, which further impact the species. In snakes, these factors are still largely unstudied, and most conservation surveys try to answer more basic questions concerning where the species is located, how many individuals there are, and the nature of the obvious threats.

In Europe the categories of most serious habitat loss are wetlands and lowlands within mountainous countries, where semi-aquatic species such as *Natrix maura* in Switzerland are particularly threatened (Hotz and Broggi, 1982). These authors also reported that 70% of the decline of *Vipera aspis* in the Geneva Basin was due to habitat destruction and that roads were thought to take a heavy toll during construction and subsequent use.

In North America, habitat loss stems from residential or agricultural development, logging and forestry practices, and impoundment of streams and rivers. However, specific data are rarely supplied. One exception is that for *Thamnophis couchi gigas* in the San Joaquin Valley of California; this species has lost at least 33% of its available habitat, primarily in the northern part of its range, to land clearing for agriculture (Hanson and Brode, 1980).

A loss of natural habitat is rarely correlated with a decline in the number of specific snakes but undoubtedly is responsible for major population changes. For instance, in southern Florida, 98% of Hendry County is in agriculture, and over 50% of Broward, Monroe, and Palm Beach counties is urban or agriculturally developed (Wilson and Porras, 1983); these counties and others in southern and central Florida continue to receive massive human population influxes. In the Coachella Valley of California, the human population increased from 12,000 in the 1940s to over 120,000 in 1979 and is projected to increase to 160,000 by 1990. This valley at one time contained an abundant reptile fauna, which has declined precipitously (W. Mayhew, Personal communication). In California's San Joaquin Valley, 618,000 acres of wildlands remained in 1976 but decreased to 170,400 acres by 1979 (19,200 acres/yr). While such figures on habitat loss may be available for a few rapidly developing areas throughout the world, the effects on reptiles, and snakes in particular, remain unquantified.

Likewise, urban sprawl affects metropolitan areas throughout the world, but only rarely are its effects on snakes noted. The Australian species *Hoplocephalus bungaroides* has declined in the Sydney area as a result of habitat loss (Cogger, 1982), and proximity to a metropolitan area has caused a decline in a number of European species (Spellerberg, 1957b; Honegger, 1978b). In North America, urban sprawl is thought to have adversely affected a wide variety of amphibians and reptiles (Campbell, 1974, and references therein), particularly the snakes *Thamnophis sirtalis tetrataenia* (San Francisco), *Tantilla oolitica* (Miami), and *Nerodia fasciata taeniata* (Florida's east coast), among others (see references in Table 15–1).

Forestry practices such as clear-cutting, intensive site preparation, and single-species management may also adversely impact snakes, though specific data are virtually nonexistent. Forests are generally managed to produce timber, and the techniques employed are rarely based on an evaluation of their effect on nongame species. Though claimed to enhance wildlife, forestry as practiced often adversely impacts many species, particularly those with specialized habitat requirements (Christman, 1983). Developing countries also face problems from intensive forestry practices and lumbering for firewood and industry even in protected reserves. In Kenya, A. Duff-MacKay (Personal communication) believes such activities could cause the decline in 12 species of forest snakes that reach their eastern limits in Kakamega Forest. He also expresses concern for *Geodipsas vauerocegue, G. procterae, Crotaphopeltis werneri, Aparallactus werneri,* and *Atheris ceratophis* in the Usambara and Uluguru Mountains in Tanzania.

Other forms of habitat destruction may impact snakes, but again few data are available (see Table 15–1). These include introducing domestic animals that cause disturbance of ground cover (Bullock, 1977; Temple, 1977), spreading oil on dunes for stabilization (Tuck, 1977), and building dams that eliminate retreats and appropriate habitats (Flury and Maxwell, 1981). Mowing grass to enhance the habitats of other forms of wildlife can result in loss of an appropriate habitat and direct killing of snakes (Dalrymple and Reichenbach, 1984; Seigel, 1986).

Malicious Killing

Snakes have always aroused intense feelings in people (Morris and Morris, 1965), whether they inhabit cities and have never seen a snake or live in extremely rural areas where snakes abound. For instance, out of 11,960 children who responded to a television questionnaire in Great Britain concerning the animal they most disliked, snakes led with 27%. Of a combined adult-child sample via a newspaper poll, 24% considered snakes the most disliked animal (Morris and Morris, 1965). Such feelings are likely to be equally intense in regions with many dangerous snakes, such as Asia and Africa.

The effects of wanton killing on wild populations of snakes has not been studied. Most of the species mentioned as being threatened by such killing either occurred in Europe, were venomous, or were large (Table 15–1). Tourists who kill *Vipera ursinii wettsteini* were thought to have threatened the existence of this small viper in the French Basses Alps, and bounty systems implemented in Italy and Greece were thought to have depleted other isolated viper populations, particularly *V. lebetina schweizeri* (Honegger, 1978b).

In the United States, bounty systems generally have been restricted to rattlesnakes (*Crotalus*). Such bounties can be traced as far back as 1719 in Massachusetts. Other states, including Iowa, Minnesota, Vermont, New York, Pennsylvania, and Wisconsin, have offered bounties (Klauber, 1972), however, some have rescinded this policy relatively recently (New York in 1971: Brown, 1984). Tioga County, Pennsylvania, continued to offer a $1 bounty through 1984 (C. Shiffer, Personal communication). Between 1949–1954 and 1960–1976, 29,147 rattlesnakes were turned in for bounties in this county alone (Galligan and Dunson, 1979).

Harmless snakes also suffer from bounty systems because virtually any snake encountered during a hunt is likely to be killed. Some harmless species may also be subject to official sanctioning of their destruction. Hotz and Broggi (1982, citing Perret-Gentil, 1977) noted that *Natrix natrix* is destroyed in the Swiss canton of Vaud because it is a fish predator.

Rattlesnake Roundups

Organized rattlesnake hunts have occurred in parts of the United States for at least 300 yr; the earliest was recorded in New England in 1680 (Klauber, 1972). Currently, they occur in the spring in Alabama, Florida, Georgia, Oklahoma, Pennsylvania, and Texas. Sponsored by civic or charitable organizations, the purpose of these hunts is to raise money and to provide recreation for local residents.

Accurate data on the number of snakes taken are difficult to obtain both because of exaggeration by local officials and because of sensitivity to criticism by environmental organizations. Kilmon and Shelton (1981) stated that in 16 yr 70,773 rattlesnakes were taken at Sweetwater, Texas, in these roundups. Galligan and Dunson (1979) reported that 751 *C. horridus* were collected in 9 yr at the Morris snake hunt, and 3205 in 17 yr at the Keystone Reptile Club hunt, both in Pennsylvania. The accuracy of these figures and the effect on rattlesnake populations are unknown.

One method of obtaining snakes during these hunts is to funnel or spray gasoline into tortoise (*Gopherus polyphemus*) burrows or rattlesnake dens in the hope of driving the snakes to the surface. In experiments using different concentrates of gasoline, Speake and Mount (1973) and Speake and McGlincy (1981) demonstrated that gassing a burrow does not necessarily drive a rattlesnake to the surface and that those remaining generally die. Other snakes also were susceptible to burrow gassing, particularly the eastern indigo snake (*Drymarchon corais couperi*).

Biocides

The use of various biocides is an inherent part of modern agriculture, forestry, weed and pest control, and warfare. While the most obvious detrimental effects on wildlife have been documented in bird populations, a growing body of literature is accumulating on the effects of some of these compounds on reptiles (summarized by Hall, 1980). Rawlinson (1981) and Honegger (1978b) discussed the possible effects of biocides on Australian and European herpetofauna, respectively.

To date, no snake's existence has been directly threatened by environmental contaminants, although it is clear that local populations have suffered declines of unknown magnitude and duration. Most contaminants have not been tested for their effect on snakes. For instance, while polychlorinated biphenyls (PCBs) are ubiquitous in wildlife, there are no reports involving snakes. This may be due to confusion in the reporting of pesticide results (Hall, 1980). Also, it is difficult to compare results between studies, because contaminants may concentrate at different rates in particular organs and because susceptibility, both long- and short-term, may vary among species.

Deleterious effects of DDT (applications of 0.2 to 4.9 kg/ha) have been reported for a wide variety of colubrids and viperids, including *Thamnophis, Opheodrys, Nerodia,* and *Agkistrodon* (see references in Hall, 1980) (Table 15–1), and the lethal effect of DDT on snakes was known as early as 1949 (Goodrum et al., 1949; Herald, 1949). Residues of DDT or its derivatives in affected snakes have been reported generally at less than 50 ppm, though Stafford et al. (1976) found concentrations of DDE in *Agkistrodon* and *Nerodia* as high as 1161.2 ppm.

Dieldrin killed snakes during tsetse fly control programs in Africa (Wilson, 1972) and, mixed with heptachlor, at concentrations of 2.2 kg/ha in the United States. Heptachlor alone administered at concentrations of 2.2 kg/ha also has killed a variety of snakes (see Hall, 1980); concentrations of heptachlor epoxide in snakes thought to have been killed by pesticides ranged from 4.2 to 54.0 ppm (Hall, 1980: Table 3).

Other environmental contaminants found to kill snakes included secondarily ingested strychnine alkaloids (Brock, 1965), malathion, and dichlorvos vapor (Rawlinson, 1981). Residues of mirex (0.04 to 17.20 ppm: Lawler and Lee-Fulgham, 1977; Wheeler et al., 1977), the results of fire ant control programs, were found to persist 18 mo in snake tissues and may adversely affect populations. Brisbin et al. (1974) reported radiocesium (x = 131.5, max = 1032.6 pCi/g) in 19 species of snakes at the Savannah River Plant in South Carolina in the vicinity of a nuclear reactor effluent stream.

EXOTIC SPECIES INTRODUCTIONS

The effects of introduced feral mammals on the fauna of Round Island and of the toad, *Bufo marinus,* on Australian snakes were previously noted. Likewise, the mongoose, *Herpestes auropunctatus,* is thought to have contributed to the extinction or decline of certain species of snakes and other indigenous wildlife on many Caribbean islands (see Caribbean and Other Islands, p. 491).

Little is known concerning the effects of introduced invertebrates on snake populations. However, in the southeastern United States, the imported red fire ant *(Solenopsis invicta)* is a ubiquitous pest. While evidence is circumstantial, in Alabama there appears to have been a serious decline in populations of egg-laying reptiles that has not been noted in live-bearers. Mount (1981) believed that these declines may be attributed to fire ant predation on eggs and neonates of such ground dwelling snakes as *Heterodon, Micrurus,* and *Lampropeltis calligaster.*

TRADE

Extensive trade in reptiles has existed at least since the 1920s and much longer for sea turtles and crocodilians (Honegger, 1978b). There are currently two major varieties of trade in snakes: the fashion industry, where snake skins are manufactured into clothing items and accessories, and the pet trade. Both are extremely difficult to gauge because of secrecy among people involved in such trades.

In the United States, both common and uncommon snakes are traded extensively. Most of these animals are sold either in pet shops or by dealers in exotic animals, and for the most part such trading is legal. However, although some snakes are products of captive breeding programs begun specifically to supply the trade, most are resident species collected from the wild with little concern for effects on the natural population. Some states, such as California, Arizona, and Utah, have legally banned the commercial collection of native snakes, but in most states, such as Florida with its wealth of unique species, commercial collection is not regulated or monitored.

In mid-1981, the U.S. Fish and Wildlife Service closed down an undercover operation that revealed massive illegal trade in both domestic and foreign protected species. Over 10,000 illegal reptiles were obtained during this "sting" operation, including federally protected species such as *Drymarchon corais couperi, Thamnophis sirtalis tetrataenia, Crotalus willardi obscurus,* and *Epicrates subflavus.* Over 1100 animals were seized, 40 search warrants were issued, and warrants were served for the arrest of 27 persons (Bender, 1981). Both amateur and professional biologists were included among those trafficking in rare snakes, and certain zoos were investigated for suspected illegal activities. The Fish and Wildlife Service estimated that up to 100,000 reptiles were shipped illegally through the U.S. mails each year (Bender, 1981).

In the United States, there are a small number of individuals who still may be considered commercial snake collectors. In Pennsylvania, Galligan and Dunson (1979) recorded interviews with 11 rattlesnake hunters, all of whom reported a substantial decline in the snake population and in the viability of dens within the last 10 yr. At one time, commercial collectors were far more numerous. In Florida in the 1940s, rattlesnake collecting employed about 120 collectors who brought in more than 20,000 snakes worth $2 million annually (Snyder, 1949).

Collection for pets is also a concern among European herpetologists, particularly affecting such species as *Vipera* and *Elaphe* (see Table 15–1). There is also illegal importation into Europe from other countries. *Python regius* has been imported into Great Britain from Ghana without proper certification (Antram, 1981).

The legal trade in live snakes also constitutes an unknown drain on wild populations. Elsewhere, I have summarized data taken from the Convention on International Trade in Endangered Species of Wild Fauna and Flora (CITES), a treaty enacted to curtail trade in endangered and threatened species (Dodd, 1986). The CITES provisions provide a means of monitoring the extent of trade, both in live specimens and in parts and products. Because the United States is a major consumer of the world's wildlife, the level of trade into the United States can provide an insight into the extent of legal trade in live snakes.

The U.S. CITES Management Authority tabulated legal trade between 1977 and 1982 (see Dodd, 1986). Because recording has become more reliable in recent years, early statistics undoubtedly underestimated the level of trade, and changes in trade between 1977 and 1982 are probably not indicative of overall trends. During this period, however, there were 228,416 legally reported CITES specimens of live snakes imported into the United States, plus an additional 86 shipments of an unspecified number of individuals. Although these species may have been exported legally, there are virtually no data on the status of any of them in the wild, so it is impossible to determine whether such trade has been detrimental to native populations.

Although not readily available, statistics from Europe and Japan (major importers) and from African, South American, and Asian countries (major exporters) also show extremely high levels of trade. For instance, Bruno (1973) recorded 14,760 colubrids and 51,210 viperids imported into Italy from 1968 to 1970 for commercial purposes. The levels of trade worldwide in both legally and illegally traded specimens of live snakes must be enormous.

If the trade in live snakes is difficult to assess, the trade in snake parts and products is almost impossible to estimate because skins can be imported or exported as pieces, finished products, or whole skins. Sometimes shipments are recorded not in article counts, but by weight, meter, or square meter lots. At the same time, species may or may not be correctly identified, shipments may include items produced from many different species, and species may be imported and re-exported many times before reaching a final destination. It is not uncommon to encounter *Boa* products imported from the Far East, or to see thousands of python skins with their country of origin listed as Singapore or Europe.

To estimate the extent of the trade, I compiled importation statistics for the five species most commonly imported into the United States that are listed under CITES (*Boa constrictor, Eunectes murinus, E. notaeus, Python molurus, P. reticulatus*). Between the years 1977 and 1982, 558,761 skins of these five species were imported, in addition to 26,807 m, 12,339 m^2, and 4931 kg of skins; data for other articles also have been tabulated and run into millions of items (Dodd, 1986). These figures do not represent some of the most common species in trade, such as *Ptyas mucosus*. Hemley (1983) reported that, during only 3 mo in 1982, 4849 skins and 98,006 products (direct imports) and 44,231 skins and 217,983 products (indirect imports) worth $3.2 million of this species alone were imported into the United States. During the same period, snake products worth over $813,000 (*Boa constrictor*) and in excess of $897,000 (*Python reticulatus*) also were imported.

Trade into European countries and Japan is also extensive, though many of the finished products are re-exported to the United States. In 1970 and between 1973 and 1978, Wallis (1980) reported domestic production of snakeskin products in France at 1,285,000 pieces, while reporting a rather "encouraging" trend in the reptile skin trade.

Certain exporting countries have become concerned about the extent of the trade in snake skins, and some such as India and Sri Lanka have banned commercial exportation. In India, Inskipp (1981) reported that, between 1971 and 1974, 118,585 raw snake skins (other than *Python*), and between 1971 and 1975, 5,034,584 tanned snake skins were exported. Between 1976 and 1979, 3,075,664 individuals skins plus 26,200 additional kilograms of tanned skins were exported. Most of these skins were *Ptyas* and were exported to Europe, Australia, and Japan. As is true for most species, all individuals came from natural populations, because no commercial breeding programs are presently underway. No data exist on either wild populations or the effects of such trade on wild populations.

BIOLOGICAL CONSIDERATIONS FOR SNAKE CONSERVATION

Because there are relatively few studies concerning successful approaches to snake conservation aside from statutory protection from collection or trade, individuals concerned with biological considerations must turn to experiences from other taxonomic groups and disciplines. Fortunately, several excellent reviews are now available: Soule and Wilcox (1980), Frankel and Soule (1981), Schonewald-Cox et al. (1983). These authors consider conservation in terms of evolutionary biology and genetics, and it is within these areas that the success or failure of conservation programs will be measured. As such, conservation is becoming more of a scientific discipline and, of necessity, is getting away from simplistic notions concerning protection.

A major constraint on the success of conservation programs, and one that is difficult to work with because of the lack of scientific study of many snake species, is that all conservation approaches are limited by the biological characteristics of the species themselves. For programs to be successful, it is necessary that as much as possible be known about the biology of the species in question. Continuous scientific study must be undertaken to ensure that conservation methods are selected within the constraints imposed by the species. In addition, before conservation programs are undertaken, the precise goals of the program should be well understood. Is the purpose to prevent immediate extinction or to provide for long-term evolutionary potential? If a captive breeding program is undertaken, what is to be done with the progeny, not only immediately but several generations hence? How long will funding be available, and is this the most effective way to use limited funds for research and management? How will the success or failure of the program be measured, and how long should it continue? These questions are not limited to programs involving snakes, and should be carefully weighed at the start of any conservation or management project.

Extinction and Genetic Diversity

The primary goal of conservation programs should be prevention of the extinction of species and, to the maximum extent possible, preservation of genetic diversity. From the discussion under GEOGRAPHICAL ASSESSMENT, it appears that very few snakes have become extinct, though many are known from few or single specimens. Priority should extend to the conservation of rare species, especially if surveys show that the rarity did not result from inadequate collecting. Maximum research and management efforts should be directed toward these species, such as *Casarea dussumieri* of Round Island.

Soule (1983) has noted that local population extinction is not the same as species extinction. Local population extinction may result from "stochastic ecological events," such as habitat destruction, and be amenable to prevention, whereas species extinction may result from regional-climatic factors, such as the widespread use of pesticides, and thus may be more difficult if not impossible to prevent. In determining status, it is essential to recognize that causal factors of decline are likely to be interrelated; rarely is a population decline the result of one direct, readily identifiable threat.

Susceptibility to Decline

Diamond (1984) has studied the biological attributes of species that might lead to extinction in populations unaffected by human activities. However, these criteria also apply to species that may be vulnerable to human actions. For instance, he predicted that, in a randomly fluctuating environment, population lifespan increases with (1) generation time or individual lifetime, (2) carrying capacity or population size, (3) intrinsic rate of increase, (4) ratio of birth to death rate, and (5) variability of population size. Variation exists because there are "species-specific determinants of extinction proneness besides population size," which may include short life spans, widely fluctuating populations, environmental susceptibility, and behavioral and social factors. Both Soule (1983) and Diamond (1984) offered predictions about the extinction proneness of natural populations; their forecasts might also be used to predict the vulnerability of species to decline, including species not yet on the verge of extinction. Groups particularly prone to decline include island species, species isolated by humans or other factors, and species subject to heavy predation, competition, or habitat alteration. Such species are also subject to demographic stochasticity, behavioral problems, and genetic problems resulting from a loss of heterozygosity or an increase in inbreeding depression, which in turn are influenced by the biological constraints of the species, i.e., demography, reproductive life span, reproductive output and sex ratios.

Diamond's (1984) literature review and theoretical predictions of factors promoting resistance to extinction confirmed that the risk of extinction decreases with increasing geographical range. Therefore, snakes with the most limited distribution are the most likely to be threatened, and many of the species in Table 15–1, particularly some of those reasonably well studied, are indeed threatened or endangered. Likewise, the risk of extinction decreases with increased population density. The most common category for concern worldwide, other than "unknown," is that the species appears "rare." Whereas some species now thought to be rare eventually may prove to be more common, other species such as *Pituophis melanoleucus ruthveni*, which has been considered rare for a long time in spite of collecting efforts, should be subjects of immediate concern, especially when also facing threats from habitat alteration.

Diamond (1984) also found that the risk of extinction decreased with variability in population size; unfortunately, so little is currently known about the population dynamics of snakes that adequate predictions concerning the importance of this factor in snake conservation are impossible to make (but see Parker and Plummer, this volume). Risk of extinction also decreases with an increased life span, so short-lived species are more vulnerable than long-lived species.

For snakes in general, biological characteristics like those discussed by Soule (1983) and Diamond (1984) are of limited use in predicting a species' vulnerability because of the lack of knowledge concerning the life history of most species. The lack of such data hampers conservation activities and will require continued reliance on surveys designed to show direct threats to a particular species, even though many species may be declining as the result of a combination of their biological constraints and both immediate and indirect threats to their long-term survival. Additional research on the life histories of snakes is essential to their conservation. Based on considerations such as those presented by Soule (1983) and Diamond (1984), it is possible to predict that some species of snakes are likely candidates for endangered or threatened status, or at least to predict which species most need monitoring and management.

The most obvious taxa of concern are those that either live on islands or are otherwise limited in geographical extent. As noted elsewhere, island species are generally those with the best available data and appear to be the most threatened group as a whole. In addition, many geographically limited species, such as European *Vipera,* also are threatened. Island species and species inhabiting limited areas should be monitored regardless of their present status, particularly if the island or area is small and impacted by human use.

A second major category of species that needs monitoring or protected status includes species that are rare or have known small populations (e.g., *Pituophis* in the southeastern United States). For species that are rare but for whom limited data are available, surveys should be conducted to determine the exact status; a conservative approach would protect them and simultaneously encourage research to determine their status. Small populations at the extremes of ranges, both altitudinally and geographically, such as European *Vipera,* are also candidates for protection and management.

MANAGEMENT OF SNAKES

Prohibitions on Take

Few proven management options have been tried in an effort to conserve snakes. Most management has taken the form of statutory or otherwise restrictive prohibitions: regulations aimed at controlling trade or collecting particular species. At times, these methods can be extremely effective in curtailing detrimental activities affecting particular species. The eastern indigo snake (*Drymarchon corais couperi*) of the southeastern United States was particularly threatened by the pet trade. When federal protection was afforded, trade dropped substantially, greatly improving the survival outlook of the species.

International trade holds potentially serious threats to many species of snakes. Most species commonly in commercial trade are listed by CITES in Appendix I or II. The intentions are to prevent trade in species that cannot sustain it and to monitor trade in those not presently threatened but potentially threatened if high levels of trade continue. Unfortunately, the trade data gathered through CITES are rarely available to biologists; the figures, even if reasonably accurate, are usually hidden in obscure government reports, and their accuracy is open to question. At the same time, the requirement that export certificates be issued only if the country of origin can certify that such trade is not detrimental to wild populations is ignored by virtually all countries, because the relevant data do not exist. Thus CITES provides access to trade data of varying degrees of accuracy and curtailed trade in the most endangered species, but it has yet to fulfill its potential as a conservation tool.

Likewise, most countries and various political subunits within countries have restrictive legislation regulating the collection of certain species, particularly those considered endangered or rare. This type of protection may prove effective in particular cases. However, as Rawlinson (1981) has noted, individual species protection is only part of conservation; indeed, it is the lesser of the two major focuses: individual protection and the preservation of essential habitat.

Franklin (1980) has discussed differences in the goals of long-term versus short-term conservation of species. Short-term conservation attempts to prevent loss of the complete genetic complement of a species (individual protection), while long-term conservation attempts to preserve evolutionary potential (ecosystem protection or at least provisions for long-term captive propagation). Unfortunately, most present conservation programs aimed at snakes appear to focus on the individual, whereas the greatest need is to preserve long-term evolutionary potential through the protection of ecosystems. The prevention of one without the other is self-defeating.

Habitat Protection

To conserve snakes, it will be necessary to conserve their habitats. Habitat protection aimed at particular species also must take into consideration the fact that entire ecosystems cannot be managed for individual species; reserves must provide for interactions, even if established primarily for a particular species. It will also be necessary to ensure that reserves are large enough to achieve the purpose for which they were established. Research on snakes therefore will be required to determine the effective population size capable of sustaining the population through time. For instance, to establish reserves for eastern indigo snakes and to be certain of the success of these reserves, it would be necessary to know seasonal variations in habitat use, population structure, recruitment and survivorship, movement patterns, and effective population size. These types of data are rarely known for most snakes and yet are vital to effective habitat protection. However, the lack of such data should never be used as an excuse to delay habitat acquisition or protection.

Once it is decided that management is necessary to conserve a species, there are few clear management options presently available for snake conservation. Research may provide clues to the methods needed to reduce certain conflicts, such as restrictions on vehicles, mowing, or prescribed burning during periods of snake migration. Johnson (1978) has provided general suggestions for habitat management to enhance snake populations. However, management options will be limited by the biological constraints imposed by the species, so research into basic life history is the first step in effective management.

Captive Propagation

As in other forms of management, before establishing captive propagation programs, goals should be clearly established. Too many propagation programs are operated under the guise of "conservation." When this really means to supply individuals with a sufficient number of pets, it is not conservation but recreational use of wildlife.

Several conditions should be met before espousing captive propagation as a conservation tool (also see Honegger, 1981a; Dattatri, 1982):

1. The species should clearly need captive propagation to ensure or enhance survival; scarce conservation funds and space for such programs must be used where needed most. Candidates especially should be species on the verge of extinction, such as *Casarea dussumieri*, whose habitat has been so altered as to make reintroduction unlikely (S. Tonge, Personal communication).

2. Proper facilities should be available for long-term programs. Zoo and laboratory space is becoming increasingly limited, and plans must be made to ensure that sufficient facilities are available to care for potentially large numbers of offspring.

3. Accurate and scientific data must be kept and made available to other researchers, preferably through refereed journal publication. In addition, a species survival plan, such as that developed by the American Association of Zoological Parks and Aquariums (AAZPA), should be maintained for individuals in breeding collections. At present, plans have been developed only for *Acrantophis dumerili* and *Crotalus unicolor,* though the AAZPA is reviewing other species for inclusion in future plans (H. Quinn, Personal communication).

4. Goals should be clearly established and should focus on preservation of the species in the wild while maintaining a genetically viable population in captivity. When animals are introduced into the wild, a suitable protected habitat should be available and released animals should be monitored to determine the success or failure of the program.

Education

Snakes are certainly one of the most misunderstood groups of animals, and conserving them will prove difficult because of public prejudices. To be effective, conservation and management programs need to educate people about snakes, their benefit to humans, and the importance of their preservation. In this regard, zoos and museums have played and can continue to play an important role in both developed and developing countries (Seshadri, 1984).

SUMMARY

The literature on the status of snakes is uneven in content, rarely reflects accurate information concerning populations, and leaves direct threats to either species or their ecosystems mostly unquantified. However, this literature provides a starting point in assessing the status of the world's snakes; 186 species and subspecies have been identified specifically as requiring conservation or management. The most often expressed cause of concern was rarity (although this was seldom substantiated by surveys) or that the reasons for a suspected decline were unknown. European snakes appear to be the best known in terms of status, and island species are the most in jeopardy as a group. Obscurity, or simply lack of adequate data, hampers the assessment of many species, particularly in Asia. With the exception of South Africa, virtually nothing is known concerning the status of African and South American species.

The chief threat to the world's snakes appears to be habitat destruction and alteration, though few studies have attempted to correlate human population growth and development with the decline of particular species. It is likely that loss of habitat is most severe in developed areas and areas with large human populations. Though statistics are incomplete, it is evident that the trade in snakes for pets and for the fashion industry is massive and is having an unknown impact on wild populations, particularly in Africa, Asia, and South America. Trade could be seriously affecting many species, and it is likely the major suspected cause of the decline in larger species inhabiting developing countries. Likewise, biocides may be having serious effects on local populations of snakes. Malicious killing, bounty systems, rattlesnake roundups, and the introduction of exotic species affect particular species or groups of species; as with other factors, few studies have measured quantitative effects.

Conservation approaches are limited by the biological constraints imposed by the species themselves (e.g., demography, sex ratios, recruitment). Yet basic biological data are lacking for most snakes. A primary goal of conservation, aside from immediate concerns of protecting known threatened species and ecosystems, should be the promotion of basic research that will lead to effective management and establishment of reserves. Goals need to be clearly established before undertaking management, and management must consider species within the context of their ecosystems.

Studies involving other taxa offer predictions as to which are most vulnerable to declines. These include island and other spatially limited species, rare species and those with small populations, and populations on the periphery of a species' range. Coupled with threats from human activities, snakes possessing these attributes are indeed those most often mentioned in the literature as subjects for protection and management. Unfortunately, there are few clear management options presently available for snake conservation other than regulating take and trade and undertaking habitat protection. Captive propagation may benefit some species, and education programs concerning snakes must be developed and expanded.

It is apparent that the questions raised when determining status and the ways of ensuring immediate survival and conserving evolutionary potential are complex and must be approached with a solid foundation of knowledge of the species and its ecosystem. Conservation activities will be successful only if based on broad scientific knowledge and undertaken within the biological constraints imposed by the species. Other than the bad public relations, the lack of information concerning the life history of most species is the greatest impediment to effectively conserving snake populations.

ACKNOWLEDGMENTS

I would especially like to thank the following individuals for their assistance in providing both advice and information during the preparation of this chapter: A. Braswell, D. Broadley, W. Brown, J. Covacevich, S. Dattatri, A . Duff-Mackay, B. Groombridge, R. Honegger, R. King, H. Lawler, H. Mendelssohn, A. Moser, K. Peterson, H. Quinn, A. Schwartz, R. Seigel, C. Shiffer, R. Shine, G. Stewart, S. Tonge, P. Vanzolini, Y. Werner, and G. Zug. S. Christman, J. T. Collins, K. Enge, F. W. King, S. S. Novak, R. A. Seigel, and J. N. Stuart provided valuable criticism of earlier versions of the manuscript.

LITERATURE CITED

Andren, C. and Nilson, G. 1979. *Vipera latifii* (Reptilia, Serpentes, Viperidae) an endangered viper from Lar Valley, Iran, and remarks on the sympatric herpetofauna, *J. Herpetol.* 13:335–341.

Anonymous. 1973a. Threatened wildlife of the United States, *U.S. Bur. Sport Fish. Wildl. Res. Publ.* 114.

Anonymous. 1973b. Endangered amphibians and reptiles of Maryland. Committee on Rare and Endangered Amphibians and Reptiles of Maryland, *Bull. Md. Herpetol. Soc.* 9:42–100.

Anonymous. 1979. Protection des amphibiens et des reptiles en Suisse, *Protection de la Nature* No. 5, Basel, Switzerland.

Antram, F. B. S. 1981. Illegal exports of Ghanian reptiles to the UK, *IUCN Traffic Bull.* 3(3/4):38.

Arnold, E. N. and Burton, J. A. 1978. A Field Guide to the Reptiles and Amphibians of Britain and Europe, Collins, London.

Bannikov, A. G., Darevsky, I. S., and Sherbak, N. N. 1978. Amphibia and Reptilia, in: The USSR Red Data Book: The Book of Rare and Endangered Species of Animals and Plants, pp. 151–172, Lesnaya Promyshlennost, Moscow. (In Russian.)

Barry, S. J. 1978. Status of the San Francisco Garter Snake, pp. 1–21, Cal. Fish and Game Inland Fish, Endang. Species Prog. Spec. Publ. 78–2.

Bender, M. 1981. "Sting" operation reveals massive illegal trade, *Endang. Sp. Tech. Bull.* 6(8):1,4.

Betts, W. W., Jr. 1979. Hard times strike the timber rattler, *Defenders* 54(1):14–19.

Biswas, S. 1982. Problems of conservation of snakes of India, in: Proc. IUCN/SSC Snake Group, First Mtg., Madras, India.

Bothner, R. C. 1976. *Thamnophis brachystoma* (Cope), *Cat. Am. Amphib. Rept.* 190:1–2.

Brisbin, I. L., Jr., Staton, M. A., Pinder, J. E., III, and Geiger, R. A. 1974. Radiocesium concentrations in snakes from contaminated and non-contaminated habitats of the AEC Savannah River Plant, *Copeia* 1974:501–506.

Brock, E. M. 1965. Toxicological feeding trials to evaluate the hazard of secondary poisoning to gopher snakes, *Pituophis catenifer, Copeia* 1965:224–225.

Bruno, S. 1973. Anfibi d'Italia (Studi sulla fauna erpetologica italiana XVII), *Natura. Soc. It. Sc. Nat. Museo Civ. St. Nat. et Acquario Civ. Milano* 64:209–450.

Brown, W. S. 1984. Background information for the protection of the timber rattlesnake in New York State, *Bull. Chic. Herpetol. Soc.* 19:94–97.

Bullock, D. 1977. Round Island: A tale of destruction, *Oryx* 14:51–58.

California Department of Fish and Game. 1980. At the Crossroads: A Report on the State of California's Endangered and Rare Fish and Wildlife, Sacramento, California.

Campbell, C. A. 1974. Survival of reptiles and amphibians in urban environments, in: Symposium: Wildlife in an Urban Environment, pp. 61–66, Planning and Resource Development Series No. 28, Holdsworth Natural Resources Center.

Campbell, H. W. 1978a. Short-tailed snake, in: Rare and Endangered Biota of Florida, vol. 3, Amphibians and Reptiles (R. W. McDiarmid, ed.) pp. 28–30, University Presses of Florida, Gainesville.

Campbell, H. W. 1978b. Miami black-headed snake, in: Rare and Endangered Biota of Florida, vol. 3, Amphibians and Reptiles (R. W. McDiarmid, ed.) pp. 45–46, University Presses of Florida, Gainesville.

Christiansen, J. L. 1981. Population trends among Iowa's amphibians and reptiles, *Proc. Iowa Acad. Sci.* 88:24–27.

Christman, S. P. 1983. Timber management is not wildlife management, in: Proc. 4th Annu. Mtg. Gopher Tortoise Council (R. J. Bryant and R. Franz, ed.) pp. 5–18, Florida State Museum, Gainesville, Florida.

Cogger, H. G. 1982. The potentially endangered snakes of Australia, in: Proc. IUCN/SSC Snake Group, First Mtg., Madras, India.

Conant, R. 1956. A review of two rare pine snakes from the Gulf Coastal Plain, *Am. Mus. Novit.* 1781:1–31.

Cooper, J. E., Robinson, S. S., and Funderberg, J. B. (eds.). 1977. Endangered and Threatened Plants and Animals of North Carolina, North Carolina State Museum of Natural History, Raleigh, North Carolina.

Covacevich, J. and Archer, M. 1975. The distribution of the cane toad, *Bufo marinus,* in Australia and its effect on indigenous vertebrates, *Mem. Qld. Mus.* 17:305–310.

Covacevich, J., Ingram, G. J., and Czechura, G. V. 1982. Rare frogs and reptiles of Cape York peninsula, Australia, *Biol. Conserv.* 22:283–294.

Dalrymple, G. H. and Reichenbach, N. G. 1984. Management of an endangered species of snake in Ohio, USA, *Biol. Conserv.* 30:195–200.

Dattatri, S. 1982. Captive propagation of endangered snakes as a conservation tool, in: Proc. IUCN/SSC Snake Group, First Mtg., Madras, India.

de Silva, P. H. D. H. 1980. Snakes of Sri Lanka, Department of Government Printing, Colombo, Sri Lanka.

Diamond, J. M. 1984. "Normal" extinctions of isolated populations, in: Extinctions (M. H. Nitecki, ed.) pp. 191–246, University of Chicago Press.

Diemer, J. E. and Speake, D. W. 1981. The status of the eastern indigo snake in Georgia, In: Proc. Nongame and Endangered Wildlife Symposium (R. R. Odum and J. W. Guthrie, eds.) pp. 52–61, Ga. Dep. Nat. Res. Techn. Bull. WL-5.

Dodd, C. K., Jr. 1986. Importation of live snakes and snake products into the United States, 1977–1983, *Herp. Rev.* 17(4):76–79.

Fitch, H. S. 1963. Natural history of the racer, *Coluber constrictor, Univ. Kans. Publ. Mus. Nat. Hist.* 15:351–468.

Flury, J. W. and Maxwell, T. C. 1981. Status and distribution of *Nerodia harteri paucimaculata,* pp. 1–73, Final Report, Rep. on contract 14-16-0002-79-917 to U.S. Fish and Wildl. Serv., Albuquerque, New Mexico.

Fogarty, M. J. 1978. Southern copperhead, in: Rare and Endangered Biota of Florida, vol. 3, Amphibians and Reptiles (R. W. McDiarmid, ed.) pp. 63–64, University Presses of Florida, Gainesville.

Frankel, O. H. and Soule, M. E. 1981. Conservation and Evolution, Cambridge University Press.

Franklin, I. R. 1980. Evolutionary change in small populations, in: Conservation Biology: An Evolutionary-Ecological Approach (M. E. Soule and B. A. Wilcox, eds.) pp. 135–149, Sinauer Associates, Sunderland, Massachusetts.

Fukada, H. 1969. Biological studies on the snakes. XIII. Preliminary estimate of population size in Tambabashi Study Area, *Bull. Kyoto Univ. Educ. Ser. B.* 36:3–9.

Galligan, J. H. and Dunson, W. A. 1979. Biology and status of timber rattlesnake (*Crotalus horridus*) populations in Pennsylvania, *Biol. Conserv.* 15: 13–58.

Goodrum, P., Baldwin, W. P., and Aldrich, J. W. 1949. Effect of DDT on animal life at Bull's Island, South Carolina, *J. Wildl. Manage.* 13:1–10.

Grant, C. 1932. Notes on the boas of Puerto Rico and Mona, *J. Dep. Agric., P.R.* 16:327–329.

Groombridge, B. 1982. Threatened Snakes of Europe, in: Proc. IUCN/SSC Snake Group, First Mtg., Madras, India.

Hall, R. J. 1980. Effects of environmental contaminants on reptiles: A review, *U.S. Fish Wildl. Serv. Spec. Sci. Rep. Wildl.* 228:1–12.

Hanson, G. E. And Brode, J. M. 1980. Status of the giant garter snake *Thamnophis couchi gigas* (Fitch), pp. 1–14, Cal. Fish and Game Inland Fish. Endang. Sp. Prog. Spec. Publ. 80–5.

Harris, H. S., Jr. 1974. The New Mexican ridge-nosed rattlesnake, *Natl. Parks Conserv. Mag.* 48(3):22–24.

Hemley, G. 1983. International reptile skin trade dependent on few species, *TRAFFIC (USA) Newsl.* 5(2):1, 7, 9, 12.

Herald, E. S. 1949. Effects of DDT-oil solutions upon amphibians and reptiles, *Herpetologica* 5:117–120.

Honegger, R. E. 1975. Red Data Book, vol. 3, Amphibia and Reptilia, IUCN, Morges, Switzerland.

Honegger, R. E. 1978a. Red Data Book, vol. 3, Amphibia and Reptilia, IUCN, Morges, Switzerland.

Honegger, R. E. 1978b. Threatened amphibians and reptiles in Europe, Council of Europe Nature and Environment Ser. No. 15, Strasbourg.

Honegger, R. E. 1980–1981. List of amphibians and reptiles either known or thought to have become extinct since 1600, *Biol. Conserv.* 19:141–158.

Honegger, R. E. 1981a. Breeding endangered species of amphibians and reptiles: Some critical remarks and suggestions, *Br. J. Herpetol.* 6:113–118.

Honegger, R. E. 1981b. Threatened amphibians and reptiles in Europe, Handbuch der Reptilien und Amphibien Europas, Akad. Suppl. Vol. Verlag., Wiesbaden.

Hotz, H. and Broggi, M. F. 1982. Rote liste der gefahrdeten und seltenen Amphibien und Reptilien der Schweiz, Schweizerischer Bund fur Naturschutz, Basel, Switzerland.

Inskipp, T. 1981, Indian trade in reptile skins, IUCN Conservation Monitoring Centre, Cambridge, United Kingdom.

Jaume, M. L. 1974. La mas rara culebra de Cuba, *Torreia (n.s.)* 35:1–8.

Jenkins, R. W. G. 1978. The status of endangered Australian reptiles, in: The Status of Endangered Australian Wildlife (M. J. Tyler, ed.) pp. 169–176, Royal Zoological Society of South Australia.

Jennings, R. D. and Fritts, T. H. 1983. The status of the black pine snake *Pituophis melanoleucus lodingi* and the Louisiana pine snake *Pituophis melanoleucus ruthveni*, pp. 1–32, Unpubl. rep. to U.S. Fish and Wildl. Serv., Atlanta, Georgia.

Johnson, T. R. 1978. Tips on the management of amphibians and reptiles on private lands, pp. 1–15, Missouri Department of Conservation, Jefferson City, Missouri.

Khan, M. A. R. 1982. On the endangered snakes of Bangladesh, in: Proc. IUCN/SSC Snake Group, First Mtg., Madras, India.

Kilmon, J. and Shelton, H. 1981. Rattlesnakes in America and a History of the Sweetwater Jaycees Rattlesnake Roundup, Shelton Press, Sweetwater, Texas.

Klauber, L. M. 1972. Rattlesnakes: Their Habits, Life Histories and Influence on Mankind, 2nd ed., University of California Press, Berkeley.

Kochman, H. I. and Christman, S. P. 1978a. Gulf salt marsh snake, in: Rare and Endangered Biota of Florida, vol. 3, Amphibians and Reptiles (R. W. McDiarmid, ed.) pp. 62–63, University Presses of Florida, Gainesville.

Kochman, H. I. and Christman, S. P. 1978b. Atlantic salt marsh snake, in: Rare and Endangered Biota of Florida, vol. 3, Amphibians and Reptiles (R. W. McDiarmid, ed.) pp. 27–28, University Presses of Florida, Gainesville.

Landers, J. L. and Speake, D. W. 1980. Management needs of sandhill reptiles in southern Georgia, *Proc. Annu. Conf. Southeast. Assoc. Fish Wildl. Agencies* 34:515–529.

Lawler, H. E. and Lee-Fulgham, R. 1977. Rattlesnake roundups, *Defenders* 52(6):360–366.

Lazell, J. D., Jr. 1967. Wiederentdeckung von zwei angeblich augestorbenen Schlangenarten der westindischen Inseln, *Salamandra* 3:91–97.

Leveque, R. 1963. Le statut actuel des vertebres rares et menaces de l'Archipel des Galapagos, *Terre Vie* 110:397–432.

Longmore, R. and Lee, P. 1981. Some observations on techniques for assessing the effects of fire on reptile populations in Sturt National Park, *Aust. J. Herpetol.* 1:17–22.

McDiarmid, R. W. (ed.). 1978. Rare and Endangered Biota of Florida, vol. 3, Amphibians and Reptiles, University Presses of Florida, Gainesville.

McLachlan, G. R. 1978. South African Red Data Book: Reptiles and Amphibians, *S. Afr. Nat. Sci. Prog. Rep.* 23:1–53.

Maxwell, T. C. 1982. Status and distribution of *Nerodia harteri harteri,* pp. 1–40, Final Report, Unpubl. Rep. to U.S. Fish and Wildl. Serv., Albuquerque, New Mexico.

Means, D. B. 1978a. Mole snake, in: Rare and Endangered Biota of Florida, vol. 3, Amphibians and Reptiles (R. W. McDiarmid, ed.) pp. 58–60, University Presses of Florida, Gainesville.

Means, D. B. 1978b. Appalachicola populations of the eastern common kingsnake including *L. g. goini,* in: Rare and Endangered Biota of Florida, vol. 3, Amphibians and Reptiles (R. W. McDiarmid, ed.) pp. 60–61, University Presses of Florida, Gainesville.

Medders, S. 1976. Serpent or supermarket? *Natl. Parks Conserv. Mag.* 50(4):18–19.

Mittermeier, R. A. 1972. Jamaica's endangered species, *Oryx* 11:258–262.

Morris, R. and Morris, D. 1965. Men and Snakes, Hutchinson, London.

Morris, M. A. and Smith, P. W. 1981. Endangered and threatened amphibians and reptiles, in: Endangered and Threatened Vertebrate Animals and Vascular Plants of Illinois, pp. 21–33, Illinois Department of Conservation, Springfield, Illinois.

Moser, A., Graber, C., and Freyvogel, T. A. Observations sur l'ethologie et l'evolution d'une population de *Vipera aspis* (L.) au nord du Jura Suisse, *Amphib-Reptilia.* In press.

Mount, R. H. 1976. Amphibians and reptiles, in: Endangered and Threatened Plants and Animals of Alabama, *Bull. Ala. Mus. Nat. Hist.* 2:66–79.

Mount, R. H. 1981. The red imported fire ant, *Solenopsis invicta* (Hymenoptera: Formicidae) as a possible serious predator on some native southeastern vertebrates: Direct observations and subjective impressions, *J. Ala. Acad. Sci.* 52:71–78.

Murthy, T. S. N. 1982. Studies and conservation of the rare snakes of the Western Ghats, in: Proc. IUCN/SSC Snake Group, First Mtg., Madras, India.

Nellis, D. W., Norton, R. L., and MacLean, W. P. 1983. On the biogeography of the Virgin Islands tree boa, *Epicrates monensis granti, J. Herpetol.* 17:413–417.

Nordstrom, G. R., Pflieger, W. L., Sadler, K. C., and Lewis, W. H. 1977. Rare and Endangered Species of Missouri, pp. 1–129, Missouri Department of Conservation and U.S. Department of Agriculture Soil Conservation Service, Jefferson City, Missouri.

Oliver, W. 1982. The coney and the yellow snake, *Dodo: J. Jersey Wildl. Preserv. Trust* 19:6–33.

Palmer, W. M. 1977a. *Crotalus adamanteus* Beauvois, in: Endangered and Threatened Plants and Animals of North Carolina (J. E. Cooper, S. S. Robinson, and J. B. Funderberg, eds.) pp. 308–310, North Carolina State Museum of Natural History, Raleigh, North Carolina.

Palmer, W. M. 1977b. *Micrurus fulvius fulvius* (Linnaeus), in: Endangered and Threatened Plants and Animals of North Carolina (J. E. Cooper, S. S. Robinson, and J. B. Funderburg, eds.) pp. 327–329, North Carolina State Museum Natural History, Raleigh, North Carolina.

Parker, H. W. 1936. Some extinct snakes of the West Indies, *Ann. Mag. Nat. Hist.* 18:227–233.

Perez-Rivera, R. A. and Velez, M. J., Jr. 1978. Notas sobre algunas culebras de Puerto Rico, *Science-Ciencia* 6:68–73.

Porras, L. and Wilson, L. D. 1979. New distributional records for *Tantilla oolitica* Telford (Reptilia, Serpentes, Colubridae) from the Florida Keys, *J. Herpetol.* 13:218–220.

Rajendran, M. V. 1982. Methods of conservation of uropeltids, in: Proc. IUCN/SSC Snake Group, First Mtg., Madras, India.

Rawlinson, P. A. 1981. Conservation of Australian amphibian and reptile communities, in: Proceedings of the Melbourne Herpetological Symposium (C. B. Banks and A. A. Martin, eds.) pp. 127–138, Royal Melbourne Zoological Gardens, Melbourne.

Rivero, J. A., Joglar, R., and Vazquez, I. 1982. Cinco nuevos ejemplares del culebron de la Mona *Epicrates m. monensis* (Ophidia: Boidae), *Caribb. J. Sci.* 17:7–13.

Roosa, D. M. 1977. Endangered Iowa amphibians and reptiles, *Spec. Rep. Preserves Board* 3, Des Moines, Iowa.

Roze, J. A. 1982. New World coral snakes (Elapidae): A taxonomic and biological summary, *Mem. Inst. Butantan (São Paulo)* 46:305–338.

Ruthling, P. D. R. 1916. Snake conservation in California, *Copeia* 37:90–91.

Saha, B. K. 1982. Snakes under pressure in the Sunderbans, in: Proc. IUCN/SSC Snake Group, First Mtg., Madras, India.

Schonewald-Cox, C., Chambers, S. M., MacBryde, B., and Thomas, L. (eds.). 1983. Genetics and Conservation, A Reference for Managing Wild Animal and Plant Populations, Benjamin/Cummings, Menlo Park, California.

Schwartz, A. and Thomas, R. 1975. A check-list of West Indian amphibians and reptiles, *Carnegie Mus. Nat. Hit. Spec. Publ.* 1.

Seigel, R. A. 1986. Ecology and conservation of an endangered rattlesnake (*Sistrurus catenatus*), in Missouri, USA, *Biol. Conserv.* 35:333–346.

Seshadri, D. 1984. To save the snake: Education and conservation at the Madras Snake Park, *Oryx* 18:79–81.

Sharma, B. D. 1982. Endangered snakes, their conservation in north western India, in: Proc. IUCN/SSC Snake Group, First Mtg., Madras, India.

Shaw, J. W. 1978. The seldom-seen snakes of Spirit Mountain, *Anim. Kingdom* 81(2):28–34.

Shine, R. and Covacevich, J. 1983. Ecology of highly venomous snakes: The Australian genus *Oxyuranus* (Elapidae), *J. Herpetol.* 17:60–69.

Skinner, H. A. 1973. Snakes and Us, East African Literature Bureau, Nairobi, Kenya.

Snyder, B. 1949. Diamondbacks and dollar bills, *Fla. Wildl.* 4(5):3–5, 16.

Softly, A. 1971. Necessity for perpetuation of a venomous snake, *Biol. Conserv.* 4:40–42.

Soule, M. E. 1983, What do we really know about extinction? in: Genetics and Conservation: A Reference for Managing Wild Animal and Plant Populations (C. Schonewald-Cox, S. Chambers, B. MacBryde, and L. Thomas, eds.) pp. 111–124, Benjamin/Cummings, Menlo Park, California.

Soule, M. E. and Wilcox, B. A. (eds.). 1980. Conservation Biology: An Evolutionary-Ecological Perspective, Sinauer Associates, Sunderland, Massachusetts.

Speake, D.W. and Mount, R. H. 1973. Some possible ecological effects of "rattlesnake roundups" in the southeastern coastal plain, *Proc. Annu. Conf. Southeast. Assoc. Game Fish Comm.* 27:267–277.

Speake, D. W. and McGlincy, J. A. 1981. Response of indigo snakes to gassing their dens, *Proc. Annu. Conf. Southeast. Assoc. Fish Wildl. Agencies* 35:135–138.

Speake, D. W., McGlincy, J. A. and Colvin, T. R. 1978. Ecology and management of the eastern indigo snake in Georgia: A progress report. Proceedings of the Rare and Endangered Wildlife Symposium (R. R. Odum and L. Landers, eds.) pp. 64–73, Ga. Dep. Nat. Resc. Tech. Bull. WL-4.

Speake, D. W., Diemer, J., and McGlincy, J. 1981. Eastern Indigo Snake Recovery Plan, U.S. Fish and Wildlife Service, Atlanta, Georgia.

Spellerberg, I. F. 1975a. Conservation and management of Britain's reptiles based on their ecological and behavioral requirements: A progress report, *Biol. Conserv.* 7:289–300.

Spellerberg, I. F. 1975b. The grass snake in Britain, *Oryx* 13:179–184.

Stafford, D. P., Plapp, F. W., Jr., and Fleet, R. R. 1976. Snakes as indicators of environmental contamination: Relation of detoxifying enzymes and pesticide residues to species occurrence in three aquatic ecosystems, *Arch. Environ. Contam. Toxicol.* 5:15–27.

Steinhart, P. 1984. Fear of snakes, *Audubon* 86:2, 8–9.

Stephan, D. L. 1977. *Lampropeltis getulus sticticeps* Barbour and Engels, in: Endangered and Threatened Plants and Animals of North Carolina (J. E. Cooper, S. S. Robinson, and J. B. Funderburg, eds.) pp. 236–237, North Carolina State Museum of Natural History, Raleigh, North Carolina.

Stewart, D. 1974. Canadian Endangered Species, Gage, Toronto.

Temple, S. A. 1977. Castaway reptiles of the Indian Ocean, *Anim. Kingdom* Aug./Sept.:19–27.

Terhivuo, J. 1981. Provisional atlas and population status of the Finnish amphibian and reptile species with reference to their ranges in northern Europe, *Ann. Zool. Fennici* 18:139–164.

Tinkle, D. W., Feaver, P. E. Van Devender, R. W., and Vitt, L. J. 1979. A Survey of the Status, Distribution, and Abundance of Threatened and Endangered Species of Reptiles and Amphibians, Rep. to Michigan Dep. Nat. Resour., Lansing, Michigan.

Tuck, R. G., Jr. 1977. Iranian amphibians and reptiles believed to merit designation as "rare" and/or "endangered" species, Rep. to DOE Committee for Rare and Endangered Species of Iran, Tehran.

Villa, J. 1984. The venomous snakes of Nicaragua: A synopsis, *Milw. Pub. Mus. Contri. Biol. Geol.* 59:1–41.

Wallis, B. E. 1980. Marketing assistance program for agricultural products from least developed countries: Market products for reptile leathers, International Trade Center, New York.

Weaver, W. G. and Christman, S. P. 1978. Big Pine Key ringneck snake, in: Rare and Endangered Biota of Florida, vol. 3, Amphibians and Reptiles (R. W. McDiarmid, ed.) pp. 41–42, University Presses of Florida, Gainesville.

Wheeler, W. B., Jouvenaz, D. P., Wojik, D. P., Banks, W. A., VanMiddelem, C. H., Lofgren, C. S., Nesbitt, S., Williams, L., and Brown, R. 1977. Mirex residues in nontarget organisms after application of 10-5 bait for fire ant control, northeast Florida, 1972–74, *Pestic. Monit. J.* 11:146–156.

Whitaker, Z. 1979. Artful catchers, deadly prey, *Int. Wildl.*, Mar./Apr. 26–33.

Wilcox, B. A., and Murphy, D. D. 1985. Conservation strategy: The effects of fragmentation on extinction, *Am. Nat.* 125:879–887.

Williamson, G. M. 1979. Canebrake rattlesnake *Crotalus horridus atricaudatus,* in: Endangered and Threatened Plants and Animals of Virginia (D. W. Linzey, ed.) pp. 407–409, Virginia Polytechic Institute and State University, Blacksburg.

Wilson, E. O., 1984. Biophilia, Harvard University Press, Cambridge.

Wilson, L. D. and Porras, L. 1983. The ecological impact of man on the South Florida herpetofauna, *Univ. Kans. Mus. Nat. Hist. Spec. Publ.* 9:1–89.

Wilson, V. J. 1972. Observation on the effect of dieldrin on wildlife during tsetse fly *Glossina morsitans* control operations in eastern Zambia, *Arnoldia* 5:1–12.

Index to Scientific Names

abacura, Farancia, 227, 303
Acalyptophis, 33
  peronii, 353
Acanthophis, 33
  antarcticus, 230, 234, 305, 308–309, 428
Achalinus, 26, 35–36
  spinalis, 36
Acrantophis, 29, 90–91
  dumerili, 504
acricus, Diadophis punctatus, 480, 489
Acrochordus, 4, 8–9, 11, 13–14, 16–21,
      26–28, 34, 94, 96, 110, 121, 450
  arafurae, 20, 228, 233, 255, 288, 303,
      315, 407, 411, 425–426, 459–460
  dehmi, 64
  granulatus, 20, 213, 218, 222, 228,
      270, 315–316, 450
  javanicus, 20, 64
acutus, Agkistrodon, 305
adamanteus, Crotalus, 145, 170, 306, 480
Adenorhinus, 91
aegyptia, Walterinnesia, 305, 315
aesculapii, Erythrolamprus, 351
aestivus, Opheodrys, 221, 229, 238, 241,
      256, 260, 262, 271, 273, 282, 287,
      304, 412
Afronatrix, 37–39, 81, 87
Agkistrodon, 43, 79–80, 86, 95, 112, 122,
      125–126, 133, 169, 278, 314, 496
  acutus, 305
  contortrix, 151, 174, 193, 197, 231,
      234, 240, 257, 268, 271, 275, 283,
      286, 305, 309–310, 314, 404, 406,
      411, 429
  contortrix contortrix, 479
  halys, 197, 257

  himalayanus, 479
  piscivorus, 231, 234, 288, 306, 314
Ahaetulla, 41, 121, 354–355
  dispar, 479
  fasciolata, 41
  nasuta, 41, 479
  perroteti, 479
  prasina, 41, 479
  pulverulenta, 41
ahuetulla, Leptophis, 351
Aipysurus, 33
  duboisii, 316
  eydouxii, 219, 353
  foliosquama, 353
  fuscus, 353
  laevis, 316, 353
Albaneryx, 64, 86
albofuscus, Lycodon, 42
alleni, Regina, 217, 256, 260, 262,
      287–289, 304, 306, 309, 407
Allolobophora, 260
Alluaudina, 40
Alsophis, 122, 186, 492
  ater, 491
  sancticrucis, 491
Amastridium, 40
Amblyodipsas, 31, 80
Ameiseophis, 65
Ameiva, 355
amethistinus, Python, 484
amethystinus, Liasis, 426
ammodytes, Vipera, 320, 429
ammodytes montandoni, Vipera, 485
ammodytes transcaucasiana, Vipera, 485
amoenus, Carphophis, 228, 255, 260–261,
      303, 412, 426

Amphiesma, 40, 81, 87
  stolata, 40
  vibakari, 40
Amphisbaena fuliginosa, 351
Amplorhinus, 40
anatolica, Vipera ursinii, 486
andamanensis, Ramphotyphlops, 484
angulatus, Helicops, 351
angulifer
  Epicrates, 303
  Epicrates angulifer, 481
angulifer angulifer, Epicrates, 481
angusticeps, Dendroaspis, 306
Anilioides, 63
Anilius, 22–24, 54, 88, 94, 97, 99
  scytale, 351
annulata
  Leptodeira, 351
  Vermicella, 305, 320
annulatus, Emydocephalus, 353
Anolis, 152, 187, 320, 355, 446
  carolinensis, 446
Anomalepis, 9, 14–15
Anomalophis, 20, 56, 61
  bolcensis, 20, 61
anomalus, Drepanoides, 351
Anomochilus, 23, 54, 94
antarcticus, Acanthophis, 230, 234, 305,
  308–309, 428
Antillophis parvifrons, 303
antiqua, Naja, 65
Aparallactus, 31, 38
  werneri, 494
Aplopeltura, 36
arafurae, Acrochordus, 20, 228, 233, 255,
  288, 303, 315, 407, 411, 425–426,
  459–460
Archaeophis, 19
  proavus, 19, 60
  turkmenicus, 19, 60
argenteus, Oxybelis, 219, 351
Argyrogena fasciolatus, 479
arietans, Bitis, 171
Arizona elegans, 228, 426
asper, Bothrops, 167
aspera, Candoia, 426
Aspidelaps, 33, 92
Aspidites, 28
  melanocephalus, 426
Aspidomorphus, 33
Aspidura, 40, 42
aspis, Vipera, 232, 276, 283, 288, 384,
  405, 408, 429, 435, 445–446, 485,
  493
Astrotia stokesii, 316, 353
atavus, Coluber, 62
ater
  Alsophis, 491
  Notechis, 257, 277

Atheris, 43, 79, 91
  ceratophis, 494
atra, Demansia, 219, 315
Atractaspis, 30–31, 78, 80, 91, 158
Atractus, 320
  elaps, 351
  major, 351
  occipitoalbus, 351
atricapillus, Parus, 144
atriceps, Echiopsis, 480
atrox
  Bothrops, 219, 306, 309, 351
  Crotalus, 169, 191, 196, 231, 306, 319,
    384, 410, 429, 447, 461
aulicus, Lycodon, 42
aureus, Plectrurus, 484
auropunctatus, Herpestes, 492, 497
australis
  Pseudechis, 484
  Simoselaps, 320
Austrelaps superbus, 230, 428
austriaca, Coronella, 255, 274, 320, 405,
  408, 427, 480
Azemiops, 43, 79, 95, 97–98, 158
  feae, 95

babaspul, Micrurus nigrocinctus, 482, 491
bai, Madtsoia, 60
beddomei, Calliophis, 479
beecheyi, Citellus, 144
beetzii, Telescopus, 485
bertholdi, Simoselaps, 305, 320
berus, Vipera, 192, 194, 221, 225, 232,
  234, 236, 240, 258, 268, 271, 276,
  280–281, 283–285, 288, 306, 309,
  320, 369, 380–381, 404–405,
  407–409, 411, 429, 451, 485
bibroni, Calliophis, 32
bicolor
  Lycodonomorphus, 37, 255, 271, 317, 412
  Parus, 144
bilineatum, Melanophidium, 482
bilineatus, Bothrops, 314, 351
biminiensis, Typhlops, 411
bistrigatus, Sibynophis, 484
Bitia, 35, 117
Bitis, 43, 79, 91, 93, 126, 171
  arietans, 171
  gabonica, 171, 479
  nasicornis, 168, 171
  olduvaiensis, 67
  schneideri, 479
  xeropaga, 479
bitorquatus, Hoplocephalus, 231
bivittatus, Python molurus, 437
blairi, Rana, 144
Blythia, 40, 42
Boa, 29, 88–89, 498
  constrictor, 168, 303, 351, 426, 499

Boaedon, 9, 11, 34, 37
  virgatus, 11
Boavus, 25, 59
Boiga, 92–93, 95–96
  cynodon, 479
  dendrophila, 303
  dighotoni, 479
  irregularis, 41, 426
  multimaculata, 479
bolcensis, Anomalophis, 20, 61
Bolyeria, 26, 91
  multocarinata, 479, 491–492
borneensis, Lepturophis, 42
Bothrochilus, 28
Bothrolycus, 36–37
Bothrophthalmus, 37
Bothrops, 43, 79–80, 86, 89, 169, 320
  asper, 167
  atrox, 219, 306, 309, 351
  castelnaudi, 351
  bilineatus, 314, 351
  schlegeli, 171
bottae, Charina, 227, 303, 426
bottae umbratica, Charina, 479
Boulengerina, 33, 92
Brachylophus, 97
Brachyorrhos, 35, 81
brachystoma, Thamnophis, 427, 485
braminus, Ramphotyphlops, 16, 185, 271, 484
Bransateryx, 63, 86
  vireti, 61
brevirachis, Tregophis, 64
brevirostris, Rhadinaea, 351
brookii, Hydrophis, 219, 257, 353
buccata, Homalopsis, 218, 220–221
Bufo, 319
  marinus, 491, 497
bungaroides, Hoplocephalus, 482, 490, 494
Bungarus, 33
  caeruleus, 479
  fasciatus, 479
  multicinctus, 306
butleri, Thamnophis, 191, 229, 237–239, 256, 318, 372, 485

Cacophis, 33, 305
  harriettae, 219, 230
  krefftii, 230
  squamulosus, 230
Cadurceryx, 27, 60
cadurci, Coluber, 62, 84
Cadurcoboa, 60
caeruleus, Bungarus, 479
caeruluscens, Hydrophis, 219, 353
Calabaria, 12, 23, 27–28, 79, 90–91
  reinhardii, 303
Calamagras, 60–61
Calamaria, 36
  gervaisi, 36

calamaria, Liopeltis, 482
calligaster
  Calliophis, 32
  Lampropeltis, 255, 303
calligaster rhombomaculata, Lampropeltis, 482
Calliophis, 31
  beddomei, 479
  bibroni, 32
  calligaster, 32
  gracilis, 32
  japonicus, 32
  kelloggi, 32
  macclellandi, 32
  maculiceps, 32
  melanurus, 32
  nigrescens, 32, 479
Calloselasma, 43
calonotus, Neelaps, 483, 490
Candoia, 29, 88, 97–98
  aspera, 426
  carinata, 426
canina, Corallus, 167–168
caninus, Corallus, 351
Cantoria, 35
carata, Echiopsis, 305
cariei, Typhlops, 67
carinata, Candoia, 426
carinatus
  Chironius, 351
  Tropidechis, 305
Carlia, 315
carolinensis, Anolis, 446
Carphophis, 86, 148, 272, 286
  amoenus, 228, 255, 260–261, 303, 412, 426
  vermis, 216, 228, 274, 282–283, 287, 303
carpio, Cyprinus, 317
Casarea, 26–27, 35, 67, 91
  dussumieri, 411, 479, 492, 500, 504
castelnaudi, Bothrops, 351
catenatus, Sistrurus, 231–232, 234, 241, 306, 314, 398, 407–408, 484
catenifer, Pituophis melanoleucus, 483
catesbyi
  Dipsas, 218, 351
  Uromacer, 355, 412, 428
Causus, 43, 79, 91–92, 98, 158
Cemophora, 403
  coccinea, 303, 402–404, 412, 479
cenchoa, Imantodes, 219, 351
cenchria, Epicrates, 218, 228, 351
cerasogaster, Xenochrophis, 40
Cerastes, 43, 79, 91, 93, 117
  cerastes, 111, 429
  cerastes cerastes, 479, 490
  vipera, 314
cerastes
  Cerastes, 111, 429
  Cerastes cerastes, 479, 490

Crotalus, 257, 398, 429, 459
   Dromicus, 480, 492
cerastes cerastes, Cerastes, 479, 490
ceratophis, Atheris, 494
Cerberus, 35, 96
   rhynchops, 218, 222, 228
cervinus, Siphlophis, 351
cetti, Natrix natrix, 482
ceylonicus, Typhlops, 490
Chamaelycus, 37
chamissonis, Philodryas, 304
Charina, 27–29, 63, 84, 86
   bottae, 227, 303, 426
   bottae umbratica, 479
   prebottae, 63
Cheilophis, 59–60
Chersydrus granulatus, 479
childreni, Liasis, 426
Chilorhinophis, 31
Chionactis occipitalis, 303, 426
Chironius, 320
   carinatus, 351
   fuscus, 351
   multiventris, 351
   scurrulus, 351
   vincenti, 491
chloroticus, Drymobius, 303, 319
Chondropython, 28, 96, 173
   viridis, 479
Chrysopelea ornata, 479
cinereus, Oligodon, 483
Citellus beecheyi, 144
clarki, Nerodia fasciata, 483
Clelia, 319
   clelia, 351
   occipitolutea, 218
clelia, Clelia, 351
cliffordi, Spalerosophis, 427, 438, 444
climacophora, Elaphe, 172–173, 270, 274
Clonophis kirtlandii, 479, 489
cobella, Liophis, 351
coccinea, Cemophora, 303, 402–404, 412,
   479
colberti, Estesius, 52
Colombophis, 23
   portai, 63
Coluber, 62, 64–65, 84, 93–95, 186, 272,
   286, 319–320, 452
   atavus, 62
   cadurci, 62, 84
   constrictor, 65, 144, 174, 197, 227–228,
      255, 262, 271, 274, 277, 280–283,
      288, 303, 318, 350, 377, 381, 383,
      397, 399, 404–405, 426, 452–454,
      459–460, 489
   constrictor constrictor, 479
   constrictor flaviventris, 479
   constrictor foxi, 479
   hippocrepis, 479
   jugularis, 320

   najadum, 320
   viridiflavus, 479
colubrina, Laticauda, 214, 222, 260, 276,
   353, 451
compressicauda, Nerodia fasciata, 483, 491
compressus, Tripanurgos, 351
concinnus, Thamnophis sirtalis, 428
confluens, Nerodia fasciata, 483
conicus, Eryx, 412, 481
Coniophanes, 41, 278
   fissidens, 218
Coniophis, 8, 22, 54–55, 57–59
   cosgriffi, 58
   precedens, 58
constrictor
   Boa, 168, 303, 351, 426, 499
   Coluber, 65, 144, 174, 197, 227–228,
      255, 262, 271, 274, 277, 280–283,
      288, 303, 318, 350, 377, 381, 383,
      397, 399, 404–405, 426, 452–454,
      459–460, 489
   Coluber constrictor, ʾ79
constrictor constrictor, Coluber, 479
constrictor flaviventris, Coluber, 479
constrictor foxi, Coluber, 479
Contia, 86
   tenuis, 479
contortrix
   Agkistrodon, 151, 174, 193, 197, 231,
      234, 240, 257, 268, 271, 275, 283,
      286, 305, 309–310, 314, 350, 404,
      406, 411, 429
   Agkistrodon contortrix, 479
contortrix contortrix, Agkistrodon, 479
Coprophis dakotaensis, 62
corais, Drymarchon, 90, 303
corais couperi, Drymarchon, 480, 489,
   496–497, 502
Corallus, 29, 88–89, 97
   canina, 167–168
   caninus, 351
   enydris, 303, 351
coronata
   Drysdalia, 230, 305
   Pseudoboa, 351
   Tantilla, 271, 398, 402
Coronella, 93, 272, 278, 320, 461
   austriaca, 255, 274, 320, 405, 408, 427,
      480
coronoides, Drysdalia, 230
cosgriffi, Coniophis, 58
couchi gigas, Thamnophis, 485, 493
couperi, Drymarchon corais, 480, 489,
   496–497, 502
cristata, Cyanocitta, 144
Crotalus, 43, 79–80, 86, 89, 117,
   168–169, 176, 278, 314, 345, 495
   adamanteus, 145, 170, 306, 480
   atrox, 169, 191, 196, 231, 306, 319,
      384, 410, 429, 447, 461

Crotalus (cont.)
  cerastes, 257, 398, 429, 459
  durissus, 90
  horridus, 171, 192, 231, 257, 275, 288,
      306–307, 369, 385, 404, 406–407,
      480, 495
  mitchelli, 398, 429
  molossus, 306, 319
  scutulatus, 169, 306, 319
  unicolor, 480, 492, 504
  viridis, 153, 171, 192, 197, 231, 234,
      257, 262, 269–271, 275, 277, 280,
      283, 288, 306, 372, 374, 381, 385,
      404–406, 409, 412, 447, 460, 480
  viridis lutosus, 429
  willardi, 306
  willardi obscurus, 480, 489, 497
Crotaphopeltis werneri, 494
Cryptophis, 33
  nigrescens, 428
cursor, Dromicus, 491
curtus, Python, 96
cyanocinctus, Hydrophis, 353
Cyanocitta cristata, 144
Cyclocorus, 40, 42
cyclopion, Nerodia, 229, 271, 309, 316,
      350, 427, 483
Cylindrophis, 9, 13, 22–24, 31, 54, 88, 94,
      131
  maculatus, 24
  rufus, 131–132
cynodon, Boiga, 479
Cyprinus carpio, 317
cyrtopsis, Thamnophis, 257, 427

dakotaensis, Coprophis, 62
Dakotaophis, 65
Dasypeltis, 34, 303, 307
  medici, 480
Daunophis langi, 66
Dawsonophis, 60
decurtatus, Phyllorhynchus, 271, 427
defrennei, Lapparentophis, 56
dehmi, Acrochordus, 64
Deinagkistrodon, 43
dekayi, Storeria, 198, 229, 256, 271, 304,
      371–372, 401
Demansia, 33, 305, 315
  atra, 219, 315
  psammophis, 428
Dendrelaphis, 96
  oliveri, 490
  tristis, 480
Dendroaspis, 33, 92–93, 194
  angusticeps, 306
Dendrocopos pubescens, 144
Dendrolycus, 37
Dendrophidion dendrophis, 351
dendrophila, Boiga, 303

dendrophis, Dendrophidion, 351
Denisonia
  devisi, 305
  fasciata, 305
  maculata, 305
  punctata, 305
  signata, 428
depereti, Palaeonaja, 67
depressiceps, Geodipsas, 40
devisi, Denisonia, 305
diadema, Spalerosophis diadema, 485
diadema diadema, Spalerosophis, 485
Diadophis, 34, 65, 83, 86, 148, 272
  punctatus, 221, 228, 240, 255, 260,
      262, 270–271, 274, 282–284,
      287–289, 303, 310, 373, 399, 427
  punctatus acricus, 480, 489
dichrous, Drymoluber, 351
dighotoni, Boiga, 479
dindigalensis, Uropeltis, 485
Dinilysia, 7–9, 11–14, 16–18, 22, 28, 35,
      52, 55, 57, 67
  patagonica, 11, 57
Dinodon, 96
dione, Elaphe, 255
Dipsas, 36, 41, 278, 303, 307
  catesbyi, 218, 351
  indica, 351
  pavonina, 351
Dipsosaurus dorsalis, 445
dispar, Ahaetulla, 479
Disteira, 33
Ditypophis, 37, 92
Dolniceophis, 65
dorsalis
  Dipsosaurus, 445
  Oligodon, 483
Drepanoides anomalus, 351
Dromicodryas, 37
Dromicus
  cerastes, 480, 492
  cursor, 491
  ornatus, 491
Dryinoides, 65, 83
Drymarchon, 175
  corais, 90, 303
  corais couperi, 480, 489, 496–497, 502
Drymobius
  chloroticus, 303, 319
  margaritiferus, 303, 319
  rhombifer, 351
Drymoluber dichrous, 351
Dryocalamus, 41
  gracilis, 480
  nympha, 480
Dryophis, 41
Drysdalia, 305
  coronata, 230, 305
  coronoides, 230
  rhodogaster, 230

Duberria, 31, 37–38
  lutrix, 37
  shirana, 37
duboisii, *Aipysurus*, 316
dulcis, *Leptotyphlops*, 305, 429
dumerili, *Acrantophis*, 504
Dunnophis, 25, 59–61
durissus, *Crotalus*, 90
dussumieri, *Casarea*, 411, 479, 492, 500,504

Echiopsis, 33
  atriceps, 480
  carata, 305
Echis, 43, 79, 91, 93
Eirenis, 93
Elachistodon westermanni, 481
Elaphe, 27, 65, 88, 93–95, 113, 126, 153,
    168, 172, 175, 186, 191, 194, 272,
    278, 320, 498
  climacophora, 172–173, 270, 274
  dione, 255
  guttata, 445, 481
  hodgsonii, 481
  longissima, 65, 481, 488
  obsoleta, 39, 144, 190, 255, 275, 303,
      405, 427, 481
  quadrivirgata, 255, 268, 272–273,
      282–284, 286, 398
  quatuorlineata, 303, 320, 481
  radiata, 481
  situla, 303, 320, 481
  subocularis, 303, 319
  taeniura, 212–213
  vulpina, 255
  vulpina gloydi, 481
Elapognathus, 33
  minor, 481
Elapoidis, 40, 42
elaps, *Atractus*, 351
Elapsoidea, 33, 92, 98
elegans
  Arizona, 228, 426
  Hydrophis, 353
  Thamnophis, 257, 271, 304, 313, 318,
      431, 435, 446–448, 459, 464
  Virginia valeriae, 486
elegans hammondi, *Thamnophis*, 427
elegans vagrans, *Thamnophis*, 427, 431,433
Eleutherodactylus, 319
Emydocephalus, 33
  annulatus, 353
Enhydrina, 121
  schistosa, 219, 230, 257, 276, 288, 308,
      353
Enhydris, 35, 96
  enhydris, 39
enhydris, *Enhydris*, 39
Entechinus, 122
enydris, *Corallus*, 303, 351

Eoanilius, 22, 24, 59
Ephalophis, 33
  greyi, 353
Epicrates, 29, 88–89, 97, 319, 492
  angulifer, 303
  angulifer angulifer, 481
  cenchria, 218, 228, 351
  inornatus, 481, 492
  monensis granti, 481, 492
  monensis monensis, 481, 492
  striatus, 214
  striatus fosteri, 481
  subflavus, 481, 492, 497
Eristicophis, 43, 95
  macmahonii, 95, 481, 490
Erpeton, 35
erythrogaster, *Nerodia*, 304, 308, 316, 350,
    427
erythrogaster flavigaster, *Nerodia*, 483
erythrogaster neglecta, *Nerodia*, 483
Erythrolamprus aesculapii, 351
erytrogramma, *Farancia*, 303, 481
Eryx, 29, 64, 66, 86, 93
  conicus, 412, 481
  jaculus turcicus, 481
  jayakari, 481, 490
  johni johni, 481
  tataricus, 255
Estesius, 6–7, 52, 54, 69
  colberti, 52
Eunectes, 8, 29, 88, 97
  murinus, 303, 351, 499
  notaeus, 499
  stirtoni, 64
euryxanthus
  Masticophis lateralis, 482
  Micruroides, 305, 315
Exiliboa, 25–26, 88
extenuatum, *Stilosoma*, 304, 485, 489
eydouxii, *Aipysurus*, 219, 353

fallax, *Telescopus*, 320
Farancia, 86
  abacura, 227, 303
  erytrogramma, 303, 481
fasciata
  Denisonia, 305
  Nerodia, 222, 271, 308, 316–317, 427
fasciata clarki, *Nerodia*, 483
fasciata compressicauda, *Nerodia*, 483, 491
fasciata confluens, *Nerodia*, 483
fasciata taeniata, *Nerodia*, 483, 494
fasciatus
  Bungarus, 479
  Hydrophis, 237, 353
fasciolata, *Ahaetulla*, 41
fasciolatus
  Argyrogena, 479
  Simoselaps, 320
feae, *Azemiops*, 95

fergusonianus, Rhinophis, 484
Fimbrios, 35–36
fiskii, Lamprophis, 482
fissidens, Coniophanes, 218
flagellum
　　Masticophis, 256, 262, 342, 427,
　　　　459–460, 482
　　Suta, 429
　　Unechis, 429
flagellum ruddocki, Masticophis, 482
flavigaster, Nerodia erythrogaster, 483
flavilata, Rhadinaea, 304
flavipunctatus, Xenochrophis, 39
flaviventris, Coluber constrictor, 479
flavoviridis, Trimeresurus, 232, 238, 258,
　　412
foliosquama, Aipysurus, 353
Fordonia, 35, 96, 117
　　leucobalia, 482
formosus, Oxyrhopus, 351
fosteri, Epicrates striatus, 481
foxi, Coluber constrictor, 479
frenatus, Uromacer, 305, 320
frontalis
　　Helminthophis, 15
　　Prosymna, 484
fuliginoides, Natriciteres, 38
fuliginosa, Amphisbaena, 351
fulvius
　　Micrurus, 212, 305, 315, 398, 411
　　Micrurus fulvius, 482
fulvius fulvius, Micrurus, 482
funerea, Rhinoclemys, 220
Furina, 305
fuscus
　　Aipysurus, 353
　　Chironius, 351
　　Liasis, 426

gabonica, Bitis, 171, 479
galbreathi, Texasophis, 62
gallicus, Micrurus, 66
garstini, Gigantophis, 60
gedulyi, Vipera, 66
Geodipsas, 40, 92
　　depressiceps, 40
　　procterae, 494
　　vauerocegue, 494
Gerarda, 35
Geringophis, 61
gervaisi, Calamaria, 36
getulus, Lampropeltis, 303, 342, 399
getulus goini, Lampropeltis, 482
getulus holbrooki, Lampropeltis, 482
getulus sticticeps, Lampropeltis, 482
Gigantophis, 7
　　garstini, 60
gigas, Thamnophis couchi, 485, 493
gloydi, Elaphe vulpina, 481

Glyphodon, 33, 305
goini, Lampropeltis getulus, 482
Goinophis, 66
　　minusculus, 66
Gongylophis, 29, 63–64
Gonionotophis, 33, 37
　　granti, 37
Gonyosoma, 39
Gopherus polyphemus, 495
gouldii, Unechis, 231, 305, 411
gracilis
　　Calliophis, 32
　　Dryocalamus, 480
　　Microcephalophus, 353
　　Tantilla, 227, 427
grahamii, Regina, 229, 304, 306, 427, 484
granti
　　Epicrates monensis, 481, 492
　　Gonionotophis, 37
granulatus
　　Acrochordus, 20, 213, 218, 222, 228,
　　　　270, 315–316, 450
　　Chersydrus, 479
Grayia, 38, 41, 90
greyi, Ephalophis, 353
grivensis, Typhlops, 63
guttata, Elaphe, 445, 481

haje, Naja, 305
halys, Agkistrodon, 197, 257
hammondi, Thamnophis elegans, 427
hannah, Ophiophagus, 192, 305, 315, 483
Haplocercus, 40, 42
hardwickii, Lapemis, 219, 237, 353
harriettae, Cacophis, 219, 230
harteri, Nerodia harteri, 483
harteri harteri, Nerodia, 483
harteri paucimaculata, Nerodia, 483
heathi, Mabuya, 225
Helagras, 61
　　prisciformis, 59
Heliconia, 171
Helicops, 40
　　angulatus, 351
　　petersi, 351
Helminthophis, 15
　　frontalis, 15
helvetica, Natrix natrix, 483
Hemachatus, 33, 92
Hemiaspis, 33
　　signata, 231
Hemibungarus, 32
Herpestes auropunctatus, 492, 497
Heterodon, 34, 65, 86, 110, 126, 403, 497
　　nasicus, 255, 273, 282–283, 286, 381,
　　　　397, 411, 427, 482
　　platirhinos, 119, 255, 271, 273,
　　　　282–283, 400, 403, 411, 427, 482
　　simus, 400

Heurnia, 96
hexalepis, Salvadora, 427
himalayanum, Scincella, 217
himalayanus, Agkistrodon, 479
hippocrepis, Coluber, 479
Hispanophis, 65
hodgsonii, Elaphe, 481
holbrooki, Lampropeltis getulus, 482
Homalopsis, 21, 35
    buccata, 218, 220–221
Homoroselaps, 30–31, 92
Hoplocephalus, 33, 278
    bitorquatus, 231
    bungaroides, 482, 490, 494
Hormonotus, 37
horridus, Crotalus, 171, 192, 231, 257,
        275, 288, 306–307, 369, 385, 404,
        406–407, 480, 495
Huberophis, 60
hudsoni, Ninia, 351
humilis, Leptotyphlops, 305, 315
Hydraethiops, 37–39
    melanogaster, 38
Hydrelaps, 33
Hydrodynastes, 110
Hydrophis, 33, 121
    brookii, 219, 257, 353
    caerulescens, 219, 353
    cyanocinctus, 353
    elegans, 353
    fasciatus, 237, 353
    melanocephalus, 353
    melanosoma, 219, 257, 353
    torquatus, 219, 237, 353
Hydrops, 40
Hyla, 320
Hypnale, 43
Hypsiglena, 35
    torquata, 303

Imantodes, 278
    cenchoa, 219, 351
    lentiferus, 351
indica, Dipsas, 351
inornatus, Epicrates, 481, 492
insularum, Nerodia sipedon, 483, 487
invicta, Solenopsis, 497
irregularis, Boiga, 41, 426
Ithycyphus, 37

jaculus turcicus, Eryx, 481
japonicus, Calliophis, 32
jarrovi, Sceloporus, 217
javanicus, Acrochordus, 20, 64
jayakari, Eryx, 481, 490
johni, Eryx johni, 481
johni johni, Eryx, 481
jugularis, Coluber, 320

kaouthia, Naja naja, 482
kargii, Vipera, 66
kasnakovi, Vipera, 486
kelloggi, Calliophis, 32
Kinosternon leucostomum, 220
kirtlandii, Clonophis, 479, 489
korros, Ptyas, 212–213
krefftii, Cacophis, 230

Lacerta vivipara, 236
Lachesis, 43, 79–80, 89, 169, 174
    muta, 171, 306, 308, 351
laevis, Aipsysurus, 316, 353
Lampropeltis, 65, 153, 175–176, 191, 278,
        313
    calligaster, 255, 303, 497
    calligaster rhombomaculata, 482
    getulus, 303, 342, 399
    getulus goini, 482
    getulus holbrooki, 482
    getulus sticticeps, 482
    triangulum, 65, 197, 255, 303
Lamprophis, 37
    fiskii, 482
    swazicus, 482
Lampropholis, 315
Langaha, 37
langi, Daunophis, 66
langsdorffi, Micrurus, 351
Lanthanotus, 12, 53
Lapemis, 33
    hardwickii, 219, 237, 353
Lapparentophis, 6–8, 52, 54, 56-57,
        67, 69
    defrennei, 56
latastei, Vipera, 429
lateralis
    Liopholidophis, 37
    Macrocalamus, 36
    Masticophis, 408, 427
lateralis euryxanthus, Masticophis, 482
Laticauda, 32–33, 89, 121
    colubrina, 214, 222, 260, 276, 353, 451
    laticauda, 257
laticauda, Laticauda, 257
latifii, Vipera, 486, 490
lebetina, Vipera, 486
lebetina schweizeri, Vipera, 486, 495
Leimadophis, 351
    reginae, 351
Leiolopisma, 315
leithi, Psammophis, 484
lemniscatus, Micrurus, 351
lentiferus, Imantodes, 351
lepta, Platyspondylia, 62
Leptodeira, 35, 41, 303
    annulata, 351
Leptomicrurus, 32
    narduccii, 351

Leptophis, 320
  ahuetulla, 351
  mexicanus, 304, 320
Leptotyphlops, 16, 19
  dulcis, 305, 429
  humilis, 305, 315
  occidentalis, 482
Lepturophis borneensis, 42
leucobalia, Fordonia, 482
leucoproctus, Ramphotyphlops, 484
leucostomum, Kinosternon, 220
Liasis, 28, 91, 96
  amethystinus, 426
  childreni, 426
  fuscus, 426
Lichanura, 27, 29, 64, 84, 86
  trivirgata roseofusca, 460
Limnophis, 38–39
lineatum, Tropidoclonion, 212, 230, 409,
  428
lineatus, Liophis, 219, 228, 358
lineolatum, Taphrometopon, 256
Lioheterodon, 37
Liopeltis
  calamaria, 482
  nicobarensis, 482
  rappi, 482
Liophidium, 37
  trilineatum, 38
Liophis, 278, 304, 319, 358
  cobella, 351
  lineatus, 219, 228, 358
  mossoroensis, 219, 228
  poecilogyrus, 219, 228, 358
  viridis, 219, 358
Liopholidophis, 37
  lateralis, 37
  sexlineatus, 37
Liotyphlops, 9, 11, 13–15
Lithophis, 60
lodingi, Pituophis melanoleucus, 483
longissima, Elaphe, 65, 481, 488
Loveridgelaps, 33
Loxocemus, 9, 22–23, 25–26, 28, 55, 79
  88, 97, 99, 131–132
lutosus, Crotalus viridis, 429
lutrix, Duberria, 37
Lycodon, 34, 40, 42
  albofuscus, 42
  aulicus, 42
  osmanhilli, 42
  ruhstrati,42
  striatus, 42
  subcinctus, 42
  travancoricus, 42
Lycodonomorphus, 37
  bicolor, 37, 255, 271, 317, 412
  whytii, 37
Lycodryas, 37
Lycognathophis, 40, 92

Lycophidion, 35, 37–38
  semiannule, 482
Lytorhynchus, 93

Mabuya heathi, 225
macclellandi, Calliophis, 32
macmahonii, Eristicophis, 95, 481, 490
Macrelaps, 31
Macrocalamus, 36
  lateralis, 36
Macropisthodon, 38
  rudis, 38
Macroprotodon, 93
macularia, Pareas, 483
maculata, Denisonia, 305
maculatus, Cylindrophis, 24
maculiceps, Calliophis, 32
madagascariensis
  Madtsoia, 57–58
  Sanzinia, 194
Madagascarophis, 34, 37, 39
Madtsoia, 7–8, 57, 60
  bai, 60
  madagascariensis, 57–58
madurensis ruhunae, Platyplectrurus, 490
maghrebiana, Vipera, 66
major, Atractus, 351
Malpolon, 93, 320
  monspessulanus, 320
marcianus, Thamnophis, 221, 233, 236–237
margaritiferus, Drymobius, 303, 319
marinus, Bufo, 491, 497
Masticophis, 110, 272, 278, 408
  flagellum, 256, 262, 342, 427, 459–460, 482
  flagellum ruddocki, 482
  lateralis, 408, 427
  lateralis euryxanthus, 482
  taeniatus, 229, 256, 262, 271, 275, 280,
    282, 304, 319, 350, 384, 404, 406,
    408, 427
Mastigodryas melanolomus, 304, 319
Maticora, 32
maura, Natrix, 304, 482, 493
maurus, Python, 64
medici, Dasypeltis, 480
Mehelya, 33, 37
melanocephala, Tantilla, 351
melanocephalus
  Aspidites, 426
  Hydrophis, 353
melanocephalus satunini, Rhynchocalamus, 484
melanogaster
  Hydraethiops, 38
  Thamnophis, 215
melanogenys, Oxyrhopus, 351
melanoleucus, Pituophis, 256, 261–262,
    268, 270–271, 275, 280, 283, 288,
    304, 318–319, 342, 350, 370, 381,
    398, 406, 408, 427, 444, 447

melanoleucus catenifer, Pituophis, 483
melanoleucus lodingi, Pituophis, 483
melanoleucus mugitus, Pituophis, 483
melanoleucus ruthveni, Pituophis, 484, 489, 501
melanolomus, Mastigodryas, 304, 319
Melanophidium, 23–24
  bilineatum, 482
  wynaudense, 482
melanosoma, Hydrophis, 219, 257, 353
melanurus, Calliophis, 32
mendax, Thamnophis, 39
merremii, Waglerophis, 219, 230, 305, 319
Mesophis, 52, 54, 69
mexicanus, Leptophis, 304, 320
Micrelaps, 31
Microcephalophus gracilis, 353
microlepidotus, Oxyuranus, 305
Micropechis, 33
Micropisthodon, 37
Microtus
  ochrogaster, 314
  pennsylvanicus, 314
Micruroides, 32, 89
  euryxanthus, 305, 315
Micrurus, 32, 65–66, 87, 89, 173, 176, 315, 320, 352, 497
  fulvius, 212, 305, 315, 398, 411
  fulvius fulvius, 482
  gallicus, 66
  langsdorffi, 351
  lemniscatus, 351
  nigrocinctus babaspul, 482, 491
  spixii, 351
  surinamensis, 351
Mimophis, 37
minor, Elapognathus, 481
minusculus, Goinophis, 66
mirus, Nigerophis, 59
mitchelli, Crotalus, 398, 429
molossus, Crotalus, 306, 319
molurus
  Python, 96, 192, 225–226, 499
  Python molurus, 484
molurus bivittatus, Python, 437
molurus molurus, Python, 484
monensis, Epicrates monensis, 481, 492
monensis granti, Epicrates, 481, 492
monensis monensis, Epicrates, 481, 492
monspessulanus, Malpolon, 320
montandoni, Vipera ammodytes, 485
monticola, Pareas, 483
Morelia, 67
  spilotes, 426
  spilotes spilotes, 482
mossambica, Naja, 305
mossoroensis, Liophis, 219, 228
mucosus, Ptyas, 484, 499
mucrosquamatus, Trimeresurus, 306
mugitus, Pituophis melanoleucus, 483

multicinctus, Bungarus, 306
multimaculata, Boiga, 479
multiventris, Chironius, 351
multocarinata, Bolyeria, 479, 491–492
murinus, Eunectes, 303, 351, 499
muta, Lachesis, 171, 306, 308, 351
Myron, 35, 96

Naja, 33, 91–93, 110
  antiqua, 65
  haje, 305
  mossambica, 305
  naja, 67, 213–214, 216, 219–220, 222, 305
  naja kaouthia, 482
  naja naja, 482
  oxiana, 482
naja
  Naja, 67, 213–214, 216, 219–220, 222, 305
  Naja naja, 482
naja kaouthia, Naja, 482
naja naja, Naja, 482
najadum, Coluber, 320
Nanus, 65
naracoortensis, Wonambi, 67
narduccii, Leptomicrurus, 351
nasicornis, Bitis, 168, 171
nasicus, Heterodon, 255, 273, 282–283, 286, 381, 397, 411, 427, 482
nasuta, Ahaetulla, 41, 479
nattereri, Philodryas, 219, 229, 304
Natriciteres, 38–39
  fuliginoides, 38
  olivacea, 38–39
  variegata, 482
Natrix, 39–40, 65, 81, 87–88, 93, 99, 121, 278
  maura, 304, 482, 493
  natrix, 65, 94, 256, 304, 320, 378, 405, 408, 444, 446, 495
  natrix cetti, 482
  natrix helvetica, 483
  natrix natrix, 483, 495
  tessellata, 65, 256, 304, 320, 446, 483, 488
  tigrina, 398
natrix
  Natrix, 65, 94, 256, 304, 320, 378, 405, 408, 444, 446, 495
  Natrix natrix, 483
natrix cetti, Natrix, 482
natrix helvetica, Natrix, 483
natrix natrix, Natrix, 483
Nebraskophis, 65
Neelaps, 33, 305, 320
  calonotus, 483, 490
neglecta, Nerodia erythrogaster, 483
Neonatrix, 65, 87

Nerodia, 65, 113, 117–118, 121, 126, 190, 198, 222, 260, 278, 308, 313, 316, 349, 384, 461, 496
  cyclopion, 229, 271, 309, 316, 350, 427, 483
  erythrogaster, 304, 308, 316, 350, 427
  erythrogaster flavigaster, 483
  erythrogaster neglecta, 483
  fasciata, 222, 271, 308, 316–317, 427
  fasciata clarki, 483
  fasciata compressicauda, 483, 491
  fasciata confluens, 483
  fasciata taeniata, 483, 494
  harteri harteri, 483
  harteri paucimaculata, 483
  rhombifera, 123–125, 129, 304, 309, 316–317, 350, 427, 444, 447, 458–460, 483
  sipedon, 213–214, 227, 229, 256, 269, 271, 273, 277, 279–282, 288, 304, 317, 384, 427, 460
  sipedon insularum, 483, 487
  taxispilota, 229, 304, 317
nicobarensis, *Liopeltis*, 482
Nigerophis, 18–19
  mirus, 59
nigrescens
  Calliophis, 32, 479
  Cryptophis, 428
nigrocinctus babaspul, *Micrurus*, 482, 491
nigroluteus, *Tretanorhinus*, 260
nigromarginatus, *Zacoys*, 486
Ninia, 40
  hudsoni, 351
  sebae, 320
nitidus, *Uropeltis*, 485
notaeus, *Eunectes*, 499
notata, *Uma*, 384
Notechis, 32–33
  ater, 257, 277
  scutatus, 231, 268, 270, 305, 409, 411, 428, 449–450, 483
Nothopsis, 35, 40
Notropis, 317
novus, *Woutersophis*, 60
nuchalis, *Pseudonaja*, 428
nympha, *Dryocalamus*, 480

oatesi, *Ramphotyphlops*, 484
obscurus, *Crotalus willardi*, 480, 489, 497
obsoleta, *Elaphe*, 39, 144, 190, 255, 275, 303, 405, 427, 481
occidentalis
  Leptotyphlops, 482
  Sceloporus, 456
occipitalis, *Chionactis*, 303, 426
occipitoalbus, *Atractus*, 351
occipitolutea, *Clelia*, 218

occipitomaculata, *Storeria*, 227, 229, 241, 256, 401, 404, 407
ochrogaster, *Microtus*, 314
Ogmodon, 33
  vitianus, 483
Ogmophis, 60–61, 66
  pliocompactus, 64
okinavensis, *Trimeresurus*, 232, 238
olduvaiensis, *Bitis*, 67
olfersii, *Philodryas*, 219, 229, 304
Oligodon, 41
  cinereus, 483
  dorsalis, 483
  taeniolatus, 483
  theobaldi, 483
olivacea, *Natriciteres*, 38–39
olivaceus, *Rhabdops*, 484
oliveri, *Dendrelaphis*, 490
oolitica, *Tantilla*, 485, 489, 494
Opheodrys, 122, 496
  aestivus, 221, 229, 238, 241, 256, 260, 262, 271, 273, 282, 287, 304, 412
  vernalis, 256, 259, 483
Ophiomorphus, 6
Ophiophagus, 33, 39, 167, 490
  hannah, 192, 305, 315, 483
Opisthotropis, 38–39
ordinoides, *Thamnophis*, 229, 304, 318, 403, 411, 427
ornata, *Chrysopelea*, 479
ornatus, *Dromicus*, 491
osmanhilli, *Lycodon*, 42
oxiana, *Naja*, 482
Oxybelis, 354–355
  argenteus, 219, 351
Oxyrhabdium, 28, 35
Oxyrhopus
  formosus, 351
  melanogenys, 351
  petola, 351
oxyrhynchus, *Uromacer*, 355, 412, 428
Oxyuranus, 33, 491
  microlepidotus, 305
  scutellatus, 305, 428, 430

Pachyophis, 6–7, 52, 54, 69
Pachyrhachis, 6–7, 12, 52, 54, 69
  problematicus, 52
Palaeonaja, 65, 67, 92
  depereti, 67
  romani, 65
Palaeonatrix, 65
Palaeophis, 19, 59–60
Palaeopython, 29, 59
Paleofarancia, 65, 83
Paleoheterodon, 65, 87
Paleryx, 59
Paracoluber, 65

Paraepicrates, 59
Parahydrophis, 33
Paranaja, 33, 92
Paraoxybelis, 65
Parapistocalamus, 32
Pareas, 36
   macularia, 483
   monticola, 483
parietalis, Thamnophis sirtalis, 442
Parus,
   atricapillus, 144
   bicolor, 144
parvifrons, Antillophis, 303
patagonica, Dinilysia, 11, 57
paucimaculata, Nerodia harteri, 483
pavonina, Dipsas, 351
Pelamis, 33, 347, 373, 425
   platurus, 257, 353, 371, 373, 425
pennsylvanicus, Microtus, 314
peronii, Acalyptophis, 353
perroteti
   Ahaetulla, 479
   Xylophis, 36
petersi, Helicops, 351
petola, Oxyrhopus, 351
Philodryas, 319, 358
   chamissonis, 304
   nattereri, 219, 229, 304
   olfersii, 219, 229, 304
Phyllorhynchus decurtatus, 271, 427
piscator, Xenochrophis, 40
piscivorus, Agkistrodon, 231, 234, 288,
   306, 314
Pituophis, 153, 172, 175, 191, 194, 272,
   278, 319, 478, 502
   melanoleucus, 256, 261–262, 268,
      270–271, 275, 280, 283, 288, 304,
      318–319, 342, 350, 370, 381, 398,
      406, 408, 427, 444, 447
   melanoleucus catenifer, 483
   melanoleucus lodingi, 483
   melanoleucus mugitus, 483
   melanoleucus ruthveni, 484, 489, 501
Plagiopholis, 38–39
platirhinos, Heterodon, 119, 255, 271, 273,
   282–283, 400, 403, 411, 427, 482
platurus, Pelamis, 257, 353, 371, 373, 425
Platyplectrurus, 24
   madurensis ruhunae, 490
Platyspondylia, 25
   lepta, 62
Plectrurus, 24
   aureus, 484
pliocompactus, Ogmophis, 64
poecilogyrus, Liophis, 219, 228, 358
Polemon, 31
polyphemus, Gopherus, 495
porphyriacus, Pseudechis, 225, 231, 409,
   411, 425. 428, 484

porrectus
   Rhinophis, 490
   Typhlops, 485
portai, Colombophis, 63
prasina, Ahaetulla, 41, 479
prebottae, Charina, 63
precedens, Coniophis, 58
prisciformis, Helagras, 59
proavus, Archaeophis, 19, 60
problematicus, Pachyrhachis, 52
Procambarus, 260
procterae, Geodipsas, 494
Prosymna frontalis, 484
Protropidonotus, 65
proximus, Thamnophis, 229, 240, 257, 261,
   428
Psammodynastes, 40, 42
Psammophis, 37, 92–93, 95
   leithi, 484
psammophis, Demansia, 428
Pseudagkistrodon, 38–39
Pseudaspis, 38
Pseudechis, 33, 194
   australis, 484
   porphyriacus, 225, 231, 409, 411, 425,
      428, 484
Pseudemys scripta, 220
Pseudoboa coronata, 351
Pseudoboodon, 37
Pseudocemophora, 65
Pseudocerastes, 43
Pseudoepicrates, 63
Pseudohaje, 33, 92
Pseudonaja, 33
   nuchalis, 428
   textilis, 305, 411, 428
Pseudorhabdion, 36
Pseudotyphlops, 24
Pseudoxenodon, 38–39
Pseudoxyrhopus, 37
Pseustes sulphureus, 351
Pterosphenus, 19, 60
Ptyas, 490, 499
   korros, 212–213
   mucosus, 484, 499
pubescens, Dendrocopos, 144
pulchra, Virginia valeriae, 486
pulverulenta, Ahaetulla, 41
punctata, Denisonia, 305
punctatus
   Diadophis, 221, 228, 240, 255, 260,
      262, 270–271, 274, 282–284,
      287–289, 303, 310, 373, 399, 427
   Sphenodon, 187
punctatus acricus, Diadophis, 480, 489
pusilla, Typhlops, 411
Python, 7–8, 28, 64, 66–67, 90–91, 96,
   125–126, 132, 225, 490, 499
   amethistinus, 484

Python (cont.)
  curtus, 96
  maurus, 64
  molurus, 96, 192, 225–226, 499
  molurus bivittatus, 437
  molurus molurus, 484
  regius, 28–29, 91, 498
  reticulatus, 96, 227, 484, 499
  sebae, 67, 484
  spilotes, 426
Pythonodipsas, 38

quadrivirgata, Elaphe, 255, 268, 272–273,
    282–284, 286, 398
quatuorlineata, Elaphe, 303, 320, 481

raddei, Vipera xanthina, 486, 490
radiata, Elaphe, 481
radix
  Thamnophis, 217, 229, 240, 257,
      259–260, 271, 370, 384–385, 397,
      410, 428
  Thamnophis radix, 485
radix radix, Thamnophis, 485
rakosiensis, Vipera ursinii, 486
Ramphotyphlops, 15–16, 320
  andamanensis, 484
  braminus, 16, 185, 271, 484
  leucoproctus, 484
  oatesi, 484
  tindalli, 484
Rana blairi, 144
rappi, Liopeltis, 482
Regina, 306, 316, 349
  alleni, 217, 256, 260, 262, 287–289,
      304, 306, 309, 407
  grahamii, 229, 304, 306, 427, 484
  rigida, 304, 306
  septemvittata, 229, 260, 273, 304, 306,
      384, 484
reginae, Leimadophis, 351
regius, Python, 28–29, 91, 498
reinhardii, Calabaria, 303
relicta, Tantilla, 304
renardi, Vipera ursinii, 486
reticulatus, Python, 96, 227, 484, 499
Rhabdion, 36
Rhabdophis, 38–40, 81, 87
  tigrinus, 256, 273, 282–284, 304, 484,
      490
Rhabdops, 38–39
  olivaceus, 484
Rhadinaea, 36, 40–41
  brevirostris, 351
  flavilata, 304
Rhinoclemys funerea, 220
Rhinoleptus, 16

Rhinophis, 8, 24
  fergusonianus, 484
  porectus, 490
Rhinoplocephalus, 33
rhodogaster, Drysdalia, 230
rhombifer, Drymobius, 351
rhombifera, Nerodia, 123–125, 129, 304,
      309, 316–317, 350, 427, 444, 447,
      458–460, 483
rhombomaculata, Lampropeltis calligaster,
      482
Rhynchocalamus melanocephalus satunini,
      484
rhynchops, Cerberus, 218, 222, 228
rigida, Regina, 304, 306
romani, Palaeonaja, 65
roseofusca, Lichanura trivirgata, 460
ruddocki, Masticophis flagellum, 482
rudis, Macropisthodon, 38
rufipunctatus, Thamnophis, 257, 428
rufus, Cylindrophis, 131–132
ruhstrati, Lycodon, 42
ruhunae
  Platyplectrurus madurensis, 490
  Uropeltis, 490
russelli, Vipera, 95, 306, 486
Russellophis, 20, 56, 61
ruthveni, Pituophis melanoleucus, 484, 489,
      501

sagittarius, Sibynophis, 484
Salomonelaps, 33
Salvadora, 65
  hexalepis, 427
sancticrucis, Alsophis, 491
sanniola, Sibon, 219, 229, 278
Sanzinia, 29, 90
  madagascariensis, 194
satunini, Rhynchocalamus melanocephalus, 484
sauritus, Thamnophis, 191, 229–230, 257,
      271, 318
sauritus septentrionalis, Thamnophis, 485
scalaris, Xenopholis, 351
Sceloporus
  jarrovi, 217
  occidentalis, 456
schistosa, Enhydrina, 219, 230, 257, 276,
      288, 308, 353
schlegeli, Bothrops, 171
schneideri, Bitis, 479
schweizeri
  Vipera, 488
  Vipera lebetina, 486, 495
Scincella himalayanum, 217
scripta, Pseudemys, 220
scurrulus, Chironius, 351
scutatus, Notechis, 231, 268, 270, 305,
      409, 411, 428, 449–450, 483

scutellatus, Oxyuranus, 305, 428, 430
scutulatus, Crotalus, 169, 306, 319
scytale, Anilius, 351
sebae
    Ninia, 320
    Python, 484
semiannule, Lycophidion, 482
semicinctus, Tropidophis, 25
semifasciatus, Simoselaps, 305, 320
seoanei, Vipera, 429
septemvittata, Regina, 229, 260, 273, 304,
    306, 384, 484
septentrionalis, Thamnophis sauritus, 485
severus, Xenodon, 351
sexlineatus, Liopholidophis, 37
shirana, Duberria, 37
Sibon sanniola, 219, 229, 278
Sibynophis
    bistrigatus, 484
    sagittarius, 484
    subpunctatus, 484
signata
    Denisonia, 428
    Hemiaspis, 231
Simoliophis, 6–7, 54, 57
Simoselaps, 33
    australis, 320
    bertholdi, 305, 320
    fasciolatus, 320
    semifasciatus, 305, 320
    warro, 484
    woodjonesi, 484
simus, Heterodon, 400
Sinonatrix, 38–40, 81, 87
sipedon, Nerodia, 213–214, 227, 229, 256,
    269, 271, 273, 277, 279–282, 288,
    304, 317, 384, 427, 460
sipedon insularum, Nerodia, 483, 487
Siphlophis cervinus, 351
sirtalis, Thamnophis, 39, 144, 155, 191,
    198, 217–218, 230, 240, 257, 262,
    270, 274, 277, 279, 281–283, 288,
    304, 313, 318, 371, 375, 381, 401,
    403–404, 408, 411–412, 428, 440,
    442, 447, 449, 460, 462–464
sirtalis concinnus, Thamnophis, 428
sirtalis parietalis, Thamnophis, 442
sirtalis tetrataenia, Thamnophis, 485, 489,
    494, 497
Sistrurus, 43, 79–80, 86, 169, 314
    catenatus, 231–232, 234, 241, 306, 314,
        398, 407–408, 484
situla, Elaphe, 303, 320, 481
Smilisca, 320
Solenopsis invicta, 497
Spalerosophis, 93
    cliffordi, 427, 438, 444
    diadema diadema, 485
Sphenodon punctatus, 187

spilotes
    Morelia, 426
    Morelia spilotes, 482
    Python, 426
spilotes spilotes, Morelia, 482
spinalis, Achalinus, 36
spixii, Micrurus, 351
squamulosus, Cacophis, 230
stansburiana, Uta, 319
Stegonotus, 39, 96
stejnegeri, Trimeresurus, 306
sticticeps, Lampropeltis getulus, 482
Stilosoma, 65
    extenuatum, 304, 485, 489
stirtoni, Eunectes, 64
stokesii, Astrotia, 316, 353
stolata, Amphiesma, 40
Stoliczkaia, 35, 37
Storeria, 148, 198, 373
    dekayi, 198, 229, 256, 271, 304,
        371–372, 401
        occipitomaculata, 227, 229, 241, 256,
            401, 404, 407
striatula, Virginia, 257, 260–261
striatus
    Epicrates, 214
    Lycodon, 42
striatus fosteri, Epicrates, 481
subcinctus, Lycodon, 42
subflavus, Epicrates, 481, 492, 497
subocularis, Elaphe, 303, 319
subpunctatus, Sibynophis, 484
sulphureus, Pseustes, 351
superbus, Austrelaps, 230, 428
surinamensis, Micrurus, 351
Suta, 33
    flagellum, 429
swazicus, Lamprophis, 482
Symphimus, 122

taeniata, Nerodia fasciata, 483, 494
taeniatus, Masticophis, 229, 256, 262, 271,
    275, 280, 282, 304, 319, 350, 384,
    404, 406, 408, 427
taeniolatus, Oligodon, 483
taeniura, Elaphe, 212–213
Tantilla, 403
    coronata, 271, 398, 402
    gracilis, 227, 427
    melanocephala, 351
    oolitica, 485, 489, 494
    relicta, 304
Taphrometopon lineolatum, 256
tataricus, Eryx, 255
taxispilota, Nerodia, 229, 304, 317
Telescopus, 93
    beetzii, 485
    fallax, 320

tenuicollis, Typhlops, 485
tenuis, Contia, 479
Teretrurus, 24
tessellata, Natrix, 65, 256, 304, 320, 446, 483, 488
tetrataenia, Thamnophis sirtalis, 485, 489, 494, 497
Texasophis, 65, 87
 galbreathi, 62
textilis, Pseudonaja, 305, 411, 428
Thalassophina viperina, 353
Thalassophis, 33
Thamnophis, 175, 186, 189, 198, 212, 214, 260–261, 278, 308, 313, 318, 373, 430, 462, 496
 brachystoma, 427, 485
 butleri, 191, 229, 237–239, 256, 273, 318, 372, 485
 couchi gigas, 485, 493
 cyrtopsis, 257, 427
 elegans, 257, 271, 273, 304, 313, 318, 431, 435, 446–448, 459, 464
 elegans hammondi, 427
 elegans vagrans, 427, 431, 433
 marcianus, 221, 233, 236–237
 melanogaster, 215
 mendax, 39
 ordinoides, 229, 304, 318, 403, 411, 427
 proximus, 229, 240, 257, 261, 428
 radix, 217, 229, 240, 257, 259–260, 271, 370, 384–385, 397, 410, 428
 radix radix, 485
 rufipunctatus, 257, 428
 sauritus, 191, 229–230, 257, 271, 273,
 sauritus septentrionalis, 485
 sirtalis, 39, 144, 155, 191, 198, 217–218, 230, 240, 257, 262, 270, 274, 277, 279, 281–283, 288, 304, 313, 318, 371, 375, 381, 401, 403–404, 408, 411–412, 428, 440, 442, 447, 449, 460, 462–464
 sirtalis concinnus, 428
 sirtalis parietalis, 442
 sirtalis tetrataenia, 485, 489, 494, 497
Thelotornis, 93, 354
theobaldi, Oligodon, 483
tigrina, Natrix, 398
tigrinus, Rhabdophis, 256, 273, 282–284, 304, 484, 490
tindalli, Ramphotyphlops, 484
tokarensis, Trimeresurus, 232
torquata, Hypsiglena, 303
torquatus, Hydrophis, 219, 237, 353
Toxicocalamus, 33
Trachischium, 40, 42
Trachyboa, 25, 88
transcaucasiana, Vipera ammodytes, 485
transvaalensis, Xenocalamus, 486
travancoricus, Lycodon, 42
Tregophis brevirachis, 64

Tretanorhinus, 34
 nigroluteus, 260
triangulum, Lampropeltis, 65, 197, 255, 303
trilineatum, Liophidium, 38
Trimeresurus, 43, 79–80, 86, 95, 169, 238
 flavoviridis, 232, 238, 258, 412
 mucrosquamatus, 306
 okinavensis, 232, 238
 stejnegeri, 306
 tokarensis, 232
 wagleri, 168
Tripanurgos compressus, 351
tristis, Dendrelaphis, 480
trivirgata roseofusca, Lichanura, 460
Tropidechis, 33
 carinatus, 305
Tropidoclonion lineatum, 212, 230, 409, 428
Tropidolaemus, 43
Tropidonophis, 96
Tropidophis, 25, 88–89
 semicinctus, 25
turcicus, Eryx jaculus, 481
turkmenicus, Archaeophis, 19, 60
Typhlina, 16
Typhlophis, 15
Typhlops, 14, 16, 63, 67, 305
 biminiensis, 411
 cariei, 67
 ceylonicus, 490
 grivensis, 63
 porrectus, 485
 pusilla, 411
 tenuicollis, 485

Uma, 384
 notata, 384
umbratica, Charina bottae, 479
Unechis
 flagellum, 429
 gouldii, 231, 305, 411
Ungaliophis, 23–26, 88
unicolor, Crotalus, 480, 492, 504
Uromacer, 313, 320, 354
 catesbyi, 355, 412, 428
 frenatus, 305, 320
 oxyrhynchus, 355, 412, 428
Uropeltis, 24
 dindigalensis, 485
 nitidus, 485
 ruhunae, 490
ursinii
 Vipera, 258, 429
 Vipera ursinii, 486
ursinii anatolica, Vipera, 486
ursinii rakosiensis, Vipera, 486
ursinii renardi, Vipera, 486
ursinii ursinii, Vipera, 486
ursinii wettsteini, Vipera, 486, 495
Uta stansburiana, 319

vagrans, Thamnophis elegans, 427, 431, 433
valeriae, Virginia, 398, 402
valeriae elegans, Virginia, 486
valeriae pulchra, Virginia, 486
Varanus, 7, 12, 336
variegata, Natriciteres, 482
vauerocegue, Geodipsas, 494
Vectophis wardi, 61
Vermicella, 33
  annulata, 305, 320
vermis, Carphophis, 216, 228, 274, 282–283, 287, 303
vernalis, Opheodrys, 256, 259, 483
Vialovophis, 59
  zhylan, 59
vibakari, Amphiesma, 40
vincenti, Chironius, 491
Vipera, 43, 66, 79, 91, 98–99, 122, 126, 171, 176, 278–279, 284, 314, 320, 461, 498, 502
  ammodytes, 320, 429
  ammodytes montandoni, 485
  ammodytes transcaucasiana, 485
  aspis, 232, 276, 283, 288, 384, 405, 408, 429, 435, 445–446, 485, 493
  berus, 192, 194, 221, 225, 232, 234, 236, 240, 258, 268, 271, 276, 280–281, 283–285, 288, 306, 309, 320, 369, 380–381, 404–405, 407–409, 411, 429, 451, 485
  gedulyi, 66
  kargii, 66
  kaznakovi, 486
  latastei, 429
  latifii, 486, 490
  lebetina, 486
  lebetina schweizeri, 486, 495
  maghrebiana, 66
  russelli, 95, 306, 486
  schweizeri, 488
  seoanei, 429
  ursinii, 258, 429
  ursinii anatolica, 486
  ursinii rakosiensis, 486
  ursinii renardi, 486
  ursinii ursinii, 486
  ursinii wettsteini, 486, 495
  xanthina raddei, 486, 490
vipera, Cerastes, 314
viperina, Thalassophina, 353
vireti, Bransateryx, 61
virgatus, Boaedon, 11
Virginia, 403
  striatula, 257, 260–261
  valeriae, 398, 402
  valeriae elegans, 486
  valeriae pulchra, 486
viridiflavus, Coluber, 479

viridis
  Chondropython, 479
  Crotalus, 153, 171, 192, 197, 231, 234, 257, 262, 269–271, 275, 277, 280, 283, 288, 306, 372, 374, 381, 385, 404–406, 409, 412, 447, 460, 480
  Liophis, 219, 358
viridis lutosus, Crotalus, 429
vitianus, Ogmodon, 483
vivipara, Lacerta, 236
vulpina, Elaphe, 255
vulpina gloydi, Elaphe, 481

wagleri, Trimeresurus, 168
Waglerophis, 358
  merremii, 219, 230, 305, 319
Walterinnesia, 33, 91, 93, 315
  aegyptia, 305, 315
wardi, Vectophis, 61
warro, Simoselaps, 484
werneri
  Aparallactus, 494
  Crotaphopeltis, 494
westermanni, Elachistodon, 481
wettsteini, Vipera ursinii, 486, 495
whytii, Lycodonomorphus, 37
willardi, Crotalus, 306
willardi obscurus, Crotalus, 480, 489, 497
Wonambi, 7
  naracoortensis, 67
woodjonesi, Simoselaps, 484
Woutersophis, 18, 60
  novus, 60
wynaudense, Melanophidium, 482

xanthina raddei, Vipera, 486, 490
Xenelaphis, 39
Xenoboa, 29, 88
Xenocalamus, 16, 30–31
  transvaalensis, 486
Xenochrophis, 39–40, 81, 87
  cerasogaster, 40
  flavipunctatus, 39
  piscator, 40
Xenodermus, 30, 35
Xenodon, 34
  severus, 351
Xenopeltis, 22–23, 25, 28, 55, 79, 88, 94, 97–98, 132
Xenopholis scalaris, 351
xeropaga, Bitis, 479
Xylophis, 35–36
  perroteti, 36

Zacoys nigromarginatus, 486
Zelceophis, 65
zhylan, Vialovophis, 59